Academic Women on the Move

Academic Women
on the Move

Edited by
Alice S. Rossi and *Ann Calderwood*

Russell Sage Foundation   New York

PUBLICATIONS OF RUSSELL SAGE FOUNDATION

Russell Sage Foundation was established in 1907 by Mrs. Russell Sage
for the improvement of social and living conditions in the United States.
In carrying out its purpose the Foundation conducts research
under the direction of members of the staff or in close collaboration
with other institutions, and supports programs designed to develop
and demonstrate productive working relations between social scientists
and other professional groups. As an integral part of its operation,
the Foundation from time to time publishes books or pamphlets
resulting from these activities. Publication under the imprint
of the Foundation does not necessarily imply agreement
by the Foundation, its Trustees, or its staff with the interpretations
or conclusions of the authors.

Russell Sage Foundation
230 Park Avenue, New York, N.Y. 10017

© 1973 by Russell Sage Foundation. All Rights Reserved.

Library of Congress Catalog Card Number: 73–76761

Standard Book Number: 87154–752–X

Printed in the United States of America by Connecticut Printers, Inc.,
Hartford, Connecticut.

For:
future generations
of women
in academe

Contents

Foreword   *Eleanor Bernert Sheldon*   ix

Preface   *Alice S. Rossi*   xi

Chapter 1   Women on the Move: Roots of Revolt   *Jo Freeman*   1

PART ONE: RECRUITMENT, TRAINING, AND EMPLOYMENT

A. Choice and Training

Chapter 2   Institutional Barriers to Women Students in Higher Education   *Pamela Roby*   37

Chapter 3   Women in the Male World of Higher Education   *Pepper Schwartz and Janet Lever*   57

Chapter 4   Women Dropouts from Higher Education   *Michelle Patterson and Lucy Sells*   79

Chapter 5   Women Drop Back In: Educational Innovation in the Sixties   *Jean W. Campbell*   93

Chapter 6   From Sugar and Spice to Professor   *Joan Huber*   125

B. Employment and Career Development

Chapter 7   Career Profiles of Women Doctorates   *Helen S. Astin*   139

Chapter 8   Status Transitions of Women Students, Faculty, and Administrators   *Patricia Albjerg Graham*   163

Chapter 9   Three's a Crowd: The Dilemma of the Black Woman in Higher Education   *Constance M. Carroll*   173

Chapter 10   The Faculty Wife: Her Academic Interests and Qualifications   *Myrna M. Weissman, Katherine Nelson, Judith Hackman, Cynthia Pincus, and Brigitte Prusoff*   187

PART TWO: WOMEN ON THE CONTEMPORARY ACADEMIC SCENE

Chapter 11	Institutional Variation in the Status of Academic Women	*Lora H. Robinson*	199
Chapter 12	Representation, Performance and Status of Women on the Faculty at the Urbana-Champaign Campus of the University of Illinois	*Jane W. Loeb and Marianne A. Ferber*	239
Chapter 13	Discipline Variation in the Status of Academic Women	*Laura Morlock*	255
Chapter 14	Sex and Specialization in Academe and the Professions	*Michelle Patterson*	313
Chapter 15	Sex Discrimination in Academe	*Helen S. Astin and Alan E. Bayer*	333

PART THREE: ACTION TOWARD CHANGE

Chapter 16	Political Action by Academic Women	*Kay Klotzburger*	359
Chapter 17	Women's Studies and Social Change	*Florence Howe and Carol Ahlum*	393
Chapter 18	Internal Remedies for Sex Discrimination in Colleges and Universities	*Margaret L. Rumbarger*	425
Chapter 19	A Little Help from Our Government: WEAL and Contract Compliance	*Bernice Sandler*	439
Chapter 20	Affirmative Action Plans for Eliminating Sex Discrimination in Academe	*Lenore J. Weitzman*	463
Chapter 21	Summary and Prospects	*Alice S. Rossi*	505
Notes on Contributors			531
Author Index			537
Subject Index			545

Foreword

In sponsoring this volume of essays, Russell Sage Foundation is seeking to make available to a rapidly growing public the first collection of systematic studies of the position of women in higher education. During the past few years, activist women have succeeded in putting the disabilities suffered by women as a class high on the national list of social injustices in need of rectification. They have dramatized their case effectively, but for the most part they have been working with impressionistic evidence, a basis too weak to refute the opposing traditionalist case or to provide the information needed to formulate intelligent remedial policies. During these same few years, academic women have been using their professional skills to examine systematically the facts of their particular situation, with a success that is evident in the following pages. Here a group of researchers, most of them female social scientists from a variety of disciplines, have collaborated to study themselves—to analyze the history and social status of women in academe, to present research findings on their recruitment and careers, to document the nature and range of sex discrimination, and to report on what remedial efforts are now being made.

The findings are important in themselves. In addition, the study as a whole demonstrates one of the most interesting of the conclusions reached. It has long been assumed, as much in institutions of higher learning as in the world at large, that women make good students but unproductive scholars. Helen S. Astin's study of the careers of women doctorates in Chapter Seven, which draws on and amplifies her earlier *The Woman Doctorate in America* (Russell Sage Foundation, 1969), provides convincing evidence to the contrary. As Dr. Astin writes, "Women who complete their training are committed to their disciplines and careers. They remain in the labor force, and they contribute as teachers and scholars." This collection of studies both illustrates and documents that conclusion, making the results of this collaborative enterprise doubly impressive.

In an important final chapter, Alice S. Rossi, one of the editors of this volume, effectually summarizes and evaluates the results of this scholarly enterprise and points out the implications the research contains for the future of women in higher education. Academe is a field in which women have traditionally played important, if subordinate roles; certainly college and university teaching has, more than most other occupations, long provided women with an attractive alternative to their traditional role as wife and mother. It is, then, not surprising that higher education should be the first field to be systematically studied, but it is to be hoped that the substantial contribution to knowledge made here will encourage similar studies of women in other occupations.

Dr. Rossi and her colleagues are to be commended for their initiative in planning this work, and for the care and skill with which they have researched, written, and edited the essays in it. The volume provides knowledge necessary, indeed indispensable, to realistic policy-making in our changing society.

ELEANOR BERNERT SHELDON

Preface

The central purpose of this book is to bring together the varied and rapidly increasing number of studies bearing on the status of women in American higher education. The contributors and the editors hope that the volume may serve as a useful reference work and a comprehensive overview of the status of academic women in 1973.

Every book has a history and I would like to introduce this one to its readers by sharing with them the history of how it came to be. Its "beginnings" can be traced to the winter of 1968. At that time, I was affiliated with the Johns Hopkins University and corresponding with my friends Pauline Bart at the University of California, Berkeley (now at the University of Illinois Medical Center) and Barbara Laslett at the University of California, Los Angeles (now at the University of Southern California) about problems confronting women sociologists. In the course of that correspondence the idea grew that we should begin to organize women within our own professional association, the American Sociological Association. A plan was set in motion to form a women's caucus at the annual convention in San Francisco in August 1969, and I took the responsibility of conducting a survey of all chairmen of graduate departments of sociology to gather information on the rank distribution by sex of the faculty in these departments. The purpose of the survey was to establish the "facts" in advance of the convention so that we would have a firm basis on which to argue our case and to avoid the expected response so comfortable to research sociologists, that we "conduct a study" before taking any action. It is also an interesting measure of the distance academic women have come in the brief period of three years that this first survey on the status of women in sociology graduate departments was undertaken with no funding at all in March 1969, while a committee on women in another academic discipline received a sizable grant from a private foundation to support a comparable survey in March 1972,

Unknown to most members of the women's caucus in sociology at the time, comparable organizing was taking place among women in the modern languages, political science, and psychology professional associations; within a few months surveys similar to ours were being conducted in a number of academic disciplines, and there was a sharp increase in the number of institutional studies being conducted to investigate the status of women on various campuses. By the summer of 1970, the American Association of University Professors (AAUP) reactivated its long dormant Committee W on the Status of Women in the Academic Profession, and I was privileged to serve as its first chairperson. It became apparent during the first year of the committee's work that a movement was escalating among academic women across the nation. We could see this in the rapid formation of local Committee W's in AAUP chapters and in the increasing number of unpublished institutional and discipline reports that began to circulate throughout academe. By early spring 1971, it was clear that one function the national AAUP committee could fill would be to gather all such reports together and present an overview of their findings.

For a time, AAUP considered sponsoring a conference on academic women and we began to search the private foundations for funds to support such a venture. Russell Sage Foundation expressed interest in supporting not a conference, which was outside the framework of its policies at the time, but an overview volume of commissioned papers under my editorship. By May 1971 the Foundation's Board of Trustees had approved a proposal for such an undertaking and by late June, authors had been commissioned to undertake the work. The selection of authors was based on two criteria: who was the best qualified person, in terms of professional expertise, to write a given chapter; and who through their political experience had become sensitive to women's efforts to improve their position in academe.

Since the concern for the status of women in academe has its roots in the emergence of the larger women's movement during the 1960s, Freeman opens the book with an account of this political background (Chapter One). The chapters which follow in Part One bring together what is known about women students in higher education: the barriers to their entry to academe (Roby, Chapter Two); the experiences of women in the male academic world (Schwartz and Lever, Chapter Three); the effects of those experiences on women's attrition rate (Patterson and Sells, Chapter Four); and the great increase in the number of women returning to higher education in the 1960s (Campbell, Chapter Five, and Huber, Chapter Six). The second section of Part One traces women's career development from student to faculty status by reviewing the profile of women doctorates in background, advancement, and employment experiences (Astin, Chapter Seven), and by examining the critical transition points from student to faculty member, and professor to administrator (Graham, Chapter Eight). Carroll (Chapter Nine) gives a sketch of the special dilemma facing black women in academe, and Weissman et al. (Chapter Ten) report a unique study of a neglected source of womanpower in academe, the faculty wife.

Part Two consists of five chapters that provide descriptive and analytic detail on many dimensions of women's status in American colleges and universities. On the basis of several dozen studies on the status of women in academic disciplines and over one hundred studies in institutions of higher education, Robinson (Chapter Eleven) and Morlock (Chapter Thirteen) examine the variation across disciplines and institutions in the position of academic women. Differences by sex in specialization within disciplines is examined by Patterson (Chapter Fourteen) and differential rewards in the form of status and salary granted women and men are explored by Loeb and Ferber (Chapter Twelve). The last chapter in this part draws upon the ACE-Carnegie national sample of 60,000 faculty, in a statistical analysis that measures the extent to which women are penalized in rank, tenure status, and salary. Since upward of sixty variables are taken into account that could contribute to the differences by sex in the reward structure, there is no other interpretation to be drawn than that with which Astin and Bayer conclude—that a pervasive pattern of sex discrimination exists in American higher education (Chapter Fifteen).

The cumulative impact of Parts One and Two probably will be a mixture of anger and despair, for the profile of the academic woman shows a career of struggle, conflicting social pressures concerning aspirations, and a pervasive pattern of sex discrimination. Part Three, in contrast, should give readers some degree of confidence in and commitment to the efforts to change the status of academic women and the structure of American higher education as it determines that status. The development of political action by academic women is traced by Klotzburger (Chapter Sixteen); the development of women's studies courses and programs is described by Howe and Ahlum (Chapter Seventeen); the attempts to develop institutional self-governing policies for the adjudication of grievances is covered by Rumbarger (Chapter Eighteen), and the concerted efforts by academic women to exert pressure on academic institutions to comply with standards of equity under law and government regulations is traced by Sandler (Chapter Nineteen) and Weitzman (Chapter Twenty).

Academic Women on the Move is above all a collaborative effort representing diverse professional skills but a common political commitment to social change in academe. Its twenty-one chapters were written by twenty-eight women and one man, and the book has been edited by two women, one whose life has centered in academe, the other in the publishing world. Our primary fields of training and expertise are diverse: nine in sociology, seven in psychology, two each in political science, economics, education, literature, history, and psychiatry, and one in classics. Although many of us combine teaching, research, and administration, our primary responsibilities lie in teaching or graduate study (sixteen), administration (seven), and full-time research (six).

We share a past and current involvement in political efforts to change the status of academic women. Twenty-four of the contributors have been active on campus committees or commissions concerned with the status of women; twenty-three have been active as members, officers, or organizers of academic discipline caucuses or independent organizations of academic women; twenty have served or are serving on national committees or organizations concerning women, and ten have held or are holding administrative posts, in or outside academe, in offices focussing on women's issues. Most of us, then, have been pioneers in the revolt of academic women during the past several years.

This profile of considerable political activity does not exhaust the range of involvement in the larger women's movement. That this volume focuses on women students and faculty in academe, does not mean that our concerns are limited to this privileged stratum of American society. Many of us have been deeply involved in aspects of the women's movement that concern poor, black, and Chicano underprivileged girls and working women. Even within academe itself, many of us have been keenly aware that the definition of the world of higher education as a "male" world is a partial definition at best, since it is "male" only if we confine our attention to the faculty and administrative ranks. As Howe and Ahlum point out, the potential for rectifiying women's status in academe lies in the fact that women represent a majority of *all* members of academe once our conception of higher education is broadened to include the whole range of white-collar clerical and technical employees and the blue-collar maintenance and service employees needed to keep an academic institution going. I would hazard the hypothesis that women at this point in history are better able than men to reach across status barriers of class, discipline, rank, or race, once they achieve a shared consensus and commitment to some common goal. It is this potential strength that has been activated as women have sought each other to collaborate in improving their own and others' opportunities.

The academic year 1971–1972 has been called the "year of the woman," but this meant as well a year of overcommitment among academic women, who perhaps like the contributors to this book have been active in the women's movement. As a result this volume has been much longer in the writing than we projected. The task of editing the manuscripts was lightened by sharing the work between Ann Calderwood and myself, although the distinction between stylistic and substantive editing that was to differentiate our respective tasks soon broke down as we processed the manuscript and discussed their strengths and weaknesses.

I suspect the editors have been experienced by the authors as compulsive perfectionists, projected superegos, relentless reminders of overdue manuscripts, and only occasionally as forgiving or indulgent friends—which is to say that the actual production of the book has followed the normal pattern of the author-editor relationship. It has only two unique features: the refreshing blend of professional and political interests that bound authors and editors together in a common commitment to the importance of the volume we were producing; and the extraordinary amount of guilt generated in authors, perhaps precisely because of the shared commitment, when life and work were difficult and deadlines could not be met.

In addition to my co-editor and the twenty-nine authors, a number of persons have shared in the creation of *Academic Women on the Move:* the researchers and activists on hundreds of campuses across the country whose studies and activities provided the substance with which our authors worked; the more than two hundred AAUP local Committee W's whose activities suggested the need for a volume like this one in the first place, and whose patience during my second year as the national committee chairperson permitted me to define the production of this volume as a contribution to the work of an otherwise rather inactive committee; Russell Sage Foundation, and in particular Eleanor Sheldon, for the swift processing and approval of the proposal and generous support; my student assistants at Goucher College, Caryl Goodman, Jennifer Hawes, and Ellen Weinberg, who helped check sources and process manuscripts as they moved back and forth in a flurry of mail between authors and the Baltimore and New York editors; President Marvin Perry and Vice President Harry Casey of Goucher College, for their intellectual support and encouragement and financial contribution in the form of an extremely low indirect-cost claim on the project budget; and Shirley Sult of John Hopkins University, whose magic touch on the keyboard transformed almost undecipherable edited manuscripts into aesthetically pleasing final copy.

And finally, on behalf of the authors and my co-editor and friend, Ann Calderwood, our thanks to friends, families, and students whose patience and understanding permitted us to get on with our tasks.

ALICE S. ROSSI

Baltimore, Maryland
October 1972

Chapter One

Women on the Move: The Roots of Revolt

Jo Freeman

DURING the early 1960s a great number of books and articles appeared about women:[1] women's history, economics and women, women's work, women in literature, the psychology of women, and the social position of women in general. Most of these works concluded that not only was women's position pretty bad, but that women were not likely to do anything about it. Women, they said, were content in their place.

There was a touch of irony in this conclusion. For not only did these new works contribute considerably to the consciousness necessary for a woman's liberation movement to develop in the last half of the decade, but they were also indicative of its imminence. Most social and political movements advertise their coming long before any but the most perceptive recognize their potential existence. One way this is done is through the printed word. More articles and books concerning women were printed outside of established women's publications in the five years that preceded the present women's movement than had been printed in the previous twenty years.

Discontent also manifests itself pathologically. The 1940s and 1950s witnessed the phenomenon of "momism."[2] Everything was mom's fault—she was trying to run her husband and was ruining her children. No one noticed that this happened at the same time women were being encouraged to return to the home and devote their lives to husband and family. Such women lived at the height of the "feminine mystique." They were told to live through others, and they did, to the dismay of everyone concerned.

Another pathology was the divorce rate. One out of every three first marriages

[1] A cursory examination of the card catalog of any large library and the indexes of major journals for books and articles on women discloses a striking decrease in their number after the mid-1920s that curves up again only in the 1960s. The years 1927 and 1959 appear to be the inflexion points.

[2] Wylie who created and popularized the term, almost gave his "subspecies" a feminist interpretation in his commentary on the twentieth edition (1955) of his infamous book. He said: "When we and our culture and our religions agreed to hold woman the inferior sex, cursed, unclean, and sinful—we made her mom. And when we agreed upon the American Ideal Woman, the Dream Girl of National Adolescence, the Queen of Bedpan Week, the Pin-up, the Glamour Puss—we insulted women and . . . thus made mom. The hen-harpy is but the Cinderella chick come home to roost; the taloned, crackling residue of burnt-out puberty in a land that has no use for mature men or women" (Wylie 1955:197).

1

ended in court. Alcoholism and drug addiction were on the increase among housewives, particularly among those with few financial worries. But the most common
sign of anxiety was a growing sense that there must be more to life than marriage
and children. It was this vague unspecified malaise that Friedan called "the problem
that has no name" (Friedan 1963). One West Coast psychologist called it a "great
reservoir of rage in women—just under the surface" (Farson 1969). What these
people lacked—the ones who wrote the books, took the drugs and felt the rage—
was a unifying idea to explain their feelings and a structure through which to communicate with each other. Instead, most women attributed their distress to personal
inadequacy.

The beginning of a social movement usually is found within existing social structures created for other ends. How a movement develops often is determined by the
nature of those structures. A cooptable communications network is a prerequisite
for movement formation. Such a network may be another organization or may exist
in common residence patterns or even informal social ties within a particular occupation or place of employment. What is important is the level of interaction in these
informal networks and the potential that exists for a cooptation of the network for
some new direction or movement.[3]

This process was seen in the emergence of the civil rights movement, which coopted networks within the southern Negro church. Similarly, the black power
movement sprang from the northern urban ghetto, students built upon their campus
bases, and peace groups have had a long organizational history. Unlike these social
movements, women have largely lacked such cooptable communications networks.
Not only are they the only "minority" to live in such complete integration with the
dominant group that they often are isolated from their own kind, but they have not
had even moderately well organized groups of their own since the 1920s. The
Women's Trade Union League, the General Federation of Women's Clubs, the
Women's Christian Temperance Union, not to mention the powerful, broad-based
National American Women's Suffrage Association (NAWSA)—which together
provided the troops of the suffrage movement—no longer exist or are a pale shadow
of their former selves. Until very recently, women simply did not have powerful
organizations of their own that were concerned with their problems as women.

A rare exception to this pattern is the National Women's Party (NWP), which
has remained dedicated to feminist concerns since its inception in 1916. The
daughter of the radical Congressional Union for Women's Suffrage (CUWS), it
was organized originally to mobilize women's voting power in suffrage states to
compel the adoption of the federal suffrage amendment.[4] Under the leadership of

---

[3] This idea is more extensively developed in Freeman 1973.

[4] Its founder, Alice Paul, had spent three years in Britain working with the militant suf-
fragettes there, and adopted from them the idea of holding the party in power responsible for
all governmental policies, and hence for the failure to pass the Anthony Suffrage Amendment.
Since the Democrats controlled the White House, the NWP worked against the election of all

Alice Paul, the NWP was responsible for most of the serious agitation (marches, pickets, jail-ins, fasts) that preceded the passage of the Nineteenth Amendment.[5] Unlike the moderates in the much larger sister organization, NAWSA—which transformed itself into the League for Women Voters in 1920—the more radical NWP decided that the battle was not yet won with the Nineteenth Amendment. From 1923 through 1972 Alice Paul and the NWP lobbied Congress to pass an Equal Rights Amendment (ERA). The ERA was proposed because the courts maintained that sex, unlike race, color, creed, national origin or religion, was a legitimate basis for class legislation and the NWP did not expect the courts to change their views. In the words of one judge, sex-based classification "had always been made, and, unless prohibited in express terms in the Constitution . . . is a natural and proper one to make" (Salt Lake City 1915). The NWP's suspicions have been borne out: the most recent relevant Supreme Court decision, in 1961, explicitly refused to apply the "equal protection" clause of the Fourteenth Amendment because sex was felt to be a "reasonable basis of classification."[6]

Until a few years ago, the Equal Rights Amendment was the best kept government secret of the century. It is safe to say that as late as 1969 even the majority of avowed feminists in this country had never heard of it nor of the National Women's Party. When the ERA finally passed Congress in 1972 the NWP still was unknown to most women. Although much of this ignorance was due to a general refusal by society to be seriously concerned with women's issues, it also reflected the style of the NWP. From its beginning, the NWP believed that a small group of women concentrating their efforts in the right places was more effective than mass

---

Democratic congressmen in suffrage states, even though many of them individually supported and voted for suffrage and the Democrats had at least voiced token support in their national convention.

[5] For full details see Irwin 1964.

[6] In *Hoyt* v. *Florida* (1961), a woman convicted by an all-male jury of murdering her husband challenged a Florida law stating that women were not required to serve on juries unless they registered such a desire with the clerk of the circuit court. The court said:

We of course recognize that the Fourteenth Amendment reaches not only arbitrary class exclusions from jury service based on race or color, but also all other exclusions which "single out" any class of persons "for different treatment not based on some reasonable classification." . . . In neither respect can we conclude that Florida's statute is not "based on some reasonable classification," and that it is thus infected with unconstitutionality. Despite the enlightened emancipation of women from restrictions and protections of bygone years, and their entry into many parts of community life formerly considered to be reserved to men, woman is still regarded as the center of home and family life. . . . This case in no way resembles those involving race or color in which the circumstances shown were found by this Court to compel a conclusion of purposeful discriminatory exclusions from jury service. . . . There is present here neither the unfortunate atmosphere of ethnic or racial prejudices which underlay the situations depicted in those cases, nor the long course of discriminatory administrative practice which the statistical showing in each of them evinced.

appeal. Ensconced in a large, ancient house near the Senate, it has been harassing Congress for half a century with a small, tightly knit lobbying operation whose members have grown old with the organization. Many people dismissed it as a joke and snidely referred to its indefatigable canvassers as "the tennis shoe ladies" but it did succeed in having the ERA go through committee every year since 1923 and be included in every Democratic and Republican platform since 1944. NWP also provided a core of knowledgeable lobbyists to aid in the addition of "sex" to Title VII of the 1964 Civil Rights Act. Despite its years of political savvy about the intricacies of congressional operation, the NWP was so isolated from any other group of active or interested women that it was incapable of catalyzing a new women's movement. It kept a small flame of feminist feeling burning dimly, but it established no roots in a potential social base. This had to be developed by external forces.

In the 1960s, two networks of communication were created in which women played prominent roles that allowed, even forced, an awakened interest in the old feminist ideas. Thus the movement has two different origins and the resulting branches differ in style, orientation, values, and forms of organization. The first of these will be called the older branch of the movement, in part because it began first, and in part because the median age of its activists has been higher. Its most prominent organization is the National Organization for Women (NOW), but it also contains such groups as the Professional Women's Caucus (PWC), Federally Employed Women (FEW), and the self-defined "right wing" of the movement, the Women's Equity Action League (WEAL). These groups are made up largely of employed women and have been primarily concerned with the problems of working women. Their style of organization tends to be formal, with elected officers, boards of directors, bylaws and the other trappings of democratic structure and procedure. They all started as top-down organizations lacking a mass base. Some have subsequently developed that base, some have not yet done so, and others do not want to develop one.

The younger branch of the movement is all mass base and no national organization. It consists of innumerable small groups engaged in a variety of activities, whose contact with each other is at best tenuous. Its composition, like that of the older branch, tends to be predominantly white, middle class, and college educated, but much more homogeneously so.

It is a common mistake to try to place the various feminist organizations on the traditional left/right spectrum. The terms "reformist" and "radical" are convenient and fit into our preconceived notions about the nature of political organization, but feminism cuts through the usual categories and demands new perspectives in order to be understood. Some groups often called "reformist" have a platform which would so completely change our society it would be unrecognizable. Other groups called "radical" concentrate on the traditional female concerns of love, sex, children, and interpersonal relationships (although with nontraditional views). The activities of the organizations are similarly incongruous. The most typical division of labor is, ironically, that those groups labeled "radical" engage primarily in educational work while the so-called reformist groups are the activists. Structure and style rather than ideology more accurately differentiate the various groups, and even here there has been much borrowing on both sides. In general the older branch has used the traditional forms of political action while the younger branch has been experimental.

As will be seen, the different style and organization of the two branches of the movement were largely derived from the different kind of political education and experiences of the women involved. Women in the older branch were trained and experienced in traditional forms of political action, while the younger branch inherited the loose, flexible, person-oriented attitude of the youth and student movements. The different structures that have evolved have been in turn the primary determinant of the strategy of the two branches. These differences often are perceived as conflicting, but in reality their essential complementarity has been one of the strengths of the movement.

THE FORMATION OF THE NATIONAL ORGANIZATION FOR WOMEN

The National Organization for Women is the oldest, largest, and best known of the organizations in the older branch of the women's movement. The forces which led to its formation were set in motion in 1961 when President Kennedy established the President's Commission on the Status of Women, at the behest of Esther Peterson, then director of the Women's Bureau.[7] The 1963 commission report, *American Women,* and subsequent committee publications documented just how thoroughly women still were denied many rights and opportunities in American society.

The major response to the President's Commission was the creation of state commissions—eventually in all fifty states. While many governors saw them as an easy opportunity to pay off political favors, many women saw the state commissions as opportunities to turn attention to their concerns. These commissions in turn researched and wrote their own reports, which varied widely in quality and depth.

The federal and state commission activity laid the ground for the future movement by providing ample evidence of women's unequal status and creating among many politically active women a climate of expectation that something should and could be done. During this time, two other events of significance occurred. The first was the publication of Betty Friedan's book, *The Feminine Mystique,* in 1963.

---

[7] The Women's Bureau was created in 1920 as a result of feminist activity at that time. Although its main concern has been with women workers, it has done an excellent job of producing reports and pamphlets on many aspects of women's situation. (Single copies of all materials are free upon request from regional bureaus.) Its *Handbook on Women Workers* is the movement's main source book on legal and economic discrimination.

An immediate best seller, it stimulated many women to question the status quo and some women suggested to Friedan that a new organization should be formed to attack their problems. The second event was the addition of "sex" to Title VII of the 1964 Civil Rights Act.

Many thought the "sex" provision was a joke—its initiator, Representative Howard W. Smith of Virginia, only wanted to make the employment section of the bill look silly and sufficiently divide the liberals to prevent its passage. However, the provision was taken very seriously by most of the female members of the House, regardless of party or politics. Representative Martha Griffiths of Michigan, the leading feminist of the House, claims she intended to sponsor the amendment, but held off when she learned of Smith's intentions as she knew he would bring another 100 votes with him. Most of the House liberals opposed the provision, arguing that it would weaken the bill, and Representative Griffiths knew it needed every vote it could get. Despite their many disagreements, both Smith and the liberal opponents played the provision for all the laughs it was worth and the ensuing uproar went down in congressional history as "Ladies Day in the House."[8]

Thanks to determined leadership by the congresswomen and concerted lobbying by the provision's supporters, "sex" was added to the bill, only to be aborted by the very agency set up to administer it. The first executive director of the Equal Employment Opportunity Commission (EEOC), Herman Edelsberg, publicly stated that the provision was a "fluke conceived . . . out of wedlock" (Edelsberg 1965). This attitude caused Griffiths to blast the agency in a speech on the House floor. She declared that the EEOC had "started out by casting disrespect and ridicule on the law" and that their "wholly negative attitude had changed—for the worse" (Griffiths 1966).

Not everyone within the EEOC was opposed to the "sex" provision. There was a feminist coterie that argued that "sex" would be taken more seriously if there were "some sort of NAACP for women" to put pressure on the government. As government employees they could not organize such a group, but they hoped someone would and spoke to several people about this idea.

Ten days after Griffith's speech, the three strands of incipient feminism were tied together and NOW was formed from the knot. On June 30, 1966 the Third National Conference of Commissions on the Status of Women, ironically titled "Targets for Action," forbade the presentation of a resolution calling for the EEOC to treat sex discrimination as seriously as race discrimination; officials said one government agency could not be allowed to pressure another. The small group of women sponsoring the resolution had met the night before with Betty Friedan, in town researching her second book, to discuss the possibility of a civil rights organization for women. Not convinced of its need, they chose instead to propose the resolution. When the conference officials vetoed it, these women held a whispered

---

[8] For a thorough documentation of this event, see Bird 1968, Chapter I. For a blow-by-blow account of the floor happenings, see *Congressional Record,* House, February 8, 1964.

conversation over lunch and agreed to form an action organization independent of government. The time for conferences was over, they felt. Now was the time to fight, and when word leaked out, twenty-eight women paid $5.00 to join the new organization (Friedan 1967). NOW's purpose was "to bring women into full participation in the mainstream of American society now, assuming all the privileges and responsibilities thereof in truly equal partnership with men."

By the time the organizing conference of NOW was held on October 29 and 30, 1966, more than 300 women and men had become charter members of the new organization. They were primarily from the professions, labor, government, and communications fields, and were between the ages of 25 and 45. Although special efforts were made to recruit academic women, and the temporary "office" of NOW was located at the Center for Continuing Education at the University of Wisconsin, very few academic women were among these charter members. According to Kathryn Clarenbach, NOW's first board chairperson, "they were scared to death —even though NOW had no reputation."[9] Nonetheless there were eight college professors and administrators among the original twenty-six board members and officers of NOW. Though few in number, they were very influential.[10]

At the organizing meeting in Washington, a statement of purpose and a national structure were hammered out.[11] The statement articulated a general philosophy of equality and justice under law, rather than specific areas for action. It also emphasized that "women's problems are linked to many broader questions of social justice; their solution will require concerted action by many groups." To research the need for specific actions, seven task forces were set up on discrimination against women in employment, education, and religion; the family; women's image in the mass media; women's political rights and responsibilities; and the problems of poor women. To handle NOW's administrative needs the office was moved to Detroit where it was run by Caroline Davis out of the United Auto Worker's Women's Committee.

NOW's activities for the following year reflected its limited origins more than its broad goals. Its main target was the executive branch where it sought to bend the might of federal power to the benefit of women. NOW's first achievement was to

---

[9] Personal interview, September 22, 1971.

[10] The employment background of the national board and officers was as follows: Board— labor, three; academe, seven; church related, one; government, two; law, two; communications, two; miscellaneous, three. Officers—labor, academe, church, and communications, one each; government, two. Most recent occupation was used as the criterion for classification, and potential cross-filing was arbitrarily eliminated. For example, two academic nuns were counted under "academe" rather than "church."

[11] The first officers accurately reflected NOW's origins. Friedan was elected as president, two former EEOC commissioners as vice-presidents, a representative of the United Auto Workers as secretary-treasurer, and seven past and present members of state commissions on the status of women were appointed to the twenty-member national board. Of the charter members, 126 were Wisconsin residents, and Wisconsin had the most active state commission.

persuade President Johnson to amend Executive Order 11246 which prohibited discrimination on the basis of race, color, religion, or national origin by all holders of federal contracts. On October 13, 1968, Executive Order 11375 became effective, amending the previous Order by the addition of "sex" and also prohibiting sex discrimination in the federal government. This stroke of the pen began a battle between the Office of Federal Contract Compliance (OFCC), set up to enforce the order, and feminist groups. It was not until January 1969 that the OFCC published *proposed* guidelines to combat sex discrimination, and not until eight months later that public hearings were held—at which the proposals were largely supported by women's groups. Nonetheless, the guidelines promulgated in June 1970 were so watered down that they seemed more harmful than helpful. Only six months before, the OFCC had issued Order 4 which outlined the requirements for affirmative action programs, with goals and timetables, to eradicate discrimination by race only. The order would apply to all contractors holding federal contracts. A secret memorandum on the administration of a sex discrimination program under the order had been prepared by the OFCC staff, but it was never issued; it was not until August 1971 that Order 4 was properly revised (Scott and Komisar 1971). (See Chapters Nineteen and Twenty of this book for further detail.)

Despite this second-class interpretation, on June 25, 1970 NOW filed a blanket complaint of sex discrimination against some 1,300 corporations receiving federal funds. The organization also joined with the Women's Equity Action League in its effort to file complaints against all colleges and universities holding federal contracts.

NOW's initial success in the amendment of the Executive Order was not matched in its continuing war with the EEOC. Even before its organizing conference, NOW's temporary steering committee had fired off telegrams to the EEOC urging it to change its ruling that sex-segregated help-wanted advertisements were not in violation of Title VII. In the following months NOW added two more demands: (1) that the *bona fide occupational qualification* (BFOQ) exemption of the EEOC not be interpreted in a way that would permit employers in states with "protective legislation"[12] to use those laws as rationales for denying equal job opportunity; and

---

[12] So-called protective legislation had been passed at the turn of the century in an attempt to curb sweatshop conditions. Originally intended to apply to both sexes, the Supreme Court declared "a violation of the right to contract" those laws which applied to both sexes but allowed those that applied only to women, on the grounds that women's "physical structure and a proper discharge of her maternal functions—having in view not merely her own health, but the well-being of the race—justify legislation to protect her" (*Mueller* v. *Oregon,* 208 U.S. 422, 1908). Though the extent and kind of protective laws differ by state, the bulk of them limit the hours a woman can work (usually to forty-eight per week) and the amount of weight she can lift on the job (generally to thirty-five pounds). Over the years the major use of protective legislation has been to prevent women from earning overtime pay, to bar their promotion to jobs in which overtime might be required, and to restrict access to jobs which occasionally require lifting more weight than the limit.

(2) that the BFOQ specifically not be interpreted to allow airline requirements that stewardesses must retire upon marriage or reaching the age of thirty-two. Hearings on these issues were held in May 1967 after much lobbying by NOW and eventually favorable rulings were obtained on the latter two demands.

The fight over the help-wanted advertisements has not yet been settled. Title VII does not specifically prohibit newspapers from having separate columns by sex or race. It prohibits employers from advertising in them. EEOC early prohibited separate columns by race but allowed "male" and "female" headings to "indicate that some occupations are considered more attractive to persons of one sex than the other" (EEOC guidelines April 22, 1966). From its first angry telegram, NOW has actively pressured the EEOC to change its ruling in order to avoid an employer by employer legal battle. NOW held conferences with commissioners, wrote letters, and testified at EEOC hearings. In December 1967, NOW organized perhaps the first contemporary feminist demonstration with a national day of picketing against the EEOC in several cities. It also filed a formal complaint against the *New York Times,* and a suit against the EEOC to force it to comply with Title VII. Finally, in August 1968, the EEOC ruled that separate want ads were a violation of Title VII and ordered newspapers to desegregate their want ads by December 1. The American Newspaper Publishers Association (ANPA) and the *Washington Star* promptly filed suit. ANPA claimed that compliance would hurt job seekers, employers, and newspapers, and that "newspapers and their advertisers are unwilling to depart so radically from a successful system." The newspaper publishers lost the first round but the district court did order the new EEOC guidelines suspended until an appeal could be decided.[13]

NOW's third initial target was much more recalcitrant than either of the other two. Title VII permitted the Justice Department[14] to enter suits when it felt there was a "pattern and practice" of discrimination and many women's groups strongly urged it to file one on sex discrimination. But justice was deaf to their pleas. It was not until July 1970 that it filed its first sex discrimination case (*U.S.* v. *Libbey-Owens, United Glass and Ceramic Workers of North America, AFL-CIO, Local No. 9*). The case was settled out of court in what many feminists and EEOC staff members felt was a "sell out" (Hole and Levine 1971:32–33). The Department claimed its lack of interest was because the EEOC had only referred one case to them, but since they had an informal arrangement with the agency to decide jointly on which cases they would file, before the EEOC referred them, it appears they did

[13] Despite the court-granted delay, the New York newspapers desegregated on schedule. This was due, in part, to a newly passed city regulation prohibiting separate listing of want ads. In early November, Consumer Affairs Commissioner Gerard M. Weisberg mailed letters to 956 New York City employment agencies saying their licenses would be revoked if they violated the new ordinance. In part, however, the newspaper's compliance was due to NOW's consistent picketing of the venerable *New York Times.* To celebrate, NOW held a "thank-you" picket of the *Times* the day it desegregated (Freeman 1969).

[14] The law was amended in 1972 to permit the EEOC itself to file in court.

not want one. As late as the fall of 1969 their lack of political sensitivity to this issue was apparent in an interview the President's Task Force on the Status of Women had with one official of the civil rights division. "We respond to social turmoil," he told them. "The fact that women have not gone into the streets is indicative that they do not take employment discrimination too seriously."[15]

By NOW's second conference in November 1967, the organization had grown to 1,200 members and lines of tension were already apparent. As the only action organization concerned with women's rights, it had attracted many different kinds of people with many different views on what and how to proceed. With only a national structure and at this point no broad base, it was difficult for individuals to pursue their particular concerns on a local level; they had to persuade the whole organization to support them. Given NOW's top-down structure and limited resources, this placed severe limits on diversity, and in turn, severe strains on the organization.

Conflict came to a head when the 1967 conference proposed a Bill of Rights for Women to be presented to candidates and parties in the 1968 elections. Five points called for enforcement of laws banning sex discrimination in employment; maternity leave rights in employment and in social security benefits; a tax deduction for home and child-care expenses for working parents; child-care centers; equal and unsegregated education; and equal job training opportunities and allowances for women in poverty. These five points presented no problem to the organization, but when some women proposed that support for the Equal Rights Amendment and repeal of all abortion laws be added, several members threatened to walk out.

Women from the United Auto Workers (UAW) opposed inclusion of the ERA not on personal grounds but because their union was against it. They said they would be forced out of NOW if the organization took a stand on the issue. Another group said they would walk out if NOW did *not* speak out. When the ERA was added to the NOW Bill of Rights, the UAW women did not resign, but they did withdraw from active participation. This action cost NOW the use of the UAW office and clerical services, compelling relocation of the national office to Washington, D.C. and creating administrative chaos in the process. Two years later the UAW reversed their stand on the ERA and the members of their Women's Committee resumed active participation in NOW.

The second major disagreement in 1967 was over the inclusion of "reproductive issues." Several women viewed NOW as an "NAACP type organization" and thought it should stick to economic and legal issues. At this time abortion repeal was not a national issue and public discussion was considered controversial. Some NOW members thought that abortion was not a women's rights issue and that support for repeal of abortion laws would only scare off potential financial contributors. Nevertheless NOW supported abortion law repeal, making it the first

[15] Interview with Benjamin Mintz, Office of Civil Rights, Justice Department, October 1969.

time "control of one's body" was stated as a woman's right. This action cost NOW its "conservative" wing a year later (Hole and Levine 1971:67–68).

In the fall of 1968 the many disagreements erupted and NOW fissioned off several new organizations. The "conservatives" announced the formation of the Women's Equity Action League which would concentrate on legal and economic issues, especially in the area of employment and education. Initially, it was concentrated in Ohio and consisted primarily of the former Ohio NOW chapters; but it would eventually make the biggest impact on academe of all the groups.

The "radicals" left because of disagreements on structure, not program. By now the younger branch of the movement was becoming publicly known as was its disavowal of traditional structure. The "radicals," most of whom were from New York, wanted to replace what they felt was NOW's "elitist" structure with decision-making positions chosen by lot. NOW's rejection of this proposal represented not only a preference for traditional forms of structure, but a certain amount of fear of the New York chapter since it had over half the national membership, and was the most active and best known of all the chapters. To many, the New York chapter *was* NOW. Chapters in other cities had gone through many false starts, forming and then collapsing in confusion and inactivity. Unlike New York City, which had easy access to the national media and many people skilled at using it, the other chapters had difficulty developing programs not dependent on the media. As the national program focused almost exclusively on legal cases or federal lobbying, the regional chapters could not easily fit into that either. By the fall of 1968, two years after NOW's founding, the chapters were beginning to get on their feet with local programs. They did not want to see the national organization taken over by New York.

As it turned out, New York did not like the proposed structural changes either and a month later rejected a move to use them in the New York chapter. At this time the three strongest proponents of these changes walked out and formed the October 17th Movement (commemorating the day they left), a group eventually known as The Feminists. Although The Feminists started as a split-off from NOW, most of their new members came from the younger branch of the movement and the group has grown to be one of the more prolific sources of radical feminist ideas.

If the conservatives walked out over programs and the radicals over structure, the third group to leave that fall departed from impatience. Since 1966, NOW had been trying to form a tax-exempt sister organization to handle legal cases modeled on the NAACP Legal Defense and Education Fund. In 1968, it was running into numerous problems and three of the lawyers—Mary Eastwood, Caruthers Berger, and Sylvia Ellison—walked out in disgust. With them they took NOW's most important legal cases, on which they had been working.[16] Eventually these lawyers

---

[16] These were *Bowe* v. *Colgate Palmolive* and *Menglekock* v. *State of California*. The former has been settled favorably and the latter is still in court. The Legal Defense Fund did not begin operation until 1971.

formed Human Rights for Women (HRW), a nonprofit, tax-exempt corporation to support sex discrimination cases.

With the departure of these lawyers, the Washington office collapsed, since they had been its prime volunteers. In an attempt to avoid a repetition of this problem, the NOW office moved to New York and hired its first (poorly) paid staff member, who serviced the organization out of her home. This was not the end of office problems, and in 1970 it moved to Chicago. As the national administrative machinery began to get into gear so that mail could be answered, referrals could be made to chapters, and program ideas could be distributed, NOW's emphasis shifted to the development of local chapters.

The next two years were spent putting together a grass-roots organization, and forming liaisons with the younger branch of the movement. In November 1969, the first Congress to Unite Women was held in New York and several others were held elsewhere during the following year. They were largely unsuccessful. Fraught with dissension, backbiting, and namecalling, they did not result in any umbrella organization to speak for the interests of all feminists. But this very failure portended some success, as feminists from both branches—but particularly from NOW —began to realize that a diverse movement might be more valuable than a united one. The multitude of different groups reached out to different kinds of women, served different functions within the movement, and presented a wide variety of feminist ideas. Although they made coordinated action difficult, they allowed an individual woman to relate to the movement in the way most appropriate to her life. Fission began to seem creative as it broadened the scope of the movement without weakening its impact. The groups agreed to disagree and to work together where possible. When NOW organized the August 26 strike to commemorate the fiftieth anniversary of the Nineteenth Amendment, it was supported by virtually every feminist group in some manner or other.

This strike marked a turning point for the women's liberation movement. It was the first time that the potential power of the movement became publicly apparent, and with this the movement came of age. It was also the first time the press gave a women's demonstration straight coverage. Weeks before they had given it a good deal of publicity, but mostly because it was a slow summer for news and this appeared to be the most entertaining event of the season. Whether encouraged by the amount of publicity or angered by its tone of wry amusement, women turned out by the thousands in cities all over the country and in two European countries. The sheer numbers shocked everyone—including the organizers—and made it clear that the movement would now have to be taken seriously.

The idea for the strike had originally been a shock to NOW and not a pleasant one. Betty Friedan announced it unilaterally in her farewell speech at the March 1970 convention. It got instant attention from the press and instant groans from NOW members who feared they would look ridiculous if only a few women supported the strike. Spurred by Friedan's announcement to do something, they first redefined the word "strike" from its usual sense, to a "do-your-own-thing" strike. This made it possible for women to participate privately, in their own homes and offices, without having to take to the streets. The strike swelled the ranks of NOW tremendously—some chapters expanded as much as 50 to 70 percent. Among the earlier members of NOW chapters, both young and older women had the same educational and professional background. Following the August 1970 strike the new members who joined the NOW chapters were younger, less apt to have college degrees, and largely embedded in the massive white collar and clerical sectors of the labor force. These new young members helped to relieve the tension between the two branches of the movement.

The August 26 strike also compelled the movement to define its goals narrowly for the first time. The entire history of the movement has been one of broadening its scope and narrowing its immediate goals—a very necessary process for any social movement. The strike was centered around three central demands—abortion on demand, twenty-four hour child-care centers and equal opportunity in employment and education. These were not viewed as the sole goals of the movement, but merely the first steps on the road to liberation. As such, they provided a programmatic structure that gave sympathizers something *to do* rather than just talk about oppression.

At the same time, NOW gained a broader conception of just how interrelated are all social phenomena and the contextual nature of women's situation. At its convention in the fall of 1971, numerous resolutions were passed establishing a feminist position on a multitude of subjects not directly related to women. This move was anticipated by NOW's original Statement of Purpose, its early support of the guaranteed annual income, and its concern with women in poverty. Nonetheless, it was a major break with the past.

In its short six-year life NOW has transformed itself far beyond the expectations of its founders. It still suffers from its original top-down structure but it is no longer a small lobbying group run out of its members' homes. In the past NOW created expectations it could not meet because its members were more skilled at using the press than organizing programs. In the last year it has begun to flesh out the skeleton of those expectations to create a powerful feminist organization with strong roots in its chapters. Friedan retired from the presidency in 1970 and was replaced by former EEOC Commissioner Aileen Hernandez. In 1971 Hernandez was succeeded by Wilma Heide, Pittsburgh chapter officer and national task force leader, a change that reflected the new trend for NOW officers to come up through the ranks. The national task forces have been increased and have begun to coordinate local efforts, so that individual projects can combine a national thrust with instrumentation on the local level.

The activity and success of the task forces vary, but among the more successful has been what was originally called the Campus Coordinating Committee. A rather inactive task force, it was taken over in 1970 by Ann Scott, an English professor at the State University of New York at Buffalo who had become interested in contract compliance and the potentiality of the Executive Order. Scott's first action was to issue 2,500 "Academic Discrimination Kits" with instructions on how to file a complaint of discrimination against one's university and how to formulate an affirmative action plan. Teaching personnel specifically were exempt from Title VII of the Civil Rights Act until it was amended in 1972, but all employees of universities that hold federal contracts—and most of them do—fall under the amended Executive Order 11246. Failure to provide an active affirmative action plan to alleviate discrimination theoretically could result in loss of all federal contracts. While the OFCC has final jurisdiction, it appoints one of the executive departments to oversee compliance for each body of contractors. For universities, this job fell to the Department of Health, Education, and Welfare (HEW).

Consequently, HEW as well as the OFCC has been the target of the barrage of complaints from some 300 campuses around the country. It is impossible to say how many of these were instigated by NOW or NOW members. The task force's policy was not to file complaints on its own but to work through local affiliates and campus groups. The "kit" provided specific information on what to do, and the task force has concentrated on providing back-up action: pressuring Congress to get HEW to investigate specific campuses; lobbying against inadequate affirmative action programs and for the application of Order 4 to sex discrimination. The latter action finally was achieved after NOW threatened a mandamus action against the Department of Labor, which has jurisdiction over the OFCC. On August 31, 1971, Revised Order 4 was issued. (See Chapter Nineteen for further detail on contract compliance procedures.)

THE GROWTH OF THE SMALL GROUPS

During the mid-1960s, unaware and unknown to NOW, the EEOC, and the state commissions, younger women began forming their own movement. Contrary to popular myth, it did not begin on the campus, nor was it started by Students for a Democratic Society (SDS). While few of its activators were students, all were "under 30," and they had obtained their political education as participants or concerned observers of the social action projects of the sixties. These projects, particularly the civil rights movement, attracted a large number of women. Many were to say later that one of the major appeals of this movement was that the social role if not the economic condition of blacks was similar to that of women. But this observation was a retrospective one. At the time most women would not have expressed these thoughts even if they could have articulated them. The few who did were quickly put down.

Whether as participants in civil rights groups, the New Left, peace groups, or in the free universities, women found themselves quickly shunted into traditional roles. One early pamphlet described these roles as those of "workers" and "wives":

the "workers" serviced the radical organizations with their typing and clerical skills and the "wives" serviced the radical men with their homemaking and sexual skills. Those few women who refused these roles and insisted on being accepted in the "realm of the mind" found themselves desexed and often isolated by their comrades (Bernstein et al. 1966).

The situation in which these women found themselves unavoidably conflicted with the ideologies of "participatory democracy," "freedom," and "justice" that they were expressing. They were working in a "freedom movement" but were not very free. Nor did their male colleagues tolerate any dissent. Generally, the men followed the example of Stokeley Carmichael, who cut off all debate on a woman's resolution at a 1964 Student Nonviolent Coordinating Committee conference by saying, "The only position for women in SNCC is prone." The problems for women in the radical movement were raised again and again over the next three years. In Seattle, members of the Socialist Workers Party (SWP) defected and formed the independent Freedom Socialist Club in 1964. The refusal of the SWP to consider "the woman question" was a major cause. Civil rights workers, housewives, and students in New Orleans formed a summer free school discussion group in 1965. Women on the 1966 Meredith Mississippi march held secret nightly meetings after they were ordered to walk on the inside of the march line and be accompanied by a man at all times.

The idea of women's "liberation" was first raised at an SDS convention in December 1965. It was laughed off the floor by the male radicals. Undaunted, some New Left women circulated papers on the issue[17] and tried to interest SDS women in organizing themselves. Although they largely failed, the workshops on women in SDS regional conferences attracted many women who were later to be instrumental in the formation of feminist groups. At the summer 1967 national conference, SDS women finally succeeded in passing a resolution calling for the full participation of women in SDS. Generalizing from their experiences (and unknowingly paralleling the developing NOW program) they also suggested that SDS work on behalf of all women for communal child care, wide dissemination of contraceptives, easily available abortions, and equal sharing of housework. More specifically, they requested that SDS print relevant literature and that the SDS paper solicit articles on women. These requests were largely ignored. Instead, the SDS organ, *New Left Notes,* decorated the page on which the women's resolution appeared with a free-hand drawing of a girl in a baby-doll dress holding a picket sign and petulantly declaring "We want our rights and we want them now!" (*New Left Notes,* July 10, 1967).

No single group or organization among these protest movements directly stimulated the formation of independent women's liberation groups. But together they

[17] "A Kind of Memo" by Casey Hayden and Mary King was circulated in mimeograph form for many months prior to the 1965 SDS convention and largely stimulated the discussion there. The essay was later published in *Liberation.*

created a "radical community" in which like-minded women continually interacted or were made aware of each other. This community provided the necessary network of communication and its radical ideas provided the framework of analysis which "explained" the dismal situation in which radical women found themselves. In this fertile field, the younger branch of the women's movement took root in 1967 and 1968. At least five groups in five different cities (Chicago, Toronto, Seattle, Detroit, and Gainesville, Florida) formed spontaneously and independently of each other. They came at a very auspicious moment: 1967 was the year in which the blacks expelled the whites from the civil rights movement, student power had been discredited by SDS, and the organized New Left was on the wane. Only draft resistance activities were on the increase, and this movement more than any other exemplified the social inequities of the sexes. Men could resist the draft. Women could only counsel resistance. For months women met quietly to analyze their perpetual secondary roles in the radical movement, to assimilate the lessons learned in free university study groups, or to reflect on their treatment in the civil rights movement. They were constantly ridiculed by the men they worked with and told that their meetings with other women were "counterrevolutionary" because it would further splinter an already badly factioned movement. In many ways this very ridicule served to increase their growing rage.

A typical example was the August 1967 National Conference on New Politics convention held in Chicago. Although a women's caucus met for days, it was told its resolution was not significant enough to merit a floor discussion. By threatening to tie up the convention with procedural motions, the women succeeded in having their statement tacked to the end of the agenda. It was never discussed. The chair refused to recognize any of the women standing by the microphones, their hands straining upward. When he instead called on someone to speak on "the forgotten American, the American Indian," five women rushed the podium to demand an explanation. But the chairman just patted one of the women on the head and told her "cool down, little girl, we have more important things to talk about than women's problems."

This was only the beginning. At the 1969 demonstrations at Nixon's inauguration, women asked and received time for two short speeches at the rally, after many objections from the men. When they tried to speak they were hooted down with cries of "take her off the stage and fuck her." This was only one among many such incidents. Despite this friction, women still continued to work within the radical community, and to use the underground press and the free universities to disseminate women's liberation ideas. Many women traveled widely to Left conferences and demonstrations, using the opportunity to talk with other women about the new movement. In spite of public derision by movement men, or perhaps because of it, young women steadily formed new groups around the country.

Although women were quick to use the underground media, they took longer to form their own. Moreover, they had great difficulty articulating their grievances in specific terms. The early Chicago women produced the first Statement of Principles of eight points only after months of work and ended by lamenting that they knew their statement was reformist, but it was the best they could do at the time (*New Left Notes* November 13, 1967). By the time the first national women's liberation gathering took place in August 1968, only five pamphlets had been written.[18]

The three-day meeting in Sandy Springs, Maryland, was limited to twenty women from six cities (Boston, Washington, D.C., Baltimore, New York, Chicago, and Gainesville, Florida) and was to be focused on clarifying the issues that were developing in the embryonic movement. The main question was whether there was a movement at all: should it remain a branch of the radical Left or become an independent women's movement? There was a rough correlation between people's political background and their initial stand on this issue. Those from the New Left favored remaining within the radical fold and those from civil rights and related experiences favored independence. Proponents of the former became known as "politicos" and the latter as "feminists." They traded arguments about whether capitalism or male-dominated social institutions and values were the enemy. The only major agreement to come out of the Sandy Springs meeting was to hold an open national conference in Chicago the following Thanksgiving, and four women from four cities volunteered to arrange it. Although notices were sent out only a month in advance, over 200 women attended from twenty states and Canada. The diversity and rapid growth of the movement were apparent at this convention and the participants returned home turned on by the *idea* of women's liberation and began to organize more and more small groups.

The influx of large numbers of previously apolitical women eventually shifted the balance of power from politicos to feminists, and an independent, autonomous women's liberation movement developed. The continuing hostility of radical men also convinced many politicos to shift to a primarily feminist position. Nonetheless the basic differences in orientation remained. The former politicos continued to see women's issues within a broader political context while the original feminists focused almost exclusively on women's concerns.

Another early disagreement centered on what to call the new women's groups. These discussions occurred primarily in New York and Chicago and revolved around a choice of "radical women" or "women's liberation." The former was favored by most because their identities were tied up with the idea of "radicalism" and they wanted to develop the concept of being radical as a woman, not just of a woman who was a radical. Since many feminists in New York also thought that the term "women's liberation" was too much an imitation of politico jargon, both

---

[18] These pamphlets were "Towards a female liberation movement" by Judith Brown and Beverly Jones; "Position paper on radical women in the professions" by Marlene Dixon; "Towards a radical women's movement" by Marilyn Salzman Webb; "Women in the radical movement: A reply to *Ramparts*" by Evelyn Goldfield, Heather Booth and Sue Munaker; and "The look is you: Towards a strategy for radical women" by Naomi Jaffe and Bernadine Dohrn.

factions agreed to call themselves New York Radical Women. Women in Seattle likewise adopted the name Radical Women as did several groups elsewhere.

The advocates of "women's liberation" liked the term not so much because of its implied identification with third world and black liberation movements, but because they wanted to define the terms of debate in what they saw as a potentially significant movement. They had been educated by the misunderstandings created by the referent, "the Negro problem," which inevitably structured people's thinking in terms of "the problem with Negroes" rather than racism and what to do about it. They were also aware of the historical "woman question" and "Jewish question" which had led to the same mistake. The problem, they felt, was not women but women's liberation, and the best way to get people to think of the problem in those terms was to label it as such from the very beginning.[19]

Women's Liberationists started the first national newsletter for the miniscule movement. The first issue came out in March 1968 as three untitled mimeographed sheets with the tag line "The voice of the women's liberation movement." By the second issue three months later, it had grown to four offset sheets and the label became the name. Under a different editor each issue, *The Voice of the Women's Liberation Movement* (*VWLM*) served as the main vehicle of communication for the growing movement for the next sixteen months. The publication came to represent the national movement to most women who read it, and the term "women's liberation" came to be used more and more frequently.

Initially, the term "women's liberation" applied only to the younger branch of the movement. Organizations such as NOW considered themselves part of a women's movement, but not a women's liberation movement. Gradually, however, more and more NOW people and other women not associated with any particular group adopted the name. Some feminists still do not like to be thought of as part of women's liberation and some of the latter do not like the term feminist, but for most the two terms are synonymous.

The original newsletter ceased publication in June 1969, but during its short life it was a useful organizational tool. Adopting an expansionist policy, its revolving editors gave most issues away free to anyone interested and placed many on book store shelves. It was supported by donations, unpaid labor, some subscriptions, and the sale of women's liberation literature at exorbitant prices.[20] Its purpose was to reach any potential sympathizer in order to let her know that there were others who thought as she did, that she was not isolated but part of a growing sisterhood. It also functioned to put women in contact with other like-minded women

---

[19] Unfortunately they did not anticipate that "liberation" would be caricatured as "lib," "libbie," and "libbest" and contribute to the woman's movement not being taken seriously.

[20] One of the early clashes of women's liberation with the radical movement occurred when the New England Free Press decided to publish women's liberation pamphlets at very low prices. While this made the materials available to a larger public, it undercut the financial base of the newsletter, which was not highly appreciated.

and thus stimulated the formation of new groups. To do this, all mail had to be answered, whether requests for literature, contacts, advice on organizing, or responses to news and articles solicited for subsequent issues. This grew to be a herculean task: the *VWLM* grew from 200 to 2,000 copies, and from six to twenty-five pages in size. It finally died because the work of keeping it up grew too great to handle and because the editors thought no "national newsletter could do justice to the role of 'voice' at the present time" (*VWLM* June 1969:25).

At the time of its demise, there were no other major movement publications. Three months later the first women's liberation newspaper, *off our backs,* was published in Washington, D.C. Thereafter the number of feminist papers and journals increased rapidly. To date there are over a hundred, and many more were started but did not survive. None of the papers are national in scope although they borrow from each other freely. Magazines range from scholarly to popular to propagandistic. Some have a policy of printing literally everything they receive, in the belief that all women have something to say and should be given the opportunity to see their work in print, while others are as exclusive as any professional journal.

In part, these numerous publications were started out of disillusionment with the straight press and the belief that only movement publications would give them fair coverage. Young feminists had been hostile to the press from the beginning—significantly more so than other social movements. Some of this hostility was due to inexperience, but most of it derived from inaccurate press coverage of the social movements and student protests in which women had been active. Unlike blacks, young white women had grown up believing that the press was as objective as it liked to portray itself. When their political experiences revealed gross discrepancies between what they saw at a particular demonstration and what was reported, they withdrew from the press in disgust. Blacks, on the other hand, had never had any illusions about the press and saw the media as a tool to be used.

Most of the media compounded this problem by treating early women's liberation activities with a mixture of humor, ridicule, and disbelief. Some of these early activities did seem funny on the surface. Yippies had utilized Zap actions and guerrilla theater as a respite from the boring ineffectiveness of mass marches. Women's liberation picked up the idea as a way to make a political point in an unusual, eye-catching manner. Some reporters looked at the serious side of these actions, but most of them only laughed. The press treated women's liberation much as society treats women—as entertainment not to be taken seriously.[21] If they thought it would be funnier, newspapers even made up their own actions, of which

---

[21] This was not true in all countries. When the Dolleminas of Holland whistled at men on the streets and held other similar actions, their local press was much more sympathetic. But there was a firmer tradition behind these acts. The Provos there had developed the idea of *ludik* actions to a fine art. These actions were intended to make people laugh and at the same time carry a political message. The press became accustomed to look for the politics and carried this over to reporting *ludik* actions by women.

the "bra-burning" episode is the most notable. There has yet to be a woman in women's liberation to burn a single bra, but this mythical act was widely reported in the press.[22] "Bra" stories and related nonincidents usually got front page coverage, while serious stories on employment discrimination were always on the women's page. Reporters commented more on their interviewees' femininity, marital status, or style of dress than on their political views; and editors ordered production to "get the Karate up front" (North 1970). Underground and New Left papers were often the worst of the lot, frequently running women's liberation stories illustrated by naked women and exaggerated genitalia.[23]

Women's liberationists dealt with the conflict between their desire for coverage and their dislike of misrepresentation by refusing to speak to male reporters. By doing so, they compelled the media to hire more women reporters and to give women journalists opportunities to report news usually denied them. Moreover, they received better coverage. Young feminists had discovered that even sympathetic men were often incapable of understanding what they were talking about because men simply had not had the same experiences as women. They did not, for example, understand women's anger at being treated as sex objects. With women reporters, however, feminists could communicate their concerns through discussions of experiences common to them that were incomprehensible to men.

Nevertheless, women reporters sometimes experienced difficulty covering the movement. Most young activists would not talk to them at all because they assumed that even women reporters from the straight press would give distorted coverage. Those who would consent to be interviewed often required anonymity and frequently demanded the right to edit the final copy, which they were, of course, denied. Reporters were tossed out of women's liberation meetings; hung up on when they phoned; at rallies their notes were grabbed from their hands and destroyed, their microphones were smashed, their cameras were threatened, and their films were stolen (North 1970). But they also found some sympathetic feminists who would talk to them at length, give them reams of material to read, arrange interviews and group discussions for their benefit, and direct them to good sources of information.

The immediate results of these policies were reflected not so much in the quality of the news stories as in their numbers. There was something intriguing about the very difficulty of covering the new movement. Furthermore, the idea that *men* were being excluded from something, especially male *reporters,* generated much more interest than women normally receive. People were *curious* as to why *men* were

---

[22] For details of how this myth developed, see Martin 1971. It should be remembered that draft-card burning was much in the news those days and many other things were going up in smoke.

[23] Sometimes women retaliated. In 1969, Berkeley women held hostage an editor of a new underground newspaper, *Dock of the Bay,* until he agreed to stop publication of a special "sextra" issue planned to raise money for the new paper.

excluded; and if the stories ridiculed feminists for discriminating in this way, many women read between the lines and flocked to join. Female reporters also joined. Initially skeptical, they often found themselves becoming much more involved in the ideas of the movement than they had ever intended. What many thought would be an ordinary story turned out to be a personal revelation.[24]

In the fall of 1969, the major news media simultaneously decided to carry stories on women's liberation, and they appeared steadily for the next six months. Quickly discovering that only women could cover the movement, editors tried to pick reporters known for their objectivity and nonfeminist views. The results were not unexpected: their female staff became politicized by what they learned. Women writers, researchers, and secretaries became conscious of their secondary role on their own publications, formed their own small groups, and began protesting for better working conditions.[25]

In setting up such groups, feminists developed certain organizing principles. The basic unit of the younger branch of the movement is the small group of from five to twenty women. The groups have a variety of functions but a very consistent style, which deemphasizes structure and damns the idea of leadership. The thousands of groups around the country are virtually independent of each other, linked only by numerous publications, personal correspondence and cross country travelers. Some cities have a coordinating committee which attempts to maintain communication among the local groups and to channel newcomers into appropriate ones. Other cities have women's centers which provide places for meetings, classes, informal gatherings, and emergency assistance to individual women. Neither centers nor coordinating committees have any real power over group activities, let alone group ideas, and most small groups are not formally associated with them.

One result of this style is a very broad-based, creative movement, to which individuals can relate pretty much as they desire, with no concern for orthodoxy or doctrine. Another result is a kind of political impotency. It is virtually impossible to coordinate a national action, assuming there could be any agreement on issues around which to coordinate one. Fortunately, the older branch of the movement does have the structure necessary to coordinate such actions, and is usually the one to initiate them as well, as NOW did for the August 26, 1970 national strike.

[24] For example, the cover stories in *Life, Time, Newsweek,* etc., were almost all personal conversion stories.

[25] *Newsweek,* in particular, illustrated all these phenomena. The person originally assigned to the story was a young writer being "given her chance." Her piece was criticized for lack of objectivity, rewritten by the male editors every week for two months, and finally dropped. In her place a free-lancer who happened to be the wife of one of *Newsweek*'s senior editors was hired. She was paid in advance, specified no undue editing, and wrote the most personal report of all. Despite the fact that it was quite different from *Newsweek*'s usual style, it was printed. In the meantime, women staffers watched these developments with great interest and made plans of their own to commemorate the occasion. They chose the day of the special issue's publication to announce that their complaint of discrimination had been filed with the EEOC.

Common characteristics of the small groups include a conscious lack of formal structure, an emphasis on participation by everyone, a sharing of tasks, and the exclusion of men. This latter policy has been, to observers, one of the most controversial aspects of the movement, but it was and is one of the least controversial issues within the movement itself. There was virtually no debate on this policy in any city at any time. Originally the idea was borrowed from the black power movement, which was much in the public consciousness when the women's liberation movement began. It was reinforced by the unremitting hostility of most of the New Left men. Even when such hostility was not present, women in virtually every group in the United States and Canada soon discovered that the traditional sex roles reasserted themselves in mixed groups regardless of the good intentions of the participants. Men inevitably dominated the discussions, and usually would talk only about how women's liberation related to men, or how men themselves were oppressed by sex roles. In all-female groups women found the discussions were more open, honest, and extensive, and gave them the opportunity they wanted and needed to learn to relate to other women.

The policy of male exclusion was continued because women felt men were largely irrelevant to the development of their movement. Their goal was to reach women, and it was both frustrating and a waste of time to have men present. Women also discovered a tactical advantage to the policy: their activities were taken much more seriously when they insisted that they only wanted to speak with women. The tactic had shock value, as it had in the early insistence that their activities be reported by women. Another result was that men formed groups of their own around the problems of the male sex role.

The basic form of political education of women came not through movement literature, but through "rap groups." In such groups, women explore personal questions of feminist relevance by "rapping" to each other about their individual experiences and analyzing them communally.[26] Unlike the male exclusion policy, the concept of rap groups did not develop spontaneously or without a struggle. The political background of many of the early feminists predisposed them against the rap group as "unpolitical" and they condemned discussion meetings which "degenerated" into "bitch sessions." Other feminists saw that the rap session met a basic need. They seized upon it and created a new institution. From a sociological perspective the rap group is probably the most valuable contribution the women's liberation movement has made so far to the tools for social change.

The rap group serves two main purposes. One is traditional, the other unique. The traditional role is the simple process of bringing women together in a situation of structured interaction. The "radical community" served this function in the formative days of the movement, but when the movement outgrew the Left there was no natural social structure equivalent to the factory, the campus, or the ghetto for maintaining interaction among women. The rap group as an artificial institution

[26] For a thorough elaboration on the function and operation of the rap group see Allen 1970.

providing some degree of structured interaction is similar to the nineteenth-century development of a multitude of women's clubs and organizations around every conceivable social and political concern. Those organizations taught women political skills and eventually served as the primary communications network for the spread of the women's rights movement. Contemporary rap groups may serve much the same function for the future development of the women's movement.

The second purpose of the rap groups is to function as a mechanism for social change. The groups are structures specifically created for the purpose of altering the participants' perceptions and conceptions of themselves and of society at large. The means by which this is done is called "consciousness-raising." The process is very simple. Women come together in small groups to share personal experiences, problems, and feelings. From this group sharing comes the realization that what was thought to be individual is in fact common; that what was thought to be a personal problem has a social cause and a political solution. The rap group attacks the effects of *psychological* oppression and helps women to put it into a feminist context. Women learn to see how social structures and attitudes have molded them from birth and have limited their opportunities. They begin to see the extent to which women have been devalued in this society and how they have developed prejudices against themselves and against other women as a result. They learn to develop self-esteem and to appreciate the value of group solidarity. It is this process of deeply personal attitudinal change that makes the rap group such a powerful tool. Most women find the experience both irreversible and contagious. Once a woman has gone through such a "resocialization," her view of herself and the world is never the same again, whether or not she continues to participate in the movement. Even those who drop out of the group or the movement carry these ideas with them and pass them on to their friends and colleagues.

While the rap groups have been excellent mechanisms for changing individual attitudes, they tend to flounder when their members exhaust the virtues of consciousness-raising and decide they want to do something more concrete. Some groups take on specific projects; some constitute themselves as organizing cells and set up other groups; some become study groups and delve more deeply into feminist and political literature; most just dissolve, leaving their members to look for other feminist activities to join. Because the groups are small and uncoordinated, they take up small tasks that can be handled on a local level. Women have set up women's centers, abortion counseling services, book stores, liberation schools, day-care centers, film and tape production units, research projects, and rock-and-roll bands. Production of a feminist publication is one of the most feasible projects for a small group to handle, which is one reason why there are so many of them. Development of a project is never the result of nationwide planning and thus reflects only the opportunities, needs, and skills of the women engaged in it.

This laissez-faire philosophy of organization has allowed the talents of many women to develop spontaneously and allowed others to learn new skills. It has also created some major problems for the movement. Most women come into the movement via the rap group and most go out from there. There is no easy way to move from a rap group to a project; women either stumble onto one or start their own. Most do neither. Once involved in a project, participation often consumes enormous amounts of time. Moreover, most groups are unwilling to change their structure when they change their tasks. They have accepted the ideology of "structurelessness" without realizing its limitations. The rap group style encourages participation in discussion and its supportive atmosphere elicits personal insight, but neither the style nor the tone of the rap group is very efficient to handle specific tasks. Essentially, this means that the movement is run on a local level by women who can work at it full-time.

Nationally, the movement is not run by anyone, and no public figure commands obedience from any part of it. But because the movement has not chosen women to speak for it, believing that no one could, the media has done the choosing instead. This has created a tremendous amount of animosity between local movement "leaders"—who would deny that they are leaders—and those labeled "leaders" by the media. The movement did not give them their platform, and it cannot take it away from them; so instead it deplores the fact that a platform exists at all.

The problem of "structurelessness" is causing several organizational crises within the movement as a whole.[27] For one, the formation of rap groups as a major movement function has become obsolete. Due to the intense press publicity that began in the fall of 1969, and the numerous "overground" books and articles now being circulated, women's liberation has become a household word. Its issues are discussed and informal rap groups emerge among people who are not formally associated with a movement group. Ironically, this subtle, silent, and subversive spread of feminist consciousness is causing a situation of political unemployment. Educational work is no longer such an overwhelming need. The younger branch of the movement has never had ways of channeling participants into other areas; now that it so desperately needs to develop those areas, it does not even know who are its participants.

The need for a program and the inability of most younger branch movement groups to formulate it has driven young women into other feminist and nonfeminist organizations. Quite a few are joining NOW, despite their original hostility to the older group. Many others are starting and joining a plethora of new organizations. All are now searching for some way to constructively act on the problems of which they have become so aware.

MOVEMENT PROLIFERATION

For the last few years the movement has been marked by an unceasing, uncoordinated fission which has been both its strength and its weakness. Each new group brings an entirely new segment of the female population under its umbrella and

[27] For a more thorough examination of why and how this problem has occurred see Joreen 1972.

exposes even more men and women to the personal reality of feminist revolt through the activities of their friends, colleagues, and relatives. Concomitantly, this diversity makes the possibility of unity more and more remote. While every feminist effort has the moral backing of the movement, very few projects are able to tap the movement's substantive strength. Most feminist organizations still consist of a handful of dedicated people and a large penumbra of hesitant sympathizers.

Predictably, lines of fission in the younger branch have been ideological and the resulting groups short lived. Their impact is left primarily in the feminist literature and in their participants' minds. Within the older branch, lines of fission have followed the other social cleavages of our society—occupation being the most significant. (The 49 percent of adult women who are full-time housewives have yet to organize in any significant way.) What follows is a rough breakdown of the new areas of expansion.

Specifically Feminist Organizations

WEAL was founded by an Ohio lawyer, Elizabeth Boyer, as a result of a split within NOW over the abortion issue. WEAL concentrates its energies on legal and economic discrimination in education and employment and makes a special effort to recruit women who already occupy positions of power. Within the first three years of its formation in 1968, it had acquired representation in more than forty states.

Human Rights for Women also emerged as a result of a split within NOW, but much less intentionally. When the three disgruntled lawyers walked out of the NOW meeting in 1968, they decided that what the movement needed was not another action organization, but a nonprofit, tax-exempt foundation through which research and legal work could be financed. Since its founding. HRW has raised money to finance feminist research projects, and produces an educational newsletter. Its major activity has been the filing of *amicus curiae* briefs in sex discrimination cases.[28]

Government and Politics

Although the state commissions on the status of women do not apply the term "feminist" to themselves, they were the first women's groups with close connections to the government, and many of them still are in operation as fact-finding and occasionally as lobbying groups.

In 1966 President Lyndon Johnson established the Federal Woman's Award Study Group on Careers for Women to recommend new ways of making government service attractive to women. In an almost exact parallel to the formation of NOW, several women from this group decided in 1968 that they would have to

[28] *Phillips* v. *Martin Marietta; Rosenfeld* v. *Southern Pacific; U.S.* v. *Vuitch;* and *Eisenstadt* v. *Baird.*

form a nongovernmental organization to fight discrimination in the government. The organizational result was the aptly named FEW, or Federally Employed Women. With chapters in fifteen cities and headquarters in Washington, D.C., FEW's chief target is the Civil Service Commission. Under a separate provision of Executive Order 11375, the commission is charged with alleviating discrimination within the government and encouraging the active search for and promotion of qualified women to higher government positions. FEW charges that the commission has not seriously enforced the provision, and that it practices extensive discrimination within its own ranks, where it acts as a compromised prosecutor, judge, and jury of discrimination complaints (Hole and Levine 1971:75–77).

At the national level there is an informal women's caucus within the Congress itself, which puts pressure on the EEOC to process sex discrimination cases, and keeps an eye on legislation relevant to women. On July 8, 1969, four Republican congresswomen sent a memorandum to President Nixon berating his administration because it had done nothing of significance in the field of women's rights. They charged that administration officials not only had avoided the issue, but several were known to be positively antiwoman. The congresswomen followed this memorandum with a list of seventeen recommendations including presidential support for new legislation, recruitment of women to top government positions, and thorough investigation into and correction of all areas of sex discrimination in and out of government. They urged enactment of the Equal Rights Amendment and supported the construction of multipurpose day-care centers for the children of working mothers. The presidential response was to appoint a Task Force on Women's Rights and Responsibilities in September 1969. Although the task force submitted its report by December, it was held up for six months because it was "too strong."

Outside the federal government, the most significant development was the formation of the National Women's Political Caucus (NWPC) in July 1971. The immediate impetus to its formation was advance preparation for the 1972 elections. Its emphasis has been to concentrate on local rather than national organization, building state caucuses to carry on most of its work. Its major aim is to elect women to public office in proportion to their percentage in the population. It was one of the most vigorous prods to the sharply increased representation of women at the national party conventions in the summer of 1972. Electing women to office was not the only concern expressed by the 324 women who attended the founding meeting of the NWPC. The caucus has also supported major legislation of concern to women, and legislation concerning the war, poverty and racism, in which it believes women have a special interest.

The Church

Since the advent of the women's liberation movement, many women's caucuses, boards, and special organizations have been formed within the Catholic Church and the Protestant denominations. St. Joan's Alliance, founded in England during the suffrage movement, started an American branch in 1965. The National Coalition of American Nuns was formed in July 1969 "to speak out on human rights and social justice" as well as to urge the ordination of women and "protest any domination . . . by priests, no matter what their hierarchical status." The Joint Committee of Organizations Concerned with the Status of Women in the Church is working for the creation of an official Office of Women's Affairs with the United States Catholic Conference. The Unitarian-Universalist Women's Federation is the most militant of the Protestant groups. Such organizations as Church Women United of the National Council of Churches and the Women's Board of the Methodist Church have been quite active on women's issues and the status of women.[29]

The Professions

There has been a great expansion of activity among women in the professions, either in caucuses within professional associations or through separate women's organizations created to advance the status of women in various fields. There is one omnibus organization, the Professional Women's Caucus which attempts to represent the more general interests of women professionals. Founded in April 1970, PWC attempts to organize professional women who feel they do not fit in elsewhere, as well as to coordinate the efforts of women's groups in professional associations.

Labor

Although several union women were active in the formation of NOW, the movement did not spread rapidly among the ranks of the female blue-collar work force. This is due, in part, to the lack of union organization among women workers which not only leaves them unprotected economically but precludes a network through which feminist ideas can spread. Activist women within the unions have not been able to use their unions to organize on women's issues since, even if women predominate in a particular local, the unions are run by men at the regional and national level. What has happened instead is that individual women have seized upon Title VII to file sex discrimination cases against both their employers and their unions. By filing such cases they have become conscious of the economic discrimination other women face and the need to organize to alleviate it. In Indiana, for instance, women involved in the suit against the Colgate Palmolive Company formed the League of American Working Women (LAWW) to lobby against so-called protective legislation, and for the ERA and other laws beneficial to working women. Through the lawyers who handled their case, they became aware of sex

---

[29] Further detail on the church as well as other new women's groups can be found in Hole and Levine 1971, and Doely 1970.

discrimination cases in other states, handled by the same volunteer feminist attorneys, and are now working to form LAWW chapters elsewhere.

On the West Coast some women formed separate unions when they found it impossible to buck the locals' male power structure. In northern California a group called Women, Inc. struck Crown Zellerbach and Fiberboard plants over their union's protest. They borrowed their idea from women who had closed down a paper mill near Seattle the previous year in protest over its discriminatory hiring practices and separate seniority lists. In their struggle, the Seattle women were refused recognition by their national union, so they decided to name themselves— Local 36-22-36.

The one union which does have a long record of activity on women's issues is the United Auto Workers (UAW), which formed a Women's Department in 1944. The UAW has funded several research projects, lobbied for laws against sex discrimination, and passed strong women's rights resolutions at all its national conventions. Though the UAW once opposed the ERA, it reversed its stand when the UAW Women's Department studies indicated that "protective" laws were more discriminatory than beneficial. Recently the Women's Department has organized a "Network for Economic Rights" (NER) in several states, as a coalition of social action groups to work on legislation prohibiting social and economic discrimination against women and other disadvantaged groups.

Academe

The first women's campus groups to emerge in late 1968 and 1969 were composed primarily of undergraduates who had some relationship to various New Left organizations. With the Left on the wane, energy was poured into women's groups and by 1970 undergraduate women's groups were ubiquitous. The undergraduate groups mirror those off campus in their focus on rap groups and educational work, but they have applied some pressure for the formation of women's studies courses, campus child-care centers, and contraception and abortion services through the student health service.

On many campuses, graduate women have formed separate groups, usually confined to their particular department or professional school. Although many of them serve much the same functions as rap groups, they also reflect the increasing concern of women graduate students about their future careers and employment. Women often are excluded from the informal networks of communication among male faculty and students through which so much information necessary to professional socialization is passed. The graduate caucuses give women a chance to share what bits of information they have and to form their own network. Similarly, they function as support groups for women who are discouraged or feel isolated in the predominantly male graduate schools. More concrete concerns are demonstrated by passing on information about jobs and fellowships, lobbying departments for more women faculty, conducting research on women, and filing formal complaints of discrimination with professional associations. The Women's Law School Caucus at the University of Chicago has sued the Law School under Title VII of the Civil Rights Act, charging that the school in its function as an employment agency has allowed firms that have explicitly refused to hire women graduates to use the Law School premises for recruitment purposes. The League of Academic Women at the University of California at Berkeley filed a federal court suit on February 15, 1972, charging sex discrimination. They seek to compel that university to appoint a percentage of women to the faculty and managerial nonacademic positions approximately equal to the percentage of qualified women in the labor force.

Until very recently, there were few groups of faculty women organized on local campuses around a concern for the position of women. Some statewide organizations of faculty women are now emerging, particularly within the large state university systems. There has been some tendency for faculty women either to join with graduate student women, to form a contingency within the local NOW or WEAL chapter, or to confine their feminist activity to their professional association's women's caucus (see Chapter Sixteen for a detailed account of the growth of these academic caucuses). During the past year there has also been a sharp increase in activity within AAUP chapters and state conferences. By spring 1972 there were well over 200 local Committee W's on the Status of Women within local AAUP chapters, and from these bases Committee W's are joining together to work within the state conference level of the AAUP structure (see Chapter Eighteen).

Associations of nonfaculty campus employees have been fewer in number and much more concentrated on job-related disabilities than any of the other campus groups. The major interest has been better pay and working conditions and an end to discrimination. Thus, many of the employee associations have focused their interests on organizing unions—with or without a feminist approach.

Despite their differences and diversity (Yale, for example, has six separate women's groups), campus groups are joining together in charging their universities and colleges with violation of Executive Order 11375. While some campus groups were formed specifically to compel an HEW investigation, many have seen this as only a part, albeit a major one, of their activities. Concern with contract compliance has brought about coalitions among women who never before considered that they had interests in common.

In the meantime, universities themselves have not been insensitive to the potential power of women's organizations. Many institutions appointed official committees on the status of women, which in turn have produced a number of reports on the status of women (see Chapter Eleven for a review of these reports). So, too, professional associations appointed official committees to examine the status of women within their disciplines. Such official studies, together with studies produced by women's action groups within the disciplines are reviewed in Chapter Thirteen. Detail and quality vary from report to report, but the basic conclusion they all point to is one that feminists have been saying all along: women thin out toward the top of any status hierarchy.

PROSPECTS FOR THE FUTURE

A review of the growth and spread of the women's movement over the past five or six years leaves an impression of both expansion and disintegration. New groups are constantly being formed, older ones slip into quiescence or dissolve in disarray. With an increase in diversity, there is an impression of diffuseness so that one is no longer sure where the movement is or what it is doing, or even what "it" is.

When and where certain aspects of the movement flourish depends on both its environment and internal group dynamics. The younger branch was able to expand rapidly in the beginning because it capitalized on New Left organizations, the interest of the media, and the presence of many members skilled in organizing the local community. Large numbers of new women who entered the movement after 1969 lacked the organizational skills of their predecessors. The ideological opposition to "leadership" and "organization" often prevented these women from acquiring the skills they lacked. Consequently, the growth of movement institutions has not gone beyond the local level and these have been inadequate to accommodate the vast influx of new members. Instead, groups form and then dissolve, stimulating a good deal of consciousness but very little action. The movement continues to grow, but remains unorganized; it pushes constantly into new areas, yet fails to consolidate its gains. Its sympathizers and supporters increase, yet it is unable to weld them into an effective political weapon. Its presence often is felt more as a local irritation than as a sharp prod for change.

The national organizations have had a different focus and different impact. The women and men who founded them had the intention and the skills to use the legal, political and media institutions to change the status of women. This they have done, within the confines of those institutions. They continue to function primarily as pressure groups within the limits of traditional political activity, from campus coalitions to the national level of politics. Their actual membership remains small, their appeal often seems limited, but their impact in the short time in which they have existed has been tremendous. They are thriving at this point because there are clearly delineated tasks to perform and because they have both the personal and political resources to use the institutional tools our society provides for social and political change. Yet these tools permit them to operate only within narrow spheres, and the skills required for effective participation limit the people who take part and the activity that can be undertaken. No movement can long survive on the institutional handouts of a hostile society and it remains to be seen whether the national organizations can exhibit the creativity to develop new resources for future growth.

While the movement spreads erratically, public consciousness expands steadily. In 1972 Louis Harris reported a "swing in attitude—and a dramatic one—is taking place among women in America today." When the Harris group asked in 1971 whether women favored or opposed most of the efforts to strengthen and change women's status in society, respondents were almost equally divided—42 percent in favor of change and 40 percent opposed. Only a year later, American women voiced their approval of such efforts by a substantial 48 percent compared to 36 percent opposed (Harris 1972:2). Harris maintains, however, that this approval is coupled with a distaste for the movement itself as "the phrase 'women's liberation' remains an emotionally charged expression with negative implications for many women" (Harris 1972:5).

This ambivalence is reminiscent of the days when many blacks as well as whites declared their support of the goals of the civil rights movement while deploring its methods. The ambivalent attitude of the public at large toward feminism stems in part from the distorted and confused image painted of it by the press, but it also reflects the fear of the unknown, tinged with the awe of the possible, that people experience when trying to comprehend the implications of new ideas. The resulting mix of foreboding and hope is exacerbated by the apparent lack of a cohesive structure, program, and ideology of the overall women's movement which would provide some guide for action.

The resurgence of feminism has tapped a major source of female energy and anger in an amazingly short period of time. Only part of that energy has been successfully channeled, while the rest of it still is expended on the private front of personal and interpersonal probings. The result is that much of the movement is proliferating underground and may seem far less powerful than it is. The complex and diverse phenomenon that is the feminist movement in 1973 represents a vast reservoir of growing feminist sentiment which only awaits appropriate opportunities to erupt into action.

REFERENCES

Allen, Pamela. 1970. *Free space: A perspective on the small group in women's liberation.* New York: Times Change Press.

Bernstein, Judi et al. 1966. Sisters, brothers, lovers . . . listen. . . . Boston: The New England Free Press.

Bird, Caroline. 1968. *Born female: The high cost of keeping women down.* New York: David McKay Co.

Congressional Record, House of Representatives. February 8, 1964, pp. 2577–2584.

Doely, Sarah Bentley (Ed.). 1970. *Women's liberation and the church.* New York: Association Press.

Edelsberg, Herman. August 25, 1965. N.Y.U. eighteenth conference on labor. *Labor Relations Reporter,* 61:253–255.

Farson, Richard. December 16, 1969. The rage of women. *Look,* 33:21–23.

Freeman, Jo. February 24, 1969. The new feminists. *Nation,* 208(8):243.

Freeman, Jo. January 1973. The origins of the women's liberation movement. *American Journal of Sociology.* 78(4):792–811.

Friedan, Betty. 1963. *The feminine mystique.* New York: Dell Publishing Co.

Friedan, Betty. April 1967. N.O.W., how it began. *Women Speaking,* 10:4.

Griffiths, Martha. June 20, 1966. Speech in the House of Representatives. *Congressional Record,* 89th Congress, 2d Session.

Harris, Louis, and Associates. 1972. *The 1972 Virginia Slims American women's opinion poll.*

Hayden, Casey, and King, Mary. April 1966. Sex and caste: A kind of memo. *Liberation,* 11(2):35.

Hole, Judith and Levine, Ellen. 1971. *Rebirth of feminism.* New York: Quadrangle.

Hoyt v. *Florida* 368 U.S. 57, 59–62, 68 (1961).

Irwin, Inez Haynes. 1964. *Up hill with banners flying: The story of the National Women's Party.* Penobscot, Maine: Traversity Press.

Joreen. 1972. The tyranny of structurelessness. *The Second Wave,* 2(1):20.

Martin, Joanna Foley. 1971. Confessions of a non bra-burner. *Chicago Journalism Review,* 4(7):11.

New Left Notes. July 10, 1967. 2(26):4.

New Left Notes. November 13, 1967. 2(39):2.

North, Sandie. March 1970. Reporting the movement. *Atlantic Monthly,* 225(3):105.

Salt Lake City v. *Wilson.* 46 Utah, 60, 69, 148, pp. 1104, 1107 (1915).

Scott, Ann, and Komisar, Lucy. 1971. *And justice for ALL.* National Organization for Women.

Voice of the Women's Liberation Movement. June 1969.

Wylie, Philip. 1955. *Generation of vipers.* New York: Rinehart.

Part One

Recruitment, Training, and Employment

A.
Choice and Training

Chapter Two

Institutional Barriers to Women Students in Higher Education

Pamela Roby

HIGHER education in America has undergone an unprecedented growth over the past fifty years. In the short span of twenty years, college enrollment has tripled, from 2.3 million students in 1950 to 7 million in 1970. Recent estimates of future growth predict a continuing increase, although at a slower rate, well into the 1980s when enrollment is expected to taper off at about 12 million (Carnegie Commission 1968; Cartter 1970). This phenomenal growth in student enrollment has been matched by a comparable increase in the number of college teachers. As seen in Figure 2.1, there has been a dramatic upturn in the number of doctorates awarded each year during the same twenty-year period that student enrollment underwent its major increase. In the post-World War II period, between 5,000 and 7,000 doctorates were granted each year. In 1970, 30,000 doctorates were awarded. Predictions of future growth vary, but even a conservative estimate foresees about 50,000 doctoral degrees awarded annually by 1980 (Cartter 1970:9).

In *absolute* terms, women have shared in this educational boom. There were some 40,000 women employed as faculty or other professional staff in higher education in the academic year 1939–1940; by 1963–1964 this had almost tripled to 110,000 women (see Table 2.1). So too, the number of doctorates awarded yearly to women has grown from 107 fifty years ago, to almost 4,000 by 1970 (see Table 2.2).

But in *relative* terms, women have lost ground in academe over the past fifty years. Just before World War II, women constituted 28 percent of the faculty and professional staff in academe, but by 1963–1964, this had dropped to 22 percent (see Table 2.1). The proportion of doctoral degrees granted to women shows a similar decrease. In the early 1920s women earned 16 percent of all doctorates. Except for the war years, there was a gradual decline in the proportion of degrees earned by women to a low of 9 percent in 1953–1954. Since then, there has been a gradual increase, but by 1969–1970, women received only 13.3 percent of the degrees awarded, still below their representation fifty years ago (see Table 2.2).

Women, then, have not benefited from the educational boom to the extent men have; they never have had more than a tentative foothold in academe except as tuition-paying undergraduate students. The overriding fact concerning women in

FIGURE 2.1. Annual Awards of Doctorates in the United States, 1919–1969, by Sex

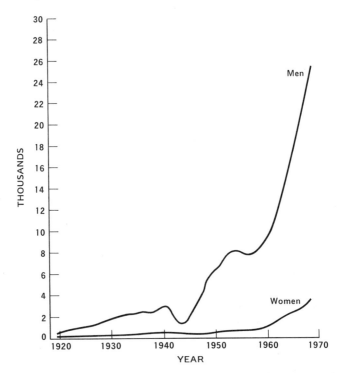

SOURCE: 1919–1947 data: National Academy of Sciences 1963: 51, 53; 1947–1970 data: American Council on Education 1971; 71.193, 71.194.

academe is their continuing *underrepresentation*. This chapter will explore the institutional or structural barriers to the entry of women into higher education and to their ability to persist there long enough to earn higher degrees. By institutional barriers we mean those policies and practices in higher education which hinder women in their efforts to obtain advanced education. These barriers include practices pertaining to student admission, financial aid, student counseling, student services, degree requirements, and curriculum.

ADMISSION

Whether and to what extent women are discriminated against in college admissions is difficult to determine. No national statistics are available on college applicants who have been rejected by institutions of higher education. We know the characteristics of those who are accepted and we can compare women enrollees with men enrollees, but we do not know if the rejection rate is higher among women

TABLE 2.1. Faculty and Other Professional Staff[a] of Institutions of Higher Education, 1939–1964, by Sex

Academic Year	Total Number	Women	Percent Women
1939–40	147,790	40,855	28
1949–50	248,749	71,286	25
1951–52	246,337	58,012	24
1953–54	268,028	61,823	23
1955–56	301,582	69,475	23
1957–58	348,509	78,496	22
1959–60	382,664	84,690	22
1961–62	427,833	94,003	22
1963–64	498,359	110,594	22

SOURCE: American Council on Education 1970:70.125.

[a] Includes full- and part-time faculty for resident instruction in degree credit and other courses, extension courses by mail, radio, TV, short courses, and individual lessons; professional staff for general administration, student personnel services, library, organized research; professional staff in elementary and secondary schools conducted by institutions of higher education. Changes in definitions and categories adopted for the 1966 and following surveys limit comparison with earlier figures.

applicants to colleges than among men applicants, nor whether this varies by type of institution.

In the absence of such information, we must examine indirect and partial evidence. Table 2.3 sets the stage for one approach to the analysis, by giving an overview of the percentage of women at various educational levels. There is full sex equity among high school graduates (women earn 50.4 percent of the high school diplomas). But the transition from high school to a college freshman class involves an immediate attrition of women: women are 44.7 percent of first-time enrollees in institutions of higher education; 43 percent of those earning bachelor's degrees; 39.6 percent of master's degree earners; and, as noted above, a mere 13.3 percent of doctoral degree recipients (see Table 2.3).

If women could be shown to perform more poorly than men in high school, this might account for the drop in the proportion of women between high school graduates and college freshmen. But this clearly is not the case. The American Council on Education (ACE) has conducted periodic surveys of entering freshmen classes of large, national, stratified samples. Their findings consistently show that women's high school academic records are superior to those of male high school graduates. Table 2.4 summarizes their results using two measures of academic performance of all 1971 high school graduates: grade point average and rank position in the graduating class. In every type of institution (with the single exception of four-year technical institutes), a much larger proportion of women than men either earned grade point averages of B+ or better, or placed in the top quarter of their class.

TABLE 2.2. Annual Awards of Doctorates in the United States, 1919–1969, by Sex

Academic Year	Total Doctorates	Number Women	Percent Women	Academic Year	Total Doctorates	Number Women	Percent Women
1919–20	560	90	16.0	1944–45	1,629	333	20.4
1920–21	660	107	16.2	1945–46	1,988	380	19.1
1921–22	780	113	14.4	1946–47	2,949	411	13.9
1922–23	1,062	157	14.7	1947–48	3,989	493	12.3
1923–24	1,124	167	14.8	1948–49	5,050	522	10.3
1924–25	1,203	203	16.8	1949–50	6,420	616	9.5
1925–26	1,438	197	13.6	1950–51	7,338	674	9.1
1926–27	1,538	230	14.9	1951–52	7,683	714	9.2
1927–28	1,617	232	14.3	1952–53	8,309	792	9.5
1928–29	1,907	320	16.7	1953–54	8,996	815	9.0
1929–30	2,058	311	15.1	1954–55	8,840	826	9.3
1930–31	2,329	356	15.2	1955–56	8,903	885	9.9
1931–32	2,397	383	15.9	1956–57	8,756	939	10.7
1932–33	2,452	345	14.0	1957–58	8,942	964	10.7
1933–34	2,692	350	13.0	1958–59	9,360	989	10.5
1934–35	2,582	363	14.0	1959–60	9,829	1,028	10.4
1935–36	2,749	419	15.2	1960–61	10,575	1,112	10.5
1936–37	2,749	405	14.7	1961–62	11,622	1,245	10.7
1937–38	2,731	420	15.3	1962–63	12,822	1,374	10.7
1938–39	2,847	411	14.4	1963–64	14,490	1,535	10.5
1939–40	3,245	421	12.9	1964–65	16,467	1,775	11.6
1940–41	3,566	405	11.3	1965–66	18,239	2,118	11.6
1941–42	3,386	418	12.3	1966–67	20,621	2,457	11.9
1942–43	2,564	390	15.2	1967–68	23,091	2,906	12.5
1943–44	1,939	328	16.9	1968–69	26,189	3,436	13.1
				1969–70	29,872	3,980	13.3

SOURCE: 1919–1947 data—National Academy of Sciences 1963:51, 53; 1947–1970 data—American Council on Education 1971a:71.193, 71.194.

Once in college, women continued to demonstrate superior academic performance. Women freshmen across all types of institutions achieved a better profile of academic performance during their first year at college than did men. Some 28.6 percent of the freshmen women compared to 19.6 percent of the freshmen men earned a grade point average of B or higher in their first year (see Table 2.5).

The same pattern continues into graduate school. Samples of graduate students show that women who reach graduate departments had better undergraduate academic records than men graduate students. Table 2.6 shows that some 37 percent of the women compared to 26 percent of the men graduate students in 1969 had undergraduate grade point averages of A— or better.

These indices of the superior academic performance of women at both undergraduate and graduate levels are important to bear in mind when we examine other

TABLE 2.3. Earned Degrees and First-Time Enrollees in Institutions of Higher Education by Level of Study and Sex: 1970

Earned Degrees and Enrollment	*Total*	*Men*	*Women*	*Percent Women*
High school graduates, 1969–1970	2,906,000	1,439,000	1,467,000	50.4
First-time enrollees in institutions of higher education, 1970	1,775,158	981,154	794,004	44.7
Bachelor's degrees requiring four or five years, 1969–1970	792,316	451,097	341,219	43.0
Second-level (master's) degrees, 1969–1970	208,291	125,624	82,667	39.6
Doctoral degrees (Ph.D., Ed.D., Eng.D., Sci.D.), 1969–1970	29,866	25,890	3,976	13.3

SOURCE: U.S. Department of Health, Education and Welfare 1972:51, 69, 90.

aspects of the educational experience of women and men in higher education. It is traditionally claimed that the rewards of higher education are based on merit. In the light of women's superior academic performance, they should receive *more* financial support in the form of fellowships and grants, be *more* likely to finish their advanced training, and be likely to secure even *better* jobs once they leave the campus. It is an open secret that none of these things have actually happened.

TABLE 2.4. High School Academic Performance of Fall 1971 Entering Freshmen, by Sex and Type of College

Type of College or University	*Percent B+ or better Average HS Grade*		*Percent Top Quarter of HS Class*	
	Men	*Women*	*Men*	*Women*
All institutions	25.1	41.1	35.1	49.7
All two-year colleges	11.1	25.6	15.5	29.3
Two-year public	11.0	26.5	15.4	30.1
Two-year private	11.8	18.2	16.9	23.3
All four-year colleges	29.9	44.3	42.6	55.6
Technical institutions	60.0	45.9	74.9	46.7
Public	17.4	39.9	30.8	54.5
Private nonsectarian	36.4	54.2	47.7	60.7
Protestant	28.9	59.0	42.4	58.9
Catholic	28.5	44.8	35.2	49.1
All universities	43.2	59.7	59.1	70.6
Public	37.2	56.8	54.9	69.0
Private	63.0	72.6	72.7	77.8

SOURCE: American Council on Education 1971b:25, 33.

TABLE 2.5. Grade Point Average during First Year of College, by Type of
Institution and Sex: 1966–1967
(In percentages)

Grade Point Average	All Institutions		Two-Year Colleges		Four-Year Colleges		Universities	
	Men	Women	Men	Women	Men	Women	Men	Women
A— or better	3.9	5.4	2.5	4.3	3.7	5.1	5.7	6.8
B or B+	15.7	23.2	14.1	21.8	14.1	23.6	17.9	23.9
B—	14.0	16.5	22.3	29.3	22.6	32.3	24.9	31.1
C+	22.1	22.0	24.3	22.5	22.2	22.8	20.0	20.3
C	34.3	27.6	37.3	32.5	34.5	26.0	31.4	25.7
D	9.9	5.2	8.5	4.0	10.6	5.3	10.3	6.2

SOURCE: Bayer et al. 1970:19.

One significant remedy to the underrepresentation of women students on all
levels is a very easy one to implement: simply admit women with academic records
that match those of men who are admitted. Though admittedly indirect evidence,
the data reviewed here strongly suggest that institutions of higher education maintain higher standards for the admission of women than they do for men. Here, too,
there are scattered bits of evidence to support the allegation that colleges and universities have "rule of thumb" if not covert quotas on sex which are followed in
the admission procedure. Dr. Peter Muirhead (at the time, associate commissioner
of education of HEW), told the House subcommittee investigating sex discrimination in higher education:

> We know that many colleges admit fixed percentages of men and women each
> year, resulting in a freshman class with fewer women meeting higher standards
> than it would contain if women were admitted on the same basis as men. At
> Cornell University, for example, the ratio of men to women remains 3 to 1

TABLE 2.6. Undergraduate Grade Point Averages of American Graduate
Students in Ph.D. Programs, by Sex
(In percentages)

Undergraduate Grade Point Average	Men	Women	Total
A or A+	9.7	13.8	10.7
A—	16.2	23.1	17.9
B+	22.6	29.4	24.2
B	18.0	16.6	17.7
B—	17.1	10.7	15.5
C+	13.4	5.7	11.5
C or below	2.9	0.8	2.4

SOURCE: Creager 1971:45.

from year to year; at Harvard/Radcliffe it is 4 to 1. The University of North Carolina at Chapel Hill's fall 1969 "Profile of the Freshman Class" states, "admission of women on the freshman level will be restricted to those who are especially well qualified." They admitted 3,231 men or about half of the male applicants, and 747 women, about one-fourth of the female applicants (United States Congress 1970:643).

When Yale University turned coeducational, the president made several speeches assuring alumni that Yale would continue to produce its usual quota of the national "leaders," and it has been no secret that women admitted to Yale have been subject to much more stringent admission reviews than men applicants.

Threat of legal action has on some occasions forced the hand of public universities on this admissions issue. In 1969, a suit that charged the University of Virginia with violation of women's rights was dropped before the court could rule because the university changed its policy to admit women in order to prevent the establishment of legal precedents through court action. At Pennsylvania State University, the faculty senate voted only in 1972 to abolish all student admission quotas for women; the undergraduate ratio of men to women had previously been maintained at 2½ to 1 (Association of American Colleges 1972:1). As Muirhead suggests, there are probably many other state colleges and universities that receive sizable amounts of public funds which still have unpublicized universitywide or departmental fixed quotas to limit the proportion of women admitted.

The use of such discriminatory quotas has been particularly prevalent in medical schools. Dr. Frances S. Norris, M.D., testified to the House subcommittee that the number of women entering medical schools has been limited to a range of 7–10 percent of the total admissions, at least in part because of the admitted prejudice of medical school admissions committees. She testified that interviews with admissions officers at twenty-five northeastern medical schools revealed that "nineteen admitted they accepted men in preference to women unless the women were demonstrably superior" (Murray 1971:251). One "corrective" device used to process admissions is to apply an "equal rejection" theory to the applicants—women applicants are separated from men applicants, and an equal proportion of each sex category is accepted, which means that women are not judged on an equal competitive basis with men. Since women have better academic records than men, and in traditionally masculine fields like medicine and law only the very best women even apply, it is clear that the "equal rejection" procedure discriminates against women. Of some 2,097 women who applied for admission to medical school in 1968–1969, only 976 were accepted (Murray 1971:251). That women constitute only a small proportion of physicians in the United States compared to women in many other countries reflects not a "shortcoming" of women, nor simply the consequence of a long history of systematic discouragement of women aspiring to medical careers, but the systematic exclusion of women by medical schools admissions committees. As Dr. Norris testified: studies of medical school admissions policies make it "apparent that the women rejected from the small female applicant pool were equal to or better than men accepted and that they were rejected because their sex quota was filled" (United States Congress 1970:511–512).

In a seven-year study of the attitudes of medical schools toward women students, Kaplan reported that "widespread prejudice is depriving the nation of urgently needed physicians." One dean is quoted as saying "I just don't like women as people or doctors—they belong at home cooking and cleaning." Another stated "I have enough trouble understanding my wife and daughter—I certainly don't want women as medical students" (*American Medical News* 1970:1).

Dinerman reports that law schools do not follow the quota system that has so notoriously restricted women from medical schools, but they:

> do admit to scrutinizing female applicants more closely for ability and motivation. Some schools give close consideration to the marital status of women before granting admission, and other schools take into account the possibility that a female student might not graduate and continue to practice. It follows that a male applicant is often chosen over an equally qualified female (Dinerman 1969:951).

In his study of female and male law school graduates, White also investigated the views of law school officials and reported that of sixty-three placement officers, forty-three believed that discrimination against women law school graduates is "significant," fourteen stated it was "extensive," and only six felt it was "insignificant" (White 1967:1085).

There is no way we can draw up a balance sheet that distinguishes the extent to which discrimination operates to exclude women from advanced graduate and professional training and the extent to which self-exclusion from advanced training results from the sex-role socialization that inhibits women's aspirations. Sewell's longitudinal study of 1957 Wisconsin high school seniors suggests that women are seriously disadvantaged compared to men because both parents and teachers are far less likely to encourage women to "aim high" in their life goals (Sewell 1971:800). By the time young men and women reach their senior year in college, women have lower aspiration levels than do men. In a nationwide sample of June 1961 college graduates Davis found that only 24 percent of the women (compared to 39 percent of the men) planned to attend graduate school the following year, despite the fact that 63 percent of the women seniors (but only 50 percent of the men) were in the top half of their graduating class. Only 14 percent of the men had *no* plans to attend graduate school at any point in the future, but a full 22 percent of the women considered their formal education at an end when they graduated from college (Davis 1964:85).

FINANCIAL AID

Compared to the admission picture, much firmer data exist on the issue of how men and women support themselves in their passage through higher education.

Much of the research on financial support was triggered by government concern for scientific manpower following the launching of Sputnik in 1957, when it was feared the United States was falling behind the Soviet Union in scientific and technological expertise. From the early 1960s on, the federal government has played a major role in stimulating students to obtain scientific and technical training, and underwriting massive programs of stipends and loans to both individual students and institutions of higher education. The periodic surveys of entering freshmen conducted by the American Council on Education have kept close watch on how students support themselves in college and graduate work. Table 2.7 summarizes the findings of its most recent survey.

TABLE 2.7. Major Sources of Financial Support of College Freshmen, Fall 1971, by Sex
(In percentages)

Sources	Men	Women
Parental or family aid	48.9	61.2
Part-time or summer employment	34.2	22.8
Scholarships and grants	18.4	20.5
Loans (NDEA, institutional, or government insured	13.8	15.9
Savings from employment	11.5	6.9
Other repayable loans	5.6	7.0
Personal military service	4.5	0.2
Parent's military service	1.9	1.8

SOURCE: American Council on Education 1971b:26, 34.

Most college students do not rely on just one source of financial support, but on two or more. Only the most privileged students from financially well-off families have their college bills covered exclusively by their parents. Many hold jobs as well as scholarships; others supplement aid from their parents with summertime employment; still others take out loans and combine study with part-time employment.

There is one major difference between women and men college students in the sources of their financial support. Parents of women undergraduate students provide a much larger share of college costs than parents of men students (61.2 percent versus 48.9 percent). Men, to a much greater extent than women, rely on their own earnings from part-time work, summer jobs, or savings (45.7 percent versus 29.7 percent). The data also suggests a slightly greater tendency for women college students to rely on loans than do men (27.5 percent to 19.4 percent). This is partially balanced by the educational benefits a small proportion of men draw from military service. In general, women show a pattern of greater dependency on parents or borrowing against their future, while men tend to draw on some means of self-support or use benefits or savings. Data are less extensive on the *amount* of financial aid men and women students receive. One national survey of 1969–1970 college sophomores who were full-time students found that the average financial aid awarded to women by institutions was $518 compared to $765 to men (Horch 1972). It is difficult to interpret this difference. More women than men receive aid from their parents, and fewer women than men from families in the lower income brackets attend college—a point we shall return to below. Whether these factors are the cause or the result of the discrepancy in the financial aid awarded to woman and men cannot be determined by these data.

The American Council on Education study mentioned above also examined students' expectations regarding barriers to completing their education (see Table

TABLE 2.8. Expectations That May Hinder College Completion among Entering Freshmen, Fall 1971, by Sex
(In percentages)

Item	Men	Women
Concern about financing education		
No concern	35.3	32.4
Some concern	55.0	56.4
Major concern	9.7	11.2
Estimate chances are very good that they will:		
Drop out temporarily	1.4	1.5
Drop out permanently	0.7	1.0
Work at outside job	33.4	32.9
Get married while in college	7.3	9.8
Transfer to another college	10.9	12.1

SOURCE: American Council on Education 1971b:23, 25, 29, 37.

2.8). Very few men and women college freshmen thought it likely that they would drop out either temporarily or permanently, and only one in ten anticipated that financing their education was a major concern. At the same time, a majority expressed "some concern" about financing their educations, and a third believed that the chances were very good that they would work at outside jobs. Women and men equally expected to contribute to their college expenses in the future. But even among the freshmen, men students were more apt than women students to be working or drawing on earnings from past employment (34.2 percent versus 22.8 percent; see Table 2.7)—a finding that may reflect both greater economic independence of boys in high school and the prolonged dependency of girls on their families until they are somewhat further along in college than their brothers. It also must be borne in mind that both the range and the pay of jobs men students are able to get permit them to contribute a good deal more than women students to the costs of their education. This may make self-support far more attractive to men than to women undergraduates.

Differences by sex in financial support of graduate study are more complex. The sources of support tend to be more varied because there are far more institutional and government stipends available to graduate students, and because graduate students have more personal expenses to meet. Many graduate students rely on a combination of employment, savings, help from their families, plus a graduate stipend or assistantship. Table 2.9 shows the results from the ACE survey of graduate students in 1969. About two-thirds of both women and men graduate students receive some type of institutional aid if they are in doctoral programs. Roughly a third of both women and men rely on the earnings of a spouse to cover some edu-

TABLE 2.9. Sources of Income of American Graduate Students, 1969, by Sex and Highest Degree Expected (In percentages)

Sources of Income[a]	Ph.D. Candidates Only		All Graduate Students[b]	
	Men	Women	Men	Women
Teaching/research assistantship	43.4	37.1	31.0	30.0
Fellowship	25.8	28.7	17.7	15.0
Spouse's job	30.1	32.5	29.3	38.5
Nonacademic job	31.5	22.9	39.2	23.9
Savings and/or investments	31.4	29.6	34.1	30.7
Aid from family	15.7	21.7	17.7	17.8
Loans (personal/government/institutional)	15.8	15.9	18.4	13.0
Other	15.6	12.8	18.3	18.2

SOURCE: Creager 1971:19.

[a] Multiple responses possible, so total exceeds 100 percent.

[b] Includes Ph.D., Ed.D., first professional and subdoctoral-nonprofessional graduate students.

cational expenses. There is a slightly greater tendency for men than women to rely on nonacademic job earnings, and for women to rely more on aid from family and spouse.

Table 2.10 compares the sources of financial support during the undergraduate and graduate school years by sex. As we noted earlier, graduate education is subsidized to a much greater extent than undergraduate education: an increase from about one in five undergraduates to two out of three graduate students. No significant sex differences are found on this dimension of support.

The differences in support by sex found at the undergraduate level are considerably blurred at the graduate level. Men continue to be somewhat more dependent than women on their own efforts, through employment and use of savings or loans, while women are somewhat more dependent on contributions from their families (most frequently, their husbands). Since women tend to marry men somewhat older than themselves and men receive better pay than women, it is clearly the case that husbands of married women graduate students are better able to contribute

TABLE 2.10. Type of Income Sources of 1971 College Freshmen and 1969
Doctoral Graduate Students, by Sex
(In percentages)

	1971 College Freshmen		1969 Ph.D. Students	
Type of Income Sources[a]	Men	Women	Men	Women
Own efforts	69.6	42.8	78.7	68.4
Family efforts	50.8	63.0	45.8	54.2
Institutional efforts	18.4	20.5	69.2	65.8

SOURCE: Computed from Tables 2.8 and 2.9.
[a] Classifications are derived from specific items in Tables 2.8 and 2.9, and are defined as
follows: *Own effort*—nonacademic job, savings, employment, loans, personal military service;
family effort—parents and spouse, parent's military service; *institutional effort*—fellowships,
teaching or research assistantships, scholarships and grants.

toward expenses than can the wives of men students. The ACE survey found that
32 percent of the women graduate students but only 20 percent of the men graduate
students reported a total family income above $12,000 a year (Creager 1971:18).

At both undergraduate and·graduate levels of higher education, women are more
dependent on their families for support of their higher education. The psychological consequences of the differences in financial dependency are crucial and have
never been examined empirically. Whether it is father or husband who contributes
to a woman's education, emotional indebtedness accompanies such support. Data
is not available concerning possible class differences in the differential support of
daughters and sons. It is likely that upper- and middle-class women are assured
financial help through their college years, but what happens to bright young women
from less well off families is not really known. If women depend more on family
support than do men, it may be that daughters in lower middle- and working-class
families are especially penalized compared to their brothers. Not only may such
families have lowered the educational aspirations of their daughters to a greater
extent than their sons, but they may consider it appropriate for sons to "work their
way" through college, but inappropriate for their daughters to do so.

That social class makes a very great difference in the probability of acquiring
some form of post-high school education has been known for a long time. Sewell
recently calculated these differential chances as follows:

> a high SES student has almost a 2.5 times as much chance as a low SES student
> of continuing in some kind of post-high school education. He has an almost 4
> to 1 advantage in access to college, a 6 to 1 advantage in college graduation,
> and a 9 to 1 advantage in graduate or professional education (Sewell 1971:
> 795).

Sewell points out that the educational chances of males are uniformly greater than
those of females at every SES level. More importantly, this advantage of men over

women increases dramatically as we move down the social class ladder. Thus Sewell estimates that the *percentage advantage of men over women* in completing college education is 28 percent among the top socioeconomic stratum but 86 percent among the bottom stratum. Comparable figures concerning attendance at graduate or professional school are 129 percent for the top and 250 percent for the bottom strata (Sewell 1971:795). Being a woman *and* coming from a lower income family are powerful deterrents to acquiring a higher education.

Even more persuasive is Sewell's conclusion that the handicaps of social class and sex are great even after academic ability is taken into account:

> The selective influences of socio-economic background and sex operate independently of academic ability at every stage in the process of educational attainment. Social selection is most vividly apparent in the transition from high school to college, but it is operative at every other transition point as well (Sewell 1971:796).

Sewell estimates that if women's opportunities for acquiring a higher education had been equalized in the cohort he studied, there would have been a 28 percent increase in the number of women who obtained some schooling beyond high school, a 52 percent increase in the number who attended college, and a 68 percent increase in the number who graduated from college (Sewell 1971:796). Since working class families are larger and have fewer resources to support all their children through college, sons frequently are singled out for higher education while their daughters take a two-year nursing course, a three-month course to qualify as a beautician, a year's secretarial course, or move directly from high school to clerical, sales, operative, and service occupations.

There is little evidence of great differences by sex in institutional financial support. However, if academic competence and performance strictly determined who receives fellowships and assistantships, more women than men would receive support, since women demonstrate superior overall academic performance. In his 1961 study of college graduates, Davis found that women were slightly less apt to apply for financial aid than men in all fields except the social sciences and the health professions (Davis 1964:204).

There are many situations in which women simply are not considered for particularly lucrative fellowships. Women represent one-third of the student body at the New York University Law School, but it took a considerable amount of pressure from the school's Women's Rights Committee before the law school would even consider women for its highly coveted scholarships, the prestigious and lucrative Root-Tilden and Snow Scholarships. As two of the women testified at a congressional hearing:

> Twenty Root-Tilden Scholarships worth more than $10,000 each were awarded to male "future public leaders" each year. Women, of course, can't be leaders, and NYU contributed its share to making that presumption a reality by its exclusionary policy (Hearings 1970:584, 588).

Murray reports a similar charge against Cornell University regarding scholarships and prizes open to arts and science undergraduates but restricted on the basis of sex. Women, it turned out, were "eligible" for only 15 percent of these annual scholarships (Murray 1971:255).

Another restriction upon the aid for which women may apply is the limitation of practically all federal scholarship and loan aid to full-time students. There is only a small difference by sex in the proportion of doctoral graduate students who are enrolled on a part-time basis (30.7 percent of the women and 26.6 percent of the men; see Creager 1971:36), but there is reason to believe that many women, particularly those who are married and carrying family responsibilities, would *prefer* to be part-time students. The pressure on graduate students to enroll on a full-time basis is itself a coercive factor that shapes the marital patterns of all couples in which one or both partners is a student. An increasing number of young husbands and wives are attempting to share family and household responsibilities equally (Astin 1969). The requirement that one partner must study or work full-time makes an equal division of familial responsibilities very difficult. Pressure on employers to provide the option of part-time work may increase in the future, if we can extrapolate from an interesting finding in the Creager study of contemporary graduate students: 70 percent of both women and men graduate students endorsed the view that "career will take second place to family obligations" in their lives (Creager 1971:68).

Those who are now part-time students are almost automatically cut off from any real chance for financial assistance. Women often are told they do not qualify or stand little chance for stipend support because "someone is already supporting them"—their husbands. Since women with higher degrees can anticipate considerably lower wages than men, it may also be the case that many women hesitate to borrow too heavily against their future earnings through loans.

One of the serious limitations of studies of financial support to women graduate students is their restriction to women who are *attending* graduate schools. Countless women may never attempt to enter graduate school because they cannot anticipate financial support from either their husbands or schools. The underrepresentation of women in graduate and professional schools is not apt to change until the perceived barriers, as well as the actual barriers, are reduced.

CAMPUS COUNSELING

Once the "entry" barriers have been hurdled the woman student faces a set of obstacles peculiar to her sex in addition to the "normal" trials that accompany advanced training. College advisors have been known to counsel women students away from rigorous, traditionally male courses of study, or away from advanced work of any kind. A woman psychologist reported a member of her department who feels strongly that "women should not be professionals" and shows no hesitation in making his view known to his women students. At another university, women students reported a professor who tells his students that "the fact that women have produced less than men professionally and artistically is an indicator of women's lesser ability." A well-meaning career services officer at Princeton suggested that "although it sounded old-fashioned, it really was a good idea for women to have secretarial skills to fall back on" (Showalter 1970:8). Harris reports the most common question women graduate students hear from their professors is "Are you really serious?" She cites a number of typical responses of faculty to graduate women:

> The admissions committee didn't do their job. There is not one good-looking girl in the entering class.
>
> A pretty girl like you will certainly get married; why don't you stop with an M.A.?
>
> You're so cute. I can't see you as a professor of anything.
>
> We expect women who come here to be competent, good students, but we don't expect them to be brilliant or original.
>
> How old are you anyway? Do you think that a girl like you could handle a job like this? You don't look like the academic type.
>
> Somehow I can never take women in this field seriously.
>
> Any woman who has got this far has got to be a kook. There are already too many women in this Department (Harris 1970:285).

Angered by such statements, University of Chicago graduate women attached a set of them to a page addressed to their professors, explaining why such comments are harmful and offensive to women:

> Comments such as these can hardly be taken as encouragement for women students to develop an image of themselves as scholars. They indicate that some of our professors have different expectations about our performance than about the performance of male graduate students—expectations based not on our ability as individuals but on the fact that we are women. Comments like these indicate that we are expected to be decorative objects in the classroom, that we're not likely to finish a Ph.D. and if we do, there must be something "wrong" with us. Single women will get married and drop out. Married women will have children and drop out. And a woman with children ought to stay at home and take care of them rather than study and teach.
>
> Expectations have a great effect on performance. Rosenthal and Jacobson have shown that when teachers expected randomly selected students to "bloom" during the year, these students' IQ's increased significantly above those in a control group. . . . It would be surprising to find that graduate students are immune to this phenomenon. When professors expect less of certain students, those students are likely to respond by producing less (Harris 1970:285).

Consistent with these expectations are the findings of one ACE survey that men

doctoral students are more apt than women students to agree that "the female graduate students in the department are not as dedicated to the field as the males" and
women are considerably more apt than men to agree that "professors in the department don't really take female graduate students seriously" (see Table 2.11).

TABLE 2.11. Attitudes toward Women Graduate Students among Doctoral
Program Graduate Students, 1969, by Sex

Item	Ph.D. Students Only	
	Men	Women
The female graduate students in department are not as dedicated to the field as male students.		
Percent agree	23.6	17.6
Professors in department don't really take female graduate students seriously.		
Percent agree	21.2	30.9

SOURCE: Creager 1971:64, 65.

An atmosphere of disparagement only compounds the normal anxiety associated
with graduate study and works against finding pleasure and success in one's work. In
the Creager study doctoral students were asked to indicate the extent to which certain types of barriers might prevent them from completing graduate work (see
Table 2.12). Both pressure from a spouse and emotional strain were more frequently reported by women than men students. Consistent with their poorer aca-

TABLE 2.12. Perceived Barriers to Completion of Graduate Work among
Doctoral Program Graduate Students, 1969, by Sex
(In percentages)

Factor	Item	Ph.D. Students Only	
		Men	Women
Ability	Academic inability will prevent completion of graduate work: Yes or maybe	20.0	15.4
Interest	Lack of interest will prevent completion of graduate work: Yes or maybe	22.9	23.3
Finances	Lack of finances will prevent completion of graduate work: Yes or maybe	35.4	37.9
Stress	Emotional strain will prevent completion of graduate work: Yes or maybe	27.5	35.3
Spouse	Pressure from spouse will prevent completion of graduate work: Yes or maybe	11.6	15.3

SOURCE: Creager 1971:40, 41, 42.

demic performance, men students more frequently than women view "academic in-ability" as a potential barrier to completion of their work. The most serious poten-tial problem for more than one-third of both women and men is the financial one. Interestingly, there is only a slight tendency for women to report pressure from their spouse more often than men students do. The largest difference by sex is the factor of *emotional strain:* 35 percent of the women students consider this a possible barrier to completion of their graduate work compared to 27 percent of the men graduate students. For a group that so often is made to feel unwelcome, whose creativity is questioned, whose motivation is held suspect, it is surprising that more women students do not report emotional strain as a barrier. One would assume that women who survived these difficulties would find easy acceptance at later stages of their academic careers, but the remaining chapters of this book report quite a dif-ferent story.

CAMPUS REGULATIONS AND SERVICES

Few undergraduate and even fewer graduate women are any longer plagued by campus regulations that traditionally restricted women's personal lives and served as a constant reminder that they were in special need of "protection." On today's campus, the controversy over the assumptions underlying such regulations focuses on the issues of contraception and abortion referral and their inclusion in health services available to women students. In the fall of 1971, American University women students staged a sit-in in the president's office in an effort to secure a campus gynecologist, after less dramatic appeals had failed. Although abortion counseling and referral continues to be a hotly debated issue, one gynecologist at an eastern university has urged these services be considered a key service for women students, since its availability may determine whether or not a woman will be able to remain a student and to attain the level of education she desires.

The second type of service that has been in great demand in recent years is child-care. It has been an uphill battle to convince institutions of higher education that such facilities are much needed by and represent a legitimate service for both stu-dents and younger faculty members that academe should provide to its constituency. One study of women who planned but were not attending graduate school indicated that the availability of child-care facilities topped the list of the factors they con-sidered most important as a condition to graduate study (U.S. Department of Health, Education and Welfare, National Institute of Health 1968:9). Despite this impor-tant finding, most colleges and universities continue to ignore the growing demand for day-care facilities.

CURRICULUM

At both the undergraduate and graduate level women students are often sub-jected to a concentrated dosage of materials formulated by and filtered through an exclusively male perspective. All too often instructors and textbook writers seem to have joined forces to keep "women in their place." Introductory sociology texts are required reading for over 100,000 students a year, but women typically are mentioned only in chapters on the family. In such chapters women are described in their "traditional" roles as full-time homemakers and mothers—roles which in fact only the upper middle classes of affluent societies can afford. "Marriage and the Family" courses rarely have subjected the modern family to a critical examination. In examining thirty-eight marriage and family textbooks published in the years 1958 through 1970, Wolf cited several examples of this:

> In summary, let us imagine the roles of man and woman in a maximally functional nuclear family. The man would play foreman to the woman's role of worker, official to her role of constituent, and perhaps priest to her role of parishioner (Winch 1965:702).

In another gem, Winch equates "masculinity" with being in the "bigtime":

> Commuting is a form of mobility, and from our analysis it follows that it is more masculine to commute than not to commute . . . there does seem to be a feeling in the suburbs that those men who are in the suburbs during the day —tradespeople, city officials, people in the services and the professions—are somehow less hardy, less he-men and less likely to be "in the bigtime" than those who "go into the city" (Winch 1965:400).

In sociological theory courses, as Friedan has noted, structural-functionalists "by giving an absolute meaning and a sanctimonious value to the generic term 'woman's role' . . . put American women into a kind of deep freeze" (Friedan 1963:118). As in Parsons' (1965) theory of social stratification, "what is" quickly becomes interpreted as "what should be."

Sociology is not alone in ignoring female assertiveness, initiative, and creativity. History, economics, psychology, and literature courses also overlook the human needs and the oppression of women as well as their past and potential achievements. In schools of medicine, engineering, and architecture, where the subject matter itself is less apt to be used to reinforce male and depress female egos, women students are nevertheless channeled into such "feminine" specialities as pediatrics, gynecology, and interior design. Women who persevere in a speciality such as surgery often find themselves blocked by hospital administrations that do not allow them to fulfill their internship requirements (see Chapter Fourteen).

Thus college and university professors place heavy emphasis on the culture and achievements of white males, which may contribute to the motivation of white male students, but dampen the motivation of blacks and women, who hear instead the implicit message, "You do not belong among those who make important decisions for or significant contributions to society. . . . If you try to become something other than a housewife or low-income worker, you will be unsuccessful."

Women today, like blacks a half decade ago, are discovering that they have a history and that there are alternatives to a male-dominated society. As women faculty members have gained experience in offering such courses, they report a change in their own attitude to the subject matter they teach, and their students' response to it. Chapter Seventeen will describe the recent upsurge of women's studies courses and programs. It should be noted, however, that a woman student is lucky if she gets one course out of ten that gives any attention to women.

REFERENCES

American Council on Education. 1970. Faculty and staff. *A fact book on higher educa-tion.* Issue 3: 70.125, 70.133.

American Council on Education. 1971a. Earned degrees by sex and control of institution. *A fact book on higher education.* Issue 4: 71.190–71.197.

American Council on Education. 1971b. The American freshmen: national norms for Fall 1971. *ACE Research Reports,* 6(6).

American Medical News. November 23, 1970.

Association of American Colleges. 1972. *On campus with women,* no. 3.

Astin, Helen S. 1969. *The woman doctorate in America.* New York: Russell Sage Foun-dation.

Bayer, Alan E. et al. 1970. The first year of college: A follow-up normative report. *ACE Research Reports,* 5(1):1–72.

Carnegie Commission on Higher Education. 1968. *Quality and equality: New levels of federal responsibility for higher education.* New York: McGraw Hill Book Co.

Cartter, Allan M. 1970. Scientific manpower trends for 1970–1985, and their implica-tions for higher education. Paper presented to AAAS Meeting, Chicago, Illinois. Mimeographed.

Creager, John A. 1971. The American college student: A normative description. *ACE Research Reports,* 6 (5). Washington, D.C.: American Council on Education.

Davis, James A. 1964. *Great aspirations: The graduate school plans of America's college seniors.* Chicago: Aldine Publishing Co.

Dinerman, Bernice. 1969. Sex discrimination in the legal profession. *The American Bar Association Journal,* 55.

Friedan, Betty. 1963. *The feminine mystique.* New York: Dell Publishing Company.

Harris, Ann Sutherland. 1970. The second sex in academe. *AAUP Bulletin,* 56(3): 283–295.

Horch, Dwight. 1972. *How college students finance their education.* Princeton: College Scholarship Service of the College Entrance Examination Board.

Murray, Pauli. 1971. Economic and education inequality based on sex: An overview. *Valparaiso University Law Review,* 5(2):237–280.

National Academy of Sciences-National Research Council. 1963. *Doctorate production in United States universities, 1920–62.* Washington, D.C.: National Academy of Sciences Publication 1142.

Parsons, Talcott. 1965. An analytical approach to the theory of social stratification. *Es-says in sociological theory* (rev. ed.). New York: The Free Press.

Sewell, William H. 1971. Inequality of opportunity for higher education. *American Sociological Review,* 36(5):793–809.

Showalter, Elaine. February 24, 1970. "Women and the university." *Princeton Alumni Weekly.*

United States Congress. 1970. Discrimination against women: Hearings before the Special Subcommittee on Education of the Committee on Education and Labor, House of Representatives, on Section 805 of H.R. 16098, 91st Congress, Second Session. (Cited in Text as Hearings 1970.)

U.S. Department of Health, Education and Welfare. 1972. *Digest of educational statistics—1971 edition.* Washington, D.C.: U.S. Government Printing Office.

U.S. Department of Health, Education and Welfare, National Institutes of Health. 1968. *Women and graduate study.* Washington, D.C.: U.S. Government Printing Office.

White, James J. 1967. Women in the law. *Michigan Law Review,* 65:1051–1122.

Winch, Robert F. 1965. *The modern family.* New York: Holt, Rinehart and Winston.

Wolf, Charlotte. 1971. Sex roles as portrayed in marriage and family textbooks: Contributions to the status quo. Mimeographed.

Chapter Three

Women in the Male World of Higher Education

Pepper Schwartz
Janet Lever

THE ENTERING college student is excited and hopeful that the next four years will bring personal satisfaction and intellectual growth. If that student is a woman, however, she typically brings with her a history of self-doubt, conflicting motivations, and anxieties about her social success, and these factors constitute psychological barriers to academic achievement. In addition, she will confront structural barriers that interfere with the quality of her undergraduate education and influence her ambition for long-term goals. The purpose of this chapter is to describe how these psychological and structural disadvantages interact to shape the unique pattern of obstacles that women face in the male world of higher education.

We will begin with a review of some of the literature on female socialization and certain studies of discrimination against women in academe. In addition, we will draw from data collected during the first year of undergraduate coeducation at Yale College in the academic year 1969–1970. Yale epitomizes the "male world of higher education" and a case study of male-female interaction and role relationships on that campus should illuminate the difficulties a woman confronts in developing a positive self-image as a scholar. And because Yale selected her first women students from an applicant pool of some of the most intellectually capable women in the nation, it was felt that a study of how the Yale experience influenced the self-image and academic aspirations of this promising group of young women would be important in evaluating women's academic potential and their difficulties in achieving that potential. Yale has a long history of being interested only in the education of young men. While women have attended the graduate schools since the turn of the century, they definitely are second class citizens, and there are few women at any rank on the faculty who can serve as role models for women students. A minor but telling point is that there were very few women's rest rooms, no gynecological service in the student health department, and little access to the gymnasium and other facilities until undergraduate women arrived on the Yale campus.

Yale presents what widely is accepted as a "male image." The architecture and ambiance of the school are very much like an old and exclusive men's club. The authors first entered Yale as graduate students in the fall of 1968, and throughout that first year we gained a good deal of insight into the nature of being a woman

57

in academe because the strongly male environment brought into focus certain features found in all institutions of higher education but less noticeable in the coed setting to which we had been accustomed. When the decision was made to admit 500 women to the undergraduate college the following year (establishing a ratio of one female to eight males), we felt that the first months of transition from a 267-year-long bastion of male scholarship to a coeducated campus would provide a rare opportunity to study the trials and adjustments of women in the university setting.

We were not disappointed. The first year of confusion, confrontation, and "infringement" of male "prerogatives" yielded exactly what men considered to *be* their prerogatives and their opinions of the women who had entered their male sanctuary of learning. We interviewed the women as well to learn how these male perspectives influenced them; their feelings about their intellectual abilities; their feelings about managing both a career and family; and the indignities or rebuffs (as well as the encouragements) they had received that they felt were specific to them as women.

PREPARATION FOR FAILURE: THE DOUBLE BIND

An important barrier to the female student's education is her fear of commitment because it may entail denying her "femininity" and lessening her "marketability" as a wife and mother. Many sociologists have noted this role crisis.

> The young girl is asked to be studious and learn, but she increasingly becomes aware that she may not be asked to demonstrate her knowledge. She is asked to be good-looking, and charming and deferential to men, yet she must go to school and compete with young men at all levels of educational training. The syndrome has a variety of labels, like cultural discontinuity or identity stress. Here is where social structural ambiguity or sociological ambivalences come in (Epstein 1970:61).

The young girl is exposed to these ambiguous expectations over and over again. She is told that her role in life will ultimately depend upon the man she marries while a young man's role is determined by what he does; yet throughout the undergraduate years, both women and men are educated alike. Of course, women often are told that their training is like an insurance policy; it is something to rely on if they fail in their real mission in life—to be married and to be a mother (Bettelheim 1962). And if a good marriage, rather than one's schooling is the key to success, then responsible parents are obliged to watch closely over their daughter's social life, encouraging her to be both the "belle of the ball" and a good student, without sensing the contradiction in such demands. The anxieties inherent in this contradiction increase as the girl grows older and passes from high school to college. One student complained of

> the double bind. You had to be intellectually assertive (in class) and play dumb (with men). You had to be ambitious and self-advancing but also sup-

portive and submissive. You had to know when to speak up and when to shut up and never get mixed up (the penalties for misjudging situations were severe: if you shut up in class you'd get a lousy grade and if you spoke up on a date he'd never ask you out again . . . both major failures). You had to be a good student and a good date and standards for the two were usually directly opposed to each other (Schneider 1971:422).

In her study of the "motive to avoid success," Horner showed that most women, either consciously or unconsciously, equate intellectual achievement with loss of femininity and, consequently, with unpopularity and loneliness. She contends that "a bright woman is caught in a double bind. In achievement-oriented situations she worries not only about failures but also about success" (Horner 1969:36–38). With few exceptions, the men in Horner's study believed that intellectual success would enhance, not inhibit, their social success, and therefore they scored relatively low on the "motive to avoid success."

The ambivalences women are likely to encounter are summed up well by a recent Yale Ph.D.:

> The woman professional must cope with the very contradictory drives of her profession and what society expects of her. Men are fortunate that professional success and social success are judged by standards which don't conflict with each other. But what of the woman professional? She is judged by one set of standards as a professional and another set of standards as a woman. She may find that success as a professional detracts from her status as a woman, and feel, as a result, that she must somehow compensate for her professional success in order to prove herself as a woman (Greene Report 1971:5).

Early socialization directly influences the course of a woman's college experience and career plans. The woman is socialized to prefer such "feminine" majors as social work, primary and secondary education, or nursing—fields compatible with the maternal role, which also pose little threat to the man in her life. This socialization is the result not only of parental encouragement, but also the counseling of high school and college teachers and career guidance agencies that so often warn women against entering such masculine fields as medicine, physical science, and theology. In her book, *The Feminine Mystique,* Friedan (1963) described such "sex-directed educators" of the 1950s as counselors who urged female students to avoid *any* career for fear of hampering their sexual adjustment and compromising their femininity.

Women are taught very early in life to value marriage more than work, and many women jeopardize their own education for the sake of their husband's training and career. Women who do not drop out of college altogether may become part-time rather than full-time students; or change campuses year-to-year as their husbands relocate; or postpone graduate school for the sake of raising a family or supporting their husband's professional studies. Of those women who do not interrupt their undergraduate training to get married, there are many who compromise the quality and intensity of their academic experience by expending a great deal of psychic energy and social time in search of a mate. Academic failure may not have as great an impact on women as on men, but should women graduate from college without being engaged to marry, their friends and families are likely to consider them "social failures."

Dating entails other complications as well. Since it is important for a girl to maintain an image of desirability (and marriageability), she will hesitate to turn down dating opportunities. Since it is the men who ask and the women who accept, the timing of dates is at the convenience of men, not of women. The woman student may have an exam or an important paper due the next day, but will hesitate to turn down a date for fear it will endanger her social life. Of course, if she "goes steady" she may be able to control her schedule a little better, but such relationships may develop prematurely into marriage which may in turn lead to leaving college short of a degree.

The struggle to be desirable and popular has important effects on women's long term goals. They often are afraid to commit themselves to such fields as law or medicine because demands of study make social life less flexible, and require long term commitments that may interfere with a boy friend's or husband's future plans.

Interested in her studies, but also concerned about retaining her sexual marketability, the well-socialized woman student is caught in a dilemma. She is never allowed to be a "success" on her intellectual merit alone. She suffers pangs of inadequacy if she is studying in her dorm on a Saturday night instead of being at a dance or party. One transfer from Vassar told us that she would hide in her room on such nights to keep others from thinking that she was unpopular.

This intense pressure toward dating and marriage, coupled with the built-in stresses of academic competition, can have a devastating effect on female friendships. As one Bryn Mawr student said,

> I became aware of how much I hated to be around only other women. It wasn't that I thought that they weren't interesting or exciting; for the most part they were the most interesting group of women I had ever known. The most important thing was being desirable enough to get a boy friend, and/or doing brilliantly, both of which made all of us terribly competitive with each other (Schneider 1971:419).

Women have been taught since childhood that they must compete with other women for the attention of men. Women engage in very few activities that promote cooperation and feelings of dependence on one another for the sake of a common goal, as do men through organized sports for example. Packer and Waggoner give a cultural explanation for the general phenomenon that intellectual women have fewer female friends than male friends:

> From adolescence on, women are encouraged to regard other women solely as potential rivals, as competitors in the dating game. Then too, since women are regarded as "incapable of abstract reasoning," frivolous, and irresponsible, a

woman with academic ambitions is often tempted to shun the company of other women in an attempt to prove to her male colleagues that she at least is "serious" about her work (Packer and Waggoner 1970:29).

It is only recently, through "consciousness raising" sessions and participation in the women's liberation movement, that many academic women have been able to overcome hostility and competitiveness with other women and strive instead to form a community of friends who work together toward the solution of common problems. An interesting recent development is the tendency for graduate students and professional women to join forces in seeking change in their school's policies and practices which discriminate against women. For many of these women, who presumably were less involved in the intense rivalry for a husband as undergraduates, this is nevertheless their first experience of sex solidarity.

THE FEMALE INTELLECT

One of the most harmful effects of female socialization is the preference so many academic women show for intellectual companionship with men rather than with women. Self-doubt about one's intellectual ability is inextricably linked to feelings of self-hatred for having been born female. Women have been accused of being their own worst enemies. Riesman makes this point in his introduction to Bernard's book, *Academic Women:*

> The evidence lies in the tacit league of educated housewives accusing working mothers of neglecting their families, or the preference of women college students for men teachers, or the dislike of women to be "bossed" by other women . . . (Bernard 1964:15).

Many of these prejudices are predicated on stereotypes about the female intellect. These same stereotypes narrow the woman student's choice of college curriculum and postgraduate vocation. For many years we have heard the claim that women excel in verbal skills and are inferior in mathematical ability. Their choice of college majors is restricted further by the widespread belief that they lack the rigorous analytic thinking required for law, engineering, and the physical sciences. When a woman succeeds academically, both male and female friends maintain it is because she is diligent, rather than exceptionally smart or creative. A woman from Brandeis told us:

> At Brandeis women were getting better grades and ruining curves. It's not a question of the women being brighter, it's more a question of the women being able to sit down and memorize some things and conquer it. Whereas men tend to form more concepts and things in a wider view of life—which I think is probably better in the long run.

Even if there appears to be some truth to the assertion that the female intellect displays less originality and creativity than the male intellect, we need not assume that this is because women are innately less intelligent. It is early patterns of female socialization that determine adult behavior. Little girls are rewarded for conformist behavior, for sitting quietly and patiently at tasks until they are completed (both requisites for diligent study habits); but they are discouraged from being competitive, self-assertive, independent, and dominant in their interaction with other children (traits shown to be crucial in raising IQ's) (Maccoby 1971:250). These latter traits play a critical role in creativity in intellectual tasks. Young boys far more than young girls are apt to be encouraged to take risks in both physical and mental endeavors, and risk-taking is another important component of original, creative thinking.

Maccoby suggests a further explanation for women's lack of intellectual creativity. Since those girls who show qualities of dominance and active striving are engaging in sex-inappropriate behavior, they pay a high psychic cost for their intellectual success by suffering high anxiety levels. Maccoby links this high anxiety level to the lower levels of productivity among academic and professional women. Psychological research suggests that anxiety "is especially damaging to creative thinking, for it narrows the range of solution efforts, interferes with breaking set, and prevents scanning of the whole range of elements open to perception" (Maccoby 1971:253). It is interesting to note that the very traits women are encouraged to develop— risk-avoidance, dependency, and low assertiveness or competitiveness—contribute to the observed tendency for college women to perform poorly in the classroom, and thus they are less likely than men students to be perceived by their instructors as outstanding young scholars.

WOMEN AT YALE

The responses of Yale undergraduate men to coeducation, and the women students' reactions to the Yale environment, put in sharp profile many of the long-term influences we have charted in the brief review of sex-role socialization that precedes college entrance. In our study, we interviewed a stratified random sample of fifty men and fifty women, drawn equally from the four class years and the twelve colleges on campus. (Yale is organized into residential colleges much like the Oxford and Cambridge systems in England.)

Yale women, like women elsewhere, vocalized doubts about their identity, their competitive instincts, the relationship of their work to their future as wives and mothers, and their capabilities as scholars. The great majority accepted the premise that their scholarship differed from male scholarship. A junior transfer from an all-woman's school noticed a difference in her classes at Yale and attributed it to the masculine way of doing things:

> I find classes more active here than at Manhattanville. It's probably caused by
> social conditioning—males are trained to think that they should be assertive
> in their roles and that by contesting something they're performing their role,
> being more male, in a way.

Many of the men we interviewed agreed that aggression in the classroom was a male prerogative:

> This girl's classroom discussion was unfeminine. She was authoritative and uncompromising, and those are really masculine traits.

Some women who accepted the traditional definition of the female intellect, felt guilty when they achieved more than "real femininity" would allow. One transfer from a state university told us of her utter relief at being out of the academic spotlight:

> The whole intellectual atmosphere is so terrific. At my first school, I was the only one who read the *New Yorker*—not that I'm such a super brain, but I was there. Here I'm just able to be with people like me and it was such a relief to be, for the first time, the stupidest one in the class. What a fantastic feeling.

Other women, comfortable with social limitations on their intellectual power, were nervous in the face of "rate busters." Women who "came on too strong" in the classroom were embarrassing. It was acceptable and admirable to do well, but it was somewhat out of place to enter into intellectual competition with men. Women who were intellectually aggressive were seen as somewhat deviant. They were people who were compensating for other needs. Women should be quietly competent. If they were brilliant, they were supposed to take great pains to guard against losing their femininity. Some women were happy that they did not have to measure up as the intellectual equals of Yale men. A transfer student was relieved that as a girl, she was outside the bounds of real intellectual competition at Yale:

> I'm not competing with anyone here, but I feel that men here have a built-in power struggle. It doesn't manifest itself in the struggle for higher grades but even when they're sitting at a table, there's a competition for who can make the wittiest comment. Competition is in social intercourse; classes are peripheral as far as that goes. The girls I'm friendly with aren't at all competitive. Most of them are involved with guys . . . for women, that's more significant.

It was easy to see how the women's self-images were reinforced. Many Yale men felt that a woman could not measure up to a man intellectually, at least not in the important ways. One senior felt that women were ill equipped to take full advantage of the Yale experience:

> I don't think Yale women will get as much out of a Yale education as Yale men. I mean, a girl studies all night and goes off to the library and comes back and goes to bed at twelve o'clock, light out, and goes to all her classes and studies. Great. What for?

The Yale men we interviewed felt that the women didn't know how to handle learning with "style." Many times a man felt put off by a woman who acted too aggressive in class, or who didn't know how to handle an agrument with scholarly acumen. The women didn't know how to play Yale "word games." When they got into serious battles they earned a good deal of contempt for being "uncool." Again, it was another "damned if you do, damned if you don't" situation.

Men often belittled and assumed a position of tolerance and condescension toward women who were excited about their work. A junior told us his observations on male tractability:

> In classes when one of these girls really takes odds with an opinion, there is some competition. But usually, the male will just give in. He feels, "Oh well, she doesn't know what she's talking about." Or, he may just believe in social deference, you know, "Oh well, let her have her way."

When women students realize that they are not being taken very seriously, they are even more affected by the psychological fears they have brought with them. Why play the male game if you are denied male rewards? Women watch men argue with one another, play word games, and try to win one another's respect. When they try to compete, a whole new set of rules and sanctions is introduced. Frequently, they find that their entry into the male debate simply is ignored. One sophomore woman talked about her experiences when she tried to be a "man among men":

> I had been to Betty Friedan's lecture and I was discussing it with my boy friend and some other guys at the dinner table. And whenever I made a point, they would say, "That's ridiculous." You know, they would say it matter of fact, like they knew it wasn't true. A boy who'd been to the lecture was there and he would say, "Wait a minute, that is true." And he would explain. Sure enough, all the boys would be quiet and listen to him and say, "Oh yeah, you're right, we didn't realize that." But anything I said, because I wasn't asserting it in a feminine manner, you know, I was trying to use my logic and just assert it as a human being, it wasn't well received . . . more and more I'm seeing that in order to convince any man of your point you have to do it in a cute way. . . . If men want to make a point, they make it and that's the end. They don't have an approved manner and certain style.

Most men believed that the top intellects at Yale were men. The few exceptions, like the female "super scientist types," were considered beyond the pale. Nevertheless, we spoke to quite a few men who said they did like having women in their classes and who specified the "qualifications" of a good female classmate. First there was the "feminine viewpoint" or the "other perspective." Second, there was the feminine attitude—that is, graciousness and support. A woman was expected to contribute, not exhibit, and she was supposed to be supportive to the class and its group objectives. If she was too outstanding, she was abrasive.

We had a conversation with a sophomore who summarized this viewpoint:

> The feminine viewpoint—which I hold exists—is something that is worth having in any profession, but it's not worth having if it's given by a goddess

who knows what you don't know and it's not worth having when it's given by an idiot who doesn't know anything. It's worth having when it's given by somebody relatively equal to yourself.

(Interviewer: What is a goddess?)

A goddess is a girl who transferred here from Radcliffe for the novelty of the thing and because she had straight 800 Boards and was number one in her class and broke the norms on the National Merit Scholarship test, and probably built her first computer at the age of seven. I know a couple like that. Only one here, but she seems pretty human. She accepts her brains, and says, "Well great, I'm brighter than most of the guys, but let's not show it outside of the classroom." So she's pretty good about things like that.

(Interviewer: What about a guy like that?)

I don't hate it much in a guy. I guess I'm a product of my society. If I get shown up by a guy, well, I've had a fighting chance and he's smarter than I am. If I get shown up by a girl, it's a blow to my ego—I'm not supposed to be shown up by girls. I try to be open minded, but that's the way I feel.

The imposition upon women of the "feminine viewpoint" was a common female complaint. A junior was rather bitter about her relegation to one specific purpose in classroom discussions:

We were discussing Lolita's character in English class and they asked me as a woman how it is possible that there would be such a woman at age twelve. And that kind of thing isn't fair. It's obviously intellectually unfair.

Some of the women felt that both male students and male faculty were very self-conscious with women in their classes. Professors as well as students had firm assumptions about what was female and what was male intellect. A junior from Brandeis told us this story:

The only special treatment I get is the special treatment women get all over the place. Not just Yale. In one class, Statistics, I wrote that intuitively it should be one way, but actually it was another. The teacher asked if that was "woman's intuition?" I went up to the guy and bitched about it; he just sort of hedged and stuff. He mentioned on the next test that the girls' mean was higher than the boys' and I said, "Oh whoopee." He's very nice but he's very self-conscious about the whole thing.

Sometimes the confusion was due to sexual tension. A junior from Smith related a particular class experience with which she had to deal:

The only time I was treated differently in classes was in a small group psych course this semester—a T-group. I was the only girl. Everybody said they wanted to rape me. It was run by a Freudian.

Hazards and biases notwithstanding, most women were pleased and excited with the intellectual climate, especially those from girls' schools or women's colleges. They found a stronger intellectual climate and praised the spirit of discourse they found at Yale. A sophomore from Smith told us that it was vastly different from her old school:

> At Smith it seemed to me that whenever you were in class and a girl made a point, you didn't really care much about what she was saying. I don't know if it was because she was a girl, or because the teacher was usually a man and you're more interested in what he had to say. But here I have a polemic attitude with everyone. You defend your position and back it up with logic, and it's much more dynamic, you know, really alive.

A student from Wellesley agreed:

> Nobody talked in my classes at Wellesley. Most of the women never challenged the professor. He was some sort of paternal father figure up there. You could ask him to rephrase or clarify something, but nobody ever said, "That's absurd" like they do here. Guys here will say something is wrong and there will be a running debate.

The authors were disheartened, although not surprised, to hear more women than men articulate their dislike of female professors. A sophomore transfer from Wellesley told us,

> My own personal dislike is women professors. I avoid them whenever possible. The ones I've had at Wellesley just haven't been as good and, well, I just like male professors, especially the ones you get to know better. . . .

Another girl explained exactly what she felt was wrong with the "feminine style of teaching":

> I admire women professors and I think they can be as good as men. But I think generally women might find it hard to be as exciting a lecturer because they can't kid around as much and they don't get as creative. The women I've heard usually rely on their notes, what's prepared, and it's less ladylike for them to kid around or get passionately involved and start yelling or something. It doesn't seem quite the style of women.

And several people just felt that there was more magic between people of the opposite sex—even in the classroom. They were accustomed to using "feminine ploys" to make life easier, and they didn't like being robbed of that kind of interaction. As one girl said,

> Girls who don't want women professors because they're not "good" or because they're not "dynamic" are putting up a front. I want men teachers because they're easier to get along with. There's a flirtation.

Unfortunately, when women students frame their interaction with their male professors in a sexual context, they undercut their intellectual presentation as well as damage their confidence in their own intellectual skills. By showing deference to the male authority figure, by consuming what he teaches without question, and by resorting to coquettish roles to obtain favors and establish friendships, women students neither learn of their real capabilities in the neuter role of student, nor do they challenge their male professors to perform to the best of their ability.

CAREERS AND MARRIAGE

Not only does the women students' preference for male professors reflect their inability to develop a strong self-image as a scholar, but their more general preference for male leadership and male professionals is indicative of some of the problems these students will have in building an image of themselves as "career women." At Yale, both men and women students doubted the ability of a woman to play a dominant role. A junior transfer from Vassar believed that some things —and male leadership was one of them—were immutable:

> I don't have any proof but there's a feeling that men have always been heading things here and that things aren't going to change. I mean women can come here and be coeds, but I think it would sort of boggle their minds if a woman was placed in a position of leadership that has always been filled by a male.

The male monopoly of leadership positions is not limited to Yale. In 93 to 98 percent of the 200 coeducational institutions Oltman surveyed in 1970, men filled the offices of president and vice-president (Oltman 1970:14–15). Even on the undergraduate level, women who might want to fill leadership roles soon come to understand that such positions are closed to them. The best they can hope for are the lower offices in the student government. More often the only prestigious positions in which they find other women are those of beauty queen, cheerleader, and fraternity sweetheart!

Women at Yale, like most women, accepted the presumption of male leadership. The women exhibited anxiety about female intrusions into any traditionally male career. They distrusted female doctors, lawyers, and professors, even when they admitted that they had no rational basis for doing so. One girl was ambivalent but admitted that at an emotional level she reacted negatively to female professionals:

> I admire a woman doctor in that it's such a commitment in terms of time and all that training and sacrifice. But I tend to, well, I don't trust them as much. Thinking about it, my honest reaction is not to want a woman doctor. Maybe I'm just used to all that reassuring masculinity. Maybe there's even some jealousy with a woman who's achieved that much. And females have a notorious lack of trust for one another.

These kinds of feelings create a very frightening situation for the female student. Ostensibly, she is in college to be educated in order to make a contribution to society. But she is unsure of how much she really has to offer and is threatened by the women who prove that it can be done. What if she decides that she too can be capable and outstanding? How will that affect her future as a wife and mother? What will happen if she decides to be a doctor; will that take her out of the marriage market? Surely she has heard remarks like the one this male senior made, and it makes her fear her own amibitions:

> I do think there are some careers that are not suitable for women. I would, for instance, be very afraid of a female lawyer, as I am definitely afraid of a female doctor. Any profession that's taken a lot of educational development along with personal rigor. I don't like the fact that women are able to achieve more than I do. It's one of those middle echelon things. Either teaching, where they are filling a semimaternal role, or in an executive secretary type office. I'd be wary of an executive.

Men, in no uncertain terms, tell the undergraduate female that male dominance must be maintained. A senior was quite specific:

> I would not like my wife to be in the same career. If she beat me out, I don't think I could take it. I would like her to have many of the same interests as myself. I'd like her to be in English at a state university while I was in English at Yale. I'd want her to appreciate my superiority. I'd want to overcome her with my superior learning. I am being facetious but not entirely. Let's be frank about this. I do have to be superior over the girl that I would marry.

Even the men who wanted their wives to work doubted that they would want a woman who was committed to a time-consuming, emotionally demanding *career*. A job was one thing, but a career was another. In particular, they worried about *losing control* over their wife or the family economy. One underclassman told us about a girl whom he liked but with whom he would not get serious:

> A girl I was dating seriously wants to be a corporation lawyer. She'll make a lot more money than I will. Frankly, that's a very big factor in the way I treat her and the way I will treat her in the future. I want to be superior in earning power and stature. So I keep it sort of cold and I don't let the relationship get too serious. I respect her but I don't want that situation.

Thus the women students worried, with justification, about how they could commit themselves to a career and reconcile it with marriage and a family; they did not want to do injustice to one or the other or both. They were afraid to choose a profession that might conflict with their own and their peers' definition of femininity. They were afraid of the implications of "professionalism." A professional is a leader who helps direct other people's lives; therefore, if the professional is a woman, a great many of her traditional roles are violated. She may be regarded as taking on "masculine" traits, forsaking her place as a loved and protected object, and attempting to dominate and direct men's lives, i.e., she is negating her womanhood. This is the image of the "career woman" and it is obvious why most women have trouble identifying with what is understood to be the life style of such a woman. Horner's (1969) research suggests that the women most prone to the anxieties we have discussed, those who ranked highest on the "will to fail," were also the women with the highest intellectual abilities. That is, the most capable women are the most chastised by this double bind.

Of course, some women escape most of these self-doubts and have a healthy self-respect both as an intellect and as a woman, but they are constantly challenged in this self-respect. If by some fluke they miss the message that they should be inferior to their male partner, they nevertheless cannot help but note the kind of women intelligent men typically favor. Some of these women are shocked and upset when they discover that men are not using the same criteria in judging women that women use to judge men. They may become depressed over the fact that many men they know do not think that a woman's mind is an essential consideration in their relationships. One girl put it this way:

> What I don't understand is how Yale guys can be content to date girls from New Haven College. That just really appalls me. I want my husband to be bright. Don't they care whether the girl is smart or not? I was talking to this guy about attributes in people to marry. I told him my husband would have to be on my intellectual level. He asked what that had to do with marriage. I couldn't believe it.

STUDENT-FACULTY RELATIONS

If the woman student is able to deal with the pressures from her peers, her family, and her counselors, she still must face the assumptions and expectations that faculty and other members of the university community reserve for women students. She must cope with being introduced as "cute" and praised as a "decorative object" (a compliment she has never heard applied to her male colleagues), and face professional prejudices about the kind of work academic women produce. If she pushes to prove her dedication and her unswerving ambition, she will be labeled as neurotic. She is fenced in by almost every person she meets. Their assumptions and interpretations concerning her behavior frequently become self-fulfilling. The student is encouraged to doubt herself, her work, and her suitability for creative effort, but she is rewarded for being a "cute young thing." With this kind of psychological support, it is amazing that so many women do persevere, go on to graduate school, and continue to think of themselves as whole women, original and intellectual.

In our personal experience as graduate students at Yale, we assumed that we could give parties, be social, and still be regarded as serious students. But we found that some people in the department began to expect us to take responsibility for all social functions, and at the same time we began to be taken less seriously as academics. In order to recover lost ground, we had to come on hard and aggressive even in casual conversations with members of the faculty. It seemed that the easiest way to prove commitment to intellectual endeavors was to become a one-dimensional, masculinized caricature.

Many women find that as they leave undergraduate and enter graduate school, their sexual status becomes more and more important. Unlike the more protected position of the undergraduate, the graduate woman is sexually approachable in the eyes of the faculty. The sexual component of interaction is more readily acknowledged and sometimes barter systems emerge. The professor trades power and entré into his status category for an affair (or at least sexual bantering) and the woman gives her favors (or the expectation of her favors) for an informal relationship with someone who might never give her any attention if the sexual element were not present. Of course, this presents hazards for long-term professional relationships. Because of the well-known propensity of male professors and women graduate students to become involved with one another, faculty wives often resent their husbands' extended research or writing projects with an attractive female student. A friend of ours at another university netted a very exciting job with a professor on a Friday afternoon and by the following Monday morning she was fired. Apparently the professor's wife doubted his motives or his will power. In any case, the wife was determined that he find someone else—that is, a qualified *male*—for the job.

Men may avoid taking on women students as assistants and collaborators in order to *prevent* any conflict with their wives. In effect, then, there is a tendency toward a polarization in the relationships between faculty men and women graduate students. Some professors may maximize their sexual bargaining power, while at the other extreme there are faculty men who deny promising female students the attention they deserve for fear of arousing the suspicions of their wives and colleagues.

While we would not deny that sexual awareness of the other is always present in heterosexual relationships, we emphasize that it is particularly double-edged in the academic situation. An attractive female student may interpret any interest in her work as having a sexual component and she may rely on this factor to help her through her education. In the long run, this can only be debilitating because the student needs to know she is being encouraged by virtue of her intellect, not by virtue of her sexual interest. It is only the former kind of recognition that will help her develop as a professional who is committed to her field.

Unfortunately, women who enter the coeducational environment soon learn that the school will not make the same kind of investment in them as in their male students. Male professors rarely take them on as protégés and their names are not passed along the informal communications network that is so essential to getting a good job. Besides the avoidance syndrome used as a defense against insinuations of sexual interest, the simple fact is that many professors do not feel that they derive status from cultivating a female disciple. Part of a male professor's reluctance to train female students to continue his line of research stems from his fear that women will place family commitments before professional commitments, or that they may give up their careers altogether. In addition, there are some professors who believe that women do not have the intellectual capabilities of men, and that all efforts toward the higher education of women are a waste of both time and resources.

Male professors encourage male students, and give them the "outside-the-classroom" support that in reality determines the course of a person's academic career. In a recent letter from one professor to another, the head of a department noted all the excellent male students that his department was training. Then he said, "if you're interested in a female student, (so-and-so) is good." In other words, women are in a separate category. They may be used to make a department appear diverse, teach women's subjects, or, more recently, to comply with the demands of the Department of Health, Education and Welfare so as not to risk the loss of federal funds.[1]

Tokenism and blatant discrimination are still the rule. There are numerous examples of insensitivity to the ideal that women should be regarded as professional *equals,* and this is demonstrated when we observe both formal and informal hiring practices. For instance, in a 1971 recruitment letter from a sociologist at the University of Chicago, the writer informed departments that while they already had their "woman," they would be willing to interview other female applicants, but were primarily interested in hiring a "black Negro." The important fact about this instance was that very few departments complained about the implications of a letter of this kind. Of course, complaints would be rather futile. But, it is through just such informal correspondence, at professional conventions and in conversations among old friends that graduate students' names are passed around. Generally the only time a woman's name becomes part of this system is when the department is looking for a "woman."

One place the woman student might be expected to look for professional help and encouragement is to women faculty members. But, as we know, there are very few women on faculties to serve as guides and role models, and those women are grossly underrepresented on committees that make decisions crucial to the women students' academic careers. At Yale there are only 43 women on a faculty of 839, and only 2 women hold tenured rank (Greene Report 1971).

Not only are there few women faculty members on campus, but many of them do not think that women as a group need special attention. They have an "I made it, so can they" attitude. Very few of the female students we spoke to cited any women who had directly influenced their intellectual self-esteem or inspired them to achieve. As one sophomore transfer from Wellesley said:

---

[1] Eighty percent of the nation's institutes of higher education legally could be compelled to revise their employment practices (Robinson 1971:1).

> I can think of many men I admire—Senator Eugene McCarthy for one. But it's really strange. I've followed the women's movement and things like that, but I can't think of one particular woman I'd like to be. I really can't. Well, maybe my mother, but no one in public life.

However, even though students felt career women were suspect, they were anxious to meet such women and talk with them. Most women students found some flaw in every woman they could think of that made the nominee unacceptable as a model. Their criteria for role models were directly related to their ideas of femininity. One junior felt that the professional women she had known were "denying their femininity and were extremely hard. They constantly had to compete with males." It is important to note that the Wellesley transfer quoted above mentioned nothing about Senator McCarthy's competence in his private role as a family man, but like most women we interviewed she demanded competence from female role models in both their public and private lives, thereby lowering the number of women she could admire.

Older, accomplished women do not seek out recognition from women students as "role models" by initiating friendship and support in the student's struggles with psychological and structural obstacles. This vacuum is seen as a serious problem by many women professionals who have an interest in seeing women students succeed in academe. We asked Elga Wasserman, special assistant to the president on the education of women at Yale, what she thought the university's role should be in helping female students. She said,

> I have become aware of how insensitive Yale can be to the aspirations and needs of women. We have a Career Counseling Office which tells students essentially what the requirements for admission to different schools are. They have business people visit and if you want to sign up for an interview, you can. I have made the point that this is not enough for women. "Well, why not?" they ask. "Are our girls going to be different from the boys?" That seems to me to be concealed discrimination.
>
> Liberal as well as conservative members of the faculty are often equally reactionary on this point. They expect women to live up to male expectations. To have the same career pattern. If they can't do it, tough luck! In my view, that is a very antifeminine outlook.
>
> Both are reducing the options for women in a culture which is not really totally equal. Men have role models from the time they are little children. Girls, unless their mothers work, have hardly any. There are no women on this faculty to speak of. Few students know women lawyers, women doctors, or women professors. We must provide role models. Since our society is dominated by men, we must compensate by bringing women, as well as men, into the university community. Students must be helped to overcome the stereotyped view of working women who are represented as some sort of caricature on TV. We are all familiar with the image of the working woman who

snatches everyone's husband or who ends up as a spinster, or at least a neurotic. Eventually, if she lands a man, she changes, and of course, lives happily ever after.[2]

WOMEN'S COLLEGES

One might think that the opportunity for contact with female faculty and for the flowering of female intellect would be greater at women's colleges than at co-educational colleges. While they are idealized as environments supportive to women's needs, actually they are dominated by male faculty who have, it may be assumed, the same assumptions about and expectations of women students as do male faculty at colleges such as Yale. Although 92 percent of all undergraduate women students are enrolled in coeducational institutions (Harris 1970), the women's colleges, especially the Seven Sisters schools, are important symbols of women's intellectual achievement. Barnard, Bryn Mawr, Mount Holyoke, Radcliffe, Smith, Vassar, and Wellesley still attract a large proportion of the most qualified women in the country, but the Gourman Institute ratings show that all women's schools are at least 200 points (on an 800 point scale) below their men's schools counterparts (Harris 1970). Far from giving their students the drive and intellectual curiosity that might justify sex-segregated schools, they provide an insulation from the competition and striving of the outside world. A Yale transfer student from Mills reevaluated her own education and challenged the theory that sex-segregated classrooms were less inhibited and thus more intellectually exciting:

> At Mills they went by the myth that if women separate themselves from men for four years they're going to be able to develop as individuals, whereas in the presence of men they would be intimidated and inhibited. And I think that is really a myth. Take class discussions for example. Whereas women should participate, supposedly because men aren't there, instead there was a lot of apathy.

An article by Schneider about women at Bryn Mawr noted parallel responses:

> The only thing that has made my last year at Bryn Mawr bearable has been women's liberation. . . . Until women's lib, I thought of Bryn Mawr as a cloistered retreat from anything real. (Student, class of 1972)

> The most outstanding part of my "Bryn Mawr experience" was Haverford— to get a Haverford boy friend whom I could be an extension of and whose achievements and respect and friends I could acquire by association. . . . My

[2] More recently we asked Dr. Wasserman if the women faculty members still felt that giving extra attention to the needs of women was unnecessary. Dr. Wasserman told us that the campus climate had changed rather drastically. Women faculty had gone through a great deal of "consciousness raising" and now saw their role as women and as women faculty members in a different light. There seemed to be a much stronger affirmation of their need to be role models and to relate to the women students who came to them for guidance.

reputation at Haverford was of primary importance and fundamentally shaped my self-image. (Class of 1968)

We were totally brainwashed by *that place* to have this incredibly gullible self-image as part of a tradition which gave its alumnae competitiveness in the name of high-standards, self-hate in the name of critical analysis, cocktail-party-ese in the name of well rounded education, elitist snobbery in the name of talent and creative ability! (Class of 1968)

Who were our models? Professors. . . . And except for a few token women (mostly eccentrics from another age) these professors were *men*. . . . (Class of 1965) (Schneider 1971:419–421)

Women's colleges were established because women could not obtain an education elsewhere. Many men's colleges opened their doors to women during the late nineteenth century only because of shrinking enrollment; women were acceptable since they were tuition-paying students who could ease the financial burdens of the colleges. More recently, Yale, Princeton, Dartmouth, and many of the minor Ivy League schools have also been encouraged to accept female students, at least on an exchange basis for quite different reasons. Women were needed to attract the best male applicants, who increasingly were choosing coeducational colleges rather than spending four years in male monasticism. The "geisha girl theory of coeducation" did not mean that these schools recognized women's right to the same kind of education and preparation for a lifetime career as men. It merely meant that the presence of women on campus would augment the daily regimen of male leaders-to-be by simplifying their access to women as companions and future wives.

CONCLUDING REMARKS

The academic circumstances of women students are paradoxical. It is not difficult to see that women are faced with problems specific to their sex. They are thought to be less "creative." On the other hand, they are expected to handle, without institutional help, all the additional responsibilities that their feminine role requires and still rank respectably close to the men in their class. They receive little counseling; they are notoriously shortchanged on financial aid at most schools (if they are married or have children they are almost "unfundable"); and they are expected, as a matter of course, to take care of the needs of the men in their lives, and if married with a family, to assume most of the child-rearing responsibilities. Sometimes these differences in treatment are supported to a bizarre degree. A visiting woman professor at Yale was living in an apartment in the Hall of Graduate Studies when she quite accidentally discovered that the single male professors in the building were receiving maid service while she was not. The university refused to provide maid service because she was a woman! After much discussion it was decided that she would receive maid service just like all the other professors, but that the maid absolutely would not make her bed. After all, *that* truly was a woman's own responsibility!

Most campus administrators impose such restrictions and inconveniences on women without considering the injustice of their policies. For example, there have been graduate women at Yale since 1892, but until the school went coeducational on the undergraduate level, the approximately 900 women who lived on and around the campus never had adequate health care. Yale had no gynecological services. Other small but significant insults were common. Women often were assigned the poorest housing facilities. The only residence that is not gothic, luxurious, and impressive is Helen Hadley Hall—a hall that until 1971 was used exclusively to house graduate women.

From admission to graduation the majority of female students find themselves second-class citizens on the college campus. Nationally, women undergraduates need an A or A– average to be accepted to graduate school while men can enter with a B average (Harris 1970). The interaction of a debilitating psychological inheritance and a discriminatory educational system would seem to be crippling to women students in the male world of higher education, yet women are awarded approximately 40 percent of the nation's bachelor's degrees, 34 percent of all master's degrees, and almost 12 percent of all doctorates (1968 *Handbook of Women Workers*). And at Yale, despite the school's male leadership ethos, only fifteen women or 3 percent of the women undergraduates left during the first year of coeducation—a drop-out rate lower than that of the men students! At the end of the first semester of the academic year 1969–1970, the women's grade point average was slightly higher than the men's. Furthermore, in questionnaires returned by 115 of Yale College's 180 first female graduates, 46 percent stated that they planned immediate postgraduate or professional studies, a figure identical to that of their male counterparts.

The authors were pleased by this high percentage figure, since our research in 1969–1970 had found women extremely confused about the issue of "life after graduation." At that time, the majority agreed with this sophomore transfer from Wellesley:

> I feel like I'm trying to straddle both worlds. Personally I know if I want to be fulfilled that I want to get married and have children. At the same time, after going to school for such a long time and going to Yale and being told that I have a mind and that I should do more than get married and have a baby, I know that I want to be more than a suburban wife. I really don't know how I'm going to handle it.

Our findings supported those of earlier studies. Komarovsky's study of Barnard women in 1968 also showed a tremendous conflict over the question of postgraduate training, especially in the case of those women who planned to marry (Komarovsky 1973). Likewise, Epstein reported that women at a recent convention at

Bennington College showed no clear vision of their future, rejecting both the image of homemaker and that of the working woman (Epstein 1970:65). These women, as women students everywhere, were looking for some model that would justify the struggle that they were going through, but they were having trouble finding one. There are few alternative models that confirm one's sense of sexual self and still encourage competitive and intellectual endeavor. Meanwhile the securities and comforts of family life and "volunteer service" beckon.

Many women interpret these experiences and anxieties as personal failures. They worry that *they* are not bright enough or highly motivated enough to succeed; they do not see their problems as problems of all women students. Their women friends may have taken less ambitious routes and they wonder if they are kidding themselves in not having done the same. Until recently, there has been no one who would take the time to tell them otherwise—no one to say that medicine is not a "masculine" field, no one to say that they are capable of excellence in work and intellectual contributions.

In the last few years the philosophy of women's liberation has begun to give at least some psychological support to women who have entered the male world of higher education. Female studies are not yet "respected" by everyone, but the need and desire for them have been so great that many universities have instituted some kind of program. The passage of the Equal Rights Amendment and the recent investigations by federal agencies of university employment policies have given women a new understanding of what has been systematically denied them. While the educational structure is still anything but supportive, there are changes underway. In the meantime, academic women must continue to depend on their own resources and form alliances with other women to combat the psychological and institutional barriers to their intellect and potential for achievement.

REFERENCES

Bernard, Jessie. 1964. *Academic women.* University Park: Pennsylvania State University Press.
Bettelheim, Bruno. 1962. Growing up female. *Harper's,* 225 (1349):120–128.
Epstein, Cynthia Fuchs. 1970. *Woman's place.* Berkeley: University of California Press.
Friedan, Betty. 1963. *The feminine mystique.* New York: Dell Books.
Greene Report. 1971. A report to the president from the committee on the status of women at Yale. New Haven, Connecticut.
Harris, Ann Sutherland. 1970. The second sex in academe. *AAUP Bulletin,* 56(3): 283–295.
Horner, Matina S. 1969. Women's will to fail. *Psychology Today,* 3:36–38, 62.
Komarovsky, Mirra. 1973. Cultural contradictions and sex roles: The masculine case. *American Journal of Sociology,* 78(4):873–884.
Maccoby, Eleanor. 1971. Women's intellect. In Arlene S. Skolnick and Jerome H. Skolnick (Eds.), *Family in transition.* Boston: Little, Brown and Company, pp. 242–254.

Oltman, Ruth. 1970. Campus 1970—where do women stand? *American Association of University Women Journal,* 64:14–15.

Packer, Barbara, and Waggoner, Karen. 1970. Yale and the new sisterhood. *Yale Alumni Magazine,* 33:26–31.

Robinson, Lora. 1971. The status of academic women. Syracuse, N.Y.: ERIC Clearinghouse on Higher Education, Review 5.

Schneider, Liz. 1971. Our failures only marry: Bryn Mawr and the failure of feminism. In Vivian Gornick and Barbara K. Moran (Eds.), *Women in sexist society.* New York: Basic Books, pp. 419–435.

U.S. Department of Labor, Women's Bureau. 1968. *1968 handbook of women workers.* Washington, D.C.: U.S. Government Printing Office.

Wasserman, Elga. 1970. Coeducation 1969–70. A progress report from the University Committee on Coeducation. New Haven, Conn.: Yale University Press.

Chapter Four

Women Dropouts from Higher Education

Michelle Patterson
Lucy Sells

A GREAT DEAL has been written in recent years on the problem of attrition in higher education, but few studies have probed into the situation of the woman dropout. Furthermore, the more recent national investigations have focused only on the college level (e.g., Astin 1972; Astin and Panos 1969; Trent and Medsker 1968).[1] In contrast, this chapter examines students who enter higher education —both college and graduate school—but who do not complete their course of study. Its aim is to shed some light on the factors that have a differential impact upon the propensity of women and men to drop out.

Despite the fact that the sexes do not differ significantly in intelligence or academic ability, the educational attainment of women is considerably lower than that of men (Folger, Astin, and Bayer 1970). The proportion of women completing degrees beyond high school is smaller than the proportion of men, and declines with each higher degree. Women receive over 40 percent of all bachelor's degrees, about one-third of all master's, and only about 10 percent of all doctorates.

Part of the difference in the educational attainments of women and men is explained by socioeconomic status (SES). Trent and Medsker (1968) found that at the low SES level, only 40 percent of the most able high school students went on to college, while 60 percent of the least able students from high SES backgrounds continued their education. Feldman and Newcomb (1969) report a 1957 study that found that the lower the SES, the smaller the percentage of women (relative to men) who attend college. This finding recently was confirmed by Werts (1966). In a comparison of 76,015 boys and 51,710 girls, controlling for high school grade average and father's occupation, Werts found that the college entrance rates of boys and girls of high SES were very similar, but that among low SES students, boys were much more likely than girls to go to college. The ability measure revealed a similar pattern. Boys and girls of high ability were about equally likely to continue their

AUTHOR'S NOTE: The authors wish to thank Mrs. Janet Mitchell, director of dissertation fellowships, Woodrow Wilson Fellowship Foundation, for making the data from the Mooney study (1968) available to us for secondary analysis.

[1] Astin does look at college dropouts by sex and it is on his data that we will rely for our discussion. For the defects of the other studies cited, see Astin (1971:1).

79

education, but among students with poor high school academic records, boys were more likely than girls to continue. Moreover, Werts found an interaction between the independent variables, suggesting that low grades are a greater deterrent to college attendance for low SES girls than for high SES girls.

These facts are not surprising in light of Kohn's studies (1959a; 1959b) showing that working-class and middle-class parents differ in their expectations for sons compared to daughters and in the degree to which they treat boys and girls differently. Gordon's analysis (1969) of educational opportunity survey data demonstrated that the variable most strongly correlated with sex for ninth-graders was the parental aspiration index: boys were much more likely than girls to picture their parents as holding high educational expectations for them, although the girls earned higher grades. Results from these studies suggest that the influence of significant others, documented by Sewell and his colleagues (Sewell, Haller, and Portes 1969; Sewell, Haller, and Ohlendorf 1970) is more important for women than for men, although perhaps in a different way.

Sewell's (1971) recent work confirms this conclusion. He found that women were most seriously disadvantaged relative to men in the level of their teachers' and parents' encouragement and their own educational aspirations. On the other hand, the women had the advantage of achieving better high school grades and, in seeming contradiction to their lower educational aspirations, they had somewhat higher occupational aspirations.

On the whole, however, Sewell's model tends to predict higher average educational attainment for women than they actually achieve. He suggests the discrepancy is due to effects immediately following high school and therefore not included in his model, since socialization and family effects already were manifest in women's levels of performance, aspirations, and significant others' influence—all of which he measured during the high school years.

It is possible, however, that there may be factors at work among females during the high school years that are not taken into account by Sewell's recursive model. Some years ago, Coleman (1961) suggested that the Chicago area high school girls he studied were caught in a "double bind" in wanting to meet their parents' and teachers' expectations of good performance, but also fearing that conspicuous achievement would cause them to lose popularity with boys. More recently, Horner's research has refined this idea:

> A bright woman is caught in a double bind. In testing and other achievement-oriented situations she worries not only about failure, but also about success. If she fails, she is not living up to her own standards of performance; if she succeeds she is not living up to societal expectations about the female role. Men in our society do not experience this kind of ambivalence, because they are not only permitted, but actively encouraged, to do well (Horner 1969: 38).

For women, then, the desire to achieve often is contaminated by the motive to avoid success. Femininity and individual achievement often are viewed as two desirable but mutually exclusive goals. "Whereas men are unsexed by failure . . . women seem to be unsexed by success" (Horner 1971:106).

This chapter centers on those women who do continue their education beyond high school but who fail to attain a college or advanced degree. We may expect that the same pressures which lower the proportion of women who *apply* to colleges and graduate schools will be brought to the campus by those who are admitted.

THE COLLEGE DROPOUT

The problem of defining drop-outs is a difficult one. As Astin noted,

> There can never be a wholly satisfactory definition of the term *dropout* until all students either obtain their degrees or die without obtaining a degree; any former student can, in theory, go back to school at any time to complete his degree (Astin 1972:6).

To cope with this problem, Astin developed four measures of student persistence for his study of college dropouts: (1) returned for at least a second undergraduate year; (2) received the bachelor's degree (or equivalent); (3) received the bachelor's degree or was still enrolled for work toward the degree; (4) received the bachelor's degree, was still enrolled for work toward the degree, or had transcripts sent to another institution. Each of these measures is in some respects unsatisfactory but they represent a reasoned attempt to cope with this difficult problem.[2]

Using these measures, Astin collected data on 51,721 students randomly selected from 217 institutions. All of the respondents entered college in 1966 and were followed up in 1970. Unfortunately, most of the results from this survey were not broken down by sex. The data that show the dropout rates for women and men in four-year colleges is presented in Table 4.1.

The nationwide attrition rate for women college students was not significantly different from that of men. Indeed, women were slightly more likely (49 percent versus 45 percent) to have obtained the bachelor's degree within four years of entering college. These figures closely parallel those reported by Astin and Panos (1969) for freshmen entering four-year colleges in 1961 and followed up in 1965: 56 percent of the males and 55 percent of the females had neither dropped out of their original college nor changed colleges during the four-year period.

Astin's findings are more revealing, however, when the gross rates for women and men are broken down to show the effects of sex on the propensity to drop out of college when the students are matched on ability. Astin sorted the women and men into nine ability groupings based on two variables that are known to predict

[2] For a discussion of the shortcomings of each of these measures, see Astin (1972:4–5).

TABLE 4.1. National Dropout Rates for College Students by Sex
(Class of 1970, Four Years after Entering College)

Percentage of Students Who:	Men	Women	Total
Did not return for a second year	21	23	22
Did not receive a degree	55	51	53
Did not receive a degree and were not enrolled	39	44	41
Did not receive a degree, were not enrolled, and did not request that a transcript be sent to another institution	16	22	19

SOURCE: Astin 1972:10, Table 2.

attrition: scores on a test of academic aptitude (SAT) and average grades in high school (Astin 1971). The distribution of women and men across the nine ability categories was consistent with well-known differences between the sexes: women earn substantially higher grades in high school (89 percent receive A's or B's compared to 75 percent of the men) but slightly lower test scores than men (48 percent of the women scored at the high level compared to 55 percent of the men).

Table 4.2 presents the performance of nonblack women and men in each of the nine matched groups on Astin's third measure of attrition: whether the student did not receive the degree and was not enrolled after four years.[3] Although the data presented in Table 4.2 is based on one measure, the same general pattern was found for each of Astin's four definitions of dropouts.

The data show that for every one of the matched ability groups, women had a higher dropout rate than men. In every case but one (low aptitude test score and an A grade average), the difference in the dropout rates between women and men was greater than the 5 percent by which women's dropout rate (on this measure) exceeds men's rate nationally. These figures seemingly contradict the earlier ones which presented women's and men's completion rates as fairly close to one another.

The explanation for the apparent discrepancy lies in the fact that women make better grades in high school but score lower on standardized achievement tests. Table 4.3 gives the distribution of nonblack male and female college students over the nine ability categories. At each aptitude score level, the data show that women are *better qualified* than men by virtue of their grades. One would expect, in contrast to the attrition rates cited above, that the dropout rate for women would be noticeably *lower* than that of men.

Most of the research on attrition, however, has shown that, aside from ability, sex is one of the best predictors of dropping out (Astin 1971). It is difficult to

[3] This measure was selected for two reasons. First, it is neither the most stringent nor the most liberal as an empirical definition of attrition; and second, it is the measure that we will use in examining graduate school attrition.

TABLE 4.2. College Dropouts by Sex and Selected Ability Measures
(Class of 1970, Four Years after Entering College)

Aptitude Test Interval[a]	Average Grade in High School[b]	Did Not Receive Degree, and Not Enrolled (*in percentages*)	
		Men	Women
Low	C	60	67
Low	B	45	56
Low	A	43	44
Middle	C	57	65
Middle	B	42	51
Middle	A	33	43
High	C	46	57
High	B	33	40
High	A	22	31

SOURCE: Computed by authors from Astin 1972:18, Table 5.
[a] High includes all students with SAT Verbal plus Mathematical scores above 1,054; Middle includes all between 838 and 1,054; low includes all below 838.
[b] A includes A+, A, and A—; B includes B+, B, and B—; C includes C+, C, and D.

TABLE 4.3. Average High School Grades of College Students by Aptitude Test Scores and Sex (Four-Year Colleges and Universities, Class of 1970)

Aptitude Test Interval[a]	Average Grade in High School[b]	(*In percentages*)	
		Men	Women
Low	C	60	34
Low	B	37	60
Low	A	3	6
		100	100
Middle	C	38	16
Middle	B	55	67
Middle	A	7	17
		100	100
High	C	12	4
High	B	59	55
High	A	29	41
		100	100

SOURCE: Computed by authors from Astin 1972:16, Table 4.
[a] High includes all students with SAT Verbal plus Mathematical scores above 1,054; middle includes all between 838 and 1,054; low includes all below 838.
[b] A includes A+, A, and A—; B includes B+, B, and B—; C includes C+, C, and D.

specify the precise factors associated with sex that account for its predictive power. Bayer (1969) has shown that not only do marital and family plans exert an independent effect on the educational aspirations of high school girls, but that for women they are also the best predictors of attrition from college (Bayer 1968). Even so, marital and family plans, along with the more than thirty other variables employed by Bayer, failed to account for even 30 percent of the variance in women's attrition versus persistence. Further research clearly is needed to determine what as yet unspecified factors have a differential impact on women's and men's persistence in college.

THE GRADUATE SCHOOL DROPOUT

The literature on graduate school attrition reveals two consistent patterns: women are more likely than men to drop out, and students of both sexes are more likely to fail to complete doctoral programs in the humanities and social sciences than in the physical sciences (Berger 1967; Joseph 1971; Mooney 1968; Tucker, Gottlieb, and Pease 1964). Unfortunately, none of these studies has attempted to determine what factors operate to produce the differential dropout rates for women and men.[4]

Our discussion of graduate school attrition is based primarily on a secondary analysis of data collected by Mooney (1968). In 1966 Mooney gathered information from graduate school histories of the 7,498 graduate students who were awarded Woodrow Wilson Fellowships between 1958 and 1963. Of these nearly 7,500 students, 28 percent, or 2,113, were women. Each year Woodrow Wilson Fellowships are awarded to approximately 1,200 individuals selected from about 10,000 students nominated by the faculty members of their undergraduate colleges. This introduces an obvious bias since the Woodrow Wilson recipients have unusually excellent undergraduate records and because they have expressed a desire to become college teachers. This bias, however, should serve to understate the extent of attrition, rather than overstate it.

Mooney (1968) analyzed the data for the 3,542 Woodrow Wilson Fellows of 1958 through 1960. Defining "success" as having received the Ph.D. by 1966, and "failure" as attending graduate school for six to eight years without completing the Ph.D., men were found to have succeeded more often than women: 41 percent of the male students had received the doctorate within the six to eight year time period, compared to only 16 percent of the women.

Tucker et al. (1964) found that the mean time for completion of the doctorate was 11.7 years in the humanities and 7.3 years in the physical sciences. It seems unrealistic, therefore, to measure "success" against a maximum of eight years of

---

[4] The Tucker et al. (1964) report was a national study designed to investigate variables that might be associated with the attrition of graduate students. Much of their analysis focuses on the constellation of attitudes that comprise the commitment of the graduate student. They did not report their findings by sex, however, so this potentially valuable information was lost.

graduate study. Since women are more heavily represented in the humanities, an eight-year cutoff introduces a sex-linked bias into the attrition rates.

For purposes of our secondary analysis of the Mooney data, we have therefore operationalized the dropout concept as follows: dropouts are those 1958–1963 Woodrow Wilson recipients who had not completed the Ph.D. by 1966 and were not enrolled in graduate school in that year. One problem with this definition is that it includes, as dropouts, students who may have merely interrupted rather than terminated their graduate training—that is, Woodrow Wilson Fellows who did not register for graduate school in the follow-up year (1966) but who may have re-enrolled in the years since 1966. To the extent that interrupters are counted as dropouts the attrition rate will be overstated. This problem, however, does not appear to be very serious. The data show that 98 percent of the Woodrow Wilson Fellows who did not register for their second year of graduate training and 91 percent of those who failed to return for their third year were still not enrolled in the follow-up year (1966). These findings indicate that there are likely to be few interrupters: the odds of an individual returning to graduate school within three to eight years are very small. Thus, the measure of the attrition rate we are using—Ph.D. not obtained and not enrolled in 1966—is likely to be a close approximation of the true rate.[5]

By 1966, 28 percent of the men Woodrow Wilson Fellows had received their Ph.D. compared to only 9 percent of the women. A similar disparity between women and men was found in a 1970 follow-up study of the first five classes of NDEA Title IV Fellows, seven to twelve years after entrance: 51 percent of the men had earned the doctorate, while only 18 percent of the women had done so (Joseph 1971). This difference in completion rates presages a corresponding difference in the dropout rates for women and men. By 1966, 44 percent of the male Woodrow Wilson Fellows and 64 percent of the women had not received their degree and were no longer enrolled as students.

It is striking that the dropout rate for these relatively elite graduate students was nearly one-half. More striking is the fact that the women were so much more likely than the men to drop out. Although the attrition rate varied across disciplines (for men, a high of 52 percent in the humanities to a low of 26 percent in the physical sciences; for women, a high of 66 percent and 54 percent respectively), the rate was *always* lower for men. Moreover, the percentage difference between women

---

[5] One note of caution should be sounded on this point. Women Woodrow Wilson Fellows are young college graduates, and to the extent that they withdraw from graduate school for childbearing and child rearing, their withdrawal period may be in excess of the three to eight years which the Mooney sample would span. The fact that women are, on the average, somewhat older than men when they attain the doctorate suggests that those women who *do* withdraw from advanced training may return after a longer interruption than their male counterparts. As a result, there is a possibility that our definition of attrition exaggerates the "real" or "final" attrition rate of women among the Woodrow Wilson Fellows.

and men was highest in the physical sciences where the dropout rate for both sexes was lowest.

Differences in ability do not explain differences by sex in anticipated dropout rates. A survey of graduate students by the American Council on Education and the Carnegie Commission on Higher Education in the spring of 1969 found that fewer women than men (15 percent compared to 20 percent) reported that lack of academic ability would prevent them from completing their graduate education (Creager 1971). Moreover, to the extent that ability was measured by the ratings given each graduate student by faculty members, women Woodrow Wilson Fellows were more able students than their male counterparts: 76 percent of the women received "excellent" or "very good" ratings compared to 66 percent of the men.

Despite these facts, a higher dropout rate for women persisted across all rating levels (Table 4.4). The dropout rate for both sexes was lowest at the highest rating level, but the dropout rate of women who received "excellent" ratings was still substantially greater than 50 percent, while less than one-third of the men with a comparable rating dropped out. Furthermore, the percentage difference between the dropout rate of women and men did not differ by faculty rating.

TABLE 4.4. Dropout Rate by Faculty Rating of Graduate Students and Sex (1958–1963 Woodrow Wilson Fellows in 1966) (In percentages)

Faculty Rating of Student	Men	Women	Total
Excellent	32	58	38
Very good	44	67	50
Average to poor	61	80	66

SOURCE: Computed by authors from data collected but only partially presented by Mooney (1968).

Parents' education and occupation were not significant determinants of the dropout rate. The effect of family income (Table 4.5) was less clear. For men, higher economic status was related to a decrease in dropout rate (from 46 percent among low income to 34 percent among high income men). For the women, on the other hand, there is no clear relation between family income and dropout rate. These data suggest that the effects of family background are mediated by other factors in the graduate school environment. While family background characteristics have an impact on the decision to attend college and graduate school, by the time the student actually embarks upon a graduate career, these characteristics are largely neutralized as a contributing influence on persistence or attrition.

Marital status, on the other hand, clearly has a differential effect on the dropout rate of women and men (Table 4.6). The data show that marriage has no effect

TABLE 4.5. Graduate School Dropout Rate by Family Income and Sex
(1958–1963 Woodrow Wilson Fellows in 1966)
(In percentages)

Family Income	Men	Women	Total
Less than $6,000	46	61	49
$6,000–$9,999	39	74	45
$10,000–$14,999	35	63	43
Over $15,000	34	71	45

SOURCE: Computed by authors from data collected but only partially presented by Mooney (1968).

on male graduate students: the dropout rate is 45 percent for single men and 44 percent for those married before they received fellowships. Marriage is not so neutral in its impact on women: the attrition rate for married women is 9 percent higher than that for single women. Two may be able to live as cheaply as one, but being the student half of a married couple is worse than being single for the female graduate student.

Being married means more than sharing a life and household with a spouse; for a woman, it means an increase in responsibility for home maintenance and child rearing. We have found no direct evidence of the influence of housework or child rearing per se upon attrition, but there is some indirect evidence that the sheer time spent on housework is much greater for married women than married men or single persons of either sex. The Women's Caucus at the University of California at Berkeley recently conducted a study of the differential effect of parenthood on women and men graduate students in one large department at that school (Gribben 1971). The results showed that if a woman was married but had no children, she spent fifty hours a week on household chores. If she was married with children, she spent sixty hours on household duties. Single men and women, on the other hand, spent about fifteen to twenty hours on household work a week. Married men, including those with children, devoted less than ten hours a week to housework.

TABLE 4.6. Graduate School Dropout Rate by Marital Status and Sex
(1958–1963 Woodrow Wilson Fellows in 1966)
(In percentages)

Marital Status	Men	Women	Total
Single	45	59	48
Married before fellowship	44	68	50

SOURCE: Computed by authors from data collected but only partially presented by Mooney (1968).

It is not surprising then, that several studies found marital and family status was the best predictor of women's attrition rate (Folger, Astin, and Bayer 1970; Davis 1962; Campbell et al. 1969).

The actual influence of parenthood upon graduate school attrition cannot be ascertained from the Mooney data. Although data were collected on the number of children each Woodrow Wilson Fellow had as of 1966, there is no way of determining when these children were born, in order to relate them to the graduate school experience of their parents. As a result, we can not tell what difference the presence of children makes in the differential propensity of women and men Woodrow Wilson Fellows to drop out.

The Carnegie Commission research indicates that marriage can be helpful to the woman graduate student in at least certain respects (Creager 1971). More than one-fourth of the women in the sample reported that their spouse's income was their primary source of support during graduate school, compared to slightly less than 16 percent of the men (see Chapter Two for tables summarizing these results). This greater support from spouses also was reflected in the fact that only one-half as many women as men supported themselves primarily by holding non-academic jobs (10 percent compared to 19 percent). Identical percentages (48 percent) of women and men supported themselves primarily by fellowships, teaching assistantships, or research assistantships, and women were not significantly more likely than men to indicate that lack of finances would prevent their completion of graduate work (38 percent versus 35 percent). Moreover, Davis (1962) found that there was no significant relationship between concern about financial problems and dropping out of graduate school.

On the whole it appears that women's higher dropout rate is not a result of financial difficulties. The figures in Table 4.7, however, seemingly give the lie to this conclusion. They very clearly show that the presence of fellowship support for women in their second year of graduate school reduces their drop-out rate by more than one-fourth. Second-year fellowship support is also associated with a lower drop-out rate for men, but the impact is not nearly as great. How can these data be reconciled?

It may be that second-year fellowship support signifies more than financial help to a woman graduate student; financial aid may indicate a degree of commitment to and faith in her on the part of the institution, which has a symbolic meaning far beyond the mere dollars granted. Creager (1971) reports that women were more likely to cite emotional strain (35 percent versus 27 percent) and pressure from spouse (15 percent compared to 12 percent) as a factor that would prevent their finishing graduate school. Moreover, nearly one-third (31 percent) of the women reported that they believed the professors in their department did not really take women graduate students seriously. It may be that financial support from their institution helps to counteract the additional pressures on women graduate students by conveying to them the message that their department does take them seriously,

TABLE 4.7. Graduate School Dropout Rate by Second-Year Fellowship Support in Graduate School and Sex
(1958–1963 Woodrow Wilson Fellows in 1966)
(In percentages)

Second-Year Support	Men	Women	Total
None	49	70	56
Any	35	44	36

SOURCE: Computed by authors from data collected but only partially presented by Mooney (1968).

which would account for the lower dropout rate for those women who receive second-year support.

For women especially, the first two years of the graduate school experience seem to be critical. For those women who survived until the third year, the dropout rate was 46 percent, 18 percent less than the overall rate for women. For men the corresponding figure was 34 percent, a 10 percent reduction in the dropout rate. After the second year, then, the contrast between women and men in attrition rates was reduced, although men were still more likely to persevere.

When this finding is coupled with data on the dropout rates for those students who received fellowship support, the second year appears to be critical to women's persistence in graduate school. At least for these Woodrow Wilson Fellows, the additional pressures that women graduate students experience—whether they be external, such as from spouses, or internal, such as the motive to avoid success—may be effectively mediated by a tangible indication of institutional support during the second year of graduate school.

CONCLUDING REMARKS

It is clearly the case that the attrition rate of women is higher than that of men at both the college and graduate school levels. What is surprising is how little empirical research has been done to explore the factors contributing to this waste of human skill and energy. Only in the last few years has there been some research comparing women and men dropouts from college. Research on the attrition of women in graduate school is even more scarce. We have noted that the national surveys on this subject are noteworthy primarily for their failure to control for sex. We do not know the effects, for example, of marital plans, parenthood, commitment, and career orientations on the differential propensity of women and men to leave graduate school before completion of the degree.

Women are now attaining the undergraduate degree in proportions comparable to men. But it is graduate and professional schools in the United States that today serve as the port of entry to careers of prestige, power, and financial reward. Unless women are able to navigate the channels of graduate school, they will not be able to take their places at the helm of society. We need the research that will chart the shoals in their passage through our graduate and professional schools.

REFERENCES

Astin, Alexander W. 1971. *Predicting academic performance in college.* New York: The Free Press.
Astin, Alexander W. 1972. *College dropouts: A national profile.* Washington, D.C.: American Council on Education.
Astin, Alexander W., and Panos, Robert J. 1969. *The educational and vocational development of college students.* Washington, D.C.: American Council on Education.
Bayer, Alan E. 1968. The college drop-out: Factors affecting senior college completion. *Sociology of Education,* 41:305–316.
Bayer, Alan E. 1969. Marriage plans and educational aspirations. *American Journal of Sociology,* 75:239–244.
Berger, Alan S. 1967. *Longitudinal studies on the class of 1961: The graduate science students.* Chicago: University of Chicago, National Opinion Research Center, Report No. 107.
Campbell, Rex et al. 1969. *Missouri graduate education: Assessment, needs and institutional plans.* St. Louis: Missouri Commission on Higher Education.
Coleman, James S. 1961. *The adolescent society.* New York: The Free Press.
Creager, John A. 1971. *The American graduate student: A normative description.* Washington, D.C.: American Council on Education.
Davis, James A. 1962. *Stipends and spouses: The finances of American arts and science graduate students.* Chicago: University of Chicago Press.
Feldman, K. A., and Newcomb, T. M. 1969. *The impact of college on students.* San Francisco: Jossey-Bass.
Folger, John K., Astin, Helen S., and Bayer, Alan E. 1970. *Human resources and higher education.* New York: Russell Sage Foundation.
Gordon, Chad. 1969. *Looking ahead: Self-conceptions, race and family factors as determinants of adolescent achievement orientations.* Washington, D.C.: American Sociological Association.
Gribben, Suzanne. 1971. Preliminary findings of women's caucus questionnaire. Berkeley: University of California English Graduate Association.
Horner, Matina S. 1969. Woman's will to fail. *Psychology Today,* 3:36–38, 62.
Horner, Matina S. 1971. Femininity and successful achievement: A basic inconsistency. In Michele H. Garskof (Ed.), *Roles women play: Readings toward women's liberation.* Belmont, Calif.: Brooks/Cole, pp. 97–122.
Joseph, Charlotte B. 1971. *A report on the first five classes of NDEA Title IV fellows, by sex.* Washington, D.C.: U.S. Government Printing Office.
Kohn, M. L. 1959a. Social class and parental values. *American Journal of Sociology,* 64:337–351.

Kohn, M. L. 1959b. Social class and the exercise of parental authority. *American Sociological Review,* 24:352–366.

Mooney, Joseph D. 1968. Attrition among Ph.D. candidates: An analysis of a cohort of recent Woodrow Wilson fellows. *Journal of Human Resources,* 3:47–62.

Sewell, William H. 1971. Inequality of opportunity for higher education. *American Sociological Review,* 36:793–809.

Sewell, William H., Haller, Archibald O., and Ohlendorf, George W. 1970. The educational and early occupational status attainment process: Replication and revision. *American Sociological Review,* 35:1014–1027.

Sewell, William H., Haller, Archibald O., and Portes, Alejandro. 1969. The educational and early occupational attainment process. *American Sociological Review,* 34:82–92.

Trent, J. W., and Medsker, L. L. 1968. *Beyond high school.* San Francisco: Jossey-Bass.

Tucker, Allan, Gottlieb, David, and Pease, John. 1964. *Attrition of graduate students at the Ph.D. level in the traditional arts and sciences.* East Lansing: Michigan State University, Office of Research Development, Publication No. 8.

Werts, Charles E. 1966. *Sex differences in college attendance.* Evanston, Ill.: National Merit Scholarship Corporation Reports, 2(6).

Chapter Five

Women Drop Back In: Educational Innovation in the Sixties

Jean W. Campbell

WOMEN are not yet assured equality of employment in higher education or equal access to achievement and leadership roles within the educational establishment. But there is progress—some of which was generated a decade and more ago in a creative period of feminist activity similar in many ways to the movement today. An examination of this earlier period may heighten our sense of continuity within the feminist movement and thus strengthen its base of support.

The present political, economic, and cultural conditions not only give rise to but make possible for the first time in history "the kind of change in role expectations and psychological orientation women's liberationists have been talking about. It does not mean only women's rights, it means the emancipation of both men and women from a sex-dominated archaic division of labor and from the values that sustain it" (Lerner 1971:248). With this distinction in mind, we can trace the postwar changes in women's education as a response to the changing needs and demands of women, and examine the seeds of the present women's movement.

In the fifties, a growing belief in higher education for all, dramatized by the enthusiastic return of veterans to the campuses, gradually generated a renewed interest in women's education. McGuigan (1970:112) has noted that the much remarked-upon drop in recent years from prewar highs in the percentage of women earning higher degrees and participating in professional academic roles is related to the quotas set by institutions of higher learning in the mid-forties to absorb men on the GI bill. In our anxiety to dismantle the war machine and absorb veterans into the economy, we severely curtailed women's admission to higher education and sent them home from wartime jobs. Women did not protest their declining opportunities nor did they foresee that in a few years there would be fewer models of leadership and fewer women who felt justified in a commitment to achievement and equality. While demographic analyses have thrown some light on the postwar status of women (Oppenheimer 1966; Rossi 1970), the genesis of popular attitudes concerning women's role and status in the 1950s remains to be studied by social historians.

During this period, scholarly interest in the education of women was delineated by the activities of the American Council on Education and sustained by the abiding concern of the American Association of University Women. A landmark conference sponsored by the American Council on Education in 1957 explored many present-day themes and produced *The Education of Women—Signs for the Future* (David 1959). Statistics concerning the number of women enrolled in higher education, their employment, and life span, and the discontinuities in their lives were made clearly apparent. The president of AAUW, Anna Hawkes, noted, "There is . . . evidence for the fact that, of the brightest high school graduates who do not go on to college, two-thirds are women. In light of the lack of sex difference in college aptitude and high school performance, this is an appalling waste" (David 1959:31).

Mary Bunting, president of Radcliffe, suggested in 1967 that her observation more than a decade earlier concerning the fate of bright high school students was an important determinant in her work in institutional innovations responsive to women's life styles. At the 1957 American Council on Education conference, Bunting asked, "Is it not entirely possible that a great deal of inefficiency in women's education can be attributed to a pattern that forces full-time study from 18 to 22 followed by full-time homemaking from 23 to 33?" She suggested combined study and homemaking over an eight-or-ten-year period so that "when the last child goes off to school, they will be ready for jobs worthy of their talents and education. The chance to choose an interesting vocation is one that the intelligent and the educated should have, and one that many women have been denied" (David 1959:106). The Vassar study by Sanford (1956) with its wealth of insight into academic motivation in women, Douvan's work on adolescent girls, and other research informed the (ACE) conference. Discussions of the career development of women, based on now-outmoded assumptions concerning sex differences, seem less useful to the present-day reader except to underscore the continuing search for the bases of a viable theory of women's career development.

The problems examined in this recent but almost forgotten past are alive in women's education today. Presumably there was as wide agreement at the 1957 conference as there would be today with Harold Taylor, former president of Sarah Lawrence College, when he declared,

> I will argue, however, that over this past half century there has been a slow growth of awareness that in order to achieve the complete emancipation of women, not only is it necessary for women's education to be of a quality equal to that of men, but it must be of such a character that women may have an opportunity to grow to their stature as women without the psychological handicap of taking secondary roles in relation to men (David 1959:83).

The ACE Commission on the Education of Women, established in 1953, published a bulletin, *The Education of Women,* from 1958 to 1961, and the Council sponsored one more important conference in 1962—the "Itasca Conference"—before withdrawing from active leadership in the deliberations surrounding women's education.

The Education of Women was succeeded by *Women's Education,* published by The American Association of University Women until 1966. Together with the newsletter of the Center for the Study of Liberal Education for Adults, this publication kept a short generation of educators in touch with research on women's education, publications, and all matters relating to programs for the "continuing education of women," much as *Women Today* or *The Spokeswoman* are now serving educational innovators in the absence of a more specialized newsletter.

Between 1957 and 1962, the federal government through the National Manpower Council reports, *Womanpower* (1957) and *Work in The Lives of Married Women* (1958), represented a continuing influence in favor of educational programs better suited to the needs of women, particularly those returning to the work force. President Kennedy's appointment of a Commission on the Status of Women in 1961 (U.S. Department of Labor 1963a) and the increasingly vigorous development and dissemination of statistics by the Women's Bureau of the Department of Labor played a critical role in shaping a concern for and understanding of the growing importance of women to the work force and the employment potential presumably resting in educated women with incomplete or outmoded educations. Educational institutions were urged to develop special programs, facilities, and services to accommodate women in the mainstream of education "to be sure that education is available to mature women at suitable times and places and in a manner appropriate for adult experience and patterns of life" (U.S. Department of Labor, Women's Bureau 1963b:51).

During this period, roughly as the decade turned and unfolded, there was a joining of interests much like that of today. Experimental programs in colleges and universities multiplied. Conferences, articles, commercial and university television programs proliferated. And women talked with each other in living rooms throughout the country. To be sure, there was no talk of sexism or consciousness-raising —words of the future—but there were endless examinations of the loss of, or the failure to develop identity, the sacrifice of self to a truncated role, the uncertainty about the effect of work on children, the dawning comprehension that the fit between women's needs and the means to an education was poor indeed. The struggle continues. But during that time, a self-awareness on the part of educated women who were calling for freedom of choice in how they lived and for full access to opportunity coincided with job shortages, and the combination provided the conditions for a remarkably innovative period in women's education. The major innovations are usually (and loosely) thought of as "continuing education programs" or the "continuing education movement."

The ACE conference at Itasca in 1962 was devoted entirely to "continuing education" and the report contains descriptions of the early programs (Dennis 1963). Although the spirit of the meeting was quiescent by today's standard (". . . it may be wiser to [effect change] with 'soft-tongues' than with over-ardent demands"), this conference focused attention on the importance of developing special programs for women and recommended that "each institution develop a plan . . . most suitable for the individual institution. . . . The pilot projects differ greatly. Their pattern is that they have no set pattern, but only a goal—happier and more useful women" (Dennis 1963:147, 149).

The lack of a set pattern persists. Continuing education programs are astonishingly varied, which accounts in part for the strength of the movement and explains in part the difficulty of describing it and assessing its impact.

The awareness of class differences in motivation and attitudes toward education and employment, and sensitivity to the educational needs of working class women have accompanied the continuing education movement; but the early development of continuing education programs focused on the barriers to achievement by middle-class, educated women and their right to self-fulfillment through creative work. Emphasis was placed on institutional changes that would accommodate a combination of roles over a woman's lifetime. In this sense, continuing education meant adjusting the educational system to the demands of women's dual role, taking for granted interruptions in their formal education and providing as a matter of course for their reentry into the system. In her discussion of changes in selected continuing education programs, Addis distinguished women's continuing education programs from adult education programs: "Reference to programs for women should be interpreted as avenues for *resumed* education" (Addis 1967:16). In another study of continuing education programs, Jacobson noted:

> Mature women students, adult women students, women students . . . are used interchangeably to mean those women who have returned to *formal* [italics added] education after an interruption of any number of years. . . . This is not so much an age group as a situation group. It is a group differentiated from the usual 18 to 21-year-old standard undergraduate college student, continuing her formal education from high school to college, or even into graduate school without any significant interruption. This group of women would be starting or continuing their education after the age of 21, and often at a much more advanced age (Jacobson 1969:12).

The term continuing education has other meanings. It may be useful to mention them briefly since our discussion is not limited to those programs providing for reentry to formal education. Continuing education for both women and men has come to be synonymous, in some cases, with "adult education" and thus separated from the mainstream educational process. It also commonly is equated with professional renewal education, programs instituted primarily for on-the-job practitioners, i.e., nurses, doctors, lawyers, management personnel, social workers. So, too, "refresher" courses for former practitioners of particular vocations, i.e., nursing, or training programs for the untrained in specific skills, or work-study arrangements of various kinds often are described as continuing education programs.

From the first, then, different patterns for continuing education were available for the consideration of educators. The early leaders, intent on discovering the most effective way to educate women and help them use their talents and training, received financial assistance from major foundations, particularly the Carnegie Corporation which gave major support to three different approaches: The Radcliffe Institute of Independent Study, The Center for Continuing Education of Women at Sarah Lawrence College, and the Minnesota Plan at the University of Minnesota.

The Radcliffe Institute for Independent Study (Bunting 1961), which even now inspires emulation (Commission on Education at Mather and Adelbert Colleges 1970:33), was established in 1960 independently of the regular degree program of Radcliffe and Harvard. Essentially a program to support the independent projects of women who exhibited potential for outstanding achievement—scholars, artists, and women with a commitment to the community—the Fellowships for Independent Study Program was combined with the illustrious Radcliffe seminars which had flourished and sustained educated women in the Boston area for ten years before the institute was established. Counseling and advisory services were provided for aspiring women and educators; and the desirability of program evaluation was anticipated by provision for a research staff. In time, the institute developed additional scholarship programs, designed with a flexibility not widely practiced by the educational establishment. Assistance to part-time students admitted to colleges and universities within a three-state area as well as the provision of fellowship support to medical students in various stages of part-time training and internships dramatizes the abiding philosophy of Bunting and the institute's first director, the late Constance E. Smith, that women can successfully combine education with family responsibilities and need not abandon or even interrupt the former if institutions provide the necessary support (Smith 1968).

Another visionary leader, Esther Raushenbush (1961, 1962), with financial support from the Carnegie Foundation and the provision of physical facilities by Sarah Lawrence College, opened the Center for Continuing Education of Women (Richter and Whipple 1972). The center invited adult women back to Sarah Lawrence College, legitimizing in an institutional sense the interruptions to education and career caused by early marriage and family responsibilities. Women responded in overwhelming numbers. Through the center, Sarah Lawrence admitted women with some college experience to a transitional period of course work conducted apart from the student body, after which they could enroll as regular students. This was an imaginative response to the women's loss of confidence that typically occurs after having been away from school for some length of time. Unhappily, the Sarah Lawrence program was described in the media as a "second chance" education, and thus anticipated endless plays on the concept of "rusty ladies." The implication of second class studentship of such programs still plagues the issue of women's education.

The Minnesota Plan, launched in 1960, was the first continuing education program for women in a large university. The plan was a comprehensive program (Schletzer et al. 1967) that brought together a wide variety of services and instruction for women of all ages. Sparked by the creative ideas and leadership of Virginia Senders, Elizabeth Cless, and Vera Schletzer, the program set before the public the critical issue in women's education as then conceived: institutions must be redesigned for greater flexibility given the inevitability of marriage for most women and their continuing, if not greater, educability after their social and biological roles have been clarified. The model of higher education for men is not adequate for developing the talents of women.

Under the auspices of the Office of the Dean of Women and the leadership of Kathryn Clarenbach, the University of Wisconsin launched its program for women in 1963. A Department of Education of Women was created to assist the prospective mature woman student on her return to serious study and to help her with placement in professional employment. The department also was concerned with reaching undergraduates. Until 1968 Wisconsin was distinguished by the Carnegie-supported E. B. Fred Fellowship program (Thompson and Sager 1970) which encouraged and supported returning women graduate students. In recent years the program has become part of the Center for Women's and Family Living Education in the Extension Service. The center has a broad agenda that includes legislative action and support for affirmative action in employment. Dorothy Miniace at the University of Wisconsin-Milwaukee Office of Continuing Education also was among the first to develop an outstanding comprehensive counseling service, primarily for women but available to men and couples as well (Office of Continuing Education 1972).

With Kellogg Foundation support and the direction of Priscilla Jackson, the Michigan State University-Oakland Extension Service initiated an imaginative noncredit program essentially based on conferences and a specially designed testing program for the Detroit suburban community. Known primarily for its "Investigation into Identity" program and its training and use of volunteer leaders to carry the program to a wider audience of women, the Oakland Continuum Center has broken ground for countless "self-discovery" programs. The Continuum Center also included a day care program from its beginning.

Another pioneer, Louise G. Cain at the University of Michigan, drafted a proposal for a multipurpose Center for Continuing Education of Women, administered through the Office of Academic Affairs. When it opened in 1964, the center was charged by the university to provide a wide range of services for women returning to the regular graduate and undergraduate credit programs and to recommend policies and changes in requirements and procedures that might be necessary for women to return successfully. The Michigan center (discussed more fully in a later section) initially was supported largely by alumnae fund raising.

This sampling of leaders and their programs is illustrative of an impressive roster of women educators on the move in the early 1960s. Also active were Betty Jane Lloyd (1967) at Margaret Morrison Carnegie College; Mary Iverson at Syracuse; Virginia Henderson at Pennsylvania; Ruth Osborn (1967) at George Washington;

Jean Pennington at Washington University; Dorothy Strawn at the University of Washington; Helen Schleman and Cecilia Zissis at Purdue; Caryl Kline at Pittsburgh; Alice Smith at Radcliffe; Freda Goldman at the Center for the Study of Liberal Education for Adults and later at Rhode Island; Jane Berry, Margaret Fagin and Nell Greenwood at Missouri; Bert Loewenberg at Sarah Lawrence; Constance Threinen at Wisconsin, and many more.

This sample also suggests the geographical range and styles of innovative programs for women. Each institution borrowed generously from the other as well as establishing new directions in education to meet the special needs of their constituency. Sarah Lawrence continued to pioneer in the area of interinstitutional arrangements for part-time professional training. For example, a four year part-time program was established in conjunction with the New York University Graduate School of Social Work (1965–1969). Elizabeth Cless created the Center (now, Office) for Continuing Education for the Claremont (California) Colleges to include men as well as women and developed a new master's degree in liberal studies with appropriate proseminars and academic placement for the nontraditional student (Cless 1969).

The University of Missouri system for continuing education of women, with offices in the extension services at coordinate campuses and regional offices, represents the broadest state coverage in the country. Berry and Epstein (1963) at the University of Missouri-Kansas City campus were among the first to question women about their aspirations and intentions to continue their education. Fagin (1971) at the University of Missouri-St. Louis has made the College Level Examination Program available to women across the state and significantly increased the use of these tests among adult women. (CLEP, a program introduced by the College Entrance Examination Board in 1965, offers a national examination service similar to the College Proficiency Examination Program of the New York State Education Department [CPEP]. The service measures achievement in five basic areas of the liberal arts and twenty-seven introductory college subjects, and may be useful in awarding college credit for unconventionally acquired knowledge.)

In 1960 Rutgers University instituted a mathematical retraining program for women because of the need for more mathematics teachers and more mathematically trained personnel in industry. Scholarship, counseling and placement were part of the program. At about the same time Wellesley initiated a program to retrain women chemists. Supported by a National Science Foundation grant, the Institute in Chemistry enabled women five to twenty years beyond their first degrees to return to work in the field by pursuing half-time graduate study leading to the master's degree. Exempt from tuition and fees, eligible for tax-free stipends for child care, transportation and supplies, these returning chemists carried out individualized plans of study. The Rutgers and Wellesley retraining programs no longer exist, although Wellesley subsequently developed a continuing education program, modeled to an extent on the Sarah Lawrence program. Women whose academic careers have been interrupted and who wish to matriculate at Wellesley are carefully selected and counseled into the regular curriculum. After two semesters as continuing education special students, the women can become degree candidates.

In 1965, Betty Kaynor and others in the Miami (Florida) area pioneered a community-based service which coordinates information from various educational institutions and community services and provides guidance and a wide range of programs for women with varying interests. In 1969, the council became part of Miami-Dade Junior College; it is a model communitywide service designed to encourage women to continue their education at all levels.

For years Rosalind Loring at UCLA has developed imaginative daytime extension programs and career training options for women. A UCLA humanities course for adult women on the urban crisis is a recent model program (University of California 1970).

Catalyst, a New York-based nonprofit national organization founded in 1962 by Felice Schwartz, pioneered the now familiar model of retraining and placing educated women in positions suffering a shortage of trained personnel, such as teaching, social work, and the sciences. Its broad objective was "to bring to our country's needs the unused capacities of intelligent women who want to combine family and work." A subsection of the organization, Catalyst on Campus, designed to alert undergraduates around the country to the need to plan for new life styles, was ahead of its time. Catalyst has been effective in calling attention to the need for different employment patterns, and in demonstrating that many women will be relatively more productive as part-time teachers and social workers than as full-time workers (Catalyst 1968, 1971). It recently sponsored a self-help book (Schwartz et al. 1972) for women returning to the work force and, with Ford and Kellogg Foundation support, has laid plans for developing a national network of part-time job services.

Ruth Van Doren has directed the Human Relations Center at the New School for Social Research (New York) since the mid-1960s. As the scope of the center broadened to emphasize human relations skills and community services, the name of the center was changed in 1971 to the Human Relations Work-Study Center. The present name of the center calls attention to the close relationship between continuing education for women and the need for human services in the community that has characterized the movement since its beginning. An early example of this close relationship between community service and women's education is the Barnard College Community Service Workshop, designed in 1966 (with Higher Education Act support) to steer mature educated women into acutely needed community service. Under the aegis of the Barnard placement office, the workshop was an outgrowth of a general vocational guidance program operated in cooperation with six other women's colleges—the Carnegie-supported Seven College Vocational Workshops. More recently, Barnard set up a comprehensive Women's Center which offers women's studies, vocational guidance, and help in obtaining fellowships or loans (Barnard College 1971).

Roosevelt University in Chicago, one of the forerunners in establishing a flexible degree program for adults age 25 and older, emphasizes concentrations that train students to work actively with urban problems and provides supervised internships in community service. (Roosevelt is one of several institutions which have phased out an exclusively women's program in favor of a coeducational program supported by individual counseling.)

The use of the term "new careers" grew out of the idea that educated women were available who could be trained to provide needed professional services. The National Institutes of Mental Health project developed by Rioch et al. (1964) to train housewives as psychotherapists through a two year part-time study program was a promising example. But problems concerning licenses and credentials arose and few programs of this kind developed in spite of the successful training experience of this group of women. A few programs to create new subprofessions, such as Colorado's "physician assistant," have been developed, but are not geared to the needs of the educated adult woman who has had little work experience.

The Women's Talent Corps, created in 1965 as a nonprofit corporation (and funded by OEO) under the leadership of Audrey Cohen, was designed to train nonworking, low-income women for jobs in their neighborhoods. The development of this Corps into the College for Human Services, accredited by the Regents of the State of New York, was a landmark in continuing education for women. Devoted to new careers and career ladders for the disadvantaged, the college offered a subsidized, innovative, two-year work-study program, emphasizing the "closest possible relationship between classroom and field work and creating an interdisciplinary college-level curriculum based on concepts from the social sciences and humanities" (Hortenstine 1971:21). In a review of continuing education for disadvantaged women, Hortenstine describes the College of Human Services in the modal terms used for earlier programs: the need for services, if not so much the availability of jobs, and "a vast reservoir of unused talent . . . in the neighborhoods" (p. 20). Recently the college has shifted its focus to a master's level program on the same model.

There are many federally supported "new careers" programs. For example, the University of Michigan School of Education sponsors a subsidized work-study degree program for twenty-one Detroit teacher-aids who need not meet admissions requirements and whose job levels increase as their knowledge increases. At the end of four years they are fully qualified teachers. Programs such as this one may not find their place in a directory of programs, but they set the stage for many that do. Tufts has designed a continuing education for women program to include and subsidize low-income women and provide various institutional adjustments and supportive services.

Another program of particular interest is the Quo Vadis School of Nursing in Canada, a school created solely for adult women. Such a school offers an example for study of the special teaching and learning problems of this special population (McLean and Lucas 1970).

EVALUATION RESEARCH

The variety of continuing education programs for women is evident; research concerning the organization of these programs is not. Two studies, however, are useful. A descriptive study (Mayhew 1970) of four comprehensive university centers—Michigan, Oakland, Minnesota, and Wisconsin—gives some sense of both similarity and variety in continuing education programs. At the time of Mayhew's study, two of the programs were in the extension services of their universities, one in the Office of the Dean of Women and one in the Office of Academic Affairs. Two sought to reach women mainly through extension services: classes, conferences, and community programs. The other two provided services primarily to women who sought them. However, counseling services and motivational programs are common to all, and interinstitutional cooperation is characteristic. The institutions permit part-time enrollment but all of them have difficulty in establishing acceptance of credit by examination and/or experience, and more flexible scheduling of classes. All offer tutorial assistance or training in study skills. All but one offer refresher courses and a range of noncredit classes. Other common program features are a newsletter, a library of vocational materials, placement services, scholarships and other financial aids. Mayhew also reports the major barriers to continuing education for women as expressed by the four program directors: societal attitudes, financial problems, adequate flexibility in admissions, credits and class scheduling.

The earlier and somewhat more sophisticated study by Addis (1967) explored and specified certain problems encountered in the organization and articulation of programs. Examining the institutions that responded to the 1962 AAUW survey, Addis found eighteen suitable for study. Nine were selected for site visits and thorough analysis. They represented "public and private universities, technical and liberal arts colleges for women, residential and nonresidential, large and small, prestigious and nonprestigious, and more than one which had originated as a 'night school.'" In her search for administrative problems created by the adoption of new programs for women, Addis examined a broad range of programs for women re- suming education.

Addis found that uncertain financial and faculty support were the two most serious problems encountered in the programs she studied. It was clear that top-level administrative commitment was essential to the success of these programs (see also Mayhew 1970:232). Fewer problems were found when the execution of plans for a center remained in the jurisdiction of those who did the chief planning. The prestige accruing to programs receiving outside support, whether from foundations, government, or special fund-raising efforts, lent support to the theory that successful innovation in higher education is accelerated through a combination of "inside" and "outside" forces.

Addis' major recommendations stress the need for more information about adult women, particularly to build faculty understanding of the needs such women have for continuing education programs. Students also need more information to assist their academic orientation and personal readjustment to a new pace and mode of living; and counseling is an essential element for continuing education program success. Programs may include new course offerings or special classes designed for retraining but not related to degree programs. In these cases, faculty understanding and support are especially necessary to the continuing success of the program since they take time and budget from competing interests. The study strongly suggests that continuing education programs might profitably serve a male as well as a female clientele: "If women are seen as needing special orientation, it would still be possible to offer such special services without denying men total access to the new opportunities" (Addis 1967:293).

In neither the Addis nor the Mayhew study is there an indication that homogeneous classes are needed by adults in the transitional period of orientation to a degree program. Yet numerous colleges have instituted separate classes for the women students during the first year of their reentry. Hruby suggests this is "for the protection of the women against their own fears during this period" (Hruby 1968:1), but there is no indication that this policy is based on findings that establish its necessity. The situation at Sarah Lawrence, in which older women attend separate classes for the first twenty credit hours, may be unique because of the demanding nature of its small classes and tutorial method. Under such circumstances, some women "are afraid of the freedom" inherent in the "free selection of courses, of independent study, of discussions in classes and in conferences" (Richter and Whipple 1972:26). In contrast, in an experimental evening program of classes at the University of Michigan it was found that some heterogeneity of age and sex was preferred by students and faculty alike (Wulp 1971).

The evaluation of the New York State Guidance Center for Women is an indispensable study for both students and program directors (Raines 1969). This model center, organized by Esther Westervelt with state funds (a "first") and now a part of Rockland County Community College, had a "positive impact on the vast majority of its counseling clients" (Raines 1969:70). The evaluation report recommends a network of Adult Guidance Centers in the community colleges of the state of New York. As Westervelt (1968) has suggested, the community college may be the catalyst for effective growth of continuing education programs. Consistent with a modest trend in the late sixties, the report recommends that "women" be dropped from the title. At the same time it stresses that "it would be very important for new Centers to emphasize *particular* concern for assisting adult women. This need for special emphasis stems from a societal tradition that has been nonsupportive of developmental needs of women outside the house" (Raines 1969:73).

The trend to open to men continuing education programs for women is not as apparent today as it was a year or two ago. The new feminism and "affirmative action" have widened the possibilities for compensatory services to women, postponing for a while, perhaps for a long while, the impetus to integrate the women's experimental programs.

PROFILE OF RETURNING WOMEN STUDENTS

Who are the women returning to school? Why do they return? How do they fare? Characteristics of returning women vary somewhat with each program, but an examination of even one program in some detail is enlightening. The University of Michigan Center for Continuing Education of Women is a good example of programs that serve large university communities and are geared to the unique needs of their particular university—in this case a highly decentralized group of nineteen schools and colleges. The center is a service to the state and welcomes *all* women; at the same time it recognizes that there is a self-selection factor operating upon those who do come because of the unique nature of and the particular services offered by the center. Two out of three women return to school although one out of three postpones enrollment for a time. Not all of these women attend the University of Michigan when they do return.

As a part of the Office of Academic Affairs, the Michigan center reaches across the university and through all academic levels in seeking to lower the barriers or change university policies for qualified women with family or job commitments. The center provides information, counseling, referrals, a library, scholarships and grants-in-aid, an evening program of regular credit courses, conferences, and small discussion groups throughout the year, a series of publications, consultation with counselors and programs on other campuses, services to promote research on women's education and development and scholarship in women's studies. Those center participants attending the university are qualified mainstream students. Except for certain licensing programs, some professional schools and a few graduate departments, students may be on a part-time basis; they may transfer credits of any age; and they may establish their own residency apart from their husband's. Some have received credit by examination, and some have had residency requirements waived and credits transferred beyond the stated limit. Summer independent reading courses and other independent study programs are available as well as a degree program that entails no fixed course requirements.

In 1964–1965 approximately 500 women came to the Michigan center for individual consultation. The typical woman was 37 years old, married, living in the area, with a professional or student husband, two or three children, some college, or more likely than not a bachelor's degree. She wanted to prepare for employment (approximately 85 percent of the women gave this as a reason for attending the center); and she needed help in thinking through her job possibilities, in selecting an educational program appropriate to her goals, and in dealing with technical problems of admissions, registration, convenient class scheduling, and financial assistance. She was very likely to be interested in some phase of education, in the social sciences, humanities, or in social work or library science as a career. Surprisingly, as many women expressed an interest in business administration as in nursing and health (10 percent). Also 2 percent were interested in law, 4 percent in mathematics and engineering, 8 percent in the physical or natural sciences, and a negligible number in medicine.

To date, more than 4,000 women have talked with counselors at the center and the participant profile has changed. There is now a greater diversity of background among the women who come to the center. The average participant is remarkably younger (36 percent are under 25 in contrast to an earlier 7 percent); is more likely to be single, divorced, or widowed (30 percent compared to 14 percent); has fewer children (1.6) than the typical participant of even five years ago. She more often needs money to finance her education and she is somewhat more likely to be employed when she comes to the center. Her educational achievement, the kind of help she requests from the center (except for more financial assistance), and her interest in preparing for a good job have remained about the same. Very few women are interested in courses without credit, in volunteer work, or solely in self-improvement. There is a slight increase in interest in nontraditional fields for women and a slight shift away from public school teaching, but essentially the fields of interest remain those traditionally associated with women.

The center designs its programs with the changing needs of women in mind, and presumably this will determine to some extent who utilizes the center. Changing expectations among the under-thirty age group concerning education and life styles (for example, joint planning of student couples, willingness to postpone marriage and child bearing, a desire to reduce or eliminate periods of interruption in education) probably are reflected in these statistics.

Consider the "returning woman" in 1971 who describes her return in these terms:

> After graduating . . . in 1966 . . . I deserted academia and set out to learn about the Real World . . . as I became aware of injustices, my energy and sense of outrage grew. . . . Autumn of 1968 was my choice point . . . many of my friends became radical, and either left town or left my circle of friends. . . . Everywhere, it seemed, my peers were dropping out, turning against the Establishment with increasing bitterness and violence. . . . The choice, in retrospect, was to join that groundswell of radicalization completely and wholeheartedly . . . or search elsewhere for a way to act . . . my beliefs in non-violence had grown too strong for me to jump drastically with the leftward swing. But, unfortunately I shared the bitterness of that movement too strongly for me to influence my rapidly changing friends to act other than they saw fit. For the next year and a half I wandered, mentally . . . in the spring of 1970, these mental efforts showed some results . . . it became clear to me that those of us in my generation who still have positive goals and a belief in the worth of all persons, should act, strongly and quickly. And I began to see a sense of direc-

tion when I realized that my interest in children, learning, and education was growing. . . .

Today the returning woman may be one who dropped out to assess her goals and life style rather than one who dropped out to marry and bear children.

Whatever the reason for dropping out, when a woman returns to a degree program, she is serious and highly motivated. The investment of time, money, and energy required is not for the casual student. A 33-year-old wife and mother of two, finishing her fifth year in architecture said:

> It is often remarked, when the subject of my involvement in architecture arises, that I am very lucky because someday I will be able to design my own home. I suspect that I elicit this reaction because I am a woman in an essentially "male" field and many people seem able to countenance the idea of a woman architect in terms of single family houses but not in terms of, say, high-rise office buildings or schools, or urban redevelopment projects. This is a serious misconception, one which I fervently hope I do not continue to encounter, especially on a professional level. Although I am sure I might enjoy designing my own home someday, I will certainly not have devoted five years of arduous work and study plus several more of on-the-job training and experience to the ultimate end of designing one private home.

Another woman, of similar age, divorced, with two children and a part-time job, and just about to complete her undergraduate degree after six years of part-time work is clearly not a casual student:

> May I suggest that the [scholarship] committee broaden their search to include the returning woman student with sagging motivation, due perhaps to average or low grades, or due to the lack of opportunity to make a creative or scholarly contribution? God knows, there are days when I feel creative if I put a cherry on the dessert for dinner, in spite of the fact that I am blessed with a stimulating and interesting job. Please don't lose sight of the fact that for many women, simply going to college is a feat in itself.

A reason very often given for returning to school is the need for a "feeling of achievement" or sense of competency. For some women this is a comment on the loss of self-esteem accompanying the traditional roles of housewife and mother. For others it is simply a recognition of the value of a fully certifiable training. A professor of political science, acting head of her department and currently sought after in the competition for women academic administrators, stated:

> I decided that I would return to school after twenty years and get a Ph.D. in political science so that I could teach in a college. I went because I really felt that more education would give me a useful skill, and also I think that from a personal, psychological view, I did want something more when my children, who are now eleven, fifteen, and sixteen, would be gone. I was bored with volunteer politics; twenty years of volunteer politics is enough!

Equally forthright, another, somewhat younger student in political science who is teaching part-time at a community college explained:

> I came to the Center . . . and I said to the counselor, "I feel I have twenty or thirty good years ahead of me. I've gone through the organizations. I like to play bridge, but I can't play all the time. I don't enjoy housework. My house is not really a problem. What am I going to do from nine to three with me [sic]? I would like to do something part-time. I feel I can contribute, I can be kept interested, and I would be quite unhappy without some sort of outside interest. . . ." We started sorting things out together, and she guided me and let me make up my own mind in a very successful fashion. This is why I am now pursuing political science in graduate school. . . . I hope one day to be equipped to teach at a community college.

These returning women had to learn to be persistent and to overcome initial fears:

> I really suffered from a feeling of inadequacy. The first few months were very difficult for me . . . I had tremendous feelings of doubt. I was reading material I couldn't understand. I couldn't find the words in the dictionary because they simply have a new—I hate to say jargon—but let's say an entirely new mode of expression. Until I had my mid-semester and discovered that I could keep up with these young kids, I lived in a state of anxiety.

The returning women observed that there are new ways of learning and teaching. A woman in American Civilization said:

> I try to put it all together and make it my own so that I can think about it intelligently and make comparisons: here are the trends going through and here is where the trends don't go through. . . . This is hard, but this is also challenging and far more worthwhile than the old type of, you know, "Here's the word—now give it back to me."

The women had to come to terms with problems of choice and priorities. A sociologist now teaching behavioral science to medical students said:

> Seeing one's life in a kind of broad perspective, seeing the roles . . . making sure that you really have set up priorities . . . makes it possible for you to decide what to drop, what to keep on doing, and what is going to come first. I put my family first. School comes second and it often comes second with a big sigh because there are so many more things you would like to do. . . . This compromising with excellence is a very, very difficult thing to come to terms with.

Besides their strong motivation, seriousness of purpose, persistence, adaptability, and industry, the returning women were eager and enjoyed learning for its own sake: "And after just one course in art history, I was hooked. I knew that I had been a misplaced person all these years."

They expressed concern about the effect of their activities on their children, but their concern was essentially to provide good substitute care. The woman returnee recognized the inconclusive nature of the data on children and working mothers, and rationalized her activities: "I think this interest . . . in furthering . . . education is going to be the greatest thing in correcting the child-centered home." On the other hand, women ". . . *do* have guilt feelings. This is par for the course. You step out in fear and trembling and hope that what you are doing is not going to starve yourself or your husband or your children."

The attitudes of husbands were understood to be important. The supportive and interested husband or one who appreciated his wife's enhanced earning power was singled out:

> I would just like to say that I just recently moved from a small town where *The Feminine Mystique* was known as a dirty book. They questioned me when I took it out of the library. . . . So, I just went back to school, and I find that as I grow interested in what I am learning and go home and talk to my husband about it. . . . He has developed pride in what I am doing. Frankly, I think he was a little tired of hearing me say, "What's new at work today?"

Returning women without husbands were particularly likely to elicit their children's cooperation and support in organizing their lives. To encourage other women, one center participant wrote a three-page "how to" statement in which she explained her family management techniques, and the convictions concerning human fulfillment on which they are based.

There is little doubt that returning adult women perform well in school. Fagerburg (1970) found that they perform better than other women students including very young returnees. In a University of Michigan report on grades over a three-year period, the grade-point averages of married women students were found to be higher than any other students. A recent survey of the center participants indicates that 91 percent earned grades as good as or better than their earlier records (Markus 1972).

Women reported that family responsibilities and lack of money were the major barriers to returning to school. But some experienced discrimination as a barrier. An engineering student said,

> One of the things that always comes up is the salary discrepancy. . . . We had a discussion of the number of companies that will not even interview women at all. . . . Their complaint . . . is that a woman . . . will not stay because she will get married. . . . I *am* married, I *have* three children . . . but the attitude is not too terribly different toward me. . . .

There was some concern about the generation gap. A study at Mundelein (Hruby 1968) indicated that young students thought the older ones were all right if they didn't dress and act too young. A few women were sensitive to the younger students, believing they would be rejected as "over thirty," fearing contempt or hostility. But most women reported that the younger students accepted them and even asked them for counsel, though the latter sometimes resented how hard the returning women were motivated to work and how intensively they could work since they were taking fewer courses.

In the last ten years, attention has focused so strongly on the compensatory needs of the returning adult woman that many educators have forgotten a major concern of the early programs and their imitators: to provide models and preplanning for undergraduate women: "To date there has been little of the expected benefit to undergraduate women from having them share a campus with the mature women being educated" (Addis 1967:292). Such well-known programs as the Minnesota Plan and the Span Plan at Purdue (Office of the Dean of Women 1971) focus attention on the undergraduate with discussions and educational information. Michigan takes its Arrow program (1972) for undergraduate women into the residence halls and encourages students to use the center.

SCOPE OF CONTINUING EDUCATION PROGRAMS

Information concerning the number of programs for returning women in the nation's colleges and universities and the number of women participating in them is limited. In 1962, a survey of 1,167 accredited colleges, junior colleges, and universities in the United States was made by the American Association of University Women's Educational Foundation. At that time, approximately 300 institutions indicated that they had programs designed especially for returning women or that they provided for the admission and special needs of these women in the regular academic program (Kelsall 1963). Succeeding editions of a listing prepared by the Women's Bureau of the Department of Labor indicated that there were 375 such programs by 1968 and 436 by 1971. Of those, 212 programs existed on the college and university level by 1968 and 376 by 1971.

Special counseling services are built into a number of college and university programs (Dowding 1971). Of the 192 institutions studied by Jacobson (1969), sixty-three offered special counseling programs. Two-thirds of the institutions which did not have special programs nevertheless indicated that regular counseling services were available to returning women. Sixty-six institutions expected such a program to be established. Only twenty-two indicated they thought a special counseling program for adult women would never be established in their institutions.

The American Association of University Women report, "Campus 1970—Where Do Women Stand" (Oltman 1970), based on a survey of 454 institutions, indicated that less than 50 percent of these institutions made any institutional adjustments to fit the special needs and even fewer had special programs for returning women, but almost all indicate that they make it possible for women to return to a degree program. Leland (1969) suggests that "at the decade's close nearly a quarter of our institutions of higher learning had at the very least begun some special response to the unique educational and occupational situations of women."

There is little doubt that the number of programs will continue to increase. Women's "felt needs" are apparent and, as yet, not adequately met. According to the 1971 report on continuing education programs from the Women's Bureau, between 1950 and 1959 school enrollment rose from 26,000 to 311,000 among women 25–29 years of age and from 21,000 to 215,000 among women 30–34 years. Although enrollment figures for women 35 years of age and over will not be available until the 1970 census data are released, there is no doubt that a significant number in this age group are college students (U.S. Department of Labor, Women's Bureau 1971:2).

There is no way to relate these numbers to institutions with special programs for women. Although centers like Michigan keep careful records of those women who use their services, even these do not account for all of the women who return to their institutions. Educational institutions have not kept records according to age, much less according to patterns of dropout and reentry. Recently, however, affirmative action programs have encouraged better record keeping.

The number of "participants" in the University of Michigan's service is probably quite similar to that in other university programs. Over an eight-year period approximately 4,000 women have received individual counseling at Michigan; many have had more than one interview. Some return intermittently but repeatedly as their situations change. In 1971 the number of women seeking appointments for individual guidance increased by 43 percent over 1970. Each year, the various programs (i.e., conferences, conversations, brown bag lunches) may bring 500 to 1,000 more in contact with some supportive and, hopefully, aspiration-stretching experience.

THEMES IN CONTINUING EDUCATION PROGRAMS

More interesting than size and growth are the common concerns and themes running through continuing education programs. Important among these are the need for flexibility in educational institutions, counseling, career development opportunities, and the availability of part-time jobs, day-care, and financial assistance, as well as for continuing research and evaluation of such programs. As Leland comments,

> In these special programs for women there appears to be an openness to new methods and patterns of learning which if studied and tested might offer alternative models to colleges and universities which now resist change for lack of sufficiently convincing demonstrations of effectiveness (Leland 1969:16).

In the catalog of concerns of the continuing education movement, the introduction of more flexibility in the educational system is paramount. In responding to the needs of adult, highly motivated students, the movement for continuing education for women has in a quiet, not very visible way been the bellwether for certain demands now being made by students, blacks, and disadvantaged groups. As Mattfeld (1971) pointed out, the forces moving the educational system today are asking essentially the same questions that motivated the move for adult women's education a decade ago. We must thank the young graduates' effective challenge to establish education over the last several years for

> wider acceptance of individualized programs, the abolition of compulsory courses, distribution and major requirements, and fixed residence requirements, the validation of credit toward the degree of work satisfactorily completed at other institutions, the introduction of credit for field work, the arts, and life experience, the loosening of the four-year-full-time in the ivy-tower-attitudes to permit both acceleration and extension of the degree program to suit individual student's needs. All of these features were established early on as necessary ingredients of continuing education programs for women (Mattfeld 1971:4).

Mattfeld's remarks suggest that more effective change has taken place on our campuses than is probable, but they do point up forces that will maintain continuing education for women in the mainstream of educational reform:

> There is a great emotional surge, among educators and the lay public alike, toward a postsecondary educational system with more flexibility than heretofore and with more options from which the individual should be able to choose, regardless of age or circumstance (Commission on Non-Traditional Study 1971:99).

The provision of supportive counseling is of central importance to continuing education. In the 1960s major efforts were channeled into considerations about the counseling of adults, and a number of workshops were conducted—notably the AAUW summer workshop of 1966 (see References page 119 for reports of other workshops). Counselor bias was explored, particularly by Schlossberg (1968), Troll (1968), and others at Wayne State University. In the case of many programs, problems encountered in counseling returning adult students dramatized the urgent need for improved counseling for girls and undergraduates, and the Women's Bureau developed a series of regional conferences on "counseling girls toward new perspectives" (U.S. Department of Labor, U.S. Department of Health, Education and Welfare, 1966).

Today's consciousness-raising techniques and peer counseling have generally moved all counselors toward feminism. One of them speaking to the American Personnel and Guidance Association said,

> I think females need to be actively pushed . . . females need to be confronted when they harbor unrealistic visions of the traditional role and their own futures, and . . . females must be encouraged to explore the nebulous routes to self-esteem which involve varieties of multiple commitments. Essentially the

counselor must design some program that tells women about women (Pringle 1971).

Another common theme in the counseling centers of continuing education programs is the strong concern for career development, job development (particularly part-time), and placement. Among the first to publish information on part-time job opportunities was the Alumnae Advisory Center in New York (Schwartz 1964). The Michigan experience suggests that virtually all women are interested in using their education on a job, and counseling at the center has always integrated decisionmaking about education with information about jobs and employment trends. As a service to the many struggling programs, the Center published *Careers for College Women* (1968), a bibliography of free and inexpensive vocational materials.

Part-time jobs for women, like day-care centers for children, was an ever-recurring theme in the sixties. It seemed likely that women who carried both home and work responsibilities, whether disadvantaged or privileged, would profit from the option of part-time employment during their children's early years. As convincing evidence accumulated that indicated the critical importance of the child's early development, the interest in part-time permanent jobs flourished.

Radcliffe's attention to the need for part-time jobs was reported in *The Next Step* (White, Albro, and Skinner 1964). The center at Michigan published its *New Patterns of Employment* (1966), and later repeated the theme of part-time employment in *Women in Action* (1969). The University of Missouri prepared for the Missouri Department of Labor and Industrial Relations a *Guide for Development of Permanent Part-time Employment Opportunities—Girls and Women* (Berry et al. 1969). Much earlier, Senders at Minnesota (1961) and Raushenbush (1961) had set the tone for attention to this matter, and when Bunting became a member of the Atomic Energy Commission, she encouraged the creation of a part-time job project in the agency. Later, under Secretary John Gardner, the idea flowered in the Department of Health, Education and Welfare and Elsa Porter gave distinguished leadership to the Professional and Executive Corps. The corps was made up of professional women recruited and placed in part-time professional jobs identified especially for this program. The results to date of this prototypical demonstration are reported in *Good Government* (Silverberg and Eyde 1971). The well-known partnership teaching program, initiated in the Boston area by the Women's Educational and Industrial Union, redirected thinking about the usefulness of women working part-time on work teams.

Women themselves maintain that greater availability of part-time education and jobs would increase their numbers in the professional market (U.S. Department of Health, Education and Welfare 1968). Institutional resistance, pervasive mythologies against working women and the fluctuating demand for "marginal" workers and job innovations have combined to keep part-time job options chiefly confined to seasonal, temporary, or noncareer ladder positions. Nevertheless, in spite of the recent economic downturn or because of it, employers have begun to understand that economies rather than extra cost may be the salient feature of part-time employment.

Small private enterprises with catchy names like "New-time" are appearing. As already noted in this chapter, Catalyst and FEW are demonstrating the feasibility of employing professional women in a variety of jobs on short-day or short-week arrangements. The center at Michigan has had a long-standing interest in part-time job development, working with the Michigan Civil Service on a demonstration project and with the university in regard to its affirmative action program to increase the number of women employed part-time in high level positions.

Academic women have been divided, if not on the desirability, at least on the dangers of institutionalizing part-time employment. Some women reject the idea outright. In their view, true equality is not possible for those women who combine roles, and society must be redesigned to eliminate the necessity to carry dual roles. Some feel it is a matter of strategy to demonstrate women's equality with men by competing without such institutional "compensations" as part-time employment. Others fear that part-time work is a hazard to real achievement. In general, it seems that most academic women are searching for the formula that will provide the opportunity to pursue a first-class academic career during their childbearing years. The Harvard University Faculty of Arts and Sciences report on the status of women at Harvard reflects the difficulties in such a search (1971:38). The American Association of University Women (1971) in their guidelines on sex bias assume regularly employed part-time faculty, and insist that these faculty receive professional benefits and be employed at ranks and salaries commensurate with full-time personnel. Some professional caucuses are on record in support of such a ruling and other professional caucuses are working toward its acceptance by their associations.

Interest in day-care—certainly the recognition that quality day-care is essential both to women's professional achievement and to a healthy society—has been another common concern in continuing education. But there has been far more concern than action. The University of Minnesota initiated and then abandoned day-care arrangements; Oakland University has coordinated a day-care center; a number of community colleges have developed day-care and child-care training centers. However, the initiative and leadership for such centers have come primarily from those concerned with disadvantaged mothers and children. The women's liberation movement finds it especially difficult to understand why there has not been more attention given to day-care in the continuing education movement. Perhaps the motivation to organize day-care centers was less compelling to those devoted to "bending institutions to women's needs" than to those devoted to eliminating sex roles. It is more likely that continuing education programs, which on the whole are small and somewhat marginal, have not had the political strength to induce their institutions to support day-care programs.

Providing financial assistance for returning women is another major concern shared by continuing education programs. The Radcliffe scholars' program was predicated on the need to "buy time" for distinguished scholars and achievement-oriented women. Efforts small and large (and sometimes the former have been the most heroic) to seek out funds for women students have marked all women's programs far more than efforts directed toward other forms of support. Fellowships and scholarships to neutralize the high cost of education for returning women, especially for part-time students are scarce.

In the early 1960's, the Danforth Foundation inaugurated a program to attract women to college teaching and to locate educated women not presently using their education. The American Association of University Women worked toward meeting the same needs in its College Faculty Program, through which members raised money to be given to women attending institutions within their states. Because of the shift in economic circumstances and the college-teaching job market, the College Faculty Program no longer exists. Danforth, with a brief pause for recouping capital, persists. One Michigan state senator, without conspicuous legislative allies, has sponsored a bill providing state funds for adult, part-time women students.

The Michigan center provides two sources of financial assistance to women. One is a share in state-supported funds which are granted by the Center in small amounts for educational costs (including baby-sitting), in cases (mostly part-time) where the need is critical and other resources inadequate or unavailable. The second is the CEW Scholarship Program for which it solicits non-university funds. Both resources are expanding, but the more important challenge has been to eliminate the full-time requirement as a guideline for all-university financial assistance. In spite of administrative support this goal has not yet been fully achieved, partly because of federal policy.

The need for research and evaluation of continuing education programs for women has been a matter of growing concern. By 1967, when the Oakland Continuum Center, supported by the Kellogg Foundation, called a national continuing education conference for program leaders and research-oriented women, it was apparent that their energy and ingenuity needed a firmer base. There were no new hypotheses; few new directions were noted. Still some distance from understanding the gathering momentum of female discontent, this assemblage of program leaders nevertheless made a significant contribution by assessing the need for basic and comprehensive research about women's position in our society—the heart of women's studies as well as intelligently planned educational programs and services. From this meeting the idea of a consortium of continuing education programs took shape—to mine the data concerning programs for women; to avoid unnecessary duplication of studies; to make optimal use of limited national resources for storing data and retrieving information; to communicate and order research findings; and in general, to provide the base of support for better research.

In 1971 a major cooperative effort, with Johnson Foundation support, brought the National Coalition for Research on Women's Education and Development into being, supported by thirteen institutions and advisory and scientific support committees (see *Description* 1971). The combination of research-oriented and service-oriented planning was a bold concept. Open to all educational institutions or education-related agencies, the Coalition intends to encourage and support a broad program of basic as well as program-oriented research.

Other institutions also have expressed research-oriented interests. The Research Center at Alverno College is a focus of conferences on continuing education. The Women's Action Program of the Department of Health, Education and Welfare has promoted research—notably, a major study on the barriers to women in higher education, soon to be reported by the Educational Testing Service. The College Research Center, now part of the Educational Testing Service in Princeton, New Jersey, continues to serve its women's college members. The American Council on Education is assessing issues in women's education and its Office of Research may become an important resource for research on women.

Although little research has come from the continuing education movement as such, these programs have been informed and influenced by research on achievement in women, sparked by Horner's insight into the "fear of success"; Maccoby's continuing experimentation and integration of research on sex differences; the examination by Newcomb and others on the effect of the undergraduate experience; Rossi's (1970) conceptualizations of women's role and career development; and numerous studies in physiology, economics, and adult development. One of the major features of the feminist movement is the increasing interest of women scholars in research on women. Comprehensive women's programs will increasingly draw upon and incorporate this research potential.

Continuing education programs do know something about who returns to school and the changing nature of this population (Schletzer et al. 1967; Davis et al. 1966; Burton 1968; Withycombe-Brocato 1970; Likert 1967; Fagerburg 1970; LeFevre 1971; Richter and Whippel 1972; Markus 1972; and others). Some centers have collected demographic information about their students; some, like Michigan, have interview protocols and will shortly report follow-up studies. There has been some investigation of the returning woman's attitudes toward education and work and some attempt to relate this information to personality measures. However, studies of the adult woman student who combines roles and whose education is punctuated with interruptions are few.

Longitudinal studies of women returning to school, the problems they face, and the effect of educational discontinuity on goal completion and career development are subjects wide open for investigation. Data on how well older women graduate students do in comparison to younger students or to male students are critically important in gaining acceptance for programs geared to women's needs and capabilities. Continuing education counselors have a special interest in career development, particularly in the career development of successful women. The Radcliffe

Institute, one of the few programs with a research staff, has had a long-standing research interest in the career development of advantaged women (Kahne 1971).

CONCLUDING REMARKS

This brief history and summary of major themes in women's continuing education suggests both the vitality of the programs and some of their problems. Women interested in studying this movement in greater detail may be referred to Fought's history (1966), the Westervelt and Fixter annotated bibliography (1971), and the Astin et al. bibliography on research (1971). An older summary of research (Leland and Lozoff 1969) is especially useful, as are the *Current Information Sources* #22 (Continuing Education of Women 1968), and #32 (1970) available from the Eric Clearinghouse on Adult Education at Syracuse and the Resource Center on Women of the YWCA. Many programs, like that of Michigan's, have libraries of materials useful to students.

This survey is not just an historical exercise. Stubborn barriers to the completion of interrupted education are still very much apparent: the lack of widespread quality day-care, the instability of part-time work and study arrangements, the inability to relocate, and the cost to a family of two educations. While innovative, achievement-oriented women show an increasing willingness to postpone marriage and children (Tangri 1971) and to explore alternative life styles, most women will continue to marry before their life goals are clarified. Many will continue to combine roles with insufficient institutional support for some time to come. (Discussions of current research in Center for Continuing Education 1971 are useful in this connection.)

In working with hundreds of women—uncertain, eager, serious, and motivated—continuing education program leaders have become poignantly aware of the absence of academic role models, the low priority of concern for women as professionals and top-level administrators, the declining status of women in jobs as the numbers of working women rise (to 38 percent of the labor force) and their age increases. (In 1970, there were almost as many women workers 45 to 54 years of age as there were 20- to 24-year-old women workers—the peak working years.)

The dramatic accomplishment of continuing education in the sixties was the practical assistance afforded individual women. However, the institutional change brought about by these programs, impressive in an absolute sense, has been disappointing. "By no means has the early challenge of the 1960s been fulfilled. Seldom have our colleges shown any more flexibility or enlightenment with regard to women than a host of other societal institutions" (Leland 1969:15).

Perhaps the accelerating rate of change somewhat disguises the very real institutional consolidation of the ideas and reforms of continuing education programs (Campbell 1970). Academic women who are increasingly concerned with eliminating discrimination in admissions, financial assistance, and employment, and who are encouraging scholarship in women's studies are well aware of the importance of institutionalized part-time study programs and day-care arrangements.

It must not be supposed that continuing education programs have been unaffected by the writings and spirit of the "second wave of feminism." While continuing education programs are essentially adaptive, seeking wider opportunities, compensatory support, and greater access to the academic system, they are nevertheless subject to the criticism implied by Lerner with which this chapter opened. Their leaders are in the tradition of political and institutional *reform*. They must ask themselves if they wish to be a part of a "civil rights" movement which may in the long run fall short of fundamental social change, or if they wish to work for reform sufficient to secure a viable equality. Will they contribute stability and continuity to a gradual change that will someday develop a constituency and a ground for broad acceptance of feminist principles—freedom to be one's self, to choose a way of life, to achieve, to share, to nurture?

A major focus (and accomplishment) of women's continuing education programs has been helping the individual woman take the next step to grow on her own terms. The movement *is* vulnerable to the question of what benefits a woman gains if she comes to expect what is denied her by society. But most criticism of the programs is superficial. A recent radical critique of adult women's education (Merideth and Merideth 1971) suggests no *specific* reform that was not already a major concern of continuing education programs, except support of alternative forms of living (already common in many college and university communities), and affirmative action in employment.

If continuing education programs evolve into more inclusive educational programs, they undoubtedly will exert considerable leadership. Women's action groups such as NOW and WEAL, women's professional and political caucuses, the proliferation of commissions on the status of women, "guidelines" on sex bias, and the panoply of techniques for concerted and forceful action have changed the university world for some women. But these developments, which may open more opportunities, have not lessened the need for models of education that make sense to *all* qualified and motivated women students. Even more than a decade ago, women must now examine how education can more effectively nurture their talents and raise their aspirations. If the major function of continuing education programs is to help create educational alternatives that in no way discriminate, enormous changes in policy and patterns of support by the educational community are required.

Just such far-reaching changes have been proposed to the educational establishment in recent reports from the Carnegie Commission on Higher Education (1971), the Assembly on University Goals and Governance (1971), and the U.S. Department of Health, Education and Welfare, Office of Education (1971). The work of the Commission on Non-Traditional Education (1971) and the Panel on Alternative Approaches to Graduate Education, supported by the Council of Graduate

Schools and the Educational Testing Service, will give additional impetus to change.

Present programs and services for women are innovative and energetic, but in all cases somewhat marginal to the educational power structure and, by their own definition, compensatory. These programs have a clear view of the need for change but few allies with the same vision, although an increasing number of top-level administrators are speaking out. For example, Lyman of Stanford, speaking to his alumni fund raisers,

> hinted that part-time opportunities might have to be broadened in the future.
>
> While the University clearly will continue its strong commitment to undergraduate education, he said: "less and less will Stanford be concentrating its energies on the education of persons between the ages of 18 and 21."
>
> He explained that "People will do other things between high school and college partly because they want a break in the educational lockstep, partly because they will feel somewhat freer to postpone college until such time as they have a clearer idea of what they might wish to get out of going there."
>
> Meanwhile other people will be seeking to come back to learn new skills, or to learn things that would enrich their growing leisure or to restore their critical capacities (*Stanford Observer* 1971:1).

Women will have to put great energy into urging broad-based, long-term planning to accomplish such educational reform, and must be prepared for a monumental lack of collegial interest in their major concern—a reexamination of the basic structure of the college and university.

If the major goal of these programs is elusive, how will they carry on in their present stance as "interveners," as agencies pointing to the special needs of women in higher education? Insofar as measures are compensatory, they are not central. Insofar as they are not central, they require the constant attention of the compensatory agency to ward off the effects of competing pressures. Simply opening the doors and keeping them open to students who must carry out their educational program at a slower pace than those who can give it their full-time attention can be a very demanding enterprise when it goes against institutional mores. Strengthening a compensatory program is not the answer as much as developing a broader base of support which can move the "compensatory" concerns to a more central position in higher education. This, in fact, is what Lyman implied in his predictions of the changed use of universities by future students, male as well as female.

Some women question the desirability of compensatory programs out of ignorance of the barriers to equal opportunity. Other women feel they should ask no favors, that women cannot demand both equality and special treatment. These women, of course, are opposed by those who feel they have too long blamed themselves instead of the system for difficulties in educational and employment achievement.

The most nettling problem is the intractable one—the rate of change—which demands a continual restatement of assumptions concerning everything from demographic data to projected employment needs, from the state of the economy to relative social goods. Before one set of expectations can be institutionalized, attention has shifted to another.

All of these problems are overshadowed by the threat of decreasing support for higher education and the competition for "new" money. Limited budgets and the rising demand for education will, perhaps, force fundamental changes and flexibilities in the system that will benefit women. The problems seem formidable, but women's programs are expanding conceptions of what is possible and what constitutes a comprehensive program. Their efforts to enlarge opportunities for women and to encourage women to use these opportunities will be increasingly effective as all women learn to use the moral power of the democratic ideal.

REFERENCES

Addis, M. E. 1967. Problems of administrative change in selected programs for the re- ← education of women. Ph.D. dissertation, Harvard University.

American Association of University Women, 1971. Standards for women in higher education—affirmative policy in achieving sex equality in the academic community. Washington, D.C.: Author. Mimeographed.

American Association of University Women Educational Foundation. 1966. *Counseling techniques for mature women.* Washington, D.C.: Author.

Assembly on University Goals and Governance. 1971. A first report. Cambridge, Mass.: The American Academy of Arts and Sciences.

Astin, Helen S., Suniewick, Nancy, and Dweck, Susan. 1971. *Women: a bibliography* ← *on their education and careers.* Washington, D.C.: Human Service Press.

Barnard College. 1971. The women's center. New York. (Brochure.)

Berry, Jane, and Epstein, Sandra. 1963. *Continuing education of women—needs, aspirations and plans.* Kansas City, Mo.: The Division for Continuing Education of the University of Kansas City.

Berry, Jane, McCarty, Edward R., Bates, Jean M., and Terrill, Hazel J. 1969. *Guide for development of permanent part-time employment opportunities for girls and women.* Kansas City: University of Missouri.

Bunting, Mary I. 1961. The Radcliffe Institute for Independent Study. *Educational Record,* 42:19–26.

Burton, Lisbeth K. 1968. A follow-up study of the mature women clients at the University of Colorado Women's Center, 1964–1966. Master's degree dissertation, University of Colorado.

Campbell, Jean W. 1970. Change for women—glacial or otherwise? In *Women on Campus: 1970.* Ann Arbor: University of Michigan Center for Continuing Education of Women.

Carnegie Commission on Higher Education. 1971. *Less time, more options.* New York: McGraw-Hill Book Co.

Catalyst in Education. 1968. *Part-time teachers and how they work, a study of five school systems.* New York: Author.

Catalyst. 1971. *Part-time social workers in public welfare.* New York: Author.

Center for Continuing Education of Women. 1966. *New patterns of employment.* Ann Arbor: University of Michigan.

Center for Continuing Education of Women. 1968. *Careers for college women.* Ann Arbor: University of Michigan.

Center for Continuing Education of Women. 1969. *Women in action.* Ann Arbor: University of Michigan.

Center for Continuing Education of Women. 1971. *Women on campus: 1970—a symposium.* Ann Arbor: University of Michigan Center for Continuing Education of Women.

→Center for Continuing Education of Women. 1972. ARROW program for undergraduate women. Ann Arbor: University of Michigan. (Brochure.)

Cless, Elizabeth. 1969. A modest proposal for the educating of women. *The American Scholar,* 38:618–627.

Commission on Education at Mather and Adelbert Colleges. 1970. *Report.* Cleveland, Ohio: Case Western Reserve University.

Commission on Non-Traditional Study. 1971. *New dimensions for the learner—a first look at the prospects for non-traditional study.* New York: Author.

Continuing Education of Women. 1968. *Current information sources,* No. 22. Syracuse, N.Y.: ERIC Clearinghouse on Adult Education.

→Continuing Education of Women 1970. *Current information sources,* No. 32. Syracuse, N.Y.: ERIC Clearinghouse on Adult Education.

David, Opal D. (Ed.). 1959. *The education of women—signs for the future.* Washington, D.C.: American Council on Education.

Davis, Natalie Zemon, Grimshaw, J., Mandell, E., Prentice, A. S., and Warkentin, G. 1966. A study of 42 women who have children and who are in graduate programmes at the University of Toronto. Mimeographed.

Dennis, Lawrence E. (Ed.). 1963. *Education and a woman's life.* Washington, D.C.: American Council on Education.

Description of the National Coalition for Research on Women's Education and Development, Inc. 1971. New York: State University of New York at Stony Brook.

Dowding, Nancy E. 1971. Summary of results of questionnaire survey of counseling services for women students sent to 1,850 collegiate institutions in the U.S. Parma: Cuyahoga Community College, Western campus. Mimeographed.

Fagerburg, J. E. 1970. A comparative study of undergraduate women in relation to selected personal characteristics and certain effects of educational interruption. Ph.D. dissertation, Purdue University.

→Fagin, Margaret C. 1971. Analysis of the performance of adult women in Missouri on three general examinations of the college level examination program. *Adult Education Journal,* 21:148–165.

Fought, C. A. 1966. The historical development of continuing education for women in the United States: Economic, social and psychological implications. Ph.D. dissertation, Ohio State University.

Harvard University Faculty of Arts and Sciences. 1971. Report of the committee on the status of women. Cambridge: Harvard University.

Hortenstine, Anne. 1971. Continuing education for disadvantaged women. Unpublished paper, Duke University.

Hruby, Norbert. 1968. The generation gap: Its impact on Mundelein from within. Chicago: Mundelein College. Mimeographed.

Jacobson, R. F. 1969. The organization and administration of special counseling programs for adult women in colleges and universities. Ph.D. dissertation, University of Southern California.

Kahne, Hilda. 1971. Women in the professions: Career considerations and job placement techniques. *Journal of Economic Issues,* 5(3):28–48.

Kelsall, Ann. 1963. The continuing education of women: New programs, old problems, fresh hopes. In Joseph V. Totaro (Ed.), *Women in college and university teaching, a symposium on staff needs and opportunities in higher education.* Madison: University of Wisconsin, School of Education, and the Johnson Foundation, pp. 19–29.

LeFevre, Carol. 1971. The mature woman as graduate student: A study of changing self-conceptions. Dissertation abstract, The University of Chicago. Mimeographed.

Leland, Carole. 1969. Structures and strangers in higher education. In *An imperative for the seventies: Releasing creative woman power.* St. Louis: University of Missouri (St. Louis), pp. 15–18.

Leland, Carole A., and Lozoff, Marjorie M. 1969. *College influence on the role development of female undergraduates.* Final project report, Stanford Institute for the Study of Human Problems. Washington, D.C.: Educational Resources Information Center (ED. 026 975).

Lerner, Gerda. 1971. Women's rights and American feminism. *The American Scholar,* 40:235–248.

Likert, Jane (Ed.). 1967. *Conversations with returning women students.* Ann Arbor: University of Michigan Center for Continuing Education of Women.

Lloyd, Betty Jane. 1967. A ten-year report: Margaret Morrison Carnegie College projects related to the changing role of women. Pittsburgh: Margaret Morrison Carnegie College. Mimeographed.

Markus, Hazel. 1972. Continuing education of women: Factors influencing a return to school and the school experience. Unpublished paper. University of Michigan.

Mattfeld, Jacquelyn A. 1971. A decade of continuing education—dead end or open door. Unpublished manuscript, Brown University.

Mayhew, Harry C. 1970. An analysis of comprehensive continuing education programs and services for women at selected midwestern universities. Ph.D. dissertation, Ball State University.

McGuigan, Dorothy G. 1970. *A dangerous experiment—100 years of women at the University of Michigan.* Ann Arbor: University of Michigan Center for Continuing Education for Women.

McLean, Catherine D., and Lucas, Rex A. 1970. *Nurses come lately. The first five years of the Quo Vadis School of Nursing.* Etobicoke. Ontario: The Quo Vadis School of Nursing.

Merideth, Elizabeth, and Merideth, Robert. 1971. Adult women's education: a radical critique. *Journal of the National Association of Women Deans and Counselors,* 34:111–118.

National Manpower Council. 1957. *Womanpower*. New York: Columbia University Press.

National Manpower Council. 1958. *Work in the lives of married women*. New York: Columbia University Press.

New York University Graduate School of Social Work. 1965–1969. *Annual reports on the Westchester project in graduate education for mature women*. White Plains, N.Y.: New York University.

Office of Continuing Education. 1972. *A matter of degree*. Milwaukee: The University of Wisconsin.

→Office of the Dean of Women. 1971. *Span plan program for women*. West Lafayette, Ind.: Purdue University.

Oltman, Ruth M. 1970. *Campus 1970: Where do women stand?* Washington, D.C.: American Association of University Women.

Oppenheimer, Valerie. 1966. The female work force in the United States: Factors governing its growth and changing composition. Ph.D. dissertation, University of California, Berkeley.

Osborn, Ruth H. 1967. *Continuing education for women*. Washington, D.C.: George Washington University College of General Studies.

Pringle, Marlene. 1971. Counseling women. *Caps Capsule*, 4:11.

→Raines, M. R. 1969. *An appraisal of the New York State Guidance Center for Women*. New York: State University of New York.

Raushenbush, Esther. 1961. *Unfinished business: Continuing education of women*. Washington, D.C.: American Council on Education (reprint from *Educational Record*, 42:261–269).

Richter, Melissa L., and Whipple, Jane B. 1972. *A revolution in the education of women —ten years of continuing education at Sarah Lawrence College*. Bronxville, N.Y.: Sarah Lawrence College.

Rioch, Margaret J., Elkes, Charmian, and Flint, Arden A. (Undated, but probably 1964.) *NIMH pilot project in training mental health counselors*. U.S. Department of Health, Education and Welfare, National Institute of Mental Health. Mimeographed.

Rossi, Alice. 1970. *Women in the seventies: Problems and possibilities*. Pittsburgh, Pa.: KNOW, Inc.

Sanford, Nevitt. 1956. Personality development during the college years. *Journal of Social Issues*, 12(4).

Schletzer, Vera M., Cless, Elizabeth L., McCune, Cornelia W., Mantini, Barbara K., and Leoffler, Dorothy. 1967. *Continuing education of women—a five year report of the Minnesota Plan*. Minneapolis: University of Minnesota.

Schlossberg, Nancy. 1968. Is adult counseling different? Unpublished paper given at Conference on Adult Counseling. Wayne State University—Merrill-Palmer Institute.

→ Schwartz, Felice N., Schifer, Margaret H., and Gilotti, Susan S. 1972. *How to go to work when your husband is against it, your children aren't old enough—and there's nothing you can do anyhow*. New York: Simon & Schuster.

Schwartz, Jane. 1964. *Part-time employment—employer attitudes on opportunities for the college trained woman*. New York: Alumnae Advisory Center.

Senders, Virginia L. 1961. The Minnesota plan for women's continuing education: a progress report. *Educational Record,* 42:270–278.

Silverberg, Marjorie, and Eyde, Lorraine. 1971. Career part-time employment: Personnel implications of the HEW professional and executive corps. *Good Government,* 88(3):11–19.

Smith, Constance E. August 31, 1968. Career development of advantaged women: An institutional case study. Paper read at the American Psychological Association 76th Annual Meeting, Washington, D.C.

Stanford (California) *Observer.* October 1971, p. 1.

Tangri, Sandra. September 4, 1971. Occupational aspirations and experiences of college women. Paper read at the American Psychological Association 79th Annual Meeting, Washington, D.C.

Thompson, Marian L., and Sager, Lawrence. 1970. *Report on the E. B. Fred fellowship for mature women, 1963–1968: a program in continuing education.* Madison: University of Wisconsin, University Extension.

Troll, Lillian E. 1968. Age, sex, and social class variables in counseling adults. Paper read at the Conference on Counseling Adults, Wayne State University—Merrill-Palmer Institute.

U.S. Department of Health, Education and Welfare. 1968. *Special report on women and graduate study.* Resources for medical research report no. 13. Washington, D.C.: U.S. Government Printing Office.

U.S. Department of Health, Education and Welfare, Office of Education. 1971. *Report on higher education.* Washington, D.C.: U.S. Government Printing Office.

U.S. Department of Health, Education and Welfare, Public Health Service. 1971. *Equivalency and proficiency testing.* Washington, D.C.: U.S. Government Printing Office.

U.S. Department of Labor, Women's Bureau. 1963a. *American women.* Washington, D.C.: U.S. Government Printing Office.

U.S. Department of Labor, Women's Bureau. 1963b. Why continuing education programs for women. Washington, D.C. Mimeographed.

U.S. Department of Labor, Women's Bureau. 1971. *Continuing education programs and services for women, pamphlet 10 (revised).* Washington, D.C.: U.S. Government Printing Office.

U.S. Department of Labor, Women's Bureau, and U.S. Department of Health, Education and Welfare. 1966. *Counseling girls toward new perspectives—a report of the Middle Atlantic Regional Pilot Conference* (held in Philadelphia). Washington, D.C.: U.S. Government Printing Office.

University of California, Los Angeles, Department of Daytime Programs and Special Projects. 1970. *The humanities: tools for solving the urban crisis—a program for mature women.* Los Angeles: University of California.

Westervelt, Esther M. 1968. *Releasing women's potentialities—the two year college as catalyst.* Proceedings of a conference held at Rockland Community College. Albany: State University of New York.

Westervelt, Esther, and Fixter, Deborah. 1971. *Women's higher and continuing education: An annotated bibliography.* Washington, D.C.: College Entrance Examination Board.

White, Martha S., Albro, Mary D., and Skinner, Alice B. (Eds.). 1964. *The next step:*

A guide to part-time opportunities and study for the educated woman. Cambridge, Mass.: Radcliffe Institute of Independent Study.

→ Withycombe-Brocato, C. J. 1970. The mature woman student: Who is she? Ph.D. dissertation, United States International University.

Wulp, Patricia. 1971. Report on the CEW evening program. Ann Arbor: University of Michigan Center for Continuing Education of Women. Mimeographed.

BIBLIOGRAPHY

Berry, Jane, Kern, Kenneth K., Meleney, Elaine K., and Vetter, Louise, 1966. *Counseling girls and women—awareness, analysis, action.* Kansas City: University of Missouri.

Brewster, Kingman, 1970. The involuntary campus and the manipulated society. Washington, D.C.: American Council on Education (reprint from *Educational Record,* 51:101–105.

New England Board of Higher Education and The Center for the Study of Liberal Education for Adults, 1965. *Proceedings of the conference on the training of counselors of adults.* Winchester, Mass.: New England Board of Higher Education.

Pietrofess, John S., and Schlossberg, Nancy. 1972. Counselor bias and the female occupational role. In Nona Glazer-Malbin and Helen Youngelson Waehrer (Eds.), *Women in a man-made world.* Chicago: Rand McNally.

Pringle, Marlene. 1971. Counseling women. *Caps Capule,* 4:11.

Proceedings from The First Catalyst on Campus Conference. 1964. *A program proposal.* Pittsburgh: Margaret Morrison Carnegie College.

Raushenbush, Esther. 1962. Second chance: new education for women. *Harper's Magazine,* 225:148–151.

Thompson, Clarence H. (Ed.). 1967. *Counseling the adult student. Proceedings of a pre-convention workshop.* Washington, D.C.: Commission XIII, American College Personnel Association.

Thompson, Clarence H. (Ed.). 1968. *Counseling adults: contemporary dimensions. Proceedings of a pre-convention workshop.* Washington, D.C.: Commission XIII, American College Personnel Association.

U.S. Department of Labor, Women's Bureau, 1969. *Handbook of women workers.* Washington, D.C.: U.S. Government Printing Office.

Chapter Six

From Sugar and Spice to Professor

Joan Huber

A PERSON who maintains a self-definition with no social support is mad; with minimum support, a pioneer; and with broad support, a lemming. Most of us are lemmings. We accept or change our ideas about rights and duties only when we perceive social support for doing so.

In the United States, social and occupational identities are closely related; a person is what he or she does. Occupations are ranked in order of their prestige and pay and this ranking becomes part of our identity. To explain and justify the wide variation in occupational income and prestige, the ideology of equal opportunity holds that the rewards a person receives are deserved because hard work and brains determine success or failure. But the gap between the ideal and reality is great: black men and white women earn about one-half to two-thirds, and black women earn only about a quarter of the pay of white men. Systematic discrimination accounts for most of this variation. Sometimes the subordinated themselves claim that they experience no discrimination and this fact occasionally is used as evidence that none exists. Social scientists are not surprised when those who are discriminated against accept prevailing social definitions and explanations. To understand certain basic assumptions of one's society as illusions is a lonely business and only those who have the courage of pioneers can face up to it. I am no pioneer. My self-definition has been largely a response to events of my own time. This essay briefly recounts my attempt to redefine my social rights and duties, supported by social conditions which made traditional work roles so uncomfortable that the search for alternatives became necessary.

Let us briefly examine some broad technological and demographic changes which have made traditional roles obsolete and then focus on the specific events of the last fifty years which have affected the social identity of women of my generation who grew up in the Depression years. Although I am a statistical rarity as an academic woman in a male occupation, this account will stress aspects of self-definition common to many women.

In traditional societies most labor is domestic or agricultural and people work where they live. Industrialization requires wage labor away from the home but

AUTHOR'S NOTE: This chapter is a slightly revised version of an article first published by *The Notre Dame Journal of Education,* 2(4), Winter 1972.

the wages typically are so low that both women and children work in order to provide for the family. By the late nineteenth century, the dramatic rise in real income enabled families to subsist on the wages of only one earner and women stayed home to perform unpaid labor. In the transition from rural to urban society, however, the birthrate fell and in the twentieth century birth-control methods became so reliable that rational family-planning was possible. At about the same time, economic growth required an enormous pool of skilled labor. Women could be induced to work for about half the wages of men with a similar level of training or education; hence, the clerical segment of the work force became predominantly female. The twentieth century thus brought a high demand for female labor along with an increasing ability to control pregnancy and a decreasing desire for large families. These technological and demographic facts set the stage for the women's movement.

Specific events of the last fifty years affecting women's roles include the Depression of the thirties. As expected in hard times, the birthrate fell sharply. At the same time, married women often were fired because they did not "need" the money. Thus, women were discouraged both from working and from having large families. Meanwhile, the influence of Freudian psychology made women feel responsible for taking care of their children's egos and cleaning up their ids. Women were caught in a double bind: if they didn't stay home, they were bad mothers; if they did, their children were likely to become victims of pernicious momism.

World War II had an apparently opposite effect: women swarmed into the work force and even into the armed services, but not for long. The birthrate usually rises after all wars and World War II was no exception. For the first time in history the inverse relation between family income and number of children was reversed when the upper middle class took to procreation with a vengeance. A better demonstration of lemming-like behavior would be hard to find. Family togetherness was, as the popular magazines asserted, a way of life for the sophisticated moderns of the postwar world. In practice, this meant that mommy, after spending all week with the kids, could spend the weekend with the kids and daddy. The experience was alleged to be richly rewarding and to have a cement-like effect on family relationships. Doing fun things with daddy and the kids gave the ultimate substance and meaning to a woman's life.

As the togetherness generation grew up, an alarming fact appeared: a nasty generation gap separated the mommies and the daddies from the kids who, contrary to expectation, showed signs of laziness, ingratitude, and total irresponsibility as indicated by the way they messed up their rooms, wore their hair, and spent their parents' money. Moreover, the availability of liquor and pot gave many middle-class parents a degree of contact with their friendly local police that they had not anticipated. Parents of the Depression generation nervously asked themselves what had gone wrong and almost unanimously described the situation with one word: permissiveness.

For adult white males, the decade of the sixties was a real loser: blacks, teenagers, and women got out of hand at the same time; not all of them, but enough to make the decade very noisy. The assorted demands were varied but common themes included a fundamental questioning of systems of social stratification and the family, and a strong desire for social change. By the end of the decade, pollution was an additional problem that threatened not only the organization of the American economy but possibly the future of life on our planet. The bearing of the population issue on women's identity problems can hardly be overestimated. A large family has become a sign of social and moral irresponsibility rather than a monument to the energy and endurance of a selfless woman. Although this country is rich and can (if one ignores obligations to the rest of the world) afford to keep a class of persons whose main function is to provide domestic service for males, the traditional maternal aspects of the female role are so changed that the ancient arguments for keeping women at home do not apply. New role definitions are evolving, along with new ideas of appropriate occupations and life styles for men and women, new personal and family relations, and new modes of socializing children. Stimulated by these larger events, my own identity has changed considerably in the last twenty-five years and I shall trace the changes here: a short history of a lemming.

With a twin sister I was born in 1925 in a small town in the midwest. My grandparents had farmed but in my parents' generation the dominant occupation was teaching. My parents always expected me to go to college so I cannot claim to have chosen, inspired by the Protestant ethic, to live the austere life of a college student. Before I was born, my mother had been a dedicated fifth-grade teacher; and with total recall of the songs, stories, and projects of her childhood and teaching days she enriched our minds with great energy. In other respects our rearing was similar to that of girls of our parents' occupational and income level. The most impressive aspect of this socialization was the capacity to sweep unpleasant facts about a girl's future under the rug.

Girls are socialized with double-talk because no one has ever demonstrated the relationship of doing well in school to domestic service. Since housewives' activities are not inherently interesting, a lot of fast talking is required to convince little girls that they face a great future. I should like to report that at an early age I noticed the vast discrepancies between what people said and what they did, and reacted in moral outrage; but I climbed no infant barricade. Far from it; I liked being a girl. I liked pretty clothes and I liked playing with dolls. Boys led a dull and colorless life in brown corduroy knickers and grey sweaters, and they were always hitting things.

While my father went off to a roll-top desk in an office with an interesting smell of formaldehyde, my mother's activities did not inspire emulation. On Mondays she disappeared into the basement, wearing an old pair of rubber galoshes and a slightly raveled sweater, to do the family wash. Dirty clothes first were boiled in a big copper tub, stirred with a stick worn smooth. Sometimes the tub would boil dry and you could smell charred underwear all over the house. Handkerchiefs were put in a crock with some Clorox and swished around to remove the mucus. I thought that cleaning the mucus off a dirty handkerchief was unpleasant, especially when the user had a heavy cold. When I told my mother this, she replied that Kleenex was too expensive. Putting clothes through the wringer was most exciting because the newspapers constantly carried tales of an unwary child whose fingers or arm had been caught in the machine. But the basement was damp and dark, with spiders on the beams, and the job took all day. On Tuesdays, mother would stand all day long in the kitchen ironing, only taking time out to make lunch and dinner and wash up. Some jobs like decorating Christmas cookies and Easter eggs were fun. Others were bad: when the cat threw up and you could see the worms crawling in the vomit, she sent us off to scrub our hands while she cleaned up the mess.

Clearly, those jobs had to be done and neither my mother nor anyone else questioned that it was her responsibility to do them. But the value of the work was obvious when my sister and I found that we could get out of practically any job by claiming that we needed to practice the piano, cello, violin, or do homework. Schoolwork obviously outranked housework. I have always been grateful to my mother that she ignored my messy room (most of the time) and let me get my work done.

The same inconsistency between our childhood education and future role was apparent in high school. As captain of the debating team and editor of the school paper, I demonstrated that Susan B. Anthony and all those brave women had not lived in vain. But the occupations most frequently mentioned to me were those of teacher and librarian. No one told me outright that to aspire to the diplomatic corps was fatuous, but I was thoroughly exposed to the view that, as a girl, I should have a realistic occupation because my husband might die and I might need to work, and that I could always find a job teaching no matter where I lived. In grade school I had liked the idea of becoming a teacher but by the time I was in fifth grade, I noticed that the perfect grade to teach was always the one in which I currently was enrolled. By the time I was in high school, simple extrapolation led me to conclude that teaching would be attractive only if the students were grown up and interested in assorted ideas. But college teaching was not what my advisors had in mind.

In college the ambivalence about the future permeated the fabric of women's lives. Most of us expected to marry. A few spoke seriously and sincerely of the joys of homemaking, especially if they were in home economics and had devoted great energy to learning to scrub carrots and pare apples to make Waldorf salad and other delicacies. A more common response was wry resignation; occasional cracks could be heard about the utility of a college education for a career in the kitchen. We were told that our education would make us better mothers, although no one explained how knowing anything about the Icelandic Eddas or the Duino Elegies would improve the ability to communicate with a five-year-old. Most of us regarded the pious pronouncements about our civilizing influence on the next generation as pure treacle designed to give everyone the good feeling that ours was the best of all possible worlds.

I was ambivalent but I played the game. I finished college at nineteen and married at twenty. Admitted to a top graduate school, I didn't go on because it seemed sensible to defer a Ph.D. till after the children I wanted were grown. Although my name had come to represent someone who was able to manage her life as an adult, I changed it without thinking much about it because there was no choice. This was the way things were. I began to act out the role of housewife, confronted by a spate of low-level technological problems.

An example will help the reader who has never learned a semiskilled trade to understand what housewives do, hence what is involved in a change of identities. A pressing problem in the cotton age was to learn to iron a shirt without scorching the collar. Like flying an airplane, the procedure is easy once you have mastered it although it is less exhilarating. To do the job properly requires about twenty minutes. The damper and more heavily starched the shirt, the more likely that you will scorch it. Moreover, if the shirt is too damp, ironing it may require up to an hour for if you fail to get it completely dry it will relax limply the moment you have ceased paying any attention to it. And an overstarched shirt will not only abrade the skin right off the wearer's neck but give him the look of a martial character in a comic opera. But if you iron it when it is too dry, it will remain gullied with wrinkles and advertise to the world that your unfortunate husband has an incompetent wife. Furthermore, proper starch should be heavy for the collar, lighter for the cuffs, and lighter still for the body of the shirt. Making the starch is tricky because, unless it is stirred vigorously at just the right moment, ineradicable lumps appear and you must throw it out and start over. If you decide that a clean shirt every day is more than a man needs, then you must learn how to remove the extra accumulation of dirt from the collar; that is, you must learn to use Clorox. If you do not use enough, the collar will remain an earthy shade of yellowish-grey but if you use too much, it will disintegrate. This is why shirts sent out to the laundry are always white but do not last very long. Actually, what a housewife is learning to do is to find minimax solutions to a wide variety of problems. Even women of modest intelligence become extraordinarily adept at rapid solutions involving a host of variables. Unfortunately, the problems themselves are trivial.

I had plenty of company. The pressure on women to devote themselves to domestic concerns was enormous at that time. During the Depression and the war many families had deferred having children until times were better. The sudden release of pent-up wishes for family life isolated the young woman who had no one with whom to discuss the number of stitches her episiotomy had required, or what should be done if the baby's b.m. was green. (If you are sure he hasn't eaten any crayons—the consequences are colorful but harmless—call the doctor right away.) Second, the depression that many economists had expected in the transition to a peace-time economy did not occur and, for the middle classes, job security was high and income was growing at a steady rate. Many women found that they were being kept in a style to which they were not accustomed and hence they expanded their activities to include gracious living, a concept extolled by the women's magazines. A three-color layout would show a willowy creature dressed in a velvet hostess gown putting the finishing touches on a six-course dinner for eight. In practice, gracious living meant that, with the aid of a mixmaster and a dishwasher, you were supposed to emulate the life style of a middle-class Victorian Englishwoman who had a nanny, a tweenie, a cook, and a parlormaid to help her. Gracious living could, however, keep a woman fully occupied at home, for an unlimited number of hours can be spent preparing excellent food, keeping the table linens spotless and the silver gleaming, arranging a stunning centerpiece, and choosing an amusing little rosé. The message was clear: no woman ever need be bored at home. Something is wrong with a woman who is not gloriously happy performing these delightful functions.

Nowhere at that time do I recall reading an honest statement about what it meant to be a housewife. Women were told that they were destined to play warm, motherly, nurturant, friendly, companionable roles—but they never were advised of the price. The fact is that a married woman has little control over her own future because so much depends on the occupational performance of her husband. A married woman either must remain passive and hope that things will turn out all right or attempt to control the outcome by influencing her husband's performance; in plainer terms, she must do nothing or try to control another person to attain the ends she seeks. Either choice is profoundly unsatisfactory. In most marriages, the important life decisions either are made by the husband or are made as a consequence of his occupational performance: which job to take, which city to live in, what kind of house or neighborhood to live in—in short, just about everything that matters. To speak of a marriage of equal partners in such circumstances is fatuous. A career as a homemaker means that a woman, even if she is bright and works very hard, will spend about twenty years at a semiskilled blue-collar job in preparation for another thirty years of domestic service with a little amateur social work on the side. Her job performance will have little influence on her share of income, prestige, and influence. The marriage and family texts do not describe the situation in these words because it might sound a little like a system of forced labor. However, the discrepancy between what people say and what they mean is even greater in another role which is chosen or foisted upon the great majority of women: motherhood, the most important job in the world.

Mothers are important because they take care of children, the hope of the future, or so people say. I agreed and, as the months of my first pregnancy passed, I had no doubts about the rightness of having or adopting a baby, nor about the fact that the job of rearing them devolved mainly on women. But I was curious to know how I would feel, home alone all day with a baby. Almost a quarter of a century later I still hold the maternal role in such esteem that to admit that I was sometimes bored and lonely is hard to do. Nevertheless, spending almost all one's waking hours in the company of preschool children requires sound nerves, a good imagination and—what many women do not have—the desire to spend almost all one's waking hours in the company of preschool children.

In the fifties, as today, the middle-class woman who left her preschoolers and went off to school or work was suspected of sacrificing their psyches to her own needs. Women who stayed home with their babies would declare with a hint of piety that they would not have anyone else bringing up their babies, no indeed; their educations were not wasted one bit because a child needed an educated mother who could guide its growth intelligently and teach it to be creative and out-going. In fact, colleges offer almost no training in child rearing for either men or women, and the enrichment of children's lives usually excludes a discussion of Edward Albee or existentialism. Actually, the idea that mamma should stay home with the kiddies changing diapers and dishing out the applesauce lest they feel rejected and come to a bad end is a myth designed to keep women out of the labor market, using guilt as a mechanism of social control. No one really cares who wipes up the spilled milk. Other persons perform this service for the children of the Queen of England and no one worries about how her children will turn out. Indeed, the diapers of almost all upper class children are changed by someone other than the mother and no evidence shows that these children turn out worse than others, nor does one hear an outcry about maternal neglect.

Moreover, society appears to care little whether poor women can stay home and take care of their babies, for in most states the Aid to Dependent Children (ADC) grants are so small that a mother cannot buy adequate food, let alone the other things that children need. Indeed, ADC grants are much lower than welfare grants to the blind, the disabled, and the elderly although no evidence explains why ADC families need less than others. Unfortunately, many Americans seem less moved by a systematic concern for the needs of children than by a fear that educated women may get uppity and try to compete in the job market.

Although some aspects of the role of mother may be emotionally rewarding, it is not very rewarding economically. The value of women's unpaid services is less than the wage of an unskilled male laborer. Indeed, should a mother be out of commission and have to be replaced, anyone with a good disposition and a strong back will do. In a tight labor market, a strong back is a sufficient qualification. Substitutes for mothers receive almost the lowest wages in this society. One may, of course, argue that a mother's real worth is in personal terms—that she cannot be emotionally replaced. This argument is unanswerable. Neither can a father be replaced. Still, the knowledge that one's economic contribution is worth less than the minimum wage does not enhance self-esteem.

The next stage in the development of my identity also involved unpaid labor, in the community. Volunteer work may be loosely defined as white collar busywork that no one cares enough about to pay for. This fact is a tautology, the implications of which never are clearly spelled out to the women who do the work. Going to one's neighbors with a packet of official receipts, collecting for heart, cancer, and polio can give you a real sense of fulfillment, especially if you ignore the fact that the richest nation on earth could easily afford to support research on such diseases without sending volunteers around with tin cans. I shall illustrate the good works one could do in those days in order to clarify the effect of such activity on one's identity.

My first invitation to serve as a volunteer came from the ladies' auxiliary at the local hospital. They asked me to serve as a pink lady, so-called because they wore crisp, coral-colored cotton jumpers. The job specs called for sorting mail twice a day before carrying it to the patients and fending off visitors who, unless closely watched, would herd themselves in quantity into the room of the hapless patient. The job attracted wives of prominent businessmen who felt a need to help suffering humanity. I found that the nurses disliked tripping over us, and I quit with the discovery that 80 percent of the time there was nothing to do.

As a Den Mother for the Cub Scouts, I agreed to inculcate a set of virtues—I can no longer remember which ones—into a group of young males who otherwise would have been outdoors playing by themselves. A certain latitude was permitted the Mother in choice of activity and my Den went for an inordinate number of nature walks in the hills back of town because (a) it kept them from wrecking the living room and (b) I liked messing around in ponds hunting frogs as much as they did. Some days it rained and we had to do something indoors. Three such meetings were occupied by taking them to the home of a woman who made ceramics and charged almost nothing to teach the Den to make clever ashtrays as Christmas gifts for their parents. As my charges galloped down her cellar steps and elbowed their way among the pottery, her soft voice and sweet smile demonstrated that saints still walk this earth. The boys broke only three items.

A very different sort of activity was that of the American Association of University Women whose purpose was to study and then act on significant issues. The difficulty was that women who really liked to study and act were out in the real world doing just that. The national leadership tried to involve local AAUW branches with a host of issues but the women preferred the study and practice of gourmet cooking which they considered to be basically intellectual because some of the recipes were French. As a vehicle for even a modest degree of action at the local level the AAUW was not very satisfactory, leading one of my friends to formulate the drip-drip theory of social change: if you drip water on a rock long enough, one day it will be eroded. The theory provided little emotional comfort but it was intellectually satisfying.

To attend a meeting of the Parent-Teachers' Association always gave a warm glow because it proved that one was really interested in a child's progress and was the right kind of parent; besides, it could temporarily allay one's anxiety about what was going on at school. The real function of the PTA was to provide a captive audience that could be coopted by the superintendent and the principal to legitimate the school's need for more money. Since the schools always needed money desperately, school administrators were very gracious to parents who worked for the PTA. It made us feel good to be told that our participation was crucial to the cognitive and emotional development of our children. At one point in my career as a volunteer, I rose to dizzying heights of local power as president of both the AAUW and the PTA. My name often appeared on the woman's page of the local newspaper, amidst reports of engagements, golden wedding anniversaries, and really exciting new cookie recipes.

Churches are financed mainly by pledges but a common way of raising additional funds is through women's guilds, which hold rummage sales and bazaars. The rummage is provided by members who clean out their closets once or twice a year, give the really good things to friends and relatives, and the rest to the church to sell to people who can afford only the castoffs of the higher income strata: aging underwear, dresses, frayed shirts, a cracked object of art, and a kitchen pot with a loose handle. One might suppose that working at a rummage, playing Lady Bountiful, politely dispensing items to the poor would gratify one's ego. In fact, the experience is corrosive because it increases the awareness that, by any standard of decency, our society is not very moral, nor were *we,* in selling worn-out socks to the poor at five cents a pair.

The church bazaar, however, was fun. Groups of women met several times a month to make pretty little things to sell to other women who wanted to buy pretty little things. Some of the items were handsome but others were latter-day versions of the antimacassar. I contributed my share. With common pins I stuck sequins into styrofoam balls to make tree ornaments; made Christmas wreaths out of pine cones and arrangements of weeds, lacquered and gilded; and knitted hats for skiers. My prize contribution sold very well: argyle socks for babies, in pink and blue. As everyone said, they were just darling. They were also useless because any healthy baby would kick them off in two minutes. Once I computed the return on the time we spent making our wares and found that we worked for about four cents an hour. The money would be sent to the vestry, earmarked for a special item such as a dishwasher for the church kitchen. But the work ostensibly generated a feeling of togetherness which could hardly be measured in dollars.

When the children entered junior high and stopped coming home for lunch, I asked myself at the end of that year what had been accomplished. The answer reminded me that graduate school was now or never. I dropped most of the volunteer activities and began driving to the nearest university, a round trip of about 150 miles. I changed universities for the Ph.D. and the round trip was 200 miles. After more than 100,000 miles of driving and hard work, I earned the degree. In those five years my social identity was transformed.

I lived on the far edges of two worlds separated not only by miles but by social definitions. The professors were naive about the lives that business and corporation people lead and the corporate types had no idea that graduate school requires a seven day work week or else. Both worlds defined me as pleasant but eccentric. The professors felt that taking courses was, on the whole, a worthy enterprise and one kindly man informed me that he had had a housewife in a course a year earlier and she even received an A. The local people were sympathetic too. "Aren't you finished yet?" they would inquire in concerned tones after I had been commuting about a year. "Well, I guess it's just hard trying to keep house and go to school." Yet marginality has an enormous advantage: one becomes aware of the social givens that other people take for granted. I was forced to become aware of institutionalized sexism.

Even in graduate school the future had to be swept under the rug when a woman thought about finding a job. Many women were stymied by the nepotism rule and, if this did not stop them, by the rule that the university will not hire its own graduates. A married man can find a job and move with his family. A married woman has different options: she may obtain a post outside her department in an obscure corner of the university; she may become part of a low paid labor reserve, called upon when the department is shorthanded or needs someone to teach introductory courses; worse, she often may be called to teach, but refused tenure, retirement, and other rights; she may commute to another town; she may have another baby and go back to the PTA for another ten years; or she may end the marriage and hunt for a job on the same terms as men. I was lucky and found a job 100 miles away. I commuted for two years to a part-time job because I could not make the trip every day. Then my marriage ended and I became a full-time worker.

I like my new identity because I no longer have to pretend that everything is all right when I know that it is not. At times I feel a little like a house-nigger when my colleagues anxiously ask if everything isn't really all right. My colleagues like to think of themselves as kindly creatures who certainly don't want to do women in. Many of them grasp the idea of sexism quite easily, although others have difficulty with it. A number of my male colleagues were uneasy, for example, when I remarried and retained my maiden name. Many find it hard to apply their sociological insights to concrete problems; that is, they do not see the inconsistencies between what they say and what they do. The discrepancy is especially obvious in those radicals whose desire to press for the total transformation of society stops abruptly at the kitchen door.

When I was about 18 I told my father that I really didn't want to spend the rest of my life doing housework. As a long-time follower of Norman Thomas, he replied that I was snobbish: if poor women had to do such work, on what grounds did I consider myself to be above it? I reminded him that he did not feel obligated to be a ditch digger because he was a man; why did I have to do housework all my life because I was a woman? He looked quite surprised. Then he said slowly, "I don't know."

The old answers will not do. Social arrangements can be devised where no person —black, poor, female—automatically inherits the dirtiest jobs at the lowest wages. The fact that the dirtiest jobs have the lowest wages is man-made and can be changed. The social and technological changes that spawned the women's movement will continue to be felt. Increasingly, women will find their lives trivialized if the old institutions deny them full identity as mature human beings. Both men and women can and must devise new institutions to create new options for all humans.

B.
Employment and Career Development

Chapter Seven

Career Profiles of Women Doctorates

Helen S. Astin

WOMEN doctorates constitute a unique group in that they are a small minority among the female population as a whole. Less than half of all female high school graduates enroll in college, about half of this number graduate from college, and of those who graduate one in a hundred go on to obtain the Ph.D. The career development of women doctorates, the career choices they make, their productivity and contributions, and the rewards they receive, are all important considerations in appraising the status of academic women. Moreover, it is crucial that we have an accurate knowledge and understanding of the highly educated woman's career profile in order to counsel wisely and plan appropriately for the generations of young women to come. The current changes in academe, in the life styles of women, and in the aspirations of young women indicate that the pool of women with highly specialized training will increase. Thus, documenting the recent trends in the training and career patterns of various cohorts of doctoral recipients is essential.

This chapter first examines the choices that women make with respect to fields of specialization. What fields of specialization do women most often choose? How do they differ from the fields men are more likely to choose? What are the personal characteristics and early experiences that determine the kinds of field choices women make?

Next, we will discuss the career patterns of women doctorates, comparing their employers, job functions, and job mobility with those of men. Their achievements and their rewards as measured by academic status and salary also will be examined. The last section of this chapter deals with trends in the employment patterns of women and men doctorates between 1960 and 1970.

The information presented here is drawn from a variety of sources, although most of the data are derived from *The Woman Doctorate in America* (Astin 1969), a comprehensive study of the career development of women doctorates in America. This study was based on a sample of 1,979 names, representing all the women who earned doctorates in 1957 and 1958, and was secured from the Office of Scientific Personnel of the National Academy of Sciences, which maintains records of all recipients of research doctorates at all universities in the country. A questionnaire entitled "Survey of Women Doctorates" was mailed during December 1965 and February 1966. From the total of 1,958 mailed questionnaires (21 cases had been omitted from the mailing list due to a clerical error) 1,547 women returned completed questionnaires.

Moreover, 106 additional women completed a shorter version of the questionnaire. These questionnaire data were linked to data collected from the same women upon completion of the doctorate, and from their high schools which provided information on their early achievements and aptitudes.

This chapter also draws extensively on the National Academy of Sciences' series of reports on career patterns (Harmon 1965; National Academy of Sciences 1968). These reports are invaluable in their contribution to the discussion of the careers of doctorate cohorts since 1935. They were based on data collected from 10,011 doctorates, of whom 1,045 were women, who obtained the degree in the years 1935, 1940, 1945, 1950 and 1960. The Career Patterns Questionnaire, mailed in 1963, requested that these men and women detail what they had been doing during each fifth year following completion of their degree. Where were they living? For whom were they working? At what were they working? What was their academic status, and what were their earnings? Some questions on family background and stipend support during graduate training also were included.

In many of the analyses that follow, we shall draw on the data from both of these sources, referring to *The Woman Doctorate in America* as the study of women doctorates and to the National Academy of Sciences reports as the study of career patterns.

Additional data on the employment prospects and employers of different doctorate cohorts since 1960 were provided by the National Academy of Sciences' Office of Scientific Personnel (1970). These data, here referred to as employment trends, are based on the yearly surveys of earned doctorates conducted by the Office of Scientific Personnel in cooperation with the graduate deans of all United States institutions that grant research doctorates. Two questions in the survey were utilized in tabulating data on comparative trends in the employment status of women and men doctorate recipients over time: "How well defined are your postdoctoral plans, i.e. have you signed a contract, do you have a postdoctoral fellowship, or are you negotiating?" And, "What type of employer are you going to work for, e.g. educational institution, government, industry?" This information was tabulated by field for doctorate recipients in 1960, 1965, 1967, 1968, 1969, and 1970 (Astin 1971).

CAREER DECISIONS AND EDUCATIONAL TRAINING

This section examines the field choices women make and compares them with the ones men make. It also explores the determinants of various career choices. Finally, the types of institutions that women doctorates attend, women's sources of financial support during graduate training, and their postdoctoral fellowship experiences are discussed.

TABLE 7.1. Doctorate Production in 1960 and 1970 by Field of Specialization

Fields	1960			1970		
	Total N	Percent Male	Percent Female	Total N	Percent Male	Percent Female
Natural Sciences						
Mathematics	291	95	5	1,218	94	6
Physics and astronomy	530	97	3	1,657	97	3
Chemistry	1,078	96	4	2,223	91	9
Earth sciences	253	99	1	509	97	3
Engineering	794	99.6	0.4	3,432	99.5	0.5
Agriculture and forestry	414	98	2	914	98	2
Health sciences	156	93	7	488	86	14
Biochemistry, biophysics, physiology, molecular biology	421	88	12	1,255	85	15
Anatomy, cytology, entomology, genetics, microbiology, embryology	385	89	11	948	82	18
Ecology, hydrobiology	35	94	6	140	96	4
Botany, zoology, general biology	317	86	14	819	84	16
Social Sciences						
Psychology	772	83	17	1,883	76	24
Anthropology and archaeology	77	82	18	225	72	28
Sociology	162	83	17	506	82	18
Economics and econometrics	352	96	4	971	94	6
Political science and international relations	238	91	9	634	90	10
History	364	91	9	1,092	87	13
English and Humanities						
English and American language and literature	386	78	22	1,093	69	31
Modern foreign language and literature	214	74	26	784	67	33
Classical language and literature	45	87	13	86	70	30
Philosophy	135	83	17	350	87	13
Speech as a dramatic art	143	83	17	267	85	15
Fine arts and music	148	82	16	254	70	30
Business administration	140	98	2	584	98	2
Religion and theology	146	95	5	212	95	5
Education	1,548	81	19	5,836	80	20
Total (all fields)	9,734	89	11	29,436	86.5	13.5

SOURCE: Data from the National Academy of Sciences, Office of Scientific Personnel, 1970.

Fields of Specialization

In 1970, 13.5 percent of all doctorates were awarded to women, an increase of about 2.5 percent over 1960. Out of twenty-six field categories, however, women constituted 10 percent or more of the pool in only sixteen specialized fields. In the remaining ten field categories, women constituted a smaller proportion, ranging from a low of less than 0.5 percent in engineering to a high of 9 percent in chemistry (see Table 7.1).

There were some noteworthy changes between 1960 and 1970 in the top five fields most preferred by women. In 1960, education ranked third in popularity, but by 1970 it had dropped to sixth place and fine arts was third. Both philosophy and speech were less often chosen by women as fields of specialization, and anatomy and cytology, botany, zoology, and general biology had become more popular. Classical languages and literature had also risen in popularity from a total of 13 percent in 1960 to 30 percent in 1970. Finally, the proportion of women in health sciences had doubled from 7 percent to 14 percent by 1970. The fields that remained almost exclusively male were: engineering, business administration, agriculture and forestry, physics and astronomy, and earth sciences.

If we group these twenty-six fields into four major categories—natural sciences (biological and physical sciences), social sciences (including psychology), arts and humanities, and education—the differences between women and men with respect to field of specialization become clearer (see Table 7.2). Whereas women were

TABLE 7.2. Distribution of Men and Women Doctorates of 1970 by
Field of Specialization
(In percentages)

Field of Specialization	Women (N = 3,961)	Men (N = 25,475)
Natural sciences	24	52
Social sciences	23	18
Arts and humanities	21	12
Education	31	19
	99	101

SOURCE: Data from the National Academy of Sciences, Office of Scientific Personnel, 1970.

distributed about equally among the four major categories, more than half the men were in the natural sciences, and the smallest proportion (12 percent) were in the arts and humanities.

It is somewhat difficult to explain these differences in choice of field of specialization. Traditionally, women have differed from men not only in educational attainment but also in the fields they choose. For example, over one-fourth of undergraduate women plan to enter teaching, and similar proportions of men expected to go into business or engineering (American Council on Education 1971). It is unclear just how much these differences are attributable to differences in aptitudes and interests, and how much they are attributable to societal expectations that constitute educational and occupational barriers against women, and the psychological consequences of these expectations.

Determinants of Career Choice

Studies of the determinants of career choice are very important, not only because they contribute to our understanding of a significant facet of human behavior, but also because they may indicate how these determinants are amenable to change. Our knowledge about this aspect of women and work is limited since most theory and empirical research on career choice has focused on men. Nevertheless, some of the factors that affect the career decisions of women have already been identified. For example, studies of high school and college women indicate that women with high socioeconomic backgrounds and high mathematical aptitudes are more likely to plan careers in the sciences and the professions than in other fields (Astin 1968; Astin and Myint 1971).

With respect to women doctorates two major questions emerge: To what extent are women doctorates similar to, or different from, other college-educated women in their aptitudes, family background, and early interests in a particular field? How do women doctorates who have specialized in one field differ from women who have chosen some other field?

The undergraduate majors of women doctorates are very different from those of college-educated women in general. For example, comparing the undergraduate majors of the women doctorates of 1957 and 1958 with the majors of women who graduated in 1957, we observe the following: slightly less than 7 percent of the 1957 college-graduate women took their baccalaureate degree in one of the natural sciences, whereas 27 percent of women doctorates had, as undergraduates, majored in one of the natural sciences. Moreover, 42 percent of the 1957 college graduates had majored in the arts and humanities, compared with 26 percent of women doctorates. Women who later achieved the doctoral degree tended to score about 1 to 1½ standard deviations above the mean on measured abilities while in high school. Moreover, they were high achievers and enjoyed scholarly endeavors (Astin 1969).

Some of the early determinants of career choice among women doctorates were identified in the study of women doctorates. The longitudinal data collected on the sample made it possible to examine the personal characteristics as well as the educational and home experiences of these women and to relate them to their particular fields of specialization. The antecedent variables in these analyses were the subject's date of birth, father's and mother's employment statuses (working or nonworking) while the woman doctorate was growing up, measured intelligence, high school rank, grades in high school mathematics and science courses, and citizenship status at the time of doctoral completion.

First, the subject's age was found to be related to her choice of field. There was a larger proportion of younger women in the natural sciences than in the humanities and in education. Several factors may account for this finding. The woman natural scientist may have made an earlier career decision, pursued graduate training at an earlier age, and completed her training without major delays or interruptions. Or certain employment constraints may have persuaded her to postpone taking a job until she had completed her graduate training.

Second, women who were citizens of foreign countries at the time of doctoral completion were more likely to have chosen the physical sciences, whereas those who were American citizens were more likely to choose careers in the social sciences and in education. It is difficult to interpret this finding solely on the basis of cultural differences—that foreign women do not believe as do American women that it is unfeminine to choose a career most often chosen by men. Another possible explanation may be that the sample is biased; in other words, a disproportionate number of foreign women with interests in the physical sciences choose to come to this country because of its greater technological and educational facilities.

The third factor related to choice of field was the woman doctorate's early skills and achievements. For example, women who specialized in the physical sciences received good grades in mathematics while in high school, whereas the biological scientists typically received high grades in the sciences. Social scientists scored highest on aptitudes as measured by intelligence tests, although psychologists tended to be the lowest early achievers of all the groups, as reflected in their low high school class rank.

A working mother was a differentiating factor with respect to career choice only for women who chose psychology as their field of specialization. This finding, too, is difficult to interpret without further research. What is the precise role and influence of the working mother on her children and their career aspirations? Does she represent a model to follow, i.e., because the mother has been employed, is the daughter more likely to want to work? Or is it the personal qualities that relate to the mother's decision to work that create an atmosphere conducive to her daughter's high educational and vocational aspirations? These are important issues in any inquiry into career development in women.

In brief, early achievements and interests, parent-child interactions, and mother's career interests and commitments seem to be highly influential factors in a young woman's decisions about her education and career.

Graduate Education and Stipend Support

The majority of women in the study of women doctorates reported that their primary reason for obtaining the doctorate was that they needed it to pursue their desired career. A third of the women were also persuaded to continue their training beyond the bachelor's or master's degree because they found their studies interesting in themselves.

Women and men doctorates seemed to have equal access to quality institutions. Of the women doctorate recipients, 29 percent received their training at the "top ten" institutions,[1] a proportion roughly equal to that of men with similar training. In a recent study of psychologists employed at universities (Astin 1972), 27 percent of both the men and the women psychologists were found to have received their training at the top ten universities. Actually, this finding is not particularly surprising, in that the women who continue on to graduate school and who receive their doctorates are highly qualified. Moreover, a higher proportion of women than men doctorates have exceptionally high aptitude scores (Harmon 1961).

The study of career patterns reveals that 46 percent of the women doctorates had some stipend support during graduate training: 12 percent had received government support (i.e., Public Health Service, National Science Foundation, National Institutes of Health, National Institute of Mental Health, or Office of Education fellowships), while 34 percent had received institutional support either in the form of an assistantship or a scholarship, and 50 percent had to use their own savings or accept financial support from their family or spouse. The differences in types of financial support received by women and men are shown in Table 7.3.

TABLE 7.3. Sources of Stipend Support for Doctorates of 1950–1960 (In percentages)

Source	Women (N = 482)	Men (N = 5,757)
Government	12	22
Institution	34	36
Own savings or support from family or spouse	50	42
Other	4	No Information
	100	100

SOURCE: National Academy of Sciences 1968.

Postdoctoral Fellowships

The number of doctorates who receive postdoctoral fellowships has increased over time. Among the doctoral recipients of 1960, 7 percent of the men and 6 percent of the women received such fellowships. By 1970, these proportions had more than doubled to 15 and 13 percent respectively (Astin 1971).

Independent of sex, the proportion of doctorates pursuing postdoctoral study

[1] Columbia, University of California at Berkeley, Yale, Cornell, University of Illinois, Stanford, University of Michigan, Chicago, Harvard and U.C.L.A.

varied considerably according to field of specialization. For example, a very high proportion of the doctorates in biochemistry, biophysics, physiology, and molecular biology (41 percent) received postdoctoral fellowships, whereas fewer than 1 percent of doctorates in philosophy, English and American language and literature received postdoctoral fellowships (Astin 1971). Moreover, the number of postdoctoral fellowships available in the sciences (particularly in the biosciences) had increased, whereas the number in the arts and humanities and in professional fields had diminished (National Academy of Sciences 1968). Women in the biological sciences were the most likely ones to have been postdoctoral fellows, and the women in education the least likely. These differences in fields probably reflect both the availability of funds and the degree of emphasis on postdoctoral research in a given discipline. In the survey of career patterns, 18 percent of all the women doctorates in contrast to 16 percent of the men doctorates in all cohorts received postdoctoral fellowships; a slightly larger proportion of single women than married women were recipients. Among the early cohorts (1935, 1940, and 1945), 21 percent of the single women and 14 percent of the married women had been postdoctoral fellows: among the later cohorts (1950, 1955, and 1960), 17 percent of the single and 21 percent of the married women had received postdoctoral fellowships.

Both female and male students who received support from their institutions and those who held postdoctoral fellowships were more likely to have academic careers later on (National Academy of Sciences 1968). One may speculate that experience as a teaching assistant (one common form of institutional support) or postdoctoral fellow (which often requires residency at an academic institution) enables the student to develop skills appropriate for employment in academe. Then, too, the same aptitudes and motivation that predict selection for an assistantship or postdoctoral fellowship also may predict academic employment.

Of the women respondents to the survey of women doctorates, a total of 18 percent had held postdoctoral fellowships; 21 percent of the married women compared with 17 percent of the single women were recipients. This difference may be more a matter of circumstance than of preference. The husband of the typical married woman doctorate is himself a professional or academic man, and if he is employed at an institution that has an antinepotism regulation, his wife—unable to find employment at the institution—has no alternative other than to apply for a postdoctoral fellowship. Furthermore, when the woman doctorate's husband takes a sabbatical leave outside their home community, she may apply for a fellowship in order to keep up with her career if employment opportunities are limited in their new location.

Only a fourth of the women fellowship recipients became fellows immediately after completing their degrees in 1957/1958. At the time of the survey (1965), seven to eight years after the doctorate, 4 percent were fellows but the large majority, 71 percent, were postdoctoral fellows some time between 1958 and 1964

This timing suggests that some women may decide to become fellows not so much out of choice, but because they have been unable to find other suitable employment.

Younger women, and those who had received scholarships or fellowships during graduate study, were most likely to have been postdoctoral fellows. This finding suggests that selection committees may be impressed by women whose motivation manifests itself in early achievement. Such women would also be the ones who continue their education with few interruptions—another factor which may explain their younger age.

CAREER DEVELOPMENT

The aspects of career development explored in this section are the type of employer chosen by women doctorates, the job functions the doctorates perform, and the rewards they receive. In addition, their scientific and scholarly productivity is examined and the continuity and discontinuity of their careers is discussed.

Employers of Women Doctorates

According to our data sources, the work context that women doctorates most frequently choose after receiving the doctorate is academe. For that matter, men doctorates, too, choose academe over government, business and industry, and other categories.

Looking at employment trends since 1960 (see Table 7.4), we find that the distribution of recent doctorate recipients in industry, government, and nonprofit organizations has remained the same; while educational institutions have steadily attracted more graduates: from 60 percent of the men and 73 percent of the women doctorates in 1960, to 68 percent of the men and 82 percent of the women doctorates in 1970. Self-employment decreased from 11 percent for men and 15 percent for women in 1960 to 3 and 5 percent respectively in 1970. The greatest employment differences by sex were found in business and industry, where a much larger proportion of men than women were employed. In 1970, 16 percent of the men but only 3 percent of the women had accepted positions in business and industry (Astin 1971). The difference is explained largely by differences in the fields chosen by women and men. That is, business and industry employ a far higher proportion of doctorates in the natural sciences than doctorates in arts and humanities, and (as we noted earlier) the natural sciences are dominated by men, whereas proportionally fewer women choose this field, tending to specialize instead in the arts and humanities.

In the study of women doctorates, too, the subjects were asked to indicate their first and current (i.e., 1965) employers. The results are presented in Table 7.5.

The observed differences between the findings presented in Tables 7.4 and 7.5 may be attributed to: (a) differences in the definition of categories: i.e., in the study of career patterns, a category labeled "other" was included under which was

TABLE 7.4. Trends in the Type of Postdoctoral Employer of Men and Women Doctorates, 1960–1970 (In percentages)

Type of Employer	1960 (N = 9,734)		1965 (N = 16,341)		1967 (N = 20,385)		1968 (N = 22,916)		1969 (N = 25,721)		1970 (N = 29,436)	
	Men	Women	Men	Women	Men	Women	Men	Women	Men	Women	Men	Women
Educational institution	60	73	61	71	61	71	61	70	67	81	68	82
Industry/business	18	3	14	3	15	2	15	3	17	3	16	3
Government	8	5	6	4	7	4	7	5	9	6	10	6
Nonprofit	3	3	3	5	3	4	3	4	3	4	3	4
Other (including self-employment)	11	15	15	16	14	18	14	19	4	7	3	5
Postdoctoral study	7	6	11	10	11	10	11	10	14	13	15	13
Unknown status	2	3	4	6	4	5	4	4	5	7	5	7

SOURCE: Data from the National Academy of Sciences, Office of Scientific Personnel, 1970.
NOTE: Unknown postdoctoral study and status are figured as percentages of total. Types of employer are figured as percent of total minus postdoctoral study and status unknown.

TABLE 7.5. Type of Employers of Women Doctorates
(In percentages)

Type of Employer	First Job after the Doctorate (N = 1,482)	Job as of 1965 (N = 1,480)
Business and industry	3	3
Government	6	6
Nonprofit organization	5	5
Academe[a]	81	80
Clinic or hospital	4	3
Self-employment	1	4
	100	101

SOURCE: Data abstracted from Astin 1969.
[a] This category includes universities, four-year colleges, junior colleges, and secondary and elementary school systems.

subsumed "self-employment" and "elementary and secondary school systems"—these types of employment were subsumed under the category "academe" in the study of women doctorates; and (b) differences in employment patterns depending on the year in which the subjects' first job was obtained. The study of career patterns goes back only to the 1960 cohort, whereas, the woman doctorate study examines the first job of the 1957 and 1958 cohorts.

The distribution of current employers of all doctoral cohorts (1935–1960) in 1963, as revealed by the career patterns study (Harmon 1965), is shown in Table 7.6. A greater proportion of women than of men were employed by colleges and

TABLE 7.6. 1963 Employers of Doctorates Who Received Their Degree between 1935–1960
(In percentages)

Type of Employer	All Doctorates[a] (N = 10,017)	Women Doctorates (N = 1,053)
College/university	59	66
Business/industry	15	4
Government	8	7
All others[b]	18	24
	100	101

SOURCE: Data abstracted from Harmon 1965, Tables 4 and 27.
[a] Ninety percent of the "all doctorates" category are men.
[b] This category includes elementary schools, high schools, foreign employment, self-employment, and "no response."

universities, and a greater proportion listed their employer as "other," a category which includes elementary and secondary education.

In the same study, shifts in and out of academic and nonacademic careers were analyzed, and the proportion who remained in academic or in nonacademic positions throughout their career was reported. In the case of both women and men, 49 percent had been employed in academe continuously. However, 23 percent of the men, as compared with 15 percent of the women, had been working in nonacademic jobs since receiving the doctorate. By the time of the survey, 19 percent of the women, as compared with 13 percent of the men, had shifted from nonacademic to academic careers. In general, then, women doctorates were more likely than men doctorates to take academic jobs immediately after completing the doctorate and to remain in those jobs longer. Moreover, single women were more likely than married women to remain continuously in academic positions and to shift from nonacademic to academic jobs.

The observed differences between women and men with respect to shifts between academic and nonacademic employers may be attributed in part to differences in the fields they choose. Men, being more inclined to specialize in such fields as engineering and the physical sciences, have a wider range of employers from which to choose. Some of the differences may also be attributed to the expressed interests of women and men. In a recent survey of academic women and men, 90 percent of the women indicated that they were primarily interested in teaching, whereas only 73 percent of the men said that this was their dominant interest (Bayer 1970).

The differences between single and married women may be attributed to the obstacles raised against married women: antinepotism regulations and the husband's mobility. Fifty-five percent of married women doctorates, as compared to 68 percent of single women doctorates, are in "always academic" positions (National Academy of Sciences 1968). Moreover, a married woman typically follows her husband if he decides to accept a position that necessitates moving to another area; and this often results in an interruption in the wife's academic career and in her entering into a nonacademic career since this may be the only suitable employment in the new location. Of the married women doctorates, 12 percent shifted from academic to nonacademic positions, compared to 7 percent of the single women (National Academy of Sciences 1968). In the study of the women doctorates, "husband's mobility" was listed as the third greatest barrier to career development.[2]

Work Activities of Women Doctorates

In the study of women doctorates, subjects were asked to indicate the proportion of time they spent at various work activities: teaching, research, administration, and services to clients. The typical woman doctorate spent about half of her working

[2] "Finding adequate domestic help" and "employer discrimination" were the two greatest barriers.

time teaching and about a quarter of it in research. The remaining quarter was almost equally divided between administration and services to clients (Astin 1969). The division varied somewhat according to field: women in the social sciences, arts, and humanities spent a greater amount of time in teaching and women in the natural sciences devoted more time to research. Moreover, a large proportion of the women in education devoted more time to administrative functions than did the rest of the women doctorates, partly because of their age and longer career experience. One may also speculate that women administrators in education are generally more acceptable to their male peers, or, perhaps, that men in education are less competitive, thus giving women in education a greater chance than women in other fields to advance to administrative posts.

The doctorate cohorts of 1935–1960 were asked a similar question in the study of career patterns. The proportions of doctorates who spent 50 percent or more of their work time on specified job activities are listed in Table 7.7. From these percentage distributions it is evident that more women than men, single or married, spent a greater proportion of their time teaching.

TABLE 7.7. Work Activities of Doctorates of 1955–1960 (Percent who spend 50 percent or more of their work time on specified job activities) [a]

Job Activities	All Doctorates[b] (N = 4,136)	Single Women Doctorates (N = 148)	Married Women Doctorates (N = 200)
Teaching	34	49	41
Research	46	25	47
Administration	12	11	6

SOURCE: Data abstracted from Harmon 1965, Table 31.
[a] Percentages do not add up to 100 percent because other functions, such as consulting, clinical services, and so on are not included.
[b] Ninety percent of the "all doctorates" category are men.

An examination of the differences in work activities between single and married women doctorates reveals some interesting patterns. Although more single women were involved in teaching and administration, more married women were involved in research, a finding which may reflect the presence of certain limitations imposed on married women regarding academic appointments. For example, married women, because of antinepotism regulations, tend to hold research appointments at research institutes affiliated with universities. That more single women performed administrative functions is, in part, a reflection of differences in the field choices of single and married doctorates. A higher proportion of women in education are single: 53 percent as compared with 38 percent in all other fields combined (Astin 1969). Moreover, a larger proportion of women in education performed administrative functions (32 percent) as compared with all other women doctorates, of whom only 12 percent were involved in administration (Astin 1969).

Rewards for Professional Performance

Status and rewards for professional or academic performance traditionally have been measured by academic rank and by salary level.

Salary. The salaries of women doctorates—whether they were in academic or non-academic jobs—were considerably lower than those of men (Harmon 1965; National Academy of Sciences 1968). In 1963, the mean salary of academic men was $11,222, compared with $8,768 for academic women. The mean salary of non-academic men was $14,321, compared with $9,103 for nonacademic women. These reported averages were based on all cohorts (1935–1960).

Single women in both academic and nonacademic posts earned close to $2,000 more than did married women, a difference that may be explained on the basis of age, experience, and work activities. Within the various cohorts, single women were somewhat older and were more likely than married women to be in administration (Astin 1969; Harmon 1965). Moreover, these figures do not take into account the employment of many married women doctorates on a part-time rather than a full-time basis—another factor that may account for the salary differential.

Doctorates who had been continuously employed in nonacademic positions earned the highest salaries; those who had shifted from academic to nonacademic careers earned the second highest salaries. The poorest paid were those who had shifted from nonacademic to academic careers, a group that probably includes many persons who decided to go into academic work because they were more interested in the work itself than in its monetary rewards.

Insofar as primary work activities are concerned, doctorates who spent more than half their working time in administration earned the highest salaries, those involved in research came next, and those whose time was spent primarily in teaching were paid the lowest salaries. These differences were observed across all cohorts and within each cohort, indicating that the differences cannot be accounted for on the basis of the age and experience of the doctorates.

The two highest paid fields were engineering and physics, and the three lowest paid were languages, literature, and zoology.

In summary, all of these factors that determine salary—academic or nonacademic employment, work activity, and field of specialization—negatively affect women more than men. Women are more often in academic careers than nonacademic ones, and they are more likely to be in teaching than administration or research. Women also constitute a very small proportion of physical scientists, who have the best-paid careers, and a disproportionately large number of those in the humanities and the arts, which are the lowest paying fields.

Rank. Rank in academe represents achievement and stature. Invariably, women were found to occupy the lower ranks, as Table 7.8 demonstrates.

TABLE 7.8. Ranks of Academic Women and Men in 1963
(In percentages)

Rank	Early Cohorts (1935, 1940, 1945)			Later Cohorts (1950, 1955, 1960)		
	All Ph.D.'s (N = 2,564)	Single Women (N = 174)	Married Women (N = 181)	All Ph.D.'s (N = 3,655)	Single Women (N = 163)	Married Women (N = 191)
Professor	69	76	56	22	25	16
Associate professor	25	22	31	44	50	36
Assistant professor	5	2	8	26	21	33
Instructor	1	—	5	8	4	15
	100	100	100	100	100	100

SOURCE: Data abstracted from National Academy of Sciences, Office of Scientific Personnel 1968, Table 24.

Although the finding that married women did not fare as well as did either men or single women was to be anticipated, the finding that higher proportions of single women reached the professorial ranks than did men was unexpected. One would have expected women, whether single or married, to fare less well than men because of sex bias against women in general. It is also interesting to note that there was a higher proportion of persons in the humanities at the professional rank than in other fields; that is, in the study of career patterns, 75 percent of the humanities doctorates of 1935, 1940, and 1945 had attained the rank of professor by 1963, whereas only 65 percent of the biological scientists and 58 percent of the social scientists occupied professorial ranks. Similar differences among fields were observed in the study of women doctorates (Astin 1969). A greater proportion of women doctorates in the arts and humanities were professors than were women in other fields.

Since these data were not controlled for type of institution, this finding may be attributable to institutional differences rather than to differences between fields. There is some indication that, among academics, a larger proportion of bioscientists (11 percent) are employed by universities than by two-year and four-year colleges (4 and 5 percent respectively). Conversely, there is an overall higher proportion of humanities specialists at colleges (24 percent) than at universities (13 percent) (Bayer 1970). Since competition for professorial rank undoubtedly is greater at the university level, these factors may explain the overall differences between fields with respect to rank achieved. Ideally, however, one ought to test this surmise by examining differences in rank both by field and type of institution.

In their study of the career progress of natural and social scientists, as measured by rank and salary, Bayer and Astin (1969) concluded that beginning rank was unrelated to sex but that, over time, women social scientists were promoted less rapidly than men. However, this was not the case for women in the natural sciences. The implication of their findings is that differences in the academic reward system are more a reflection of field than institution.

Scientific and Scholarly Productivity

Traditionally, rank and salary in academe are based on scholarly productivity rather than on training, ability, or teaching effectiveness. The use of the publications criterion is unfortunate for two reasons: (1) Despite its quantifiability, the criterion is not particularly appropriate for rewarding achievement in an educational environment; teaching effectiveness would seem a far better, even if more difficult to measure, criterion; (2) it affects women adversely, since they tend to publish less and devote more time to teaching (see Table 7.9).

However, when we examine the productivity of women doctorates in general, as compared to academic women, we observe that the former had published an average of four to five articles, that 75 percent had published at least one, and that

TABLE 7.9. Publications and Research vs. Teaching Interests of Academic Women and Men
(In percentages)

Publications and Interests	Women	Men
A. *Articles Published*		
None	63	39
1–4	26	30
5–10	6	12
11–20	3	8
21 or more	2	11
	100	100
B. *Teaching-Research Interests*		
Primarily research	2	5
Both but lean toward research	9	22
Both but lean toward teaching	29	36
Primarily teaching	61	37
	100	100

SOURCE: Data abstracted from Bayer 1970. They are based on all higher education teaching faculty, independent of degree held.

13 percent had published eleven or more. Natural scientists were the most productive, 92 percent having published at least once, and 24 percent having eleven or more articles to their credit. Moreover, those in academic settings appear to be slightly more productive than those in other work settings (see Table 7.10).

The quality of the institution from which a woman received the doctorate seems to be associated with productivity, over and above the woman's own interests and aptitudes in research and writing (Astin 1969). This influence may, to some ex-

TABLE 7.10. Productivity of Women as Measured by Articles Published in Field of Specialization and Work Settings

Field	All Work Settings (median)	Academic Settings (median)	Never Published (percent)	Published 11 Articles or More (percent)
Natural sciences	5.80	6.00	7.8	24.3
Psychology	2.88	4.00	26.3	9.8
Social sciences	3.40	3.08	25.3	10.7
Arts and humanities	1.30	1.50	33.6	10.4
Education	2.52	2.99	32.3	7.3
Total, all fields	3.26	3.54	24.7	13.0

SOURCE: Data abstracted from Astin 1969, Table 24.

tent, be explained by two factors. First, women attending distinguished institutions are likely to model themselves on the faculty, most of whom are known to colleagues through their publications. Second, women who are attracted to elite and competitive institutions may be more motivated and research oriented to begin with, and thus more productive in their careers.

Taking books instead of articles as the criterion of productivity, we found that women in the arts and humanities had written more books than women in other fields (Astin 1969). Another intriguing finding is that women married to academic men were more likely to have published books, whatever their field of specialization. Perhaps this was a way for these women to maintain their scholarship while temporarily out of the labor force because of family responsibilities. Or perhaps their work represents collaborative efforts with their husbands. In short, we would suggest that situational determinants rather than personality characteristics make women doctorates married to academic men more productive than single women or women married to nonacademic men. The association of productivity and marital status to rank and salary is examined more thoroughly in Chapter Fifteen.

Some authors (e.g., Bernard 1964) have attributed the lower scholarly productivity in writing of women as compared with men, to differences in employment setting. Women are more likely to teach at four-year colleges than at universities and, consequently, to have heavier teaching assignments that leave them less time for research and writing. Furthermore, funding agencies are more willing to allocate funds to a scholar at a university than to one at a four-year college. One should not, however, exclude the importance of the different work activity interests of women and men that probably operate over and above the external barriers that hinder a woman's research and writing.

Continuity in Career Development

In examining patterns of career development, it is essential that we give some attention to continuity and discontinuity, the reasons for dropping out of the labor force, and the effects of such interruptions on career progress.

The woman college graduate's career development usually is characterized by a pattern of initial entry, interruption for bearing and rearing children, and reentry at a later age (Mulvey 1963). This typical pattern has often been used by educators and employers to justify discriminatory practices against women. The career development of highly educated women, however, does not follow this pattern. The survey of women doctorates revealed that 91 percent of the women doctorates of 1957 and 1958 were in the labor force seven or eight years later. Of these, 81 percent were working full time and only 10 percent were employed on a part-time basis. Seventy-nine percent of the women had never interrupted their careers; for the rest of the group, the median interruption was a mere fourteen months.

The married woman doctorate who was fully employed typically had married before she had completed the doctorate. Thus, these women learned how to cope with dual roles early in their careers. Moreover, there may be certain personality characteristics that are related both to early marriage and the ability to work even though one has preschool children. One such characteristic may be simply one's level of energy.

The woman doctorate whose mother worked while she was growing up was more likely to be employed full-time at the time of the survey, suggesting that the mother's ability to handle both roles encouraged the daughter to do likewise. Moreover, a working mother may promote greater independence in her children, since she is around less and therefore is not as likely to intrude in their lives. In short, it would seem that career commitment (as measured by full-time employment) requires independence and an ability to handle dual roles successfully.

Women who had held assistantships and postdoctoral fellowships were also more likely to be employed full-time later on, as were women who had taken a full-time job immediately after receiving the doctorate (see Astin 1969, Table 17). These findings suggest an early commitment to career development. An additional determinant of full- or part-time work was the income of the doctorate's husband. It is interesting that, even among highly educated and motivated women, economic factors influence employment decisions.

In summary, women doctorates as a group demonstrate a strong career commitment. Within the group, however, there exists considerable variation with respect to career involvement and persistence. Home and personal factors, as well as predoctoral and postdoctoral experiences all influence the woman doctorate's decisions about her career.

EMPLOYMENT PROSPECTS

In the last several years, a good deal of anxiety has been expressed over the question of surplus Ph.D.'s. Some authorities (e.g., Cartter 1970) have contended that the system is producing from 30 to 50 percent more doctorates than can be used effectively in the 1970s and early 1980s. The report of the Commission on Human Resources and Higher Education (Folger, Astin, and Bayer 1970) takes a more optimistic view of the prospects for the employment of doctorates up to the mid-1980s and, in some fields, even into the 1990s. Another report concluded: "The data indicate a tightening of the job market but give little evidence of appreciable unemployment among the Ph.D.'s" (National Academy of Sciences 1970:937).

To discover the extent to which any tightening of the job market may affect women more than men, we examined the employment patterns of doctorate recipients in 1960, 1965, 1967, 1968, 1969, and 1970. The analysis was carried out separately by sex and by field for the fields in which women constitute at least 10 percent of the doctorate population (Astin 1971). The National Academy of Sciences doctoral files, from which the data were derived, include all recipients of doctorates for each fiscal year. We were concerned with two questions: (1) whether a doctorate had signed a contract for the year following her or his completion of the degree, and (2) if so, with what type of employer.

An examination of the employment status of the most recent cohort (1970) indicates that men do not seem to be experiencing the tightening of the employment market as much as the women doctorates. The proportion of men with signed contracts in 1970 has dropped by 4 percentage points from what it was in 1960; for women, however, the drop was 8 percentage points. That is, in 1960, 73 percent of the new women doctorates had signed contracts, whereas only 65 percent had done so in 1970 (see Table 7.11).

TABLE 7.11. Trends in the Employment Status of Men and Women Doctorate Recipients, 1969–1970
(In percentages)

Year Earned Degree	Sex	Employment Status				Post-doctoral Study[a]
		Signed Contract	Negotiating	Seeking/No Prospect	Other	
1960	Men	82	8	6	4	7
(N = 9,734)	Women	73	8	12	7	6
1965	Men	80	8	5	7	11
(N = 16,341)	Women	72	9	10	9	10
1967	Men	81	7	4	7	11
(N = 20,385)	Women	73	9	10	9	10
1968	Men	80	7	5	8	11
(N = 22,916)	Women	70	9	12	9	10
1969	Men	79	8	7	6	14
(N = 25,721)	Women	67	9	16	8	13
1970	Men	78	8	9	5	15
(N = 29,436)	Women	65	10	17	8	13

SOURCE: Data from the National Academy of Sciences, Office of Scientific Personnel 1970.
[a] Postdoctoral study is figured as a percent of total, and the percentages of employment status are figured as percent of total minus those with postdoctoral fellowships.

In the natural sciences, the greatest change in employment occurred in biochemistry and biophysics, and in anatomy, cytology, entomology, genetics, microbiology, and embryology combined.[3] Between 1960 and 1970 the drop in employment of men was 2 percentage points; for women it was 22 percentage points (see Table 7.12). In the social sciences, with the exception of anthropology, fewer women in 1970 than in 1960 had signed contracts, although this did not hold true for men, who fared better in 1970 than in 1960 in all social science fields except psychology. Of the women in the humanities and education, those in philosophy and classics had the hardest time obtaining jobs in 1970. The men suffered no such difficulty:

[3] The groupings of fields used here are those employed in the doctoral files of the National Academy of Sciences.

TABLE 7.12. Employment Status of Men and Women Doctorates in Selected
Fields, 1960–1970
(In percentages)[a]

Fields[b]	Men			Women		
	1960	*1970*	*Change*	*1960*	*1970*	*Change*
Health sciences	70	74	+4	67	64	−3
Biochemistry, biophysics, physiology, molecular biology	75	73	−2	79	57	−22
Anatomy, cytology, entomology, genetics, microbiology, embryology	77	77	0	70	48	−22
Botany, zoology, general biology	79	77	−2	62	53	−9
Psychology	80	79	−1	69	61	−8
Anthropology and archaeology	73	85	+12	55	68	+13
Sociology	86	88	+2	78	72	−6
History	81	83	+2	71	66	−5
English and American language and literature	91	86	−5	73	71	−2
Classical language and literature	72	90	+18	67	65	−2
Philosophy	78	85	+7	73	52	−21
Speech	89	86	−3	79	78	−1
Fine Arts	80	78	−2	60	66	+6
Education	84	76	−8	79	69	−10
Total all fields	82	78	−4	73	65	−8

SOURCE: National Academy of Sciences, Office of Scientific Personnel 1970.
[a] Percentages indicate proportions that had signed a work contract following doctoral completion.
[b] Included are only fields in which women constitute at least 10 percent of the doctoral pool.

85 percent of the men in philosophy and 90 percent in classics had signed contracts, compared with 52 and 65 percent of the women in these respective fields.

An increasingly greater proportion of both women and men doctorates signed contracts with educational institutions, rather than with other types of employers. However, more women than men in the health fields signed contracts with industry, business, and nonprofit organizations in 1970 than in 1960.

Fewer social scientists signed contracts with industry in 1970 than in 1960. On the other hand, more women psychologists in 1970 found employment in industry, business, and government than did men psychologists. Even women in the humanities tended to shift employers. Fewer women in philosophy, speech, and fine arts signed contracts with educational institutions in 1970 than did in earlier years. Moreover, a greater proportion accepted positions in industry, and some of those in fine arts accepted employment in elementary or secondary school systems, or became self-employed.

In short, then, when the job market starts to close down, women are more likely to suffer than men. Moreover, an expansion occurs in the types of employers with which women find positions. This change may result from the greater competition for academic jobs, but it may also be attributable to a greater willingness on the part of these employers to accept women among their ranks. If such is the case, we should welcome the change, since it means that women doctorates will become more visible in the larger community, and that they will have an opportunity to contribute to areas other than the academic sectors of our society.

SUMMARY

Although women doctorates still constitute a small proportion of the total doctorate pool, their numbers have grown steadily over the past decade. Women constitute at least 10 percent of the doctorates of most fields. A few fields however, such as engineering, physics, and earth sciences, have remained masculine strongholds.

Women doctorates differ from other college-educated women in their interests, aptitudes, and career development. Four times as many women doctorates majored in one of the natural sciences as undergraduates, and women doctorates score about 1 to 1½ standard deviations higher on measured aptitudes and on achievement as measured by grades than do their less highly educated contemporaries. In brief, women doctorates have strong interests in the natural sciences, very high scholastic aptitudes, and outstanding academic achievement.

About a third of the women doctorates did their graduate work at better-known institutions, and slightly less than half received some kind of financial aid for their graduate education. Moreover, about 18 percent of all women doctorates became postdoctoral fellows at some point after completing the degree.

Although women doctorates differ somewhat from men in their choice of fields, the educational experiences of the sexes are very similar. About the same proportion of women and men obtain their doctorates from prestigious institutions. They receive similar kinds of financial aid. The same proportion of women as men pursue postdoctoral studies. The career development of men and women doctorates, however, follows a somewhat different pattern. The status as well as the monetary rewards that men receive are greater by far than those that women receive. Even though the majority of women and men doctorates are employed by academic institutions, far fewer women are found in nonacademic positions. In academe, women are promoted more slowly and receive much lower salaries.

Independent of sex, persons in administration and in nonacademic posts receive the highest salaries. Moreover, physical scientists are the best paid of the specialist groups. By the choices they make regarding field of specialty, and activity within that field (and one wonders if they are, indeed, free choices), women often lose out on the benefits dispensed by the educational system.

Nevertheless, women who complete their training are committed to their disciplines and careers. They remain in the labor force, and they contribute as teachers, scientists, and scholars. Even though the system has not assisted women who have home and family responsibilities in addition to their professional responsibilities, and though it has not rewarded professional women equitably, academic women have demonstrated stamina, persistence, and devotion to their commitments.

One hopes that greater awareness of the status of professional women—both in the past and today—will encourage institutions to establish conditions that will facilitate the contributions of academic women.

REFERENCES

American Council on Education, Office of Research. 1971. *The American freshman: National norms for fall 1971.* Washington, D.C.: Author.

Astin, Helen S. 1968. Career development of girls during the high school years. *Journal of Counseling Psychology,* 15:536–540.

Astin, Helen S. 1969. *The woman doctorate in America.* New York: Russell Sage Foundation.

Astin, Helen S. 1971. Comparative trends of the employment status of men and women doctorate recipients over time. Paper delivered at AAAS meeting in Chicago, 1970.

Astin, Helen S. 1972. Employment and career status of women psychologists. *American Psychologist,* 27(5):371–381.

Astin, Helen S., and Myint, Thelma. 1971. Career development of young women during the post-high school years. *Journal of Counseling Psychology,* 18:369–393.

Bayer, Alan E. 1970. College and university faculty: A statistical description. *ACE Research Reports,* 5(5). Washington, D.C.: American Council on Education.

Bayer, Alan E., and Astin, Helen S. 1968. Sex differences in academic rank and salary among science doctorates in teaching. *Journal of Human Resources,* 3:191–199.

Bernard, Jessie. 1964. *Academic women.* University Park: Pennsylvania State University Press.

Cartter, Allan M. December 1970. Scientific manpower trends for 1970–1985 and their implications for higher education. Paper read at the annual meeting of the American Association for the Advancement of Science, Chicago.

Folger, John K., Astin, Helen S., and Bayer, Alan E. 1970. *Human resources and higher education.* New York: Russell Sage Foundation.

Harmon, Lindsey R. 1961. High school backgrounds of science doctorates. *Science,* 133: 679–688.

Harmon, Lindsey R. 1965. *Profiles of Ph.D.'s in the sciences.* Career Patterns Report No. 1. Washington, D.C.: National Academy of Sciences.

Mulvey, Mary Crowley. 1963. Psychological and social factors in prediction of career patterns of women. *Genetic Psychology Monographs,* 68:309–389.

National Academy of Sciences, National Research Council, Office of Scientific Personnel. 1970. Employment status of recent recipients of the doctorate. *Science,* 168:930–939.

National Academy of Sciences, Office of Scientific Personnel, Research Division. 1968. *Careers of Ph.D.'s: Academic versus nonacademic.* Career Patterns Report No. 2. Washington, D.C.: Author.

Chapter Eight

Status Transitions of Women Students, Faculty, and Administrators

Patricia Albjerg Graham

DISCUSSIONS about the status of women in higher education have become as contagious as cholera and just about as popular with predominantly male faculties and administrations. The scarcity of women in the upper echelons of academe has triggered heated arguments not only from women's activist groups but also from male faculty and administrations facing investigations from the Department of Health, Education and Welfare.

The discussion that follows is a reflective one; it is not a report of research findings. Other chapters of this book deal with recent research and current analyses of the status of women in various fields and divisions of the academic community. This chapter will discuss two crucial junctures in a woman's academic career: the transition from graduate student to faculty member and from faculty member to administrator. These are important transitions for both women and men in the academic world, but they present peculiar difficulties for women.

The most important single observation about women in the academic world is that their numbers decrease dramatically as the importance of the post increases. Women constitute 41 percent of the undergraduates, 13.5 percent of the doctorate recipients, about 2 percent of the full professors at leading graduate schools of arts and sciences, and no woman holds the position of president of a major coeducational university. When women are found on college faculties, they tend to be concentrated in those fields thought to be particularly suitable for women, i.e., social work, education, home economics, nursing, and library service. In administrations they are most likely to be located in the offices of dean of women or dean of students, positions low in status in the university hierarchy.

At the beginning of one's teaching career, it is quite common to be both a graduate student and a faculty member. This is a period when the transition from student to faculty is obscure. Unlike physicians and lawyers who enter their professions with degrees, many young women and men begin their college teaching careers before they have completed their doctorates. However, this double status is not expected to continue very long if the young college teacher hopes to advance in the profession. Once the doctorate is achieved, the part-time lecturer or full-time instructor expects to be promoted immediately to assistant professor with full professional and faculty status. Just as some persons are both graduate students and teachers, some persons are both teachers and administrators. A department chairman usually is both teacher and administrator. In many colleges, the academic dean teaches a course or two in addition to administrative responsibilities.

The transformation from graduate student to professor, particularly when accompanied by completion of the doctorate, is universally regarded as an enhancement of one's status. There is less general agreement that the move from faculty to an administrative position is a comparable increase in status and depends, of course, on the institution and administrative position. The offer of the presidency of a good college or the influential deanship of an important school of a major university still is regarded in most academic circles as highly desirable. But there are many other administrative positions in academe about whose incumbents it is sometimes uncharitably observed, "He's all washed up as a scholar, so he's taken a deanship."

One final observation about status transitions for both women and men: In order to become a faculty member, one must have been a graduate student, but to become an administrator, one need not have been a faculty member. Thus, faculties are composed of persons who have had a common prior experience—graduate school; but administrations are not comparably homogeneous. They are made up of persons of more varied academic attainments and experiences. Ordinarily, however, the top academic administrative positions are held by former faculty members. The status transitions under discussion, then, apply to all faculty members but only to some administrators.

The status of women in academe reflects society's expectations of women. When they are young, women are likely to have status comparable to men their age, but as they grow older the discrepancy between their status and that of their male counterparts increases dramatically. With advancing years, men move into positions of higher status and women remain behind in the lower echelons of academe. There are at least two general explanations for the slow advance of women compared to that of men. When young, both women and men occupy positions subordinate to older, more experienced, more distinguished practitioners in their fields. As men grow older they attain levels of equality with their senior colleagues with relative ease; but it is much harder for a woman to do this. The social expectation, conscious or unconscious, is that she remain in a relatively subordinate status. Nor does her advancing age seem inconsistent with this status. In a highly competitive world, men are expected to move naturally into assertions of equality with older men. But when a woman adopts this behavior, everyone, including other women, puts down their papers and stares.

Another explanation is that academic positions of power and prestige have been defined with men in mind. It often is taken for granted that a major administrative job requires collateral duties in the form of entertainment, and it is assumed that these duties will be carried out by the incumbent's accommodating wife. The traditional idea of what can be expected from a young assistant professor is clearly a male-oriented concept. The heavy pressure of duties—teaching, preparing new courses, getting on with that first book or set of articles—are required at the same time women normally would bear and rear children. If women are to participate on an equal basis with men the conditions of their academic employment must be redefined.

Women who wish to achieve the status of graduate student face increasingly fewer difficulties than their predecessors. Graduate school professors who once vowed that they would not have a woman graduate student in the department have either retired or shut up. Occasionally, however, an anachronism may be encountered. A young woman recently elected to Phi Beta Kappa in her junior year at a women's college, spent her senior year at a coeducational institution where her new husband was also a senior. In her senior seminar in English it was clearly acknowledged that she was the outstanding student in the class, although all of the other students were men. At the end of the term, her professor (male) queried the students about their plans for the following year, encouraging them in their decisions about graduate study in English, professional school, and so on. When he came to the young woman, he smiled and said, "Well, we all know where you'll be next year—at home looking after your husband." She was stunned by his assumption that her academic days were over, that simply because she was female and married she should have no further formal study. In fact, she had received a national fellowship for graduate school and was intending to work for a doctorate in English.

The shift from college to graduate school is in some ways a difficult one for young women, for at that juncture many recognize for the first time that their future careers may be very different from those of most men. Nonetheless, the shift from undergraduate to graduate status for women does not entail the greater psychic shock that comes later when the young woman obtains her first professional position. A graduate student, after all, is a student, a nonassertive role that is consistent with what is expected of a woman. For many young women, graduate study is an intentional prolongation of a nonassertive life and an evasion of the conflict between women's traditional role and the assertiveness required by a career.

Toward the end of graduate school studies the young woman no longer is able, whether she wishes to or not, to cling to the comfortable status of student, a searcher of truth at the foot of the wise professor. This status appeals to some young women and to an even larger proportion of those professors (generally male) at whose feet she searches. It is not surprising that many male professors regard with enthusiasm the prospect of bright, young, and often attractive women earnestly following their academic researches along lines suggested by the professors. Who of us would not rejoice in intelligent and eager students appreciatively exploring our ideas?

But when the young woman ventures into the job market to secure a teaching position in a college or university, she faces the classic obstacles that have limited women's full participation in American academic life. First, she must contend with the myths that surround women's careers. It is conventionally assumed that the young academic woman will not be as steadfast as a man in commitment to her job—an assumption which ignores the research of Astin, who found that 91 percent of the women receiving doctorates in the mid-fifties were employed seven years later (Astin 1969:57).

Another myth is that women in higher education may be good teachers (look at their large numbers in the elementary and secondary school ranks!), but they do not do research, and research is indispensable to a career in the senior ranks of scholarship. That such a conclusion is unwarranted is shown by numerous studies, at least one of which points out that women doctorates actually publish more than men doctorates (Simon et al. 1967:221). Other studies indicate that academic women, victims of heavy teaching assignments, publish despite this handicap (see Chapter Fifteen). Furthermore, it is not clear how many women could publish but do not do so because of certain social and psychological pressures brought to bear because they are women. In any event, the question cannot be settled by tabulating mere numbers of items on bibliographies, since such quantitative indices are no guides to quality.

A third myth surrounding women doctorates is that if they are married they cannot be expected to undertake really demanding professional positions. A chairman of a history department at a West Coast state university recently explained, "We just have difficulty believing that a married woman is really serious about her job. Surely she is more interested in her family." He added that his department was quite willing to appoint single women (presumably those whom they deemed unlikely to marry), but they were dubious about the married ones.

Most of the problems affecting the single woman doctorate, such as the pressure to publish, also apply to the married woman doctorates, often to heightened degrees. There is no question that the married woman doctorate must run a more difficult course than her unmarried counterpart. Recent studies indicate that single women Ph.D.'s are hired for the more lucrative jobs and that they earn an average of $2,000 more annually than married women doctorates (Leive 1972; Harmon 1968). This pay differential may be explained, in part, by the higher proportion of older women among single doctorates and by the fact that a greater proportion of married women are employed part-time. Although Harmon's studies also show that women who were married at the time they obtained the doctorate have academic records that are superior to their male counterparts and to single women, the fact is that a much higher proportion of single women than married women doctorates achieve full professorships. The percentage of women doctorates who marry has increased over the last thirty-five years, but the percentage of those who are unmarried is still startlingly high. Of the women who received doctorates in 1935, 47 percent never married. Except during the 1950s, the percentage of those remaining single dropped about 2 percent every five years. In 1969, the last year for which figures are available, 40 percent of all women doctorates have never married (Harmon 1968; Astin 1969). The increase in the number of married women Ph.D.'s is not rapid but it is real, and it is the married scholars who face the more serious problems of advancement in academe.

Academic women like all other women often are ambivalent about academic success. We would suggest, however, that this is particularly true of married women. A young married woman doctorate is concerned not only about achieving success as such but also about the effect of her academic achievement on her husband. Most women are reluctant to achieve positions of higher status than their husbands, particularly when both are likely to be employed in the same line of work. A male professor of economics may find it enhancing to his ego if his wife is a successful artist or actress, but it is more difficult to accept if she is a more able economist than he. And when such a wife receives a grant or fellowship for their joint sabbatical and he receives no grant at all, tensions may arise, or so many believe.

One way of insuring that the academic husband's status will be higher than his academic wife's is to allow the husband's job opportunities to determine where the family lives. The wife then is left to locate whatever job she can in the area of her husband's school. Generally, high status institutions of learning do not look with enthusiasm on faculty wives seeking academic employment in their preserves, simply because they were not *invited* to the institution, as were their husbands. For many men, an academic wife is almost a handicap to consideration for first-rate appointments. The attitude of many a dean or chairman is that the best candidate is the one who must be lured with difficulty from a distant institution. The faculty wife occasionally may be useful for pinch-hitting but she usually is not regarded as a full-fledged professional. Let her find a job at the local community college or maybe the high school can use her! This difficulty is much less serious when she is still in graduate school. It is easier to find an acceptable graduate program wherever her husband might go than to find an acceptable teaching job. The situation is far more serious if the young woman is already a college teacher, and it is most serious of all for the woman administrator.

Another obstacle to the married woman doctorate is the nepotism rule, written or unwritten, that still prevails on many campuses. Although more and more institutions are now willing to employ two members of the same family, few regard with enthusiasm the prospect of husband and wife serving in the same department, particularly if they are equally qualified. Since many academic women meet their husbands in graduate school the probability of husbands and wives being in the same field is very high (the proportion of women doctorates married to doctorates in the same field is very high in all fields except education, where women are less likely to be married). In such cases the wife rarely is appointed, and far more rarely, given the superior appointment. Typically, she takes a job at another, less prestigious institution or works part-time as a "research associate" at her husband's school.

Many people in the academic world are familiar with the horror stories about departments that disintegrate because a married couple dictated policy for all the other department members. Some alarming instances of husband-wife domination of a single department have undoubtedly occurred. There is also the problem of tenure. Many departments are reluctant to hire a young couple at the assistant professor level for fear that both (or even worse, that only the wife) will meet the standard for tenure six years later. "What can we do?" they ask, "We can't possibly promote her and not him. It would ruin their marriage!" Of course, the couple can be warned upon appointment that tenure may not be possible for either or both of them. The department need not shoulder any responsibility for the security of their marriage.

What often is overlooked in discussions of nepotism are the advantages that accrue to the university that practices a policy of hiring, promoting, and paying both husband and wife at positions appropriate to their training and talents. The potential for institutional loyalty from couples is very great, simply because so few other institutions hire both husband and wife. Another advantage for couples in the same field is the greater opportunity for cooperative research. The greatest gain however, is that both the husband's and wife's academic aspirations are taken equally seriously by their colleagues, thus undercutting the likelihood of domestic tension which often occurs when a woman feels that her professional interests are being ignored.

Even at those universities that do hire a husband and wife at roughly equal positions, salaries frequently are not equally appropriate to rank and qualifications. Sometimes this policy is justified on the grounds that husbands without working wives require a larger salary. In other instances, the policy reflects the poor bargaining position of the couple. Finally, many husband and wife teams themselves are reluctant to press for equitable salaries simply because they are sensitive to the fact that the university is sending two checks to their family and only one to others.

A common problem which some young married women doctorates face as they enter academe concerns the interruption of professional life by pregnancy and maternity. Although university administrators are accustomed to coping with male professors who suffer nervous breakdowns, coronaries, or other ailments they frequently are aghast at the need to establish policy guidelines for pregnant faculty members. One reason why institutions may find the professor with the coronary a less difficult problem than the professor expecting a baby is that he is likely to be a senior man in the institution whom the administration knows well and values highly. Furthermore, his problem is one that the dean recognizes might befall him. The pregnant professor, on the other hand, probably is in the junior academic rank and has not yet become well established on the campus. Moreover, male administrators tend to assume that the responsibilities of child rearing fall to the mother, after the fashion of their own wives in the years when their children were small.

Implementing a progressive maternity leave policy would entail a serious challenge to the social customs that have governed these administrators' personal lives.

The problem of pregnancy and maternity leave for women faculty affect relatively few members of faculty women. Women doctorates tend to have fewer children than other women. Their childless ratio, according to one study, was double the national norm. Those who did have children had fewer than the national average. Nevertheless, a significant number of young women faculty members do have children—most typically, they are born early in the woman's career. One of the more serious problems faced by the married woman professor with children is the lack of time. There are just not enough hours in the day to do all she must do. A recent UNESCO study revealed that the average working mother had 2.8 hours of free time on a typical weekday compared with 4.1 hours for the working father (*New York Times* 1967). Women doctorates in the United States average about 28 hours per week on household tasks. Although we are fond of talking of the great advances gadgetry has made to free women from domestic tasks, the working mother's concern for her children is not eased by her automatic washer-dryer or her dishwasher. None of her electrical household appliances will take care of a sick child. What that mother needs, and what she finds increasingly difficult to find is household help—persons who are competent and reliable, who will help her in caring for her children and running her house. While day-care centers are a partial solution they do not solve the problem of household chores nor provide care when a child becomes ill.

These problems are accentuated in the suburban setting. More and more Americans live in outlying suburban areas, and it has become more and more difficult for women to find jobs that do not take them away from home for long periods of the day. Since many a woman must spend up to three hours daily commuting to her school, the amount of energy she has left at the end of a day for domestic chores is small indeed, and little or no time and energy is left for research and other scholarly activities. Domestic help is notoriously difficult to find in suburban communities. Moreover, in many suburban communities there are no convenient public places where one can spend a pleasant evening, and the overtired woman is expected to provide the serene environment in which friends can spend a delightful evening. An obvious solution is simply to reduce one's social life to the barest minimum, but this common way of dealing with the problem simply works another kind of hardship on the professional woman and her family.

Most of the problems limiting a woman's progression through professorial ranks similarly retard her entry into administration. A graphic example is Columbia University, which has granted more doctorates to women than any other school in the country. Currently, 38 percent of the entering graduate students and 19 percent of the doctorates are women, while only 3.5 percent of the full professors and none of the top administrators at the level of dean or above is a woman—except Martha Peterson, president of Barnard College, the women's undergraduate college of the university.

The few women in administration are likely to be assigned to "women's" tasks. The top woman administrator in most American coeducational colleges and universities is the dean of women, now often referred to as the associate dean of students. She is likely to be one of those administrators who has not followed the faculty-to-administration path. She typically has done specialized graduate work in guidance or student personnel administration, taken a low-level and peripheral job on the administrative staff of a college or university and has reached the position of dean of women without ever having been a member of the teaching faculty. Such a background is not likely to permit her to move into a major power position within the university. Within the last year a number of institutions have promoted junior women faculty members to junior administrative positions. Whether they eventually will move into senior positions remains to be seen.

Several factors inhibit those women who *are* members of the teaching faculty and thus represent possible candidates for administrative posts, in moving to upper-level administrative positions in greater numbers. A woman may shrink from the inevitable isolation she will feel when she joins an all-male group of top administrators. There is less financial incentive to enter administration since very few women professors have sole or primary economic responsibility for an entire family. Or it may be that the relatively few women who receive doctorates are more intent upon a scholarly life than men, some of whom appear to seek a degree as a union card not only to faculty membership but also to administrative posts. Many women, particularly those with families, may resist being drawn into the "office" regimen of administrative work with its less flexible schedules and inevitable time-consuming absences from home. The overall demands on a woman professor's time are great in terms of classroom teaching, lecture preparation, and research work, but these activities often can be scheduled at times and places convenient to her. And she does have her summers relatively free. This is not the case for the woman administrator who is expected to spend 9 A.M. to 5 P.M. in an office five days a week, forty-eight weeks a year. Nor does a woman administrator have a wife to assist her in the social and community obligations so often regarded as a male administrator's duty.

Violation of cultural stereotypes may be another factor working against women faculty members moving into upper-level administrative positions. It generally is assumed that women can make their best contributions in positions subordinate to men. Hence the university administrator's job description is almost invariably drawn with a man in mind, particularly a married man whose wife can provide auxiliary social support. Moreover, administrators are expected to be independent and assertive, behaviors understood as "tough and bitchy" when displayed by women, but "clear-headed and attentive to detail" when found in a man. Tolerance for men's behavior is a good deal broader than it is for that of women. Men are permitted their idiosyncracies of whatever sort, but women are expected to maintain a much more precarious balance between conspicuous competence and tactful femininity. Manifestations of independence and autonomy are expected in a male executive; their presence in women makes some male colleagues cringe.

There is a widespread belief that men will not work for women, and that women generally do not wish to either. Grounds for these common assertions are not frequently cited, and facts often point the other way. For example, at two colleges which regularly have had woman presidents (Barnard and Wellesley), men have consistently numbered around 40 and 50 percent of the faculty, and have never seemed to mind serving under a woman president. It is often charged that women will not support female candidates for administrative positions, and there may be some truth in this contention. Men who try to enlist the aid of successful women in promoting other women for similar responsible positions occasionally are surprised to discover that women at the top are reluctant to help their "sisters" up the ladder. The few women who have "made it" may prefer to believe that they have succeeded strictly on the basis of their own merit and that any failure to succeed on the part of other women is simply due to ability. As a consequence such women, many of whom have nearly cut themselves off from other women professionally and have defined themselves and their jobs by masculine standards, are often resistant to any special efforts to recruit more women to top administrative posts. Thus, reluctance to support other women provides men with a justification for not supporting them either. Some counterweight to this discouraging tendency has been achieved in recent years by those younger women (and some older ones, as well) who have come up from the ranks and who are displaying greater support for their "sisters," a term and an idea that have achieved legitimacy through the current women's movement.

Women at high administrative levels deal principally with men since they form the vast majority of senior academic administrators. These men rarely have worked with women *their own age* in positions of equal responsibility. Many academic men have not worked with women on an equal basis since their undergraduate days. At the very beginning of their careers, perhaps, some men may have worked with women on levels of relative equality. But in their middle and later years the gap between the two sexes in the professional field widens rapidly. So the woman administrator not only has a new job to learn and new relationships to cultivate, she must also legitimize the authority of her office, and gradually break down the resistance of her male associates to taking supervision and direction from a woman. It is not easy for most men to change their assumption that women are bossed, not bosses.

Senior academic ranks and administrative posts should not be such demanding posts as to force a woman (or man) to lose her humanity. It is no wonder that many able women are discouraged from making the move from faculty to administration. It is a rare person, woman *or* man, who is able to handle a responsible administrative position without being threatened by its dehumanizing aspects.

It is not surprising that so few women find their way to top faculty and administrative positions even if we count the recent efforts of a few universities to appoint women to previously all-male administrations. If society is to take the educational opportunities of its women as seriously as it does those of its men, then it must broaden the options open to women. From the entering student to the top administrator, academic institutions must become truly coeducational. Tokenism has no place at any level of higher education today.

REFERENCES

Astin, Helen S. 1969. *The woman doctorate in America: Origins, career, and family.* New York: Russell Sage Foundation.

Harmon, Lindsey R. 1968. *Careers of Ph.D.'s academic v. nonacademic. A second report on follow-ups of doctorate cohorts, 1935–1960.* Washington, D.C.: National Academy of Sciences.

Leive, Loretta. April 24, 1972. *Refuting myths about women microbiologists.* Paper presented at the American Society for Microbiologists, Philadelphia.

New York Times. March 5, 1967.

Simon, Rita J., Clark, Shirley M., and Galway, Kathleen. Fall 1967. The woman Ph.D.: A recent profile. *Social Problems,* 15:221–236.

Chapter Nine

Three's a Crowd:
The Dilemma of the Black Woman in Higher Education

Constance M. Carroll

FOUR YEARS AGO, if anyone had said to me that the black woman in higher education faces greater risks and problems now than in the past, I doubt I would have taken the remark seriously. I would have marveled at the rhetoric and pointed to federal legislation enacted on the crest of the civil rights movement of the 1950s and 1960s, and nodded proudly at the few blacks in token ("you've got to begin somewhere") positions in major institutions. I would have pointed to such outstanding black women as Mary McLeod Bethune, Mary Church Terrell, Coretta King, and Shirley Chisholm. "A great deal still needs to be done," I would have said, "but blacks, including black women, have come a long way."

In 1972, after four years of teaching and working in a university administration, I would nod my head in ready agreement if the same remark were made. My mind was changed not by startling new studies or surveys on the subject—indeed there are none—but by personal experience and by listening to accounts of black women educators and administrators across the country. Black women in higher education are isolated, underutilized, and often demoralized. They note the efforts made to provide equal opportunities for black men and white women in higher education, while they somehow are left behind in the wake of both the black and feminist movements. The intent of this chapter is to assess the situation of black women in higher education—undergraduates, faculty, and administrators.

CIVIL RIGHTS AND THE BLACK WOMAN

In the past two decades, a wealth of material has appeared on the subject of blacks in higher education; but most of these studies concern only black men. This is understandable since the great majority of blacks who have received advanced degrees in higher education are men. In a 1968 survey of doctoral and professional degrees conferred by black institutions (see Table 9.1), it was found that 91 percent were awarded to black men, only 9 percent to black women. Such data militate

AUTHOR'S NOTE: I am grateful for the useful discussion and criticism of Dr. Konnilyn Feig and Dr. Rebecca Carroll.

173

TABLE 9.1. Professional Degrees Conferred by Black Institutions in 1968 by Sex and Field of Specialization

Field	Number of Degrees	Men (percent)	Women (percent)
Medicine (M.D.)	125	85.6	14.4
Dentistry (D.D.S.)	84	95.0	5.0
Law (LL.B.)	146	90.4	9.6
Veterinary Medicine (D.V.M.)	29	96.5	3.5
Theology (Th.D.)	45	97.8	2.2
Total number and overall percentages	435	91.0	9.0

SOURCE: Jackson 1972a.

against the general assumption that black women have been included, on an equal basis with men, in the movement toward equal rights and increased educational and employment opportunities.

The few black women in academe today feel isolated because they *are* isolated. Jacqueline Johnson Jackson summarizes the situation well:

> Even if the facts were narrowed to higher education only, it is still true that black females have been severely disadvantaged. In 1940, a slightly *larger* number of black males (25 years and older) were more likely to complete four or more years of college than their female counterparts. Twenty years later, the pattern had reversed, when a very small percentage of black females in that same age group had completed higher school grades than had black males. By 1970, though, a larger percentage of black males (21 years and older) had completed four or more years of college (Jackson 1972b:102).

Even though black women enter college in roughly the same or often larger proportions than do black men (see Table 9.2), black men are more likely to receive an advanced degree beyond the Master's degree and thereby gain access to positions in colleges and universities. One has only to glance at the faculty or staff directory of any university or college to note the absence of black women. My own institution, the University of Pittsburgh, represents a microcosm of this nationwide situation (see Table 9.3). Eight per cent of the professional staff are black, and a slightly larger proportion of the white staff members than of the minority staff members are women (17 percent compared to 14 percent). The most significant contrast is the difference in rank distribution—white men and black men markedly exceed white women and black women at the upper ranks. White men constitute 50 percent of the associate or full professor ranks, black men 31 percent, white women 19 percent, and black women 3 percent. Clearly, sex is more of a handicap than race in the upper ranks of the teaching staff at the University of Pittsburgh, and

TABLE 9.2. Proportion of Black Students in College Freshman Classes, Fall 1971, by Type of Institution and Sex (In percentages)

Type of Institution	Men	Women
Coeducational Colleges		
Nonsectarian	12.0	13.3
Catholic	2.9	3.5
Single Sex Colleges		
Nonsectarian	5.3	16.9
Catholic	3.0	3.1
Predominantly Black Colleges	94.7	97.5

SOURCE: American Council of Education 1971:55.

the disproportion between the sexes is far greater for blacks than for whites. Among whites, men are about two and a half times more likely than women to be in the upper ranks, but among blacks, men are ten times more likely than women to enjoy higher status.

Consistent with this profile is the tendency for women of both races to be dis-

TABLE 9.3. Full-Time Professional Staff at the University of Pittsburgh, Fall 1970, by Race and Sex

Rank	White Men No.	White Men %	White Women No.	White Women %	Minority Men[a] No.	Minority Men[a] %	Minority Women[a] No.	Minority Women[a] %
Full professor	420	27	25	7	21	17	—	—
Associate professor	355	23	42	12	17	14	1	3
Assistant professor	483	31	128	38	43	36	16	50
Instructor	196	13	91	27	27	22	11	34
Assistant instructor	45	3	29	9	6	5	2	6
Lecturer or teacher	68	4	20	6	7	6	2	6
Total teaching ranks	(1,567)		(335)		(121)		(32)	
Research associate or professional librarian	38	2	58	15	12	9	6	16
Total professional staff	(1,605)		(393)		(133)		(38)	
Total faculty (by race)	(1,998)				(171)			
Percent female (by race)	17				14			

SOURCE: Computed by author from university catalog.
[a] Predominantly black.

proportionately represented in such nontenured or "marginal" academic statuses as research associate or professional librarians. Much the same picture holds in the instance of administrative posts. These positions are far more likely to go to black men than black women—a difference also found among white academics. Jackson is right in saying,

> One must . . . understand that black males have had greater access to the more prestigious institutions of higher learning. This means that the occupational opportunities of black females have been limited (Jackson 1972b:102).

This situation is not unique to institutions of higher learning. The black woman's status in higher education mirrors her impact on the national scene. One can leaf through the now famous 1971 *Ebony* roster of America's 100 leading blacks and find the names of only *nine* women. The problem is clear. New surveys and data are not necessary to document what is painfully manifest: Mary Church Terrell, Jeanne Noble, and Shirley Chisholm notwithstanding, the black woman has been excluded from institutions of higher education as she has been excluded from all other opportunities.

For the most part, black women college graduates have moved into areas that traditionally have been "open" to them, e.g., elementary and secondary education, social work, and nursing. The United States Bureau of the Census survey of population employment in 1960 showed that among employed black women, 5 percent were public school teachers; 19 percent were nurses; 5 percent were in social work; and 3.2 percent were health technicians. In comparison, 1.1 percent were employed by colleges as presidents (notably Bennett, a black woman's college), professors, and instructors; 0.1 percent were lawyers or judges; 0.3 percent were physicians and surgeons (U.S. Bureau of the Census 1964). I see the same trends among black women students whom I counsel, either because they were guided into these areas or because they believe that these are the only areas open to them.

Even in those areas where their numbers are large, black women rarely receive the same promotional advancements as black men. In public school systems few become principals and even fewer are promoted to upper administrative posts. The same is true in social and government agencies. This is not the case for black men, who are usually given positions in which they can be highly visible in an agency's or institution's "crusade" for equal employment or affirmative action. For some uncanny reason, a black woman at a board meeting is not thought to have the same "visibility" as a black male. It would be easy to say that white men who control these agencies and institutions can identify more easily with black men and thereby practice an "unconscious" sexism within their affirmative action programs. We are all familiar with the shock value of the joke:

—I saw God last night.
—Really? What's he like?
—Well, *he's* a *woman* and she's *black!*

When one ponders this testimony to what the white male really feels to be his most polar opposite, one wonders how far we have come and how far we can really expect to go. The strongest antagonism in the joke is the *God: woman* equation; that is, the tension between sexual "opposites" (male language) appears to be greater and more difficult to transcend than the antagonism between the races.

There is no more isolated subgroup in academe than black women. They have neither race nor sex in common with white males who dominate the decision-making stratum of academe; black males in academe at least share with white males their predominance over women. Even in black educational agencies and institutions, there is a disproportionately greater number of black males than black females in important positions. At the University of Pittsburgh, for example, there are only three women among the seventeen faculty members of the Black Studies Department. No calculator is necessary to count the number of black women holding responsible appointments in the NAACP, the Urban League, black colleges, black studies departments, and minority programs in white institutions. Where they *are* found, women tend to be at lower salaries and to wait longer for promotion through the *cursus honorum*.

> When occupational comparisons are made, it becomes quite clear that black women have *usually had the greatest access to the worst jobs at the lowest earnings*. Black females have consistently been in the minority among black physicians, college presidents, attorneys, architects and other high level positions (Jackson 1972b:102).

It is clear that when translated into actual opportunities for employment and promotional and educational benefits, the civil rights movement really meant rights for black men, just as, historically, the rights of men have referred to the rights of white men.

In this framework, black women feel their academic opportunities are limited, that there are barriers to their futures in higher education and a built-in isolation in an academic career. Unlike white and black men who more frequently are selected for apprenticeships or assistantships to male "people developers," black women have had very few models or champions to encourage and assist them in their development. Black women have had to develop themselves on their own, with no help from whites or black men, in order to "make it" in academic institutions. This has taken its toll on black women in all areas of life and work.

UNDERGRADUATE WOMEN

In talking with black women undergraduates, I have noticed an almost fierce single-mindedness in their preparation for careers. More than half express a desire to pursue careers in "traditional" areas, e.g., education, social work. With very few exceptions, they insist that they are fully prepared to pursue these careers despite plans for marriage. These findings are consistent with those found by Ladner (1971), Noble (1956), and others. Black women undergraduates feel the pressures of both racial and sexual discrimination, and choose education and the hard struggle of career mobility as the "way out." Yet, they have few role models with whom to identify in developing healthy self-concepts. The great majority of their professors are white men, or, if they take black studies courses, black men. Rarely do they see black women in responsible academic or administrative positions; and so students must look to each other for support and role models. As a result, they often form peer groups similar to extended family structures.

In their survey of black students at predominantly white universities and colleges Willie and Levy (1972) found that the greatest degree of social mobility and "freedom" among black students exists in large institutions, particularly those in which the black student population is sizable.

> On campuses where black populations are relatively small and the social lives of their members are limited to interaction with other black students, the black-student groups take on the character of extended families; when this occurs, all relationships, including those that might otherwise be secondary, become intensely personal. The black students who make unlimited claims upon each other find such relationships sometimes supportive, but they also find them sometimes stultifying and confining (Willie and Levy 1972:52).

Willie and Levy also demonstrate that even on large campuses, the situation is far from ideal. Black men have more freedom than black women to date both black and white students.

> While nearly all blacks on white campuses often feel isolated and confined, it is the black women who feel it most heavily . . . our data indicate that the dating situation may be a function of the absence of opportunities (Willie and Levy 1972:76).

The black women undergraduates with whom I have spoken confirm these assertions. They feel locked-in socially, are not awarded leadership roles in black student groups, do not see impressive role models with whom to identify, and as a result, they turn to their studies in the hope of escaping their dilemma some time in the future. In this respect, they are not unlike the small groups of black students on small campuses.

BLACK WOMEN PROFESSORS AND ADMINISTRATORS

The sheer paucity of black women among the faculty and administration in colleges and universities tends to force black women into a small, isolated community. My own appointment is in the College of Arts and Sciences, which puts me in touch with most academic departments of the university. Nevertheless, with the exception of black studies and minority programs I never come in contact with another black woman professor or administrator in my day-to-day activities. This seems to be typical for most of the black women in similar positions. There is no one with whom to share experiences and gain support, no one with whom to identify, no one on whom a black woman can model herself. It takes a great deal of psychological strength "just to get through the day," the endless lunches, and meetings in which one is always "different." The feeling is much like the exhaustion a foreigner speaking an alien tongue feels at the end of the day.

In the wake of the HEW investigations of several hundred universities for noncompliance with the federal guidelines concerning equal treatment of minorities and women, black women have raised their level of expectations and aspirations, just as black men and white women have done. Affirmative action programs and recruitment programs have sprung up across the country, spotlighting the inequities and proposing solutions to them. Colleges and universities have stepped up their hiring of black women in the same way they have gradually increased the roster of black men. They have been recruited to fill secretarial positions, to staff black studies and minority programs and, in rare cases, junior administrative posts. Overall, however, significant change has not yet occurred. In 1971, the total number of minority women faculty at the University of Pittsburgh was 57 (including part-time faculty), representing 1.8 percent of the total faculty of 3,043; the number of minority males in 1971 was 180, or 5.9 percent of the total faculty. There has been an increase of blacks of both sexes since 1970, but the rate of increase has been far greater for men than for women. Viewing these developments, black women feel a sense of frustration and hopelessness. It seems that just as civil rights in the 1950s and 1960s for the most part benefited black men, so affirmative action programs in the 1970s may largely benefit black men and white women.

When black women question this disparity in representation, responses range from "we can't find them" to what may be called the "two-steps behind" syndrome. No black has ever accepted the "we can't find them" response. Black men, when seriously sought, have been found, encouraged, and promoted. In some cases, they have multiplied so rapidly, one begins to think twice about denouncing spontaneous generation. Everyone now knows that when an institution is seriously recruiting in a framework of (budgetary) reward and punishment, its minority deficiencies can easily be repaired. Obviously, no serious efforts have been made until very recently and on a very limited scale to recruit or promote black women to important staff, faculty, or administrative positions in institutions of higher learning. If these institutions are to pursue an equitable policy that will not result in the demoralization of any of their constituency, *they must recruit and promote black women at the same rate and in the same proportions as black men in all areas of the academic structure.*

Another objection often raised that is even more disturbing is the "two-steps behind" philosophy, which mitigates against equal benefits for black women on the fallacious assumption that discrimination has had far more serious repercussions for black men than for black women: black women must now take a back seat to the black man as he "catches up." I have received such remarks and they seem to be fairly common even now. One writer rebuts it candidly:

> It must be pointed out at this time, that black women are not resentful of the rise to power of black men. We welcome it. We see in it the eventual liberation of all black people from this oppressive system of capitalism. Nevertheless, this does not mean that you have to negate one for the other. This kind of thinking is a product of miseducation; that it's either X or it's Y. It is fallacious reasoning that in order for the black man to be strong, the black woman has to be weak. Those who are exerting their "manhood" by telling black women to step back into a submissive role are assuming a counter-revolutionary position. Black women likewise have been abused by the system and we must begin talking about the elimination of all kinds of oppression (Beal 1970:343–344).

Black women have grown sensitive to this discrimination within discrimination, but their protests have not yet been translated into affirmative action on their own behalf. The black woman is told that black man has fared far worse from racial discrimination than she has; that when black men could find no work at all, she could always be a maid for "Miss Ann" or find some employment with "Mr. Charlie." Recent studies show that such arguments are based on false assumptions and incorrect data (Wright 1972:13–15). One would be hard pressed to say which is the more demoralizing circumstance: unemployment or servitude. The black woman will never rediscover *her* pride and *her* identity by learning to be second class a second time. Universities, black and white, must take these issues into serious consideration if the ultimate goals of *human* freedom and equal opportunities are to be reached.

BLACK WOMEN'S LIBERATION AND HIGHER EDUCATION

The rise of women's liberation and the protests of third world women in the late 1960s and early 1970s provided another framework in which black women could evaluate their relationship to black men and white women. From the outset, the women's liberation movement, at least philosophically, has sought to embrace and speak to the concerns of all women. This in itself is an impossible task because of the infinite complexity and variety of women in this country. As a goal, it represents the true cross-cultural and cross-racial orientation which was and is the basic unifying force in the movement. The danger in such an ideal arises when individuals or groups attempt to put it into practice without first dealing with its implicit assumptions. With regard to black women, for example, the women's movement has attempted to transcend rather than confront the racial tensions and the complexities resulting from the black woman's involvement in the movement. I have sat through meeting after meeting in which after a black woman raises objections to certain of the movement's directions and orientations, the inevitable "reverential silence" sets in and then the discussion simply proceeds as before. Promises are often made to study the situation of the black woman and she is reassured that the movement has her interests at heart because "she is a woman." *But black women are different from white women.* Their situation is more than a parenthetical remark in a chapter which supposedly includes them.

Black women understandably have mixed feelings about women's liberation. At first glance, the women's movement casts an all-too-familiar picture. The black woman finds herself in a special category in yet another white-dominated group— a division that in many ways mirrors society as a whole and toward which she has some deep-seated hostility. Many black women feel that the life experiences and life styles of white women in the movement are dramatically different from theirs.

> Another major differentiation is that the white women's movement is basically middle class. Very few of these women suffer the extreme economic exploitation that most black women are subjected to day by day. It is not an intellectual persecution alone; it is not an intellectual outburst for us; it is quite real (Beal 1970:350–351).

Statistics bear out this point: 50 percent of all black women work in contrast to 42 percent of all white women, and black women work in lower status jobs and at lower pay than white women. These facts account in part for black women's view of work as more of a necessity than an "opportunity," and that in turn may contribute to the misunderstandings and disagreements between black and white women.

The black woman sees that her numbers are few among the general membership of the women's movement, and nonexistent among its national leadership. She often is told that many of the problems she raises are problems of all blacks and, as such, are not the special concern of the women's movement. Why, for example, should a new women's studies center with limited funds finance course offerings on black women when there is already a black studies center or department? Can academic issues affecting black women even legitimately be separated from those affecting her race? These important questions and their implications have gone unanswered for the most part or relegated to black women to work out themselves.

A black woman's view of teaching methods and scholarship will also be different from those of her white counterpart. My own academic training has been in Classics and I have found, for example, that black women students, much more than white women students, understand and can identify with the situation of Medea. When the chorus agree that the plight of *all* women is dismal, Medea makes some distinctions that are intrinsic to grasping one of the central issues of the play.

> Surely, of all creatures that have life and will, we
> Women are the most wretched.
> Still more, a foreign woman, coming among new laws,
> New customs, needs the skill of magic, to find out what

> Her home could not teach her . . .
>   But the same arguments do not apply to you and me.
> You have this city, your father's home, the enjoyment of
> Your life, and your friend's company. I am alone, I
> Have no city; now my husband insults me. I was taken as
> Plunder from a land at the earth's edge. I have no
> Mother, brother, nor any of my own blood to turn to in
> This extremity (Euripides 1964:24–25).

The black woman in higher education is not unlike Medea. She is inexperienced in the system, just as most of her peers and family have traditionally been excluded from it. Black even more than white women need "magic," that is, superior ability, in order to receive equal opportunities.

Prior to my experience with the Chancellor's Advisory Council on Women's Opportunities at the University of Pittsburgh and my experience and involvement with the women's movement, I had unquestioningly accepted what I conceived to be the black woman's role. I functioned by the tacit formulae followed by all black women who wish to succeed in a man's (both black and white) world:

You must be *better qualified* than the men.

You must be *more articulate.*

You must be *more aggressive.*

You must have *more stamina* to face inevitable setbacks.

You must have *more patience,* since you will advance *more slowly.*

Above all, you must remain *feminine* and *not appear threatening.*

I have found that black women share these dicta with white women. However, black women have an extra step in the syllogism which white women do not have, that is, *they must also be better than white women.* It is this seldom discussed fact which has generated bitterness toward white women in general. In a power ladder, the white woman is seen to be two steps removed from the power, but the black woman is three steps removed. The black woman cannot help being cautious in allying herself with a "privileged competitor."

Recognizing these similarities and differences, the black woman's experience could add richness and depth to many areas of higher education. In a women's studies curriculum, for example, the black woman's experience should be depicted and studied in contrast to the white woman's experience, for the benefit and growth of both black and white students. This approach would also increase the involvement of black women faculty in such programs. Iris Murdoch's book *The Time of the Angels* is an example of a starting point for such a venture. Pattie O'Driscoll symbolizes the experience of many young black women who, surrounded by white women and men in academe, find themselves in a unique and dehumanizing situation. Her situation is poignantly summarized: "[A]s a child she had not distinguished between the affliction of being coloured and the affliction of being Pattie . . . whiteness seemed to join all the white people together in a cozy union, but blackness divided the black, each into the loneliness of his own special hue" (Murdoch 1971:22–23).

Among the faculty and administrative ranks, black women face even more complex problems. Institutions have responded initially to the women's movement with twice the "deliberate speed" with which they responded to the black movement, for white women are far more numerous in faculty and administrative positions than are either minority men or women. Institutions often have met the double threat of the black and the women's movements by pitting the two groups against each other. Everyone who has worked in compliance and affirmative action programs knows that this is a favorite institutional ploy. Blacks and women often are lumped together in the competition for the same famous "slice of the pie," the same positions, and the same benefits. This ploy, in a period of financial crisis heightened by the pronouncements and activities of HEW has caused new tensions and rivalries to arise. I do not know how many times I have gone to meetings on women's opportunities and institutional change where I have heard avuncular remarks to the effect that women would have to be patient since so much money had to be spent on providing more opportunities for minority candidates. I then hear the same administrators admonishing black groups to be patient since the women were using up so much money. The ploy evidently works, for I know of no institution where the women's groups and black groups have publicly allied to put an end to such divisive tactics; and I know of no institution where *significant* gains have been made for both white women and minority women and men. A bridge between these two groups is sorely needed for the benefit of both.

Caught between the claims of the women's movement and the black movement the black woman is being sorely pressed to define her political allegiances. While she has learned that involvement in the black movement has not led to a significant advancement of black women, strategically her association with the women's movement places her in an extremely awkward position and often damages her credibility among her black friends and colleagues. I have often been criticized for "deserting" the black cause and lessening the chances for black advancement in working for the causes of women. Yet, once in the women's movement, I find that many of my concerns and different needs are ignored, overlooked, or rarely discussed due to the powerful myth of an all-embracing sisterhood.

Some black women who have struggled with these conflicts have decided that the only solution is secession from both movements in favor of a third group exclusively devoted to the concerns of black women. This route seems to ensure "purity," pride, identity, clarity in issues, and solidarity; but strategically it is the one most fraught with peril. By its aloof stance, a third movement is, in effect, disavowing both the women's movement and the black movement. Unwittingly, it turns these other movements into unnatural enemies. Black women in this isolated position have forced themselves into a whole system of moves and countermoves which cannot fail to damage the other movements; at the same time, they invite institutional attempts to "slice the pie" yet a third way. My objection to this alternative is not ideological, nor am I suggesting malintent on the part of these women. I share their frustration and their impatience. But I have seen the resentment and fear engendered within and by these women faced with a dilemma, constantly at cross-purposes with themselves and others, as they stand alone to fight for what no one else will fight for quite hard enough.

Just as in some African myths of creation, the black woman has been called upon to create herself without model or precedent. She has had enough experience to know that, unless it changes, she can never comfortably or confidently fit into the white-oriented women's movement. At the same time, she has been held back, overlooked, and chided enough to know that all of her problems cannot be answered in the male-oriented black movement. She has had enough experience with institutional behavior and strategy to know that a third interest group (at least at this time) is lethal to the movements which, to a certain extent, have her concerns at heart.

There seems to be only one feasible course, one productive but difficult and lonely road if the black woman is to achieve concrete benefits at the end of her struggle. She must be the gadfly who stings both movements into achieving their goals— prodding the women's movement into confronting its racism and working doubly hard for the concerns of black women; and prodding the less volatile black movement into confronting its inherent sexism and righting the injustice it has done to black women. The black woman must work doubly hard in both movements; she must become the sorely needed bridge between them if their goals are to be translated into reality. The two movements must become "company" in affirmative action in order for the goal of human rights in higher education to become a reality.

REFERENCES

American Council of Education. 1971. The American freshman: National norms for fall 1971. 6(6), Washington, D.C.: Author.

Beal, Frances M. 1970. Double jeopardy: to be black and female. In Robin Morgan (Ed.), *Sisterhood is powerful.* New York: Vintage Books, pp. 340–353.

Euripides. 1964. *Medea.* New York: Penguin Books.

Jackson, Jacqueline J. 1972a. Black women and higher education. Mimeographed.

Jackson, Jacqueline J. 1972b. Where are the black men? *Ebony,* 27:99–106.

Ladner, Joyce. 1971. *Tomorrow's tomorrow—the black woman.* Garden City, N.Y.: Doubleday & Co.

Murdoch, Iris. 1971. *The time of the angels.* New York: Bard Books.

Noble, Jeanne. 1956. *The Negro woman's college education.* New York: Columbia University Press.

U.S. Bureau of the Census. 1964. *U.S. census of population: 1960 characteristics of the population.* Washington, D.C.: U.S. Government Printing Office.

Willie, Charles, and Levy, Joan. 1972. Black is lonely. *Psychology Today,* 5(10):50–80.

Wright, Doris. 1972. On black womanhood. *The Second Wave,* 1(4):13–15.

BIBLIOGRAPHY

Drake, St. Clair. 1971. The black university in the American social order. *Daedalus,* 100(3):833–897.

Dubois, W. E. B., (Ed.). 1969. *The Negro American family.* New York: New American Library.

Feig, Konnilyn. 1972. Myths of female liberation. University of Pittsburgh. Mimeographed.

Ferris, A. 1971. *Indicators of trends in the status of American women.* New York: Russell Sage Foundation.

Miller, Albert H. 1971. The problems of the minority student on the campus. *Liberal Education,* 55:18–23.

Slaughter, Diane T. 1972. Becoming an Afro-American woman. *School Review,* 80(2): 299–317.

Chapter Ten

The Faculty Wife:
Her Academic Interests and Qualifications

Myrna M. Weissman, Katherine Nelson, Judith Hackman
Cynthia Pincus, Brigitte Prusoff

UNDER POLITICAL pressure both from women's groups and government officials, colleges and universities recently have begun to develop affirmative action plans to increase the representation of women on their staffs. Sometimes this is done willingly, with strong support from the chief administrator, an example of which is Kingman Brewster, president of Yale University, who expressed his "personal commitment to the training, employment and promotion of qualified professional women" (Taylor 1971).

In many other instances, however, there is great reluctance on the part of universities to seek out and hire more women. One hears in many places the claim that there are no qualified women to be found. In point of fact, a number of qualified and interested women not only are available, but right at the universities' own back doors. They are the educated wives of the universities faculty members. The academic potential and employment interest of faculty wives as a group never has been explored. It was for these reasons that we undertook a survey of the employment and educational status and interests of the faculty wives at Yale University (Nelson et al. 1972).

Ten departments, selected as a representative sample of the university composition as a whole, were chosen for the study.[1] Mail questionnaires were sent to the wives of all the faculty members, and to all the women on the faculty in the ten departments. The faculty women in the departments surveyed were included as a comparison group to the sample of faculty wives. The total sample consisted of 408 women, of whom 381 were faculty wives and 27 were faculty women. In all,

AUTHORS' NOTE: This research was partially funded through the office of Elga Wasserman, special assistant to the president for the education of women, Yale University. Data collection was assisted by Elizabeth Barrnett of the Yale School of Nursing and by the staff of the Information and Counseling Center for Women, Yale University Women's Organization, New Haven, Connecticut.

[1] The ten departments sampled were: Political Science, Psychology, History, English, Chemistry, Mathematics, Music (School and Department), The School of Art and Architecture, the Law School, and the Department of Surgery, School of Medicine.

282 (69 percent) questionnaires were returned,[2] 262 from faculty wives and 20 from women on the faculty.

GENERAL CHARACTERISTICS

The median ten-year age range of the faculty wives was 30 to 39 with 16 percent over 50 and 21 percent in their twenties. The great majority of the respondents (77 percent) had one or more children or a mean of 2.1 children living at home. Family size varied with the educational level of the wife, those women at higher educational levels having fewer children. Husbands of the women sampled occupied ranks from research associate and lecturer to full professor, with 58 percent in nontenured and 42 percent in tenured positions (representative of the proportion of tenured to non-tenured faculty for the university as a whole). Geographical mobility among these academic families was high—the median number of moves from one geographic area to another was three moves in ten years, and two of these moves were for the purpose of the husbands' career development.

EDUCATIONAL STATUS AND INTERESTS

The median educational level of the faculty wives was "some" graduate work, and 151 (57.7 percent) of the faculty wives had some training beyond the B.A. (see Table 10.1). Sixty-eight (26 percent) had masters degrees and twenty-eight (10.7 percent) held the Ph.D. or LL.B. degree. Nationally, one woman out of every 100 college graduates receives a Ph.D.; in this sample of 208 college graduates the proportion was almost thirteen times this average (Astin 1969). If our sample was an accurate cross-section of the total female population at Yale, faculty wives with a Ph.D. or LL.B. degree represent as many as 160 women in the university community.

In addition to the 45 women enrolled in study, 119 women (45 percent of the total group) were interested in further study. This constitutes a total of 66 percent (164) of the group who either were studying or were interested in further study. The greatest demand was for study at the M.A. level (36.1 percent), with a substantial number interested in the Ph.D., LL.B., or M.D. degree (25.6 percent). Many of the women interested in master's and doctoral level study wished to study part time and most cited new career goals as at least one of their reasons for study.

Many of the respondents interested in returning to complete their education were over 30. They had interrupted their careers to rear their children, and were now interested in part-time work or study. Graduate study was the subject of many

---

[2] The Psychology Department had a higher than average response rate (88.6 percent), while the Mathematics and Art and Architecture Departments had the lowest response rates with 52.4 percent and 44.9 percent, respectively.

TABLE 10.1. Educational Status of Faculty Wives

Highest Educational Level Achieved	Number	Percent of Total
High school graduate or less	9	3.5
Technical training or some college	45	17.0
B.A. degree	57	21.8
Some graduate work	55	21.0
M.A. degree	68	26.0
Ph.D. degree	23	8.8
LL.B. degree	5	1.9
Total	262	100.0

of the additional comments of the respondents. Some older women interested in part-time study expressed ideas about how their qualifications might be evaluated:

> I would like to see the university encourage women of my age to prepare for a new career. I endorse the procedure that allows a woman to enroll in a course and acceptance in the graduate program contingent on her performance in that trial seminar. This seems a better way to screen those "over thirty" than the Graduate Record Exams, or a college record that dates back twenty years—or more.

Others commented on the problems encountered in reentering study programs:

> I would like to return to school for my Ph.D. only if I could do so on a part-time basis. . . . I would hope that if attitudes toward the value of part-time graduate work could be changed this would be reflected not only in admission policies but in financial aid policies as well. It is almost impossible to get financial aid for part-time study currently.

In addition to the cost of further study and the need for part time study, there were other difficulties these women encountered with interrupted study. Problems of geographical mobility were evident in a number of comments:

> I am *not* in favor of the university accepting any faculty wife for study, regardless of qualifications. I would like to see, however, part-time study opportunities made available to qualified women, since faculty salaries are so low that many wives want to earn some money. It would also be useful if the university would at least investigate and possibly accept the study a wife may have begun at another university—providing standards and performance are high.

And,

> As you must know, faculty wives are in many ways more handicapped than other women in pursuing careers. I have found that one of the most serious barriers to our career development is the restriction on part-time study which

most graduate programs maintain. Very few women can study full time during the child-raising years and many even afterward (many have other family responsibilities, such as aging or sick parents and others, depending on husbands' position and schedule). Moving from one community and one state to another can be disastrous for the faculty wife's career, and I think especially for the kind of career that depends on a network of relationships, status and recognition earned through work with colleagues.

EMPLOYMENT STATUS AND INTERESTS

One hundred twenty-six (48 percent) of these faculty wives were employed, 14.9 percent on a full-time and 33.2 percent on a part-time basis. Employment status was closely related to the women's educational level. Although 72.2 percent of the women with less than a bachelor's degree and 59.7 percent with a bachelor's degree were not employed, only 25 percent of the Ph.D. and LL.B. degree holders were not employed.

Non-working wives were asked about their interest in employment. Forty percent of all the unemployed women, regardless of educational level, planned to look for work within the next two years. Almost half of the women with less than a bachelor's degree, but only one-third of the women with graduate training and only one of the women with a Ph.D. or LL.B. degree said they were not interested in employment at that time. The unemployed wives in the Ph.D. or LL.B. group indicated that they were not working because there was no work available either full- or part-time, no work in their field or at their level, or no work within a convenient location. Six of the seven unemployed wives with Ph.D.'s were looking for employment. Thus unemployment of the most highly educated faculty wives was related to a lack of suitable jobs, not to a lack of interest. Among those women who were unemployed but interested in employment, the overwhelming demand was for part-time work. This was true for all educational levels, including the Ph.D. level.

The faculty wives reported a number of additional job qualifications including competency in foreign languages, computer programming skills, musical or artistic competency at a professional level, academic and nonacademic publications, membership in professional societies, and a substantial number of academic and professional honors.

Consistent differences in employment interest and status were found among educational achievement groups. The more highly educated the woman the more likely she was to be working, to be looking for work, or to plan on working later. Although there was a strong interest in part-time work at all levels, the more highly educated group was most likely of all to be interested in full-time work.

Looking at employment status and interest for the total sample we found that 199 of the 262 faculty wives sampled (75.9 percent) either were employed or planned to look for employment in the near future. This is an astounding percentage, even higher than one would expect on the basis of the general increase in employment among well-educated married women over the past few decades.

THE PH.D. AND LL.B. WIVES

Faculty wives who held the Ph.D. or LL.B. degree were compared with the sub-group of women faculty who were not faculty wives. The faculty wives included thirty-four women with the Ph.D. or LL.B. degree whose husbands were on the faculty. More than one-third of these women also held a faculty appointment. The faculty women included thirteen women who had either the Ph.D. or LL.B. degree and, if married, whose husbands did not hold faculty appointments at the university. Women with the LL.B. degree were included as this is the highest degree required for academic positions in the Law School, which was one of the departments sampled.

The outstanding difference between these two groups was that the faculty women had been sought out for their positions, while the faculty wife found her job through her own efforts, in contrast to her husband who had been sought out by the university.

Twenty-three of the thirty-four faculty wives with a Ph.D. or LL.B. degree were working in academic settings (sixteen at the university and seven at other colleges and universities). Four of the thirty-four wives were working outside academe and seven were unemployed. The thirteen faculty women not married to members of the faculty or who were single were compared with the Ph.D. or LL.B. wives who were working at a university or who were currently unemployed (see Table 10.2). The employed faculty wives tended to be slightly older than both the faculty women, most of whom were in their twenties, and the unemployed faculty wives, who had an even higher proportion of women in their twenties than did the employed wives. Eleven out of the thirteen faculty women (84.6 percent) had no children, compared with 17.4 percent of the working wives and 14.3 percent of the non-working wives. A third of the faculty wives were employed at the university part time, while none of the faculty women held part-time positions. This may be due to the fact that the wives were slightly older, were married and had children.

We did not obtain information about degree-granting institutions, grades, recommendations, and estimates of professional promise for these groups. However, in terms of academic or professional honors the three groups of women were very similar. A substantial number of faculty wives, whether employed or not, had one to five academic publications and nonacademic publications, including books, to their credit. A larger proportion of faculty women than faculty wives had published more than five works, and a great proportion of these were academic rather than nonacademic publications. Quite likely this reflects a difference in career patterns. Some academic jobs encourage publication, while others do not (Graham 1970; Astin 1969). One faculty wife with both academic and nonacademic pub-

TABLE 10.2. Comparison of Faculty Women and Faculty Wives with Ph.D. and LL.B. Degrees

| | Faculty Women N = 13 | | Faculty Wives with Ph.D. or LL.B. Degrees[a] | | | |
| | | | Working at a University N = 23 | | Not Working[b] N = 7 | |
	N	Percent	N	Percent	N	Percent
Age						
20–29	7	53.8	2	8.7	2	28.6
30–39	1	7.7	11	47.8	4	57.1
40–49	5	38.4	8	34.8	0	0
50 and over	0	0	2	8.7	1	14.3
Number of Children						
None	11	84.6	4	17.4	1	14.3
One	0	0	6	26.1	0	0
Two and over	2	15.4	13	56.5	6	85.7
Work Status						
Part-time	0	0	8	34.8	—	—
Full-time	13	100.0	15	65.2	—	—
Qualifications						
1–5 academic publications only	5	15.3	13	56.5	2	28.5
Over 5 academic publications	7	53.8	6	26.1	0	0
Nonacademic publications	1	7.6	3	13.0	1	14.2
Professional honors[c]	6	46.1	13	56.0	3	42.8
University Position						
Secretary	0	0	1	4.3	—	—
Fellow or instructor	2	15.4	3	13.1	—	—
Research associate	0	0	8	34.8	—	—
Assistant professor	7	53.8	7	30.4	—	—
Associate professor	2	15.4	1	4.3	—	—
Professor	2	15.4	0	0	—	—
Administration	0	0	3	13.1	—	—

[a] Four women with LL.B. degrees were excluded because they were not working at a university.
[b] One nonworking wife with a LL.B. degree included here was a doctoral student.
[c] Professional honors include Phi Beta Kappa, fellowships, etc.

lications to her credit commented that the temporary and insecure nature of her academic position left her with periods of unexpected unemployment. She did free-lance writing during these periods to maintain an income instead of preparing her own academic work for publication as she would have preferred.

Of the faculty wives with the Ph.D. or LL.B. degree, nearly 80 percent were employed and 70 percent were employed at universities. All but one of the unemployed, however, said that they were seeking employment and would accept a suitable job if it could be found. One unemployed LL.B. wife was a doctoral student. The unemployed Ph.D. wives who were seeking employment tended to be younger than the employed wives, possibly reflecting the increasingly tighter job market for new Ph.D.'s.

The academic positions held by faculty women and faculty wives were compared. Of the faculty women, 84.6 percent held academic "ladder" positions compared to only 34.7 percent of the faculty wives whether employed by Yale or other universities and colleges. One of the wives with a Ph.D. was employed as a secretary at the university. When only those faculty wives employed by the university were considered, our comparison of their ranks with those of faculty women was even more striking. Only one faculty wife was in a "ladder" position; most of these women were research associates. Both the faculty women and wives expressed concern about the possibility of academic advancement. However, faculty wives expressed additional dissatisfactions about their particular academic positions: having limited teaching opportunities, being expected to assume certain service functions (such as having to run various routine tests for the laboratory, rather than being able to devote that time to their own research), and being overqualified for their jobs.

Did the groups differ in their personal goals and ambitions? We asked respondents to indicate what their homemaking and career plans had been as a teenager, college student, newlywed, and during the past two years. The responses of the two groups were nearly indistinguishable. However, the faculty wife group had been more career oriented; in high school, 90 percent of the faculty wife group planned a full-time career compared to 75 percent of the faculty women group. Since 1969, the shift has been to a greater interest in full-time career and marriage: two-thirds of the faculty wives and all of the faculty women stated that they were interested in full-time careers.

It has been well documented that women are underrepresented in academe whether or not they are faculty wives, and the data do not suggest that faculty women who are not faculty wives have been able to obtain their positions with ease. Nevertheless, they are sought after by universities. When Ph.D. faculty wives are compared with this highly selected group of women on the faculty, the two groups appear similar in life goals, backgrounds, job preparation, and career orientation. They differ primarily in their university positions and in full-time employment status.

PART-TIME ACADEMIC WORK AND STUDY

Our data showed a considerable demand for part-time academic employment and graduate study, especially by married women with children at home. Despite changing patterns—and we expect that they will continue to change—and regardless of their career aspirations, the women sampled considered care of their home and family to be their responsibility, not their husband's. These women did not accept for themselves the recent movement toward greater involvement of married men in the home and a less compulsive career orientation for both men and women. The emphasis in our sample on women carrying most of the responsibility for home and family may be related to the age of the respondents, to preselection factors operating in the university, or to other unidentified characteristics of the respondents.

Some women were able to manage domestic responsibilities and carry on a full-time career as well—if their families were small, and their husbands cooperative, if they had household help and a high level of physical and mental energy. However, a large proportion of our sample felt they needed, for short or long periods during their careers, to take part-time positions if they were to continue their careers at all. This finding should not be taken to imply that women should not carry on demanding academic careers for which they are otherwise qualified. Rather, it implies that employers should be flexible in meeting the needs of this group of women. It is particularly instructive to consider the life goals of the professional and academic women in this sample at varying times during their lives. Although 75 percent now want full-time careers in addition to their marriage, less than 60 percent wanted careers when they were first married.

Some of the faculty wives who were working full-time would have preferred some flexibility in their appointments.

> I enjoy my work tremendously; however, if part-time work at the ranks of regular teaching, with full faculty recognition, associated benefits, and leaves after an equivalent amount of work, and so on became available, I would find my life a little less hectic. I am quite confident that I can deliver the same quality work as my male colleagues, but am equally sure I cannot deliver the same quantity. This may affect me adversely when it comes time for reappointment. If it were possible for me to work part-time without destroying my chances for advancement, I would consider that alternative very seriously indeed. Being the hub of a family and working full-time is just a hair's-breadth short of impossible—and this has nothing to do with the [un]availability of child care. It is more a question of how much one human can *be* rather than of how many things one has time to do.

SUMMARY AND CONCLUSIONS

Our sample of faculty wives represented a diversity of interests and included a substantial number of highly educated, academically inclined, career-minded women. Most of these women either were working or studying and the majority of those who were not working or studying planned to do so in the near future. Their greatest demand was for part-time work and study. The more educated the woman, the more likely she was to be working outside the home or to plan on working in the future.

The interests of the faculty wives in activities outside the home reflect a similar trend in the general population. While many wives had strong career goals before marriage, many shifted their goals toward homemaking after marriage. After some years of marriage they became interested in finding ways of combining a career with homemaking responsibilities. This trend is reflected in the strong interest in returning to school of the "over thirty" group. While many faculty wives desired part-time work and study during their active child-rearing years, others (particularly the most highly educated) were interested primarily in full-time work. These diverse responses reflect the fact that women's needs and interests vary both with individual characteristics and with the stage of family responsibilities. The problem of interrupted careers and study was common to most of the women. These interruptions were the result not only of child-rearing patterns but of the geographic mobility required by their husbands' careers.

Contrary to the expectations and fears of many academics, these women showed a strong concern for maintaining high academic standards. Many of them stated that only well-qualified women should be admitted to graduate programs or promoted to faculty positions. They did not feel that they should be given special privileges by the university by virtue of their husbands' positions; neither did they feel they should be penalized. Many women were sensitive to nepotism rules which had discriminated against them in the past. Some expressed the feeling that they were overqualified for their jobs but were unable to negotiate for better ones because they could not leave the area.

The problems faced by these faculty wives in establishing or reestablishing careers are similar to those faced by women in any relatively isolated academic community. The university is the major source of education, as well as the major consumer of educated workers, male and female. Moreover, formal and informal employment policies often exclude or discriminate against the spouse of a faculty member. Flexible university policies that are sensitive to the career patterns of all women will insure the increased participation of women at all levels. Faculty wives represent only one pool of talented women who will be available to take advantage of new opportunities in academe. Universities have little need for concern that there will not be enough qualified women available for these positions.

REFERENCES

Astin, Helen S. 1969. *The woman doctorate in America.* New York: Russell Sage Foundation.

Graham, Patricia A. 1970. Women in academe. *Science,* 169:1284–1290.

Nelson, Katherine, Weissman, Myrna M., Hackman, Judith, Pincus, Cynthia, and Prusoff, Brigitte. 1972. The Yale faculty wife: Her employment and educational status. Report available from Katherine Nelson, Department of Psychology, Yale University, 333 Cedar Street, New Haven, Conn. 06510.

Taylor, Charles H., Jr. 1971. Memorandum to Yale faculty and professional staff. Yale University, Office of the President, New Haven, Conn.

Part Two

Women
on the Contemporary
Academic Scene

Chapter Eleven

Institutional Variation in the Status of Academic Women

Lora H. Robinson

[T]oday's university should be the last place to tolerate discrimination of any sort, either overt or by the perpetuation of destructive social attitudes through sheer apathy. In fact, the university's educational responsibility requires it to be particularly sensitive to such attitudes. In its capacity as a test lab for ideas, the university must maintain a ceaseless program of self-evaluation, for, if it does not, it risks depriving its students of choice by passing on such attitudes unquestioned (State University of New York at Buffalo 1970:4).

INSTITUTIONS of higher education presently are under fire for perpetuating society's generally low valuation of women and for treating women unfairly. That a pattern of discrimination against women exists in academe is evident in the numerous studies on the status of academic women that recently have become available. These reports vary considerably in depth and breadth, but collectively they provide an illuminating profile of the current status of academic women.

This chapter updates and expands a review of these reports by the author for the ERIC Clearinghouse on Higher Education (Robinson 1971). In 1971 data were available for sixty-six colleges and universities. The number of reports has doubled in the intervening year, and these additional reports also will be summarized. The studies cover many facets of faculty women's status, but only those factors considered prime attributes of status will be reviewed. They include: institutional participation rate, departmental participation rate, rank, initial appointment level, marginal appointments, promotion, tenure, salary, and administrative activities. When possible, we will examine the range of institutional variability of each dimension.

The primary sources for our data are the 125 campus reports listed in the section, "Institutional Data Sources," at the end of this chapter. In some instances a single report covers more than one institution, so the 125 reports actually contain data for 145 schools. Very few reports covered all nine of the status variables under review, nor were the topics covered in an identical fashion. Because we will review only data similar in variable definition and measurement, sample size will vary by topic, that is, by attribute of status.

AUTHOR'S NOTE: The author wishes to thank the ERIC Clearinghouse on Higher Education for the use of its facilities in the preparation of this chapter.

199

INSTITUTIONAL PARTICIPATION RATE

The most basic datum of all institutional reports is the actual number of women on their faculties. Nationally, about 20 percent of all college teachers are women ("Highest percentage. . ." 1970). At the sixty-five schools for which data were available, the participation rate for women ranged from 2 to 35 percent. Eighty percent of these institutions (all are coeducational) reported *lower* participation rates than the national average. At more than half the schools women constituted less than 16 percent of the faculty.

What could or should be the proportion of women on a particular faculty is a complex and difficult question that most reports attempted to answer. Though the need for a standard by which to establish an equitable participation rate was acknowledged by all, there was great variation in choice of criteria. The most common procedure was to compare the proportion of women on the faculty of a particular college or university with the national average of 20 percent. Some schools compared their participation rate against measures of *expected* participation, based on various definitions of the labor pool of qualified women.

The University of Arizona report is a good example of a more complex evaluation of the degree of utilization of women. The report first compared the percent of women graduate students at the university with the percent of women faculty, on the assumption that the graduate student pool represented potential faculty women. A survey of the degree levels of men faculty as listed in the university catalog revealed that a large proportion (18 percent of tenured faculty men, 33 percent of men assistant professors, and 90 percent of men instructors) did not hold advanced degrees. In light of this, the report assumed the graduate student female pool was a reasonable criterion against which to assess the participation of women on the faculty. Women represented 38 percent of the graduate students and 13 percent of the faculty, indicating underutilization of women by a factor of roughly three. The same comparison was made within departments, with similar results.

Next it was argued that the potential availability of qualified women could be gauged by the number of women chosen for the 1969–1970 Woodrow Wilson Dissertation Fellowship Program. Those chosen for fellowships are among the top predoctoral students in their fields. Selected fields illustrating the underrepresentation of women on the faculty thus determined are shown in Table 11.1.

Since neither graduate students nor fellows reflect the number of available trained academic women, another estimate was used. The percentages of Ph.D.'s granted nationally to women in the 1940's, 1950's, and 1960's were compared to the actual proportion of women doctorates among all UA faculty (see Table 11.2).

The Columbia University report provides a second example of methods used to evaluate women's representation on faculties. It compared the current ranks of women and men faculty who had earned their doctorates in the 1960s. The average female assistant professor received the doctorate in 1965; the average male assistant

TABLE 11.1. Women among Woodrow Wilson Fellows and Faculty at the University of Arizona by Field of Study or Department (In percentages)

Field of Study	Woodrow Wilson Fellows (women)	University of Arizona Faculty (women)
Anthropology	80	8
History	25	0
English	43	34
Modern languages	80	12
Philosophy	10	0
Government	33	0

SOURCE: University of Arizona 1970:4.

TABLE 11.2. Actual versus Expected Proportion of Women on the Faculty of University of Arizona by Rank (In percentages)

Rank	Actual	Expected
Full professor	4	13
Tenured faculty (full and associate)	5	10
Assistant professor	6	11
All faculty	5.5	11

SOURCE: University of Arizona 1970:3.

professor in 1966. Well over 50 percent of the men who received the doctorate in 1963 or 1964 are associate professors; none of their female counterparts have been promoted to that position. If Columbia women faculty who received their doctorates in the 1960s were distributed by rank in the same proportion as were Columbia men faculty in 1970 there would be three full professors, nine associate professors, and thirteen assistant professors. The actual distribution of women and men is shown in Table 11.3. The authors note that Columbia's current faculty figures show a lower percentage of women at all ranks than does Parrish's 1962 study of the distribution and numbers of women faculty in ten high endowment and ten high enrollment institutions of higher education.

The preceding reports recognized that many factors determine the distribution of women college teachers. But, regardless of the criterion employed to determine the pool of qualified academic women, report after report found fewer women than should be expected.

A rather unique criterion was that utilized by at least two other reports, the University of Maryland at Baltimore and the University of Pennsylvania, which maintained that women should comprise the same proportion of faculties as they do in

TABLE 11.3. Actual and Expected Distribution of Columbia University
Faculty by Rank and Sex

Faculty Rank	Men No.	Men (%)	Women No.	Women (%)	Expected Number of Females
Full professor	30	(15)	0	(0)	3
Associate professor	74	(38)	1	(4)	9
Assistant professor	91	(47)	24	(96)	13

SOURCE: Columbia University 1970, Appendix 1.

the total population—51 percent. The argument for this standard was that any alternate criterion had already been "sexually conditioned," i.e., it would reflect the effect of sex discrimination. The total population standard is appealing but hardly practical since external factors will continue to effect the representation of women on college faculties.

Women's representation on college faculties varies as a function of specific characteristics of higher education institutions. Some of the correlates of variation in representation include: type of institution (two-year, four-year, or university); quality of institution (elite or nonelite); and sex composition of the student body (single-sex or coeducational).

Women comprise 25.6 percent of the faculty at two-year colleges, 22.7 percent at four-year colleges and 14.8 percent at universities ("Highest percentage . . ." 1970:5). Bernard (1964) suggests that this pattern reflects sex differences in extent of training and type of employment choices. Since fewer women than men receive the doctorate, they are less likely to be found at universities that require the degree for appointment. Yet Bayer's data (1970:13) show that the proportion of women faculty at four-year colleges who hold the doctorate (30 percent) is practically the same as at universities (28 percent). In contrast, a larger proportion of men faculty who hold the doctorate are found at universities (61 percent) than at four-year colleges (46 percent).

Bernard also suggests that women are more interested in teaching and therefore prefer appointments at colleges rather than universities. This view has long been held and Bayer's data tend to support it. Table 11.4 shows that women express a greater interest in teaching than do men. This difference is far more pronounced in universities than in four-year colleges. In contrast, Henderson's (1967) comparison of men and women *doctorates* established no differences by sex in preferences for research, teaching, and counseling.

Some researchers have found women *not* to differ in their choice of employing institution. However, Henderson found that women were not able to secure positions in the type of institution that they preferred in the same proportion as were

TABLE 11.4. Teaching versus Research Interests of Faculty, by Sex and
Type of Institution, 1969 (In percentages)

Teaching-Research Interests	Four-Year Colleges		Universities	
	Men	Women	Men	Women
Heavily in research	2.5	1.2	6.9	3.0
Both, lean toward research	14.3	8.2	31.9	12.1
Both, lean toward teaching	37.6	30.5	38.2	31.3
Heavily in teaching	45.5	60.1	23.0	53.5

SOURCE: Bayer 1970:15.

men. Significantly, more women than men did not even apply to preferred institutions. Henderson did not attempt to establish the extent to which this fact accounted for differences in job placement. Women justified their actions on the basis of nepotism rules, inability to relocate, their belief that women simply would not be hired there and that women would not be able to secure jobs even if they did apply.

The second notable factor that affects the distribution of women among types of institutions is, whether or not an institution is "elite." Of the reports reviewed, information on women's participation rate in the total faculty was available for thirteen of the twenty schools classified "elite" (so defined on the basis of endowment and enrollment) by Parrish (1962). For these thirteen schools, women's participation rate was 2 to 17 percent, half the range for the entire distribution of the coeducational schools whose reports we have examined (2 to 35 percent). Women's representation was below 10 percent in nine of the thirteen "elite" schools. When these elite schools were excluded from the total distribution of the sixty-five schools, the lower limit of the range of distribution in nonelite schools was raised from 2 to 6 percent and the median rate of participation was raised from 13 to 18 percent.

There is a difference by sex in participation rates at single-sex colleges. Women's colleges have a far greater proportion of women on their faculties. As shown in Table 11.5, the percentage of women faculty members of five nonelite women's colleges ranged from 23 to 58 percent—all above the national average. In exclusively male schools, the number of faculty women is quite restricted. Women's representation on the faculties of four nonelite men's schools ranged from 1 to 8 percent (see also, Wilcox 1970; Schuck 1969; and Harris 1970). Of the thirteen elite schools, two recently became coed; one formally restricts women's enrollment, another traditionally has had few women students; and one traditionally has maintained a coordinate institution for women. These five predominantly male institutions all fall below the 10 percent participation rate for women faculty, and four

ABLE 11.5. Proportion of Women on the Faculty, by Type of Institution

Type of Institution	Number of Schools	Range (percent women)
Men's colleges (nonelite)	4	1 to 8
Elite schools (all coed)	9	2 to 17
All coed schools (including elite)	65	2 to 35
Women's colleges (nonelite)	5	23 to 58

SOURCE: Robinson analysis of institutional reports.

of the five fall below 5 percent. Thus, the lowest participation rates for women faculty among both elite and nonelite institutions are in male or predominantly male schools.

The institutional variation in the proportion of women on the faculty has been accepted by many as the way things *should* be, since that is the way they *are*. This becomes apparent when institutions compare their rate of participation with other "comparable" schools. Implicit in the comparison is the preconception, "since others are similar, it justifies the way we find things here." For example,

> the situation at Harvard is only slightly worse than that at other major universities. At the University of Chicago in the spring of 1969, 11 out of 475 full professors were women, 16 out of 217 associate professors, 16 out of 308 assistant professors, and 15 out of 102 instructors. At Berkeley in the spring of 1970, 2% of all full professors, 5% of all associate professors, and 5% of all assistant professors were women (Harvard 1971[3]:2).

Harvard is not the only institution to make this type of comparison. The University of Chicago takes a similar approach:

> Women constituted 7.3 percent of the regular teaching faculties in the spring of 1969. . . . The overall figure is considerably below the average for all universities . . . , but it compares favorably, so far as we have been able to ascertain, with those universities which, like The University of Chicago, view themselves as "elite" (University of Chicago 1970[1]:1).

So, too, the University of Pennsylvania compared itself to the University of Chicago. And as the cycle continues the comparisons reinforce and perpetuate the status quo.

More commonly, campuses compared women's participation rate on their campus with the overall national rate. Reports from Baldwin-Wallace, Cornell College, Eastern Kentucky University, Indiana State University (2), the University of Akron, and the University of Oregon are examples of this approach. The conclusions usually drawn from such a comparison were that if a school employs women at a rate above the national percentage, it was employing them at an acceptable rate. Indiana State University provides an example of such a rationale:

Table 1 discloses that approximately 24 percent of the faculty are women and that this percentage has been somewhat consistent throughout the past six years. According to data reported by the American Association of University Women, "Nationally, women comprise 22 percent of the faculty. . . ." If these data are reliable, it appears that Indiana State employs an appropriate percentage of women to the faculty (Indiana State University 1970[2]:3).

In this instance, women's participation rate was considered acceptable, but most of the reports that employed this standard did not find their institutional participation rates to be favorable.

As pointed out above, both the selection and rationale of appropriate standards by which to establish participation rate may be fallible when attempting to evaluate the status of women. We would suggest that women's standing must be examined with respect to a wide-ranging number of variables. Admittedly, the percent of women on a campus faculty is only a gross indicator of the status of those women. In fact, no report limits its analysis of women to this factor. The reports also contained a breakdown of the participation data into other such categories as departments, areas, schools, divisions, or colleges within a university, and rank. Some of the categories—for example departmental and rank breakdowns—directly reflected the standing of women at a given institution.

DEPARTMENTAL PARTICIPATION RATE

Some reports examined the status of women faculty in every department. More often figures for only selected departments were presented. Departments that traditionally have been considered women's departments, such as nursing and home economics, and those in which women very rarely are employed such as engineering (i.e., the extremes in women's participation rate) were deleted in many studies.

The most common standard for comparison between departments was the percentage of women among doctorates granted in the field or fields covered by a department. Pools of women graduates were determined from yearly Office of Education reports on the number of degrees awarded nationally, the number of degrees earned by women at the top ten institutions, and the number of degrees awarded by field at the reporting institution. Other figures utilized for purposes of comparison were the number of female graduate students in the department, female Woodrow Wilson Dissertation Fellows by fields, female B.A. majors and female undergraduate majors in various fields. Regardless of the standard used, departmental staffing across campuses showed a general pattern of underutilization of women.

From over sixty different fields cited in various reports, thirteen were selected that appeared most frequently and could be most clearly differentiated. Table 11.6 summarizes the data from 354 departments within these fields, showing: (1) the range of women's participation by department; (2) the percent of doctorates

TABLE 11.6. The Departmental Participation Rate of Women Faculty in Thirteen Selected Fields

Fields	Departments (n)	Percentage of Women on Departmental Staff: Range[a]	Degrees Earned by Women Nationwide, 1967–1968[b] (percent)	No. of Departments Employing Below Nationwide Total of Earned Degrees[a]	No. of Departments Employing Above Nationwide Total of Earned Degrees[a]
Biology	(22)	0 to 50	29.0	20	2
Chemistry	(31)	0 to 14	8.0	28	3
Economics	(25)	0 to 11	5.8	17	8
Education	(20)	0 to 46	20.3	9	11
English	(32)	0 to 50	27.4	24	8
History	(31)	0 to 29	13.0	26	5
Mathematics	(30)	0 to 27	6.0	17	13
Music	(23)	0 to 33	14.5	11	12
Philosophy	(29)	0 to 20	9.1	25	4
Physics	(25)	0 to 5	8.8	25	0
Psychology	(37)	0 to 40	22.5	36	1
Sociology	(27)	0 to 21	18.5	24	3
Speech	(22)	6 to 40	18.5	10	12
		Mean number of departments:		20.9	6.3

[a] From Robinson analysis of institutional reports.
[b] From Hooper and Chandler 1969.

awarded nationally in 1967–1968 to women by fields; and (3) the number of departments that reported employment percentages of women faculty above or below the national average. In biology, for example, women earned 29 percent of the doctorates in 1967–1968, but in the twenty-two institutional reports indicating women's representation on the faculties of biology departments twenty departments fell below this figure.

Departments varied widely in women's representation, from none to 50 percent. The general trend was to employ women at rates lower than their proportion of earned degrees in respective fields. As suggested by the averages shown at the bottom of Table 11.6, women's participation on faculties of these thirteen departments are more than three times as likely to be below as above their proportion nationwide (20.9 versus 6.3). Seventy-seven percent of the 354 departments fell *below* the national figure. In only three fields—education, music, and speech— were the number of departments employing women above the nationwide rate equal to or greater than those employing women below the nationwide rate. Women are underemployed in those fields in which a significant number of them earn degrees, and those in which they are relatively scarce (e.g., psychology and physics, respectively). Systematic exclusion seems particularly evident in such fields as psychology and sociology where a significant number of women earn degrees, yet only one of thirty-seven psychology departments and three of twenty-seven sociology departments employed women above the rate at which they earn degrees. Thus, the institutional reports demonstrate systematic exclusion of women both in their overall proportion of total faculty and in a selected number of departments.

RANK

Two methods of comparison tend to predominate in the analysis of rank in the institutional reports: (1) the sexual composition of each rank ("within rank"); and (2) the distribution of the ranks within each sex ("within sex"). The second approach is less frequently encountered than the former (28 "within sex" in contrast to 68 "within rank" comparisons).

"Within sex" comparisons reveal striking differences in the distribution of rank. Nationally, 21.6 percent of all college and university faculty members are full professors, 20.7 percent associate professors, 28.3 percent assistant professors, and 19.9 percent instructors (Bayer 1970:13). If one assumes that this distribution represents the way ranks *should* be divided among a given faculty, the percentages of women who hold positions at every rank except assistant professor are quite discrepant. Bayer's data (shown in Table 11.7), show that women are below the national percentages in the top two ranks, about equal in the third rank, and well above the national figure in the rank of instructor.

Overall, about half of all male faculty are in the top two ranks, compared to no more than one fourth of all female faculty. This trend has repeatedly been found in

TABLE 11.7. Academic Rank Distribution by Sex and Total Faculty, National Sample 1969 (In percentages)[a]

Rank	Men	Women	Total
Professor	24.5	9.4	21.6
Associate professor	21.9	15.7	20.7
Assistant professor	28.2	28.7	28.3
Instructor	16.3	34.8	19.9

SOURCE: Bayer 1970:13.
[a] Percentages do not add up to 100, because categories of "no ranks designated," "lecturer," and "other" are not shown.

studies by discipline (Wilcox 1970; Simon and Rosenthal 1967; Schuck 1969; and Rossi 1970b) and in all of the individual institutions reviewed here. At Stanford University, for example, 50 percent of the men are professors or associate professors, but fewer than one-tenth of the women hold these ranks. Sixty-seven percent of all women are research associates, instructors, or lecturers, whereas only 28 percent of the men are at these ranks. This trend is repeated at the University of Oregon where 32 percent of the men and 5 percent of the women are professors, and 76 percent of the women and 45 percent of the men are in the lowest two ranks of assistant professor and instructor.

As noted earlier, the "within rank" comparison is more commonly found in the institutional reports. The number of ranks examined varies from report to report. Some reports provided the numbers of women in every faculty position at their institution. One such example is the Harvard University (3) report for which a table of all appointments was prepared. The following is a composite list of the types of positions which were examined in the reports under review: laboratory associate or assistant, preceptor, adjunct, lector, tutor, fellow, associate, postdoctoral fellow or assistant, lecturer or special lecturer, acting or assisting instructor, emeriti, regents' professor, distinguished professor, guest investigator, visiting faculty, and various labels usually applied to those still in graduate training. Given the diversity of titles, it is fortunate for purposes of comparison that the four common faculty ranks—instructor, assistant, associate and full professor—are used across all institutions.

The four common faculty ranks were used in compiling the following percentages from fifty institutional reports covering sixty-eight coeducational schools. Since the California State Colleges were not reported on individually, they were considered as one case in the summary statistics. Table 11.8 summarizes the institutional report distribution in the percentage of women for each of the four academic ranks.

Women consistently comprised less than 10 percent of the full professors (forty-two of fifty reports). They constituted more than 30 percent of the associate pro-

TABLE 11.8. Distribution of Selected Institutional Reports in the
Percentage of Women by Rank

Percentage of Women on the Faculty	Professor	Associate	Assistant	Instructor
0 to 10	42	29	14	6
11 to 20	7	17	24	7
21 to 30	1	3	11	12
31 to 40	0	1	1	12
41 to 50	0	0	0	10
51 to 60	0	0	0	3
Total reports[a]	(50)	(50)	(50)	(50)

SOURCE: Robinson analysis of institutional reports.
[a] Fifty reports covering sixty-eight schools.

fessor rank in only one report; in forty-six of fifty reports, women comprised 20 percent or less of all associate professors. Women comprised 30 percent of the assistant professor rank in only one case, yet in fourteen reports they constituted 10 percent or less. Women sometimes comprised over 50 percent of the instructor rank (three of fifty cases), yet in six instances, they comprised 10 percent or less. There seems to be a relatively fixed ceiling on women's participation in the upper three ranks. *Only the rank of instructor shows significant variability in the participation rate of women across schools.* These overall figures concur with those of other studies (Beazley 1966; Bernard 1964; Parrish 1962), which show that women comprise more of the lower than the upper levels of faculty hierarchies. Individual reports often illustrate with graphic "pyramids" the decreasing percentages of women as a function of rank.

At Indiana State University (1) a unique approach was used to examine the rank standing of the sexes. Both the "within sex" and the "within rank" distribution methods were analyzed statistically. Assuming either that women would appear in

TABLE 11.9. Within Rank and Within Sex Distribution of Faculty, Indiana State University (In percentages)

Rank	Within Rank		Within Sex	
	Men	Women	Men	Women
Full professor	85	15	18	10
Associate professor	84	16	27	18
Assistant professor	80	20	37	31
Instructor	60	40	19	42

SOURCE: Indiana State University 1970(1):2, 6.

each rank with a constant frequency of about 20 percent or that they would be distributed throughout the ranks in the same proportion as men, the distributions shown in Table 11.9 would have occurred randomly in less than one in over a thousand instances. Thus, the distribution of women throughout the ranks is not likely to have occurred by chance.

APPOINTMENT LEVEL

The fact that women more frequently than men are found at the lower academic levels may be, in part, a function of differences in initial appointment levels. Unfortunately, little data on appointment level is available in the institutional reports. What little information there is indicates that appointment levels do vary by sex.

Five of the institutional reports dealt with initial appointment level by sex. Table 11.10 summarizes the pattern of appointment at three of these institutions: in each case, women rarely are appointed to the professorial ranks and men typically are appointed to the ladder positions in the faculty hierarchy. The report from the University of Washington indicates that, on the average, women were hired

TABLE 11.10. Initial Appointment Level by Sex for Selected Institutions (In percentages)

Institution	Type of Appointment	Men	Women
Eastern Illinois University (1970:1)	Hired at professorial ranks	67	32
University of Washington (1970:17)	Hired at professorial ranks	84	34
	Hired at instructor and lecturer ranks	16	66
University of Pittsburgh (1970[3]:18)	Hired at professorial ranks	68	28

one rank lower than men. At the University of South Florida (2), no women doctorates were hired for 1970–1971 and women's percentage of the "new hires" was less than their percentage of the current faculty. At the University of Pittsburgh (3), the median entry level for men in the fall of 1969 was assistant professor, and for women it was one grade lower. Data from the Bureau of Institutional Research at the University of Minnesota indicate that women start at a lower rank than men. Table 11.11 which presents the most detailed information on rank distribution by sex at initial appointment found in the institutional reports, also indicates that the modal appointment for women is instructor, and for men, assistant professor.

TABLE 11.11. Rank of 1969–1970 Full-Time Instructional Staff at the
University of Minnesota at Time of Initial Appointment, by Sex

	Male		Female		Total	
						Percent women
Initial Rank	No.	Percent	No.	Percent	No.	of total
Instructor	461	26.1	128	54.9	589	21.7
Assistant professor	792	44.7	78	33.5	870	9.0
Associate professor	365	20.6	19	8.2	384	4.9
Professor	152	8.6	8	3.4	160	5.0
Total	1,770	100.0	233	100.0	2,003	11.6

SOURCE: University of Minnesota 1971(3):12.

Not only did very few reports contain information on appointment levels, but none of them examined initial appointments of women and men who held the same degrees. However, there are a few studies which suggest that even in the case of doctorates, women do not fare as well as men in initial appointment. Henderson (1967) found that the first appointments of women doctorates were at a lower rank than men or at a lower salary than men doctorates at the same rank (see also, University of Chicago (2); Simon and Rosenthal 1967).

Two studies give evidence of the kind of treatment women seeking academic employment can expect to receive. Simpson (1968) set out to determine employing officials' treatment of qualified women. A questionnaire was designed to explore discriminatory employment choices and generally derogatory attitudes toward women. Deans, department chairmen, and faculty in selected academic fields at six Pennsylvania institutions were sampled. Pairs of resumes were submitted to administrators with descriptive material held constant: only the names and photos were alternated on the two forms. An employment preference rating scale ranging from "strongly preferable" to "strongly unpreferable" followed each resume. Generally derogatory attitudes about women were assessed on a twelve-item "Open Subordination of Women Attitude Scale." The purpose of the scale was to determine if potential employers who reject academic women also place "women-in-general" in a subordinate position.

Simpson found that the respondents did exhibit discriminatory attitudes toward academic women: men received more frequent and higher preference ratings than equally qualified women, although a clearly superior female was selected over a less outstanding male candidate. The academic position of the respondents did not affect their choices, e.g., deans did not differ from departmental chairmen. Furthermore, respondents who evidenced discriminatory employment choices also held more negative attitudes toward women in general.

Furthermore, Simpson isolated certain variables which appeared to affect the discriminatory choices. First, the field of employment was an important variable.

Equally qualified women were more likely to be chosen over male candidates in fields which typically have a high female employment rate; while in fields traditionally low in female employment rate, even superior females received significantly fewer choices. The sex, age, and experience of the respondents also had an effect on the employment selection of female candidates. Women respondents were more likely to choose women, as were respondents over 60 and those under 30 years of age. So, too, respondents with less than five years of academic experience and those with over twenty years were most apt to choose female candidates.

A similar study was conducted by Fidell (1970). Descriptions of the professional behavior of eight young psychologists were sent to chairmen of every degree-granting psychology department in the United States. The names and reference pronouns in the descriptions were alternately varied by sex. Fidell found that in the case of seven out of eight "candidates" women were offered lower levels of appointments than men, and were rated as less desirable in six out of eight instances. Results of these studies suggest that the best women stand a chance of being hired but at a lesser position than inferior men. It is no wonder that women aspiring to be college teachers are counseled on the hazards that lie ahead.

MARGINAL APPOINTMENTS

Many reports highlighted a second aspect of appointment that restricts the careers of academic women: the tendency to appoint women to positions variously referred to as marginal, "soft-line," irregular, nonladder, part-time, exceptional, or fringe. The number of such positions is almost limitless, to which the great variability in the job titles attests.

The Columbia University report points out that although women are almost invisible in the regular faculty ranks, they constitute the majority of part-time employees. In twelve out of seventeen departments at Sacramento State College, women constituted a greater percentage of the part-time than of the full-time faculty. The most extreme case was a department in which women constituted 5 percent of the full-time but 50 percent of the part-time faculty. At Harvard (2) women constitute a higher percentage of the irregular than of the regular faculty appointments. The same pattern was found at Michigan State University where women account for 52.3 percent of the temporary faculty (assistant instructor through professors) in contrast to 11 percent of the faculty under tenure rules.

Although the number of women in higher education increases once these marginal positions are taken into account, their status does not. Such positions rarely offer salaries, fringe benefits, access to tenure, or access to other university resources equal to that concomitant to regular positions. The Yale report gives a good explanation of how marginal positions restrict the careers of women:

> The concentration of women in the positions of lecturer and instructor has important implications for their academic careers. These faculty do not have voting privileges at faculty meetings and are often not eligible for the full

range of faculty benefits, such as Morse fellowships, leave privileges or TIAA. In addition, these appointments are usually one year contracts which offer little security in terms of job and research stability. Although the appointment may continue for a number of years the continued uncertainty and ambiguity of position are not conducive to planning and conducting research (which is a prerequisite for promotion). Since instructors and lecturers are hired primarily for teaching responsibilities research must necessarily be wedged into free time. The result is a vicious cycle; women are placed in marginal positions and so burdened by the positions that they have little opportunity to do the work of a productive scholar. In contrast, the scholarly work of those on the tenure ladder is encouraged by relatively lighter teaching loads, leaves, sabbaticals, job security and especially University support for research (Yale 1970 [2]:7–8).

A number of reports commented on the fact that women are virtually entrapped in marginal slots. This was the position of the Brown University report:

> It is our contention that women qualified for faculty status are particularly likely to occupy such positions (Teaching Associates) with a faculty-like aura but without the responsibilities or privileges of true faculty rank. While most male Research Associates hold that rank on a short-term basis for the pursuit of post-doctoral research, . . . many women who have long had the doctorate hold the position of Research Associate on a final basis (no hope of advancement), apparently because they are women or because they are faculty wives. These women are denied not only the status and salary of regular faculty appointment, but also the security of such appointments; even when they are working on a three-year grant, they often have one-year appointments (Brown University 1970:2).

Of the 153 temporary faculty women at Michigan State University, thirteen had been employed for ten years or more. One of the instructors had taught twenty-five years, and two assistant professors had taught twenty-four years. Many academic women have occupied what can only be called "permanent temporary" positions in higher education.

The drawbacks to marginal appointments noted thus far have relatively clear cut consequences. Beyond them is the more subtle realm of psychological consequences. Although there is no "hard" data on the psychological impact of being relegated to a marginal, nonladder status, there has been speculation about its effect. The Harvard (2) report points out that the restriction of women to marginal appointments outside of the "real" system is likely to lead to feelings of inferiority and isolation on the part of women in these positions. Given the status insecurity and politically powerless nature of marginal appointments, women who occupy them are hardly likely to view themselves as highly valued members of the academic community.

This is *not* to say there are no prestigious marginal positions in academe, for there are several. Joint appointments are one example. On the face of it, a joint appointment simply means receiving pay from more than one department or academic unit. In fact, it means filling two part-time positions. At some institutions, those who hold joint appointments have higher average salaries than those who hold a full-time faculty position in one department. High salary is itself an index of how valued is the shared person. Most joint appointments are held by males, so that academic institutions already have shown high regard for "shared" men. Yet the same institutions have done little to adopt policies which would upgrade the prestige and salary of certain part-time positions primarily held by women.

Sometimes women are in an inferior position to men even when they hold the same special faculty title. For example, a faculty title may have a double meaning, one for men and another, inferior one, for women. The Princeton report notes just such a situation in the case of the university's "visiting" staff members who fall into two groups. The first group consists of staff members who actually are affiliated with other institutions but serve at Princeton on a part-time basis or while on leave from their home institution. The second group consists of people not affiliated elsewhere, but employed at Princeton only on a short-term basis. An informal survey of persons classified as "visiting" revealed that men tend to predominate in the first category and women in the second.

Two studies attempted to account for the fact that women occupy a higher percentage of fringe than of regular teaching positions. The Stanford report considered both age and marital status as possible explanations for the cluster of women in the junior ranks. The data did not support either factor as an explanation. Two other explanations—preference for teaching activities and field of concentration— were postulated, but were not explored. The investigating committee at Chicago (1), utilizing interview information, concluded that fringe positions were desired by both the women who held them and their departmental chairmen. Such positions, it was found, provided needed flexibility in employment. Although Chicago found advantages in the fringe system for both the university and women, most other reports claimed the advantages were only for the university.

The existence of so many women in fringe positions supports the not uncommon claim that women are in positions which often exclude them from the regular operations of the academic community, and is additional evidence of the inferior status of women in academe.[1]

PROMOTIONS

The fact that women are plentiful in the lower ranks and scarce at the higher ranks constitutes indirect evidence of discrimination with respect to promotions. However, promotions have been investigated directly in a number of ways. Four-

---

[1] For a general discussion of women's marginality in academe, see Bernard (1964), Simon and Rosenthal (1967), Rossi (1970a), the University of Chicago (1970[1]), and the University of Oregon.

teen institutions covered this aspect of women's status in their reports. Such a variety of methods were used, however, that it was impossible to extract summary statistics. Consequently, we must take a case approach to illustrate the ways in which institutional reports analyzed women's promotion patterns.

Since promotion is so important an aspect of one's career, it might seem strange that only fourteen reports dealt with it. There seem to be a number of reasons for this lack of coverage. In many instances, authors of the reports simply did not have access to information concerning promotions. Omission of such data, then, did not mean that the author failed to recognize its importance; many reports recommended further studies which would include promotional analyses. Second, the study of promotions involves delicate assessment difficulties, since there are a number of criteria that enter deliberations concerning promotion. Given the difficulty of this task, it is not surprising that the analysis of promotions was so seldom covered in the institutional reports.

One type of analysis examined the time spent at a given rank. Such a comparison assumes that those appointed to a given rank are equally qualified and that there are no differences by sex in professional attributes which are relevant criteria for promotion. For example, Connecticut College found that at each rank women were more likely than men to have had the doctorate when they were first appointed. Yet, women had spent more time at each rank than men. Furthermore, women doctorates waited an average of four and a half years longer than men doctorates before achieving the rank of full professor. A similar trend was found at the University of Washington. Doctorate and nondoctorate women hired below the rank of assistant professor waited twice as long as their male counterparts for promotion to assistant professor. The average length of time at the assistant professor rank since appointment or promotion was about twice as long for women, considering the date of appointment for those with the doctorate or the number of years since the degree was completed for those hired without the doctorate.

Promotion at the University of Indiana at Bloomington was investigated by comparing the average length of time in a given rank before women and men faculty were recommended for promotion by their departments, and the average length of time in rank before they actually were promoted. The investigators found that for a three-year period women were in rank about 1.23 years longer than men before being recommended for promotion and 1.59 years longer than men before they actually were promoted.

> A differential in the number of years in rank preceding recommendation for promotion implied that the discrimination occurred at the department level. The data suggested this to be the case. The number of years in rank before actual promotion would be based upon the number of years before recommendation plus time when the promotions were denied. An increase in the differential from years to recommendation to the years to promotion would point to supra-departmental committees and officials as locus of discrimination. As

noted above, women were in rank 1.23 years longer before recommendation and 1.59 years longer before promotion. The difference between these two figures was quite small, indicating that, by comparison with the time before recommendation by department, the time to actual promotion conferred by higher offices was not significant. . . . The results indicated that women are promoted more slowly than men. It is possible that women met the standards of teaching, research, and service necessary for promotion more slowly than men but the burden of proof would be on the University (Indiana University, Bloomington 1970[1]:28).

Every institutional analysis of promotion that examined length of time in rank showed that women progress through the ranks at a significantly slower rate than men.

The other primary technique in analyzing promotions was the comparison of the number or percentage of women who were promoted, with the number or percentage of women who reasonably should have been promoted. At times, these studies are difficult to interpret simply because it is difficult to determine whether the numerical standard assumed is a reasonable or logical one.

The Indiana State University (2) report used more than one standard of comparison. In their first analysis, promotional information covered a six-year span. During this period, 21 percent of the women faculty received promotions. This percent was contrasted to the total percent of women on the faculty (24 percent). The same comparison was carried out by rank. The percentage of women receiving promotions was compared to the percentage of each rank comprised by women. The proportion of women who attained the ranks of full, associate, and assistant professors exceeded the proportion of that rank which was female, 15 to 11 percent, 16 to 14 percent and 39 to 22 percent, respectively.

These figures are misleading, however, in suggesting that women are receiving their fair share of promotions, when in fact no such determination can be ascertained from the information given. In this case, the proportion of rank which is female is inappropriate as a standard of comparison since it logically cannot be applied simultaneously to both males and females. It would have been more appropriate to compare the percent of women and men who attained the ranks of full, associate, or assistant professor.

In fact, the second analysis by the Indiana investigators is just this. They compared by rank the percentage of women's and men's applications for promotion which were approved. It was found that for the past four years, 27 percent of the male and female applicants achieved the rank of full professor; 54 percent of the male and 49 percent of the female applicants received associate professorships; 47 percent of the men and 74 percent of the women received assistant professorships. Of the total, 50 percent of the women and 41 percent of the men received the promotions for which they applied. These rates appear to be exceptional when one considers that women's applications constituted only 20 percent of the total. The report does not explore why so few applicants were so successful in attaining

their promotions. One might postulate, however, that the women were more qualified than the men.

The University of Minnesota report contains a unique analysis of promotion.
This study compared the number of promotions received by women to the number
expected based on the promotion experience of men adjusted for initial rank, years
of service, and present degree held (see Table 11.12). Of the differences between

**TABLE 11.12. Expected and Observed Promotions for Full-Time Women
Faculty by Rank, University of Minnesota 1969–1970**

| | *Number* | | *Percent* | |
Initial Rank	*Expected*	*Observed*	*Expected*	*Observed*
Instructor	72.5	65	56.6	50.8
Assistant professor	50.9	39	65.3	50.0
Associate professor	13.9	15	73.2	78.9

SOURCE: University of Minnesota 1971(3):13.

expected and observed promotion rates, only that found for assistant professor was
statistically significant ($p < 0.05$). No explanations were offered to explain the
curious results—two ranks in which the observed was less than expected, the third
and highest rank in which the expected was less than the observed. On the basis of
these findings it appears that the biggest promotion hurdle for women is between
the assistant and associate levels.

The most elaborate analysis of promotions was conducted at the University of
California at Berkeley. A catalog study of two time periods (1920–1940; 1950–
1969) compared each woman's promotion and attrition rate with that of a male
counterpart. It was found that promotion opportunities for women were more
limited than for men. The proportion of women promoted was lower at all ranks;
and women waited longer for their promotions. A more detailed study was made
of regular faculty in the College of Letters and Sciences. Year of birth, year of
doctorate, and department were taken into account. The observed rate of advancement based on promotion to tenure, average number of steps advanced per year,
and the highest step achieved was lower for women than for men.

Many would assert women's slower promotion rate lies with women themselves rather than with the promotion process. The implication is that institutions
hire women, retain them (many reports found lengthier terms of service for
women than men), and promote them (albeit more slowly) even though they are
"less qualified" than men. This hardly seems likely. In fact, many would argue that
since women must surmount discrimination they must have better qualifications
than men to win their initial appointment, and must prove themselves again and
again in order to make progress in their careers. The factor cited most frequently
as the crucial explanation of differences by sex in rate of promotion was that women

do not publish as much as men. Research and publication activities currently are given more credit than teaching and service activities in evaluating faculty, although all these factors are considered. Given the priority of publication over other professional activities, and the belief that women scholars are less productive, it is not surprising that lower publication rates are cited so frequently as the cause for women's lower academic status. The idea that women publish less than men is currently being challenged. Bernard concluded that "if enough variables are controlled, sex differences in productivity are reduced to almost insignificance," and that university or college position is a better predictor of publication rate than sex (Bernard 1964:154). Simon, Clark and Tifft (1966), Simon, Clark and Galway (1967), and Simon and Rosenthal (1967) provide clues to differences in publication rates. For example, Simon and Rosenthal found that married women doctorates outproduced married men, and both unmarried men and women doctorates. Fidell (1970) presented preliminary findings indicating that differences in publication rates that favor males in psychology may be found exclusively at the full professor level; at lower ranks women published more than their male counterparts. Henderson (1967) found that although women doctorates were similar to men doctorates in teaching assignments, published works, and satisfaction derived from work, women advanced slower in rank. Hargens (1971) found that sex accounted for 1 percent or less of the variance in academic productivity in the fields of mathematics, political science, and chemistry. However, it will be difficult to dispel the notion that women produce less than men, despite increasing evidence to the contrary.

Urging women to publish more does not mean that they will reap the rewards of higher rank and better positions. There is evidence that their present standing, based on current rates of publication is less than should be expected. Figures supplied by the University of California at Berkeley indicate this to be true:

> suppose one accepts the current publication rates of women as an estimate, presumably conservative, of their potential publication rate, and suppose one assumes that publication rate is the principal basis for employment. Then women are under employed at prestigious institutions, especially at Berkeley. The top decile academic institutions, on the basis of prestige, employ 29.1 percent professorial rank persons who have published at least ten articles, 40.1 percent who have published less than ten, and 30.8 percent non-publishers. If these ratios of employment are applied to women, according to their *present* publication rates, the top decile institutions should have employed 12.7 percent women in their professorial ranks. Actually, they employ only 8.8 percent women while Berkeley employs only 3.6 percent women, meager indeed by this standard (University of California at Berkeley 1970:35–36).

To date, no definitive study has been conducted which takes into account the various indices of merit. Still the weight of evidence which exists provides a great deal of support for the notion of differences in promotions as a function of sex.

Because of the importance of promotions to one's academic career, it seems imperative for institutions to investigate the topic in more detail.

TENURE

Some of the institutional reports examined tenure in association with women's rank and department. Although tenure usually is granted at the associate and full professor rank, there are many exceptions. Many assistant professors have tenure while some associate professors do not. How these exceptions operate as a function of sex has not been systematically studied. If one assumes that tenure is granted at the rank of associate professor, the figures on rank reviewed above would indicate that women usually constitute less than 25 percent of the tenured faculty. In fact, at only ten of forty-eight institutions with data on rank do women comprise more than 25 percent of the tenured faculty. However, statistics from Bayer's (1970) national study indicate that it is misleading to take the upper two ranks as indicative of tenure. He found that 25.1 percent of women faculty held the ranks of professor and associate professor, yet 37.5 percent reported having a regular appointment with tenure, which suggests that many women at lower ranks have achieved tenure. (Comparable figures for men are 46.4 percent and 48.8 percent.)

It is difficult to get a clear picture of the composition of the tenured faculty from the available institutional reports. If we reject the notion that tenure automatically is conferred with a given rank, there are two means for determining tenure: (1) the direct mention of the rank at which tenure routinely is achieved at a given institution; or (2) separate tenure figures presented by sex. In the fifteen institutions for which the percentage of women and men who held tenure (regardless of rank) could be computed, there was no instance in which tenured women equalled or exceeded tenured men. Differences between the percentages for tenured males and females ranged from a low of 8 to a high of 40 percentage points in favor of men.

Some reports, while covering tenure, did not present data in a way that permitted their inclusion in the above comparisons. In other cases, tenure was considered only in passing when discussing women in marginal positions, since tenure seldom is granted to those in nonladder academic positions. Other reports simply mentioned the fact that there were few tenured women on their campus. Considering the importance of tenure to college teachers, it is somewhat surprising that institutional reports did not pay more attention to this variable. A really satisfactory investigation of differences by sex in tenure simply did not exist in the reports surveyed.

SALARY

Salary is perhaps second to rank in importance as an indicator of status, and this factor received a great deal of attention in institutional reports. The concept of equal pay for equal work clearly is of central concern to groups investigating the status of women in academe and the economy at large. Twenty-nine reports covering fifty-five schools touched on this vital "pocketbook" issue.

Some studies were highly sophisticated, and held a number of variables constant in order to account for differences in pay. One complete campus report is discussed in Chapter Twelve, and a national faculty sample is discussed in Chapter Fifteen of this book. Although some institutions regarded salary data as "private," the importance of the topic and the presentation of data in summary rather than individual form served to overcome a great deal of reticence.

More than one national study has shown that women college professors generally earn less than men (Bayer 1970; Scully 1970). Our review of reports from individual institutions supports this national trend. There was evidence that women are paid less in fifty-one out of fifty-five schools, while four schools found no conclusive evidence of differences in pay on the basis of sex.

A number of studies focused on the salaries of women and men at different ranks. The mean was the statistic most commonly employed, although the median probably improves the relative status of women with respect to men. As the Simmons College report points out:

> The median salary as a position or location average is used for comparing income distributions in order to avoid the undue influence of large incomes. However, the median salary is not an appropriate measure for this report. If it were used, it would ignore the influence of large incomes received by full professors holding chairmanships. Since more than two-thirds of full professors are males and more than three-fourths of chairmanships are held by males, the use of the median would defeat the very purpose of this report. To a large extent it would conceal the sex salary differential (Simmons College 1971 [2]:3).

This argument applies to most institutions, since a pattern of unusually high salaries for some men in the senior ranks is very prevalent in higher education.

While salaries were most commonly presented by rank, some reports explored other factors on which the sexes varied that may have influenced salary. Two approaches were used, the first of which attempted to establish the relationship of one variable to another. More rarely, the interrelationship of a number of variables was accounted for statistically. On the other hand, it seems justifiable to assume that differences in salaries at each rank by sex substantiate differential treatment. This was the view put forth by Kansas State Teachers College:

> We must assume that there have been at least some minimal standards in placing individual faculty members within certain ranks, even if these standards have not been applied consistently among the various departments. Therefore, at least in theory, male instructors and female instructors should have essentially similar qualifications. If their qualifications are not essentially similar— that is, if there is a wide disparity in their qualifications, one of them is holding the wrong rank (Kansas State Teachers College 1970:3).

As noted here, the most common format in reporting salary data was to present mean salary by rank and sex. Table 11.13 summarizes the reports which gave data in this fashion. In each case, the difference between men's and women's average salaries was computed. The actual differences between their mean salaries ranged from $63 to $4,065. There was only one instance in which women's mean salary was greater than men's: this difference of $255 occurred at the rank of instructor. With this exception, Table 11.13 shows all salary differentials by dollar amount and academic rank.

TABLE 11.13. Distribution of Institutional Reports by Extent to which Men's Mean Salary Exceeded Women's, by Rank

Extent to which Men's Mean Salary Exceeded Women's (in dollars)	*Academic Rank*			
	Instructor	*Assistant*	*Associate*	*Full Professor*
Less than $100	2	1[a]	—	—
$100–400	6[a]	3	2	—
$401–800	1[b]	3[b]	6[b]	2
$801–1,200	2	5	3[a]	2
$1,201–1,600	1	2	1	—
$1,601–2,200	—	—	2	4[b]
$2,201–2,800	1	—	.—	1
$2,801–3,400	—	—	—	2
$3,401–4,000	—	—	—	1
More than $4,000	—	—	—	1
Total cases	13[c]	14	14	13[d]

SOURCE: Robinson analysis of institutional reports.

[a] One of these cases represents fourteen two-year institutions in a particular state system.

[b] One of these cases represents thirteen four-year institutions in a particular state system.

[c] There was only one instance in which women's mean salary was greater than men's. This case occurred in the instructor rank and was omitted from this table.

[d] There were no full professors shown for the fourteen two-year institutions. Therefore, there is one less case than there should be in this category.

Table 11.13 shows that the largest dollar differences occur at the full professor rank. There also is a marked tendency for the disparity in pay to increase in a direct ratio to an increase in rank, and for the lowest rank to show considerable variance. The data in the table are typical of the salary analyses contained in institutional reports. They consist of salary comparisons for women and men by one or more academic units or groupings. For example, in a faculty survey at the University of Kansas (2), salaries were compared by rank, academic division, and for new faculty appointees. The average difference in compensation across five ranks was $2,064 in favor of men. Differences between ranks, lecturer through professor, ranged from $331 to $2,993. No regularly appointed female full professor was paid even the average salary of a male full professor. The School of Education was singled out as the division in which differentials were especially marked. Furthermore, there were no women in six of the ten departments in which the average salary was over $15,000 per year. Among the new faculty appointees for 1970–1971, the salary range was higher for men at each rank except that of lecturer. Only one woman was appointed full professor, and that was at a salary $1,000 lower than for any of the eight men appointed to this rank.

A number of other studies explored not only the academic units illustrated in the case of the University of Kansas, but certain professional characteristics that have a direct bearing on salary levels such as highest degree attained, type of work activity, age, and years employed. The AAUP chapter survey conducted at the University of Akron is the most complete example of this type of analysis.

A total of 156 (out of 300) AAUP members responded to a survey designed to explore salary differentials at the University of Akron. Data were collected on the highest degree attained, total years of work experience in primary and related work activities, academic rank, college or division, age, sex, and salary. Characteristics of the respondents indicated that the sample was a close approximation to the total university population. Starting from an overall male-female salary difference of 25.5 percent in favor of males, analysis of various professional characteristics were made to see if the difference still remained. It was found that both the means and the medians of female salary were less than those of males at all *ranks,* even though males had less average work experience and were younger than their female counterparts. When men and women of equivalent degree attainment were compared, the pattern of differential pay by sex was maintained rank by rank. Furthermore, the salary earned by a female with the highest degree (e.g., Ph.D., M.D., Ed.D.) was almost identical to the salary earned by a male with only a master's degree. Regardless of the professional criteria on which the subjects were matched, the pattern of salary differences by sex remained.

A third group of studies utilized more sophisticated statistical techniques to analyze both academic units and professional characteristics. Studies of this type are rare among institutional reports. A salary study done at the University of Indiana at Bloomington (2) serves as a good example.

Data were compiled from faculty salaries paid in December 1968, as well as information on individuals' professional qualifications that might affect earnings: type of appointment, rank, division, level of education, and experience. These factors were subjected to a "least squares" analysis, and it was found that "a woman equivalent to a man in terms of all other variables included in the regression equation could expect to earn about $100 per month less than a man" (University of Indiana at Bloomington 1969[2]:5).

The overwhelming conclusion to be drawn from the latter two types of analysis is that as a faculty member a woman is very likely to be paid less than her male counterpart. One instance was even found of a woman listed in the official faculty directory of her institution who was not being paid at all. Given the importance of economics in our society, it is not surprising that institutional reports have devoted so much attention to this aspect of women's status in higher education. It will surely remain high on the priority list of those concerned with the status of faculty women.

ADMINISTRATION

Women in administration are a separate topic altogether. Many administrative posts traditionally are filled by faculty personnel and many administrative functions are linked closely to the responsibilities of college faculty.[2] Oltman's findings in a study of 454 corporate members of the American Association of University Women indicate a conspicuous lack of participation by women in administrative areas:

> Women are most often found in positions which have minor relationship to policy-making and are at a middle-management level or which involve sex stereotypes. . . . in 34 schools (all coeducational) there are no women department heads and the mean number of women department heads in all schools is less than three per institution. . . . Women holding department chairmanships are found mostly in home economics, physical education, English, languages, nursing and education. . . . Women at 35 percent of the schools are said to be represented on almost all faculty committees and boards. . . . They are less likely to be represented on committees for guidance, scholarships, judicial problems, long range planning, institutional research, admissions, educational or advisory policy, or to be advisers to campus organizations (Oltman 1970: 14–15).

Of the coeducational campuses surveyed by Oltman, 93 to 98 percent employed only men in the positions of president, vice-president, director of development, and business manager during the past three years; 82 percent have placed only men in the positions of dean of students, director of counseling, and college physician; 72 to 79 percent placed only men in the positions of associate or assistant academic dean, academic dean, director of placement, and director of financial aid. Women trustees average one in eight among all the schools sampled.

Data on this aspect of women's status in academe is sparse, nonuniform, and generally lacking in depth in the institutional reports. Two trends were stressed: (1) the higher the position, the fewer the women; and (2) administrative units typically are headed by men and staffed by women.

In fifteen reports covering twenty-nine schools, the participation figures for "top" administrative positions[3] ranged from zero to 14 percent. Fourteen of the twenty-nine schools reported women's participation rate in administration below

---

[2] See Harris (1970) and Bernard (1964), for a general discussion of this aspect of the link between faculty and administration.

[3] It is difficult to determine the exact nature of top administrative positions. Comparability is difficult to determine when the titles of top administrative positions differ across institutions. Furthermore, some reports failed to specify the positions being included in those referred to as top posts. In general, top administrative positions refer to levels above department chairmen.

7 percent. One school considered the possibility that more women than men refused administrative opportunities when offered them. Yet when a number of administrative officers were asked about this, no mention was made of such reluctance on the part of women to assume administrative duties.

Percentages may be misleading, especially when dealing with an attribute that is rare. Administrative positions are a small number of the total jobs held within a given institution, and this must be taken into account when evaluating the status of women in academic administration. For example, to say that women are 10 percent of an administration may mean very little if the school administrative staff numbers ten. Hiring one more woman could greatly increase women's participation rate in administration whereas the appointment of one new teacher would hardly increase the faculty rate at all. If we keep base population in mind, it becomes apparent how severely women have been curtailed in administration. Their percentages barely reach half the range found for their participation rates in the total faculty.

The segment of administration in which women are found also is a pertinent issue. The few women administrators are found in traditionally women's fields. This was true at the University of Kentucky where women deans were in home economics and nursing, and women departmental chairmen were in dental hygiene and medical technology, and home economics.

It is also pertinent to point out that administrative titles can be misleading, since women rarely are in positions of "real decision-making authority." For example, at Purdue University 215 women and 527 men were classified as administrators, but most of the women were almost completely lacking in high-level administrative authority. Forty-three were classified as administrative officers, the majority of whom serve in the residence hall kitchens, and the remaining 172 were administrative assistants. Only the dean of women and the dean of the School of Home Economics held positions of authority.

Finally, women do not participate in the administrative career ladder as do men. The Princeton report points out that women tend to *remain* in administrative positions which are *beginning* posts for many men. The rank of administrative assistant, so often a first step in an administrative career for men, frequently is a position women achieve at the end of their careers as a "reward for long and faithful service" to the university, often as office personnel.

Participation in the faculty governing body and its committees is an intrinsic aspect of the faculty role. Information is scanty on this important dimension of academic politics and power. Henderson (1967) found that women served less often and on less prestigious committees than men. Only eleven reports mentioned the participation of women on committees and a sampling of observations reveal their participation rates are very low. For example, over the past ten years at the University of Chicago (1) only two women appeared on the list of university boards, committees, and council appointments, of which there are between 100 and 110 per year. At the University of California at Berkeley, the percentage of women appointed to selected senate committees in the last fifty years ranged from zero to 1 percent. Their participation was zero on twelve and less than 1 percent on twenty-two of the twenty-three committees. When the low participation rate of women in the standing committees of the university senate was noted at the University of Pittsburgh (3), the chancellor urged the inclusion of qualified women. In the next year, however, the number of women increased by only one.

Other aspects of the status of women in academe that institutional reports considered were policies on "in-bred" hiring, nepotism, maternity leaves, sabbaticals, released time, leaves of absence, institutional grant funds, and fringe benefits such as child care facilities, insurance policies, health benefits, and retirement systems. Of these, policies on nepotism have so far received the greatest attention.

REPORT RECOMMENDATIONS

Many institutional reports made recommendations designed to improve the status of faculty women on campus. These varied in elaboration from those offering fairly broad, sweeping statements, generally exhorting the university to do or not do certain things, to more specific recommendations of programs, procedures, formulas, or operations. There was a general call for the remedy of current inequities, for mechanisms to monitor these remedies, and for more detailed studies of various aspects of women's status. Most recommendations evolved directly from findings of reports. On occasion, other topics were covered that were related to conditions faced by women workers, such as lack of child care facilities or the insecurity of part-time positions.

Many reports recommended increasing the number of women on the faculty and administration. Several reports discussed the criteria for hiring, and others delved into the process of increasing the number of women. Sometimes simple quotas were proposed, taking into account the availability of qualified women. Selection of equally or more qualified women in preference to men was urged.

Nepotism regulations were mentioned, either directly or indirectly, as a factor operating against the appointment of women. Some recommended the complete abolition of current policies; some recommended revision of policies to specify working rules to be followed when relatives are employed at the same institution; others urged that the fact that antinepotism regulations do not exist at their institution be made known and adhered to by all. Some reports urged that the only criteria for employment be merit, while others urged that the criteria for employment specifically exclude sex, and financial and marital status.

Two other topics commonly covered in report recommendations concerned "in-bred hiring" and part-time employment. Although only one school specifically recommended the removal of "in-bred hiring" policies, this topic received some attention in those reports that dealt with the discrepancy between the number of women trained and the number hired at their institution, and by those that suggested that graduates are a valid estimate of the availability of qualified women. Several schools recommended expanding part-time employment at the professorial ranks to allow more women to participate in the academic labor market and to allow more flexibility of career patterns for both women and men.

The correction of salary inequities frequently was advocated. As with hiring, reports recommended that criteria not related to professional qualifications be eliminated when considering appropriate salary levels, or in correcting existing inequities. Simmons College (2) recommended that criteria used to evaluate female faculty who teach in fields in which the masters degree constitutes the highest professional degree should not differ from those used to evaluate faculty in the traditional arts and sciences departments. Most reports called for special funds to equalize salaries.

At least a dozen reports made recommendations concerning the review of and procedures for promotion and tenure. In general, the proposals on procedures would benefit both women and men. For example, they called for specific criteria for promotion that are restricted to actual performance in instruction, research, and service, and that are applied uniformly to all staff members. Often it was urged that information be collected and disseminated regularly and systematically. Reasons for department decisions should be recorded and provided to the applicant. Effective grievance machinery should exist and be given prominent publicity. All grievance committees that make recommendations on tenure and promotions should have some women members. The reports suggested that the incentive system for administrative decision makers, especially at the departmental level, should promote actions which would redress inequities. One way to encourage action by administrators would be to make the attainment of equal treatment for women and ethnic minorities one criterion for their own promotions. Finally, reports suggested that a body should be created with power to review reappointments on a campuswide basis.

Several other work conditions frequently were mentioned. Many reports made recommendations concerning day care provisions, leave policies (especially parental or maternity leaves), and insurance benefits. More unique recommendations covered the use of the faculty club, health services, invited lectureships, honorary degrees, artists-in-residence, university publications, affirmative action plans, meetings and class scheduling, and committee membership. All reports urged a general reexamination of institutional policies as they affect women.

The mechanisms suggested for the implementation of proposals were varied and many were unique. Essentially three types of approaches were suggested—periodic reporting or review procedures; the addition of women to significant policy and decision-making committees already in existence; and the creation of a specific body charged with certain responsibilities and goals.

It is not known exactly how many of the proposals which appeared in university reports actually have been implemented at their respective institutions. Given the nature of the issue, many of these schools probably have instituted some mechanism to meet some of the needs of women.

CONCLUDING REMARKS

The reports reviewed here provide a wealth of information on the status of faculty women on campuses across the nation. It is fitting to close with brief comments on both the contribution and limitations of these studies.

Probably their greatest contribution is the consistent documentation of sex discrimination against faculty women on the nine dimensions of status summarized in this review. On the negative side, many reports tried to cover too many facets of academic life without covering any in sufficient detail. It would have been better to select three or four important aspects of status and review them thoroughly. Of course, the number of topics that can be covered adequately by an investigating group ultimately will depend on their resources. Many of the reports were prepared by groups new to the research enterprise and working with very limited financial resources. Under these circumstances, the best approach would have been to focus in depth on a few important variables. Of the nine status indices reviewed in this chapter, the one most lacking in depth is that of promotions. Given its significance to academic careers, differences by sex in academic promotions should receive much more attention in future reports. Care should be taken to provide information on both women and men. In some institutional reports, data were presented on women only, and there was no way of knowing whether women were better or worse off than men at the same school.

Reports should be written in such a way that those not familiar with institutional procedures can understand the significance of the findings presented. Is a particular job title an esteemed one or not? Are particular committee members elected or appointed? Does one apply for promotion or wait to be recommended? Explanations which provide a contextual framework for the variable in question would aid in interpreting the data presented.

Report recommendations should not be too wide ranging. We would suggest that recommendations be limited to those aspects of women's status analyzed in the body of a given report. By focusing in depth on specific areas for remedial action, the steps to be taken will be clearer and more likely to serve as an impetus to action.

REFERENCES

Achbar, Francine, and Bishop, Pam. April 5, 1970. Harvard probed for discrimination against women. *Boston Herald Traveler,* 3:1ff.

Bayer, Alan E. 1970. College and university faculty: a statistical description. *ACE Research Reports,* 5(5). Washington, D.C.: American Council on Education.

Beazley, Richard. 1966. *Numbers and characteristics of employees in institutions of higher education.* Washington, D.C.: U.S. Department of Health, Education and Welfare, Office of Education, National Center for Educational Statistics.

Bernard, Jessie. 1964. *Academic women.* University Park: Pennsylvania State University Press.

Fidell, Linda S. 1970. Empirical verification of sex discrimination in hiring practices in psychology. *American Psychologist,* 25(12):1094–1098.

Hargens, Lowell, L., Jr. 1971. The social context of scientific research. Ph.D. dissertation, University of Wisconsin.

Harris, Ann S. 1970. The second sex in academe. *American Association of University Professors Bulletin,* 56(3):283–295.

Henderson, Jean C. G. 1967. Women as college teachers. Ph.D. dissertation, University of Michigan.

Highest percentage of women teachers at two-year colleges. July 17, 1970. *Higher Education and National Affairs,* 19:5.

Hooper, Mary E., and Chandler, Marjorie O. 1969. *Earned degrees conferred: 1967–68, part A—summary data.* Washington, D.C.: U.S. Department of Health, Education and Welfare, Office of Education, National Center for Educational Statistics.

Oltman, Ruth M. 1970. Campus 1970—where do women stand? *American Association of University Women Journal,* 64(2):14–15.

Parrish, John B. 1962. Women in top level teaching and research. *American Association of University Women Journal,* 55(2):99–107.

Robinson, Lora H. 1971. *The status of academic women.* Washington, D.C.: ERIC Clearinghouse on Higher Education.

Rossi, Alice S. 1970a. Discrimination and demography restrict opportunities for academic women. *College and University Business,* 48(2):74–78.

Rossi, Alice S. 1970b. Status of women in graduate departments of sociology: 1968–69. *The American Sociologist,* 5(1):1–12.

Schuck, Victoria. 1969. Women in political science: Some preliminary observations. *Political Scientist,* 2(4):642–653.

Scully, Malcolm G. February 9, 1970. Women in higher education: challenging the status quo. *The Chronicle of Higher Education,* 4:2–5.

Simon, Rita J., Clark, Shirley M., and Galway, K. 1967. The woman Ph.D.: A recent profile. *Social Problems,* 15(2):221–236.

Simon, Rita J., Clark, Shirley M., and Tifft, L. L. 1966. Of nepotism, marriage, and the pursuit of an academic career. *Sociology of Education,* 39(4):344–358.

Simon, Rita J., and Rosenthal, Evelyn. 1967. Profile of the woman Ph.D. in economics, history, and sociology. *American Association of University Women Journal,* 60(3):127–129.

Simpson, Lawrence A. 1968. A study of employing agents' attitudes toward academic women in higher education. Ph.D. dissertation, Pennsylvania State University.

Wilcox, Thomas. May 1970. The lot of the woman: A report on the National Survey of Undergraduate English Programs. *Bulletin of Departments of English,* 25:53–59.

BIBLIOGRAPHY

Batten, James K. April 25, 1970. Bias issue embroils Harvard and HEW. *Washington Evening Star*, 115:A-2.

Bazell, Robert J. 1970. Sex discrimination: campuses face contract loss over HEW demands. *Science*, 170(3960):834–835.

Collins, J. 1969. Women in the universities. *The Radical Teacher*, 0:13–14.

Grouchow, Nancy. 1970. Discrimination: women charge universities, colleges with bias. *Science*, 168(3931):559–561.

Hawkins, Ruth R. 1969. The odds against women. *Change in Higher Education*, 1(6): 34–36.

Logan, Albert A., Jr. July 6, 1970. Universities told they must grant equal opportunity to women. *The Chronicle of Higher Education*, 4:5.

Miller, Susan B. June 30, 1971. Female academicians claim careers curbed by male chauvinists. *The Wall Street Journal*, 177:1, 16.

Rebelling women—the reasons. April 13, 1970. *The U.S. News and World Report*, 69: 35–37.

Wentworth, Eric. June 22, 1970. Women seek equality in universities. *The Washington Post*, 93:A–15.

Appendix
Institutional Data Sources

Many of these documents appeared in the first review on academic women (Robinson 1971) with both an annotation of their contents and detailed information about their accessibility. Many of the sources have been entered into the Educational Resources Information Center's (ERIC) system, and therefore may be purchased from the ERIC Document Reproduction Service. *Research in Education,* available in the reference section of many libraries, should be consulted for an abstract of the particular document of interest along with ordering instructions. The ERIC Clearinghouse on Higher Education, The George Washington University, Washington, D.C. 20006, also houses all of the documents listed in this section.

Akron, University of.
> Van Fleet, David D. December 1970. Salaries of males and females: A sample of conditions at the University of Akron. 9 pp.

Amherst College.
> Achbar, Francine, and Bishop, Pam. April 1970. Harvard probed for discrimination against women. *Boston Herald Traveler.*

Arizona, University of.
> Sigworth, Heather. July 1970. Supplemental letter on the University of Arizona. 6 pp.

Assumption College.
> Achbar and Bishop. 1970.

Baldwin-Wallace College.
> Institutional Analysis Committee. June 1971. Status of women at Baldwin-Wallace. 8 pp.

Boston College.
> Achbar and Bishop. 1970.

Boston University.
> Achbar and Bishop. 1970.

Brandeis University.
> (1) Achbar and Bishop. 1970.
> (2) Murray, Pauli. June 1970. Discrimination against women: Hearings before the special subcommittee on education of the committee on education and labor. Statement of Dr. Pauli Murray, professor of American studies, Brandeis University. Washington, D.C.: House of Representatives, pp. 328–341.

Bridgeport, University of.
> Anon. [1971.]* [Salary data.] 5 pp.

* All brackets are estimated dates, titles, etc.

Brooklyn College, City University of New York.
>   Babey-Brooke, Anna M., and Amber, R. B. July 1970. Discrimination against women in higher education. A 15-year survey. Promotional practices at Brooklyn College CUNY: 1955–1970, all ranks—tenured and untenured. 26 pp.

Brown University.
>   Brown University Chapter of the American Association of University Professors. October 1970. Report of the AAUP committee on the employment and status of women faculty and women graduate students at Brown. 22 pp.

California State Colleges. (Dominquez Hills, Fullerton, Hayward, Kern Co., Long Beach, Los Angeles, San Bernardino, California Polytechnic—Pomona and San Luis Obispo, Chico State, Fresno State, Humboldt State, Sacramento State, San Diego State, San Fernando Valley State, San Francisco State, San Jose State, Sonoma State, and Stanislaus State)
>   Anon. [1970.] Employment status of women in the California State Colleges. 4 pp.

California State College at Fullerton.
>   The National Organization for Women and Woman's Liberation, California State College at Fullerton. June 1970. [A report on the status of women at the California State College at Fullerton.] 18 pp.

University of California. (Berkeley, Davis, Irvine, Los Angeles, Riverside, San Diego, Santa Cruz, San Francisco, and Santa Barbara)
>   (1) Anon. [1969.] Representation of women among the high level administrative posts within the University of California, all campuses. 1 p.
>   (2) Card, Emily. July 22, 1970. Women faculty at the University of California— summary of testimony before Senate Education Committee, California State Senate. 2 pp.

California, University of, at Berkeley.
>   Academic Senate Subcommittee on the Status of Women. May 1970. Report of the subcommittee on the status of academic women on the Berkeley campus. 79 pp.

California, University of, at Irvine.
>   Task Force on the Status of Women. Fall 1970. Task force on the status of women at University of California, Irvine. 31 pp.

California, University of, at Los Angeles.
>   Harris, Ann S. 1970. The second sex in academe. *American Association of University Professors Bulletin.*

Carnegie-Mellon University.
>   Anon. [1970.] Survey broken down by sex of Carnegie-Mellon University appointments at an academic level higher than graduate student. Taken from the official published directory for 1969–1970. 1 p.

(East) Carolina University.
>   Faculty Affairs Committee. [1970.] Faculty affairs committee report: Analysis of faculty salaries (1969–1970). 9 pp.

Case Western Reserve University.
>   Ruben, Alan Miles, and Willis, Betty J. 1971. Discrimination against women in employment in higher education. *Cleveland State Law Review,* 20(3):472–491.

Chicago, University of.
>   (1) The Committee on University Women. May 1970. Women in the University

of Chicago—report of the Committee on University Women. Chicago: The University Senate. 125 pp.
(2) Freeman, Jo. 1969. Women on the social science faculties since 1892. 14 pp.
Clark University.
Achbar and Bishop. 1970.
Colorado, University of, at Boulder.
Minturn, Leigh. May 1970. Inequities in salary payments to faculty women. 6 pp.
Columbia University.
Columbia Women's Liberation. Spring 1970. Report from the Committee on Discrimination against women faculty. *Barnard Alumnae,* 59:12–18.
Connecticut College.
Committee W. [1970.] Report to AAUP by Committee W on the status of women at Connecticut College. 3 pp.
Cornell College.
Committee on the Status of Women. [1970.] A report of the Cornell College Chapter of the AAUP: Committee on the Status of Women. 3 pp.
Cornell University.
Francis, Barbara. [1970.] The status of women at Cornell. 6 pp.
Detroit, University of.
Action Committee for Federal Contract Compliance in Education. April 1971. [Formal charge of sex discrimination lodged by Women's Equity Action League.] 1 p.
Fisk University.
Action Committee for Federal Contract Compliance in Education. June 1971. [Formal charge of sex discrimination lodged by Women's Equity Action League.] 2 pp.
Florida, State University System of. (Florida A & M University, Florida Atlantic University, Florida International University, Florida State University, Florida Technological University, University of Florida, University of Northern Florida, University of South Florida, and University of West Florida)
Anon. April 1970. State University system of Florida. 1 p.
(South) Florida, University of.
(1) AAUP Committee on Employment Status of Academic Women. April 1971. Employment status of academic women committee: Faculty report. 64 pp.
(2) AAUP Committee on the Employment Status of Women. November 1970. Status of women committee: Faculty report. 31 pp.
(3) MacKay, E. M. February 1971. Portions of current study of T and R faculty women. 6 pp.
Georgetown University.
Anon. July 1971. The pattern in Georgetown University faculty employment for the year 1970–1971. 1 p.
Harvard University.
(1) Anon. [1969.] Harvard statistics. 7 pp.
(2) Bynum, Caroline W., and Martin, Janet M. June 1970. The sad status of women teaching at Harvard or "From what you said I would never have known you were a woman." *Radcliffe Quarterly,* 54:12–14.
(3) Committee on the Status of Women. April 1971. Report of the Committee on

the Status of Women in the faculty of arts and sciences. Cambridge, Mass.: Faculty of Arts and Sciences. 96 pp.

(4) The Women's Faculty Group. March 1970. Preliminary report on the status of women at Harvard. 16 pp.

Holy Cross College.

Achbar and Bishop. 1970.

(Eastern) Illinois University.

Anon. [1970.] Discrimination against women teachers at Eastern Illinois University. 2 pp.

(Southern) Illinois University at Carbondale.

Klaus, Michelle S. July 30, 1971. HEW team coming to investigate: Faculty women to file complaints. *Southern Illinoisan.*

(Southern) Illinois University at Edwardsville.

Committee on Female Concerns. [1971.] Report of Committee on Female Concerns. 3 pp.

Illinois, University of, at Champaign-Urbana.

Ferber, Marianne, and Loeb, Jane. November 1970. Rank, pay, and representation of women on the faculty of the Champaign-Urbana campus of the University of Illinois. 28 pp.

(Western) Illinois University.

Anon. May 1970. Sexual equality at W.I.U.? 2 pp.

Indiana State University.

(1) Anon. [1970.] Evidence of discrimination against women at Indiana State University. 13 pp.

(2) Hardaway, Charles W. [1970.] The status of women on the faculty of Indiana State University. 29 pp.

Indiana, University of, at Bloomington.

(1) AAUP Committee on the Status of Women. January 1971. Study of the status of women faculty at Indiana University, Bloomington campus. 55 pp.

(2) Berry, Sara, and Erenburg, Mark. [1969.] Earnings of professional women at Indiana University. 21 pp.

Johns Hopkins University.

Alexander, Anne. 1970. Who's come a long way, baby? *The Johns Hopkins Magazine,* 21(2):11–15.

Kansas State Teachers College.

Committee on the Status of Women. [1970.] KSTC Chapter of American Association of University Professors, Report 1 of Committee on the Status of Women. 16 pp.

Kansas, University of, at Lawrence.

(1) Associated Women Students Commission on the Status of Women. [1970.] Reports of Associated Women Students Commission on the Status of Women: 1969–1970. 30 pp.

(2) Committee W. [1970.] Report of Committee W (Status of Women). 3 pp.

(3) The Office of Academic Affairs. [1970.] The University of Kansas faculty salary study—1970–1971. 15 pp.

(Eastern) Kentucky University.

Riffe, Nancy L. April 1971. Committee W—AAUP, EKU chapter. 5 pp.
Kentucky, University of.
  Anon. [1970.] The status of women at the University of Kentucky. 31 pp.
Louisiana State University.
  Action Committee for Federal Contract Compliance in Education. December 1970.
  [Formal charge of sex discrimination lodged by Women's Equity Action League.]
  1 p.
Loyola University.
  Action Committee for Federal Contract Compliance in Education. December 1970.
  [Formal charge of sex discrimination lodged by Women's Equity Action League.]
  1 p.
Maryland, University of, at Baltimore.
  The New University Conference. April 1970. The status of women at the University
  of Maryland, Baltimore County. 9 pp.
Maryland, University of, at College Park.
  Sandler, Bernice. Fall 1969. Sex discrimination at the University of Maryland. 12
  pp.
Massachusetts Institute of Technology.
  Achbar and Bishop. 1970.
Massachusetts, University of, at Amherst and Boston.
  Achbar and Bishop. 1970.
Miami, University of.
  Anon. April 12, 1970. UM faculty dominated by males. *The Miami Herald.*
Michigan State University.
  Office of Institutional Research. July 1970. A compilation of data on faculty women
  and women enrolled at Michigan State University. 55 pp.
Michigan, University of.
  (1) Shortridge, Kathy. April 1970. Women as university nigger: How the 'U'
      keeps females in their place. Pittsburgh: KNOW, Inc.
  (2) Shortridge, Kathy. May 1970. [Women at the University of Michigan.] 5 pp.
Minnesota, University of, at Twin-Cities.
  (1) Council for University Women's Progress. December 1970. Academic women
      at the University of Minnesota (Minneapolis-St. Paul): Their number and
      departmental affiliation. 11 pp.
  (2) Minnesota Planning and Counseling Center for Women. May 1970. Research
      on the status of faculty women—University of Minnesota. 15 pp.
  (3) Subcommittee on Equal Opportunities for Faculty and Student Women. April
      1971. Report of Subcommittee on Equal Opportunities for Faculty and Stu-
      dent Women. 18 pp.
Missouri, University of, at Kansas City.
  Anon. [1971.] University of Missouri at Kansas City—information taken from
  UMKC Bulletin, 1971–1972. 1 p.
Mount Holyoke College.
  Achbar and Bishop. 1970.
New Hampshire, University of.
  Achbar and Bishop. 1970.

New York, State University of, at Buffalo.

    Scott, Ann. May 14, 1970. The half-eaten apple: A look at sex discrimination in the university. *Reporter.* 8 pp.

Northeastern University.

    Achbar and Bishop. 1970.

Northwestern University.

    Houston, Susan. [1970.] Faculty women at Northwestern University College of Arts and Sciences. 2 pp.

Notre Dame University.

    Stidham, Greg. April 2, 1971. Less than three percent. *The Scholastic,* 112:12–13.

Ohio State University.

    Ruben, Alan Miles, and Willis, Betty J. 1971. Discrimination against women in employment in higher education. *Cleveland State Law Review,* 20(3):472–491.

Oregon, University of.

    Ad Hoc Committee. [1970.] The status of women at the University of Oregon. Report of an Ad Hoc Committee. 20 pp.

Pace College.

    Anon. [1970.] [Pace College faculty.] 14 pp.

Pennsylvania State University.

    Action Committee for Federal Contract Compliance in Education. February 1971. [Formal charges of sex discrimination lodged by Women's Equity Action League.] 3 pp.

Pennsylvania, University of.

    Committee on the Status of Women. March 1971. Women faculty in the University of Pennsylvania. 36 pp.

Pittsburgh, University of.

    (1) Advisory Council of Women's Opportunities. November 1970. Progress report to the chancellor. 14 pp.

    (2) Anon. Spring 1969. Number of women holding top level administrative positions at the University of Pittsburgh. 1 p.

    (3) The University Committee for Women's Rights. November 1970. Discrimination against women at the University of Pittsburgh. 70 pp.

Princeton University.

    The Task Force on Equal Academic Opportunities. April 1971. A preliminary report on the status of women at Princeton University. 22 pp.

Purdue University.

    Metzler, Cindy. [1970.] The status of women at Purdue University. 9 pp.

Rhode Island, University of.

    Achbar and Bishop. 1970.

Rockefeller University.

    Rockefeller University Committee of Women. [1970.] Status of academic women at the Rockefeller University. 1 p.

Rutgers University. (The State University of New Jersey System: Rutgers, Douglass and Livingston Colleges in New Brunswick, The College of South Jersey [Rutgers-Camden], and Rutgers-Newark)

    (1) Anon. [1970.] Statistics of Rutgers College. 7 pp.

(2) Boring, Phyllis Z. 1971. Distribution of women faculty at Rutgers University. *American Association of University Professors Council of Rutgers Chapters Newsletter,* 2(6):1–3.

(3) Boring, Phyllis Z. 1971. Salary differential and the women faculty members at Rutgers University. *American Association of University Professors Council of Rutgers Chapters Newsletter,* 2(5):1–3.

(4) Selick, Barbara. 1971. Women want Rutgers men to lib a little. *The Home News,* 93(199):1, 49.

(5) Smith, Georgina. [1971.] Summary-survey of faculty career patterns. 7 pp.

(6) Staff writer. May 9, 1971. Rutgers women charge bias. *Newark Sunday News.*

Sacramento State College.

Anon. [1970.] Statistics on women at Sacramento State College. 2 pp.

Salem State College.

Achbar and Bishop. 1970.

San Diego State College.

Jancek, Camilla. [1969.] Women in teaching at San Diego State College, 1968–1969. 2 pp.

Simmons College.

(1) Achbar and Bishop. 1970.

(2) American Association of University Professors' Salary Committee. March 1971. Sex discrimination at Simmons College—AAUP report. 6 pp.

Smith College.

(1) Anon. [1970.] A report important to the future of Smith College: The status of women faculty in academic departments in Smith College in 1969–1970. 4 pp.

(2) Personal correspondence to Dr. Florence Howe, Goucher College, Towson, Maryland. March 1970. 4 pp.

South Carolina, University of.

Action Committee for Federal Contract Compliance in Education. November 1970. [Formal charges of sex discrimination lodged by Women's Equity Action League.] 1 p.

Southern Methodist University.

Action Committee for Federal Contract Compliance in Education. December 1970. [Formal charges of sex discrimination lodged by Women's Equity Action League.] 1 p.

Stanford University.

Siegel, Alberta E., and Carr, Ronald G. March 1969. Education of women at Stanford University. In *The Study of Education at Stanford: A Report to the University,* 7:81–100. Stanford: Stanford University.

(Middle) Tennessee State University.

American Association of University Professors' Chapter. [1970.] An internal salary study of Middle Tennessee State University for the academic year 1970–1971. 10 pp.

Tennessee, University of, at Knoxville.

Anon. [1970.] The University of Tennessee, Knoxville, academic staff. 4 pp.

Texas, University of, at Austin.

(1) Office for Institutional Studies. December 1970. [Tables of salary rates.] Pp. 55–62.

(2) Rogoff, Regina, et al. July 1971. [Formal charge of sex discrimination against the University of Texas at Austin.] 30 pp.

Tufts University-Jackson College.

Achbar and Bishop. 1970.

Virginia Public Colleges. (Longwood, Madison, Old Dominion, and Radford College; Richmond Professional Institute, now part of Virginia Commonwealth University; University of Virginia—Clinch Valley, Eastern Shore, Lynchburg, and Patrick Henry; Virginia Military Institute; Virginia Polytechnic Institute; Virginia State— Norfolk and Petersburg; College of William and Mary—Christopher Newport and Richard Bland; Community Colleges—Blue Ridge, Central Valley, Dabney Lancaster, Danville, John Tyler, Northern Virginia, Virginia Western, and Wytheville)

Peninsular Chapter of the New University Conference. 1971. Women in Virginia higher education. 35 pp.

Virginia Polytechnic Institute.

Anon. [1971.] Status of women at Virginia Polytechnic Institute and State University. 11 pp.

Washington, University of.

The Associated Students of the University of Washington Women's Commission. October 1970. Report on the status of women at the University of Washington: Part 1, faculty and staff. 48 pp.

Wayne State University.

Anon. [1970.] Fact sheet. 5 pp.

Wellesley College.

Achbar and Bishop. 1970.

William and Mary, College of.

Action Committee for Federal Contract Compliance in Education. November 1970. [Formal charges of sex discrimination lodged by Women's Equity Action League.] 1 p.

Willamette University.

Action Committee for Federal Contract Compliance in Education. May 1971. [Formal charges of sex discrimination lodged by Women's Equity Action League.] 6 pp.

Wisconsin, University of, at Madison.

(1) Anon. [1970.] University of Wisconsin, Madison Campus 1969–1970. 2 pp.

(2) Central University Office of Planning and Analysis. 1971. Final report on the status of academic women. 490 pp.

(3) Women's Research Group. [1969.] Women at Wisconsin. Beaver Dam, Wisc.: National Organization for Women. 20 pp.

Yale University.

(1) Anon. [1970.] Yale faculty. 1 p.

(2) Yale Faculty and Professional Women's Forum. March 1971. Women on the Yale faculty. 33 pp.

(3) The Yale Faculty and Professional Women's Forum, Yale Non-faculty Action Committee, Yale Law Women's Alliance, Yale Medical Women's Association,

Yale Graduate Women's Alliance, Yale Public Health Women, and the Yale Sisterhood. May 1971. Sex discrimination at Yale: A document of indictment. 77 pp.

The following institutional reports arrived too late to be included in the analyses for this chapter; however, they are available at the Clearinghouse on Higher Education.

Carnegie-Mellon University.
    Commission on the Status and Needs of Women. November 1971. Final report of the Commission on the Status and Needs of Women at Carnegie-Mellon University. 150 pp.
Delaware, University of.
    Dahl, K. H. 1971. Report on women at the University of Delaware. 35 pp.
Illinois State University.
    The Research Committee, Women Faculty Association. 1971. The status of women faculty at Illinois State University, 1970–1971. 44 pp.
Illinois Wesleyan University.
    Calabrese, Maureen. January 1972. The academic women—case study: IWU. A report to the personnel council from the Sociology of Women Seminar. 30 pp.
Ohio State University.
    Ad Hoc Committee on the Status of Women. April 1971. Report of the Ad Hoc Committee to review the status of women at The Ohio State University. 358 pp.
Rutgers University.
    Dinnerstein, Dorothy. May 1971. Some discrepancies between the situations of male and female faculty members Newark College of Arts and Sciences of Rutgers University: A preliminary analysis. 19 pp.
Stanford University.
    Miner, Anne S. November 1971. Academic employment of women at Stanford. 10 pp.
Syracuse University.
    Wheeler, Elliot S. March 1971. Report on the status of full-time women teaching faculty. 5 pp.

Chapter Twelve

Representation, Performance and Status of Women on the Faculty at the Urbana-Champaign Campus of the University of Illinois

Jane W. Loeb
Marianne A. Ferber

RECENTLY adopted federal guidelines require that colleges and universities with federal contracts be able to demonstrate that their employment policies afford equal opportunity to women and to provide affirmative action plans to correct sex-based inequities if such are found to exist. A case study of compliance of one institution should prove helpful to others. While the university examined is in certain respects typical only of large state schools, the methods used should be applicable to other colleges and universities as well. This chapter, then, summarizes data bearing on the extent to which the Urbana-Champaign campus of the University of Illinois has complied with these guidelines. Specifically, representation of women on the faculty and in the administration was investigated, and the rank and pay of men and women faculty were compared. Because low publication rate and interrupted career patterns possibly accounted for the low representation, rank, and pay of women, the productivity of men and women was compared as well.

REPRESENTATION, RANK AND PAY OF WOMEN ON THE FACULTY

Several reports compiled from university records summarizing data on representation, rank, and pay of female faculty preceded this study. Carey (1969) found that in the fall of 1968, 11.8 percent of the academic faculty at Urbana were women. However, only 3.7 percent of the full professors and 9.4 percent of the associate professors were women, while they constituted 16.8 percent of all assistant professors and 33.7 percent of all instructors (see Table 12.1).

Carey's data also indicated that the mean salary for women at each rank, whether on nine-month or eleven-month appointments, was lower than that for men. The mean salary for women varied from 99.6 percent to 76.2 percent of the mean male salary, depending on rank and type of appointment (see Table 12.2).

Data summarized by Tousey (1970) indicated that similar salary differentials existed for the 1969–1970 academic year. Tousey also compared the average nine-

TABLE 12.1. Full-Time Faculty, by Rank, Type of Appointment, and Sex, Fall 1968

Rank	Type of Appointment (in months)	No. Men	No. Women	Women as Percent of Rank
Professor	9	623	23	3.7
	11	235	10	
Associate professor	9	318	41	9.4
	11	175	10	
Assistant professor	9	317	56	16.8
	11	142	39	
Instructor	9	99	36	33.7
	11	72	51	

SOURCE: Data abstracted from Carey 1969.

TABLE 12.2. Mean Salaries of Full-Time Faculty, 1968–69

Rank	Type of Appointment (in months)	Men	Women	Mean Salary of Women as Percent of Mean Salary of Men
Professor	9	$18,581	$15,474	83.3
	11	20,512	17,930	87.4
Associate professor	9	13,256	11,654	87.9
	11	14,845	14,790	99.6
Assistant professor	9	10,983	10,050	91.5
	11	12,900	11,628	90.1
Instructor	9	9,043	7,708	85.2
	11	10,722	8,168	76.2

SOURCE: Data abstracted from Carey 1969.

month salary of men and women doctorates, as of October 1969, within colleges and within some departments. In all colleges and in most departments for which adequate comparative data were available, salaries of male doctorates exceeded those of female doctorates holding the same rank (see Table 12.3). In addition, Tousey found that the rate of advancement of women through the ranks tended to be slower, on the average, than that of men in the same college (see Table 12.4).

Given the fact that there are few women on the academic staff of the university, that they are chiefly clustered in the lower ranks, are paid less and promoted more slowly than men, this report is addressed to the following questions: (1) Is the number of women on the faculty commensurate with the number available in the labor

TABLE 12.3. Mean 1969 Salary of Doctorate Men and Women by College and Rank (In Dollars)

College		Instructor	Assistant Professor	Associate Professor	Full Professor
Agriculture					
Total	Male	$10,993	$11,336	$13,266	$16,873
	Female		8,200	11,990	16,374
Home Economics					
	Male		12,177	12,400	
	Female			12,139	16,683
Education (all depts.)					
Total	Male		11,890	13,815	18,815
	Female		11,936	12,522	16,658
Special Education					
	Male		11,688	15,071	19,651
	Female			14,307	18,950
Fine and Applied Arts					
Total	Male	9,000	11,795	12,719	18,346
	Female			12,167	14,006
Liberal Arts & Sciences					
Total	Male	9,587	11,205	13,705	20,326
	Female	8,282	10,551	12,794	17,820
English					
	Male	9,750	10,445	13,907	20,365
	Female	9,200	10,255	11,752	14,600
Mathematics					
	Male		10,806	13,180	20,881
	Female	7,200	10,365	13,643	
Speech					
	Male		11,528	14,021	17,690
	Female		10,639		18,500
Physical Education					
Total	Male		11,184	13,738	18,885
	Female	10,000	10,902	12,745	17,730
Library					
Total	Male		10,715	13,665	18,478
	Female	7,790	10,204	11,029	16,029
Graduate School					
	Male		12,956		18,041
	Female		10,204		18,200
Departmental Libraries					
	Male		10,496	13,530	
	Female	7,790		11,029	13,858

SOURCE: Data abstracted from Tousey 1970.

TABLE 12.4. Mean Rate of Rank Advancement

College		Instructor to Assistant Professor		Assistant Professor to Associate Professor		Associate Professor to Professor	
		Years	Sample	Years	Sample	Years	Sample
Agriculture	(Female)	5.64	14	7.77	13	7.17	6
	(Male)	3.71	51	5.40	166	5.53	123
Education	(Female)	5.33	3	6.27	15	3.50	4
	(Male)	3.88	16	3.68	60	4.50	50
Fine and	(Female)	5.80	5	7.00	10	6.00	7
Applied Arts	(Male)	4.51	61	4.80	97	5.58	83
Liberal Arts &	(Female)	5.58	26	6.00	14	6.40	5
Sciences	(Male)	3.06	144	4.35	266	4.75	183
Physical	(Female)	6.00	7	7.67	6	2.00	1
Education	(Male)	4.39	23	6.57	14	5.10	10
Library	(Female)	7.27	26	9.42	12	8.60	5
	(Male)	5.53	19	4.62	13	10.67	6
Number of colleges in which women remain in rank longer than men		6 of 6		6 of 6		3 of 6	

SOURCE: Data abstracted from Tousey 1970.

market? (2) Is the number of women appointed to administrative positions commensurate with their number on the faculty? (3) Is the disproportionate recruitment and promotion of men justified by lower productivity of women faculty? (4) Are the salaries and ranks of women commensurate with their experience and productivity? (5) Is the rate at which women are advanced through the ranks commensurate with their experience and productivity?

REPRESENTATION OF WOMEN IN THE LABOR MARKET VERSUS REPRESENTATION OF WOMEN ON THE FACULTY

The percent of doctorates awarded nationwide to women in selected fields in 1967–1968 and the percent of women in the assistant professor rank, and assistant, associate, and professor ranks combined in Urbana departments in the 1969–1970 academic year are compared in Table 12.5. Ten departments had at least as many female assistant professors as would be found if they had been hired in numbers reflecting the proportion of 1967 women doctorates nationwide. These data do not, however, prove that these departments did not discriminate in hiring. In many cases the relatively high proportion of women at the assistant professor rank may have been a result of their low rate of promotion to higher ranks. In thirteen other departments, the sex ratio among assistant professors was below that among recent doctorates.

TABLE 12.5. Comparison of Doctorates Awarded to Women Nationwide
(1967–1968) with Faculty Positions Held by Women at University of Illinois
(In percentages)

Department	Doctorates Awarded to Women (1967–1968)[a]	Rank of Women Employed at University of Illinois	
		Assistant Professor or Higher (1969–1970)	Assistant Professor (1969–1970)
Anthropology	24	0	0
Art	34	4	4
Chemistry	8	2	7
Educational Administration	8	0	0
Educational Psychology	28	11	26
Elementary Education	42	18	33
English	27	20	28
French	38	12	17
German	24	25	25
History	13	3	14
History and Philosophy of Education	19	9	0
Journalism	16	0	0
Library Science	32	43	40
Linguistics	21	11	0
Mathematics	6	9	21
Music	14	9	8
Philosophy	9	0	0
Political Science	11	10	20
Psychology	22	5	7
Secondary Education	17	19	0
Sociology	18	8	8
Speech	18	24	33
Zoology	15	5	18

[a] Data abstracted from Hooper and Chandler 1969.

REPRESENTATION OF WOMEN IN ADMINISTRATIVE POSITIONS

The extent of female representation in the administration was estimated by computing the number of men and women listed in the 1969–1970 Staff Directory as holding administrative positions. Table 12.6 presents the representation of women on Urbana's college committees. Several colleges were omitted because they had so few women faculty, or because data were not readily available. Generally, representation of women on committees was not proportional to their numbers on the faculty. Since many committee memberships included women students, the representation of women faculty probably was overestimated by these figures. An examination of the rank of members within committees and the relative importance of the various committees might well reveal an even greater inequity in representation.

TABLE 12.6. Representation of Women on College Committees (In percentages)

College	Percent Female Faculty[a]	Committee Positions Held by Females (including students)
Agriculture	15	9
Education	21	7
Fine and Applied Arts	10	14
Liberal Arts and Sciences	12	3
Physical Education	32	20
Library Science	59	50
Graduate College	5	4
Communications	2	4[b]
Veterinary Medicine	4	3[c]

[a] Data abstracted from Tousey 1970.
[b] Excluding the Alumni Relations Committee, the percent is 0.
[c] Excluding the Library Committee, the percent is 1.

Of the deans, heads, chairmen, directors, and coordinators of colleges, departments, offices, and other administrative units, their assistants (excluding assistants *to*) and associates, only 7 percent were female. Only four of the more than eighty-five teaching departments were administered by women. None of the colleges had even one female dean. Since 4 percent of the full professors and 9 percent of the associate professors were women, it is clear that women were underrepresented in administrative posts. Finally, it should be noted that the staffs of the chancellor and president were exclusively male.

PRODUCTIVITY OF WOMEN AND MEN FACULTY MEMBERS

The low number of women assistant professors relative to the number of women doctorates nationwide cannot be regarded as evidence of discrimination if women doctorates either (1) fail to seek work or (2) are less productive than men in terms of their accomplishments in publishing, teaching, honors received, and so on. Similarly, their low rate of appointments to administrative positions would not be evidence of discrimination if they are less productive than men. The possibility that women fail to seek work has been investigated for a national sample of doctorates and found not to be the case: all but a small minority of women with doctorates remain in the labor force (Simon et al. 1966).

Published sources yielded some data concerning productivity of the Urbana faculty. A list of faculty publications, published annually, was one such source. The *Advisor,* a student publication that described the results of a questionnaire on teaching effectiveness distributed voluntarily by some faculty members to their students, was another. In order to gather additional data for a comparison of the productivity of women and men faculty members, a questionnaire was distributed in the spring of 1970 to 186 women holding the rank of at least instructor at the Urbana campus and to a sample of men matched on department and rank. When several matches were possible, men were selected randomly. The sample of 186 women represented about half the women at academic rank, and all for whom matching males were available. The requirement that a matching male exist eliminated women in a number of departments, including home economics, library science, and social work. Returned questionnaires numbered 278, or 75 percent of the initial sample.

Information requested included department; rank; number of years spent at each rank at the university; highest degree obtained; date of degree; institution granting degree; age; sex; number and type of publications since 1965 and over the respondent's lifetime; number of full-time equivalent years in academic or other professional positions; number of professional honors received since 1967; present contract (nine- or eleven-month, full- or part-time); and present salary.

Publications of Women and Men Faculty

The publications of the 186 women and 186 men from 1966 through 1968 were compared. Table 12.7 shows that women published slightly more bulletins and technical reports, edited volumes, and reviews, while men published slightly more books and articles. These findings are not strictly comparable however. About 15 percent of the women in the sample worked part-time, compared to about 1 percent of the men. If one assumes that research output of a part-time employee would be proportionally lower than that of the full-time employee, women's productivity is under-

TABLE 12.7. Publications of 372 Women and Men at the University of Illinois 1966–1968

Type of Publication	No. Published		Women's Publications as a Percent of Men's
	Men	*Women*	
Books	21	18	85.7
Books edited	4	7	175.0
Articles	197	174	88.3
Bulletins and technical reports	8	21	262.5
Reviews	48	53	110.4

SOURCE: Data abstracted from university list of faculty publications.

estimated by these data. In addition, some of the sample were not at the university during the entire period studied and work published elsewhere was not credited to them.

Because of the difficulties inherent in this comparison the questionnaire data on lifetime publishing productivity were also investigated. It was expected that date of degree, number of years of full-time academic employment, age, and highest degree obtained would be the major factors accounting for variability in total articles published. If men and women performed unequally when these factors had been accounted for, differential productivity would be indicated. The analysis was based on the 197 women and men for whom all requisite data were available. Using the technique of stepwise multiple correlation it was found that sex did not account for differences in total number of articles published.

Nevertheless it seemed possible that highest degree, degree date, age, and years of employment might exert a different influence on productivity of men than that of women. Therefore, the interactions between these factors and sex were examined as additional variables. One was significant: sex by degree date. Men who obtained their degrees in 1964 or earlier tended to have outpublished women with the same degree date, age, and years of experience. However, women with more recent degrees tended to have outpublished their male counterparts. Regression coefficients at two stages of the stepwise procedure, i.e., with and without the significant interaction term, are listed in Table 12.8.

TABLE 12.8. Regression Coefficients for Prediction of Articles Published in Lifetime

Variable	Unstandardized Regression Coefficients without Interaction	Unstandardized Regression Coefficients with Interaction
Highest degree (4 = Ph.D., 3 = Post M.A., 2 = M.A., 1 = B.A.)	2.47[a]	2.28[a]
Degree date (last 2 digits, e.g., 47)	−0.30	1.19[b]
Years academic employment (FTE)	0.76[b]	0.66[b]
Age	−0.24	−0.22
Sex (2 = male; 1 = female)	3.60	67.83[b]
Sex × degree date		−1.05[b]
Dependent variable intercept	12.69	−76.74
Multiple R	0.45	0.52

[a] $p < 0.05$.
[b] $p < 0.01$.

Although these data are not advanced in support of a policy which would recruit young women in preference to young men, they lend absolutely no support to the recruitment of men in preference to women. In terms of article production, an older woman is a known quantity while a younger woman is, it appears, a good risk.

Teaching Effectiveness of Women and Men Faculty

In order to provide an index of teaching effectiveness, the mean ratings received by those members of the sample listed in the 1968 and 1969 *Advisor* were calculated. In 1968, the men's mean was 3.28, while women received a mean of 3.31. In 1969, the men's mean was 3.08 and the women's mean, 3.07. These data suggest that the sexes did not differ in teaching effectiveness as perceived by their students.

Professional Experience of Women and Men Faculty

Full-time equivalent years of nonacademic and academic employment were examined for the 259 subjects who reported experience, degree date, and age. It was expected that degree date and age would be the primary factors accounting for variability in years of experience. If women accumulated fewer years of experience than men after these factors had been taken into account, the conclusion that women are more likely to have their careers interrupted or to work part-time would be warranted.

Using the technique of multiple correlation, sex and the interactions of sex with the other predictors were found to have no significant relationship to either measure of experience once age and degree date were taken into account. Regression coeffi-

TABLE 12.9. Regression Coefficients for the Prediction of Years of Professional Experience

| | *Unstandardized Regression Coefficients* | |
| | *Criterion:*
Years of
Professional Employment | *Criterion:*
Years of Academic
Professional Employment |
Variable		
Sex	−7.90	−3.90
(2 = male; 1 = female)		
Degree date	−0.19	−0.26
(last two digits, e.g. 47)		
Age	0.64[a]	0.34[b]
Sex × Degree date	0.06	−0.01
Sex × Age	0.13	0.15
Dependent variable intercept	−1.90	11.08
Multiple R	0.90	0.84

[a] $p < 0.01$.
[b] $p < 0.05$.

cients are listed in Table 12.9. A 39-year-old with a degree dated 1960 would be predicted to have accrued about one year more professional experience if male than if female. This statistically insignificant difference suggests that women do not experience part-time or interrupted careers as frequently as is generally assumed.

It should be pointed out, however, that the method of sampling may be sufficiently biased to mask real differences by sex. Both women and men were sampled from among currently active faculty members. Women who drop in and out of the labor market would be underrepresented in such a sample. Administrative records might provide clearer data on the relative job stability of women and men.

In sum, data on publications, teaching effectiveness, and experience suggest that women were not measurably less productive or less stable as employees than men. Hence, their relatively low representation on the faculty and in the administration cannot easily be justified.

SALARY AND RANK AS FUNCTIONS OF EXPERIENCE, PRODUCTIVITY, AND SEX

The existence and extent of sex-based inequalities in pay and rank were investigated, using the questionnaire data described above. Inequality may manifest itself in several ways. For one, the reward structure may be the same for both sexes, with a journal article advancing one's rank and pay at the same rate regardless of sex, while a constant salary or rank increment might be added for men. In technical terms, the slopes of the regressions of salary and rank on the multiple predictors might be equal but the intercepts different for the sexes. A second mode may be inequalities that exist in the reward structure itself, with articles, books, or honors, etc., advancing men at a more rapid rate than women. Both possibilities were investigated, using a stepwise multiple correlation procedure. Indices of merit and experience were used first, then sex was introduced into the equation. Finally, terms representing the interaction of sex with experience and merit indices were allowed to enter the equation according to their predictive power.

Subjects examined for sex-based salary inequities were the fifty-nine male and sixty-nine full-time women faculty members who answered all requisite questions. Predictors of salary were the mean 1968–1969 nine-month salary for department and rank, number of years at the university at that rank, highest degree obtained, appointment type (nine- or eleven-month), full-time equivalent years of professional experience, publications since 1965, and honors received since 1967.

Inequalities in rank were investigated in two ways. First, rank itself was predicted from merit, experience, and sex indices, and their interactions. In order to investigate the rate of advancement through the ranks, a weighted total of the number of years spent at each rank was established, and this variable was predicted from the number of years employed at the university, experience, merit, and sex, and the interactions of sex with the other indices. Subjects in the investigations of rank were the 148 full-time faculty members—72 women and 76 men—who answered all requisite items. Predictors of both salary and rank included the number of years at the university at a rank of at least instructor, highest degree, date of degree, lifetime publications, number of years of professional experience, and honors.

It might be expected that subjects returning completed questionnaires would tend to be those members of the original sample who believed discrimination existed, and hence that the sample might overrepresent women, particularly women at lower ranks. When this possibility was examined it was found that the final samples were not seriously biased in this regard (Loeb and Ferber 1971).

Salary

Table 12.10 lists multiple correlations and unstandardized regression coefficients at two stages in the stepwise prediction of salary. The first set of coefficients is applicable to a predictive equation including all merit indices and sex. The second set of coefficients defines a predictive equation to which all interactions of sex with merit indices which are capable of significantly increasing the accuracy of prediction have been added. The coefficient of 0.81 in the first set of coefficients can be interpreted as meaning that each dollar more that a department has for its mean salary at a given rank will result in an individual in that department and rank being predicted to have $0.81 more salary. Furthermore it can be seen that the extra two-month summer employment is worth, on the average, $1,413.57 in the prediction of a faculty member's salary.

Sex significantly increased the predictability of salary ($F = 6.68$, $df = 1/113$, $p < 0.05$) beyond that afforded by mean salary for department and rank, nine- or eleven-month appointment information, and the multiple indices of experience and merit. The unstandardized regression coefficient for sex, 845.96, can be interpreted as the average yearly dollar value of masculinity in this sample. The statistical significance of this coefficient signifies that if salary were predicted without the sex variable, the drop in the multiple R would be significant.

Beyond the factor of sex, two interaction terms were capable of adding significantly to the prediction of salary: Sex $\times$ Bulletins ($F = 4.49$, $df = 1/112$, $p < 0.05$) and Sex $\times$ Years at Rank ($F = 5.36$, $df = 1/111$, $p < 0.05$). The positive regression coefficients for these predictors indicate that both of these factors predict more salary dollars for men than for women. Table 12.11 lists the predicted salary differences for men and women as a function of bulletins and number of years at rank. It can be seen that among those who have not published bulletins and technical reports, the sexes are about equal in pay when they first enter a rank, but the predicted discrepancy is around $800 after five years. For producers of bulletins and technical reports, the discrepancies are greater of course.

The mean salary in the derivation sample for the salary prediction was $12,361.39, and the discrepancy predicted for the sexes was $845.96. A raise of 7 percent for

TABLE 12.10. Multiple Correlations and Unstandardized Regression Coefficients for Prediction of Salary

Variable	Unstandardized Regression Coefficients without Interaction	Unstandardized Regression Coefficients with Interactions
Mean salary for department and rank	0.81[a]	0.79[a]
Years at present rank	60.99	−203.54
Highest degree	594.43[a]	537.84[a]
(4 = Ph.D., 3 = post M.A., 2 = M.A., 1 = B.A.)		
Appointment type	1413.57[a]	1534.71[a]
(2 = 11 mo., 1 = 9 mo.)		
Years of professional experience	46.59	41.80
Books published (since 1965)	−278.73	−215.57
Books edited	−438.05	−460.25
Bulletins and technical reports published	10.91	−307.29[b]
Reviews published	−36.21	−36.18
Papers read at meetings	179.64[a]	139.74[a]
Journal articles published	−45.10	−37.15
Other publications	4.35	5.44
Total number of honors	335.91[a]	334.80[b]
Sex	845.96[b]	−190.31
(2 = male; 1 = female)		
Sex × Bulletins published		291.11[b]
Sex × Years at present rank		198.54[b]
Dependent variable intercept	−3517.94	−1759.61
Multiple R	0.87	0.88

[a] $p < 0.01$.
[b] $p < 0.05$.

women might be considered a rough estimate of adequate salary equalization. Since women who publish bulletins and technical reports and women who have spent several years at one rank are more underpaid than other women, it is important that sex-based inequities be reviewed on an individual basis.

Seven percent may be a rather low estimate of discrepancies which exist. Katz (1971) found a residual sex difference of $2,242 in the salaries of a sample of faculty members from selected Urbana departments after adjusting for a number of merit and experience factors. Several aspects of the present study which may have produced a relatively low estimate should be mentioned. First, the use of merit indices assumes that opportunities to achieve merit are equally available to both sexes. Actually, honors such as research grants, fellowships, journal editorships, and election to office in professional organizations may be more readily available to men than to women. To the

TABLE 12.11. Predicted Salary Differentials as a Function of Bulletins Published and Years at Present Rank

	Years at Present Rank				
No. of Bulletins	1	2	3	4	5
2	$590.45	$788.99	$987.53	$1,186.07	$1,384.61
1	299.34	497.88	696.42	894.96	1,093.50
0	8.23	206.77	405.31	603.85	802.39

extent that the merit and experience indices used in this study are themselves discriminatory, rank and pay inequities are underestimated by the present data. Second, salaries were predicted from the mean salary for an individual's department and rank. Thus, the reported sex difference in pay refers to individuals of the same rank, and hence does not reflect the extent to which slower promotion through the ranks has depressed salaries for women. Third, the current report is based on an incomplete sample of departments. Some very poorly paid, predominantly female departments were omitted by the sampling technique. It may be that the presence of males in a department tends to elevate not only the average salary but the salaries of female members of the department as well. Thus women in departments not sampled because matching men were not available may be more underpaid than women in the sample.

Rank

Sex itself did not add to the prediction of rank, after degree date, years at the university and the merit and experience indices had already entered the equation ($F < 1.0$). One significant interaction emerged, however: Sex $\times$ books ($F = 9.16$, $df = 1/133$, p < 0.01). Table 12.12 lists unstandardized regression coefficients for the prediction of rank. The predicted rank of a male who had published one book is one-tenth of a rank beyond that of a female author; additional books are expected to advance males two-tenths of a rank more than females.

Sex did not add to the power of the experience and merit indices to predict weighted total number of years at the university ($F = 1.60$). However, three of the interaction terms did increase predictability of this criterion ($P < 0.05$): Sex $\times$ Books Published, Sex $\times$ Books Edited, and Sex $\times$ Articles Published. Table 12.12 lists the coefficients and indicates that while having published books and articles tended to advance men through the ranks more quickly than women, having edited books advanced women more quickly than men. Whether it is advantageous to be male or to be female will depend on one's pattern of publications. Hence, the publication record of the 206 individuals who answered the item on lifetime publications were examined and the contribution to predicted weighted total years of their books, books edited, articles, and sex was calculated twice, once assuming masculinity and once assuming

TABLE 12.12. Unstandardized Regression Coefficients for Prediction of
Academic Rank and Weighted Total Years at the University

Variable	Academic Rank	Weighted Total Years at the University
Years at present academic rank at the University of Illinois	0.02	2.61[a]
Highest degree obtained (last two digits, e.g. 47)	0.50[a]	1.32[b]
Degree date	−0.02[b]	0.06
Books published over entire lifetime	−0.20[b]	−2.01[b]
Books edited	0.05	4.28[b]
Bulletins and technical reports published	−0.01	0.08
Reviews published	−0.00	−0.08
Papers read at meetings	0.03[a]	0.28
Journal articles	−0.00	−0.11
Other publications	0.02[b]	0.07
Years of professional experience	0.02[b]	0.01
Total number of honors	0.06	0.00
Sex (2 = male; 1 = female)	−0.10	−0.52
Sex × Books published	0.22[a]	2.03[b]
Sex × Books edited		−2.48[b]
Sex × Articles		0.18[b]
Dependent variable intercept	1.56	−13.03
Multiple R	0.84	0.97

[a] $p < 0.01$.
[b] $p < 0.05$.

femininity. Of this group, 62 percent would be expected to advance more quickly if
male, while 8 percent would advance more quickly if female.

Two factors often advanced in explanation of the relatively low rank and pay of
academic women are their fewer number of publications and less professional experience. However, after both of these factors had been taken into account, women still
were found to receive lower salaries and rank than men. Several arguments might be
raised to account for this without invoking discrimination in explanation, but they
amount to such unlikely explanations as assuming that women publish inferior bulletins and technical reports, books and articles, but edit superior books; or that women
write the kind of publications less likely to be rewarded in their particular departments.

SUGGESTIONS FOR FURTHER STUDY

It is unlikely that these data based on the academic years 1968–1969 and 1969–
1970 will accurately reflect the representation or rank and pay levels of women on the

faculty in 1972–1973. Pressure from HEW has already led to the review of salaries earned by most women on the academic staff, and some increases have been awarded. On the other hand, budgetary pressures in higher education have contributed to a recent contraction in the academic job market. The problem at the University of Illinois has reached crisis proportions, and numerous terminal contracts have been issued to nontenured staff. Since a higher proportion of men than women are tenured, the proportion of women on the faculty may decrease to below that reported in this study. In order to prevent women from bearing more than their share of the budget cuts, the data on representation must be continuously monitored. When the university once more is able to resume hiring, it will be necessary to monitor the sex ratio of new additions to the faculty.

Additional questions concerning faculty rewards which might profitably be investigated include the extent to which the quality of publications by men and women differ, if at all, the extent to which differences in the ability of faculty members to attract outside offers may be responsible for salary differences, and the extent to which financial need, as reflected by marital status and number of dependents, is responsible for sex differences in salary. Evidence analyzed elsewhere (Ferber and Loeb 1972) suggests that men married to faculty women are paid less than other faculty men, and that married women are paid less than single women.

Future investigations might well include information concerning offers of advancement by institutions other than one's present employer. It is reasonable to expect outside offers to women to occur less frequently because it is assumed that married women are less willing to move. Moreover, outside offers may involve smaller salaries for women than for men because the competition for women has not been as keen as for men; hence, the effects of such offers on salary and rank should not be partialled out in any statistical investigation of sex discrimination. Nevertheless, the extent to which outside offers are discriminatory and influence salary would be worthwhile information. If hiring practices at other institutions have a major impact on salary at a given institution, a one-shot salary equalization will not produce permanent effects; rather, periodic equalizations may be necessary.

An examination of quality of publications also would be a worthwhile refinement in future studies. The quality of articles and reviews might best be measured in terms of the quality of the journal in which they appear. Papers delivered at meetings might similarly be rated by ranking the prestige of the sponsoring organization. No comparable solution suggests itself for ranking books. They might, however, be ranked as beginning, intermediate, or advanced texts, or nontexts, if general agreement can be reached as to the relative merit of these categories.

The argument is often encountered that while women may not experience interrupted careers, they tend to be less stable employees than men because they are expected to follow their husbands. The main flaw in this argument is that if the husband were expected to stay in his job the problem would not arise. It is true that institutions lose women faculty because their husbands obtain better offers elsewhere, but institutions also keep some women who could obtain better offers at other institutions but remain because their husbands remain. Thus, it might be hypothesized that average tenure does not differ for women and men; and this easily could be determined by examining institutional employment records.

SUMMARY

The data concerning one university's faculties indicated that women are hired less frequently than their numbers in the labor market would lead one to expect. They hold lower ranks than men, and their salaries are lower than those of men holding the same rank. The data also suggested that women are underrepresented on administrative committees and in administrative positions. A comparison of the productivity of men and women faculty indicated that there is little difference between the sexes in publication rate or in prior professional experience. Thus, failure to recruit women as actively as men cannot readily be justified.

REFERENCES

Carey, Robert C. 1969. *A study of academic salaries at the University of Illinois, men compared with women. Part II: Fall 1968 salary.* Urbana, Ill.: University Bureau of Institutional Research.

Ferber, Marianne A., and Loeb, Jane W. 1972. *Professors: Productivity and rewards.* Champaign, Ill.: University of Illinois.

Hooper, Mary E., and Chandler, Marjorie O. 1969. *Earned degrees conferred: 1967–68, part A—summary data.* Washington, D.C.: U.S. Department of Health, Education and Welfare, Office of Education, National Center for Educational Statistics.

Katz, David A. 1971. The determinants of faculty salaries and rates of promotion at a large university. Ph.D. dissertation, University of Illinois, Urbana.

Loeb, Jane W., and Ferber, Marianne A. 1971. Sex as predictive of salary and status on a university faculty. *Journal of Educational Measurement,* 8:235–244.

Simon, Rita J., Clark, Shirley M., and Tifft, Larry L. 1966. Of nepotism, marriage, and the pursuit of an academic career. *Sociology of Education,* 39:344–358.

Tousey, Walter C. 1970. *Females at the Urbana campus of the University of Illinois.* Urbana, Ill.: Office of Administrative Studies.

Chapter Thirteen

Discipline Variation in the Status of Academic Women

Laura Morlock

IN THE BRIEF three-year period from the spring of 1969 to the spring of 1972, approximately thirty studies were conducted on the status of women in fourteen academic disciplines. These studies were sponsored by commissions established by professional associations of particular disciplines, by women's caucuses within the associations, and by independent organizations structured along disciplinary lines. Since the studies were generated out of concern about sex discrimination, they tended to cover many of the same factors such as hiring, promotion, salary, tenure, and rank. The chief concern of the studies was to establish the comparative status of women and men within academic disciplines. There was little coordination among researchers except for occasional consultation on problems of sampling, questionnaire design, or data analysis.

Despite their independent origins, the studies were based primarily on three similar data sources: direct compilations from official association records and publications; mail questionnaires sent to college and university departmental chairpersons; and surveys administered to individual graduate students, faculty, or association members. Some studies examined conditions in a variety of departments and institutions, others focused on graduate departments only; some surveyed only women, while others included both women and men.

The major concern of this chapter is the extent to which there are similarities and differences among academic disciplines in the status and career development of women. The specific career dimensions that will be covered are: participation rate; rank distribution; nonladder appointments; tenure patterns; initial appointment level and the hiring process; promotion rate; work load in teaching, research and administration; scholarly productivity; salary; and degree of participation in professional associations. Attention also will be given to variation among academic fields in women's perceptions of sex discrimination.

Since there was no coordination among disciplines in the design of the surveys, reports vary in the size of their samples, the nature of the sampling, the time period in which the study was conducted and the kind of information solicited. This unevenness may provide cues for future investigations into the status of women. Then, too,

AUTHOR'S NOTE: I would like to thank Alice Rossi and Lora Robinson, as well as many women in professional commissions and caucuses, for assistance in collecting information for this chapter.

there are a number of academic disciplines that have not yet undertaken studies of the status of women in their professions. It is hoped that this review will aid them in their research.[1]

WOMEN IN GRADUATE PROGRAMS

The transition from undergraduate to graduate student typically is a step from a world in which a woman is almost equally represented with men in the student body, to a world in which she is part of an increasingly smaller minority: women were about 43 percent of graduating seniors in 1970, 40 percent of students granted master's degrees, but only 13 percent of students earning doctorates. These general statistics can be misleading, however, for once a woman begins her graduate career she is much more likely than during her undergraduate days to move in the circumscribed sphere of her own department. Moreover, this sex ratio differs from discipline to discipline.[2]

Table 13.1 illustrates both the tremendous variation across disciplines in the proportion of women among students, and the progressive decline in the proportion of women in all fields at each successive degree level: the proportion of women among master's degrees recipients in 1969–1970 varied from 83 percent in library science to 7 percent in physics, while the proportion of women among doctorates shows only half this range—from 40 percent in library science to less than 3 percent in physics.

Several studies suggest that the failure of women to attain doctorates in proportion to their numbers in graduate programs is due, in part, to the lower aspiration levels of women students, whether resulting from personal preferences, ambivalent career aspirations, various social and cultural pressures, or discouragement from others. For example, surveys in psychology (Torrey 1971), sociology (Rossi 1970), and political science (Schuck 1969) found that women constitute a larger proportion of students working toward the M.A. than those seeking the Ph.D. degree (see Table 13.2).[3] These data also indicate that aspiration levels alone do not account for the lower percentages of women among doctorates awarded, for in all three fields the

[1] To facilitate access to the research studies themselves, the alphabetized list of references at the end of this chapter is supplemented by a list of studies organized by academic discipline. An index of topics covered in this chapter (e.g., rank distribution of faculty with doctorates), for each discipline, also is included in the Appendix.

[2] Women constitute 55 percent of the graduate students in modern languages, between 30 and 38 percent in American studies, anthropology, psychology, and sociology, and 18 percent in political science. But their proportions fall to 8 percent in law and medical programs, and 5 percent in physics.

[3] Rossi (1970:3), however, found that differences by sex in the proportions seeking the Ph.D. disappear almost completely in "top prestige" sociology departments. In a study of women in the University of Michigan political science department over the past fifteen years, Stokes (1970:36–38) found the proportion of women among graduate students has decreased, but the aspiration level has increased: a decade ago 90 percent of women students were master's degree candidates, but in 1968–1969 nearly half of the women enrolled in graduate study already had a master's degree and were pursuing a Ph.D.

TABLE 13.1. Number and Proportion of Bachelor's, Master's, and Doctor's Degrees Awarded to Women in 1969–1970, and Proportion of Doctorates Awarded to Women in 1920–1968 for Selected Fields

Field of Study	Bachelor's Degrees 1969–1970		Master's Degrees 1969–1970		Doctorates 1969–1970		Doctorates 1920–1968	
	No.	Percent	No.	Percent	No.	Percent	No.	Percent
Library Science	968	91.8	5,436	83.1	16	40.0	18[a]	32.7[a]
Foreign Languages and Literature	15,884	73.6	3,247	62.7	293	33.5	2,736	28.6
English and Literature	37,833	67.0	5,176	61.0	373	31.0	3,146	24.1
Anthropology	2,050	55.2	295	44.4	58	27.0	447	22.1
Psychology	14,741	43.5	1,566	38.0	372	22.3	4,026	20.2
Education	124,819	75.0	14,145	55.3	1,196	20.3	10,280	20.3
Sociology	18,403	59.7	677	37.3	104	19.5	931	17.6
American Studies	699	58.5	107	46.3	8	16.3	23[a]	19.3[a]
Biological Sciences	10,514	27.9	1,844	31.6	469	14.3	6,245	12.1
History	15,066	34.6	1,655	32.7	137	13.2	1,635	13.5
Philosophy	1,086	19.0	121	16.6	44	12.3	525	12.9
Political Science	5,158	19.9	442	21.0	56	10.7	585	8.4
Medicine					713[b]	8.5[b]		
Mathematical Sciences	10,317	37.4	1,674	29.6	96	7.8	747	7.2
Chemistry	2,116	18.2	477	22.5	167	7.7	2,060	5.8
Economics	1,877	10.9	247	12.4	52	6.5	612	5.5
Law					852[b]	5.6[b]		
Physics	329	6.2	158	7.2	37	2.6	456	2.6

SOURCES: Hooper and Chandler 1970; Office of Education, National Center for Educational Statistics 1968, 1969, 1971; National Academy of Sciences 1963 and 1967. Fields are listed in descending order according to the proportion of women among Ph.D.'s awarded in 1969–1970.
[a] Figures are for 1967–1969 only.
[b] Figures and percentages are for "first professional degrees."

proportion of women among Ph.D. students is greater than among Ph.D. recipients. The parity indices in Table 13.2 compare the degree to which the percentage of women among graduate degree recipients approaches the percentage of women who seek degrees. If the proportion of women graduate students equals the proportion of women among degree recipients, the parity index would be 100 percent. Most of the indices, however, fall below this figure. Table 13.2 also shows lower parity indices at the Ph.D. level than the M.A. level for all three fields, as well as a tendency for women in psychology to be less likely to achieve the degrees they desire than their sisters in sociology or political science.[4]

[4] For a discussion of differential dropout rates of women students see Chapter Four in this volume.

TABLE 13.2. Percent Women among Graduate Students Enrolled in Selected Disciplines, Students Seeking M.A. and Ph.D. Degrees, and M.A. and Ph.D. Recipients, 1969–1970

| | Percent Women among: | | | |
Discipline	Graduate Students Enrolled	Degrees Sought	Degrees Awarded	Parity Index[a]
Psychology (Torrey 1971)	38 M.A.	53	38	72%
	Ph.D.	35	22	63%
Sociology (Rossi 1970)	33 M.A.	37	37	100%
	Ph.D.	30	20	67%
Political Science (Schuck 1969)	18 M.A.	21	21	100%
	Ph.D.	15	11	73%

SOURCE: Hooper and Chandler 1970.

[a] The Parity Index is defined as $(\frac{x}{y})$ 100 where

x = percent women among degrees awarded
y = percent women among degrees sought

Our central concern in this chapter, however, is with women who were successful as graduate students by earning their degrees and moving on to an academic career. Our primary focus will be on the question of whether the discipline in which they elected to spend their professional lives made a difference in their academic experiences.

WOMEN FACULTY

Participation Rates by Field

Nationally, women comprise approximately 19 percent of all college and university faculty (Bayer 1970:7). As we would expect from differences by discipline in the distribution of women among graduate students and degree recipients, the proportion of women faculty members varies greatly by field. For example, women constitute 37 percent of all faculty in modern languages, but only 3 percent in physics (see Table 13.3).

Several nationwide surveys have found that the distribution of women varies by level of institution and departmental prestige.[5] As Table 13.4 indicates, these dif-

[5] Bayer (1970:7) found that nationally women constitute about 26 percent of the faculty in junior colleges, 23 percent in four-year colleges, and only 15 percent in universities. In an earlier study by Parrish (1962:99–107) it was found that women comprised about 10 percent of the faculty in twenty leading universities, compared to 23 percent of faculty in higher education as a whole.

TABLE 13.3. Proportion of Women on the Faculty in All Departments, Departments with Doctoral Programs and High-Prestige Departments, for Selected Disciplines (In percentages)

Discipline	All Departments	Ph.D. Departments	High-Prestige Departments
Modern Languages (Howe, Morlock, and Berk 1971; Morlock 1972)	37	25	
Psychology (Torrey 1971)		17	
Anthropology (Vance 1970a)	15		
Sociology (Rossi 1970; Patterson 1971)		15	8
Political Science (Schuck 1969)	8		
Philosophy (Wilson 1971)	7		
History (Ad Hoc Committee 1971)	6[a]		
Law (AALS Special Committee 1970)	4		
Physics (Committee on Women 1972)	3[b]	2	1
National sample (Bayer 1970)	19	15	

[a] Estimated from data for three groups of history departments including departments in co-educational liberal arts colleges, women's colleges and graduate departments.
[b] Includes four-year colleges and universities—no junior colleges.

ferences also are reflected in each discipline. Although women in modern languages are 37 percent of the total faculty, they are only 25 percent of faculty in doctorate granting departments. Similarly, in physics the proportion of women declines from 3 percent in all departments to 2 percent in those with doctoral programs to 1 percent in doctoral departments with high prestige.

We would expect some differences in the participation of women by level and quality of institution due to the lower proportions of women among Ph.D. recipients. But a recent study of anthropology faculty (Lander 1971:6) provides some evidence that these differences persist even after controls are introduced for degree attained and prestige of degree. When comparisons were made between women and men faculty with doctorates from sixteen leading institutions, 30 percent of the men, but only 9 percent of the women, were teaching in high prestige departments.

The range of faculty with part-time appointments varies by sex and discipline: among men faculty, the proportion with part-time appointments ranges from 11 percent (modern languages) to 27 percent (law), while among women faculty, the range is 23 percent (modern languages) to 42 percent (psychology). The last two columns of Table 13.4 highlight the distribution of women among full-time compared with part-time faculty: the proportion women is approximately twice as great among part-time as among full-time faculty in all disciplines except law.

It has often been argued that women faculty may serve an important function as role models, as well as provide encouragement and support to women students. A study of political science departments (Schuck 1969:646) found that in small departments a larger proportion of women on the faculty is associated with a larger

TABLE 13.4. Percentages of Men and Women Faculty with Full-Time and Part-Time Appointments for Selected Disciplines

Disciplines	Women Faculty		Men Faculty		Percent Women among:	
	Full-Time	Part-Time	Full-Time	Part-Time	Full-time Faculty	Part-time Faculty
Anthropology (Vance 1970a)	11–15				14	30
Law Schools (AALS Special Committee 1970)	71	29	73	27	4	4
Modern Languages (Howe, Morlock, and Berk 1971)	77	23	89	11	33	54
Physics (Committee on Women 1972)[a]	68	32	87	13	4	11
Psychology (Torrey 1971)[b]	58	42	76	24	13	26
Sociology (Rossi 1970)[b]	65	35	84	16	11	27

[a] Percentages are based on data from colleges with either undergraduate or master's programs. University faculty are not included.
[b] Percentages are for faculty in graduate departments only.

proportion of women undergraduate majors, but as departments grow larger, this pattern does not hold. The study also shows a slight tendency toward a greater proportion of women graduate degree candidates in departments where women are faculty members. A study of sociology graduate departments (Rossi 1970:10) shows a distinct relationship between the proportions of women among faculty and Ph.D. candidates: 57 percent of the departments in which women constitute at least 10 percent of the faculty have a high proportion of women among Ph.D. candidates, but only 28 percent of the departments in which women comprise less than 10 percent of the faculty, have a high proportion of women among doctoral students. It is impossible to know the extent to which these figures reflect the impact of women faculty on women students, and to what degree they indicate a tendency for departments who welcome women to the faculty to provide a more encouraging atmosphere for women students as well.

Faculty Rank

It has long been known that women are far less numerous in the upper than in the lower ranks of the academic hierarchy. Bernard reported in 1964 that sex distribution by rank varied according to type of institution and discipline, but that differences by sex persisted even among women and men with similar qualifications. The more recent surveys conducted by academic disciplines support and elaborate these earlier findings. Table 13.5 shows a steady decline in the proportion of women at each rank up the academic hierarchy—a pattern characteristic of all nine disciplines reviewed here. This decline is most striking in law schools where the proportion of women full professors is one eighth their proportion as instructors or lecturers, and in sociology where the proportion of women full professors is only one-fifth their proportion within the lowest rank. In anthropology, microbiology, physics, and political science the proportion of women full professors is one fourth to one third their percentage as instructors and lecturers. Only in modern languages, and especially English, is this tendency of diminishing proportions somewhat less noticeable.

TABLE 13.5. Proportion of Women, by Rank, for Selected Disciplines (In percentages)

Discipline	Research Associates	Instructors-Lecturers	Assistant Professors	Associate Professors	Full Professors
English (Wilcox 1970)	—[d]	38	36	25	24
Modern Languages (Howe, Morlock, and Berk 1971)	—[d]	50	33	28	19
Microbiology (Leive 1971)	—[d]	35	19	15	8
Anthropology (Vance 1970a)	22	24	19	14	7
Sociology (La Sorte 1971b)[a]	—[d]	30	18	13	6
Political Science (Schuck 1969)	14[b]	17	9	7	4
History (Ad Hoc Committee 1971)[c]	—[d]	—[d]	8	6	4
Law (AALS Special Committee 1970)	—[d]	16	6	5	2
Physics (Committee on Women 1972)	4	6	3	2	2

[a] Includes only full-time faculty.
[b] Includes "other" appointments.
[c] Percentages computed from data for three groups of sample departments in preliminary and final reports from the Ad Hoc Committee on Women in the [History] Profession.
[d] No information.

It is difficult to compare the rank distributions of women across disciplines without also taking into consideration the availability of qualified women to fill these positions. If we assume that the Ph.D. is a minimum criterion for advancement to full professor and that women candidates for this rank must come from the pool of doctorates produced during the past five decades, then we can compare disciplines by how well they have utilized qualified women.[6] To facilitate this comparison, for each field a "parity index" has been constructed that measures the degree to which qualified women have received appointments at the highest rank. As Table 13.6 indicates, the proportion of women full professors in both modern languages and physics is about three-fourths as large as their proportion among all doctorates in these fields. The parity index is much lower in political science (48 percent) and extremely low in anthropology, history, and sociology: in these fields the index suggests a utilization of women at the full professor level of only one-third their availability.

[6] One further assumption here is that among women doctorates in each field the proportion who desire academic positions is approximately equal.

TABLE 13.6. Relative Parity of Women among Full Professors Compared to Doctorate Pool, by Selected Disciplines

Academic Disciplines	Number of Doctorates Awarded to Women 1920–1968[a]	Percent Women among Doctorates Awarded 1920–1968	Lowest Percentage of Women among Doctorates Awarded for Any Five-Year Period[a]		Percent Women among Full Professors	Parity Index I (based on 1920–1968 percentage women)[b]	Parity Index II (based on lowest percentage women)[c]
			Period of Lowest Percentage	Percent Women			
Modern Languages[d]	5,882	26.0	1950–59[e]	19	19	73%	100%
Anthropology	447	22.1	1940–44	16	7	32%	44%
Sociology	931	17.6	1950–54[f]	13	6	34%	46%
History	1,635	13.5	1950–54	9	4	30%	44%
Political Science	585	8.4	1950–59[e]	6	4	48%	67%
Physics	456	2.6	1950–69[e]	2	2	77%	100%

[a] See Table 13.2 for sources.

[b] Parity Index I is defined as $\left(\frac{x}{y}\right) 100$ where

x = percent women among full professors

y = percent women among doctorates awarded 1920–1968

[c] Parity Index II is defined as $\left(\frac{x}{z}\right) 100$ where

x = percent women among full professors

z = the lowest percentage of women among doctorate recipients for any five-year period from 1920–1968

[d] Includes both English and modern foreign languages.

[e] Percentage of women among doctorates remained at lowest point for several consecutive five-year periods.

[f] Women also constituted 6 percent of doctorates in sociology in 1920–1924 and 1930–1934.

Of course it could be argued that the proportion of women among doctorates produced during the last five decades is an unrealistic base for comparing their percentages among the highest faculty ranks. For it is reasonable to suppose that the majority of faculty who are now full professors received their doctorates during the 1940s and 1950s—a period in which the proportion of women among Ph.D.'s awarded was lower in almost all fields than at any time before or since.[7] Therefore a more conservative estimate for the availability of women would use the lowest percentage of women among doctorates produced during the past few decades. When we compare disciplines on a second parity index incorporating this more stringent standard, we find that only in modern languages and physics are the proportions of women among full professors equal to the lowest possible estimate of their availability. In anthropology, sociology, and history the percentages of women who received Ph.D.'s during the lowest periods of women doctorate production still were more than twice as large as the percentage of women full professors.

It is difficult to explain these differences by discipline in the professional achievement of qualified women. One hypothesis might be that the variation is attributable to differences in the personal circumstances of women by academic field. Several disciplinary studies have noted the special problems of married women in academe. Certainly the attempt to combine family responsibilities with professional activities is more likely to create career discontinuity and lack of mobility for women than for men.[8] Indeed, a much larger proportion of women than men elect not to combine

[7] Explanations offered for this trend include the effects of the depression and the aftermath of World War II, and a popular view throughout the late 1940s and 1950s that women's talents were best utilized in the home. See Bernard 1964.

[8] Research in several fields has documented these effects on women's academic careers. Harmon's study of doctorates (1968:71–73) notes that married women are almost twice as likely as single women to move back and forth between academic and nonacademic positions, suggesting that marriage and family responsibilities may cause career disruptions and require more frequent job changes. A survey of women librarians in academic settings finds that one in seven women left library work for six months or more due to marriage or family responsibilities (Schiller 1969:1100). A recent study of microbiologists (Kashket and Huang 1972) reports that 29 percent of the women versus 19 percent of the men have experienced discontinuities in professional careers. Of those women with disrupted careers, half report they would have worked had child care been available. A survey of women physicists on college faculties (Committee on Women in Physics 1972: Appendix D) found that 32 percent experienced discontinuous careers, due primarily to family responsibilities and maternity. Of these women, one-third would have continued work if child care had been available, and one-half would have remained working if they could have obtained part-time positions.

Of course, these studies of current faculty members do not indicate the numbers of women with interrupted careers who have not returned to academe. Although we do not have data of this nature by discipline, Astin (1969) has found that among those women who received doctorates in 1958–1959, 91 percent currently are working and 80 percent have experienced no disruptions in their careers since receiving the Ph.D.

Family responsibilities not only create more interruptions for women than men, they also impose greater limitations on mobility. For example, a recent survey of microbiologists (Kash-

TABLE 13.7. Faculty Marital Status, by Sex, for Selected Disciplines (In percentages)

Discipline and Sex	Marital Status		
	Currently Married	Divorced, Separated, Widowed	Never Married
Sociology (Patterson 1971)[a]			
Men	90		
Women	57		
Psychology (Keiffer and Cullen 1970)			
Men	80	5	15
Women	55	20	25
Physics (Committee on Women 1972)[b]			
Men			
Women	46		
Microbiology (Kashket and Huang 1972)			
Men	89		
Women	44		
National sample (Bayer 1970)			
Men	87	3	10
Women	47	12	40

[a] Data are for faculty in graduate departments only.
[b] Data are for women in four-year colleges only; universities are not included.

academic with marital and parental roles: women are much less likely than their male colleagues to be married, and if married less likely to have children (Bayer 1970). As Table 13.7 indicates, women in psychology and sociology are somewhat more likely to be married than women in either physics or microbiology. Although we have data on the rank distribution and availability of women in only two of these fields—sociology and physics—it is interesting to note that physics has both a higher proportion of women doctorates who have achieved full professorships and a lower percentage of married women.

Married women whose husbands are in academe are especially likely to be affected adversely by restrictive employment policies. Approximately 35 percent of all col-

ket and Huang 1972) asked those men and women with professional spouses whether their husbands or wives support their career ambitions with enthusiasm, with ambivalence, with reluctance, or not at all. Although 81 percent of the women versus 72 percent of the men feel that they are supported with enthusiasm, 90 percent of the women with enthusiastic support from their husbands responded that they would move for professional reasons only if their spouse could obtain satisfactory employment before relocating. In contrast, 50 percent of those men with enthusiastic support from their professional wives said they would move under any circumstances, and 26 percent would move with the hope that their wives eventually also would find satisfactory employment. Similar findings were reported in a recent survey of women physicists on college faculties (Committee on Women in Physics 1972: Appendix D).

leges and universities currently have specific rules prohibiting nepotism in the hiring of faculty (see Oltman 1970).[9] Strong evidence is provided by a recent study of modern language departments (Morlock et al. 1972) which showed that such regulations do limit appointments for women.[10] As Table 13.8 indicates, departments

TABLE 13.8. Proportion of Women at Each Rank in Modern Language Departments, by Type of University Nepotism Rules (In percentages)

Rank	Written Antinepotism Regulations	Unwritten Antinepotism Regulations	Regulations Prohibiting Supervision by a Relative	No Antinepotism Regulations
Instructor or lecturer	38	28	42	35
Assistant Professor	17	15	24	30
Associate Professor	13	15	15	18
Full Professor	7	5	8	10
Total	18	17	21	23
Number of departments	(64)	(37)	(32)	(95)

SOURCE: Morlock et al. 1972. Reprinted by permission of the Modern Language Association.

which are bound by university antinepotism policies (written or unwritten) tend to have lower percentages of women at all ranks in comparison to departments which are not subject to such rules. Departments bound by regulations prohibiting the *supervision* of one relative by another (e.g., a husband who is a chairman recommending for promotion a wife who is a departmental staff member) tend to fall between those departments with and those without antinepotism regulations in respect to proportions of women at each rank. Furthermore, among those departments which are not restricted by university rules (see Table 13.9), those with antinepotism policies of their own have lower proportions of women full-time faculty at each rank than departments without such regulations.[11]

[9] Such regulations are found most often at large schools, least often on small campuses and at private and women's colleges. One study (AALS Special Committee on the Status of Women 1970) found that 45 percent of all law schools are subject to such restrictions in hiring.

[10] Among the departments surveyed in 1971, 27 percent are part of universities with written antinepotism rules which prohibit the employment of both a husband and wife as faculty members; 15 percent are subject to similar, although unwritten, policies; and 13 percent report written rules which do not restrict the employment of relatives, but which do prohibit the participation of relatives in decisions which affect the other's terms of employment. In addition, among those departments which are not bound by universitywide and antinepotism rules, 17 percent have departmental policies against the hiring of both a husband and wife.

[11] Several studies questioned women concerning the impact of nepotism restrictions on their careers. A survey of women physicists in universities (Committee on Women in Physics 1972: Appendix G) finds that 22 percent of married women commented on hardships worked

TABLE 13.9. Proportion of Women at Each Faculty Rank by Type of
Departmental Nepotism Regulation (In percentages)

Rank	Unwritten Antinepotism Regulation	No Antinepotism Regulation
Instructor or lecturer	32	33
Assistant Professor	21	25
Associate Professor	12	18
Full Professor	7	9
Total	20	22
Number of departments	(25)	(116)

SOURCE: Morlock et al. 1972.

In addition to employment policies, other factors such as academic level and departmental quality have an important impact on the rank distribution of women faculty. Table 13.10 shows that in several disciplines at all ranks the percentage of women is lower in doctorate granting departments than in all departments combined; and in most fields there is a further decrease when we examine only those doctorate-granting departments with high prestige.

Our discussion up to this point has focused on comparing disciplines according to the proportion of women at each rank, which we have viewed as a function of the percentage of women within the pool of doctorates produced over the past few decades within each field. We may achieve a somewhat different perspective by holding aside questions concerning the proportion of women faculty, and instead examine the way those women who have achieved positions in academe are utilized and rewarded in comparison to their male colleagues.

Table 13.11 reflects marked differences by field in the percentage breakdown of

---

by antinepotism restrictions. Simon and Rosenthal (1967:127–128) report that among a sample of women who received Ph.D.'s between 1958 and 1963, about 15 percent of the married women feel their careers have been affected by nepotism rules. These women have not been unable to locate positions; rather, "they have been unable to find the type of job at the level of institution and at a salary to which they aspire and for which they appear to be professionally competent." In a comparison of productivity by sex they find that women who complain of nepotism restrictions have a greater number of publications than other women, whether single or married, or their male colleagues.

In view of the demonstrated restrictions which antinepotism rules can place on the careers of married women, it is encouraging to find evidence that the proportion of institutions with such policies appears to be diminishing. Oltman (1970) reports some liberalizing of nepotism regulations in public institutions over the past decade. In addition, a survey of modern language departments (Morlock et al. 1972:10) finds that among those departments that function under written or unwritten rules which prohibit the employment of more than one family member, approximately one-third report discussions underway at the university level to eliminate or amend these policies.

TABLE 13.10. Proportion of Women by Rank and Academic Discipline in All Departments, Ph.D.-granting Departments, and Departments with High Prestige (In percentages)

Discipline and Type of Department[a]	Instructors- Lecturers	Assistant Professors	Associate Professors	Full Professors
Modern Languages (Howe, Morlock, and Berk 1971)				
Total	50	33	28	19
Ph.D. programs		17	13	7
Psychology (Torrey 1971)				
Total[b]				
Ph.D. programs	33	17	11	7
Sociology (Rossi 1970, La Sorte 1971b)				
Total	30	18	13	6
Ph.D. programs[c]	27	14	9	4
High prestige[c]	34	5	5	1
Political Science (Schuck 1969)				
Total	17	9	7	4
Ph.D. programs[d]	5	6	6	2
High prestige[d]	5	7	5	1
History (Ad Hoc Committee 1971)				
Total[e]		8	6	4
Ph.D. programs		2	2	1
Physics (Commission on Women 1972)				
Total	6	3	2	2
Ph.D. programs	6	2	2	1
High prestige[f]	3	1	1	1

[a] "Total" includes those departments which offer the bachelor's, master's, or doctorate as the highest degree. High-prestige departments are a subset of departments with Ph.D. programs.

[b] No information.

[c] Percentages include full-time faculty only. High prestige category includes top seventeen departments.

[d] Only the nine "largest producers of doctorates" are included in the first category. The high prestige category includes the top eighteen departments, some of which are also top doctorate producers.

[e] Percentages computed by combining three sample groups of departments listed in the preliminary report.

[f] Includes top ten physics departments.

TABLE 13.11. Academic Rank Distributions, by Sex, for Selected Disciplines (In percentages)

Discipline and Sex	Research Associates	Instructors-Lecturers	Assistant Professors	Associate Professors	Full Professors	Parity Index (for full professors)[a]
Physics (Committee on Women 1972)						64%
Men	3	12	33	24	28	
Women	4	27	32	19	18	
English (Wilcox 1970)						64%
Men		26	32	20	22	
Women		36	35	15	14	
Law (AALS Special Committee 1970)						61%
Men		3	13	22	62	
Women		13	22	28	38	
Political Science (Schuck 1969)						45%
Men	6[b]	11	32	20	31	
Women	10[b]	25	33	16	14	
Microbiology (Leive 1971)						45%
Men	6	24	21	20	29	
Women	20	17	27	22	13	
Modern Languages (Howe, Morlock, and Berk 1971)						38%
Men		32	31	17	21	
Women		54	26	11	8	
Sociology (La Sorte 1971b)						37%
Men[c]		14	32	24	30	
Women[c]		32	38	19	11	
National Sample (Bayer 1970)						36%
Men	6[b]	20	28	22	25	
Women	7[b]	39	29	16	9	

[a] The Parity Index is a measure comparing the distributions of men and women at full professor rank. If the percentages of men and women were equal, the index would register 100 percent; percentages below this figure indicate the extent to which the proportion women falls below that for men. The index is defined as $(\frac{x}{y})$ 100 where

x = proportion women who are full professors
y = proportion men who are full professors

[b] Includes "other appointments."

[c] Percentages in sociology are for full-time faculty only. Figures for other disciplines include all faculty members.

both women and men faculty across ranks. For example, the percentage of men who are full professors ranges from 62 percent in law schools to 21 percent in modern language departments, while the percentage of women at this rank varies from 38 percent in law to 8 percent in modern languages. In spite of these differences among fields in the proportion of faculty at each rank, the position of women in relation to their male colleagues within the same field is remarkably constant from discipline to discipline. With few exceptions, women are more likely than men to hold the ranks of instructor and assistant professor and less likely to hold appointments in the two upper ranks. But the parity index reveals a range across disciplines in the *degree* of status difference between the sexes. Thus, women in sociology and modern languages are about one-third as likely as their male colleagues to achieve the rank of full professor (a proportion close to the national norm), but women are approximately two-thirds as likely to attain this rank in physics and English.

Differences by sex in educational attainment account for some portion of the imbalance in rank distribution between women and men. Nationally, 22 percent of women faculty and 46 percent of men hold the Ph.D. There are, however, differences by discipline in Ph.D. attainment by sex. Women in philosophy and anthropology faculties are nearly as likely as men to have the Ph.D., while men in modern languages are twice as likely to have the Ph.D. as their women colleagues (see Table 13.12).

By confining our attention only to those faculty with Ph.D.'s we find that differences by sex in status are reduced somewhat, although substantial discrepancies still exist at the ranks of assistant and full professor (see Table 13.13). Again there are differences by field: the Ph.D. improves the level of parity between men and women

TABLE 13.12. Percentage of Faculty Members of Selected Disciplines with Ph.D. Degrees, by Sex

Discipline	Men (Percent)	Women (Percent)	Ratio: Women to Men
Philosophy (Wilson 1971)	57	54	0.95
Anthropology (Vance 1970a)[a]	53	49	0.92
Physics (Committee on Women 1972)	65	48	0.74
Sociology (La Sorte 1971b)[b]	71	46	0.65
Modern Languages (Howe, Morlock, and Berk 1971)	50	25	0.50
All disciplines: national sample (Bayer 1970)	46	22	0.48

[a] Figures include percentages of men and women who obtained a Ph.D. from one of the fourteen major degree-granting institutions in anthropology.
[b] Percentages are calculated only for full-time faculty listed as sociologists in the National Register.

among full professors in modern languages and physics, but seems to make little difference in microbiology or sociology. Table 13.14 combines the indices from Table 13.11 and Table 13.13 to facilitate comparison.

TABLE 13.13. Academic Rank of Faculty of Selected Disciplines with Ph.D. Degrees, by Sex (In percentages)

Discipline	Sex	Instructors-Lecturers	Assistant Professors	Associate Professors	Full Professors	Parity Index: (Full Professors)[a]
Physics						82%
(Committee on Women 1972)	Men[b]	3	33	26	34	
	Women[b]	9	34	22	28	
Philosophy						72%
(Wilson 1971)	Men	6	30	25	39	
	Women	10	41	21	28	
Modern Languages						68%
(Howe, Morlock, and Berk 1971)	Men	5	33	24	38	
	Women	14	35	25	26	
Microbiology						49%
(Leive 1971)	Men	3	30	28	39	
	Women	9	42	30	19	
Sociology						38%
(Rossi 1970)[c]	Men	1	31	26	42	
	Women	8	54	22	16	

[a] The Parity Index is defined as $(\frac{x}{y})$ 100 where

x = proportion women who are full professors
y = proportion men who are full professors

[b] Four percent of men and seven percent of women are research associates, research assistants or "other."

[c] Includes only full-time faculty in graduate departments. Other disciplines include both full-time and part-time faculty in all departments.

Disciplinary studies have sought explanations for disparities in rank by examining differences by sex among faculty not only in educational attainment but also in the prestige of the department from which the doctorate was acquired, in academic specialty, marital status, and publication rates. In a study of sociology graduate departments, Patterson (1971:230) found no difference by sex among faculty in respect to the prestige level of departments from which the Ph.D. was earned. Nonetheless, 72 percent of the men and only 41 percent of the women in these departments held appointments at the ranks of associate or full professor. Much the same pattern was found in a study of anthropologists (Vance 1970b).

TABLE 13.14. Parity Indices for All Full Professors and Those with Ph.D. Degrees for Selected Disciplines[a]

Discipline	All Full Professors	Full Professors with Ph.D.'s
Physics	64%	82%
Microbiology	45%	49%
Modern Languages	38%	68%
Sociology[b]	37%	38%

[a] Parity indices are taken from Tables 13.11 and 13.13.

[b] For sociology, problems arise in comparing the two indices, for the first is based on data for all full-time full professors in all departments (La Sorte 1971b), while the second is based on information for full professors with Ph.D.'s in graduate departments only (Rossi 1970). In the other disciplines, both indices are based on a single sample of departments.

Patterson (1971:231) explored the possibility that women in sociology graduate departments may experience rank inequity because they have specialized in different areas than their male colleagues. This was clearly not a factor, however, for she found only slight differences by sex in sociological specialties.

The impact of marital status on rank attainment has been investigated for women doctorates in the natural and social sciences, humanities, and education (Simon, Clark, and Galway 1967:228–229). The largest rank differences between women and men were found at the level of associate professor in each of the four fields. In addition, Simon, Clark, and Galway report that married women were less likely than unmarried women to have been promoted to the rank of associate professor in either the natural or social sciences, and less likely than unmarried women to have atained the rank of full professor in all four academic areas.

Hoffman et al. (undated:3) examined the extent to which sex differences in rank among psychologists could be accounted for by different publication rates. In a comparison of twenty-five women who were relatively well known through their publications, with a sample of twenty-five equally eminent men, they found that 87 percent of the men, but only 35 percent of the women, held full professorships.

Part-Time Appointments

We have observed that women are a significant proportion of part-time faculty. As Table 13.15 makes clear, for the four fields in which we have data by type of appointment, the proportion of women is higher at all ranks for part-time positions than for full-time appointments, with the single exception of instructors in psychology. Furthermore, when the relative positions of women and men part-time faculty are compared with differences by sex among all appointments, it is clear that compared to men faculty the status of part-time women is better than the status of full-time faculty women (see Table 13.16). Table 13.17 combines the indices from

TABLE 13.15. Proportion of Women among Part-Time and Full-Time
Faculty, by Rank, for Selected Disciplines

Discipline and Type of Appointment	Instructors- Lecturers	Assistant Professors	Associate Professors	Full Professors
Modern Languages (Howe, Morlock, and Berk 1971)				
Part-time	56	56	33	38
Full-time	46	32	28	18
Difference	+10	+24	+5	+20
Psychology (Torrey 1971)[a]				
Part-time	33	25	17	11
Full-time	37	15	10	7
Difference	−4	+10	+7	+4
Sociology (Rossi 1970)[a]				
Part-time	33	31	16	7
Full-time	27	14	9	4
Difference	+6	+17	+7	+3
Physics (Committee on Women 1972)[b]				
Part-time	10	15	7	14
Full-time	7	3	4	5
Difference	+3	+12	+3	+9

[a] Data are based on graduate departments only.
[b] Percentages are based on data for faculty in colleges with either undergraduate or master's programs. University faculty are not included.

Table 13.11 and Table 13.16 to facilitate comparison of the relative utilization of women part-time professors to all full-time professors for these disciplines. Although improvement in the position of part-time women is noticeable in all three fields, it is especially apparent in physics where among part-time faculty, women are more likely than men to have attained the rank of full professor.

Nonladder Appointments

It has been noted that among natural and social scientists women are much more likely than men, and married women more likely than single women, to hold such nonladder positions as research associate (see Simon, Clark and Galway 1967). Disciplinary studies have found that research associateships are held by 6 percent of the men and 20 percent of the women in microbiology. The sex ratio of research associateships in other fields are: 6 versus 10 percent in political science, 3 versus 4 percent in physics (see Table 13.11) and 6 versus 9 percent in sociology graduate departments (Rossi 1970:6). Several studies show that women are also more likely to hold titles below the level of research associate. In microbiology, 10 percent of the women, but only 2 percent of the men, hold the position of research assistant (Leive

TABLE 13.16. Academic Rank Distributions for Part-Time Faculty, by Sex, for Selected Disciplines (In percentages)

Discipline and Sex	Rank				Parity Index (for Full Professor)[a]
	Instructors-Lecturers	Assistant Professors	Associate Professors	Full Professors	
Physics (Committee on Women 1972)[b]					125%
Men	46	23	15	16	
Women	39	32	8	20	
Modern Languages (Howe, Morlock, and Berk 1971)					57%
Men	80	8	5	7	
Women	85	9	2	4	
Sociology (Rossi 1970)[c]					56%
Men	52	16	9	23	
Women	70	20	5	5	
Psychology (Torrey 1971)[c]					36%
Men	43	17	18	22	
Women	64	18	11	8	

[a] Parity Index is defined as $(\frac{x}{y})$ 100 where

$x =$ proportion women among part-time full professors
$y =$ proportion men among part-time full professors

[b] Percentages are based on data for faculty in colleges with either undergraduate or master's programs. University faculty are not included.

[c] Data are based on graduate departments only.

TABLE 13.17. Parity Indices for All Full Professors and Those with Part-Time Appointments for Selected Disciplines[a]

Discipline	All Full Professors	Part-Time Full Professors
Physics	64%	125%
Modern Languages	38%	57%
Sociology[b]	37%	56%

[a] Parity indices are taken from Tables 13.11 and 13.16.

[b] For sociology, problems arise in comparing the two indices, for the first is based on data for all full-time full professors in all departments (La Sorte, 1971b), while the second is based on information for part-time full professors in graduate departments only (Rossi 1970). In the other two disciplines both indices are based on the same sample of departments.

1971:59). Similarly, 33 percent of the women, but only 11 percent of the men in immunology hold "catch-all" titles outside the faculty ladder (Committee on the Status of Women [Immunology] 1971:4).[12]

Tenure

Differences between academic men and women in the attainment of faculty ranks are reflected in tenure patterns. Nationally, about half of all faculty men, but only 38 percent of all faculty women occupy tenured positions (Bayer 1970). The proportion of men with tenure is lowest in four-year colleges and highest in universities, while the proportion of tenured women is highest in two-year colleges and lowest in universities (see Table 13.18).

TABLE 13.18. Proportion of Faculty with Tenure, by Sex,
for Selected Disciplines (In percentages)

Discipline	Men Faculty with Tenure	Women Faculty with Tenure	Tenured Faculty who are Women
National sample: total (Bayer 1970)	49	38	
Two-year colleges	47	42	
Four-year colleges	44	38	
Universities	52	35	
Modern Languages (Howe, Morlock, and Berk 1971)			
All departments	43[a]	33[a]	30
Graduate departments			22
Psychology: graduate departments (Torrey 1971)	60	45	11
Sociology: graduate departments (Patterson 1971)	67	33	29
Medical schools (Committee on Women's Immunology 1971)	39[b]	19[b]	5[b]

[a] Percentages are computed from unpublished tables.
[b] Percentages are based on data from the combined faculty of ten medical schools.

As we would be led to expect from our findings on sex differences in academic rank, tenure patterns vary not only by type of school but also by field. Although in all four disciplines that report tenure patterns, men are more likely than women to oc

[12] It also may be true that women are more likely than men to be employed in departments outside their own field. In a study of anthropologists, Fischer and Golde (1968:341) found that although women in 1965 were 18 percent of all new teachers in anthropology, and 10 percent of full-time faculty members in graduate departments, they were 25 percent of anthropologists found in departments other than anthropology.

cupy tenured positions, the proportion of tenured men varies from approximately one and a quarter times the percentage of women in modern languages to twice the percentage of women in sociology graduate departments and medical schools. Patterson (1971:228–229) found that both women and men in high prestige sociology departments are more likely to have tenure than their colleagues at less prestigious institutions, but the greater proportion of men than of women who hold tenure remains about the same regardless of the prestige ranking of the department with which they are affiliated.

The differences by sex in tenure and rank that we have observed are but two indications of differences in the career patterns of academic women and men. In their efforts to understand the process by which these differences occur, several researchers investigated whether women are more likely than men to be hired initially at lower ranks, and whether once hired, women are promoted more slowly.

Hiring and Initial Appointments

Nationwide studies to determine whether differences by sex exist in initial faculty appointments report somewhat mixed results. A survey of 7,500 new college teachers appointed in 1964 found that, in comparison to their male colleagues, women were appointed at lower ranks, received lower salaries, and were assigned heavier teaching loads (Brown 1965:163–165).[13] These women, however, were less qualified academically than men: they were only half as likely to hold a doctorate degree, had published less and were somewhat less likely to have received their degree from a high prestige graduate school.

It obviously is desirable to compare women and men with similar educational qualifications. One study of recent doctorates in the natural and social sciences concluded that beginning academic rank is *not* related to sex, although initial salary differentials between women and men do exist regardless of rank, major field of specialty, or work setting (Bayer and Astin 1968). However, in an even more equally matched group of women and men college teachers who had received Woodrow Wilson Fellowships, Henderson (quoted in Robinson 1971:2–3) found that when compared to men with equivalent qualifications, women doctorates obtained their first appointment at a lower rank and at a lower salary for the same rank.[14]

[13] Furthermore, women filled disproportionately high percentages of the positions at the least prestigious schools and were underrepresented in schools with high prestige. In general, they had fewer job options from which to choose than their male counterparts.

[14] These differences could not be explained by differences by sex in qualifications, institutional preferences, subject specialization, teaching level, or type of institution. In addition, Henderson found that men had three times the initial job offers, and were better able than women to attain the positions they preferred. Not surprisingly, more women than men expressed dissatisfaction with their first job.

Disciplinary studies in anthropology (Lander 1971) and history (Ad Hoc Committee 1971) echo Henderson's findings. Among recent Ph.D.'s in anthropology, women were less likely than their male peers to receive appointments as assistant professors, but more than twice as likely to be hired in the nonladder position of research associate (see Table 13.19). Differences between women and men doctorates in history are even more striking: women were six times more likely than men to be hired as instructors or lecturers, and only about half as likely to receive assistant professorships.

TABLE 13.19. Rank of First Faculty Position after Obtaining Ph.D. in Anthropology and History, by Sex (In percentages)

	New Ph.D.'s hired as:		
Discipline	Research Associate	Instructor-Lecturer	Assistant Professor
Anthropology (Lander 1971)			
Men	8	18	55
Women	20	19	40
History (Ad Hoc Committee 1971)			
Men		5	77
Women		32	47

There also are data for young historians that show parallel differences in starting salaries. The median salary in 1970 for these recent Ph.D.'s was between $10,000 and $12,000. However, 66 percent of the men but only 35 percent of the women fell within this salary bracket. In contrast, 51 percent of the women but only 15 percent of the men in 1970 were earning salaries of less than $10,000. These figures are particularly surprising in light of the fact that the women were, if anything, better prepared than their male cohort: about one-third of the women in contrast to only one-fourth of the men earned their doctorates at one of the ten top-ranking departments in the country.

The Ad Hoc Committee on Women in History concluded that "the first job poses a greater problem for women than for men, and . . . it constitutes one of the most acute pressure points in the career development of women historians" (Ad Hoc Committee 1971:17). There are a number of reasons for this. Although almost all men and women found employment, differences by sex existed both in the kind of position obtained and the respondents' reasons for accepting these jobs. For example, of those who found jobs in teaching or academic administration, men were more likely than women to be employed at four-year colleges (33 percent versus 24 percent) and in state universities (43 percent versus 28 percent). In contrast, women were much more likely than men to have accepted positions at junior colleges (9 percent versus 2 percent), and at private universities (16 percent versus 11 percent).

Women and men also differed in the range of opportunities they had with respect to their first jobs. In all, 54 percent of the employed men, but only 26 percent of the women, had received more than one job offer. Of the men, 55 percent, in contrast to 37 percent of the women, credited their placements to the aid of their dissertation supervisors or the departmental or university placement services. Whether these differences were the result of favoritism to men, indifference, or the inability of women for personal reasons to take advantage of placement services, it is clear that institutional aids in job placement were not as useful to women (Ad Hoc Committee 1971:19).

When men and women were asked to rank in importance their reasons for accepting their current job, over half of the women listed job scarcity, location, and "failure of spouse to be relocated elsewhere." Men also listed job scarcity and location, as well as a wide range of other considerations not important to women. For example, women regarded salary as unimportant in their decision twice as often as men, and also were less likely than men to take into consideration library facilities, chances for future promotion, and institutional prestige. The committee concluded that "for women, the constraint posed by their lack of mobility was clearly the paramount factor in their decision" (Ad Hoc Committee 1971:21).

The Committee on Women in Physics (1972:B–2) compared employment plans of women and men degree recipients at the time of receiving their degrees for the period 1958–1970, and concluded that married women had more difficulty in locating a position than either single women or men.[15] Converse and Converse (1971: 346–347) also found that more women than men encountered problems in initial job placements in political science. They report that women expressed much lower levels of satisfaction with their first jobs than men, and these differences were even more marked among those holding the doctorate.

Some hope for improvement in initial placements for women is provided by a recent study of new appointments in modern languages (Morlock et al. 1972). This survey of departments reports that the proportion of women among new faculty appointments for the 1971–1972 academic year was greater than the proportion of women currently on the full-time staff for all ranks except instructor or lecturer. Furthermore, at the level of assistant professor the increase was substantial: although women are only 21 percent of all full-time assistant professors in modern language departments, they are 31 percent of new appointments at this rank—a percentage equal to the average proportion of women among doctorates for the last

---

[15] They found that at the time of receiving their degree the percentages of those with definite commitments for gainful employment were 60 percent for married men, 46 percent for single men, 45 percent for single women, and 40 percent for married women (Committee on Women in Physics 1972:B-4).

five years. Twenty-one departments, or 9 percent of the sample queried, reported that they recently had made special efforts to consider women for faculty openings.

Promotion

Several studies suggest that, once appointed, women advance more slowly than men up the academic hierarchy. In a study of 10,000 women and men who received doctorates between the years 1935 and 1960, Harmon (1968:87) found that when those who had always worked in academe were compared, the rate at which women achieved the status of full professor was slower than that for men, a disparity that varied somewhat by field. The average lag ranged from two to five years in the biosciences up to as much as a decade in the social sciences. Harmon also found a difference by marital status. Single women, in general, led their married women colleagues by five to ten years, and at each time period under study 10 percent to 20 percent more of the single than married women had achieved the rank of full professor. (See Chapter Seven for a review of this study.)

A study of more recent science doctorates also found differences by field in promotion rates (Bayer and Astin 1968). The very small proportion of women in the natural sciences tended to receive promotions comparable to their male colleagues. However, among social scientists, a greater proportion of whom are women, men tended to be promoted more rapidly than their female counterparts.

Even when such factors as type of work and publication rate are held constant, women are promoted more slowly. Henderson reports that careers of women fellowship recipients advance more slowly than those of men even though the two groups are similar in their publication rates, teaching loads, and the degree of satisfaction they report in their work (quoted in Robinson 1971:8).[16] Studies in sociology, psychology, microbiology, anthropology, and political science all provide additional evidence that women advance less rapidly than men, even after controls are introduced for such factors as level or prestige of degree, or productivity rates.

Patterson (1971:229) found that women in graduate sociology departments are half as likely to attain senior positions as men, and furthermore, those who achieve such positions must wait at least a decade longer than men for promotion to the senior level. Although more than three-fourths of the men achieve tenure by their forties, the majority of women (55 percent) do not attain tenured positions until

---

[16] Simon, Clark, and Galway (1967:229), in a study of doctorates employed full-time who received their degrees between 1958 and 1963, report that when the proportion of tenured women are compared by year of degree, initially men receive tenure earlier than women, but this difference between men and *unmarried* women decreases over time, and when those doctorates who received their degree in 1962–1963 are compared, the proportions of single and married women with tenure are higher than the proportion of their male cohort. Simon et al. view this reversal for the sample as a whole as a consequence of the tendency for women in education to receive tenure early.

their fifties (see Table 13.20). Patterson reports that marital status has little effect on the age at which men achieve tenured positions. For women, however, marital status has a significant impact: the majority of single women attain tenured positions by their fifties while married women must wait until their sixties before the majority advance beyond the rank of assistant professor. (See Chapter Fifteen for further detail on differences by sex in tenure attainment.)

TABLE 13.20. **Percentage of Faculty with Tenure in Sociology Graduate Departments, by Age and Sex**

Age	Men	Women
Under 40	29	10
40–49	79	34
50–59	97	55
60 or older	100	67

SOURCE: Patterson 1971:229.

Similar findings are reported by Hoffman et al. (undated:2–3) in their study of American Psychological Association Fellows in the areas of general and experimental psychology. Their data indicate that among those fellows who received the Ph.D. prior to 1950 and who now hold a faculty rank, 30 percent of the men but only 7 percent of the women are full professors. The men in this sample worked an average of 10.8 years after obtaining the doctorate to achieve this status, while the women worked 15.2 years from the time they obtained the Ph.D. to their appointment to full professorship.

A survey of microbiologists (Leive 1971:59) also reports that a longer time is required for women Ph.D.'s to reach a given rank than their male colleagues. For example, twice as many men as women have achieved the rank of full professor, and men are three times more likely to reach this rank within five to nine years after obtaining their degrees (see Table 13.21).

A study of career progress among anthropologists controlled for both the impact of academic degree and its prestige value. Vance (1970b:8–10) compared five-year cohorts of women and men who received Ph.D.'s from fourteen selected anthropology departments within the last thirty years. She concluded that in every cohort a substantially greater number of males had reached the level of full professor by the time of her study. For example, of those in the 1940–1944 cohort, men were four times more likely than women to have attained the rank of full professor (see Table 13.22). Men also far outpaced women in more recent cohorts. Of those who attained their doctorates in 1960–1964, five times as many men as women are full professors.

Converse and Converse (1971:346) compared the career progress of women and

TABLE 13.21. Time Required for Men and Women in Microbiology with
Doctoral Degrees to Reach a Given Rank (In percentages)

	Instructor or Lecturer		Assistant Professor		Associate Professor		Full Professor	
Years since Degree N =	Men (32)	Women (17)	Men (348)	Women (82)	Men (326)	Women (58)	Men (454)	Women (38)
0–1	44	35	17	10	2	5	3	—
2–4	19	23	49	32	10	7	3	1
5–9	28	18	28	44	41	33	16	6
10–19	6	6	4	11	44	40	32	53
20–29	0	18	1	2	2	14	32	29
30 or more	3	0	1	1	1	3	16	11
Rank distribution by Sex								
Men (N = 1160)	3		30		28		39	
Women (N = 195)	9		42		30		19	

SOURCE: Leive 1971:59. Data reprinted by permission of the American Society for Microbiology.

TABLE 13.22. Percentage of Women and Men Holding Ph.D.'s from
Fourteen Selected Anthropology Departments Who Have Reached the Rank of
Full Professor, by Year of Degree

Year Degree Granted	Women	Men
1940–1944	20	79
1945–1949	57	91
1950–1954	40	80
1955–1959	35	64
1960–1964	3	16
1965–1970	0	2

SOURCE: Vance, 1970b:10. Reprinted by permission of the author.

men political scientists, controlling not only for degree level, but also for rate of
productivity. In their sample of doctorates with full-time appointments, they found
time lags in the promotion rate of women at every rank. However, differences by
sex were greatest in respect to the time required to achieve the ranks of associate
and full professor. They report that when controls for productivity were introduced,
these differences diminished somewhat but were not completely eliminated.

In summary, consensus exists among studies in a variety of disciplines that
women advance up the academic ladder at a slower rate than their male counterparts. Furthermore, these differences in professional achievement are not merely re-

flections of differences by sex in degree level, prestige of degree, or rates of productivity.

Teaching, Research and Administration

Nationwide studies of faculty members have found that women spend considerably more time in teaching than their male colleagues who are more likely to combine teaching duties with research or administration (Harmon 1965; Bayer 1970; Oltman 1970). These differences by sex are reflected in several disciplinary studies. Leive (1971:58–59) reports that 18 percent of women in contrast to only 8 percent of men microbiologists spend the majority of their time teaching. Half of the men but only one-third of the women devote at least 10 percent of their time to administrative duties. Similarly, La Sorte (1971b:305–306) found that although the great majority of sociologists with doctorates combine other duties with teaching, twice as many women as men report only teaching activities, while twice as many men are engaged in administration in addition to teaching.

Most disciplinary studies report very low percentages of women in top administrative posts. For example, the proportion of women among department chairpersons is 3 percent in college physics departments (Committee on Women in Physics 1972:Appendix D), 1 percent in graduate sociology departments (Rossi 1970:11), 5 percent in American studies programs, and none in American studies departments (Chmaj 1971:56). Lander (1971:6) found that 39 percent of the men in anthropology have at some time served as departmental chairmen, compared to 16 percent of the women. Even in academic fields where women are a large majority, they are underrepresented in administration. For example, although men are only 33 percent of academic librarians, they comprise 79 percent of all deans of library schools (Kronus and Grimm 1971:4–5) and 95 percent of the chief librarians in seventy-four large college and university libraries (Schiller 1969:1098).

Studies in sociology and modern languages explored sex differences in teaching patterns by type of department. Howe, Morlock, and Berk (1971:464) found that women in modern languages are more likely than their male colleagues to teach only undergraduates, while men are three times more likely than women to teach graduate students exclusively (see Table 13.23). Differences of this magnitude were found both in departments with master's programs and in departments that award the doctorate. Rossi (1970:6) reports that women in sociology graduate departments are twice as likely as men to teach only undergraduates and half as likely as men to teach graduate students only. However, she found that these differences diminish with increasing departmental prestige. For example, in high prestige departments the proportion of women teaching undergraduates exclusively is more than twice that of men, but women and men are equally likely to teach only graduate students.

TABLE 13.23. Teaching Level of Faculty in Modern Languages and Sociology, by Type of Program, and by Sex (In percentages)

Discipline, Type of Program, Sex	Teaching Level		
	Undergraduate Only	Undergraduate and Graduate	Graduate Only
Modern Languages:			
All departments			
Men	65	29	6
Women	86	12	2
B.A. programs[a]			
Men	89	11	—
Women	97	3	—
M.A. programs			
Men	55	36	9
Women	76	22	2
Ph.D. programs			
Men	39	50	11
Women	65	31	4
Sociology:			
All graduate departments			
Men	25	67	8
Women	55	41	4
High prestige			
Men	13	80	7
Women	31	62	7
Above average prestige			
Men	22	70	8
Women	48	31	13
All others			
Men	29	63	8
Women	58	39	3

SOURCES: Howe, Morlock, and Berk 1971:464 for Modern Languages; Rossi (1970:6) for Sociology.
[a] Departments which award the B.A. as their *highest* degree.

Patterson (1971:231), found that differences by sex among graduate sociology faculty in respect to the level of students taught become more striking when examined in conjunction with academic rank. Although there are no substantial differences in level of teaching between untenured and tenured men, significant differences exist between junior and senior women faculty: all of the tenured women teach at least some graduate students, but 46 percent of the untenured women (compared to 18 percent of the untenured men) teach undergraduates only. Patterson (1971:231–232) also found that men are more likely than women to teach courses in their academic specialties: 56 percent of the men compared to 42 percent of the women teach the majority of their courses in their specialty areas. Again, there are only slight differences between untenured and tenured men in this respect, but for women tenured status is related to the percentage of courses taught within their areas of specialty.

Scholarship and Rates of Productivity

From the data reviewed so far we should expect women to have lower rates of scholarly productivity when compared to their male colleagues. Women on the average are less apt to hold doctorates, more likely to carry a heavy teaching load, and less likely to be engaged in research. Furthermore, these differences between time spent in research and teaching are greater in universities than in two-year or four-year colleges. In other words, *women are most likely to spend less time in research than their male colleagues in precisely those institutions with the best research facilities.* It is not surprising, then, to find that in a national sample of faculty (Bayer 1970:15), women lag behind their male counterparts in the number of professional articles published: 39 percent of the men compared to 63 percent of the women have published no scholarly articles at all. At the other extreme of productivity, 11 percent of the men versus 2 percent of the women have published twenty-one articles or more. As we would expect, differences in publication rates are greater in universities than in junior or senior colleges.

Research reports in American studies, anthropology, immunology, political science, psychology, social work, sociology, and experimental biology lend some support to Bayer's findings, although there are differences by discipline. As indicated in Table 13.24, the percentage of articles by women is less than the proportion of association memberships held by women in American studies, anthropology, political science, psychology, and social work. Differences are less striking in sociology.[17] In contrast, the publication rate for women in experimental biology is higher than we would expect, and much higher in immunology.

These differences between the natural sciences and other fields are echoed in research on recent doctoral recipients. Among women and men faculty in the social sciences, humanities, and education who received their Ph.D. between 1958 and 1963, men published slightly more articles than women, but women in the natural sciences published at rates equivalent to their male colleagues (Simon, Clark, and Galway 1967:230–231). The same study found no significant differences by sex in the mean number of books published. Despite the widespread belief that academic women have difficulty combining family responsibilities with their careers, married women in this sample published more articles than single women, and produced more books than either single women or men.

[17] In contrast to the Committee on the Status of Women in Sociology which found a somewhat lower publication rate for women than for men, Clemente (1972, Table 24), after examining the publication records of Ph.D.'s in sociology for the period 1940–1970, concluded that sex does *not* exert an independent influence on productivity rates.

TABLE 13.24. Proportion of Women in the Membership of Professional Associations and among the Authors of Journal Articles and Book Reviews (In percentages)

Discipline	Professional Association Membership	Journal Article Authors	Book Reviewers
Social Work (Rosenblatt 1970)[a]	66.0	40.0	35.0
Psychology (Hoffman undated)[b]	25.3	15.0	
American Studies (Chmaj 1971)[c]	18.5	5.4	
Anthropology (Fischer and Golde 1968)[d]	17.6	6.6–17.4	
Sociology (Committee on Status of Women 1972)[e]	15.0	12.5	
Immunology (Committee on Status of Women 1971)[f]	8.4	17.0	
Political Science (Schuck 1970)[g]	7.3	3.1	1.9
Experimental Biology (Association of Women in Science undated)[h]	7.1	8.5	

[a] Percentages represent the proportion of women of the National Association of Social Workers, 1968; and the proportion of women authors and book reviewers in five social work journals, 1964–1968.

[b] Percentages represent the proportion of women among American Psychological Association members, 1970; and the proportion of articles with at least one woman author among a random sample of 3,100 articles listed in the *Psychological Abstracts* over a ten-year period.

[c] Percentages represent the proportion of women among the membership of the American Studies Association, 1970; and the proportion of women among the authors listed in the *American Quarterly*, 1960–1971.

[d] Percentages represent the proportion of women of the American Associates of Current Anthropology, 1968; and range in the percentage of publications by women in the *American Anthropologist*, 1955–1964.

[e] Percentages represent the proportion of women among the "active fellows" in the American Sociological Association, 1970; and the proportion of authors who are women in three major sociology journals, 1967–1970.

[f] Percentages represent the proportion of the general membership in American Association of Immunologists and the proportion of authors who are women in the *Journal of Immunology*, 1969–1970.

[g] Percentages represent the proportion of women of the total membership in the American Political Science Association, 1968; and proportion of women authors of articles and book reviews in five political science journals, 1959–1970.

[h] Percentages represent the proportion of women of the total membership in the Federation of American Societies for Experimental Biology, 1969–1970; and the proportion of authors who are women of articles in the January 1970 issues of *Journal of Nutrition, American Journal of Physiology, Clinical Chemistry, Endocrinology, Metabolism, American Journal of Clinical Nutrition, PSEBM, Journal of Biological Chemistry,* and *Federation Proceedings.*

The Simon study reports much smaller productivity differences between women and men than most of the disciplinary reports or the national faculty study. These differences may be due to the fact that the study is restricted to relatively recent doctorate recipients, which would suggest that the gap in publication rates between women and men is narrowing. On the other hand, it may be that productivity rates by sex widen at later stages of academic careers. Indeed, there is some evidence from the Converse and Converse (1971) study of political scientists that differences in productivity rates between women and men increase during the middle years of the academic career, and then decrease somewhat later.

Converse and Converse (1971:343–347) examined the productivity rates of women and men political scientists with respect to articles and books published, and unpublished papers presented at professional meetings. They found that men out-produce women by a factor of approximately two to one, even when statistical controls are introduced for the greater frequency of part-time positions for women and their fewer years, on the average, of professional work experience. In a more detailed analysis, they plotted productivity rates for women and men full-time faculty with Ph.D.'s by years of professional work experience (see Figure 13.1). Among

FIGURE 13.1. Cumulative Research Productivity for Political Scientists by Sex for Full-time Academics with Doctorates

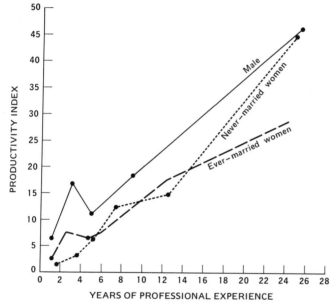

SOURCE: Converse and Converse, 1971:344. Reprinted by permission of the American Political Science Association. The Productivity Index was created for each faculty member by giving each unpublished paper a weight of 1, each published article a weight of 2, and each published book a weight of 8.

relatively new faculty members differences in productivity favor the men, but are fairly small. These differences widen when women and men are compared at increasing levels of professional work experience. It is clear that these differences are not simply a result of time taken by women from the early career years for child rearing and other family responsibilities, for there is little difference in productivity during the first fourteen years of professional experience between women who are currently married or have been married, and those who have never married. However, when faculty members are compared in the later stages of their careers, differences in productivity between men and married women become increasingly greater, while differences between men and women who have never married diminish considerably.

Salary

A wide variety of studies show that in the aggregate, academic women are paid less than their male colleagues. A recent national sample of faculty (Bayer 1970: 14–16) indicates that 63 percent of all women but only 28 percent of all men earn less than $10,000 during an academic year. In addition, women show less satisfaction with their salaries and are more likely than their male counterparts to express their dissatisfaction if they are employed at universities than at two-year or four-year colleges. Studies by the National Education Association (1966:52–53) and Brown (1965:162–170) also showed that women faculty are paid less in the aggregate than men. The investigators attribute part of the salary differential to the fact that women faculty are concentrated in colleges as opposed to universities where salaries tend to be higher, and in regions of the country that have lower average salaries. In addition, Brown found that women tend to be concentrated in low paying fields, rather than in the scientific disciplines where salaries are relatively high.

Salary differences persist even among women and men with equal educational attainment. Harmon (1968:91–98) found that among doctorates who have always worked in academe, the geometric mean of single women's salaries is about $500 per year less than that for men, while the differential for married women is about $700 a year. Simon, Clark, and Galway (1967:225–228), found that among more recent doctoral recipients employed in both academic and nonacademic settings, men earn approximately $700 a year more than women. However, they found some variation by sex and by academic field, ranging from a differential of more than $1,000 per year in education and $800 in the natural sciences, to about $400 a year in the humanities.

In an earlier study (1968) and in the detailed analysis reported in Chapter 15 of this volume, Bayer and Astin conclude that across all work settings, fields and ranks, women receive lower salaries than male colleagues with equivalent work experience, although these differences are less in the social sciences than in the natural sciences.

Table 13.25 shows more recent salary data from the 1970 National Register of Scientific and Technical Personnel for a number of disciplines in the social and natural sciences. Separate salary figures for women and men faculty are not available, but we can compare median salaries for women with salaries for the total sample, most of whom are men. Among all scientists employed in educational institutions, the salaries of women expressed as a proportion of total salaries vary from 71 per-

TABLE 13.25. Median Annual (Calendar Year) Salaries of Natural Scientists and Social Scientists Employed in Educational Institutions and Reporting Teaching as Their Primary Work Activity, by Field and by Sex

Field	Scientists Employed in Educational Institutions			Scientists Reporting Teaching as their Primary Work Activity		
	Total[a]	Women	Women's Salaries as Percent of Total	Total[a]	Women	Women's Salaries as Percent of Total
Linguistics	$13,000	$11,600	89	$12,000	$11,300	94
Psychology	16,000	13,800	86	15,000	13,400	89
Anthropology	15,500	13,000	84	13,900	13,000	94
Computer sciences	14,300	12,000	84	15,200	—[b]	
Physics	13,500	11,100	82	14,000	—[b]	
Sociology	15,000	12,000	80	13,300	11.000	83
Statistics	16,500	13,000	79	16,500	—[b]	
Political science	15,300	11,600	76	13,000	11,000	85
Biological sciences	17,000	12,600	74	17,000	13,200	78
Economics	18,000	13,100	73	16,000	12,000	75
Mathematics	13,700	10,000	73	12,200	10,000	82
Earth and marine sciences	14,100	10,100	72	13,300	—[b]	
Chemistry	12,000	8,500	71	14,200	10,600	75
All Fields	15,500	12,000	77	15,000	12,000	80

SOURCE: National Science Foundation 1972.

[a] Data for men only are not available, but in most cases, the proportion of women in each field is so small, that the median salary for the total may be considered very similar to the figure for men only.

[b] No median was computed for groups with fewer than twenty-five respondents reporting salary.

cent in chemistry to 89 percent in linguistics. However, this category of scientists includes not only those engaged in teaching, but those primarily involved in the generally more lucrative activities of research and administration—areas in which, as we have already observed, men are more likely to predominate. In order to test whether part of the salary difference by sex is due to the greater involvement of men in better paying activities, we can examine only the salaries of those scientists who reported teaching as their primary work activity. In every field, women's salaries are relatively closer to men's if we limit the comparison to faculty who are primarily teachers rather than including the entire staff.

Several surveys of equally qualified women and men have found differences in starting salaries for the first faculty position held after receiving the doctorate (see Henderson, quoted in Robinson 1971:23; Association for Women in Mathematics 1971; and Ad Hoc Committee on Women in the [History] Profession 1971). A larger number of studies report increasing salary differences for women and men at each rank up the academic hierarchy. The most recent national survey of median faculty salary differentials by sex favor men by more than $400 among instructors and lecturers, $550 among assistant professors, $700 among associate professors, and $1,100 among full professors (see Table 13.26). Recent salary data for faculty in microbiology (Leive 1971), modern languages (Howe, Morlock, and Berk 1971) and physics (Committee on Women in Physics 1972) also show greater salary differences favoring men at each increase in rank. Of the three disciplines, salaries are highest for both women and men in microbiology, where the differences by sex are also most substantial: women earn an average of $1,000 a year less as instructors or lec-

TABLE 13.26. Median Salaries (Academic Year) of Faculty, by Rank and Sex, for Selected Disciplines (In dollars)

Discipline, Year of Study, Sex	Rank			
	Instructors-Lecturers	Assistant Professors	Associate Professors	Full Professors
Microbiology 1970 (Leive 1971)				
Men	$11,000	$14,000	$17,400	$22,800
Women	10,000	12,800	14,600	17,200
Salary difference	−1,000	−1,200	−2,800	−5,600
Modern Languages 1970 (Howe, Morlock, and Berk 1971)[a]				
Men		10,500	12,500	16,500
Women		9,500	11,500	13,500
Salary difference		−1,000	−1,000	−3,000
Physics 1971 (Ad Hoc Committee 1972)				
Men[b]	9,418[c]	11,000	13,500	18,000
Women	9,766[c]	10,000	12,170	16,170
Salary difference	+348	−1,000	−1,330	−1,830
National sample 1965–1966 (National Educational Association 1966)				
Men	6,864	8,446	10,064	12,768
Women	6,454	7,870	9,322	11,649
Salary difference	−410	−576	−742	−1,119

[a] All salary figures for modern languages are approximations to the nearest $500. For example, the majority of male assistant professors earn between $10,000 and $10,999, indicated in the table by $10,500.

[b] Median salaries indicated in category "men" are for men and women combined. However, because women are only 2–6 percent of all ranks, the figures are very close to salaries for men alone.

[c] Salaries are computed by combining figures given for lecturers and instructors.

turers, and $5,600 a year less as full professors. The same pattern, though less extreme, is found in modern languages and physics.

La Sorte (1971a) reviewed the salaries of a sample of full-time teaching faculty at colleges and universities during the 1967–1968 academic year in five fields that have substantial numbers of women: mathematics, chemistry, psychology, sociology, and biological sciences. La Sorte reports lower median salaries for women in all five fields at both high and low ranks. Salary differentials varied from $100 per year for associate and full professors of biological science to $1,700 a year for associate and full professors of mathematics (Table 13.27). In three fields—psychology, chemistry, and mathematics—salary inequities were found to increase with higher rank.

TABLE 13.27. Median Salary Differentials between Faculty Men and Women, by Rank, for Selected Fields (In dollars)

Field	Full Professors and Associate Professors	Assistant Professors, Instructors and Lecturers	All Ranks Combined
Mathematics	$1,700	$ 900	$1,200
Chemistry	1,500	1,200	1,500
Psychology	1,000	600	1,200
Sociology	1,000	1,000	1,700
Biological sciences	100	600	1,000

SOURCE: La Sorte 1971a:271. Data is for the 1967–1968 academic year. Reprinted by permission of the *Journal of Higher Education*.

A survey of modern language departments (Howe, Morlock, and Berk 1971: 464–465) concluded that, in the aggregate, women earn lower salaries than men for at least two reasons: women faculty members are more likely to be employed by departments that pay lower salaries to both women and men; and women earn less than male colleagues at equivalent ranks in the same departments. In a comparison of modern language departments that award the A.A., B.A., M.A., and Ph.D. as their highest degree, the data clearly indicate that women comprise a larger proportion of the faculty in those departments which pay lower salaries (Table 13.28). For example, the median salaries of women full professors in Ph.D. granting departments are $4,000 to $7,000 higher than similarly ranked women in A.A. or B.A. departments; but women are about four times more likely to be full professors in departments that grant A.A. or B.A. degrees than in departments with doctoral programs. However, Table 13.28 also shows that in most cases *the median salary for women is lower than that for men at the same rank in the same type of department.* Median salary is higher for men than women in ten of the twelve comparisons by sex in Table 13.28. Even when each department in the sample was analyzed separately, the majority reported lower median salaries for women than for men at equivalent ranks in their department.

TABLE 13.28. Median Salary Ranges[a] by Type of Appointment for Modern Language Departments with A.A., B.A., M.A., and Ph.D. Programs

Highest Degree Awarded by the Department	Assistant Professors			Associate Professors			Full Professors		
	Men	Women	Percent Women	Men	Women	Percent Women	Men	Women	Percent Women
A.A.	$10,500	$ 9,500	29	$12,500	$11,500	32	$11,500	$10,500	26
B.A.	9,500	9,500	35	11,500	10,500	35	14,500	13,500	28
M.A. or M.A.T.	10,500	9,500	24	12,500	12,500	25	16,500	15,500	19
Ph.D.	10,500	10,500	17	13,500	12,500	13	18,500	17,500	7

SOURCE: Howe, Morlock, and Berk 1971:465. Reprinted by permission of the Modern Language Association.
[a] Salary ranges in this table are indicated by the middle figure in the range. For example, $10,500 indicates a range of $10,001–$10,999.

Several studies have tried to account for salary inequities between women and men on the basis of factors other than sex. La Sorte (1971a:271) investigated the impact of academic degree, work activity in addition to teaching, geographic region, years of professional experience, and age, on salary differentials for high and low ranks in five disciplines. Regardless of the control variable introduced, salary differentials in favor of men persisted in all five fields at high and low ranks with the single exception of associate and full professors in the biological sciences. The differentials ranged from $400 to a high of $1,700. After comparing salary differentials for selected years since 1959, La Sorte found that concomitant with the rapid increase in salaries over the past decade, there had been an increase in the aggregate salary differential between women and men, with a slight tendency for the salary gap to widen at each higher rank.

In her survey of academic and nonacademic microbiologists, Leive (1971:59–60) found salary differences between women and men at all degree levels, occupational categories, ranks, and in almost all geographic regions. She hypothesized that the lower status of women results from the dampening effect of family responsibilities both on time allotted to career development, and on commitment to the profession. Older single women earned somewhat higher salaries than their married counterparts; but married women without children seem to have little or no advantage over their peers with children. In any event, salary differences between women that can be attributed to family responsibilities are small compared to the salary differences between women and men. (See Chapter Fifteen for a detailed statistical analysis of differences in salary by sex.)

Converse and Converse (1971:342–345) report that in the aggregate, women in political science receive only about 60 percent of the remuneration awarded their male colleagues. In their attempt to explain this large difference they explored the impact of a wide range of factors, including differences in part-time and full-time work loads, degree held, age, professional work experience, marital status, number of academic honors, size of employer institution, and scholarly productivity. Several of these factors—part-time work load, degree held, and scholarly productivity—account for a significant portion of the income differential. However, the authors conclude:

> Nevertheless, there remains an income decrement for females relative to males who are comparable to them in a wide range of regards. It is particularly marked for women who have married, but appears to be present even for women who have never married and whose career trajectories are thus most like those of their male colleagues. Such women in the profession seem to receive only about 90 percent of the income given comparable males (Converse and Converse 1971:345).

Among women and men in political science who hold doctorates and have produced an equivalent number of books, articles, and papers, the average salary gap between men and single women is $1,400 and between men and ever-married women the difference increases to $3,600. Even when the amount of professional experience is added to degree and productivity, the salary differential between men and women still remains fairly substantial.

Discrimination

We have reviewed studies in discipline after discipline that document the lower status of academic women—differences that have not been erased even after introducing statistical controls measuring academic ability or scholarly achievement. Yet it is impossible to deduce from this data that the residual difference in status between women and men is the result of discrimination. In a study of 7,500 faculty members, Brown (1965:166–168) concludes that even after making allowances for differences between women and men in research productivity, the top 60 percent of institutions in his study hire a lower percentage of women than would be expected from their proportion among publishing scholars. Yet Brown reasons that at least part of this discrepancy is due to the fact that women prefer schools that pay less and are less prestigious, either because they place greater emphasis on teaching, elect to serve as faculty in women's and other small colleges, or because they impose greater geographic constraints on the types of jobs they will accept. Furthermore Brown argues that in keeping with their perceived family obligations, women may desire lighter work loads than men, and often are not subject to the same motivation for prestige as are their male colleagues (see Bernard 1964).

In order to evaluate these arguments, it is necessary to turn to studies that have tried to measure more directly the extent to which discrimination is a barrier to women's advancement. Several studies have questioned departments concerning discriminatory attitudes and practices. For example, Wilcox (1970:53–54) surveyed English department chairmen for indications of reservations about hiring women. He reports that 86 percent of all English departments "flatly assert that they have no tradition or policy against appointing women," and about 90 percent of those departments that profess to have no bias do in fact have some women faculty among the full-time members of their staffs. Although Wilcox finds that the great majority of these women are found in the lower levels of the faculty hierarchy, he concludes that, "It may well be that what imbalance there is can be attributed to the fact, so often noticed by those who are averse to hiring women, that more women than men drop out of the profession or fail to pursue their professional careers with full energy and dedication."

Other researchers, however, reach less sanguine conclusions concerning the departmental appointment process In a study of deans, department chairmen, and faculty members at six Pennsylvania institutions Simpson (quoted in Robinson 1971) found that administrators exhibited discriminatory attitudes in their more frequent choice and higher preference ratings of resumes with men's names over those of equal quality carrying the names of women. In a similar study (Fidell 1970), heads of 155 psychology departments read descriptions of job applicants with either male or female names, rated them according to their desirability, and indicated the rank at which they would be offered a position. Fidell found that, in general, descriptions of women in comparison to those of men with equivalent qualifications elicited less desirable ratings and appointment offers at lower levels. In a seven-year study of medical schools Kaplan (in Norris 1971) concluded that while all schools have an official policy of accepting women and men students on the basis of merit, a small number clearly are opposed to the presence of women in medicine, and a larger number are prejudiced against women students with children.

A number of studies have attempted to gauge the extent of discrimination in academe by questioning women, and sometimes a control group of men, about their observations and experiences. Astin (1969) found that 33 percent of the women doctorates in her study believed discriminatory practices had affected their careers adversely, and 40 percent felt they had not received the same salary as men with comparable training and experience. In addition to differential salaries, these women were concerned with promotion, tenure, and seniority policies based on sex. Astin notes that "Women who were professionally active, who published a great deal and who had been recognized for professional achievement tended to report experiences with employer discrimination more frequently" (Astin 1969:148).

Additional data on perceptions of discrimination is supplied by disciplinary reports. Fifteen percent of full-time women physicists (Committee on Women in Physics 1972:Appendix D) believe that they occupy a position lower than they deserve because of discriminatory factors (see Table 13.29). In a survey of academic

TABLE 13.29. Perception of Impact of Sex Discrimination upon Women's Academic Careers, by Discipline

Discipline	Percent Women Who Believe Sex Discrimination Has Affected Their Careers
American Studies (Chmaj 1971)	85
Anthropology (Lander 1971)[a]	66
Psychology (Keiffer and Cullen 1970)	41
Physics (Committee on Women 1972)	15
National Sample (Astin 1969)[a]	33

[a] Includes only women with Ph.D. degrees.

psychologists (Keiffer and Cullen 1970:5), 41 percent of the women and 55 percent of the men mentioned discrimination against women in discussing their own particular academic history or in describing institutions familiar to them. Both women and men were more likely to mention discriminatory practices if their spouse also was a psychologist. Lander (1971:8) found that half of the women in anthropology feel that their sex was a negative factor in their graduate school careers. In addition, 66 percent of the women faculty with Ph.D.'s believe that the fact that they are women has been a disadvantage in their employment history, a view not affected by the rank they have achieved. In a survey of faculty in American studies programs and departments, Chmaj (1971:x) noted that 85 percent of the women respondents believed they had experienced discrimination in their careers. In contrast to psychology faculty, men in American studies were less likely than women to perceive sex discrimination in salary, tenure, job classifications or hiring (see Table 13.30).

TABLE 13.30. Perceptions of Sex Discrimination among
American Studies Faculty, by Sex

	Percentage Who Perceive Discrimination	
Area of Discrimination	Women	Men
Salaries	51	20
Tenure	30	13
Job classifications	26	8
Hiring	15	10

SOURCE: Chmaj 1971.

In a recent poll of new history faculty concerning perceived prejudice in graduate school, the majority of both women and men felt their departments had been "neutral" with respect to sex in dealing with graduate students, although women were less likely than men to perceive neutrality (Ad Hoc Committee 1971:14–17). Both women and men were most concerned about discrimination in the areas of fellowships, admissions, and support from teaching jobs, and least concerned about possible problems in securing a faculty sponsor for the dissertation. Men were less likely than women to perceive sex discrimination in all potential problem areas except that of securing a dissertation sponsor (see Table 13.31).

In the most comprehensive study of perceived discrimination, the Committee on the Status of Women of the American Political Science Association questioned samples of women and men APSA members and graduate students for evidence of discrimination based on sex (Converse and Converse 1971). Women faculty were asked to indicate the degree of difficulty, if any, that they had encountered as women in regard to types of opportunity and rewards in graduate education, teaching, research, and administrative opportunities. Men faculty were asked, for the same set of items, whether they believed women encountered discrimination because of sex. Women and men graduate students were asked about their personal

TABLE 13.31. Perceived Discrimination in History Graduate
Departments, by Sex

Area of Discrimination	Percent Who Perceive Either a Strong Degree or Some Degree of Discrimination	
	Women	Men
Fellowships	42	22
Admissions	35	18
Support from teaching job	34	22
Job placement aid	29	14
Faculty contact	27	15
Student contact	20	8
Securing faculty sponsor for dissertation	5	8
Other	41	10

SOURCE: AHA Ad Hoc Committee on Women 1971:15.

experiences in graduate school and questioned about their observations and expectations concerning discrimination in teaching, research, and administration.

Two general patterns emerge from a comparison of responses (see Table 13.32). First, items related to teaching elicited more reports of discrimination than either graduate training or research. Among women graduate students, for example, the highest ranked of twenty-three items on perceived discrimination were the eight teaching items: consideration of job applications, appointment to teaching positions, initial rank assignment, promotion, tenure, salary, fringe benefits, and participation in school or departmental decision-making. For the other three respondent groups, five to seven of the teaching items appeared highest on the lists.

A second pattern that emerged from the data was a clear-cut "generation gap" in the responses of the four groups. Graduate students were more likely to perceive or anticipate discrimination based on sex than either professional women or men. The difference in degree of perceived discrimination was negligible between the two samples of men but there was a wide disparity in perceptions of discrimination between women graduate students and women professionals; women graduate students were the most apt of all to perceive sex discrimination.

Several possible reasons for such a difference are discussed by Converse and Converse (1971:332–333). The majority of items of concern to women graduate students tap areas in which they feel they will encounter resistance or prejudice in the future. However, even in view of the much lower concern of women professionals, it is difficult to dismiss the students' apprehensions as groundless. For one reason, proportionately more women graduate students are located at large institutions, where women are even more sharply underrepresented on the faculty than in the

TABLE 13.32. Variations in Perceived Discrimination by Career Aspect* for Graduate Students and Professionals in Political Science

Male Professionals	Female Professionals		Female Graduate Students	Male Graduate Students
		—2.12—		
			JOB CONSIDERATION	
		—2.06—		
			PROMOTION TEACHING APP'T	
		—2.00—		
		—1.94—		
		—1.88—	SALARY TENURE	JOB CONSIDERATION
		—1.82—	INITIAL RANK	
JOB CONSIDERATION		—1.76—		TEACHING APP'T
		—1.70—		
TEACHING APP'T		—1.64—		
		—1.58—	DECISION-MAKING	PROMOTION
		—1.52—	FRINGE BENEFITS	
	JOB CONSIDERATION	—1.46—	Placement Service *Grant Application*	
SALARY		—1.40—		TENURE
	SALARY	—1.34—		
PROMOTION		—1.28—		SALARY
	TEACHING APP'T	—1.22—		INITIAL RANK DECISION-MAKING Placement Service *Grant Application*
TENURE		—1.16—	*Secretar. Assist.* Financial Support	
Grant Application	PROMOTION	—1.10—		

Male Professionals	Female Professionals		Female Graduate Students	Male Graduate Students
INITIAL RANK	Placement Service			Financial Support
	Financial Support INITIAL RANK	—1.04—	Journal Public. Comman. Press Publ. Research Time	
		—0.98—		Later Profess. Inter. FRINGE BENEFITS
Financial Support		—0.92—	Profess. Support Later Profess. Inter. U. Press Public.	Grad. Admission Secretar. Assist. Dep't Admission Profess. Support
Placement Service DECISION-MAKING Grad. Admission	TENURE DECISION-MAKING	—0.86—		Research Time Comm. Press Public.
		—0.80—	Dep't Admission Grad. Admission	
Profess. Support FRINGE BENEFITS Later Profess. Inter.	Later Profess. Inter.			
Secret. Assist.	Profess. Support Grant Application FRINGE BENEFITS	—0.74—		Degree Candidacy Journal Public. U. Press Public.
	Research Time Secret. Assist. Teaching Fellow	—0.68—	Teaching Fellow	
		—0.62—		
Dep't Admission Camm. Press Public. Research Time		—0.56—	Exams, Thesis Degree Candidacy	Teaching Fellow
Teaching Fellow Journal Public.	Grad. Admission Exams. Thesis	—0.50—		
Degree Candidacy	Dep't Admission Degree Candidacy	—0.44—		Exams, Thesis
U. Press Public.		—0.38—		
	Journ. Public. U. Press Public.	—0.32—		
	Comm. Press Public.			
Exams, Thesis		—0.26—		

* The full items which were posed for rating in terms of "degree of problems . . . felt . . . because of sex" were as follows:

For *graduate instruction:* "Standards for admission to graduate school"; "Standards for admission to your graduate department"; "Financial assistance, scholarships"; "Candidacy to advanced degree"; "Performance expected in examinations or thesis"; "Conduct of undergraduate or discussion sections"; "Placement service"; "General support of professors"; and "Follow-up interest of professors."

For *Teaching:* "CONSIDERATION OF JOB APPLICATIONS"; "APPOINTMENT TO TEACHING POSITIONS"; "INITIAL RANK ASSIGNMENT"; "PROMOTION"; "TENURE"; "SALARY"; "FRINGE BENEFITS (e.g., TRAVEL AIDS, LEAVES, SECRETARIAL ASSISTANCE)"; "PARTICIPATION IN SCHOOL OR DEPARTMENTAL DECISION-MAKING."

For *research:* "Grant of fellowship applications"; "Secretarial assistance"; "Allowance for research as part of 'load' "; "Leave of absence or other research arrangement"; "Publication in professional journals"; "Publication by University presses"; "Publication by commercial presses." For each of these items the respondent was invited to indicate whether sex-related problems were "blatant," "moderate," "slight," or "none" if relevant to the individual. Items are located in according to mean responses to the item based on simple integer scores (0–3).

SOURCE: Converse and Converse 1971:331. Reprinted by permission of the American Political Science Association.

profession as a whole. In addition, professional women cannot simply be regarded as a projection of these graduate students some years later, for these older women are those who have achieved some measure of success in the profession. Excluded are those who left the discipline at various stages of their careers, among whom we might expect to find higher levels of perceived discrimination than among women who have remained in the field. Furthermore, Converse and Converse found some evidence that professional women are not fully aware of sex discrimination, for male political scientists were more likely to report discrimination against women than the women themselves. Converse and Converse suggest that "these male political scientists are by and large the 'gatekeepers' of the discipline, and could be expected to have the most direct and realistic view of the processes which surround the passing of the gates." The data support this interpretation. Male professionals perceive more discrimination than their women colleagues in precisely those "gatekeeping" areas of admissions, job applications, and appointment to positions, and research, grant or fellowship applications.

It is important, however, not to overemphasize disagreement between the sexes as to absolute levels of discrimination, for these differences are dwarfed by strong consensus among all four samples concerning the stages in a professional career at which such discrimination as exists tends to concentrate. All four groups are most likely to perceive problems for women as centering not only within academic teaching, but more specifically at the gateways that represent access to standard teaching roles. Discrimination with respect to the consideration of applications for teaching positions is rated highest of all twenty-three items by every group, and problems in appointments to teaching positions is rated a close second or third on all lists. In addition to problems at the beginning of a teaching career, later career stages also receive high reports of perceived or anticipated discrimination: salary, promotions, and tenure are placed high on the lists of all four groups, followed by initial rank assignment.

Within the area of graduate education, placement services are criticized most often by three of the groups, and are second on the men professionals' list. This concern is followed closely by perceptions of discrimination in the awarding of financial assistance and scholarships. There is also some concern with the "follow-up interest of professors," but fairly low discrimination is perceived in the area of graduate education, including school and departmental admission, the establishment of candidacy, standards expected on thesis or examinations, the conduct of teaching-fellow roles, and informal professional support.

The study of perceptions is at best an indirect method of investigating the relative positions of academic men and women. Yet it is significant that the areas of most concern to both women and men—such as hiring, initial appointments, promotion, tenure, and salary—are the same areas in which the greatest disparities between the sexes were found. It is difficult not to conclude that the perceptions of faculty and graduate students in a variety of disciplines provide some evidence that the lower status of academic women is to *some* extent the result of sex discrimination.

Participation in Professional Associations

One potential instrument for change in the status of academic women is the professional associations. It is doubly discouraging, therefore, to find that studies of a large number of professional societies indicate that women are underrepresented in positions of decisionmaking. There is a consistent tendency for women to hold a smaller proportion of offices than their proportion of the general membership (see Table 13.33). In addition, women are less likely than their male colleagues to appear on programs or present papers at national meetings. The only exception to this general pattern of participation is the American Sociological Association where women constitute 15 percent of the general membership, but 19 percent of committee members and 18 percent of current association officers. In fact the proportion of women among current officers is almost three times their representation in the past—a tribute to the Women's Caucus of the ASA which has made better representation of women a focus of activity since 1969. In general, however, we must conclude that women are underrepresented in positions of influence within professions at the national level, in addition to their relative exclusion from local channels of decision-making that affect departmental and institutional policies.

CONCLUDING REMARKS

Studies in discipline after discipline have indicated that in comparison to their male colleagues, women are more likely to receive initial appointments at lower ranks or in nonrank positions; they are promoted more slowly and receive tenure at a later age, if at all; they are less involved in administration or in decisionmaking at either the departmental or national professional association level; and they receive lower salaries. Some portion of these differences are accounted for by the fact that women are less likely to have earned doctorates, are more heavily involved in teaching responsibilities to the exclusion of research, and have lower publication rates. However, studies in several disciplines have shown that even when statistical controls are introduced for these differences in qualifications, men are more likely than their female colleagues to have appointments at higher ranks and to receive larger salaries at each rank. Together these studies provide evidence that aggregate differences between women and men faculty reported in national studies are not the result of very large differences in some academic fields counterbalanced by equality in others.

It is also clear, however, that the *magnitude* of status inequities between women and men differ by academic discipline. For example, the small proportion of women in physics, when compared to their male colleagues, seem to fare better in terms of

TABLE 13.33. Participation of Women in the Activities of National Professional Societies (In percentages)

Professional Society	Membership	Current Officers	Past Officers	Committee Members	Recent Program Participants, National Meeting	Paper Presenters at Recent National Meeting	Journal Editors
American Library Association (Kronus and Grimm 1971; ALA/SRRT compilation)	75.0		18.8[a]				30.0
American Psychological Association (Hoffmann undated)	25.3				10.1[b]	15.0	4.4[c]
American Studies Association (Chmaj 1971)	18.5	10.0[d]	3.5[e]				0.0[f]
American Sociological Association (Committee on the Status of Women 1972)	15.0	17.6[g]	6.8[g]	18.5[h]	12.7[i]		7.3[j]
American Association of Immunologists (Committee on the Status of Women 1971)	8.4	0.0	1.0	2.0[k]			
American Political Science Association (Schuck 1970a)	7.3		3.8[l]		3.2[m]	4.1[m]	0.7[n]
Federation of American Societies for Experimental Biology (Association of Women in Science compilation)	7.1	0.0[o]					2.4[p]
American Physical Society (Committee on Women 1972)	2.1[q]	0.5		0.4[r]		0.6[s]	0.3
American Historical Association (Ad Hoc Committee on Women 1971)				3.7	3.7		

a Proportion of women among eighty-five past presidents of the American Library Association.

b Proportion of women of all symposium participants at the 1970 APA Convention.

c Proportion of women of the combined editorial boards of ten journals.

d Proportion of women of the American Studies Association national council 1971.

e Proportion of women of the ASA national council 1968–1971. Percentage prior to 1968 was 0.0 percent.

f Proportion of women of the *American Quarterly* editorial board.

g Proportion of women of ASA officers and council for 1972 and for 1967–1972.

h Proportion of women of elected committee members for 1972.

i Proportion of women of total participants at the 1970 ASA meeting.

j Proportion of women on editorial boards, 1966–1971. Proportion for 1971 is 8 percent.

k Excludes Committees on the Status of Women.

l Proportion of women of APSA council members, 1920–1969. Women were 3.4 percent for 1960–1969.

m Proportion of women of all "papergivers" and discussants at annual APSA meetings, 1959–1969.

n Proportion of women of editorial boards of the *American Political Science Review* and regional journals, 1920–1969. Proportion of women for 1960–1969 was 0 percent.

o Proportion of women of all officers of the American Physiological Society of Biological Chemists, American Society of Pharmacology and Experimental Therapeutics, and the American Society of Experimental Pathology. The American Institute of Nutrition has one woman officer.

p Proportion of women of all editors on nine journals of associations affiliated with FASEB.

q Proportion of women among Ph.D. physicists in the 1970 National Register.

r Includes proportions of yearly positions on American Physical Society committees for the past ten years.

s Proportion of women among the presentations of invited papers at the APS general meetings in 1969 and 1970.

TABLE 13.34. Summary Measures on the Status of Women for
Selected Disciplines

Parity Measures	Physics	Modern Languages	Political Science	Sociology	Anthropology
Rank					
I[a]	High(100)	High(100)	Medium(67)	Low(46)	Low(44)
II[b]	High(54)	Low(38)	Medium(45)	Low(37)	—
III[c]	High(82)	Medium(68)	—	Low(38)	—
Salary					
IV[d]	High(82)	Medium[g]	Low(76)	Medium(80)	High(84)
V[e]	—	—	Medium(85)	Low(83)	High(94)
Perception of Discrimination[f]	Low(15)	—	—		High(66)
Summary Score[h]	2.6	2.0	1.8	1.2	2.5

[a] Proportion of women among full professors compared to the lowest percentage of women among doctorate recipients for any five-year-period from 1920 to 1968. (SOURCE: Parity Index II, Table 13.6)

[b] Proportion of women who are full professors compared to the proportion men at this rank. (SOURCE: Parity Index, Table 13.11)

[c] Proportion of women with Ph.D.'s who are full professors compared to the proportion of similarly qualified men who hold this rank. (SOURCE: Parity Index, Table 13.13)

[d] Women's salaries as a proportion of total salaries for scientists employed in educational institutions. (SOURCE: Table 13.25)

[e] Women's salaries as a proportion of total salaries for scientists reporting teaching as their primary work activity. (SOURCE: Table 13.25)

[f] Percentage of women who believe sex discrimination has affected their careers. (SOURCE: Table 13.29)

[g] Estimated from data in Table 13.26 which show greater salary inequities for women full professors in modern languages than in physics.

[h] The Summary Score is an average weighted by the number of ratings, in which High = 3, Medium = 2 and Low = 1.

rank than women in the modern languages or the social sciences (see Table 13.34). In addition they earn more equitable salaries than faculty women in modern languages, political science, or sociology.

The data available to us permit only limited speculation on reasons for these differences. We have found that women physicists are less likely to be married than women sociologists or psychologists, which may mean that the former are less apt to have commitments in conflict with their professional careers. It may be that women are more productive in physics than in the modern languages or social sciences. Although we do not have publication rates for women physicists, several studies have found that women in the natural sciences tend to publish more than women in other academic areas. It is also possible that women physicists work in a more hospitable environment than women in other fields, for they are less likely than women in other disciplines to believe their careers have been affected adversely by discrimination based on sex.

The last row of Table 13.34 permits a tentative overview of the relative status of women in five selected academic disciplines. The range of the summary scores is a narrow one from one to three, but the scores suggest that compared to women in the social science fields of political science and sociology, women in physics and anthropology fare better on parity measures of rank, salary, and/or perceived discrimination. It is interesting to note that sociology and political science also are the fields in which the first women's caucuses developed (see Chapter Sixteen for an account of the development of political action among women in the academic professional associations). The spur to women's political action in the social sciences may be rooted, therefore, in the relatively greater discrimination against them and in the *gap* between the professed general liberalism so often found to characterize social scientists and the lack of liberalism within the fields themselves toward women colleagues.

It is perhaps inevitable when a series of discrete studies are subjected to a review that as many questions are raised as are answered. We can not tell from the data to what extent the variation among academic disciplines in the status of women is the result of structural differences between fields and to what extent the variation is a consequence of differences in individuals who are attracted to each discipline. We have found, for example, that the levels of aspiration among women graduate students differ by discipline, but we do not know if the women students approach different fields of study with varying levels of aspiration or whether women experience varying degrees of discouragement as graduate students. While one may conclude from our review that there is ample evidence of discrimination in all the academic disciplines for which studies exist, the data do not permit us to speak to the subtler issues of internalized barriers to achievement or the respects in which the disciplines attract women and men with differing clusters of personal and social characteristics. At least one next step in building on the results of this review would be to examine the correlates of career choice by personality and by sex. Thus, the data support policies aimed at rectifying inequities by sex in such areas as initial appointment, promotion, and salary, but merely point the way to future study of the institutional factors which depress the aspirations of women. It will take knowledge of both discrimination and aspiration as well as new policies to insure for women full partnership in the academic enterprise.

Selected References by Discipline*

AMERICAN STUDIES
Chmaj 1971

ANTHROPOLOGY
Fischer and Golde 1968
Lander 1971
Lander 1972
Vance 1970a
Vance 1970b

ECONOMICS
Committee of the National Science
Foundation Report on the Economics
Profession 1965

HISTORY
Ad Hoc Committee on Women in the
Profession 1971

IMMUNOLOGY
Committee on the Status of Women
1971

LEGAL EDUCATION
AALS Special Committee on the Status
of Women in Legal Education 1970
Kramer 1970
Laurance 1971
Sassower 1970
White 1967

LIBRARY SCIENCE
Blankenship 1967
Kronus and Grimm 1971
Manchak 1971
Schiller 1970
Schiller 1969

MATHEMATICS
Association for Women in Mathematics
1971

MEDICAL EDUCATION
Kaplan (undated)
Norris 1971

MICROBIOLOGY
Kashket and Huang 1972
Leive 1971
Robbins 1971

MODERN LANGUAGES
Howe et al. 1971
Morlock et al. 1972
Wilcox 1970

PHILOSOPHY
Wilson 1971

PHYSICS
Committee on Women in Physics 1972
Lubkin 1971

POLITICAL SCIENCE
Converse and Converse 1971
Jaquette 1971
Mitchell 1969
Mitchell and Starr 1971
Schuck 1969
Schuck 1970a
Schuck 1970b
Stokes 1970

PSYCHOLOGY
Association for Women Psychologists
1970
Fidell 1970
Hoffman et al. (undated)
Keiffer and Cullen 1970
Torrey 1971

SCIENCE
Bayer and Astin 1968
Edisen 1971

* For complete citation see the list of references.

304

SOCIAL WORK
    Rosenblatt et al. 1970

SOCIOLOGY
    Clemente 1972
    Committee on the Status of Women
        1972

Davis 1969
Fava 1960
Fox 1970
La Sorte 1971a
Patterson 1971
Rossi 1970

REFERENCES

Ad Hoc Committee on Women in the [History] Profession. 1971. Final report to the American Historical Association. Mimeographed.

American Association of Law Schools Special Committee on the Status of Women in Legal Education. 1970. Statistical compilation of questionnaire responses from 76 law school deans. Mimeographed.

Association for Women in Mathematics Newsletter. September 1971.

Association for Women Psychologists. 1970. Women in psychology: A fact sheet. Mimeographed.

Association of Women in Science. (Undated.) Mimeographed.

Astin, Helen S. 1969. *The woman doctorate in America.* New York: Russell Sage Foundation.

Bayer, Alan E. 1970. College and university faculty: A statistical description. *ACE Research Reports,* 5(5). Washington, D.C.: American Council on Education.

Bayer, Alan E., and Astin, Helen S. 1968. Sex differences in academic rank and salary among science doctorates in teaching. *Journal of Human Resources,* 3:191–200.

Bernard, Jessie. 1964. *Academic women.* University Park: Pennsylvania State University Press.

Blankenship, W. C. 1967. Head librarians: How many men? How many women? *College and Research Libraries,* 28:41–48.

Brown, David G. 1965. *Academic labor markets.* A report submitted to the Office of Manpower, Automation and Training, U.S. Department of Labor.

Chmaj, Betty E. 1971. *American women and American studies.* Pittsburgh: KNOW, Inc.

Clemente, Frank. 1972. A note on sex differences in research productivity. Mimeographed.

Committee on the National Science Foundation Report on the Economics Profession. 1965. Women economists in the structure of economists' employment and salaries. *American Economic Review,* 55:59–65.

Committee on the Status of Women (Immunology). 1971. The status of women in science (with particular reference to immunology). Prepared for the American Association of Immunologists.

Committee on the Status of Women in the Profession of the American Sociological Association. 1972. The woman sociologist. Mimeographed.

Committee on Women in Physics. 1972. Women in physics: The report of the committee on women in physics submitted to the American Physical Society. Mimeographed.

Converse, Philip E., and Converse, Jean M. Fall 1971. The status of women as students and professionals in political science. *Political Science,* 4:328–348.

Davis, Ann E. 1969. Women as a minority group in higher academics. *The American Sociologist,* 4:95–98.

Edisen, Adele. 1971. AWIS explores impact of federal guidelines: A HEW forum. *AWIS,* a newsletter of the Association of Women in Science, 1:1ff.

Fava, S. April 1960. The status of women in professional sociology. *American Sociological Review,* 25:271–276.

Fidell, Linda S. 1970. Empirical verification of sex discrimination in hiring practices in psychology. *American Psychologist,* 25:1094–1098.

Fischer, Ann, and Golde, Peggy. April 1968. The position of women in anthropology. *American Anthropologist,* 70:337–344.

Fox, Greer Litton. 1970. The woman graduate student in sociology. In *Women on campus: 1970, a symposium.* Ann Arbor: The University of Michigan Center for Continuing Education of Women, pp. 32–35.

Harmon, Lindsey R. 1965. *High school ability patterns, a backward look from the doctorate.* Scientific Manpower Report No. 6. Washington, D.C.: Office of Scientific Personnel, National Research Council.

Harmon, Lindsey R. 1968. *Careers of Ph.D.'s, academic versus nonacademic: A second report on follow-up of doctorate cohorts 1935–1960.* Publication 1577. Washington, D.C.: National Academy of Science.

Hoffman, D. T., Scally, B., Deering, A., and Kott, E. (undated.) The women in psychology. Mimeographed.

Hooper, Mary Evans, and Chandler, Margorie O. 1970. *Earned degrees conferred: 1969–70 institutional data.* Washington, D.C.: U.S. Department of Health, Education and Welfare, Office of Education, National Center for Educational Statistics.

Howe, Florence; Morlock, Laura; and Berk, Richard. May 1971. The status of women in modern language departments: A report of the Modern Language Association Commission on the status of women in the profession. *Publications of the Modern Language Association,* 86:459–468.

Jaquette, Jane. Fall 1971. The status of women in the profession: Tokenism. *P.S.,* 4:530–534.

Kaplan, Harold I. (undated.) Women physicians: the more effective recruitment and utilization of their talents and the resistance to it—a seven year study. Excerpts reprinted in Norris, *Discrimination against women,* pp. 559–562.

Kashket, Eva, and Huang, Alice S. 1972. Preliminary report on the 1971 ASM questionnaire. Mimeographed.

Keiffer, Miriam J., and Cullen, Dallas M. 1970. *Discrimination experienced by academic female psychologists.* Pittsburgh: KNOW, Inc.

Kramer, Noel Anketell. 1970. Discrimination and the woman law student. In *Women on campus: 1970, a symposium.* Ann Arbor: The University of Michigan Center for Continuing Education of Women, pp. 39–41.

Kronus, Carol L., and Grimm, James W. 1971. Women in librarianship: the majority rules? Paper presented at the annual meeting of the American Sociological Association, Denver, Colorado, August 30–September 2.

Lander, Patricia Slade. February 1972. Male and female: New data from the AAA membership survey. *Newsletter of the American Anthropological Association,* 13:8–10.

Lander, Patricia Slade. 1971. Report on the membership survey of the AAA, career patterns of American anthropologists. Paper presented at the 70th annual meeting of the American Anthropological Association.

La Sorte, Michael A. April 1971a. Academic women's salaries: Equal pay for equal work? *Journal of Higher Education,* 42:265–278.

La Sorte, Michael A. November 1971b. Sex differences in salary among academic sociology teachers. *American Sociologist,* 6:304–307.

Laurance, Margaret. 1971. Statement submitted by the National Association of Women Lawyers, in *Discrimination against women: hearings before the special subcommittee on education* of the Committee on Education and Labor, House of Representatives, 91st Congress, Second Session, on Section 805 of H.R. 16098. Washington, D.C.: U.S. Government Printing Office, pp. 1120–1128.

Leive, Loretta. August 1971. Status of women microbiologists: A further report, including preliminary analysis of reasons for the lower status of women. *American Society for Microbiology,* 37:57–62.

Lubkin, Gloria B. April 1971. Women in physics. *Physics Today,* 24:23–27.

Manchak, Barbara. April 1971. Salary survey: ALA personal members. *American Libraries,* 2:409–417.

Mitchell, Joyce M. 1969. The status of women in the political science profession: Proposed elements of inquiry. Mimeographed.

Mitchell, Joyce M., and Starr, Rachel. 1971. Aspirations, achievement and professional advancement in political science: The prospect for women in the West. Paper presented at the 1971 annual meeting of the Western Political Science Association, Albuquerque, New Mexico, April 8–10.

Morlock, Laura L. and the Commission on the Status of Women in the Modern Language Association. May 1972. Affirmative action for women in 1971. *Publications of the Modern Language Association,* 87:530–540.

National Academy of Sciences, Office of Scientific Personnel. 1963. *Doctorate production in United States universities 1920–1962.* Washington, D.C.: Author.

National Academy of Sciences. 1967. *Doctorate production in United States universities.* Publication 1489. Washington, D.C.: Author.

National Education Association. May 1966. Salaries in higher education continue to grow. *NEA Research Bulletin,* 44:50–57.

National Science Foundation. 1972. *American science manpower, 1970.* A report of the National Register of Scientific and Technical Personnel. Washington, D.C.: U.S. Government Printing Office.

Norris, Frances S., M.D. 1971. Statement in *Discrimination against women: hearings before the special subcommittee on education* of the Committee on Education and Labor, House of Representatives, 91st Congress, Second Session, on Section 805 of H.R. 16098. Washington, D.C.: U.S. Government Printing Office, pp. 510–584.

Office of Education, National Center for Educational Statistics. 1968. *Earned degrees conferred, 1966–67. Part A—summary data.* Washington, D.C.: U.S. Department of Health, Education and Welfare.

Office of Education, National Center for Educational Statistics. 1969. *Earned degrees conferred, 1967–68. Part A—summary data.* Washington, D.C.: U.S. Department of Health, Education and Welfare.

Office of Education, National Center for Educational Statistics. 1971. *Earned degrees conferred, 1968–69. Part A—summary data.* Washington, D.C.: U.S. Department of Health, Education and Welfare.

Oltman, Ruth M. 1970. *Campus 1970, where do women stand? Research report of a survey on women in academe.* Washington, D.C.: American Association of University Women.

Parrish, John B. 1962. Women in top-level teaching and research. *AAUW Journal,* 55: 99–107.

Patterson, Michelle. August 1971. Alice in wonderland: A study of women faculty in graduate departments of sociology. *American Sociologist,* 6:226–234.

Robbins, Mary Louise. April 1971. Status of women microbiologists. *American Society for Microbiology,* 37:34–40.

Robinson, Lora H. 1971. *The status of academic women.* Washington, D.C.: ERIC Clearinghouse on Higher Education, Review 5.

Rosenblatt, Aaron et al. 1970. Predominance of male authors in social work publications. *Social Casework,* 51:421–440.

Rossi, Alice S. February 1970. Status of women in graduate departments of sociology, 1968–1969. *The American Sociologist,* 5:1–11.

Sassower, Doris L. 1970. Women in law. In *Sixteen reports on the status of women in the professions.* New York: Professional Women's Caucus.

Schiller, Anita R. March 1969. The widening sex gap. *Library Journal,* 95(6):1098–1100.

Schiller, Anita R. April 1970. Women employed in libraries: The disadvantaged majority. *American Libraries,* 1:345–349.

Schuck, Victoria. 1969. Women in political science: Some preliminary observations. *P.S.,* 2:642–653.

Schuck, Victoria. Fall 1970a. Femina studens re publicae: Notes on her professional achievement. *P.S.,* 3:622–628.

Schuck, Victoria. Summer 1970b. Some comparative statistics on women in political science and other social sciences. *P.S.,* 3:357–361.

Simon, Rita J., Clark, Shirley M., and Galway, K. 1967. The woman Ph.D.: a recent profile. *Social Problems,* 15:221–236.

Simon, Rita J., and Rosenthal, Evelyn. 1967. Profile of the woman Ph.D. in economics, history, and sociology. *American Association of University Women Journal,* 60: 127–129.

Stokes, Sybil L. 1970. Women graduate students in political science. In *Women on campus: 1970, a symposium.* Ann Arbor: The University of Michigan Center for Continuing Education of Women, pp. 36–38.

Torrey, Jane W. 1971. The status of academic women in psychology. Mimeographed.

Vance, Carole. 1970a. Sexism in anthropology? The status of women in departments of anthropology: Highlights of the guide tabulation. *Newsletter of the American Anthropological Association,* 11(9):5–6.

Vance, Carole. 1970b. Sexual stratification in academic anthropology. Paper presented at the 69th annual meeting of the American Anthropological Association.

White, James J. April 1967. Women in the law. *Michigan Law Review,* 65:1084–1095.

Wilcox, Thomas. 1970. The lot of the woman: A report on the national survey of undergraduate English programs. *Bulletin of the Association of Departments of English,* 25:53–59.

Wilson, Margaret. 1971. Preliminary tables from the Subcommittee on the Status of Women in the Profession, American Philosophical Association.

Appendix
Information Available on Women or Differences by Sex by Academic Discipline

Information	American Studies	Anthropology	Biological Sciences	Chemistry	Economics	Education	English	History	Immunology	Library Science	Mathematics	Microbiology	Modern Languages*	Philosophy	Physics	Political Science	Psychology	Social Work	Sociology	Law	Medicine	Reference
Graduate students enrolled	√	√											√		√	√	√		√	√	√	p. 256, footnote 2
B.A.'s, M.A.'s, Ph.D.'s, awarded, 1969–1970	√	√	√	√	√	√	√	√		√	√		√	√	√	√	√		√	√	√	Table 13.1
Ph.D.'s awarded, 1920–1968	√	√	√	√	√	√	√	√		√	√		√	√	√	√	√		√	√	√	Table 13.1
Degree aspirations															√	√		√				Table 13.2
Proportion of total faculty								√					√	√	√	√	√		√			Table 13.3
Proportion faculty—Ph.D. departments													√		√		√		√			Table 13.3
Proportion faculty—high prestige departments		√													√		√					Table 13.3
—control degree of prestige		√																				p. 259
Proportion of part-time faculty		√											√		√		√		√	√		Table 13.4
Relationship between women faculty and women students																	√		√			pp. 259, 260
Proportion women by rank	√						√	√				√	√		√	√			√	√		Table 13.5
Marital status													√		√		√		√			Table 13.7
Effect of nepotism regulations on percent women by rank														√								Tables 13.8, 13.9
Proportion women by rank: —Ph.D. departments								√					√		√	√	√		√			Table 13.10
—high prestige departments															√	√			√			Table 13.10
Rank distributions						√							√	√	√	√			√	√		Table 13.11
Proportion faculty with Ph.D.		√											√	√	√				√			Table 13.12

* Includes English and modern foreign languages.

310

Information	American Studies	Anthropology	Biological Sciences	Chemistry	Economics	Education	English	History	Immunology	Library Science	Mathematics	Microbiology	Modern Languages*	Philosophy	Physics	Political Science	Psychology	Social Work	Sociology	Law	Medicine	Reference
Rank distributions for faculty with Ph.D.'s													✓	✓	✓	✓			✓			Table 13.13
Sex differences in rank:																						
—by department prestige		✓																	✓			p. 270
—by specialization																			✓			p. 271
—by publication rate																	✓					p. 271
Proportion women by rank —part-time faculty													✓		✓		✓		✓			Table 13.15
Rank distributions for part-time women													✓		✓		✓		✓			Table 13.16
Nonladder appointments								✓			✓				✓	✓			✓			pp. 272, 274
Percentage with tenure:													✓		✓				✓		✓	Table 13.18
—by prestige of department																			✓			p. 275
Proportion women of tenured faculty:													✓		✓				✓		✓	Table 13.18
—by type of department													✓									Table 13.18
Rank of initial appointment	✓						✓															Table 13.19
Starting salaries							✓															p. 276
Hiring: problems in finding jobs							✓								✓	✓	✓					pp. 276–277
Promotion rates:		✓													✓	✓	✓		✓			pp. 278–280
—by marital status																			✓			p. 279
—tenure by age																			✓			Table 13.20
—for faculty with Ph.D.'s													✓									p. 279, Table 13.21
—by prestige of degree		✓																				p. 279, Table 13.22
—by continuity of career																	✓					p. 278
—by productivity rate																	✓					p. 280
Work loads:																						
—teaching, research, administration													✓						✓			p. 281
—top administrative positions	✓	✓							✓						✓				✓			p. 281
—level of students taught:													✓						✓			Table 13.23
—by level of department													✓									Table 13.23

Information	American Studies	Anthropology	Biological Sciences	Chemistry	Economics	Education	English	History	Immunology	Library Science	Mathematics	Microbiology	Modern Languages*	Philosophy	Physics	Political Science	Psychology	Social Work	Sociology	Law	Medicine	Reference
—by department prestige																					√	Table 13.23
—by rank																					√	p. 282
—% courses taught within specialty																					√	pp. 282–283
Productivity rates:	√	√	√					√									√	√	√	√		Table 13.24
—by years professional work experience																					√	Figure 13.1
Salaries:		√	√	√	√			√							√	√	√		√			Table 13.25
—by rank			√	√								√	√	√	√		√		√			Tables 13.26, 13.27
—by rank and level of department													√									Table 13.28
—by rank with control variables			√	√								√	√		√	√			√			pp. 288–292
Sex discrimination —in hiring							√															p. 292
—in student admissions																					√	p. 293
—perceptions of discrimination among faculty	√	√															√					Tables 13.29, 13.30
—in graduate school								√								√						Tables 13.31, 13.32
—in teaching, research, administration																	√					Table 13.32
Participation in professional associations	√		√				√	√	√							√	√	√			√	Table 13.33

Chapter Fourteen

Sex and Specialization in Academe and the Professions

Michelle Patterson

IN RECENT years a growing number of studies have documented the discrimination women in the professions and academe face in respect to rank, promotions, and salary. Aside from these disadvantages, however, it is generally assumed that women are free to pursue their professional interests in male-dominated fields. This chapter examines that assumption. It looks at one aspect of the more subtle influences of sex role conceptions upon the careers of professional women: the impact of sex differences upon choice of specialty within a profession or academic discipline.[1]

STEREOTYPING AND SEX-TYPING OF OCCUPATIONS

Not too long ago the following riddle was in fairly wide circulation: A father and his son went for a drive one Sunday afternoon. On the way, the father failed to negotiate a curve in the road and the car slammed into a tree. The father was killed instantly. An ambulance was summoned and the boy was taken to a hospital. Once at the hospital, he was immediately taken to the operating room. The surgeon entered and upon seeing the patient, exclaimed, "Oh, my God! It's my son!" How could that be?

If you try this riddle on your friends you will probably receive a variety of answers which demonstrate a rather tortured reasoning: the father was a priest; the father who was killed was an adoptive parent and the surgeon is the true father; the boy is of doubtful parentage. The answer is really quite simple and straightforward: the surgeon is the boy's mother.

Few people are able to give this simple answer because they are blinded by their image of a surgeon: surgeons are male. The stereotype of the woman in medicine is quite different: it is that of the quiet, efficient nurse in her white uniform, patiently waiting for the doctor's orders and unquestioningly carrying them out.

Stereotyping is the process by which "society establishes the means of categorizing

---

[1] There is no comprehensive body of data that breaks down specialties within fields by sex. Although the National Register of Scientific and Technical Personnel collects this information, they do not tabulate it. Therefore, only those professions and academic disciplines for which such data were available are discussed in this chapter, and the author wishes to thank all the researchers who so kindly made their data available to her. They are cited in the text.

persons and the complement of attributes felt to be ordinary and natural for members of each of these categories" (Goffman 1961:2). Not only are stereotypes disabling for the persons stereotyped, but disabling as well for the stereotyper, for they act as filters coloring all that he sees. According to Robert Merton, "Occupations can be described as 'sex-typed' when a very large majority of those in them are of one sex and when there is an associated normative expectation that this is as it should be" (quoted in Epstein 1970:152). Sex-typing of occupations, then, is actually a specialized case of stereotyping.

Work in America traditionally has been sex-stereotyped. For example, almost 99 percent of all stenographers, typists, and secretaries, and 86 percent of all elementary school teachers are women (Women's Bureau 1969). On the other hand, 97 percent of all lawyers (White 1967) and 93 percent of all doctors are men. Moreover, the pattern of job sex-typing has remained remarkably stable over time. Oppenheimer (1970) has shown that on the whole those occupations that were predominantly female in 1900 were still predominantly female in 1950. As a consequence, women and men tend to compete in relatively different labor markets, differentiated solely by sex. "Having been socialized to expect a certain niche in the occupational hierarchy, women continue to look for jobs where they know they can find them, and not to look toward areas traditionally closed to them" (Kreps 1971:3). As Epstein has observed:

> The more nearly a profession is made up entirely of members of one sex, the less likely it is that it will change its sex composition in the future and the more affected will be the performance of those few members who are not of that sex. Sex typing tends to be a self-perpetuating process operating according to the dynamics of the self-fulfilling prophecy (Epstein 1970:165).

The normative expectations that are crystallized in stereotypes express both our thoughts about the way things are, and our feelings about the way things ought to be. Hence, when an occupation is sex-stereotyped, the sex of the members of the minority becomes occupationally salient (Epstein 1970). The woman who enters the male-dominated spheres of academe or the professions, for example, will be defined as deviant; she is not what we think she should be.

Those who do not fit the stereotypes of their professions will encounter uncertainty in social interactions:

> [Such people] can never be sure what the attitude of a new acquaintance will be, whether it will be rejective or accepting, until the contact has been made. This is exactly the position of the adolescent, the light-skinned Negro, the second generation immigrant, the socially mobile person and the woman who has entered a predominantly masculine occupation (Barker 1948:33).

The woman in a male profession then, is likely to be self-conscious, burdened by the feeling that she is "on," and calculating about the impressions she is making in order to counteract the assumptions and perceptions of others (Goffman 1961:14). For example:

> Men, according to many attorneys, expect a woman to be emotional, so they read irrationality into her every word and gesture. "If a man gives the riot act to his secretary when she's made a mistake, he runs a tight ship," comments one female attorney. "Let a woman do the same thing and she's neurotic." Her female colleague agrees. "When a male attorney gets into a heated discussion over a point of law, he's a dynamic ball of fire. Should a woman attorney get equally excited, she's overwrought, easily agitated and taking the matter personally" (Dinerman 1969:953).

This occurs because, "when a system of stereotypes is well fixed, our attention is called to those facts which support it, and diverted from those which contradict it" (Lippman 1949:78).

Professional women, therefore, often tend to adopt compensating strategies to minimize the effects of their "deviance." Such strategies operate in one or both of two dimensions: the behavioral or personality dimension and the structural or career dimension. In either realm the adoption of a compensating strategy may mean trying to act as much like a man as possible to achieve acceptance as "one of the boys," or diligently conforming to the normative expectations of the feminine role. The latter strategy is more often adopted because by taking this route the professional woman may reduce the ostensible conflict between her sexual and professional roles.

Bird found that successful professional women find some way to make their sex "work for them": they carefully control their manner, and their voices, using "their femininity to slip through the sex barrier" (Bird 1968:89, 109). We should not be surprised to find that the male members of the professions encourage and support the adoption of "feminine" compensating strategies:

> [M]embers of a social category may strongly support a standard of judgment that they and others agree does not directly apply to them. Thus it is that a businessman may demand womanly behavior from females or ascetic behavior from monks, and not construe himself as someone who ought to realize either of these styles of conduct (Goffman 1961:6).

In the structural or career dimension, one such strategy is that women enter special categories or subfields within their profession that are considered acceptable or less deviant for them. In many cases certain specialties seem open to women because they comport well with woman's traditional nurturant role. Other specialties appear to be "appropriate" for women only because there already are a sizable number of women in them. A United States government publication, for example, in describing careers for women in the legal profession advises them that:

Women's opportunities seem best in those law specialties where their contributions to the field have already been recognized. Some of these are real estate and domestic relations work, women's and juvenile legal problems, probate work (about a third of all women judges are probate judges), and patent law for those who have the required training in science (Griffin 1958:12).

The data that follow document the tendency of women to cluster in the specialties where their "opportunities seem best."

MEDICINE

The medical profession is one of the few fields in which women and men are clearly sex-segregated in superior and subordinate occupations. More than 93 percent of all practicing physicians are men (Renshaw and Pennell 1971), while women constitute 98 percent of all professional nurses and 96 percent of all practical nurses in the country (Women's Bureau 1969). The chances of being treated by a woman doctor are about one in fourteen, by a woman surgeon one in forty. Table 14.1 presents a breakdown of the specialties of practicing women physicians based upon the 324,942 doctors listed in the American Medical Association's "physician master list" (Renshaw and Pennell 1971). More women—one-fifth of all women physicians —specialize in pediatrics than any other area. In contrast, only one woman in ten, compared to three out of ten men, is found in any of the surgical specialties. In comparing the expected percentage to the actual percentage of women in each medical specialty, pediatrics again stands out: three times more women are found than would be expected. Other areas in which women are substantially overrepresented are anesthesiology (2.12), pathology (1.73), psychiatry (1.88), physical medicine (2.20), preventive medicine (1.67) and public health (2.80). Women are substantially underrepresented in nine fields: cardiovascular (0.40), gastroenterology (0.33), general surgery (0.15), ophthalmology (0.47), orthopedic surgery (0.07), otolaryngology (0.18), plastic surgery (0.40), other surgery (0.06), and occupational medicine (0.44). Obstetrics and gynecology are the only surgical specialties in which women are not underrepresented. Women also are underrepresented, although to a lesser degree, in general practice where the ratio is 0.62, or slightly more than half the expected proportion. We shall have more to say about this pattern in our discussion of women in the legal profession.

The observed percentage compared to the expected percentage of women in medical specialties in which they are underrepresented or overrepresented are shown in Table 14.2. These figures are striking. Although women are a small minority in all medical specialties, the seven fields in which women are overrepresented contain almost half of all practicing women physicians—more than double the expected proportion of one in four is found in the specialties where women are underrepresented.

These figures seem to imply that women's choice of specialty is determined, in

TABLE 14.1. Fields of Specialization of Practicing Women Physicians
(In percentages)

Specialty	Observed (N = 20,304)	Expected[a]	Ratio of Observed to Expected
General Practice	12.1	19.4	0.62
Medical Specialties (subtotal)	31.9	23.7	1.35
Allergy	0.6	0.6	1.00
Cardiovascular	0.8	2.0	0.40
Dermatology	1.3	1.3	1.00
Gastroenterology	0.2	0.6	0.33
Internal medicine	10.2	12.6	0.81
Pediatrics	17.9	5.9	3.03
Pulmonary	0.9	0.7	1.29
Surgical Specialties (subtotal)	9.9[b]	27.4[b]	0.36
General surgery	1.4	9.4	0.15
Obstetrics, gynecology	6.2	6.0	1.03
Ophthalmology	1.5	3.2	0.47
Orthopedic surgery	0.2	3.0	0.07
Otolaryngology	0.3	1.7	0.18
Plastic surgery	0.2	0.5	0.40
Other surgery	0.2	3.5	0.06
Other Specialties (subtotal)	39.0	25.1	1.55
Anesthesiology	7.2	3.4	2.12
Neurology	1.0	0.9	1.11
Occupational medicine	0.4	0.9	0.44
Pathology	5.7	3.3	1.73
Psychiatry	13.7	7.3	1.88
Physical medicine	1.1	0.5	2.20
Preventive medicine	0.5	0.3	1.67
Public health	2.8	1.0	2.80
Radiology	2.9	4.1	0.71
Other specialty	3.7	3.3	1.12
Unspecified	7.1	4.4	1.61
Total	100.0	100.0	1.00

SOURCE: Renshaw and Pennell 1971:188, Table 1 (computed).

[a] This is the percentage of women that would have been observed in the specialties were the sex composition of each specialty the same as the sex composition of the profession as a whole.

[b] The sum of component specialties does not equal subtotal because numbers were rounded off.

part, by a desire to minimize role conflict. By practicing pediatrics women conform to the feminine role stereotype of caring for children. Psychiatry, another "caring" specialty, also draws large numbers of women. Perhaps not coincidentally, psychiatry ranked lowest when medical students of both sexes were asked to evaluate the relative standing of specialties within the profession (Merton et al. 1956).

TABLE 14.2. Observed and Expected Percentage of Women in Selected Medical Specialties

Specialties	Observed	Expected[a]	Ratio of Observed to Expected
Specialties in Which Women Are Overrepresented			
Pediatrics	17.9	5.9	
Anesthesiology	7.2	3.4	
Pathology	5.7	3.3	
Psychiatry	13.7	7.3	
Physical medicine	1.1	0.5	
Preventive medicine	0.5	0.3	
Public health	2.8	1.0	
Total	48.9	21.7	2.15
Specialties in Which Women Are Underrepresented			
Cardiovascular	0.8	2.0	
Gastroenterology	0.2	0.6	
General surgery	1.4	9.4	
Ophthalmology	1.5	3.2	
Orthopedic surgery	0.2	3.0	
Otolaryngology	0.3	1.7	
Plastic surgery	0.2	0.5	
Other surgery	0.2	3.5	
Occupational medicine	0.4	0.9	
Total	5.2	24.8	0.21

SOURCE: Renshaw and Pennell 1971:188.
[a] This is the percentage of women that would have been observed in the specialties were the sex composition of each specialty the same as the sex composition of the profession as a whole.

LAW

Like medicine, law is a profession whose heroics are popularized and dramatized through the medium of television. Its practitioners are depicted as clever, courageous and articulate, and almost without exception they are men. Fighting against tremendous odds, they work miracles in bringing about the ultimate triumph of justice. The women in their lives—wives, lovers, secretaries, assistants faithfully following after their heroes—are inevitably beautiful and little else.

Law is unquestionably a man's field. As in medicine, women and men in law are sex-segregated into occupational hierarchies. Ninety-seven percent of practicing lawyers are men (White 1967). On the other hand, more than 98 percent of secretaries, stenographers, and typists working in the legal field are women (Women's Bureau 1969). Many lawyers, both male and female, believe that there is something inherently masculine about the practice of law. The argument, related by Dinerman, runs like this:

> The law is born of conflict, and its practice, almost by definition, must be aggressive and warlike in nature. To be successful, an attorney must have a fighting disposition. He should have mental alertness, unusual self-confidence, a logical mind and a nonretiring personality. These qualifications, many contend, are not the type of traits normally associated with a feminine personality. Female attributes, such as softness, gentleness and pacifism, just aren't the characteristics that make for effective lawyers (Dinerman 1969:953).

For those "deviant" women who do enter the legal profession, such stereotypes are difficult to dispel. The position of women in law is well summarized by Professor Frederica Lombard of Wayne State University Law School, chairman of the Committee on Women in Legal Education of the Association of American Law Schools:

> The real problem facing women lawyers is getting a job. The discrimination is somewhat less blatantly stated now than it was seven years ago when I got out of law school, but that is the only change. And if law firms do hire women, they still shunt them into estates and trusts. They tell us we're good at working with widows and orphans (*New York Times* 1971:25).

By far the most comprehensive study of women in the law is James White's 1967 survey of 1,298 female and 1,329 male graduates of 108 of 134 accredited law schools during the period 1956 to 1965. Table 14.3 shows the response of White's sample when asked to describe their legal work at the time of the survey.

The most striking finding of this survey concerns the relative proportions of men

TABLE 14.3. Specialty of Attorneys, by Sex (In percentages)

Specialty in Law	Women (N = 654)	Men (N = 1115)
General Practice	31.4	49.0
Litigation	7.0	7.2
Corporate	5.2	3.8
Tax	4.8	3.5
Trusts and Estates	4.1	1.1
Criminal	4.1	2.1
Labor	1.8	2.2
Real Estate	1.5	1.7
Domestic Relations	0.3	0.0
Other (including nonlaw)	39.8	29.4
Total	100.0	100.0

SOURCE: White 1967:1064, Exhibit 7.

and women in general practice. Nearly half the men in the sample characterized themselves as general practitioners, compared to only about 30 percent of the women. A similar avoidance of general practice and a greater tendency to specialize was noted among women in medicine. There may be fewer women generalists in both law and medicine because general practitioners usually constitute the front line of their profession. It is the general practitioner who initially is sought out by the patient or client, and who makes the first decisions about the individual's legal or medical problems or refers the person to a specialist. The bias against the woman lawyer or physician is undercut somewhat by having the touchy matter of initial introductions or referrals handled by the male lawyer or physician the public expects. White suggests that

> the woman makes a conscious choice to avoid general practice because she believes that a special skill will reduce or overcome sex discrimination. Or, the relative absence of women in general practice may mean only that some employers hire women for specialized positions in probate, tax, and other fields (White 1967:1064).

Women in both law and medicine tend to work "in fields where they have been traditionally accepted" (Glancy 1970:26). This pattern is not surprising if choice of specialty is understood as part of a compensating strategy professional women must adopt in order to succeed in the face of discrimination. Nor is it surprising to find, as White indicates, that firms support such a strategy by their hiring practices.

Table 14.4, which presents data on the type of work actually performed by women and men lawyers, gives a better idea of the area of specialization in which attorneys actually work. According to White's study, men dominate litigation and corporate work. Women predominate, to a significant degree, in trusts and estates and domestic relations—traditional female domains in the profession (Glancy 1970; Epstein 1968; White 1967). The percentage of women White found to be engaged in litigation is somewhat surprising, given the common belief that women are rarely trial lawyers, but his data reveal nothing about the type or size of the litigation involved. Women may try cases but they may be of relatively little importance, and therefore, of low visibility.

On the whole, then, women lawyers are engaged largely in low-prestige specialties in which there is a large proportion of female clients and in which their "feminine" qualities can serve them well (e.g., domestic relations). In addition, they serve in those specialties where firms can put them in "back rooms," making sure they do not have contact with big clients who, the firms claim, would find it unacceptable to deal with women. There is some evidence that women choose these legal fields under the compulsion of their compensating strategies or under pressure from their employers, rather than out of their own interest.[2] A recent study of

---

[2] The two are not necessarily mutually exclusive, for, as we have seen, employers tend to support those compensating strategies that lead women to conform most closely to the normative expectations of the female role.

TABLE 14.4. Type of Work Performed by Attorneys, by Sex (In percentages)

Type of Work	Women (N = 575)	Men (N = 952)
Trusts and Estates	60.0	52.7
Real Estate	51.0	52.8
Domestic Relations	49.8	38.6
Litigation	45.6	58.5
Corporate	42.0	53.8
Tax	31.0	27.9
Criminal	27.7	28.0
Labor	7.3	11.8

SOURCE: White 1967:1063, Exhibit 6.

women graduates of the Harvard University Law School revealed that 36 percent of the women, compared to only 16 percent of the men, are not engaged in the position or field of law of their first choice:

> This relatively high dissatisfaction rate on the part of the women can be read in a number of ways—innate fickleness, general dissatisfaction, or some force keeping women graduates out of those occupations which they would most like to pursue . . . Both outright discrimination, and the subtle dictates of a negative attitude toward women, direct them out of litigation, labor law or corporate work. Rather than fight the system, some women change their minds and redirect their aspirations from such fields to less competitive "women's fields." The result is that many women, therefore, are not doing the kind of work they would most like to do and may be most capable of doing (Glancy 1970:29).

ACADEME

Academe is commonly thought of as less rigid and conservative than the law or medicine and, hence, more open to women. Statistically this is true, for the proportion of women in the academic disciplines is much higher than in the professions. Nevertheless, women still are a relatively small minority. Consequently, we would expect to find that the compensating strategies discussed above also affect women's choice of specialization in academe.

Social Sciences

Women college graduates constitute more than one-third of those who majored in the social sciences (Women's Bureau 1969). They represent about one-third of recipients of the master's degree in the social sciences, but just slightly more than one in ten of all doctorates in these fields (Women's Bureau 1969). Since no data are available on field of specialization of practicing academic social scientists, we will examine the fields in which women social scientists received their doctorates (Table 14.5). This is probably a close approximation to the proportions actually working in each of these fields.

TABLE 14.5. Specialty of Women Social Scientists, Based on Doctorates Earned (1960–1969) (In percentages)

Specialty	Observed (N = 2,072)	Expected[a]	Ratio of Observed to Expected
Social sciences, general	1.3	1.4	0.93
American studies	2.0	1.4	1.43
Anthropology	9.7	5.0	1.94
Area or regional studies	2.2	2.1	1.05
Economics	10.6	20.9	0.51
History	27.9	26.5	1.05
International relations	1.6	2.3	0.70
Political science or government	12.2	15.4	0.79
Sociology	19.4	12.7	1.53
Agricultural economics	0.6	6.2	0.10
Foreign service programs	0.1	0.1	1.00
Industrial relations	0.2	0.5	0.40
Public administration	1.1	1.5	0.73
Social work, social administration	8.4	2.6	3.23
All other fields	2.7	1.5	1.80
Total	100.0	100.1[b]	1.00

SOURCE: Computed by author from data in Truax 1971.
[a] This is the percentage of women that would have been observed in the specialties were the sex composition of each specialty the same as the sex composition of the discipline as a whole.
[b] Total does not equal 100.0 because numbers were rounded off.

Seven fields stand out in which women are either substantially underrepresented or substantially overrepresented. Women are underrepresented in economics (0.51), agricultural economics (0.10) and industrial relations (0.40), while they are overrepresented in anthropology (1.94), sociology (1.53), social work and administration (3.23) and the miscellaneous other category (1.80).[3] More than two out of every five women social scientists—almost double the percentage expected—are in those fields in which women are overrepresented. Only about one woman in ten—less than half the expected proportion—is in the specialties in which her sex is underrepresented.

Women in the social sciences, it appears, tend to gravitate toward fields in which they are more accepted and which are thought of as more appropriate for

[3] The U.S. Department of Health, Education and Welfare does not include psychology as a discipline under Social Sciences in its compilation of Earned Degrees Conferred. We shall consider the field of psychology later, using another source of data for our discussion.

women. These specialties—anthropology, sociology, and social work (the classic bastions for "caring" women)—may be loosely considered the people-oriented social sciences.

Anthropology

Although we labeled anthropology as a field in which women are overrepresented, a closer look at the discipline shows that this classification is purely relative. The data on which Table 14.5 is based showed that women earn more than 21 percent of the Ph.D's in anthropology. However, a study of 2,098 anthropologists listed in the *Guide to Departments of Anthropology, 1969–1970* found that women comprise only 15 percent of the faculty in anthropology departments (Vance 1970).

Interesting differences emerge when these women faculty members are examined in terms of their area of specialization within anthropology (see Table 14.6). The

TABLE 14.6. Specialty of Women Anthropologists (In percentages)

Specialty	Observed (N = 321)	Expected[a]	Ratio of Observed to Expected
Cultural	63.6	55.3	1.15
Physical	6.6	9.5	0.69
Archaeology	9.0	16.1	0.56
Linguistics	9.4	7.9	1.19
Unknown	11.5	11.1	1.04
Total	100.1[b]	99.9[b]	1.00

SOURCE: Committee on Status of Women in Anthropology, Fact Sheet, Unpublished. (Computed.)

[a] This is the percentage of women that would have been observed in the specialties were the sex composition of each specialty the same as the sex composition of the discipline as a whole.

[b] Totals do not equal 100.0 because numbers were rounded off.

majority of anthropologists are in the field of cultural anthropology, but the proportion of women working in this area is slightly higher than expected. Women are underrepresented in both physical anthropology and archaeology—the proportion in the latter is about half of that expected.

Commenting on these findings, the outgoing chairperson of the American Anthropological Association Committee on the Status of Women in Anthropology said:

> Our finding that many fewer women go into physical anthropology and archaeology did not surprise us for it is well known in the profession that they have been explicitly unwelcome in these two subfields. Archaeologists have been most rude in turning women down and telling them that they would not fit into the field situation (personal communication).

The rationale for channeling women into cultural anthropology and away from physical anthropology and archaeology is clear and is based upon an assumption of inherent sex differences. Social attitudes and stereotypes are called into play to enforce a division of labor: women being "weaker by nature" are not suited to the emotional and physical rigor of archeological field work.

Sociology

There are only slight variations between the sexes in the fields of specialization they pursue in sociology (Patterson 1971). In their study of 159 women and 194 men listed in the American Sociological Association's 1969 *Guide to Graduate Departments of Sociology,* Huber and Patterson (1970) found only three areas in which women are substantially underrepresented or overrepresented: social change and development (0.30), occupations and professions (1.65), and the miscellaneous "other" (1.78). (See Table 14.7.) Women may be underrepresented in "so-

TABLE 14.7. Specialty of Women Sociologists (In percentages)

Specialty[a]	Observed (N = 159)	Expected[b]	Ratio of Observed to Expected
Sociocultural theory	10.1	11.6	0.87
Methodology	8.2	13.3	0.62
Demography and population	6.6	5.6	1.18
Rural-urban	9.4	9.7	0.97
Social change and development	2.2	7.4	0.30
Social problems, social disorganization	8.2	8.2	1.00
Social psychology	15.1	12.1	1.25
Social structure and organization	13.8	14.7	0.94
Occupations and professions	10.4	6.3	1.65
Normative institutions	12.0	8.6	1.30
Other	4.1	2.3	1.78
Total	100.1[c]	99.8[c]	1.00

SOURCE: Huber and Patterson 1970: 17, Table 6 (computed).
[a] For a list of the components of each specialty category, see Patterson 1971:227.
[b] This is the percentage of women that would have been observed in the specialties were the sex composition of each specialty the same as the sex composition of the discipline as a whole.
[c] Totals do not equal 100.0 because numbers were rounded off.

cial change and development" for much the same reason they are underrepresented in physical anthropology and archeology: the field work environment may be presumed to be too harsh for them. Women dominate the "other" category largely because the traditional women's fields of social work and social welfare are included in this category. It is more difficult to explain women's overrepresentation in occupations and professions. Since it includes the legal, medical, occupational, and scientific subspecialties (see Patterson 1971:227), it may be that women who were discouraged from entering these male-dominated professions have contented themselves with studying rather than practicing in the field of their interest.

Psychology

The data on which Table 14.8 is based are derived from a study of 3,541 female and 19,891 male fellows and members of the American Psychological Association (APA) listed in the 1968 APA Directory (Hoffman et al. 1971). The specialties listed are actually divisions within the APA rather than strictly psychological fields.

TABLE 14.8. Specialty of Women Psychologists (In percentages)

Specialty	Observed (N = 3,998)	Expected[a]	Ratio of Observed to Expected
General	3.8	3.5	1.09
Teaching of psychology	7.1	7.2	0.99
Experimental	2.7	4.3	0.63
Evaluation and measurement	2.9	3.4	0.80
Physiological and comparative	1.3	2.0	0.65
Developmental	7.4	3.3	2.24
Personality and social	14.3	12.8	1.12
Society for the psychological study of social issues	3.3	5.9	0.56
Psychology and the arts	1.0	0.9	1.11
Clinical	14.5	12.3	1.16
Consulting	2.7	2.1	1.29
Industrial	1.0	3.4	0.29
Educational	9.4	8.7	1.08
School	8.7	3.6	2.42
Counseling	5.4	6.2	0.87
Psychologists in public service	1.5	2.1	0.71
Military	0.3	1.4	0.21
Maturity and old age	1.6	1.3	1.23
Engineering	0.3	1.5	0.20
Psychological aspects of disability	4.5	3.6	1.25
Consumer	0.4	1.0	0.40
Philosophical	1.1	1.9	0.58
Experimental analysis of behavior	1.6	2.4	0.67
History of psychology	0.8	1.3	0.61
Community	2.0	2.5	0.80
Psychopharmacology	0.6	1.4	0.43
Total	100.2[b]	100.0	1.00

SOURCE: Hoffman et al. 1971, Table I (computed).
[a] This is the percentage of women that would have been observed in the specialties were the sex composition of each specialty the same as the sex composition of the discipline as a whole.
[b] Total does not equal 100.0 because numbers were rounded off.

Nevertheless, the data should be a fair approximation of the relative proportions of women and men pursuing various specialties, since most of the divisions correspond to actual areas of specialization within the discipline.

Women are substantially overrepresented in two divisions of the APA: developmental (2.24), and school psychology (2.42). Together these two areas account for about one-sixth of all women psychologists—more than twice the expected proportion. Both of these fields fall within the sphere of women's traditional role, for both are concerned primarily with children. For the most part, the specialties in which women are substantially underrepresented—industrial (0.29), military (0.21), engineering (0.20), consumer (0.40), and psychopharmacology (0.43)— also speak for themselves. If industry, the military, and engineering are the bastions of men, then fields of inquiry about these subjects can only be thought of as the bulwarks for men. The only surprising pattern among these specialties is consumer psychology, for women are thought of as consumers par excellence. One need only read Friedan (1963) on "The Sexual Sell," however, to realize that the emphasis of consumer psychology, at least as practiced by industry, is on the home as the market-place for consumption. With its promotion of housewifery, one could hardly expect consumer psychology to be an hospitable field for professional women.

Languages and Literature

The specialty distribution of doctorates in foreign languages and literature reveals few differences between women and men (see Table 14.9). The one language in which women are substantially underrepresented is Hebrew (0.17) and this may largely be attributed to the tradition of the male Jewish scholar. The field in which women are overrepresented is French (1.42). It is worth noting that nearly seven out of every ten women in foreign languages and literature are in the three languages—French, Spanish, German—that are taught in virtually every high school and junior college in the country. The proportion of women in these languages is more than a third again as large as the expected percentage. Thus it may be that women in foreign languages and literature tend to seek those fields where they are relatively certain of finding employment on one level or another.

Physical Sciences

The data on women in the physical sciences show that it is almost meaningless to speak of women in any of the physical sciences other than chemistry (see Table 14.10). Fully three-quarters of all women who earned doctorates in the physical sciences between 1960 and 1969 received them in chemistry—a proportion one-and-a half times as large as the expected 50 percent.

We can only suggest explanations for these findings. Chemistry is a basic subject in almost every high school science program, and the same hope that exists for

TABLE 14.9. Specialty of Women in Foreign Languages and Literature, Based upon Doctorates Earned (1960–1969) (In percentages)

Specialty	Observed ($N = 1,186$)	Expected[a]	Ratio of Observed to Expected
Linguistics	11.2	13.3	0.84
Latin, classical Greek	10.8	12.2	0.89
French	26.2	18.5	1.42
Italian	1.4	1.1	1.27
Portuguese	0.3	0.3	1.00
Spanish	18.3	16.1	1.14
Philology and literature of romance languages	7.8	9.1	0.86
German	14.4	16.3	0.88
Other German languages	0.4	0.6	0.67
Philology and literature of Germanic languages	0.8	1.3	0.62
Arabic	0.1	0.1	1.00
Chinese	0.2	0.3	0.67
Hebrew	0.1	0.6	0.17
Hindi, Urdu (1961–1969 only)	0.0	0.0	—
Japanese	0.2	0.3	0.67
Russian	2.4	2.8	0.86
Other Slavic languages	1.7	1.6	1.06
All other fields	3.8	5.5	0.69
Total	100.1[b]	100.0	1.00

SOURCE: Computed by author from data in Truax 1971.

[a] This is the percentage of women that would have been observed in the specialties were the sex composition of each specialty the same as the sex composition of the discipline as a whole.

[b] Total does not equal 100.0 because numbers were rounded off.

women in French, Spanish and German—that of obtaining a position on a lower school level if higher education proves impossible—may apply in the case of chemistry as well. It may also be that because the greatest demand in the physical sciences is for chemists, female Ph.D.'s are more confident of finding jobs as lab assistants in this area. Whatever the explanation, the one undeniable fact is that women in the physical sciences demonstrate almost no variety in area of specialization.

Biological Sciences

The data on doctorates in the biological sciences show that women are either substantially underrepresented or overrepresented in seven fields (see Table 14.11). The explanation for the relatively high proportion of women in general biology is probably the same as that for the high proportion of women in chemistry and cer-

TABLE 14.10. Specialty of Women Physical Scientists, Based on Doctorates Earned (1960–1969) (In percentages)

Specialty	Observed (N = 1,179)	Expected[a]	Ratio of Observed to Expected
Physical sciences, general	0.3	0.4	0.75
Astronomy	2.5	1.6	1.56
Chemistry	75.0	50.4	1.49
Metallurgy	0.0	0.8	0.00
Meteorology	0.2	1.0	0.20
Pharmaceutical chemistry (1961–1969 only)	1.1	1.1	1.00
Physics	14.2	32.7	0.44
Geology	4.5	8.3	0.54
Geophysics	0.3	0.8	0.38
Oceanography	0.3	0.9	0.33
Earth sciences, all other fields	0.2	0.7	0.29
Physical sciences, all other fields	1.5	1.4	1.07
Total	100.1[b]	100.1[b]	1.00

SOURCE: Computed by author from data in Truax 1971.

[a] This is the percentage of women that would have been observed in the specialties were the sex composition of each specialty the same as the sex composition of the discipline as a whole.

[b] Totals do not equal 100.0 because numbers were rounded off.

tain foreign languages—general biology is taught at all levels of education. That women are found in the nutrition field in twice their expected numbers might be explained by reference to women's social role as nurturer. In fact, "nutrition" and "nurture" derive from the same Latin root, *nútríre,* which means "to feed," "to nurture"—traditional female duties.

The remaining fields, however, seem to defy rational explanation—at least by a nonbiologist. For example, why are women found in entomology in a proportion only one-third of the expected? Are we to assume that the ladylike fear of insects and crawling creatures instilled in girls at an early age persists and expresses itself in occupational choice? On the other hand, women who typically are portrayed as avid amateur gardeners (nurturers again) are grossly underrepresented in plant pathology and substantially below their expected proportion in plant physiology. In what way are women better qualified to study cells that accounts for their predominance in cytology?

CONCLUDING REMARKS: PRESSURE OR PREFERENCE

The data on choice of occupational specialty in law, medicine, and academe document a consistent differential pattern between women and men. In virtually every

TABLE 14.11. Specialty of Women Biological Scientists, Based on Doctorates Earned (1960–1969) (In percentages)

Specialty	Observed (N = 2,448)	Expected[a]	Ratio of Observed to Expected
Premedical, predental and preveterinary sciences	0.1	0.1	1.00
Biology, general	16.1	11.0	1.46
Botany, general	7.6	9.3	0.82
Zoology, general	13.0	12.8	1.02
Anatomy and histology	4.7	3.6	1.31
Bacteriology, etc.[b]	14.5	11.8	1.23
Biochemistry	19.2	15.2	1.26
Biophysics	1.3	2.4	0.54
Cytology	0.4	0.2	2.00
Ecology (1961–1969 only)	0.1	0.2	0.50
Embryology	0.4	0.3	1.33
Entomology	1.9	6.2	0.31
Genetics	2.5	3.8	0.66
Molecular biology (1968–1969 only)	0.2	0.2	1.00
Nutrition (1961–1969 only)	1.8	0.9	2.00
Pathology	0.6	1.5	0.40
Pharmacology	3.6	4.4	0.82
Physiology	6.9	6.5	1.06
Plant pathology	0.8	3.9	0.21
Plant physiology	0.5	1.1	0.45
All other fields	3.8	4.5	0.84
Total	100.0	99.9[c]	1.00

SOURCE: Computed by author from data in Truax 1971.

[a] This is the percentage of women that would have been observed in the specialties were the sex composition of each specialty the same as the sex composition of the discipline as a whole.

[b] Includes bacteriology, verology, mycology, parasitology, and microbiology.

[c] Total does not equal 100.0 because numbers were rounded off.

field, with the exception of sociology, women's specialties are readily apparent. The majority of women are found in a narrow range of specialties within their chosen profession or academic discipline. Furthermore, their specialties are generally the less prestigious ones.

How can we account for these findings? Two polar explanations are what we will call the *pressure theory* and the *preference theory*. The pressure theory posits that women in male-dominated fields are guided by significant others (relatives, teachers, practitioners, colleagues) into specialties that are considered appropriate for women. The preference theory says that women are genuinely attracted by, pulled by their own interests toward the specialties in which they are found.

The pressure theory finds some support in our data. As we noted earlier, women in anthropology who attempt to enter physical anthropology and archaeology are discouraged by male professors and even turned down by employers on the basis of sex. Much of the literature from which our data on women in law are drawn indicates that women are excluded from certain specialties and are most often found in trusts and estates and domestic relations work. We do not know what interests of power, prestige, or access to resources motivate this "combination in restraint of trade," but rationalizations for the exclusion of women from certain anthropology fields based upon the stereotype of the frail female should not remain unexamined. In the case of law, it is precisely those specialties that are most closely tied to power —corporation law and litigation—that have the lowest proportion of women. In addition to reflecting a belief that women are better at working with widows and orphans, the pressure for women to go into domestic relations and trusts and estates also may represent a desire to keep women from the citadels of power.

In the face of such pressure some women would rather switch than fight. Some simply accept what they see as the inevitable, while others conform as a consciously chosen compensating strategy, entering "more appropriate" specialties as a means of achieving greater acceptance from their colleagues and society at large. More concrete support for the pressure theory comes from the finding discussed earlier that more than twice as many women as men attorneys are *not* engaged in the legal field of their choice.

The preference theory would argue that the differences between women and men in the fields and sub-specialties they have chosen are simply evidence of different interests. While the pressure theory stresses *external* social pressures which prevent women from entering certain specialties, the preference theory stresses an *internal* process whereby women seek out a specialty consistent with a set of interests and skills they have acquired. However:

> [T]his view conveniently overlooks the fact that society has spent twenty years carefully marking the woman's ballot for her, and therefore has nothing to lose in that twenty-first year by pretending that she casts it for the alternative of her choice. Society has controlled not her alternatives, but her motivation in choosing [among those] alternatives (Bem and Bem 1970:26).

The specialty preferences that women show then, may be determined both by sex-role socialization and by women's own consciously or unconsciously adopted compensating strategies.

Clearly, we know very little about the determinants of women's career aspirations. From the data reviewed in this chapter, it seems probable that women's aspirations and career choices are the end product of a complex process of internal and external pressures. Yet only when we understand the process of career choice and its refinement into a choice of specialty will we be able to develop social policies which will help women fulfill their highest potential.

REFERENCES

Barker, R. 1948. The social psychology of physical disability. *Journal of Social Issues* 4: 28–38.

Bem, Sandra L., and Bem, Daryl J. November 1970. We're all nonconscious sexists. *Psychology Today* 4:22–26, 115–16.

Bird, Caroline. 1968. *Born female.* New York: Pocket Books.

Committee on the Status of Women in Anthropology, American Anthropological Association. Undated. Fact sheet. Unpublished. (See also Vance 1970.)

Dinerman, B. 1969. Sex discrimination in the legal profession. *American Bar Association Journal* 55:951–954.

Epstein, Cynthia F. 1968. Women and professional careers: The case of the woman lawyer. Ph.D. dissertation, Columbia University.

Epstein, Cynthia F. 1970. *Woman's place.* Berkeley: University of California Press.

Friedan, Betty. 1963. *The feminine mystique.* New York: Dell Publishing Co.

Glancy, D. J. 1970. Women in law: The dependable ones. *Harvard Law School Bulletin* 21:23–33.

Goffman, Erving. 1961. *Stigma, notes on the management of spoiled identity.* Englewood Cliffs, N.J.: Prentice-Hall.

Griffin, Verna E. 1958. *Employment opportunities for women in legal work.* Washington, D.C.: U.S. Government Printing Office.

Hoffman, D. T., Scally, B., Deering, A., and Kott, E. 1971. The women in psychology. University of Bridgeport. Unpublished.

Huber, Bettina, and Patterson, Michelle. 1970. Sexuality of sociological specialty. Paper presented at 1970 Annual Meeting of American Sociological Association.

Kreps, Juanita. 1971. *Sex in the marketplace: American women at work.* Baltimore: Johns Hopkins Press.

Lippmann, Walter. 1949. *Public opinion.* New York: The Free Press.

Merton, Robert K., Bloom, Samuel, and Rogoff, Natalie. 1956. Studies in the sociology of medical education. *Journal of Medical Education* 31:552–565.

New York Times. October 22, 1971. P. 25.

Oppenheimer, Valerie K. 1970. *The female labor force in the United States.* Berkeley, Calif.: Institute of International Studies.

Patterson, Michelle. 1971. Alice in wonderland: A study of women faculty in graduate departments of sociology. *American Sociologist,* 6:226–234.

Renshaw, Josephine E., and Pennell, Maryland Y. 1971. Distribution of women physicians, 1969. *The Woman Physician,* 26:187–195.

Truax, Anne. 1971. Fact sheet on earned doctorates by sex, 1960–1969. Unpublished. University of Minnesota.

U.S. Department of Labor, Women's Bureau. 1969. *1969 handbook on women workers.* Washington, D.C.: U.S. Government Printing Office.

Vance, Carol. 1970. Sexism in anthropology? The status of women in departments of anthropology. *American Anthropological Association Newsletter,* 11:5.

White, James J. 1967. Women in the law. *Michigan Law Review,* 65:1051–1122.

Chapter Fifteen

Sex Discrimination in Academe

Helen S. Astin
Alan E. Bayer

SEX DISCRIMINATION in academe does not begin when a woman accepts an appointment at a college or university. Rather, it is rooted in the cumulative effects of early childhood socialization for "appropriate" sex role behavior and attitudes, differential treatment and expectations of girls and boys by their parents, teachers, and peers throughout adolescence and early adulthood, and differential opportunities for admission to undergraduate and graduate school (Roby 1971; Bernard 1971). As a result, when women enter teaching careers in colleges and universities they have interests, aspirations, expectations, educational backgrounds, and experiences that differ from those of their male counterparts.

As faculty members, women experience a second barrier to equality with men: the academic reward system is biased toward behaviors and activities exhibited more often by men than women. Indeed, the academic reward system was established by men, so rewards go primarily to those women who accept and exhibit men's criteria for academic rewards. Thus, administration, research, and publications, which men engage in to a greater extent than women, receive higher rewards than teaching, to which women devote more time than men. This reward system is far from ideal and may even be dysfunctional to the educational objectives of American colleges and universities. However, the following discussion assumes the present reward system in order to assess the degree of sex discrimination in academic rank, tenure, and salary, *independent* of individual background characteristics, professional activities, and work settings.

THE ACADEMIC REWARD SYSTEM

The academic reward system is not monolithic. Indeed, it varies substantially from one institution to another and even from one department to another within an institution. For example, research activity may be better rewarded in elite colleges

AUTHOR'S NOTE: Data reported in this chapter were collected through a collaborative project of the American Council on Education and the Carnegie Commission on Higher Education with support from the U.S. Office of Education. We are particularly indebted to Jeffrey E. Dutton, Laura Kent, and Jeannie Royer for their assistance in various phases of this project.

333

and universities, administrative activity in four-year colleges, and teaching skills in junior colleges. Similarly, publication may be valued more highly in physics departments than education departments; teaching may be esteemed in the humanities, deprecated in the hard sciences; degree credentials may be relatively unimportant in literature and the arts, all important in the social sciences. Only when the differences between academic women and men in their backgrounds, professional activities, and employer institutions are taken into account can the existence and extent of sex discrimination in academe be accurately assessed.

Although evidence of sex discrimination in academe has mounted in the past several years (see especially Chapters Eleven, Twelve, and Thirteen; see also, Robinson 1971; Astin et al. 1971), most studies have been somewhat unsystematic and limited. Some investigators have taken a head count of chairmanships or professorships held by women within a discipline. Others have made intrainstitutional assessments of the proportional distributions of women and men within ranks or comparisons of average intrarank salaries of women and men. Because these studies often fail to consider such differences in professional background as degree, length of employment, field of specialization, productivity—all criteria for rewards in higher education—the unconvinced administrator or colleague can simply cite these and a host of other neglected variables, real or imaginary, as explanation of the extreme discrepancies in the position of the sexes. So, too, most research studies have introduced only a few intervening variables to explain sex differentials. For example, in a recent study of differences by sex in the salaries of sociologists, La Sorte showed that age and five work-related variables in part explained the observed differences, but he was unable to attribute the residual discrepancies directly to discrimination:

> Can [the residual discrepancy in salary] be attributed wholly to sex discrimination, that is, that women are paid unequally because of their sex without regard to accomplishment, or is the bulk of the residual explainable by nondiscriminatory factors left unexamined in this study? Other factors that could be considered, for instance, are publication record, marital status, geographic mobility, and professional commitment. . . . A control for institutional affiliation would probably further reduce the residual (La Sorte 1971:307).

Bayer and Astin also reached such a conclusion about virtually all studies completed to date:

> The lack of control for a number of relevant contingencies related to rank and salary differentials has resulted in an inability to assess adequately the presence or amount of discrimination experienced by women. . . . Salary and rank are usually related to length of time in the labor force, field of specialization, type of employer, and type of work activity. . . . [Although previous research reports] are highly suggestive of sex discrimination, such a conclusion is not justified without controlling [for these and other relevant variables] that affect academic rank and salary (Bayer and Astin 1968:192–193).

Some of the other relevant variables which differentiate between women and men in academe are examined below. The data are from a national survey of college and university teaching faculty, undertaken in the spring of 1969 by the Carnegie Commission on Higher Education in cooperation with the Office of Research of the American Council on Education (Bayer 1971).

VARIATIONS BY SEX IN BACKGROUND AND INTERESTS OF FACULTY

Women college faculty were only about half as likely as men faculty to hold a doctorate. In the Carnegie-ACE survey of faculty, 22 percent of women faculty and 46 percent of men faculty reported that they had a Ph.D. or Ed.D. Conversely, 62 percent of women and 36 percent of men faculty held an M.A. or less. The remainder held professional degrees, medical degrees, or other doctorates. Moreover, larger proportions of women than of men faculty listed their fields of specialization as humanities (21 percent versus 15 percent) or education (16 percent versus 10 percent), whereas larger proportions of men than of women were in physical sciences and engineering (20 percent versus 5 percent) or the social sciences (12 percent versus 8 percent).

The interests of faculty in teaching and research also varied by sex. Only 11 percent of women faculty as against 27 percent of men faculty indicated that they were interested primarily in research rather than teaching. Their publications also reflected these differences in interests: less than two-fifths (39 percent) of men faculty, but almost two-thirds (63 percent) of women faculty had never published an article in a professional journal.

VARIATIONS BY SEX IN ACADEMIC WORK SETTINGS

Women were more likely than men to carry heavy responsibilities for undergraduate teaching. Less than half of men teachers (48 percent) and more than two-thirds of women teachers (69 percent) indicated that their teaching was confined to undergraduates. These differences were only partly attributable to differences in job settings, the discrepancies being most marked in universities where proportionately twice as many women as men (48 percent and 24 percent) taught only undergraduate classes. Moreover, teaching loads tended to be heavier for women. While both sexes tended to be responsible for the same number of students, 63 percent of women compared with only 49 percent of men taught nine or more hours per week. These differences held constant across work settings, suggesting that women may teach moderate size classes, while men combine large undergraduate lecture courses with very small graduate seminars.

As noted here, the reward system differs appreciably from one type of institution to another. Small community colleges typically pay much lower salaries than large prestigious universities. More than half of all two-year college faculty, about two-fifths of four-year college faculty, and less than one-fourth of university faculty reported annual salaries of less than $10,000. The rank structure differs as well: the faculty survey showed that less than one-fifth of two-year college faculty, two-fifths of four-year faculty, and one-half of university faculty are either associate or full professors.

To the extent that women and men are differentially dispersed among the nation's colleges and universities, proportional differences in the rewards each sex receives might be expected. Most notable of the institutional characteristics associated with disproportionate concentrations of women and men faculty is whether the institution is a two- or four-year college or a university. While women constitute about one in five teaching faculty nationally, they are overrepresented in two-year colleges and underrepresented in universities. The survey indicated that women constitute 26 percent of two-year college faculties, 23 percent of four-year college faculties, and 15 percent of university faculties.

In the multiple regression analyses summarized below, other institutional factors as well as personal background and professional experience variables that are associated with differences in the rewards received by women and men are examined.

SAMPLE AND DESIGN

The Carnegie-ACE data were based on comprehensive questionnaire information received from 60,028 faculty members at a nationally representative sample of institutions: 57 two-year colleges, 168 four-year colleges, and 78 universities. Data were subsequently weighted to correct for sampling and response biases, producing national norms for all American college and university teaching faculty. These national estimates indicate that 19 percent of all teaching faculty in 1969 were women, 81 percent were men.

Those faculty who held regular appointments, with or without tenure, who were teaching nine or more class hours during the term, and who responded to the questionnaire items concerning sex, salary, and rank were selected from the unweighted file of 60,028 faculty members, yielding a sample of 21,856 (4,583 women, 17,273 men). For economy in processing data, women and men were "randomly" selected to yield an analysis sample of 3,438 women and 3,454 men.

Criterion Variables

Three primary criterion variables were derived from responses to the survey:

1. Academic rank (continuous variable: professor = 4; associate professor = 3; assistant professor = 2; instructor, lecturer, or other designations = 1)
2. Tenure status (dichotomous variable: tenured = 2; otherwise = 1)
3. Basic institutional salary, 1968–1969 academic year before taxes and deductions

(continuous variable: $25,000 or more $= 8$; $20,000–24,999 $= 7$; $17,000–19,999 $= 6$; $14,000–16,999 $= 5$; $12,000–13,999 $= 4$; $10,000–11,999 $= 3$; $7,000–9,999 $= 2$; and under $7,000 $= 1$)

Predictor Variables

There were four sets of predictor variables: demographic characteristics, educational background, professional/work activities, and characteristics of the institution of employment. The demographic variables were:

(a) Sex (the primary analytical variable: women $= 2$; men $= 1$)
(b) Age (over 60 $= 6$; 51–60 $= 5$; 41–50 $= 4$; 36–40 $= 3$; 31–35 $= 2$; 30 or under $= 1$)
(c) Race (three variables: white/other; black/other; Oriental/other)
(d) Citizenship (three variables: not U.S. citizen/other; naturalized U.S. citizen/other; native U.S. citizen/other)
(e) Religious background (three variables: Protestant/other; Catholic/other; Jewish/other)
(f) Current religion (four variables: Protestant/other; Catholic/other; Jewish/other; no religion/other)
(g) Father's education (advanced degree $= 7$; some graduate school $= 6$; college graduate $= 5$; some college $= 4$; high school graduate $= 3$; some high school $= 2$; eighth grade or less $= 1$)
(h) Marital status (three variables: currently married/other; divorced/other; never married/other)
(i) Number of children (three or more $= 4$; two $= 3$; one $= 2$; none $= 1$)
(j) Political orientation (strongly conservative $= 5$; moderately conservative $= 4$; middle-of-the-road $= 3$; liberal $= 2$; left $= 1$)

The educational background variables were:

(a) Highest degree held (four variables: baccalaureate or less/other; master's/other; professional or medical/other; any doctorate/other)
(b) Graduate school stipend support (three variables: teaching assistantship/other; research assistantship/other; fellowship/other)
(c) Year of highest degree (before 1939 $= 7$; 1939–1948 $= 6$; 1949–1953 $= 5$; 1954–1958 $= 4$; 1959–1963 $= 3$; 1964–1966 $= 2$; 1967 or later $= 1$)
(d) Major field (nine variables: business/other; education/other; biological science/other; physical science/other; engineering/other; social science/other; fine arts/other; humanities/other; health fields/other)
(e) Quality of higher education (a dichotomous variable indicating whether or not the highest degree was obtained from one of the top twelve institutions as cited by Cartter 1966)

The professional/work/activities variables were:

(a) Teaching department (nine variables: same variables as major field categories)

(b) Years employed in academe (30 years or more = 8; 20–29 = 7; 15–19 = 6; 10–14 = 5; 7–9 = 4; 4–6 = 3; 2–3 = 2; one year or less = 1)

(c) Years employed at current institution (eight categories: same variables as length of employment in academe categories)

(d) Amount of time in administrative activity (over 40 percent = 5; 21–40 percent = 4; 11–20 percent = 3; 1–10 percent = 2; none = 1)

(e) Teaching/research interests (lean toward research = 2; lean toward teaching = 1)

(f) Number of published articles (20 or more = 5; 11–20 = 4; 5–10 = 3; 1–4 = 2; none = 1)

(g) Number of published books (5 or more = 4; 3–4 = 3; 1–2 = 2; none = 1)

(h) Number of students taught (400 or more = 5; 250–399 = 4; 100–299 = 3; 50–99 = 2; under 50 = 1)

(i) Discourages office visits by students (no = 3; yes, but with many exceptions = 2; yes, always = 1)

(j) Salary base (included only in regression analyses where the criterion is salary: 11–12 month basis = 2; other = 1)

The institutional variables of the place of employment were:

(a) Type (three variables: university/other; four-year college/other; two-year college/other)

(b) Control (four variables: public/other; Protestant/other; Catholic/other; private nonsectarian/other)

(c) Sex composition (coeducational = 2; other = 1)

(d) Location (four variables: Northwest/other; Midwest/other; Southeast/other; West/other)

(e) Racial composition (predominantly black = 2; other = 1)

(f) Curriculum (three variables: liberal arts/other; teachers/other; technical/other)

(g) Enrollment size (1967 total enrollment, coded into eight categories)

(h) Affluence (total revenues per student, coded into nine categories)

(i) Selectivity (average ability test scores on entering students, coded into seven categories)

(j) Percentage of Ph.D.'s on staff (continuous variable ranging from 01 to 99)

(k) Size of library (number of library volumes, coded into eleven categories)

ANALYTICAL PROCEDURES

In the following analysis, the stepwise multiple regression model was used to analyze the independent strength of each variable. The differential significance or weight of variables is indicated by the relative size of the F ratios. The F ratios in the tables represent the independent contribution of each significant predictor variable. Zero-order correlations also are reported in order to illustrate how each variable relates to the criterion measures. The relationship of demographic factors, educational background, professional/work activities, and institutional variables to the three primary measures of the academic reward system—rank, tenure, and salary—were ascertained. After all significant correlates of these three criterion measures were statistically controlled for, the extent to which sex per se explained the residual variance in the criteria was determined in an effort to find whether sex discrimination exists in academe. Since the analyses were predicated on the existing reward structure of academe, however, any result suggesting the presence of sex discrimination is a conservative estimate indeed.

Second, to learn if the same predictors of the criterion measures are equally applicable to explain differentials among men and among women, stepwise regression was used separately by sex. The regression equations obtained from the analyses for one sex were applied to the data for the other sex to demonstrate in real terms what adjustments would be necessary if true equality were to be obtained within the existing reward structure.

ACADEMIC RANK

Men tend to occupy the highest ranks in academe. For example, 25 percent of our sample of men faculty were full professors, but only 9 percent of women faculty held that rank; 35 percent of women, but a mere 16 percent of men, were instructors. In part, this reflects the fact that only 22 percent of our sample of academic women had either a Ph.D. or Ed.D., as compared with 46 percent of academic men. For this analysis, tenure, salary, salary base, and sex were deleted, and all other variables were freely allowed to enter the stepwise regression equation until no additional variable could significantly predict the additional differences in rank. Of the seventy-six potentially significant predictors, thirty entered the regression equation with a significant weight, producing a multiple correlation of 0.79. These thirty variables explained 62 percent of the variance in rank. After all thirty variables were entered, the partial correlation between being a woman and holding a high rank was –0.17. That is, even after controlling for a large number of variables that account for rank differences among academic personnel, much of the differential could still be attributed solely to sex. Indeed, a comparison of the F ratios in Table 15.1 indicates that sex is a better predictor of rank than such factors as number of years since completion of education, number of years employed at present institution, or number of books published. These results clearly demonstrate the biases operating against women in academe with respect to rank.

Table 15.1 shows that the five most significant predictors of rank were degree, productivity as measured by articles published, years of employment, type of employer institution, and time spent in administrative activities. Independent of degree, faculty at two-year institutions were less likely to hold professorial ranks. Those faculty employed in humanities departments were less likely to have attained high rank even when their degree level, publications, number of years of work experience, and job setting were considered. Women and men employed by large institutions with high proportions of doctorates and many library volumes—indices of institutional selectivity and affluence—were less likely to have attained high

TABLE 15.1. Predicting the Rank of Academics ($R = 0.79$)

Variables	Zero-Order r	Direction and Significance Level in Final Multiple Regression Equation	
		Sign	F Ratio[a]
Doctorate	0.46	+	367.10
Number articles published	0.49	+	245.14
Years employed in academe	0.64	+	235.25
Two-year institution	−0.21	−	211.02
Time spent in administration	0.27	+	136.16
Year of degree	0.46	+	70.06
Age	0.54	+	65.80
Number books published	0.34	+	65.39
Years employed at current institution	0.55	+	54.71
Department: engineering	0.09	+	41.31
Bachelor's degree	−0.16	−	48.70
Master's degree	−0.37	−	40.63
Size of institution	−0.00	−	33.95
Private nonsectarian institution	0.06	−	27.47
Major in education	−0.04	−	25.30
Number of children	0.08	+	23.39
Father's education	−0.07	−	17.26
Single	−0.02	+	16.59
Roman Catholic institution	0.01	−	14.96
Degree from one of top 12 institutions	0.12	+	12.19
Number of library volumes	0.13	−	11.66
Percent of Ph.D.'s on faculty	0.14	−	10.33
Research interests	0.09	+	9.26
Political orientation conservative	0.02	−	7.86
Major in humanities	−0.07	−	7.74
Major in health fields	−0.02	+	7.48
Native-born	−0.01	+	7.16
Department: biology	0.09	−	6.94
Fellowship (graduate stipend)	0.06	+	6.35
Department: humanities	−0.09	−	4.37

Partial r[b] (sex-Female) $= -0.17$. $F = 197.02$.

[a] $F > 3.84 = p < 0.05$; $F > 6.64 = p < 0.01$; $F > 10.83 = p < 0.001$.

[b] The *partial r* expresses the relationship of sex (as a predictor) to academic rank, *independent* of all other predictor variables listed in the table.

ranks than their colleagues with similar backgrounds employed by smaller and less prestigious institutions.

In addition, faculty at private institutions were less likely to hold high ranks than similar faculty at public institutions. These findings suggest that different institutions, or different departments within the same types of institutions, promote faculty at different rates, sometimes on the basis of different criteria. Perhaps these differences may be attributed, in part, to imbalances in supply and demand. There may be, for instance, more faculty available for teaching in humanities departments, thus, greater competition for rank or recognition. Or, since sex was not controlled for, this finding may be a function of the greater proportion of women in the humanities.

Among the demographic variables that may determine individual differences in the academic reward system are marital status, number of children, socioeconomic background, and political orientation. For instance, after controlling for other factors, single faculty were slightly more likely than married or widowed faculty to attain high ranks. Since sex was not controlled for, this finding may reflect the differences between single and married *women,* as the career profiles of single women doctorates are more like those of men than those of married women doctorates (see Chapter Seven). Among those who had been or were married, however, those with large families were more likely to attain high ranks. Persons with large families may have greater motivation for high status since they need larger salaries. What the social process is which links this financial need to higher academic rank for the husbands is unknown, though it is an issue that merits future investigation.

Faculty who attained high rank were less likely to have well-educated fathers, an intriguing finding in understanding the impact of early home experiences on later achievement. This finding accords with an earlier finding that women doctorates whose mothers had worked at semiskilled and unskilled rather than professional occupations were more likely to be productive as measured by publications (Astin 1969). Astin suggested that these women's high drive was a compensatory reaction to their mothers' relatively low status. Other writers, however, have offered different interpretations: Epstein (1971) attributes the relationship of low socioeconomic background and high achievement to economic need coupled with the belief that through hard work one can achieve a high rank in the social structure.

Independent of degree, productivity, years of employment, field, and work activities, the quality of one's graduate institution had a significant impact on career success. The faculty member who received his or her degree at one of the top twelve elite institutions was likely to attain high rank sooner than those from less prestigious institutions. One interpretation of this finding is that persons who attend prestigious institutions are superior in ability and motivation to those who attend less elite graduate schools and show evidence of this difference by a greater amount of research and publications early in their academic careers. Another interpretation is that a graduate degree from a prestigious institution is in itself an important entree to career advancement in the academic world: it may offer privileged access to sources of highly rewarded positions and employers usually operate with biases toward those whose training they assume to be of high quality.

Having had a fellowship as a graduate student also predicted high rank. This finding also appears to reflect motivation and aptitude. Perhaps if direct measures of aptitudes and motivations had been available for this study, they would have more successfully differentiated faculty holding high rank than did graduate fellowships.

In sum, even after controlling numerous predictor variables which account for over 60 percent of the variance in academic rank, there remain significant differences between the sexes. When a woman attains the doctorate from a prestigious institution and demonstrates great scholarly productivity, she still cannot expect promotion to a high rank as quickly as her male counterpart.

ACADEMIC TENURE

Across all types of institutions and among all teaching faculty, 49 percent of men and 38 percent of women held regular tenured appointments. The second regression analysis dealt with the predictors of tenure and the influence of sex per se on the achievement of tenure.

Rank was the most significant predictor of tenure (see Table 15.2). Independent of rank, the length of employment at the respondent's current institution largely determined attainment of tenure. Persons teaching either at two- or four-year institutions were assured of tenure sooner than comparable persons at universities. Faculty at technological or affluent institutions were slower in attaining tenure than persons at liberal arts, teachers colleges and less affluent institutions. Discipline was also an important predictor of tenure. Compared to those in the biological sciences, education, and health-related fields, persons in humanities, physical sciences, social sciences, and business were less likely to have attained tenure, whatever their rank or length of employment. Since rank and length of employment at a given institution were the prime determinants of tenured staus, we would suggest that if women could reach high rank as often and as quickly as men, they would secure commensurate tenure.

SALARY DIFFERENTIALS

According to an earlier study, sex differentials in salary are greater than sex differentials in rank (Bayer and Astin 1968). For example, 46 percent of men faculty achieved high rank, compared with 25 percent of women faculty, but 28 percent of men faculty had a salary of less than $10,000, compared to 63 percent of women. Moreover, only 4 percent of academic women made a salary of $17,000 or more compared with 19 percent of men (Bayer 1970). Other studies suggest that differences by sex in salary can be explained on the basis of rank, years of employment, field of specialization, teaching department, productivity, and work activities. But is this conclusion justified?

In the third multiple regression analysis, we controlled for differences in salary base (whether academic or calendar year), degree, productivity, research versus teaching interests, time spent in administration, field of specialization, and a num

TABLE 15.2. Predicting Tenure of Academics ($R = 0.72$)

		Direction and Significance Level in Final Multiple Regression Equation	
	Zero-Order		
Variables	r	Sign	F Ratio[a]
Rank	0.58	+	612.88
Years employed at current institution	0.63	+	496.56
Two-year institution	0.05	+	132.43
Number of library volumes	−0.00	+	30.45
Four-year college	−0.00	+	29.91
Time spent in administration	0.21	+	19.34
Major in humanities	−0.08	−	17.09
Public institution	−0.01	+	18.44
Age	0.52	+	15.87
Single	0.02	+	12.34
Sectarian institution	0.02	+	11.16
Affluence of institution	−0.02	−	10.84
Year of degree	0.48	+	9.22
Major in physical sciences	0.02	−	8.97
Major in social sciences	0.04	−	8.61
Number of children	0.03	+	7.84
Major in business	−0.02	−	7.35
Years employed in academe	0.62	+	7.03
Jewish—current religion	−0.07	−	6.55
Technological institution	−0.03	−	6.13
Professional/medical degrees	−0.00	−	6.00
Department: fine arts	0.01	−	5.54
Number of articles published	0.29	+	4.45

Partial r^b (sex-Female) $= 0.02$. $F = 3.00$.
[a] $F > 3.84 = p < 0.05$; $F > 6.64 = p < 0.01$; $F > 10.83 = p < 0.001$.
[b] *Partial r* expresses the relationship of sex (as a predictor) to tenure, independent of all other predictor variables in the table.

ber of other background and professional work variables (see Table 15.3). The obtained multiple R of 0.80 indicates that 64 percent of the variance in salary can be explained on the basis of 33 personal and environmental variables. Even after control for rank, which carried the heaviest weight, and for all other significant predictors of salary, the partial correlation between sex (female) and salary was −0.16. A comparison of the F ratios indicates that sex was a better predictor of salary than such factors as number of years of professional employment or whether one holds a doctorate.

The three most important variables in explaining salary differentials were rank, productivity, and type of parent institution. Among full professors, those who published the most articles and books made the highest salaries. The type of institution

TABLE 15.3. Predicting the Salary of Academics ($R = 0.80$)

Variables	Zero-Order r	Direction and Significance Level in Final Multiple Regression Equation	
		Sign	F Ratio[a]
Salary base	0.19	+	340.04
Rank	0.67	+	1392.48
Two-year institution	−0.04	+	311.45
Number of articles published	0.55	+	238.81
Four-year institution	−0.11	+	84.25
Doctorate	0.37	+	79.10
Professional/medical degrees	0.11	+	73.93
Size of institution	0.21	+	73.08
Sectarian institution	−0.12	−	67.46
Major in health fields	0.11	+	56.98
Time spent in administration	0.26	+	51.67
Number of children	0.19	+	49.10
Major in humanities	−0.15	−	45.54
Selectivity of institution	0.18	+	43.08
Tenure	0.46	+	36.08
Department: humanities	0.03	+	35.49
Married	0.15	+	34.35
Year of degree	0.38	+	33.85
Number of library volumes	0.18	+	33.84
Roman Catholic institution	−0.11	−	33.02
Bachelor's degree	−0.15	−	26.04
Number of books published	0.34	+	23.17
Department: fine arts	−0.06	−	22.00
Department: engineering	0.12	+	21.97
Years employed in academe	0.49	+	21.11
Private nonsectarian institution	0.04	−	18.10
Years employed at current institution	0.40	−	14.18
Degree from top 12 institutions	0.14	+	12.38
Research assistant (graduate stipend)	0.16	+	8.22
Institution in Northeast	0.03	+	7.51
Current religion: Judaism	0.03	+	6.20
Black institution	−0.06	+	4.78
Research interests	0.14	+	4.46

Partial r[b] (sex-Female) $= -0.16$. F $= 191.52$.
[a] $F > 3.84 = p < 0.05$; $F > 6.64 = p < 0.01$; $F > 10.83 = p < 0.001$.
[b] *Partial r* expresses the relationship of sex (as a predictor) to salary, independent of all other variables listed in table.

was also important in that faculty (matched on rank and productivity) at two- and four-year institutions earned higher salaries than similar faculty at universities. Young faculty may finish their graduate training with a preference to teach at similar institutions themselves, so that the two-year colleges have to offer higher salaries in order to attract competent teachers away from the universities. A comparison of faculty at different universities showed that those employed by more prestigious institutions made higher salaries than those at less selective universities, and that large institutions paid higher salaries than small institutions. The pertinent implications of these findings for the issue of sex discrimination in salary are that, because of discriminatory hiring practices, women often teach at less prestigious and at smaller institutions. Moreover, women employed by large and prestigious institutions make less money than their male counterparts at the same institutions.

Being married and having a large family were positively related to making a higher salary, even after controlling for academic criteria such as degree, field, productivity, and work activities. Among the reasons for this finding may be that married faculty with large families press harder for raises and seek jobs that pay better. The system may also be willing to give higher salaries to people with larger families to support. Again, professional women are at a disadvantage. Significantly fewer academic women marry, and if they do, they have few or no children. When academic women are married and have large families, however, their salaries still do not equal those of married academic men with similar sized families. An administration may be willing to pay a male faculty member a higher salary on the grounds that "he has to support a family," but the same principle rarely is applied to women. On the other hand, women may be less likely to use their marital status or family size as a reason for requesting a higher salary since they may believe that there is a greater chance for being accepted by their colleagues if they deny their familial interests and financial responsibilities.

Other statistically significant, although somewhat less important, variables in predicting salary were certain fields of specialization and certain teaching departments. Faculty in the humanities received significantly lower salaries, and academics teaching in either business or engineering departments earned significantly higher salaries—independent of degree productivity and so forth—than those in other departments. In the current sample ($N = 6,892$), there were no women in engineering departments and only 3 percent of all women faculty were in business departments, while 8 percent of men taught in engineering departments and 5 percent in business departments. In contrast, 21 percent of the women faculty had majored in humanities, compared to 15 percent of the men. In short, since women are more likely to specialize and teach in less well-paying fields, or because traditionally "women's" fields are less remunerative, the overall salary differences between academic women and men become even greater.

Research interests and employment as a research assistant during graduate training also were statistically significant predictors of better salaries. Here again, women differed from men in that fewer women than men (11 percent versus 27 percent) indicated a primary interest in research; and fewer women had been graduate research assistants (19 percent of women compared with 38 percent of men).

The number of years of employment by the respondents' present institution negatively predicted high salary, implying that mobile faculty are more likely to be better paid. A change in institutional affiliation often is accompanied by a substantial salary increase, whereas those remaining at the same institution are more likely to get just the "usual" smaller annual increase. In addition, mobile professionals may have higher aptitudes and, thus, be in a position to command higher pay (Folger, Astin, and Bayer 1970).

Traditionally, the pressures against a married woman's geographic mobility are great. Moreover, women have not been and probably still are not as actively recruited by employers as men. Thus, they are more likely to remain longer with the same employer and, therefore, receive a lower salary.

In sum, women clearly hold a lower status not only by virtue of choices based on academic interests, but also because of limitations imposed upon them by the traditional sex-role system. Even when women make the same choices as men they still do not make as much money.

COMPARING RANK PREDICTORS

The following analyses assess the criteria used in rewarding the performance of academic men compared to women. We have found interesting differences in the variables that predict high rank among academic men compared to those that predict high rank among women (see Table 15.4). By applying the variables that were highly predictive of male success to academic women, we shall be able to see what kind of salary and academic rank levels women could have obtained, *if* the academic reward system was truly equitable.

Twenty-two variables entered the regression equation for the sample of male faculty with significant weights, and the R was 0.80. While a larger number of variables (26) carried significant weights in the female sample, the R was somewhat lower (0.77). This discrepancy, albeit slight, indicates greater difficulty in predicting ranks among women than among men.

For both women and men, the doctorate degree, years of employment in academe, productivity as measured by published articles and books, time spent in administration and years employed at the current institution, were among the most important variables in predicting high rank. Deterrents to rank advancement that handicap both sexes are employment at two-year institutions and teaching the humanities.

Over and above these predictors of success for both men and women, there are interesting differences between the sexes that suggest a rather different secondary cluster of "success predictors" for men and women. The type of institution—both where the individual earned his degree and where he teaches—seems to be more im-

TABLE 15.4. Predicting Rank of Academic Men Compared to Academic Women

Variables	Zero-Order r Men	Zero-Order r Women	Men Sign	Men F Ratio[a]	Women Sign	Women F Ratio[a]
			Direction and Significance Level in Final Multiple Regression Equation			
Significant Predictors for Both Sexes						
Two-year institution	−0.26	−0.16	−	240.88	−	56.24
Doctorate	0.40	0.48	+	138.03	+	241.05
Years employed in academe	0.67	0.63	+	132.26	+	68.23
Number articles published	0.48	0.43	+	103.34	+	70.67
Time spent in administration	0.25	0.25	+	71.36	+	43.95
Year of degree	0.53	0.42	+	65.37	+	18.72
Age	0.60	0.53	+	53.16	+	65.44
Master's degree	−0.37	−0.31	−	35.18	−	4.89
Number books published	0.34	0.29	+	29.86	+	24.95
Number of children	0.08	−0.17	+	22.99	−	14.22
Department: humanities	−0.10	−0.07	−	21.52	−	25.39
Years employed at current institution	0.56	0.56	+	19.44	+	40.29
Bachelor's degree	−0.14	−0.18	−	19.29	−	27.72
Political orientation: conservative	0.04	0.02	−	4.71	−	6.70
Significant Predictors for Men Only						
Number of library volumes	0.19		−	30.47		
Major in education	−0.04		−	15.04		
Department: engineering	0.06		+	12.48		
Private nonsectarian institution	0.04		−	10.46		
Degree from top 12 institutions	0.12		+	8.44		
Percent of Ph.D.'s on faculty	0.20		−	5.16		
Institution in Southeast	0.03		+	4.40		
Number of students in class	−0.11		−	4.00		
Significant Predictors for Women Only						
Size of institution		−0.11			−	48.15
Single		0.20			+	46.79
Department: health		−0.04			+	19.05
Public institution		−0.12			+	13.96
Divorced		−0.01			+	11.08
Fellowship (graduate stipend)		0.06			+	8.98
Research interests		0.08			+	8.38
Selectivity of institution		0.09			−	8.24
Liberal arts college		0.16			+	8.14

TABLE 15.4 (*cont.*)

| | Zero-Order *r* | | Direction and Significance Level in Final Multiple Regression Equation | | | |
| | | | Men | | Women | |
Variables	Men	Women	Sign	F Ratio[a]	Sign	F Ratio[a]
Native born		0.02			+	7.59
Private sectarian institution		0.04			+	6.18
Protestant background		0.01			−	4.44
				$R = 0.80$		$R = 0.77$

[a] $F > 3.84 = p < 0.05$; $F > 6.64 = p < 0.01$; $F > 10.83 = p < 0.001$.

portant for men than women. The strongest deterrent of rank advancement for men is employment at a two-year institution, with moderate additional deterrents related to this type of institution: small libraries and degrees short of the doctorate. It also helps men, but not women, to have earned a doctorate degree at a prestigious university and to teach in the engineering fields. So, too, number of children contributes to academic success for men but restricts advancement for women.

For women, advancement is facilitated by being single or divorced (though divorce is less significant than not having married), teaching at smaller, public institutions, and in the health fields. No single factor approaches the level of significance for the success of academic women as the possession of a doctorate, whereas for men, publications and number of years spent in academe reach about the same level of significance as the doctorate.

Thus a profile predictive of rank advancement for men includes a doctorate from a prestigious university, appointments of long duration in a private nonsectarian institution, participation in administration, and both private (children) and public (publications) productivity. In contrast, women advance up the ranks best if they attain doctorates, teach at small- to moderate-sized public institutions for some period of time, produce scholarly works, and have minimal demands on their time and energy (that is, have fewer children or remain single).

COMPARING TENURE PREDICTORS

Length of time with the same institution and rank were the two most significant predictors of tenure for both women and men (see Table 15.5). Once rank was controlled, it was found that persons employed at two-year institutions were likely to obtain tenure sooner than persons employed at four-year colleges or universities. In fact, for both sexes, employment at a university was negatively associated with ease in achieving tenure.

In contrast to their importance in predicting rank, fields of specialization carried

TABLE 15.5. Predicting Tenure of Academic Men Compared to
Academic Women

| | Zero-Order *r* | | Direction and Significance Level in Final Multiple Regression Equation | | | |
| | | | Men | | Women | |
Variables	Men	Women	Sign	F Ratio[a]	Sign	F Ratio[a]
Significant Predictors for Both Sexes						
Rank	0.59	0.55	+	297.66	+	284.03
Years employed at current institution	0.64	0.63	+	250.96	+	473.80
Two-year institution	0.03	0.07	+	64.53	+	56.59
Number of children	0.09	−0.14	+	24.08	−	6.30
Number of library volumes	0.03	−0.05	+	17.71	+	20.18
Time spent in administration	0.22	0.19	+	14.26	+	6.74
University	0.02	−0.08	−	9.89	−	19.46
Year of degree	0.51	0.46	+	4.29	+	7.06
Age	0.56	0.50	+	6.47	+	17.56
Single	−0.07	0.14	+	5.57	+	5.10
Significant Predictors for Men Only						
Affluence of institution	−0.00		−	7.48		
Years employed in academe	0.64		+	7.39		
Number of articles published	0.30		+	5.08		
Private nonsectarian institution	−0.02		−	4.42		
Coeducational institution	0.07		+	4.06		
Major in physical sciences	0.01		−	3.91		
Department: health	0.00		−	10.75		
Significant Predictors for Women Only						
Public institution		−0.01			+	22.97
Private sectarian institution		0.03			+	13.39
Percent of Ph.D.'s on faculty		−0.06			−	10.04
Major in humanities		−0.07			−	6.86
Major in business		−0.01			−	4.85
				R = 0.73		R = 0.70

[a] $F > 3.84 = p < 0.05$; $F > 6.64 = p < 0.01$; $F > 10.83 = p < 0.001$.

the predictive weights for tenure rather than departmental affiliation. Women who
had majored in either business or humanities were less likely to be tenured, independent of years of employment and rank, while men in the physical sciences were
slightly less likely to achieve tenure.

Men had a harder time achieving tenure in affluent and private nonsectarian institutions than in other types of colleges and universities. Women in private sectarian and public institutions were more likely to be given tenure. than women in other types of institutions. Once again, having children gives men an edge in the attainment of tenure, but penalizes women.

To summarize, tenured status was awarded both sexes on the basis of rank and length of employment at their institution. Moreover, the chances of becoming tenured were better at smaller and less selective and competitive institutions than at larger and more prestigious ones.

COMPARING SALARY PREDICTORS

Thirty-two variables entered the regression equation in differentiating men with respect to salary. These predictors yielded an R of O.81 and accounted for almost two-thirds of the variance. Among women, fewer variables (26) carried significant weights in predicting salary and resulted in a somewhat smaller R of 0.76 (see Table 15.6). Although most predictors of salary are similar for both women and men, there are some striking differences.

Rank was the most significant predictor of salary for both women and men. Employment at a two-year institution was found to be related to a high salary for both sexes, though more so for women than for men. There is an interesting contrast between men and women in the relative contribution of publications and holding a doctorate to salary level: for men, publications are more important than the doctorate, while for women, the doctorate is more important, second only to rank in determining women's salary. While field of specialization and teaching department were important determinants of salary for men, type and characteristics of employer institution were more important for women. Institutional size and selectivity were positive predictors for men and women alike.

Some additional predictors entered either the equations for men or for women, but not for both. Women who received fellowship support during graduate study were more likely to earn higher salaries than those who received other types of stipends or were self-supporting, suggesting that the factors that determine which women students receive fellowships—outstanding aptitude, high motivation, and so on—may also be important in determining who obtains higher salaries.

Men who obtained their highest degree from one of the top twelve institutions were more likely to have higher salaries than men who obtained degrees from less prestigious institutions. The same explanations offered earlier may also obtain here: either men who attend the elite institutions have certain personal characteristics or educational training that enable them to earn higher salaries, or having such a degree constitutes a kind of fringe benefit in that it impresses prospective employers and gives the graduate an added advantage in rank, salary, and so forth from the start of his career. However, this was not the case with the women's sample.

TABLE 15.6. Predicting Salary of Academic Men Compared to
Academic Women

| | Zero-Order *r* | | Direction and Significance Level in Final Multiple Regression Equation | | | |
| | | | Men | | Women | |
Variables	Men	Women	Sign	F Ratio[a]	Sign	F Ratio[a]
Significant Predictors for Both Sexes						
Salary base	0.26	0.13	+	229.42	+	67.35
Rank	0.66	0.63	+	641.82	+	506.07
Number articles published	0.54	0.46	+	96.83	+	66.14
Two-year institution	−0.08	0.03	+	95.70	+	120.70
Time spent in administration	0.26	0.24	+	30.87	+	21.56
Doctorate	0.25	0.42	+	30.74	+	95.75
Size of institution	0.25	0.14	+	25.21	+	50.60
Selectivity of institution	0.18	0.13	+	24.21	+	24.37
Department: fine arts	−0.07	−0.05	−	22.25	−	11.10
Number of library volumes	0.21	0.11	+	17.38	+	18.43
Professional/medical degrees	0.18	0.01	+	16.30	+	13.21
University	0.20	0.00	−	14.38	−	93.54
Tenure	0.47	0.45	+	14.06	+	25.93
Age	0.49	0.42	+	11.76	+	7.48
Number of books published	0.33	0.30	+	9.16	+	12.51
Bachelor's degree	−0.12	−0.19	−	6.24	−	20.74
Private nonsectarian institution	0.01	0.06	+	5.27	−	12.11
Institution in Northeast	−0.01	0.09	+	4.67	+	18.50
Years employed in academe	0.50	0.49	+	4.28	+	21.27
Significant Predictors for Men Only						
Department: humanities	−0.20		−	46.13		
Department: business	0.03		+	25.58		
Major in health	0.29		+	23.17		
Public institution	0.08		+	20.76		
Department: health	0.29		+	19.60		
Year of degree	0.46		+	18.27		
Number of children	0.16		+	14.35		
Degree from top 12 institutions	0.13		+	14.14		
Years employed at current institution	0.41		−	13.24		
Divorced	−0.04		−	11.08		
Department: engineering	0.06		+	9.33		
Affluence of institutions	0.14		−	6.27		
Research interests	0.10		+	5.17		

TABLE 15.6 (*cont.*)

| | Zero-Order r | | Direction and Significance Level in Final Multiple Regression Equation | | | |
| | | | Men | | Women | |
Variables	Men	Women	Sign	F Ratio[a]	Sign	F Ratio[a]
Significant Predictors for						
Women Only						
Private sectarian institution		−0.14			−	58.67
Roman Catholic institution		−0.10			−	41.08
Major in humanities		−0.08			−	24.87
Institution in West		0.08			+	12.80
Black institution		−0.02			+	10.66
Political orientation						
conservative		−0.01			−	7.18
Fellowship (graduate stipend)		0.08			+	4.93
				$R = 0.81$		$R = 0.76$

[a] $F > 3.84 = p < 0.05$; $F > 6.64 = p < 0.01$; $F > 10.83 = p < 0.001$.

Whether a woman receives her degree from a prestigious institution or not does not affect her career development with respect to academic rewards.

Divorced men tended to make lower salaries than either single or married men, although one might expect that they would seek higher salaries to pay alimony and child support. Perhaps divorce selects out less successful men, just as it may select out more career-committed women. Or, in their haste to relocate after the divorce, these men may be willing to accept lower salaries, especially if they are actively seeking a new position in a new location, rather than being recruited by an institution.

Marital status and number of children did not play as significant a part in differentiating women as it did in differentiating men with respect to salary. This may be attributable to the strong role that rank plays in differentiating women; as noted earlier, rank was influenced both by marital status and family size. Another explanation may be that there are strong pressures on academic woman to act as if she were sexless, familyless and childless in order to gain acceptance. Hence, even if a woman had economic pressures rooted in the size of her family, she might be less apt than a man to refer to this in requesting a salary increase.

In summary, although it is easier for both women and men to achieve high rank at a university than at a two-year institution, once rank is achieved one can expect a higher remuneration at the two-year college. Further, scholarly productivity and administrative responsibility insure higher salaries, independent of rank or type of employer institution. Nevertheless, women generally hold lower ranks and make lower salaries, however comparable are their backgrounds, work activities, achievements, and institutional work settings to those of their male colleagues.

EXTENT OF DISCRIMINATION

The last analysis compares the actual and the predicted rank and salary levels for academic women. (Tenure is excluded because it is not independently related to sex.) The regression weights of the predictor variables that emerged in the analyses of the men's sample were applied to the data for the women's sample in order to establish a minimum estimate of sex discrimination.

Table 15.7 shows the results of these analyses. If the same criteria, with the same weights, are applied in awarding rank to women as are applied to men, the average compensatory *increase in rank* would be from slightly below to somewhat above the assistant professor level, an average of one-fifth step. To award women the same salary as men of similar rank, background, achievements, and work settings would require a compensatory *average raise* of more than $1,000 (1968–1969 standards). This is the amount of salary discrimination which is *not* attributable to discrimination in rank. The amount of *actual* salary discrimination, attributable to discrimination in the types of institutions that employ women, the

TABLE 15.7. Actual and Predicted Rank and Salary Levels

	Men (*Actual*)	Women		
		Actual	*Predicted*	*Difference* (*Predicted minus Actual*)
Rank	2.465 (Midway between assistant & associate professor)	1.938 (Slightly below assistant professor)	2.140 (Somewhat above assistant professor)	+0.202 (one-fifth step in rank)
Salary	3.515 ($11,030)	2.526 ($8,580)	2.872 ($9,620)	+0.347 ($1,040)

opportunities they are given for administration or research, and advancement patterns, would substantially increase this figure of $1,000. Furthermore, the analyses accept all preceding discrimination against women as nonsex-related predictors, thus underestimating the net result of discriminatory factors which have operated against women since their childhood. Consequently, our estimates of the extent of sex discrimination in academe are *extremely conservative.*

SUMMARY AND IMPLICATIONS

Although it is clear that sex discrimination begins long before a woman enters academe as a trained professional, our focus has been limited to the academic status of women faculty compared with that of men. The emphasis has been on the sex bias that operates in the academic reward structure, independent of an individual faculty member's personal and educational characteristics, professional activities, and institutional setting, with full recognition that these factors themselves reflect differential and discriminatory sorting by sex.

Traditionally, the academic rewards of rank, tenure, and salary have been based chiefly on publication productivity and degree credentials. At most academic institutions, a person's teaching ability and interests are paid lip service only; they are not used as the primary performance criteria (Astin and Lee 1966). One reason for this omission is that publications and degrees are much more observable and quantifiable than success as a teacher. Moreover, scholarly productivity often means visibility to professional colleagues at other institutions. When colleagues are asked to rate departments within a field of specialization, their ratings are a direct reflection of faculty visibility (Cartter 1966; Roose and Andersen 1970).

In addition to demonstrating the importance of degree credentials and productivity as critical variables in the academic reward structure, these analyses also demonstrate the bearing of certain family and class background factors, professional activities, and work settings on rank, tenure, and salaries. A number of these variables, statistically significant but only moderately related to the rewards examined here, are worthy of further research exploration. Included here are such variables as political conservatism and place of birth of women faculty, qualities of the wives of men faculty with large families, and the career salience of women differing in marital status. The data presented in the tables on these factors suggest additional lines of future research inquiry to round out our understanding of the differential rewards of men and women in academe.

The institution at which one's degree is earned matters greatly in the reward structure, as do the time spent in administrative tasks and the degree of interest in research. Occupational mobility often accounts for higher salaries, although not necessarily for higher rank or tenure. Marital status and family size are important variables, in that institutions are more willing to help the married man, especially if he has a large family, although it is he who makes the heaviest demands on the reward system by choosing a job on the basis of how well it pays. The married woman, particularly if she has several children, is not so favored, even if she were not to interrupt her career to bear and rear children; indeed, the single woman faculty member is often better off. In addition, specialization, department affiliation, and type of institution are all important factors in differentiating women and men faculty with respect to ranks and salaries.

The relation of individual variables to academic rewards highlights the disadvantaged position of the academic woman, who often possesses few of the characteristics that determine academic success: fewer women than men in academe have doctorates, spend time in administration, have strong research interests, publish frequently, or are highly mobile. Moreover, they are much less apt to enter or teach in such high-paying fields as engineering, business, or physical science. When women are statistically matched with men on the variables that determine rewards, they are still apt to fall below men in rank and salary.

RESTRUCTURING THE ACADEMIC REWARD SYSTEM

Even if institutions of higher education put their houses in order in the seventies by promoting women on a basis comparable to that of men and by paying women salaries comparable to those of men with similar qualifications, there are several critical issues that remain to be faced. To rid academe of the vestiges of sex discrimination, the most visible and tangible manifestation of sex inequity, is only the first step in eliminating institutional sexism. Higher education must go beyond the rectification of discrimination to an understanding of the institutional sexism that restricts the goals and aspirations of women even before they enter the academic world.

A second critical issue that must be faced concerns the reward structure itself. It is assumed that productivity is an important and desirable characteristic in the academic world. Few people have examined how such a philosophy affects students and faculty or whether the quality of education is really better at an institution where faculty publish a great deal and are highly visible to their professional colleagues.

Some evidence suggests that students at institutions that have a high proportion of male faculty and "quality" doctorates and which emphasize productivity and research, are no more likely than students at other colleges and universities to indicate that the institution is concerned for them as individuals. Students at the former institutions are no less likely, and perhaps even more likely, to drop out, express dissatisfaction with the college experience, lower their degree aspirations, and take part in campus protests (Bayer 1970; Bayer and Astin 1972). In short, institutions may be perpetuating an academic reward system that is dysfunctional to students and could well become destructive to society in that it promotes competitiveness, discontent, and withdrawal from the world of intellect and scholarship.

Finally, the system has been detrimental and unjust to women on many counts. Women tend to teach more and to do less research. They are channeled into fields that are not particularly well paid. As graduate students, they often are not encouraged or helped to continue their education; thus, they interrupt or terminate their training more often than men. Women faculty have not been as readily accepted at selective, affluent, and large institutions. They have not been promoted to or asked to assume administrative leadership. The present system, as it is structured and as it allocates its rewards, has discriminated against women and is in need of change. The need, however, is not only for equality between the sexes, but also for an honest reexamination of a reward system that encourages faculty members to become more heavily involved in research and publishing and less interested in teaching. Such a pattern has questionable social merit and is fundamentally at odds with the educational objectives of American higher education.

REFERENCES

Astin, Helen S. 1969. *The woman doctorate in America.* New York: Russell Sage Foundation.

Astin, Helen S., Suniewick, Nancy, and Dweck, Susan. 1971. *Women: A bibliography on their education and careers.* Washington, D.C.: Human Service Press.

Astin, Alexander W., and Lee, Calvin B. T. 1966. Current practices in the education and training of college teachers. *Educational Record,* 47:361–375.

Bayer, Alan E. 1970. Faculty as determinators of students' perceptions of the college environment. Paper presented at the annual meeting of the American Association for the Advancement of Science, Chicago, Illinois.

Bayer, Alan E. 1971. College and university faculty: A statistical description. *ACE Research Reports,* 5(5). Washington, D.C.: American Council on Education.

Bayer, Alan E., and Astin, Alexander W. 1972. Faculty influences on the college environment. Paper presented at the annual meeting of the American Educational Research Association, Chicago, Illinois.

Bayer, Alan E., and Astin, Helen S. 1968. Sex differences in academic rank and salary among science doctorates in teaching. *Journal of Human Resources,* 3:191–199.

Bernard, Jessie. 1971. *Women and the public interest.* Chicago: Aldine Publishing Co.

Cartter, Allan M. 1966. *An assessment of quality in graduate education.* Washington, D.C.: American Council on Education.

Epstein, Cynthia F. 1971. Book Review. *American Journal of Sociology,* 77:359–361.

Folger, John K., Astin, Helen S., and Bayer, Alan E. 1970. *Human resources and higher education.* New York: Russell Sage Foundation.

La Sorte, Michael A. 1971. Sex differences in salary among sociology teachers. *American Sociologist,* 6:304–307.

Robinson, Lora H. 1971. *The status of academic women.* Review 5. Washington, D.C.: ERIC Clearinghouse on Higher Education, George Washington University.

Roby, Pamela. 1972. Structural and internalized barriers to women in higher education. In Constantina S. Rothschild (Ed.), *Toward a sociology of women.* Lexington, Mass.: Xerox College Publishing.

Roose, Kenneth D., and Andersen, Charles J. 1970. *A rating of graduate programs.* Washington, D.C.: American Council on Education.

Part Three

Action toward Change

Chapter Sixteen

Political Action by Academic Women

Kay Klotzburger

THE POLITICAL organization of women in academe emerged in 1969, the major purpose of which was to improve their professional status. The primary focus of academic women's groups to date has been on research concerning the status of women students and faculty within specific academic disciplines; political action directed toward national professional associations; and through these activities, the employers of professionally trained people in their respective fields. Within the spectrum of academic women's organizations, two main categories of groups may be identified: activist and advisory.

Activist women's groups or caucuses have their origins in the renewed feminist movement. The groups are independent of professional associations and function mainly as "pressure groups" in behalf of the self-interests of their members. They also function as sources of mutual help and support, encouraging members to develop positive self-concepts. "We're not content with the banality that 'better days are coming'," said one caucus coordinator. "That day was yesterday, and our group is demanding an end to prolonged discussions about the status of women." The Women's Caucus for Political Science (WCPS), the Association for Women Psychologists (AWP), and Sociologists for Women in Society (SWS) are notable examples of activist groups.

Advisory commissions (or committees) such as the Modern Language Association's Commission on the Status of Women, the American Political Science Association's Committee on the Status of Women, and the American Psychological Association's Task Force on the Status of Women in Psychology, tend to represent the more moderate segment of their professions, and give primary emphasis to issues concerning professionalism in a context of equal employment opportunity. These are official bodies, appointed by their professional associations to study and recommend changes in policy to meet the problem of prejudicial practices against women. In contrast to activist groups, advisory groups are generally gradualists who hope to quietly escort sex bias out of academe once the results of their status studies are made known to the members of their professional associations.

AUTHOR'S NOTE: I wish to acknowledge the assistance and/or moral support of Lillian Quigg, Linn Shapiro, Francis Slacker, Déja Strauss, and Audrey Wells in the preparation of this chapter.

These two types of organization are not in opposition nor do their members dissipate their energies in arguments with each other. They share the same basic belief that institutions of higher learning have supported discriminatory practices and they appeal to the democratic principle of human rights in an effort to improve woman's role in society. If a major difference does exist between them, it concerns how profoundly and how fast they believe the status quo must be altered in order to achieve their goals.

From 1968 to the end of 1971 at least fifty such groups of academic women were formed.[1] The overwhelming majority of them (82 percent) were founded in 1970 and 1971. The data base of this chapter consists of published and unpublished materials produced by or about these groups, together with intensive personal and telephone interviews with their representatives, and personal observation and participation at many of their meetings. No claim can be made that our list exhausts all the groups in existence by the end of 1971, but we are confident that it is representative of the political efforts of academic women between 1968 and 1971.

BACKGROUND OF THE ACADEMIC WOMEN'S MOVEMENT

The academic women's movement grew out of two developments during the 1960s: the larger women's movement (see Chapter One) and changes in the growth and structure of higher education. Under the stimulus of post-Sputnik channelling of federal funds into higher education during the early 1960s, the academic disciplines grew and so, too, did the professional associations. With expansion came a change in social composition. Federal support of higher education allowed persons formerly denied the opportunity for higher education to earn advanced degrees and, in turn, to join their respective professional associations.

APSA, for example, nearly doubled its membership in the early 1960s, as masses of students poured out of graduate schools. In so doing, the Association absorbed significant numbers of persons different in socioeconomic-ethnic background and sexual class from those of the predominant membership. This resulted in the creation of "elites" and "non-elites," and gave rise to internal "politics" as members organized into caucus groups devoted to reform.

In the past, professional associations were essentially "one party" instruments of scholarly expression. By 1967–1968 they were being accused by their own membership of social and intellectual insularity, and of functioning primarily as vehicles of indoctrination to their definition of scholarship. This confrontation particularly was apparent in social science associations, since social phenomena permit a wider range of interpretation than do the physical phenomena of the hard sciences.

---

[1] The list of women's groups included in this study was compiled with the help of Ruth Oltman at the American Association of University Women and Margaret Rumbarger at the American Association of University Professors, both of whom have kept records on women's groups in professional associations.

In other words, with the new members came new and diverse perspectives that had been all but ignored by the "elite" members of the associations. One association official noted:

> Newcomers, especially minorities and women, have experienced, and are still experiencing, problems beyond the ken of the typical establishment member. They want our Association to become more relevant, first, by recognizing their status within the profession as a legitimate professional problem; second, by encouraging new areas of scholarly concern; and third, by taking a forceful political stand on the social issues that concern them.

To this official, these demands are stiff since the elites who dominate the decision-making bodies of the association believe it should represent the profession as it was understood prior to the proliferation of area studies. The same association official explained:

> We are a nonprofit, nonpolitical learned society, primarily concerned with the diffusion of knowledge. It's not that the status of women is unimportant, but that our quarterly *Review,* our annual Convention, our international journal of abstracts, and our fellowship programs are simply more important aspects of higher learning.

The academic women's movement emerged out of and parallel to this resistance, adding accusations of sex discrimination by exclusion to those of ethnic discrimination, political irrelevance, and conservatism.

By the end of 1971, women's groups had been formed in thirty-three professional associations. Seventeen associations had both advisory and activist groups; twelve had only an advisory group and four had only an activist group. Table 16.1 lists the professional fields in which such groups have emerged, by type of group, and year in which they were formed. (Further details on the professional associations can be found in the Appendix to this chapter.)

Table 16.1 indicates several interesting things about the emergence of these groups. For one, they are clearly on the rise: only two groups were founded in 1968, seven in 1969: Then there was a sharp jump to seventeen in 1970 and eighteen in 1971. Of the fifty groups, 82 percent were founded in 1970 and 1971, and we would suggest that this trend in political organization has not yet peaked. Secondly, advisory groups are somewhat more prevalent than activist groups: twenty-nine of the fifty groups are advisory, twenty-one are activist. Moreover there seems to be a trend away from activist toward advisory groups: in 1969, five of the seven groups (71 percent) formed that year were activist groups, in contrast to only six of the eighteen groups (33 percent) formed in 1971. Protest by the pathbreaking caucus groups of a few years ago appears to have shifted to research and implementation, channelled through formal advisory groups.

Part of this trend reflects an expansion in the number of fields involved in women's issues. The first groups were formed in sociology, political science, his-

TABLE 16.1. Emergence of Professional Women's Groups, by Date of Formation and Type of Group[a]

| Date of Formation | Professional Field | | Number of Groups | | |
	Advisory	Activist	Advisory	Activist	Total
1968	Vocational Guidance	—			
	Modern Languages		2	0	2
1969	Political Science	Sociology			
	Philosophy	Psychology			
		Political Science			
		History			
		Modern Language	2	5	7
1970	History	American History			
	Anthropology	Population			
	Law	Training & Development			
	American Association of	Speech and Hearing			
	University Professors	African Studies			
	Library Science	Philosophy			
	Speech and Hearing	Statistics			
	American Studies				
	American History				
	Sociology				
	College Personnel		10	7	17
1971	Psychology	Mathematics			
	Engineering	Public Administration			
	African Studies	Philosophy of Education			
	Mathematics	Anthropology			
	Philosophy of	American Academy of			
	Education	Arts and Sciences			
	Population	College Administration			
	Microbiology				
	Physics				
	Public Administration				
	Chemistry				
	Cell Biology				
	Family Sociology		12	6	18
Total			26	18	44

[a] See Appendix for details on professional associations and dates of formation.

tory, psychology, and the humanities. By 1971, similar groups emerged in the sciences—microbiology, cell biology, and engineering. Because women in the social sciences and the humanities must critically examine the structure of society, they are more likely to develop and articulate a critical view of their own subordinate position within society and within their professional associations. Women in the sciences, in contrast, are much less likely to have had previous involvement in social and political causes. The increase in the number of groups is attributable, in part, to the tendency of activist groups to trigger the formation of advisory groups in the same associations. Of the thirteen associations which have both advisory and activist groups, it was the activist group which was formed *first* in nine associations. Consistent with the suggestion that women in the biological and physical sciences are less apt to be political pioneers or pacesetters, there seems to be a tendency for these women to bypass the activist group stage entirely. In the associations of cell biology, microbiology, engineering, and chemistry, for example, women's political activity began in 1971 with the formation of advisory groups.

Some fields are conspicuous by their absence from feminist political action. Business and commerce as well as the health professions are not represented in the sample of women's groups. That women in the business world are more complacent about the prevailing status quo than their academically employed sisters, and less apt to probe the problems of the social order or to assert themselves in social or political action is consistent with the general relationship between political orientation and occupation: political conservatism is highest in the fields of business and education.

Political activism also is more apparent in disciplines that are relative newcomers to academe, such as sociology and psychology. Women who enter an established field such as medicine are few in number and often have separate women's professional associations, most of which were established in the 1920s. An example is the American Medical Women's Association (AMWA). In the newer, vocationally-oriented fields, particularly those which build on the soft and technical sciences, women have chosen to join their major professional associations rather than to set up parallel associations. Since the "sex gap" can best be felt in a sexually mixed environment, it follows that demands to examine the status of women would be initiated by women in these new fields.

The academic women's movement is also influenced somewhat by the degree of male domination within a profession; that is, it tends to begin in fields where women represent at least 20 percent of the profession, and slowly moves to fields in which women represent a minority of less than 10 percent. Thus, women's groups were formed very early in sociology, modern languages, and psychology— fields in which women comprise 20 to 30 percent of association membership; whereas the most recent women's groups have developed in such fields as economics and engineering in which women comprise well under 10 percent of the membership.

This suggests that political activity begins in what might be called "resistant-supportive" associations, where the number of women is large enough to be threatening to men (especially in a tight job market), but supportive of organized activities by the women. It may be that women in fields where they are an extremely small minority experience a greater sense of isolation, and hence show greater reluctance to initiate activities that call attention to their sex. After all, women who have bucked the cultural cues and gone into a "man's field" may already feel insecure, and they may tend to cope with such insecurity by denying the relevance of their sex to their professional work. But as the movement grows, insecure and hesitant women may take strength from it, and slowly join the movement themselves. If one listens closely to conversations at professional women's meetings, one can sense a defensive note among women in professions that have not yet organized a women's group. A perception of group deficiency in 1972 may trigger political action in 1973.

A further catalyst to action for women is the subject matter of the disciplines themselves—that is, whether sex and gender roles have been legitimate variables in research and scholarship in the field. This is clearly the case in such disciplines as sociology, anthropology, modern languages, history, and psychology, all of which showed an early concern for the position of women in their respective professional associations. Women in these same fields have been the most active advocates of curriculum change, through the development of women's studies courses, new research questions on women's roles, and changes in the sex stereotype-ridden textbooks used in their fields.

There are indications that women's political activity is beginning in the fields of elementary and secondary education, and nursing. Why these women should be latecomers to political activity may be related to the fact that their fields traditionally have been women's fields. As such these women are less apt to experience sex inequities in comparison to male colleagues because any inequities apply to the entire field rather than just to the women. These fields have also attracted women who hold rather conventional attitudes concerning women's roles, although this too is changing as the ideas of the women's movement spread throughout society. It is interesting to note that *women* librarians were stimulated to political action when the library science profession attempted to upgrade its status among the professions by enticing men to enter the field. The trend toward a greater number of men entering primary and secondary school teaching also may trigger the same response among the nation's women teachers.

Table 16.2 summarizes institutional variations in women's political organization. As we mentioned, the tendency to have both advisory and activist groups is more typical of the academic than the nonacademic disciplines, particularly of the social sciences and the humanities, and of groups formed early in the history of the movement. If a single group exists, it usually is advisory. This is most characteristic of the natural sciences and the nonacademic professional fields, and the associations which founded groups more recently.

Activist and advisory groups rarely come into existence simultaneously, and the time lag between the founding of the groups within a particular association varies somewhat, depending on which type of group was formed first. On the average, the time lag between the founding of the groups is considerably shorter when the initial group is an action caucus. It rarely runs in excess of six months. In the African Studies Association the time lag was five months; in the American Math-

TABLE 16.2. Pattern of Single vs. Dual Women's Groups, by
Professional Field and Date of Group Formation

Professional Field and Date of Group Formation	Single-Group (Advisory or Activist)	Two-Group Pattern (Both Advisory and Activist)
Professional Field		
Academic Disciplines:		
Social Sciences and Humanities	2	11
Natural Sciences and Mathematics	5	1
Nonacademic Professional Fields	9	5
Total	16	17
Date of Group Formation		
1968–1969	1	6
1970	7	5
1971	6	5
Total	14	16

ematics Association and the American Speech and Hearing Association it was three months; in the American Historical Association it was only two months; and in the Philosophy of Education Society both groups were, in fact, founded simultaneously. The longest time lag between the founding of a caucus and the appointment of an official group was in the American Psychological Association, where the Task Force on the Status of Women in Psychology was formally set up nearly a year-and-a-half after the Association for Women Psychologists came into existence.

When the advisory group predated the action group, the time lag generally ran at least a year. For example, in the Modern Language Association and the American Philosophy Association a year passed before a caucus was organized; and in the American Anthropological Association, nearly two years intervened. The reasons for this significantly longer time lag are difficult to assess, but it may be that women who normally would have been involved in the founding of action groups were appointed to advisory groups. Moreover, where an advisory group already has been appointed, the function of a caucus is necessarily different: rather than calling for the establishment of an advisory group, the caucus serves a watchdog, prodding function of keeping the advisory group "on its toes" and "honest." Whether a caucus is needed might not be clear for some time.

In addition to women's organizations within professional associations, there are independent women's rights organizations concerned with professional career goals, examples of which are the Women's Equity Action League (WEAL), the Professional Women's Caucus (PWC), and the Association of Women in Science (AWIS). WEAL was formed in 1968 as a split-off from NOW, and is described in detail in Chapter Nineteen. PWC is an association of women from a variety of professions. Since its April 1970 founding it has tended, however, to speak for and to attract nonacademic professional women, particularly lawyers and business-women. AWIS was founded at the 1971 meeting of the Federation of American Societies for Experimental Biology (FASEB). Its primary goals also differ from the academic groups we have described, since its efforts are directed at governmental agencies, private foundations, and educational institutions rather than professional associations in the biological sciences.

With this historical overview of the emergence of political action among academic women behind us, we will examine in somewhat greater detail the advisory and activist groups of several professional associations. The bulk of the analysis examines both advisory and activist groups within the five professional associations in which organized activities on behalf of women first began—the Modern Language Association (MLA), American Sociological Association (ASA), American Psychological Association (APA), American Political Science Association (APSA), and American Historical Association (AHA).

FOUNDING

The emergence of action groups tended to occur at annual professional conventions. Occasionally they were stimulated by women who contributed to or reacted to a panel on a topic pertinent to women at such a convention. Sometimes women came together when they found themselves excluded from social-professional functions such as hallway conversations, luncheons, and cocktail parties. It was not uncommon for an organizing meeting to be called during the course of a convention by enthusiastic feminists. Organizing activities got underway in psychology when women gathered to hear a panel on "Women as Scientist and Subject." A discussion of career problems among members of the audience and panelists led to the conclusion that a national effort to elevate the status and influence of women psychologists was necessary, and the founding of the Association for Women Psychologists (AWP) in 1969 was the result. Not all initial organizing efforts were successful—women in economics did not succeed in founding a caucus until their third try.

A number of advisory groups began life precariously as special committees. While some were later reconstituted as standing committees, others continue to exist from year to year at the pleasure of their governing boards—that is, their status and financial subsidy are reevaluated annually. Some women see this review process as particularly vulnerable to harassment by an association, but it is difficult to judge whether this is so or whether the review is not an instance of budgetary crises in higher education. Similarly, the time lag between the disestablishment of an ad hoc study group and the formation of a standing committee has sometimes been viewed as harassment. It is reasonable for associations to distinguish between an initial research-oriented group and a subsequent watchdog group, and to constitute these differently. But because status report committees merely document discrimination and are only the beginning of reform, it is important to insist on their reformation as full standing committees of the associations.

SIZE

Action groups are in essence voluntary, mass membership associations, while advisory groups are elite, by-invitation-only organizations. The women's caucuses in our survey ranged in size from 50 to 450 members. The largest groups tend to be the oldest, and they report expectations of continued growth in the future. In contrast, the average advisory group has ten appointees. Those in our survey ranged in size from five to sixteen members, with the majority in the five to seven member range. The larger advisory groups are representative on a national scale, whereas several of the smaller groups tend to be based in one city, sacrificing geographical representation to the exigencies of a tight operating budget that cannot allow travel expenses for committee meetings.

MEMBERSHIP

The members of action and advisory groups differ in career status. At present, action groups tend to represent the younger, low career status female who is likely to be facing her most eye-opening bout with sex discrimination in higher education—job hunting; while advisory groups tend to represent the high career status female. Since action groups are open membership organizations, their membership profiles more nearly approximate that of the total female population in their associations, the majority of whom are in low-ranking positions. Beginning graduate students and established faculty women seldom join action groups. The younger students may not have reached a stage of career decision and commitment that makes professional associations relevant to them, and many already may have joined more militant women's liberation groups outside their profession. The older established women faculty, having reached some secure status in their profession, may have an investment in the status quo and therefore feel little interest in joining a group that advocates change. As activist groups gain "respectability" however, older women faculty who have experienced sex discrimination are less hesitant to join them.

Since members of advisory groups typically are appointed by the governing body of the professional associations, they tend to represent a narrower range of career types, primarily the established women in the profession. The proportion of high-ranking women is higher in advisory groups, although numerically there are, of course, more high status women in action groups. Few graduate students, minority women, nontenured women, not to mention men, were among the appointees. It was particularly rare to find an action group member appointed to an advisory group.

An example of advisory group membership is shown in Table 16.3 on the APSA Committee on the Status of Women. Although four men and one action group member are among its total membership of eleven, it falls within the prevailing pattern: almost two-thirds of the members are established women in the profession. The mean age of the committee members is 44.4 years, although the women appointees showed a wide spread in age, from their early 30s to their 60s, while men appointees were all close to the group average. With the exception of the action group representative and the black appointee, the female and male committee members graduated from equally prestigious institutions. A higher rate of men than women are presently affiliated with prestigious institutions, although the women on this committee clearly are situated better than most women within the political science profession.

Why are advisory groups primarily composed of establishment women? Associations claim that these are prestigious groups to which only high status individuals are generally appointed. Activist women, on the other hand, claim that this is the case because associations want to preserve the status quo. One activist coordinator commented:

> Advisory groups should be representative of individuals from all career levels within a discipline, but my association won't appoint people who represent dissident opinions, like feminists, due to the erroneous assumption that a feminist is a biased person who cannot possibly be an objective scholar when issues concern women. It's not that the appointers are gung ho for objective research. They're after their own bias, and their assumption is that successful women are non-feminists whose research will document little if any sex discrimination in their status reports.

> I'm really annoyed that no caucus women have been appointed to the advisory committee. Yet their studies have made our work of organizing women easier. I mean, when all those clouty women come out with studies that statistically document bias against women, it legitimatizes the charges the caucus was making without the backup research. In essence, the association's whole strategy backfired. They wanted a whitewash report. But they got a meaty report, not by us pariahs, but by the establishment women. Now the association has to do something, like it or not.

LEADERSHIP

There are several important differences between the leaders of the advisory and activist groups. It should be noted in advance, however, that the following composite profile of the leaders of the first ten groups may not be characteristic of the leaders of more recently formed groups or of the women who are now replacing the first pioneer cohort of group leaders. The typical head of an advisory group i a careerist and often a noted authority in her field at the time of her appointment. Rarely, however, is her field of scholarly research that of women. The first chairperson of the AHA Commission on the Status of Women, for example, was a specialist in the American South; the first appointed head of the APSA Committee on the Status of Women listed her major field of interest as comparative European governments. An exception to this generalization is Helen S. Astin, the present chairperson of the APA Task Force on the Status of Women in Psychology, who had several years of professional interest in and publications on women to her credit before she assumed office.

As suggested by examination of the political science advisory group, the average advisory committee leader is well over the age of 30. Her family background is middle class, midwestern, and protestant. She married late in life by current American standards, in her mid- to late-20s to an equally well educated male, who is also in academe although not necessarily in her discipline. She earned her doctorate from an excellent school before her marriage and has at least one child; she did not interrupt her academic career for child-rearing. She has published, is currently employed by a university or a research foundation, and holds an associate or full professorship with tenure, but has never served as department head. The institution at which she works ranks lower in status than the school(s) she attended.

Politically, she regards herself as an independent voter; professionally, she feels she is situated "dead center" between the right and the left. She has few interests outside her profession and almost no nonacademic affiliations. In contrast to her action group counterpart, she considers herself more of a scholar than an activist and has a relatively low level of consciousness on feminist issues. When asked for her own definition of "feminism," she is all but speechless. Although she is aware of the existence of sex discrimination, it seems painful for her to share her experience with others and she frequently denies that she herself has experienced any discrimination. Not infrequently she defines discrimination against women as merely exclusion and does not regard women's status in society as in any way oppressive.

Taken by surprise at her appointment to her association's advisory committee, she is reluctant, at first, to accept the position because she is highly sensitive to her colleagues' opinion of her. She does not want them to consider her one of those "flaming women's libbers," and she is equally concerned that a position as an "advocate researcher" will tarnish her credentials as an "objective scholar." Finally, however, after prolonged rationalization that the appointment will offer her possibly the only chance to "serve" a worthy cause for a short period of time, she accepts. Without exception, she later discovers that her appointment has helped her professionally, mostly by enhancing her visibility among her peers.

The characteristics of the action group coordinators may come as a surprise, for many people have considered such women to be very radical indeed. In many ways they are not dramatically different from their advisory group sisters. One important

TABLE 16.3. Status Characteristics of Members of the Committee on the Status of Women in the Profession, American Political Science Association (APSA)

Member	Date of Appointment	Affiliation	Rank/Title	Degree Granting Institution	Date of Birth[a]	Publication(s) in Professional Journal
Josephine Milburn, Chairperson	3/69	Simmons College, University of Rhode Island	Associate Professor	Ph.D., Duke University 1956	1928	Yes
Peter Barach	5/69	Temple University	Professor	Ph.D., Harvard University 1952	1918	Yes
Philip Converse	5/69	University of Michigan	Professor, Program Director, University of Michigan Survey Research Center	Ph.D., University of Michigan	1928	Yes
Warren Ilchman	5/69	University of California at Berkeley	Associate Professor	Ph.D., University of Cambridge 1959	1934	Yes
Marion Irish	3/69	American University	Professor	Ph.D., Yale University 1939	1909	Yes
Kay Klotzburger, Action Group Member	11/69	Rutgers University, New York University	Lecturer/ Graduate Student	Ph.D. Candidate, New York University	1938	No
Joyce Mitchell	3/69	Mount Holyoke College	Professor	Ph.D., University of California at Berkeley 1964	1930	Yes

Member	Date of Appointment	Affiliation	Rank/Title	Degree Granting Institution	Date of Birth[a]	Publication(s) in Professional Journal
Jewel Prestage	3/69	Southern University	Professor	Ph.D., University of Iowa 1952	1931	No
Susanne Rudolph	3/69	University of Chicago	Associate Professor	Ph.D., Radcliffe College 1953	1930	Yes
Victoria Schuck	9/69	Mount Holyoke College	Professor	Ph.D., Stanford University 1937	1909	Yes
Irene Tinker	9/70	Federal City	Assistant Professor	Ph.D., London School of Economics 1954	1927	Yes

[a] Mean age is 44.4.

difference, however, is the much greater diversity among the activist leaders. For example, the professional types range from the advanced graduate student, totally outside the power structure of her professional association, to the mature professional woman with tenure and a national reputation beyond her field.

But like the advisory group women, the typical activist leader is over 30 (although not quite as old as the typical advisory group head), midwestern, and protestant, married to a highly educated man, and has at least one child. She received her doctorate from a relatively "good" rather than "excellent" university and is employed at a reputable college or university that is on a par with her Ph.D. degree-granting institution. Unlike the advisory group leader, the activist leader tends to be a junior faculty member without tenure. None are department heads. Although she did no scholarly research on women in the past, this is now an area of intense interest to her and she has undertaken or is about to undertake such a project.

The social and economic profile of the activist leader is also interesting: she tends to be from the lower middle class and now lacks any religious affiliation. In fact, she tends to be an atheist—one described herself as a "proseletyzing atheist." Though married now, she tends to have been divorced at least once. She has a much more heightened level of social and political consciousness and is affiliated with several groups outside her profession, including women's rights groups. She is less well known in her field and has not published as often as the average advisory group leader, in part because in combining political action with scholarship she has had far less time to devote to research interests. Her teaching load is heavy because she is still at the early phase of her academic career and because she is at institutions in which teaching loads are heavy. In addition, her family is quite young with more demands on her time and energy.

The action group coordinator tends to be an only child or to have had a brother, younger or older, who often was given educational opportunities at the expense of her schooling, only to squander it in her view and end up in a job requiring manual dexterity rather than scholarship. Perhaps because of this early experience with sex discrimination within the family, she is deeply and irrevocably committed to a feminist perspective which she has no trouble defining.

Interestingly, the activist's mother is less likely to have been a working (or professional) woman; thus, the activist is her family's first career woman. As a result, her female role-models are more apt to be other women within her profession than women in her immediate family. It is not clear what her mother's influence has been: whether the activist woman was encouraged to develop career commitment and high aspirations by her mother (or both parents), or whether the activist women experienced their mothers as negative models to be avoided in their own life plans.

In terms of political affiliation, the activist falls between the Democratic party and party independence; she is a self-defined "liberal" in her professional sphere and a self-defined "radical" in the women's movement. Ironically, her professional colleagues tend to perceive her as a "radical," while her women's movement sisters generally regard her as a "liberal."

The average caucus founder possesses the basic characteristics attributed by social scientists to "leaders." She demonstrates remarkably strong self-assurance and verges on being a charismatic personality to her immediate associates. Yet in the present political climate she is somewhat reluctant to play a dynamic leadership role for fear the group's members might perceive her as an "elitist." Moreover, she is concerned that her work with the group will siphon off so much of her time that she will be prevented from pursuing her research and publishing activities, thereby creating a conflict between her work for the betterment of women and work for her own economic and professional advancement.

She is concerned also that her activities might brand her a "radical" or "trouble-maker" within her profession and thus hurt her future employment opportunities. After all, she reasons, she struggled to form a group that is not only a thorn in the side of the power structure of her professional association, but is in many ways inimical to preserving its status quo. Yet as understandable as her worries are, they have not been borne out. The average action group coordinator, like her advisory group sister, has found that her activities have enhanced her visibility among her peers, and, in addition, given her access to invaluable organizational experience which she readily concedes is a set of opportunities few women possess.

The perspective of the action group leader tends to differ somewhat from the majority of the members of her group. Whereas the leader is involved in a broad spectrum of feminist activities and speaks of substantial social changes taking place in America through the efforts of the feminist movement, the action group members are hesitant about taking their reform beyond the boundaries of their professional association and the issue of sex equality in employment. In other words, the average action group founder tends to be a bit visionary, a humanist with a personal mission to work for the freedom of all women while many members of her group tend to work more for themselves, hoping, it seems, that through their caucus activities they will be better able to "buy into" the status quo.

BUDGET

Both action and advisory groups function on very slim budgets. Since action groups operate outside the power structure of their associations, they receive no association money at all. What funds they have are derived principally from membership dues which generally range from $3.00 to $10.00 per annum, depending on the professional status of the member (graduate student to professor). A few members usually contribute amounts in excess of the dues schedule; and it is quite common for officers to absorb their own operating expenses, for phone calls, mail, and travel to meetings. Nevertheless, action groups rarely report coffers in excess of $400, and only manage to survive from annual meeting to annual meeting by operating piggyback fashion—that is, by using certain facilities available through other organizations or offices.

Most advisory groups receive operating and research funds from their associations although they are modest—sometimes no more than a token $100 to $300 to cover telephone and mail expenses. Notable exceptions are the MLA Commission which was funded initially to the tune of $3,000; the AAA Committee which received $2,500 during its first two years, supplemented with $3,300 of foundation grant monies; and the APSA Committee which was appropriated over $30,000 for research and travel, during the 1969–1971 period.

Some women have charged that advisory groups on the status of women are victims of fiscal harassment. Our research does not confirm these charges conclusively. However, if money can be viewed as an index of association commitment, then the fact that the total amount of money appropriated to *all* the advisory groups surveyed did not exceed $50,000 suggests a minimal commitment. Moreover, the APSA committee accounts for three-fifths of this total, so that the remaining two-fifths represents the amount received by thirty-two other association advisory groups.

STRUCTURE

Both action and advisory groups are task-oriented groups. Advisory groups generally follow modified hierarchical patterns with one person designated head and all members assigned specific tasks. Since the members are intellectual equals, a clear cut chain of command is missing. Nevertheless, the typical working relationships often reflect a formal authority pattern more than an informal influence pattern that develops in situations where people have frequent face-to-face contact. Advisory groups meet infrequently, due to geographic dispersion and limited budgets. Although it might be correct to say that the hierarchical pattern is undermined when these groups hammer out recommendations for action by their associations, this depends upon the ideological and personality composition of the particular group.

Organizational structure among action groups is a far more complicated matter and an issue of great concern to their members. Since many caucus women feel that organizational structure implies hierarchy, which they perceive as oppressive, they are quite hesitant about permitting their structure to become formalized. They believe it is ludicrous to form an organization to fight oppression that is itself oppressive. Many would agree with a political scientist who said:

> No organization engaged in the politics of equality should establish hierarchical offices that permit their holders to arrogate power to themselves, often without the approval, or knowledge, of the membership.

Yet some organizational structure is necessary if the group wants to be representative of its constituency. In other words, no action group can seriously claim to speak for a sector of a profession, however broad, unless it is sufficiently well organized to recruit members and to select its leaders democratically.

Since action groups do not want to mimic the traditional patterns of authority of professional associations, it is of special interest to examine their experiments in developing new organizational structures and operating techniques. A symbolic first step is taken in this direction with the substitution of the title "chairperson" or "convener" for "president." It is not uncommon to find several officers titleless. The Association of Women in Psychology, for example, has formed an Implementing Board of titleless members; and in its early days, the Women's Caucus for Political Science operated with an executive committee of five, only one of which, the National Chairperson, carried a title. The first National Chairperson of this group noted:

> Even that was more of a concession to outside pressures such as the news media which sought official statements from a *bona fide* spokesperson for the Caucus, and the APSA, which considered it easier to consult with only one representative from the group, than from any internal pressures.

However, the current trend in the women's action groups seems to be a slow change from informal to formal organizational structure: that is, from the earliest stage when the groups had no ongoing formal activities between annual meetings, through a stage with some minimal structure (usually national officers and a few task-oriented committees but no constitution), to a stage at which constitutions are drafted to spell out the specific functions of the group and the selection and responsibilities of its officers and committees. Of the twenty-one action groups in our survey, nine were self-defined as informal and twelve as formal. Only two— the Sociologists for Women in Society (SWS) and the Association for Women in Psychology (AWP)—had adopted constitutions by the end of 1971. In neither of these latter two cases was the structure notably hierarchical, although SWS had opted for calling its officers by traditional titles. Among formal caucuses that lacked constitutions, it was typical to find decision-making power distributed among as many members as possible. In theory at least, this was to prevent anyone from using an office as a personal power base. Of course, to work effectively this scheme demands the polling of the delegated/elected membership by mail before any major policies are implemented, a time-consuming and, given the slim budgets of action groups, expensive job. Other schemes used by formal caucuses to check the usurpation of authority by any one person involve the rotation of offices. Finally, it should be noted that although no rules precluded it, all of the conveners of action groups in our sample voluntarily stepped down after a two-year period—usually in a state of total collapse. In most cases their successors were elected, although not necessarily by the total membership, as some groups bent to the need of selecting leaders at annual meetings. In the newer groups where the rewards of office-holding are minimal and the amount of work very heavy, officers are by and large self-selected. Of the total number of offices in all the action groups in our sample, the great majority are presently filled by volunteers.

In general, the more formalized an action group is, the more independent it is of its professional association. Nevertheless, it cannot sustain itself completely, since it is neither large nor wealthy, nor well known enough to provide its members with the same professional services and contacts as the parent association. It tries hard to effect a sensitive ordering of its priorities. In their early stage, independent action groups played politics with their parent associations, but recently they have shown a tendency to a greater professional orientation, encouraging their members to pursue their careers vigorously and, where applicable, encouraging the development of research on women. This is symbolized by the frequent renaming of these groups as they move into their more formal stage of organizational development. The Women's Caucus of the ASA became the Sociologists for Women in Society, a name implying not only a broader membership base than female sociologists, but also concerns that go beyond interest group politics within the association, and even the profession itself.

There is an irony in this trend: Established to pressure parent associations to assume a variety of tasks related to the problems of women in the professions, some of the action groups now assume many of these tasks themselves. They, not the associations, develop rosters of qualified women, run child-care centers at annual meetings, or sponsor panels on women in the professions. To gain the representation of feminist women in the governing councils of their associations, they run candidates in association elections, not unlike a third political party. Thus, the groups become more independent by vigorously serving the needs of their members that the professional associations fail to serve, and in so doing, become a routinized although informal part of that association. Moreover, the members develop increasingly stronger self-interest in the continued existence of the action group to the point that one wonders if the problems of women in the profession will ever be solved, since the group now depends upon those problems to exist.

Nevertheless, the advantages of formal structure (and perhaps of a constitution) are that the work of the group is organized in determined ways that assure opportunities for participation by many members and that an executive and committee system is created to permit the group to carry ongoing responsibilities that serve the political and career interests of the membership. While it is true that some of the "radicalism" and much of the spontaneity of an action group is lost as it evolves from an informal to a formal structure, formal structure is necessary if the group is to develop long range goals and the tactics to achieve them. Informal structure that maximizes flexibility and spontaneity is important when a group makes its political debut in a professional association. Beyond that initial confrontation, the campaign to effect real change in the profession and in the parent association calls for a large enough membership base and mechanisms for planning and action to assure that women's voices will continue to be heard and to be taken seriously.

ACTIVITIES

The major activities of action groups are *to organize* women to advance their professional status and to encourage scholarly research on women, while the goals of advisory groups are to *research* the status of women, to *announce* their findings, and to *recommend* action by associations on matters affecting that status. Advisory groups have no enforcement powers, and hence, may be characterized as "social influence" organizations; that is, they are groups whose major purpose is not to serve a constituency, but rather to develop proposals for social change. Action groups also serve this purpose, but in addition, they furnish services and activities of benefit to their members; hence they may be characterized as "social influence and self-improvement" organizations. While there is some overlap between advisory and action groups in both goals and activities, action groups represent a broader range of activities.

Over the past three years, the major activity of advisory as well as activist groups has been the sponsoring of resolutions on the status of women for implementation by the governing councils of their associations. The other activities of advisory groups center around their research and mandates. It is important to note that when resolutions have been adopted by the associations, advisory groups move into a second phase of activities designed to encourage the implementation of those resolutions. In sociology, the caucus had conducted research and submitted many resolutions *before* the advisory committee was established. The ASA ad hoc committee has, therefore, visited selected sociology departments across the country in a planned effort to raise the level of consciousness among faculty members to the presence and the effects of sex discrimination. Similarly, the MLA Commission has published "how-to" pamphlets on the status of academic women that describe resources available to women who believe they have experienced sex discrimination, and give useful information on how to find legal assistance or take a case to court. The MLA Commission has also been instrumental in putting together several collections of designs for women's studies courses.

The range of activities engaged in by action groups cover the following:

1. Legitimating the problem of sex discrimination by:
    a. Adopting a formal statement opposing discrimination on the basis of sex.
    b. Establishing an official committee to research and report to the association on the status of women in the profession.
    c. Allocating funds, facilities, and publications space for communication among women in the profession.
    d. Holding association meetings in places that do not practice discrimination against women.
    e. Sponsoring a series of scholarly panels/conferences on women's perspective.

2. Encouraging of the recruitment of women by:
   a. Working to end discriminatory practices in the admission of women students by academic departments.
   b. Endorsing the principle of equitable stipend support regardless of sex (with allowances for child-care support).
   c. Encouraging the development of part-time programs of study.
   d. Encouraging the reevaluation of career counseling that channels women into sex-stereotyped fields.
   e. Allocating special funds for graduate education for women.
3. Eliminating obstacles to women's career development by:
   a. Encouraging the recruitment and promotion of women faculty (including an open employment system) by academic departments.
   b. Supporting the principle of equal salaries and fringe benefits for equal work.
   c. Working to eliminate antinepotism rules.
   d. Encouraging part-time faculty appointments (with proportionate salaries, fringe benefits, promotion, and tenure) and easy transitions between full- and part-time appointments for both men and women.
   e. Encouraging the establishment of child-care facilities at employing institutions and providing appropriate facilities at association meetings.
   f. Endorsing nondiscriminatory maternity and parenthood leave policies by employing institutions.
   g. Operating a placement service without discrimination against women in the profession.
   h. Working to eliminate discriminatory practices by all fund granting agencies; and for the equitable representation of women on all research funding review committees.
   i. Instituting a system of anonymous publication reviews of manuscripts.
   j. Encouraging employers to hire on the basis of professional qualifications and job characteristics only—i.e., ceasing all inquiries into sex, age, family status, and family planning in job interviews.
   k. Encouraging employers to cease requesting marital and parental status information on job application forms.
   l. Crosslisting women on the basis of their married and single names in the association directory.
   m. Assuring equitable representation of women in the formal activities of the association, including legislative councils, advisory committees, editorial boards, and convention meetings.
   n. Encouraging the equitable representation of women in policy-making positions of academic departments.
   o. Encouraging academic departments to make special efforts to place qualified women in top faculty and administrative ranks where current studies reveal the greatest discrimination against women.
4. Developing research and teaching on the topic of "women" by:
   a. Encouraging academic departments to establish women's studies courses.
   b. Encouraging academic departments to examine present course curricula with a view to adding materials relating to women.

   c. Encouraging publishers, libraries, and academic departments to review all printed materials with a view to eliminating sex-role stereotyping.

   d. Supporting, stimulating, and recognizing the legitimacy of undertaking research concerning the role and status of women in society.

5. Implementing of the adopted resolutions by:

   a. Establishing a roster of qualified women for employment referral and participation in the various functions of the profession.

   b. Actively supporting Executive Order 11246, as amended by Executive Order 11375, and HEW Affirmative Action Guidelines.

   c. Appointing a staff assistant on the status of women to the association's headquarters.

   d. Establishing the official standing committee on the status of women, allocating to it sufficient research and administrative funds.

   e. Developing procedures to censure employers who fail to furnish data necessary to evaluate the status of women in their institutions.

   f. Developing sanctions to be applied in cases of proven discrimination by employers.

   g. Developing procedures to investigate individual cases of alleged sex discrimination brought to the attention of the association—e.g., establishing liaison with AAUP.

   h. Making information available on legal recourses open to or providing legal counsel for women who wish to file sex discrimination complaints against their employer.

   i. Developing accreditation evaluation guidelines for academic departments and training programs with respect to sex discrimination.

   j. Distributing endorsed resolutions to academic departments and the association's full membership; and publishing them in the association's journal or newsletter.

   k. Actively supporting the amendment of federal civil rights laws to cover professional women.

   l. Developing criteria for evaluating progress in achieving equality for women.

6. Maintaining the organization by:

   a. Publishing newsletters, abstracts, and research findings on women.

   b. Recruiting members.

   c. Providing facilities for the companionship of women during professional conventions.

   d. Running candidates in association elections and pressuring for the appointment of members of the group to association committees.

   e. Establishing decision-making mechanisms and governing document(s).

A CASE STUDY

It is difficult to gauge the overall effectiveness of the action and advisory groups since each group operates within an internal environment and with an order of events peculiar to its professional association. For this reason, it may be helpful to trace the activities of one action group. The Sociologists for Women in Society (SWS) offers a broad range of experiences to examine because it is the oldest academic caucus and has undergone the transition from an informal caucus to an independent association.

SWS is an outgrowth of the earlier Women's Caucus of ASA. The caucus was announced in June 1969 and made its public debut three months later in September 1969 at the annual ASA convention. Despite some internal conflicts over ideology and tactics, the caucus emerged from its official founding as a cohesive entity of liberals and radicals. That a liberal-radical coalition held together may be due to the foresight and administrative skill of its founding coterie, a group consisting of both liberal and radical graduate students and two faculty members, including the group's first president, Alice Rossi.

The Caucus existed informally without any ongoing structure between annual ASA meetings for a year and a half. In February 1971, it was reconstituted as a formal organization, complete with a constitution and a new name, Sociologists for Women in Society. During most of the early period, in fact until December 1970 when the ad hoc Committee on the Status of Women in Sociology was established, the caucus operated as the only group within both the sociology profession and other academic fields that was concerned with women's issues.

At the time of the caucus' founding, Rossi was a well known and respected sociologist who had written several essays on sex equality. Whether one considers her an "élite" within the field (a debatable point since she has lent her scholarship to challenging the status quo), it can be said that unlike most other caucus coordinators, she had some degree of authority from which to operate. At the time the caucus was founded, Rossi's husband was serving as secretary of the ASA. Subsequent to the caucus' founding, Rossi herself was appointed to the editorial board of the association's professional journal, an appointment she regards as a gesture in response to the women's caucus pressure.

If indeed she enjoyed elite status within her profession, it did not always work to her favor. One would expect an activist group bent on upsetting the status quo to welcome a respected scholar into their ranks. Yet not all the radical women who gathered at the 1969 ASA meeting accepted Rossi, for many felt that while she could lend legitimacy to their demands, she could just as easily be coopted by the establishment. Moreover, they felt that no matter how radical her ideology was, she was adverse to radical strategies, preferring to play the game of cooperative politics rather than confrontation politics.

Uncertain about the kind of reception their demands for greater opportunities for women in the field would receive, Rossi prepared for the ASA convention. First, she contacted a group of sociology graduate students at the Berkeley campus who had formed a caucus in their department and had been meeting regularly during the 1968–1969 academic year. This was an ideal base from which to operate since the 1969 ASA convention was to be held in San Francisco. Next, she conducted a mail survey on the status distribution of women faculty in graduate departments of sociology and wrote a paper on its findings for distribution at the ASA convention. Reasoning that if the membership responded favorably to caucus demands they would call for a study (which would mean the passage of another year before any action could begin), the caucus decided to conduct the study *in advance* of their political debut. "Then we could say that we'd already surveyed the graduate departments and with this as a base, let's get moving," she commented. "Besides, there might have been more resistance from department chairmen to giving out facts on the status of women in their departments *after* our first political action."

The study cost little except in terms of time. It was well worth the effort in the eyes of the caucus since the study took the ASA hierarchy by surprise. Moreover, it was soon published in *The American Sociologist,* so the results could reach great numbers of sociologists who did not attend the convention. In contrast to the other early caucuses in the social sciences, the women's caucus in sociology first gathered empirical data, which strengthened the political demands the caucus made on the professional association.

The radical sociologists held their counterconvention in a church across the street from the hotel at which the ASA meetings were held. As a consequence, two women's caucuses sprang up simultaneously: the radical women's caucus and the "hotel women's caucus." One test of Rossi's mediation between the two groups arose over the seemingly innocuous issue of a meeting room. Conscious of the tremendous interest in the women's activities which had been generated among ASA members during the first days of the convention, Rossi requested a larger meeting space for the caucus' first meeting. This request was first refused by the ASA president, but later granted when he was confronted with an onerous threat to disrupt the ASA proceedings. The granting of this request-turned-demand caused consternation among the radical women, as well as several hundred ASA members who suddenly found themselves displaced from a ballroom. The radicals were upset because the resolution of the issue had avoided a confrontation with the police, which would have occurred if the meeting had been held as they expected and wanted in the hotel's ground floor lobby.

The ballroom meeting took place in an atmosphere of mounting tension. Rossi chaired the meeting which was attended by more than 500 people. Although no organizational issues were settled and the issue of an election was never faced, the meeting furthered the commitment to form a women's caucus, and to present resolutions on the status of women to that evening's ASA business meeting. The resolutions, drafted earlier by members of the Berkeley caucus and Rossi, were general but hard-hitting statements aimed at putting the ASA on record against sex discrimination in academe. The radicals now demanded certain substantive changes in exchange for their endorsement of both the resolutions and the women's caucus. In particular, they wanted a resolution for a long-range goal of increasing the proportion of women in sociology to 50 percent, reflecting the proportion of women in the total population—a figure that would triple the current number of women sociologists. Clearly, this goal implied greater changes within the profession than a goal of an unspecified "increase" in representation. To the moderates, the 50 percentile figure was unrealistic since it projected a model of the best of all possible worlds—not the proper task for a political caucus concerned with change in the immediate future. Nevertheless they agreed to include the radical demand.

That evening Rossi delivered the group's presentation at the ASA business meeting, calling for the adoption of ten resolutions "in spirit." Since the resolutions spoke to such provocative issues (for 1969) as the inclusion of the topic of sexism in the curriculum, college and university-based child-care centers, and parental leave for both women and men, Rossi was startled by an immediate motion from the floor to call the question. In seconds she left the stage in the silent aftermath of a unanimous vote in the caucus' favor, yet she felt deflated:

> In the short range you feel a sense of loss. We'd lost the possibility for an educative dialogue by playing the game. Since we hadn't violated the bylaws, no one stood up and made a screamy speech saying that these resolutions can't possibly be endorsed. The membership seemed relieved that it hadn't had to spend too much time on women and could move on to discuss "real" issues.
>
> But I'm not sure that's the case for the long run. This may be self-delusion, but I think the association has moved well on women since 1969, partly because we used the right tactics from the start. Many women thought it was inappropriate to submit resolutions at ASA business meetings. To the radicals, that was going the establishment route; while to some of the moderates it was "unladylike." But I felt that this was the beginning of something and that you don't use ultimate tactics first.

At the September 1970 ASA convention in Washington, D.C., the Caucus got down to specifics, advocating the establishment of an official Committee on the Status of Women with the understanding that it would not be primarily another fact-finding body. Instead, it was to be mandated to devise ways to implement the resolutions endorsed the preceding year and strengthened at the 1970 convention.

The resolution calling for the establishment of an ad hoc committee was passed at the convention and an initial membership of six was appointed by the ASA president during the next three months. In keeping with the wording of the resolution, the ad hoc committee was to "include some members from a list suggested by the Women's Caucus." In behalf of the caucus, Rossi submitted the names of four women candidates, three of whom were appointed by the president, who himself chose another three persons. The president turned down the caucus' request for the appointment of a graduate student, but a year later when the advisory committee made the same request, a female graduate student was added bringing the Committee to a total of seven members. Until the addition of the student, the committee was composed of "established" members of the profession, including two men. Since one of the caucus' nominees became chairperson of the committee and another nominee was a member of the caucus, relations between the two groups have been close and informed.

Between the 1969 and 1970 ASA meetings, the caucus was held together by Rossi and her committee circle of friends. By September 1970, however, it had become apparent that an organizational structure was needed to carry the group from convention to convention. Again the radicals rebelled: Was not Rossi, in ef fect, proposing to set up a hierarchy when the caucus ostensibly was opposed to traditional organizational methods and the oppression that arises from them? Rossi's answer was "no." A formal structure was needed if the group was to be representative and if the many tasks it wished to assume were to be distributed evenly and carried through during the months between conventions.

On February 13, 1971, at a meeting of twenty women held at Yale University, the Women's Caucus of the ASA dissolved itself and reformed as Sociologists for Women in Society. "We were self-selected. We came from all parts of the country. We paid our own way. We covered the gamut in age, interests, ideology, commitment," wrote one participant. The purposes of the newly formed organization were stated as follows:

> The SWS is dedicated to maximizing the effectiveness of and professional opportunities for women in sociology; exploring the contributions which sociology can, does and should make to the investigation and humanization of current sex roles; and improving the quality of human life.

> To implement the above purposes, SWS is committed to taking action to: a) urge the examination of assumptions underlying sociological work about the nature and roles of women and men; b) collaborate with other social and biological scientists in reviewing research on sex differences and assumptions underlying such research; c) actively promote research, experimentation and education on alternative sex roles and improvement in the quality of human life; d) educate and sensitize the sociological profession and the public in social, political and economic problems of women; and e) actively press for equality of opportunity for women and men within the profession of sociology.

The group adopted a constitution and elected temporary officers for the organization that succeeded the Caucus. No issue taxed the group's sisterhood more than the name of the group. The word "caucus" was being dropped since it referred to the two years when the group did not recruit members and its operating base was drawn from ASA members attending conventions. Besides, the tasks of the group were now expanding to include research, sex discrimination cases, and job market problems of women, as well as political action within the ASA and the discipline at large.

"The Association of Women Sociologists" was too restrictive since membership was to be open to men who accepted the purposes of the organization. The proposed "Association for Women in Sociology" was rejected by the radicals, who could not accept the idea of investing energy in an organization on behalf of such a small constituency as the women members of the ASA. One participant described the name selection process as follows:

> After several combinations of key words, the final selection—laughable as we found it, completely acceptable to no one—was: Sociologists for Women in Society. It is a terrible name, for where else does one find women, but in so-

ciety? And one of the most wonderful things we did after accepting the compromise name that suited no one was to laugh hilariously at ourselves. It was clear that we understood—and accepted—all our disabilities.

Since the February 1971 meeting, SWS has evolved into a very special kind of federation. By the fall 1971 ASA convention in Denver, the SWS executive committee had developed new ways to assure closer ties between regional association women's action groups and the national SWS. Only the president is open to nominations on a national level. The other officers are tied into the regional sociological associations, in a random, rotating fashion, so that none of these slots can be used to build up a personal power base. Since the number of SWS officers equals the number of regional caucuses, the posts are put into a hat and each regional caucus draws an office and becomes responsible for nominating candidates for that national office. Thus, in a given year the first vice president might come from the mountain region, while the treasurer might come from the southern region. Since candidates for a given office are drawn from the same region, geographic dispersion is assured.

SWS is not a typical formal organization. It is trying to retain a radical-liberal coalition and to be innovative in its search for the right combination of hierarchy and member participation. While it has some organizational structure, it is fully participatory at the committee level where all but the committee chairperson may freely move in and out of positions of responsibility. The active work of SWS is divided among nine standing committees: policy, job market, discrimination, social issues, publications, research, education, nomination, and finances and membership. The chairperson of each committee is elected, but she draws volunteers from members in her geographic area rather than from all over the country. It is hoped that this committee structure not only will facilitate cohesive and efficient committees, but will cost little to operate and will provide many flexible entry points for women to become visible in the larger organization.

At present, SWS has about 610 members, which makes it one of the largest action groups in academe. Asked what were SWS's most important achievements to date, Rossi replied:

> First, the instituting of change in the ASA without any backlash. Second, the lessening of the feeling of competition among women. I have seen the beginning of a solidarity among women sociologists, who take pride in being together instead of feeling that if you are not with a male sociologist you couldn't possibly be having a good time.

CONCLUDING REMARKS

The academic women's movement is surprisingly devoid of radical politics. The goals of the movement are moderate, if not conservative, in comparison with other neofeminist organizations that attack the sexist nature of American society. Academic women's groups are concerned almost exclusively with women's status *within* their professions. Their primary goals are to insure equal opportunity and to increase the participation of women in established professional groups. Having been outside for so long, they want access to the system rather than to change it. Such groups rarely set goals that go beyond the self-interests of women as professionals.

Actions by academic women's groups encompass liberalism—the politics of who gets what—and modified radicalism—the process of politicizing or raising consciousness. Neither orientation desires the destruction of existing institutions: the liberal thrust aims at power, e.g., a seat on a policy-making council of the professional association; while the radical thrust aims at conflict through which to communicate ideas, polarize opinions, and stimulate change within the professional association. The major aim, then, of academic women's groups, regardless of their positions on the radical-liberal spectrum, is the rooting out of certain manifestations of sexism from the institutions within which they operate, not the destruction of those institutions.

Within the context of these goals, the movement has been effective. First, the movement has demonstrated phenomenal growth in terms of both numerical size and breadth of representation. Second, the movement has had a profound impact upon academe, pushing through what amounts to a plank on women's rights in the professions. Third, it has served to sensitize women to their common problems and to their need to work cooperatively to solve them. Fourth, it has helped women to develop greater self-confidence by exposing them to organizational and professional experiences that were previously off-limits, such as delivering papers at annual meetings of professional associations. Fifth, the academic women's movement has fostered women's studies in the college curriculum.

These results are all the more impressive when we consider that the movement was founded by, and is composed of, that segment of the population who have been conditioned to avoid success and/or to work primarily toward the success of others. Given this, the organization of professional women in their own self-interest is to be especially commended. To criticize academic women, as many do, for being more concerned about equality for themselves as professionals than about equality for all women is to forget the great personal and professional risks these women have taken, or believe themselves to be taking, often for the first time in their lives. Furthermore, their attempts to seek solutions to their own problems as women serves the important function of broadening their understanding of the problems of *all* women. It is too early to tell if this identification with *all* women will foster broader political action by academic women.

Demands for equality and justice should not be considered radical and it is somewhat surprising that the academic women's movement has been so branded by the professions. Three possible explanations are suggested. First, the more activist members of the movement have chosen the symbolically radical caucus as an organizational form. Second, women's rights activities are often considered professionally unethical since academe tends to believe that scholars sufficiently aroused to engage in political causes are not objective. Third, men are chiefly responsible for this charge and it is not clear if they are using scholarship or traditional assumptions about female behavior as their standard of judgment. In the view of many men, women earn advanced degrees as a hobby and attend association meetings to bask in the learning of superstar males or to decorate book display booths.

But it is to the advantage of professional associations to encourage rather than to discredit women's groups. Advisory groups give the associations a good civil rights image. By generating contention, action groups encourage interest in the associations and increase attendance at professional meetings. Very simply, women's groups are a vehicle for breathing new life into half-dead institutions.

Action and advisory groups are concerned with making professional associations into more participatory institutions in which women can function on a par with men. This often conflicts with the functioning of the associations as political systems whose major preoccupation is the preservation of their organizational structure with all its inequities. Further conflict is introduced when the women's groups themselves are divided as to whether their goal is to be fundamental change in the academic system resulting in a new kind of education and a new kind of professional, or whether their goal is to be limited to a professional restructuring which will simply allow women to compete for the rewards currently awarded to men.

In theory, advisory groups are in a position from which they can observe and inform academic women of the viewpoint of the professional center—the establishment. What advisory groups actually do should reflect what those in power are willing to do for women as a "minority" group. If action groups were the academic arm of the feminist movement as a whole, then the difference in achievement between advisory and action groups might measure the resistance of the establishment to feminist goals. In practice however, the two types of groups are remarkably similar: advisory groups represent rhetoric, while action groups represent (mild) protest.

The fact that more advisory groups than action groups were found in our sample is no doubt indicative of the common tactic of attempting to allay dissidents by offering them something short of access to political power—a tactic that has backfired in this instance. For while it is true that advisory groups on the average are not as aggressive as action groups, they nonetheless have been active. The men who appointed the advisory groups apparently did not know that even if women who believe that they have not felt the brunt of discrimination were appointed—on the assumption that they would not uncover discrimination—they, almost without exception, are women who take their assignments seriously, often working harder than men would in comparable positions. These women have produced impressive studies and their documentation of discrimination has more clout than reports produced by dissidents.

Although the research of the advisory groups has done much to legitimatize the issue of women's rights, the reports often are concerned more with the past and the present than with the future. Even their impressive empirical studies do not always indicate what must be done to alleviate existing conditions. For this reason, the institutionalization of advisory groups as standing committees will not accelerate the liberation of women unless the committees evolve beyond their current role as fact-finding bodies. Moreover, stronger mandates for implementation are needed from associations and this in turn may develop if action groups continue to press their associations. More appointees with heightened consciousness of the discriminatory treatment of women also are needed, preferably from the ranks of action groups. The appointment of men to the advisory groups may sensitize them to the problems of professional sexism and, in turn, sensitize their colleagues. Finally, associations should consider appointing a full-time staff person to work exclusively in conjunction with advisory groups. (Such an office is already to be found within the AHA and the APA.) This would serve to eliminate the time-consuming processes of selecting new appointees and briefing them on past actions of the group.

Action groups must also become more effective. Being outside the power structure of their respective associations, they obtain and maintain a voice in association affairs only by strong organization and pressure. Much of the success of an action group depends on how well it uses its outcast status as a means of protest. An action caucus must maintain its independence from the professional association. Although it may ask the association to institute scholarly panels on women, to place qualified women on advisory committees, or to nominate women for council elections, it is not asking to be absorbed as an official unit of the association, thereby allowing the association to choose its officers and/or mandate its duties.

The success of action groups in this role varies. Overall, caucuses do best when they approach their criticism and couch their demands in professional terms. The psychologists, for example, have had considerable success in calling attention to the ways in which their discipline conditions women to certain social roles. In retrospect, however, they have been called politically naive for introducing a laundry list of fifty-two resolutions to the APA convention in 1970, none of which were passed because their staggering volume discouraged the membership, including AWP sympathizers. The political scientists, on the other hand, have notched several victories in their dealings with the APSA. WCPS, for example, is the only action group in our sample that has participated in association election campaigns, running—successfully in one case—its own candidates in opposition to the official APSA slate. But it has been far less successful in defining operational goals for itself beyond that of playing politics with the parent association.

Action groups also have suffered from intragroup factionalism often caused by a willingness to accept a polite endorsement of feminism in exchange for membership dues. A growing membership runs the risk of internal conflicts, followed by less effectiveness as an organization and loss of some active members. No action group, regardless of its record of achievements to date, seems strong enough to survive a splintering of its members and a consequent loss of talent.

Action groups must be wary of certain situations which appear to represent victory but actually may be quite meaningless. For example, an association may sponsor an all female panel at an annual meeting. Although the panel may be part of the regular program, it may be in essence a "ghetto" panel that may be scheduled at an inconvenient hour and set up in a far corner of the convention hotel. In the long run, more is achieved by securing the representation of women on several different panels, than by one or two all female panels.

Finally, action groups must be wary of headcounts by sex. The appointment of several women to various study groups can be quite meaningless if the appointees really do not represent women's interests. Little progress can be expected from an association that has appointed a dozen "Aunt Sallys."

It is possible that some academic women's groups are on their way to becoming "radical chic" social clubs, run primarily by women who want to promote their own status rather than the status of women as a group. It is also possible that academic women will realize that their rapidly rising status is artificial, propped up by the existence of their groups. Take the groups away and women, no matter how competent, may lose their visibility in the profession.

The academic women's movement is not the vanguard of contemporary feminism, yet there is a growing recognition and admission among its participants of the sexist nature of American society. It is no longer necessary to tell academic women that their inferior status is not their personal fault but a social problem. This is all to the good, for members of the movement must transcend their immediate concerns in order for the movement to survive and flourish.

There will be no sex equality until there are fundamental changes in American economic, family, and professional structures. Although few participants in academic women's groups seem to have a conception of feminism this broad, the force of the movement remains strong. Even if action and advisory academic groups function only to force men to move over to make room for women, restructuring necessarily will have to occur in many institutions. And academic women, whether they realize it or not, will have been a part of important social change.

Appendix

Women's Groups within Professional Associations, by Type of Group and Date of Formation

Professional Association	Advisory Group	Action Group
African Studies Association (ASA)	Women's Steering Committee (3/71)	Informal Women's Caucus (10/70)
American Anthropology Association (AAA)	Committee on the Status of Women in Anthropology (2/70)	Informal Women's Caucus (11/71)
American Association for the Advancement of Science (AAAS)		Women's Caucus of the AAAS (12/71)
American Association of Law Schools (AALS)	Committee on Women in Legal Education (3/70)	
American Association of University Professors (AAUP)	Committee W (reactivated, 4/70, originally founded, 1919)	
American Chemical Society (ACS)	Women's Chemists Committee (9/71, originally named Women's Service Committee and founded 1927)	
American College Personnel Association (ACPA)	Women's Task Force (12/70)	
American Economics Association (AEA)		Informal Women's Caucus (1969; formal organization came in to being in 1972)
American Historical Association (AHA)	Committee on the Status of Women in the Profession (2/70)	Coordinating Committee on Women in the Historical Profession (12/69)
American Library Association (ALA)	Social Responsibilities Round Table, Task Force on Women (6/70)	
American Mathematical Society (AMS)	Committee on the Status of Women (4/71)	Association of Women Mathematicians (1/71)

Professional Association	Advisory Group	Action Group
American Philosophical Association (APA)	Subcommittee on the Status of Women in the Profession (12/69)	Informal Women's Caucus (12/70)
American Physical Society (APS)	Committee on Women in Physics (4/71)	
American Political Science Association (APSA)	Committee on the Status of Women in the Profession (3/69)	Women's Caucus for Political Science (9/69)
American Psychological Association (APA)	Task Force on the Status of Women in Psychology (1/71)	Association for Women in Psychology (9/69)
American Society for Microbiology (ASM)	Committee on the Status of Women Microbiologists (5/71)	Informal Women's Caucus (1/71)
American Society for Public Administration (ASPA)	Task Force on Women in Public Administration (5/71)	Informal Women's Caucus (3/71)
American Society for Training and Development (ASTD)		Women's Caucus of ASTD (5/70)
American Sociological Association (ASA)	Ad Hoc Committee on the Status of Women in Sociology (12/70)	Sociologists for Women in Society (2/71, originally named Women's Caucus of ASA and founded 6/69)
American Speech and Hearing Association (ASHA)	Subcommittee on the Status of Women (11/70)	Caucus on the Status of Women in the ASHA (8/70)
American Statistical Association (ASA)		ASA Women's Caucus (12/70)
American Studies Association (ASA)	Commission on the Status of Women (12/70)	
Association of American Colleges (AAC)	Project on the Status and Education of Women (9/71)	
Association of Asian Studies (AAS)	Committee on the Status of Women in Asian Studies (1971)	Informal Women's Caucus (10/71)

Professional Association	Advisory Group	Action Group
Institute of Electrical and Electronics Engineers (IEEE)	Committee on Professional Opportunities for Women (2/71)	
Modern Language Association (MLA)	Commission on the Status of Women (12/68)	Women's Caucus for the Modern Languages (12/69)
National Council on Family Relations (NCFR)	Task Force on Women's Rights and Responsibilities (10/71)	
National Educational Association (NEA)	Temporary Committee on the Status of Women (1970)	Informal Women's Caucus (1970)
National Vocational Guidance Association (NVGA)	Commission on the Occupational Status of Women (11/68)	
Organization of American Historians (OAH)	Committee on the Status of Women (12/70)	Coordinating Committee on Women in the Historical Profession (4/70, same group in AHA)
Philosophy of Education Society (PES)	Committee on the Status of Women (4/71)	Women's Caucus (4/71)
Population Association of America (PAA)	Committee on the Status of Women in the Profession (4/71)	Women's Caucus (4/70)
Society for Cell Biology (SCB)	Task Force on Women in Cell Biology (11/71)	

Chapter Seventeen

Women's Studies and Social Change

Florence Howe
Carol Ahlum

INTRODUCTION

THE most conspicuous signs of the women's movement on campus are the women's studies courses and programs that have mushroomed during the past two years. By December 1970, there were 110 courses, and two women's studies programs at San Diego State College and Cornell University.[1] Neither of these programs was degree granting, but each offered a roster of elective courses, and in each institution one or more women had been hired to develop the program. One year later, in December 1971, we knew of 610 courses, more than a dozen of which were graduate courses, while a few were high school ones; and fifteen women's studies programs, five of which were degree-granting, one, in addition, was an M.A. program (Ahlum and Howe 1971). The academic year 1972–1973 will see further rapid development: we have learned of approximately 300 new courses in the months since December 1971; we know of seventeen institutions at which discussions about women's studies programs are underway; new master's programs have been established at Sarah Lawrence College (in women's history) and at San Francisco State College. More important, perhaps, are the courses beginning to appear in high schools and the curriculum being developed for elementary schools.

In short, it is hardly necessary to proselytize on behalf of women's studies: the phenomenon exists. A new and more insistent problem is how to organize, or institutionalize, the courses that are appearing as if by magic on campus after campus across the country; how to understand their appearance, how to gauge their direction.

What we are witnessing, of course, is a movement, and movements are political in essence. Movements may have unified organizational support or direction, but

AUTHOR'S NOTE: We wish to acknowledge the assistance of grant number RO-5085-72-54 from the National Endowment for the Humanities. Florence Howe is project director and Carol Ahlum research associate; the title, "Literature, History, and the Education of Women."

[1] The Modern Language Association's Commission on the Status of Women in the Profession published, for distribution at the December 1970 convention, a list of those courses under the title "Current Guide to Female Studies."

they do not always need them. The current women's movement is, in fact, a classical instance of a movement without unified organization or direction. Nationally, for example, there exists no single association of faculty women, nor of academic women in general. It is difficult if not impossible to find organized efforts that reach across professional disciplines or beyond the confines of individual campuses. No one person or group has said, "Let's organize women's studies across the country." Indeed no organization could have produced the proliferation that has occurred in the space of two years.

The ease with which the proliferation has occurred suggests several hypotheses: the tendency in higher education toward fadism; the relative flexibility of individual faculty offerings, within customary departmental guidelines—an improvement, perhaps, over conditions of a decade ago; the presence of women faculty on campus, sensitive, alert, even possibly committed to the women's movement; and of course, the power of that movement itself.

Particularly in departments of English, sociology, and history, individual faculty members have been relatively free to inaugurate new courses, with or without departmental or general institutional approval. The bulk of the 800 or 900 courses currently being taught in women's studies are separate courses introduced into traditional departments or, in fewer cases, into law and other professional schools. Such an infusion—"The Role of Women in Economic Life," "The Sociology of Women," "The History of Women in the U.S.," "Images of Women in British Literature," "Women in Cross-Cultural Perspective"—can only enliven departmental offerings; indeed, in some instances, they have drawn students' registration beyond the wildest dreams of a chairman.

Women's studies *programs,* on the other hand, have been slower to develop. The term has been used to name any structure beyond individually instituted or department-instituted courses, and the range of existing programs is very broad: among the fifteen in progress on campuses, it would be difficult to find a pair that duplicate each other in aims, organization, relationship to the university, and so on. The best definition possible, therefore, is that a program exists when some body (either a group of women teaching women's studies courses or the institution itself) declares that a group of courses *is* a program. Since the idea of programs raises administrative and political as well as educational questions, we reserve such discussion for later in the chapter.

It is important to underscore at the outset the pioneering nature of women's studies. Among the pioneers themselves there is ambivalence about goals as well as means. Shall programs and publications be called "female" studies, "women's" studies, or, increasingly these days, "feminist" studies? Skeptics have declared the movement a fad that will pass or, less flattering still, an effort at self-aggrandizement. Our sense is that campus feminists are explorers, often of the past as well as the present and the future. We believe that the movement will divest itself of fadism, discipline itself against self-aggrandizement and continue to make strides as a serious movement for educational and social change.

What gives us confidence? We are encouraged by our visits to campuses; the seminars on women's studies we have attended on some twenty campuses; the several dozen conferences held this year and last or about to occur; our correspondence with hundreds of women engaged in research and new curricular design; and the essays feminists—women and men—are writing about their explorations in teaching (see References). The emphasis on teaching methods and on the development of new curricular materials also strengthens our confidence. For the women's movement in its distinctive form—the small consciousness-raising group —is a *teaching* movement. The movement's primary aim has been to educate women and men about the stereotypic images they hold of themselves and each other. That institutionalized education in the United States should become conscious of the way in which girls and boys, later women and men, are socialized (often stigmatized) into roles seems to us essential. To change the education of women (and men) is one broad purpose of women's studies.

Feminists interested in change, however, have not neglected the past: women's history permeates women's studies at every level, in most disciplines. Students are reading Catherine Beecher, Mary Lyons, Emma Willard, and M. Carey Thomas, as well as suffragists, feminist labor leaders, and feminist writers. Again and again the same intellectual and political questions arise: Why did such splendid women not accomplish all they wished or might have? What happened to the energy of the nineteenth century feminist movement? Why are we having to "do it all over again today"? It is clear, for example, that nineteenth century feminists fought as hard and as long for education as they did for suffrage. At the beginning of the nineteenth century an ordinary woman could not go to high school and even an extraordinary one could not go to college, certainly not to a professional school. And most teachers were men. By the end of the nineteenth century, it was possible for middle class women to go to high school, most of higher education had opened to economically privileged women, and even professional schools had opened doors a crack. Teaching in elementary schools and, increasingly, in secondary schools had become a woman's profession. The accomplishments of nineteenth century feminists with regard to education for women were profound.

Yet these institutional changes were accomplished without striking at the heart of beliefs about the nature of woman's inferiority and her second "place" or "role" in the social and political order. Educational institutions accommodated themselves to the presence of women, either alone or in the company of men, without changing their fundamental views of the comparative educability of women and men. We know now that education per se does not change the status of women with regard to men, but merely the status of women with regard to other women. Education has not served to change either women's images of their own inferiority or men's images of women as inferior creatures. The education of women thus far has produced accomplished or "successful" women who, if they function in a patriarchal social order as "tokens" of possibility, also serve to remind us of the severe limitations thereof. Women's studies may provide one useful corrective to tokenism.

WHERE DID THE IDEA COME FROM?

The Student Movement and Educational Reform

Women's studies is not an isolated phenomenon, though a decade ago those words were not on the lips of even the most disgruntled academic, whether student or teacher, female or male. A decade ago students and faculty were complaining of irrelevant courses and especially of the fragmentation of the curriculum that left students feeling untaught and faculty feeling ineffective. The division of knowledge into arbitrary capsules called history or economics, psychology or sociology, and the organization of specialists into structures called departments were two essentials of the modern multiversity and even of the liberal arts college. As student or faculty member you had to fit yourself into one of those cubicles; you were a "nineteenth century British" member of a college or university English department, you were a major in "macro-economics" or "social psychology." Connections between economics and literature or psychology were not a proper subject for the aspirations either of student or professor. Boxes were boxes and labels were labels.[2]

It is possible to trace the complaints about curriculum made by students and faculty through the first half of the sixties, but it is not until 1965 that the first "free universities," organized by Students for a Democratic Society (SDS) and similar groups, began to function on such campuses as San Francisco State College, the University of Pennsylvania, Bowling Green, and the University of Washington.[3] The free university movement that flourished for several years on several hundred campuses fed into the academic world a number of educational reforms, including the idea of the "experimental college" harbored by the university or created anew in the wilderness. For our purposes, the most essential contribution

---

[2] The exception to the generalizations maintained is "American Studies," though it, too, is a relatively recent phenomenon and its reputation has been not unmixed. The existence of American studies programs and departments, it should be noted, has provided an institutional precedent for newer ethnic or area studies. Alternatively, at some institutions, black studies and women's studies have been subsumed under the department aegis of American studies.

[3] Indeed, *The American College*, published in 1962 (ed. Nevitt Sanford), is a product of a decade's work—the fifties. It reports, in essence, the "failure" of higher education to make an impact on the students that pass through its doors and out into the world. Coincidentally, Students for a Democratic Society published also in 1962 *The Port Huron Statement*, a sixty-page pamphlet that reaches a similar conclusion. For a full discussion of these reports as well as the free university movement see Lauter and Howe (1970: Chap. 4).

of the free university and experimental college movement is curricular innovation and reform.

It was not only boredom that drove students at Berkeley to complain of feeling like IBM cards. It was not simply the size of the multiversity nor the remoteness of the faculty from teaching. It was the experience first of direct participation in the civil rights movement, especially in southern freedom schools where the curriculum engaged students and teachers both with the necessities and realities of social change. What *were* living conditions in Mississippi? Courses engaged students in factual reporting, statistics-gathering in neighborhoods and surrounding regions. And why were black people in Mississippi living in poverty? Thus, the study of history aimed at understanding a current social disorder. On the heels of Mississippi summer came the war. Why could students learn nothing on their campus about black people and less than nothing about the Far East and a strange place called Vietnam? This is what students were asking in 1965, in free university literature and in leaflets written to promote "teach-ins." Early in 1966 courses sprang up on the war, on conscientious objection and pacifism, on black history. As early as 1966, at the Free University of Seattle (founded by University of Washington students) there was a course on women's history.[4]

Free university courses were distinct from "regular" college courses chiefly in their source and function, but also in their teaching and learning styles (anti-authoritarian, nondirective, collective rather than competitive). These matters are of importance to women's studies, as we shall make clear later in this chapter. The courses grew out of the interests of students; they were meant to serve the needs of those students. Such needs might be intellectual: why are we in Vietnam? what *is* the history of pacifism? Or they might be practical: how to throw pots, fix an engine, stay out of the draft, write a television script, organize a free school. Obviously they might also become courses in long-range strategies for change, as are some current women's studies courses. To read today the titles of courses offered in a free university catalog in the mid or late sixties would surprise few of us, for much of it has been absorbed into the "regular" curriculum, whooshed up by the vacuum of traditional departments, when it has not resulted in the creation of new ones. We may now take for granted courses on China, the war, peacemaking, Marxism, the Far East. Students may "get credit" for writing workshops or other "applied" courses, as well as for what has come to be known as "field studies" —the course that may be an activist project off campus in the community.

As the academic arm of a student political movement, free universities also focused substantial attention on black or other ethnic minorities in the United States. The history and culture of blacks, Chicanos, Caribbean peoples, Asians,

[4] We understand, of course, that on a few campuses in the sixties several women were teaching such courses as women's history—Annette Baxter at Barnard is a prominent example. We would argue, however, that her action was then a private, rather than a public or "movement" concern.

working-class people and, eventually, women, appeared with regularity in catalogs across the country. In some free universities, such courses were related to organizing efforts among the population in nearby communities. At San Francisco State's Experimental College, for example, courses in black history and culture and involvement in black communities led to demands for a black studies program and for other institutional reforms. In short, the free university movement's interest in third world and ethnic studies, and the increasingly vocal demands of a black political movement in the 1960s, preceded the development on campus of black studies departments. It is also perfectly clear that these and other ethnic studies departments reflect the changing social order in the United States and pressures to alter the elitist content and form of college education. If we are a democratic, open society of diverse people, students, blacks, Chicanos, and now women have been saying, let's see some of this openness, democracy, and diversity.

It is possible to understand the movement for educational reform as a movement to reveal the diversity within American society, to counter the uniformity of white, middle-class, male-dominated institutions and models.[5] It is possible also to understand the movement for educational reform as an attempt to gain at least intellectual control of the complex society in which we live, that is, by focusing the learning process on connections and interrelationships rather than on separate "disciplines." If we are talking of studies that prepare students not for particular jobs but rather for living a life, it makes as much sense to define an area of undergraduate study as "black studies" or "women's studies" as it does to define that area as "history" or "literature." Certainly size of subject area or intellectual scope has little to do with distinctions between the two types of categories. The primary distinctions are the ones that students hit upon a decade ago when they talked and wrote about the evils of specialization that prevented ordinary people from solving problems or understanding complex social issues.

Departments of history or English, for example, are organized to be as inclusive as possible. Undergraduates in literature choose a random series of courses that may range in time through a thousand years, if the geographical limitation is Britain and the United States, or 2500–3000 years if the offerings include "world" literature or history. Rarely does a student of literature pick up more than a thin sense of chronology; more often, the message in literature courses is of "timelessness," as though literature did not spring from the particulars of people's lives, their class, race, national origins and religion, and of course their sex. Similarly, history departments are caught between "coverage" of bodies of historical data and teaching students how history is written, from whence history springs. Of course, the source material of history is frequently "literature." Similarly, it is difficult to understand the emergence of "the novel" in the eighteenth century without a review of a changing social order in Europe.

[5] For an enlightening discussion that supports this thesis indirectly, see Rossi 1969:3–6, 16.

Students of women's studies or black studies will face other equally complex problems. The intellectual "cut" is diametrically different. To study the history and culture of black people or women in the United States is to confine yourself to a narrow geography, a relatively brief unit of time, and to one major issue, race or sex. But of course these issues are connected to all others, as are the issues of class for example; and hence, studies move properly into other disciplines. This emphasis is strikingly similar to the old liberal arts notion of a "rounded" course of study; at the same time, the focus is distinctive and eliminates the effects of fragmentation. Students do not move from course to course gaining a "smattering" of introductions to traditional bodies of knowledge; rather, they use tools and perspectives of various "disciplines" to understand at least one aspect of the social order, say women's history and social role in the United States. But, of course, even with so narrow a definition, the perspective is broad and may extend itself indefinitely, even as does the study of literature. For example, one may study Indian women, black women, working-class women in the United States, or one may focus on comparative, cross-cultural studies. In short, the intellectual ordering of area or ethnic studies may be different from the study of literature or history per se, but many of the same patterns of focus and perspective apply in both cases. To argue that literature, sociology and political science are definable, distinct, limited, and hence legitimate areas of study, but that area or ethnic studies are too broad and impressionistic, is unsound.

The immediate problem confronting institutions developing women's studies programs is the need for trained faculty, both with respect to curriculum and methodology. Our graduate schools still are producing narrow specialists in traditional disciplines. The pressures on young faculty members to conform to departmental standards, to publish in the usual journals, is still strong. It is not surprising, therefore, to find among young women teachers the anxiety of those taught to be psychologists, say, or historians, and hence, allegedly unable to think about or deal with literature, much less with connections between psychology and literature. For some time to come, team-taught courses will have to compensate for the narrowness of traditional training and provide interdisciplinary approaches to curriculum.[6]

The "Politics of Coeducation"

If it is possible to view women's studies as part of a general attempt to reform college curriculum, it is also clear that the women on campuses have been quick to seize the opportunity. And of course they were present to do so. For more than a century, United States higher education has been characteristically coeducational: we have preached the rhetoric of equality for women in our colleges and universities as we have not (until recently) for blacks and other minorities. Whatever

[6] Of the 610 courses listed in *The New Guide to Current Female Studies* (Ahlum and Howe 1971), 71 are team-taught by 174 faculty members, 20 of whom are male.

their status, however they may be regarded by themselves or others, women in the United States attend college at proportions (42 percent) unusual for Western countries. The number of women *employed* by a college or university is typically greater than the number of men, if one considers not only faculty (20 percent) but secretaries, clerks, librarians, housekeepers, cooks, maids, and the wives of graduate students, faculty, and administrators. In short, the presence of women in mass numbers (however invisible they may have been, and felt themselves to be in the past) provides a powerful force for change. Women do not have to be "recruited" to campuses; in most cases, they are an overwhelming presence.

On the other hand, the first effect of the women's movement on campus was to cause women to study their status there (see Chapters Eleven and Twelve). While discriminatory patterns were evident both in hiring and promotion, such studies also pointed to the presence of more complex problems. The attrition rate among graduate women students, for example, could not be explained simply by charging "discrimination." The fact that women high school graduates enter college with higher achievement records than male students, and yet set lower vocational goals for themselves clearly can not be dealt with by an Equal Opportunity Employment officer. Indeed, when one sets side by side the increasing proportions of women who do complete high school and go on to college, with the diminishing proportions who go on to graduate or professional schools, the question of "discrimination" in higher education becomes a problem for relatively few women. The massive problem is a more complex one altogether: the control not over whether a highly motivated woman can get a job but over the processes of education whereby only relatively few women emerge as highly motivated when and if they graduate from college. The crucial issue in women's education, therefore, is their aspiration.

While aspiration is a function of multiple social factors in the development of young women, important among them is the total school and college experience.[7] College officials, like public school officials, maintain that girls and boys, women and men, are treated exactly alike in classrooms and by educational institutions. Indeed, in most classrooms, females and males hear the same lectures, read the same books, do the same assignments, take the same examinations. But the *content* of the curriculum is male-biased; women are absent or are presented in passive, limited, and limiting roles. In addition, the treatment of males and females is distinctly different with regard to such subjects as physical education, and with regard to student activities outside the classroom, and health, housing, or counseling policies. In effect, the "sexual politics" of schools is no different from that in the world outside.

[7] It is not possible here to review the literature on sex bias and the public schools. See Florence Howe, "Sexual Stereotypes Start Early," *Saturday Review*, October 16, 1971, pp. 76-82, 92-94; also *Report on Sex Bias in the Public Schools*, New York Chapter of National Organization for Women, 1971; also the entire February 1972 issue of *School Review*, 80(2).

Let us consider the classroom first. When history is taught, it is the history of male warriors, rulers, tradesmen, investors, explorers. When literature is studied, it is the literature of male writers recording *their* lives, *their* perspective—*Huck Finn* and *The Portrait of the Artist as A Young Man* are classic examples (Trecker 1971a; Showalter 1971b). Psychology reflects the male experience and male points of view. Until recently, most courses in social inequality examined inequality with regard to race, religion, ethnicity, and class, but not sex. Courses on marriage and the family assumed the inevitability of the maternal role. The perspective of theology, art, history, music, political science is parallel. The implicit curricular message to women students has been simple: *men* work, write, and make history, psychology, theology; women get married, have babies, and rear them.

Outside the classroom, the message is explicit. There is the perhaps trivial matter of collegiate sports, worth mentioning here only because it illustrates how systematic and fundamental is the differential treatment of girls and boys from childhood on with regard to physical exercise. Just as boys are expected to play baseball and football, and girls to avoid these sports, so are young women quite openly sex-typed for particular vocations, further reinforced by teachers' comments or expectations or those of the guidance counselor. A broad range of university policies and practices as recently surveyed by the American Association of University Women, included student leadership. Men at institutions with a student population of over 10,000 held 92 percent of the top elected positions during the years 1967–1970, and on all but women's campuses, men are likely to hold "all positions with much power and influence," whether elected or appointed (Oltman 1970:9). The position of men on campus also is reflected in the different possibilities offered male and female graduates, even if they hold similar career goals. Women interested in publishing, for example, typically begin as secretaries, whereas men begin as editorial assistants or sales personnel.

Women's studies is part of a broad effort to develop interdisciplinary studies. In particular, it is related to ethnic studies in its focus on the history, culture, and the status of a social group. The rapidity with which women's studies has developed on campuses can be ascribed both to the presence of women in relatively large numbers, especially among graduate students and junior faculty; to numerous studies of the status of women on campus and in the professions; and to the failures of curriculum and other aspects of collegiate and university life. The immediate justification for women's studies is the narrowness of the traditional male dominated curriculum, geared to support the life goals of men and to undermine the idea that women might hold similar life goals or might wish to explore new directions for human achievement and social reward. The alleged equal treatment of women in the classroom itself is one of the causes of women's inferior social role and condition. Women and men have been taught, by example and by the content of the curriculum, that men strive and succeed; but that with rare exceptions, women do not. All men on campus are potential achievers and one would not wish to take that away from them. One would only wish for women the same privilege of hope and achievement.

COURSES

We would not have written this chapter at all, were it not for one unique aspect of the academic women's movement. From the very beginning, women were interested in and willing to share syllabi, bibliographies, and general plans for courses and programs. In our office alone, over the past two years, there has been a lively correspondence with some 500 people. Indeed, the press of such correspondence in the spring and summer of 1970 led us to the idea of publishing lists of those people teaching women's studies courses so that they might correspond with *each other*, but the list doubled and tripled almost at once, so that by October of 1970, we knew of 110 courses. The original idea of individuals circulating their own syllabi to a small group of women around the country no longer seemed practical. The need for a "clearinghouse" was inevitable.

The review of curriculum that follows is based, therefore, on three sets of materials. First, we have a list of course titles and associated information, published most recently as *The New Guide to Current Female Studies* (Ahlum and Howe 1971). From this list one can derive gross statistics (610 courses, 200 institutions, 500 instructors, and so on), and further categorical data (there are 163 courses in departments of English, 52 in sociology, 84 in history, and so on).[8] But the most valuable materials are the syllabi themselves and the essays written by teachers of women's studies courses. A total of 137 course syllabi have been published in *Female Studies I, II, and III* (Tobias 1970; Howe 1970; Howe and Ahlum 1971). In our files we have an additional 250 syllabi plus those for most courses offered by women's studies programs. A total of eleven essays have been published in *Female Studies II* and *IV* (Howe 1970; Showalter and Ohmann 1971). Another large group (fifteen essays) were prepared for a conference entitled "Women and Education: A Feminist Perspective" held at the University of Pittsburgh, and published as *Female Studies V* (Siporin 1972). A dozen discrete essays have been published during the past two years, and our files contain another dozen unpublished papers. Like the total number of courses that have appeared in so brief a period, the number of essays is astonishing.

Some 610 courses are distributed across 197 institutions, about half of which are located on the east coast, nearly a quarter in the midwest, and a somewhat smaller number on the west coast.[9] Twelve institutions are located in the south

[8] While we have received information about some 200 additional courses, these are not yet organized for publication.

[9] The listing in *The New Guide to Current Female Studies,* on which we have based our statistics, is a good example of eastern chauvinism, or at least of poor communication between east and west coasts. A recent trip to the west coast has brought to light several facts, too late

The number of courses at individual institutions ranges from one or two (the most numerous category) to thirty-three at the State University of New York at Buffalo where there is a "college" of women's studies. Nearly one half of the institutions offering women's studies courses are universities granting the doctorate; a quarter are four-year coeducational colleges. The final quarter is divided among women's colleges (thirty-five); men's colleges (three); and two-year colleges (fourteen).

There are no hard data on the numbers of students attending women's studies courses. But it is our impression from correspondence, visits to campuses and essays that registration is generous, ranging from the 300 students in the opening Cornell course, and 150 in a sociology course taught by Arlie Hochschild at Santa Cruz in the spring of 1971, to courses and seminars of 30 or fewer. Syllabi rarely are specific either about the level of the course or the number of students anticipated. Most of the students are women, though in large "general" courses men may constitute 10 percent of the class. Many courses include "token" males and at several male institutions (Dartmouth, Rutgers, M.I.T.) women's studies courses have been organized exclusively or predominantly for male students (Knowles 1971; Robinson 1970).

There are also no hard data on the status of teachers of women's studies courses, but again it is our impression that many, if not most, are graduate students or junior faculty. We also know that for some dozen of these teachers, professional careers have been disrupted by their interest in developing new courses and by their ability to attract numbers of students thereby.[10] On the whole, these courses are taught by women in just under nine out of ten cases (532 out of 600).

The subject of teaching styles merits a separate essay. We can do little more than report our impressions (culled from correspondence, visits, and essays) that, in general, teachers are transfigured by the experience of teaching even *one* women's studies course. They report shifts in their views of a discipline, as well as changes in their teaching styles and their *ability* to teach. They also report a strengthened commitment to the women's movement, to the lives of women beyond the campus. Finally, they report a heightened intellectual and political understanding of the multiple aspects of women's studies. Quite naturally too, while women's studies teachers feel a heightened sense of their own creative *power,* they sense also a certain polarization of attitudes of other faculty and administrators toward them.

In large courses, lectures are a necessity, but these are usually accompanied by

---

unfortunately to do more than include them here. There are twice as many programs on the west coast as on the east coast, and at least twice as many courses (in programs or not) as listed in *The New Guide II* and *III* will list all these courses and programs.

[10] The sentence describes euphemistically the fate of women "pioneers" in women's studies at such institutions as Fresno State College, Wayne State University, The University of Wisconsin at Madison and Whitewater, Goucher College, etc., though it is also fair to add that several of these women have been welcome elsewhere. It may be surprising, but women have lost their jobs for developing and teaching successfully women's studies courses.

small group discussions, often quite deliberately intended as consciousness-raising experiences. Indeed, if one generalization were called for, we would say that the trend is to substitute, wherever possible, groups and group processes and coopera-tive ("collective") projects for the individual competitive ones so familiar to us in academe. None of this is surprising, given the emphasis in the women's move-ment on *sisterhood,* antielitism, leaderless consciousness-raising groups, and the power of collective decision-making and activity. What is surprising is the speed with which the movement's priorities and principles have been extended into the classroom.

Finally, a cautionary note is probably in order. Most women's studies courses were offered for the first time in the 1971–1972 academic year; many more will be offered in the academic years to come. The impressions recorded above are based largely on conversations and correspondence with those who are two-year (or longer) veterans of women's studies. Within the next several years, we will need to use some survey techniques to review and revise what we have offered here as impressions.

THE CURRICULUM

The central idea of women's studies is sex bias and the status of women. Major curricular energies have focused on definitions and analyses of sexual stereotypes in institutional life (discrimination in hiring, marriage and divorce laws, women and the church, etc.) and in history, literature, film, and other aspects of the cul-ture; on the processes of socialization and education through which stereotypes are perpetuated; and on the idea of innate sexual differences or tendencies. This focus holds true across courses in specific disciplinary departments as well as in intro-ductory and interdisciplinary courses.

Implicit or explicit in women's studies courses is a critical vision of the social subordination of women. At the very least, teachers theorize that when women (and men) become conscious of sex bias, they will be motivated to plan means of appropriate social change. Many courses focus on affecting changes in the lives of women and men. How is it possible to break the processes of socialization not only for the student studying the materials (which is what happens) but for others cur-rently in elementary schools or others still unborn? Some courses are organized with a "coda" on the future; others actually involve making that future happen. The clearest examples of the latter are new courses in law schools, in some of which law students research proposed changes in legislation or prepare arguments in defense of individual women's cases.

"Introductory/Interdisciplinary" or "General" Courses

Of necessity a women's studies curriculum assumes an interdisciplinary approach; that is, it is difficult, if not impossible to consider sexual stereotyping, status, and social change without reference to multiple aspects of women's lives, including, of course, their relationships to men. Indeed, the first courses to be organized consciously as "women's studies" courses were "general" ones. Either taught by a team of women from several departments or done as a series of lectures coordinated and integrated by a generalist or by one who taught her speciality, these courses have usually attracted large enrollments. Given the departmental nature of higher education, such courses have had to find homes in exceptional places. Continuing education programs and extension divisions have provided some space, and in several universities (Pittsburgh and California at Irvine for example), courses were offered as a special program generated by a friendly divisional dean's office. At Cornell, the former School of Home Economics (now called Human Development and Family Studies) permitted the organization of "The Evolution of Female Personality," a course that drew more than two hundred students (of whom 30 were men) and an additional 150 auditors.

The 1970 Cornell course, revised in the following years, remains one model for a rapid general survey of the area. Approximately four lectures were offered on each of six major topics: Status of Women (law, marriage, socialization, biology); History of Women; Image of Women (in popular and high culture); Family Roles, Social Ecology (urbanization, architecture and planning, black women); Prospects for Change. Nineteen lecturers contributed to the course, including members of the departments of sociology, biology, English, art, and history, as well as six visiting scholars (a professor of gynecology and obstetrics, an attorney, a member of the New York Human Rights Commission, Joyce Ladner, and Kate Millett). The emphasis in lectures, as well as in extensive readings assigned, was on the facts —what do we know—and on varieties of interpretations and points of view. While there was some attention to concerns of black women, there was generally little or no discussion of class differences or political perspectives. The concluding lectures emphasized the future for educated or "independent women" (through discussion of Mary McCarthy, Simone de Beauvoir, Doris Lessing).

Quite a different model for a large introductory course is "The History and Social Role of Women," a course offered at the University of Pittsburgh in the spring of 1970. This ten-week course focused on economic and political issues, on work rather than the family. The curriculum was organized by three women from the English, Spanish and history departments around the following topics: General Concepts of Women in Industrial Society; Nineteenth and Twentieth Century Views of Women; Class-Determined Roles of Women; Sexual Politics; The Meaning of Women's Liberation. Readings included Engels, Mill, Gilman, G. Myrdal, as well as literature by Lawrence, Lessing, Woolf, Albee, and Ibsen. The course was organized to clarify class differences among women as well as racial differences, reflecting the diversity of Pittsburgh's student body. The concluding segment of the course focused on Doris Lessing's *The Golden Notebook,* Margaret Benston's "Political Economy of Women's Liberation," and other essays from recent movement publications.

These two courses illustrate two modes of organizing general introductions to women's studies and illustrate as well several recurring patterns of most women's studies courses. The readings are remarkably diverse—for academe, that is. Typically, fiction or some other form of "literature" is mixed not only with standard women's movement works (Friedan, Beauvoir, Millett, O'Neill) but with readings in psychology, biology, history, sociology, and so on. In both courses, students kept journals; they met weekly for lectures and in small discussion groups that sometimes functioned as consciousness-raising sessions.

Such courses have continued to emerge, initiated by members of departments, divisions, schools, or entire institutions. In the fall of 1971, at a small experimental college (State University of New York/College at Old Westbury) such a course seemed the best way both to test students' interest and to initiate a faculty new to women's studies. At the University of Wisconsin, where there had been several discrete women's studies courses taught by members of the English department, Joan Roberts of the School of Education organized a graduate course called "Education and the Status of Women" in the fall of 1971. Twenty-five women professors, all "tokens" in the university's departments or schools, lectured on such topics as "Women in Philosophical Perspective," "Women in Literature," "Law," "Minority Groups," and so on. The curriculum may be compared to Cornell's: variety is the key, required readings are extensive, and written critiques required. In addition, Roberts describes an interesting term project. Students may work alone or in groups, but the group option seems favored, or at least it is the one described in most detail. Students who prefer "to read extensively, to discuss their thinking, and to raise their levels of awareness about women, [may form] *small discussion groups* of four or five students." Individuals are expected to "keep a cumulative *idea and attitude log*" weekly, in which they record "evidence that your reading, your thinking, and your feelings changed or did not change in ways that make sense to you as a person *and* a scholar." Students who prefer "action research" may form groups of from two to six, define a research problem, its methodology, implications, and so on, and proceed. Again, a report is required (Howe and Ahlum 1971: 34–35).

On some campuses, an initial women's studies course was offered by an individual faculty member as part of her regular teaching load in a particular department. Whatever the title of the course and whatever the department, in most cases the course served to introduce women's studies to the campus. When Gerda Lerner, an historian at Sarah Lawrence, designed "The Many Worlds of Women," she set out "to explore women's role, status, self-image, and history." "It was, frankly, an experiment," she writes, "in that it did not confine itself to a strict 'history of women in the United States' approach, but sought to approach the subject in a freewheeling, interdisciplinary way. This proved to be its greatest strength . . ." (Lerner 1970:86). Similarly, Lillian Robinson's literature course at M.I.T., called "The Sexual Order," focused on sexual identity, sexuality, and political relations between the sexes through the use of popular and literary materials, as well as readings in

Freud, Marcuse, Reich, Engels, Mead, Masters and Johnson, Mill, Wollstonecraft, Woolf, and latter-day feminists. Just as Gerda Lerner concluded that her students could think about the history of women more clearly after they had been provided with a generous frame of reference, so Robinson acknowledged that her approach to literature, "influenced by cultural anthropology," called for an examination of "some central sexual myths." "Literature," Robinson continues, "is both the source and the reflection of those myths" (Robinson 1970: 42–43).

"Introductory" courses in women's studies also are offered under the titles of "Philosophical Issues of Contemporary Feminism," "Sex Roles in American Society and Politics," "Psychology of Women," "The Role of Women in Economic Life." It is, therefore, unwise to generalize about women's studies courses from a cursory examination of titles alone. Understandably, in a developing area of study and research many courses may seem (or be) "introductory," especially when they function also to initiate women's studies on a campus.

Introductory courses are probably more "political"—or at least more potent—in intent and effect than other individual courses. They may, in fact, lead to the development of other courses or even to programs. Moreover, feelings of "solidarity" have been generated by large classes of women and feelings of intimacy in small groups. Equally important, perhaps, is that faculty are brought together by an interdisciplinary course. Individually, faculty members experience an increase in sensitivity and consciousness. In addition, as a University of Wisconsin syllabus pointed out, team-taught courses "provide numerous possible role models for women students."

In short, the message to students is: look here, there is a body of material, research, and theory, probably unknown to you because it is not included in the general college or university curriculum. Women have begun to look into such matters; you may do so too. Indeed, you may begin in this course, and your project may take you into a number of fields. Thus an introductory course in women's studies is political in its effect, if it sends students on to other courses with new questions.

"Disciplinary" Courses

By and large, the general pattern of curricular development has been from the "general" or "introductory" course to the "disciplinary." Half of the forty-five syllabi in our file of history courses, for example, are compensatory courses in United States history; they move chronologically through the centuries from the arrival of the *Mayflower* to the publication of *Sexual Politics;* most typically, the focus falls on the nineteenth century suffrage movement. Other history courses survey a larger historical period or European history alone. In all cases, the materials students read and the subjects they study are new to them, despite a decade or more of history courses in schools and college. The discovery of women's lives and accomplishments produces, in and of itself, an effect beyond the normal expectations of the classroom. We can describe it as *contagious energy,* both intellectual and emotional in its source and appearance. It is as though women students, reading the lives of such women as Anne Hutchinson, Lucretia Mott, Sojourner Truth, Margaret Fuller, "catch" their vital purposes, their fire and commitment. There is also some anger, as Wendy Martin writes and as our own experience has confirmed, when materials on women's lives are either difficult to find or wholly unavailable (Martin 1971:9). The bias in history texts and biographies provides further justification for study and research. Characteristic is the compensatory use of feminist writings (Wollstonecraft, Mill, Gilman, for example) and histories of feminism (Flexner, O'Neill, Sinclair, Lerner), as well as new source books (Kraditor, Schneir).

On the other hand, the writings of several feminist historians emphasize another view of history altogether, one that would not focus on major historical leaders of either sex, and would not be limited to politics or economics. "We have to create a history in which man is no longer the measure," Lerner writes, "but *men* and *women* are the measure." The "new questions" we have to ask of the past are "interdisciplinary questions" (Lerner 1972). Similarly, Linda Gordon writes;

> We need histories of many social phenomena for which there *are* sources available, but of which historians have not before seen the importance: a history of birth control, of sexual reform movements, of childraising, of women's work in their homes, of courtship, but above all we need histories of general economic, political and cultural developments from a feminist point of view (Gordon 1972:51).

Gordon's program in women's history at the Cambridge-Goddard Institute reflects her views, and Lerner has organized a program in women's history at Sarah Lawrence College. It is interesting that both programs offer M.A. degrees. At the undergraduate level, another curricular sign of new feminist thinking about history is the handful of courses on the history of the family offered not by sociologists but by historians.

Unlike courses in history, traditional literature courses are noteworthy for the presence of women as fictional characters or the subjects of men's poetic fantasies. Of ninety-six literature syllabi, fifty-eight survey stereotypes of sex roles and images of women in traditional bodies of literature, mainly fiction, and mainly American and British. A fairly frequent ploy is the contrast between nineteenth and twentieth century writers, male and female. Usually, there are more male than female writers considered; usually, the female writers are predictable (Austen, Eliot, Woolf, Plath, Lessing, and Olsen are favorites). Only rarely does the list exclude women writers entirely. Most reading lists include ideological writers, especially Friedan, Millett, and Beauvoir, and in several syllabi, topics are organized thematically to follow Beauvoir's chapters.

Just as most history courses are compensatory, most literature courses are consciousness-raising. The line between the two is probably impossible to draw, and obviously both kinds of courses accomplish both ends. But on the whole, women learn to read not new texts or those on new subject areas (as in history), but with new perceptions. Students (and teachers) may be heard to exclaim, "Now I have to go back and reread all those books I read last year—and everything else besides." In a recent essay, Nancy Hoffman, formerly at Portland State University and now at M.I.T., describes her teaching of literature as a "social" act:

> For those of us who are teachers and feminists, reading poetry is not only a private pleasure, but also a social action. We give poems to our students because we know the poems and the students, because in the public sorting out of a poem, we can participate in a communal, often unacknowledged, process of defining art while simultaneously sifting through our lives (Hoffman 1972).

More than history, at least as it is commonly taught, literature is about the lives of fairly ordinary people. For that reason, it is a primary source for cultural definitions of women. Carol Ehrlich, for example, describes her course at the University of Iowa: "depictions of the female will be related to the prevailing legal, social, sexual, and political status of women in American society" (Howe 1970: 20). Wendy Martin is more explicit:

> because [there are] few women (in fact, no women) in American fiction whose lives are self-actualizing (i.e. who have identities which are not totally dependent on men), we will attempt to analyze the social, economic, and literary reasons why women are presented as passive creatures rather than human beings who lead challenging or even risk-taking lives (Howe 1970:33).

In Martin's course, students contrast the fiction they read with the lives of such "real" women as Stanton, Wright, Fuller, Earhart. The significant *literary* questions —about the absence of "self-actualizing" women—is also an important social question. Students must think about their own lives, as well as those of historical figures and fictional ones. As Selma Burkom, formerly of Kirkland College, puts it, literature courses in women's studies foster the "explicit linking of literature and life" and for that reason their impact on students is profound (Howe 1970:16). The awareness of students moves them to increased consciousness about the lives of women and men in society, including their own personal lives; and to increased understanding of literature as a strong social, even political, force on people's lives.

Relatively rare to begin with, there are now some twenty-one courses that consider only the woman writer. Some of these also focus on stereotypes or attempt to generalize about "women's consciousness," or to "explore female experience" or "personal (as opposed to political) views of feminine problems." Several are particularly interesting augurs for future developments. Bernice Zelditch's course on women poets attempts to answer questions about the "topics" and "forms" women choose, and whether or not women write " 'important' poetry" (Howe 1970:59).

Priscilla Allen's "Rediscovery of American Women Writers" focuses on Kate Chopin, Christina Stead, and Tess Slesinger, three women with new or no reputations who may be "superior to nearly all of the lesser lights (e.g., Bret Harte, Hamlin Garland) and to many of the greater ones (e.g. Stephen Crane, Frank Norris, W. D. Howells). "And if they are," Allen continues, "how many other female artists remain forgotten . . .?" (Howe and Ahlum 1971:83). Courses like Allen's and Zelditch's move us into the "nature of literary criticism, especially the content of the established canon."

Within the social sciences, women's studies courses are both compensatory and consciousness-raising. Even more than history and literature syllabi, those written by sociologists (fifty-one), economists (six), political scientists (nine), and psychologists (fourteen) are strongly interdisciplinary. A course in economics includes units on the family and (unpaid) household labor; a course in political science includes a section on marriage and property law; a course in psychology focuses on marriage; and a course in sociology is called "The Family." Any one of these courses, moreover, might include some or all of the following topics listed in a single (sociology) syllabus: Differences between Men and Women (biological, psychological, cross-cultural); Varying Patterns of Male and Female Roles and Relations (by class, race, ethnicity), Sex Roles and the Division of Labor (economic and family institutions); The Segregation of the Sexes (friendship networks, single-sex gatherings); Relations Between the Sexes: Which Conceptual Framework? (power relationship, class, majority-minority); Attempts to Transform Sex Roles (alternatives, problems, and prospects).[11]

One third of the sociology courses, and most of the other courses in the social sciences are, not surprisingly, "general" courses, introductions to the status of women in the United States. A handful of "cross-cultural" courses broaden the survey to include women in other parts of the world. Other small groups of sociology courses focus more narrowly on "The Family—And What of Its Future?"; "The Social Dynamics of Sex Roles"; "Socialization of Women"; "The Sociology of the Women's Movement." Several psychology syllabi focus on biological and psychological theories of sex differences, some of which are openly critical of "instinct-based theories." But most survey as well such associated areas as the family, socialization, adolescent behavior, sexuality, discrimination in employment and education, and so on. By and large, syllabi in the social sciences are far lengthier than those in literature, sometimes even those in history. It is not simply the presence of detailed course outlines and itemized reading assignments; often course materials include a bulky bibliography and an elaborate list of research and action projects. In addition, such syllabi may begin with a statement of perspective or a series of strategic questions:

[11] From an unpublished syllabus by Barrie Thorne, Michigan State University, winter 1972; course title: "Sex Roles in Contemporary Society," Sociology 866, section 1.

What are the goals of this struggle—for women and for society? What are the explicit and implicit barriers to a breadth of alternative spheres for women? What the prospects for social change or the possible advantages for society of the expansion of women's roles? Is equality a realistic goal? Can society reconcile the implementation of equal rights of women with the responsibilities attendant upon the female of the species?[12]

In addition to their significant focus on the future and strategies for social change, the general impression of these syllabi is of "heaviness"—lengthy reading assignments, detailed written analyses required, and complex projects. A typical undergraduate course calls for the reading of ten books and a dozen or more journal articles, the ubiquitous journal keeping ("in which the sociology and social psychology of their own sex-based status may be recorded and interpreted"), and a research paper or project. As a group, these courses are more research-minded than literature or history courses.

NEW DEVELOPMENTS: COURSES IN PROFESSIONAL SCHOOLS

While initial courses in schools of law, education, social work, nursing, theology, and medicine have taken the form of "general" introductions to women's studies, a significant number are specialized and research and action oriented. Law courses are most interesting in this respect and far ahead of the rest. As Aleta Wallach writes of a course developed at UCLA, "We consciously tried to avoid a purely legalistic approach because we learned from the failure of 'Law, Lawyers, and Social Change,' a compulsory first year class on racial discrimination, that strict case analysis was an empty exercise" (Wallach 1972:9). The seminar (nine women, six men) time was organized, therefore, around "two material or product goals":

> 1) To bring materials to the law library as the start of a permanent collection of materials on women and 2) to prepare individual papers which would also be added to the library collection for further reference (Wallach 1972:9).

In other law courses, students work as research teams, not only on employment, family and criminal law, but on constitutional law, laws concerning "control of the body," government benefits, media, education, and public accommodations. In a course offered on the UCLA campus by Riane Eisler, students were asked to group themselves into research teams to work on such projects as the following:

> Five hundred family dissolution cases under the new (post 1970) California family law will be chosen at random. The files will be examined to determine the results (e.g. child custody, division of property, child and spousal support). Students will follow up the women in the cases. A questionnaire will

[12] From an unpublished syllabus by Beatrice Bain, San Francisco State College, spring 1971, course title: "Women as a Social Force."

be devised by the students dealing with such matters as financial credit problems, insurance, child support, child care, employment readjustment, personal readjustment, etc. The resulting evaluation of the new law should consider such questions as the husband's present exclusive control of the community property, the possibility of state funding for vocational retraining for housewives, as well as specific legislative recommendations to improve California family law (Howe and Ahlum 1971:44).

In every case, students were asked to produce "specific legislative proposals."

Graduate and undergraduate courses in schools of education seem firmly committed to research projects. Students are "encouraged to conduct a field project" and to report on progress to their peers. Such projects may involve observation of teachers in classrooms as well as investigation into parental attitudes or children's behavior. Similarly, the single example of a course offered by a school of social work (State University of New York at Buffalo, School of Social Policy and Community Services) emphasizes the word "practice" without scanting theoretical considerations. Topics for reading and discussion include: Caseworkers as Models for Identification; The Psychology of Women; The Female Caseworker—Problems of Self-Definition; Casework and Reproduction; Special Groups of Women— The Adolescent Girl, the Middle-Aged Woman; The Advocate and Social Worker Roles in Casework. The instructor, Mary Schwartz, describes her dual goals:

> The purpose of this course will be to explore the significance of certain new perspectives on women for social work practice. The emphasis is on the word "practice." Students will be expected to examine their own work in field placement. This will involve an exploration of attitudes and values and a broad look at agency practice. Casework materials will be analyzed with a view toward re-examining basic social work concepts from newly-emerging points of view. Articles from the women's liberation movement will be looked at critically (Howe and Ahlum 1971:57).

Courses in other professional schools have been slow to develop. We know of only one women's studies course in each of the following schools: nursing, medicine, home economics, city planning. Graduate courses are, thus far, similarly occasional.

ADDITIONAL TRENDS: SOME CONCLUSIONS

A handful of new undergraduate courses suggests that additional departments will continue to inaugurate women's studies in foreign languages (including classics), in art history, music, theater, film, and speech. The latter is especially interesting when combined with the history of women's speech making. Students in a course taught by Professor Martha Weisman of The City College of New York are studying the "Rhetoric of Women Activists in the United States," past and present. Other efforts at isolating more sophisticated interdisciplinary curricular segments for "advanced" or "specialized" courses have come chiefly from professors of literature and history. Maureen B. Flory, of Mt. Holyoke's Latin Department, for example, offers a course called "Roman Women: Fictional and Historical"; Annette Baxter at Barnard offers a history course called "Autobiographies, Diaries, Letters"; Jenny Knauss at Mundelein gives a history course on feminist ideological writing (from Wollstonecraft to Firestone). In a few instances—Anne Driver (history) and Florence Howe (literature) at Old Westbury, Adele Simmons (psychology) and Zella Luria (history) at Tufts—such courses are team-taught, and cross-listed in two departments.

To summarize so fluid a movement may be futile. Yet certain conclusions seem obvious, and others plausible, even though we are reporting a scant two-year development in women's studies courses. First, there is little sign of consciousness-raising courses per se; yet all courses are invariably consciousness-raising. Second, most courses are rigorous in traditional (and some in nontraditional) terms—readings, reports, papers, projects. The general tone is of an intellectual feast long denied adherents hungry for its goodies, whether historical or statistical reports or experimental studies or novels and poems by women. In our own field, where ennui tends to dominate through and beyond graduate school, the discovery or rediscovery of women writers and the review of traditional (male) literary texts currently provides the chief excitement. In a recent essay, Wendy Martin insists upon the importance of "intellectually solid" women's studies courses "to give feminism academic legitimacy" (Martin 1971:10). In sum, whether because of the inherent interest in or novelty of the subject matter, or because of the need for "legitimacy," women's studies courses have raised the consciousness of participants chiefly, though not exclusively, through the study of particular texts, reports, experiments, issues, and ideas. At the same time, through many of the syllabi and all of the essays (and our conversations with teachers and students), there is another note: courses depend upon the participants, and courses are arranged intentionally to affect those lives further in some significant manner. As Ruth Cowan recently put it, her interdisciplinary women's studies course at State University of New York at Stony Brook was judged by its participants as successful "*academic* consciousness-raising." As a descriptive term, "*academic* consciousness-raising" will probably please few partisans of women's studies, and fewer movement women or academics. We believe it is a useful term, nevertheless, despite the negative connotation of "academic" (meaning without effect or empty of value, as pejoratively: "just an academic exercise"). We think it is useful because it describes in a single phrase the tensions of women's studies that may either split the movement or provide its strength.

One reason for the ease with which the opening wedge of women's studies courses was achieved is the essential conservatism of higher education: it is always easier for departments and individuals to *add* the "new" to the curriculum than to *re-form* the "old." On the other hand, there is also in academe a tendency to control the power of the "new." We have often been asked whether we see women's studies courses as a temporary stopgap, filling a need for compensatory education only long enough to allow faculty to incorporate new materials, writers, studies, into their "regular" courses. Several years ago, we might have viewed this prospect as pleasantly inevitable. We believe now that such a view was at best short-sighted.

The predominantly male faculty and administration has not looked with favor upon women's studies, nor will it, we believe, once it is clear that such studies may change people's lives, at least by altering their expectations and demands. We think that it is realistic to expect reluctance either to incorporate women's studies materials into "regular" courses (or possibly, an incapacity to deal well with such materials), as well as a diminishing willingness to allow the proliferation of separate women's studies courses.

In one respect, clashes between advocates of women's studies courses and other faculty are inevitable. Since women's studies focuses distinctively on problem-solving (rather than on a discrete area of knowledge for its own sake), its effect should be manifest: the more "successful" the course, the more profound its impact on the lives of students going on to other courses or out into graduate school or the community. Given the maleness of higher education, as well as the male biases for the non-affective domain and against change, women's studies advocates ought to be prepared for at least several years of suspicion if not neglect and hostility.

On the other hand, there is an additional if pleasanter, tension. If academics are suspicious of "consciousness-raising" and "activist" elements in women's studies courses, movement women are equally suspicious or sometimes scornful of "academics" and their work. We regard this tension as necessary, inevitable, and even healthy for women's studies, for we believe that knowledge ought to be responsible to people and relevant to social issues. Students and teachers need to be jabbed with questions about how they are spending their time, to what problems have they given priority, whose research are they doing. Are they working for an administration or a government interested in pacifying demands or for women interested in change? Many feminist scholars whose syllabi, essays, classes, and conversations we have come to know understand this tension creatively. Whether they can manage to balance their scholarly and activist concerns and at the same time sustain and increase their base and power on the university campus remains to be seen. To a very great extent, the future lies in the direction of programs.

PROGRAMS

The geography of women's studies programs follows closely the geography of the women's movement up the west coast from San Diego to Seattle, Washington; down the east coast from New England to New Jersey and as far west as Cornell, Buffalo, and Pittsburgh. And this is no happy coincidence, for unlike single courses, women's studies programs are political as well as educational entities. Their existence usually means official recognition and physical space, often funds, and sometimes the technical status of a department, with the accompanying powers to hire personnel, organize curriculum, and recommend students for degrees. Such a program with close relationships both to the women's movement and to the general community of women on campus and off might be a formidable vehicle for educational and social change.

We say "might" for two reasons. First, the precedents for this vision of social change are not altogether auspicious; second the strategy itself may be suspect. The strategic theory for a separatist program like black studies or women's studies depends on a belief in alternative structures or parallel institutions. A similar conception lay behind the free university and experimental college movement. If the host institution cannot be changed, build a smaller one beside it, or even inside it: the alternative institution should thus be able to succor its inhabitants (students) in ways that are especially strengthening and thus turn them into "agents of change"; at the same time the alternative institution should provide its host (the university, or other departments) with a model for imitation, perhaps making change more likely. We have written elsewhere and at length about the misfirings of parallel institutions conceived as vehicles for changing large, host institutions. At San Francisco State's Experimental College, for example, the prevailing motto of the students was "blackmail the institution with quality." Needless to say, it didn't work. Theoretically, the larger, traditional unit would simply "wish" to imitate the novel, younger, obviously "superior" experiment. The theory is suspect for several reasons, but chiefly because it imagines that institutional change can occur without struggle, even without collision.[13]

What the model accomplishes is separatism, a goal that may be useful for certain short-range purposes. With reference to black studies, Nathan Hare calls these purposes "therapeutic," that is, building "ethnic confidence" (Hare 1970). It is possible to argue the necessity of separatism as a primary step toward social change. Groups need "turf"—a piece of "liberated territory"—and the space and time with which to plan for the future. Two dangers are obvious, however. First, running an "experimental college" or a department is a full-time job; second, it seems to be more difficult for an established department than for an insurgent one to maintain vital relationships with the communities around it.

For some of the reasons above, women's studies programs, in their first year of operation, do not appear to be moving toward separatist models. Perhaps they have learned hard lessons from previous educational reformers or from the experience of black studies programs. In any event, they are trying to have the best of both worlds: some separatism for the sake of building strength and community; but a continuing presence in all aspects of university life and structure.

[13] See Lauter and Howe, 1970; Chap. 4.

The dominant model of organization among programs may be described as "interdepartmental," or what Sacramento State College women call "decentralized." The pattern has been for individuals teaching women's studies courses in various departments to come together and declare themselves a "program." In several instances students, staff, and community people, including faculty wives, have joined faculty in their deliberations concerning the program's structure or center.

At Portland State University, for example, a group of women and men teachers and students met last spring to discuss the women's studies courses then being offered as part of regular departmental work. They decided to publish a "catalog," announcing courses as a group, and in effect establishing "a shadow or underground department of women's studies which was student-controlled and free of administrative interference" (Howe and Ahlum 1971:164). When the university asked the "Ad Hoc Women's Institute and Resource Center" to request official recognition, a lengthy debate preceded their sensible conclusion:

> In the end, we decided that since our proposal for a certificate program in women's studies was not likely to reach the appropriate committee of the Oregon State Board of Higher Education for at least one year, and more likely two, that we would submit a proposal *pro forma,* but would put our efforts into continuing to build our independent Women's Studies Program organically, and according to our needs (Howe and Ahlum 1971:165).

Even where programs have not been so dramatically insurgent—at Pittsburgh, Washington, Richmond, San Francisco State, and Buffalo, for example, where they asked for and received official recognition, funds, space, and some staffing—organization remains decentralized. At the universities of Pittsburgh and Washington, where women students and faculty pressed this year for official recognition of women's studies programs, they won the votes needed in committee after committee throughout the university hierarchy.[14] At Pittsburgh, the College of Arts and Sciences requested sufficient funds from the university's instructional budget for the appointments of five feminists to provide the nucleus of a women's studies program. The five would be appointed to particular departments by a joint decision of those departments and a women's studies search committee. All but the director of the new program would teach half-time in women's studies, half-time in a department. As of late spring, three women had been appointed, none at senior level.

At the University of Washington the women's studies program is located in "General and Interdisciplinary Studies," a division of Arts and Sciences that incorporates some dozen interdisciplinary programs. A search is on for a director, to be appointed jointly to a department and to women's studies. The director will co-

---

[14] It is interesting to contrast this achievement in 1971–1972 with the experience of graduate students at Northwestern University, who in 1968–1969 attempted to take a women's studies program proposal through appropriate committees where it was stripped, bit by bit, of its purpose and being.

ordinate the program, recruiting teachers from feminists on the faculty or among the graduate students. She may also, as in a number of programs, influence the recruitment and hiring of feminists useful both to departments and to women's studies. At the University of New Mexico, where a search is also on for a director of a new program in women's studies, the president has notified departments and deans that new female appointments are to be made only after consultation with the women's studies search committee.

At Sacramento State, where the women's studies program was given ultimate control over a full budget line and three-quarters of another budget line, the program has attempted, with only moderate success, to influence the selection of new faculty members. In several instances, departments preferred to appoint nonfeminist or antifeminist women to the candidates proposed by the women's studies program. Similar departmental behavior has been reported by other programs as well, and it is clear that if the decentralized or interdepartmental model of organization is to work, women's studies programs must gain the power to negotiate with departments about new appointments.

At Buffalo, where programs are called "colleges," the "College of Women's Studies" provides first, "a focused place" on campus where women can come together not only for community and solidarity but "to exchange perspectives and develop new ideas . . . new directions for research"; second, it functions also as a "base" from which "to support efforts in all the departments and professional schools to improve their curricula with respect to the needs and realities of women's lives" (Howe and Ahlum 1971:142–43). The goals of programs are dual: *to draw into* their centers, courses, and research activity students, faculty, and members of the general community; *to move outward* to affect other areas of the institution. Thus, the internal structures of women's studies programs must necessarily be somewhat fluid, a decentralized *network* rather than a traditional bureaucracy.

We find this organizational model attractive because it avoids stuffing women into a corner of the campus (or the society) "to do their own thing." Women's studies courses need centers and programs, but they need also the structures or networks that allow them to do their work in the world. Such networks might extend not only into all areas of the campus (nonacademic as well as departmental ones) but also into the community—into schools, libraries, parents' groups, and so on. Given the notion of networks, women's studies programs might organizationally avoid the isolation that academic departments ordinarily suffer; at the same time, they might also be more realistically equipped to manage their educational innovations.

Most programs have not been established with degree-granting power. The notable exceptions are the University of Washington (which conferred its first A.B. degree in June of 1972), Richmond (City University of New York), San Francisco State, and Douglass (Rutgers, New Jersey). Several California programs (Sacramento, Long Beach, and Fresno) have recently applied for the power to offer "minors." In general, however, the aim of programs has been to provide a group of elective courses, the chief educational function of which is both consciousness-raising and compensatory: to compensate for the deficiency of regular course offerings and to raise women's levels of aspiration.

Barnard's programmatic statement justifies its eleven-course program of electives:

> The question arises whether the inclusion of courses on women might upset our balanced curriculum and weaken its professional approach. If we acknowledge that the purpose of a liberal arts curriculum is not merely to provide pre-professional preparation for our students, but also to give them an appreciation of their cultural heritage, then, in an institution where women are educated, it is our duty to give them an awareness of their legacy as women. The nature of that legacy is riddled with problems of sexual definition. Since positive answers cannot be supplied, it is even more urgent to place the "women question" within many scholarly perspectives. In so doing, our students will become aware of the variety of roles women have played, of the social and economic necessities which prompted them, and also of the dilemmas women have faced and the resources they have called upon (Howe and Ahlum 1971: 140).

To make a similar point, feminists at The State University of New York at Buffalo quoted from the undergraduate catalogue—"Education must be designed to liberate students from the confines of a narrow vision, to reach full potential"—and called for the establishment of a "College of Women's Studies" that will "begin to meet our needs as women." Whatever their tone, the programs state more openly than individual courses their educational mission and/or activist commitment. Portland, for example, aims to produce women who are "intellectual activists" (Howe and Ahlum 1971:165); Goddard, women "able to act" (Howe and Ahlum 1971: 157). And at Sacramento, Portland, Washington, and Richmond the connections between programs and local women's movements are clearly announced, though the details of such relationships are not characterized.

At the same time, whether the programs are collections of discrete "electives," or whether they are organized to constitute a "major," the curricular demands on students are, characteristically, rigorous. Portland's threefold descriptions of academic purpose is typical: first, scholarly research with an emphasis on an interdisciplinary "problem-centered" approach; second, the development of new perspectives in teaching and class participation; third, the encouragement of new feminist writing and criticism (Howe and Ahlum 1971:165–166). At Buffalo, the three-pronged curriculum calls for "integration" between "knowledge" and "action": first, theoretical courses, organized around problems, history, and social change; second "study and field work courses" resulting either in research or the development of strategies for change or alternate institutions; third, "basic skills" for women—especially in "male technology traditionally denied to them" (Howe and Ahlum 1971:144). (Such skills courses—in auto mechanics, self-defense, audiotape machines, etc.—also are offered at Goddard, Laney, Richmond, and Sacramento.) In most programs, an introductory course initiates students both to an interdisciplinary approach as well as to "sisterhood," and especially into "collective" ways of working both as intellectuals and activists.

While individual courses may be innovative, a women's studies program is an additional learning ground for students, since most programs are attempting novel governing structures. Instead of operating through the usual departmental chairperson or by vesting authority in tenured members of a department, such programs have organized decision-making "boards" or "committees." Indeed, in the several instances of Sacramento, Portland, and Buffalo, there has been an agreement *not to* name a single person as "director" or "coordinator," however inconvenient or startling that may be for the university. On the Sacramento board, students have three votes, faculty two, and staff one. Portland began with a one person, one vote rule for major decisions, with meetings open to all; but as it grew in size (an enrollment of over 1,500 students during the academic year 1971–1972) they decided upon a seven-person board, and chose members by drawing out of a hat the names of those who had volunteered for such duty. At Buffalo, the governing structure is part of the experiment in innovation, with a "council of elected representatives" drawn complexly from among students in courses, from "course collectives" (i.e., groups of teachers who work together), and from staff. It is difficult to generalize about the effectiveness of the variety of governing boards in operation, especially at the end of the first (or at most the second) year of operation. But the issue is a critical one not only for internal growth and development of programs, but also as a means of ensuring the type of decentralization useful for social change.

Faculty appointed jointly to a woman's studies program and to a traditional department must be prepared to expend the political energy necessary for functioning in both worlds, as part of a network for change. Some students find themselves similarly divided and their commitment strained. In a couple of instances, attempts at new governing structures have resulted in serious "splits" within programs and decreased effectiveness in community and campus activities.[15] In all cases, the reports we have had confirm the difficulties of innovation—lengthy, time-consuming meetings, debates, strained energies and relationships, and a relatively slow process of decision making. The energy for such effort, nevertheless, has not waned.

Do we recommend working toward programs? Yes, in part because women on campuses need organizational structures within which to work for change, and not simply on short-term goals. Resistance to most forms of organization is profound both from women on campus and off. The suspicion of women in the movement about the allegedly inevitable elitism of organizations, their tendency to spur competitive drives among people, whether male or female, has in part been responsible

---

[15] See, for one account of such a split, Salper's (1971) essay on San Diego State's program.

for the erosion or demise of such large urban liberation groups as there were even a year or two ago. And while academic women are not averse to elitist organizations —indeed, they must function in them—they need more than their numbers if they are to effect institutional change in their own departments, let alone the campus as a whole, or the community. Hence, we recommend not only working towards programs, but conceiving of them in deliberately nonbureaucratic, antielitist forms.

A June 1972 release from "Women's Studies at California State University at San Francisco,"[16] reports a neatly negative decision of the "Advisory Committee" (their form of governing board): "To *not* work towards a separate 'Women's Studies' department since our major purpose is the recognition of women's important 'place' at every level in all disciplines rather than its 'special' character." And yet the same release announces not only an interdisciplinary major "with a *Focus on Women*" (twenty-eight courses from which to choose), but a similar master's program. The Advisory Committee also functions to "sponsor research proposals"; to advise "in the area of affirmative action for women faculty"; to support several adjunct organizations—the Women's Alliance (faculty) and Independent Campus Women (a student action organization). In addition, the Advisory Committee has begun to function off-campus in "related activities," a "newly organized Bay Area Consortium on Continuing Education for Women," and, with twenty colleges in the Bay area, "in the development of a center or clearinghouse of information and referral for women students." In less than two years, then, women's studies at San Francisco State has begun to take on the appearance of a "network" without diminishing its role as an intellectual center for students' new curricular interests and needs.

In general, small or moderately large campuses have sparked programs more quickly than multiversities, at least partly because of the availability of feminists on faculties and their relationship to local or national women's movements. One useful strategy for the future envisions affirmative action officers (on large university campuses especially) working closely with departments and with women's studies programs to facilitate the hiring (rather than the firing) of feminists with the energy to organize for change.

At Buffalo, the women wrote of their educational goals:

> This education will not be an academic exercise; it will be an ongoing process to change the ways in which women think and behave. It must be part of the struggle to build a new and more complete society (Howe and Ahlum 1971: 142).

Goddard's feminist studies program concludes with the hopes that their students will "leave . . . not only with a body of knowledge, but a reason for learning it, a

[16] California State University at San Francisco is the new name of San Francisco State College.

context to fit it in, but most important, a strong sense of an inner core of self that most women never develop. We want them to be able to act on the world, and in the world" (Howe and Ahlum 1971:157).

We choose to conclude on the rhetoric of idealism because that is where women's studies is at the end of its first few years. Such rhetoric will seem distinctly familiar to those who have survived the efforts of the sixties to change higher education, to place it at the service of people who need knowledge to solve their problems. Women in the forefront of academic change today build on that decade of work and hope. Because of their numbers, their willingness to learn from the past, their energy, and the breadth implicit in the feminist perspective, they may succeed where others before them have failed.

REFERENCES

Ahlum, Carol, and Howe, Florence (Eds.). 1971. *The new guide to current female studies.* Pittsburgh: KNOW, Inc.

Arnesen, Nancy. December 1971. Teaching women's studies in community college. Paper read at Modern Language Association Convention, Chicago.

Barauch, Grace. 1971. Research in psychology relevant to the situation of women. Paper presented at the conference on Women and Education: A Feminist Perspective, November 5–7, 1971, sponsored by the University of Pittsburgh and the MLA Commission on the Status of Women.

Bart, Pauline B. 1972. Why women's studies? In Rae Lee Siporin (Ed.), *Female studies V.* Pittsburgh: KNOW, Inc., pp. 94–99.

Benson, Ruth Crego. 1971. Pittsburgh diary: Reflection on USOE Institute; Crisis: Women in education. In Elaine Showalter and Carol Ohmann (Eds.), *Female studies IV.* Pittsburgh: KNOW, Inc., pp. 1–7.

Chamberlain, Kathleen. December 1971. Women students at Manhattan Community College. Paper read at Modern Language Association Convention, Chicago.

Chapman, Gretel. 1972. Women and the visual arts. In *Female studies V,* pp. 38–39.

Chmaj, Betty E. (Ed.). 1971. *American women and American studies.* Pittsburgh: KNOW, Inc.

Clarenbach, Kathryn F. 1970. Human status for women. Paper read at Midwest Association for Physical Education of College Women.

Cohen, Audrey. 1971. Women and higher education: recommendations for change. *Phi Delta Kappan,* 53:164–167.

Davis, Devra Lee. 1972. The woman in the moon: Towards an integration of women's studies. In *Female studies V,* pp. 17–28.

Farians, Elizabeth. 1971. Institute for the study, redefinition and resocialization of women: a program for colleges and universities. Available from author: 6125 Webbland Place, Cincinnati, Ohio.

Ferguson, Mary Anne. 1972. The sexist image of women in literature. In *Female studies V,* pp. 77–83.

Foster, Ginny. 1971. On being "femmes des lettres." Available from author at 5619 N. Commercial, Portland, Oregon 97217.

Ginsburg, Ruth Bader. 1971. Treatment of women by the law; awakening consciousness in the law schools. *Valparaiso Law Review*, Symposium Issue, 5(2):480–488.

Gordon, Linda. 1972. Why women's history? In *Female studies V*, pp. 49–52.

Greenwald, Maurine. 1970. Women's history in America. In Florence Howe (Ed.), *Female studies II*. Pittsburgh: KNOW, Inc., pp. 65–73.

Hare, Nathan. 1970. What black studies means to a black scholar. *Integrated Education*, 8:8–15.

Hoffman, Nancy Jo. 1971. A class of our own. In *Female studies IV*, pp. 14–27.

Hoffman, Nancy Jo. 1972. Reading women's poetry: The meaning and our lives. *College English*, 34(1):48–72.

Howe, Florence (Ed.). 1970. *Female studies II*.

Howe, Florence. 1971. Identity and expression: A writing course for women. *College English*, 32(8):963–971; abbreviated version in *Female studies II*, pp. 1–4.

Howe, Florence. 1972. Feminism, fiction, and the classroom. *Soundings: An Interdisciplinary Journal* 55(4):369–389.

Howe, Florence, and Ahlum, Carol (Eds.). 1971. *Female studies III*. Pittsburgh: KNOW, Inc.

Knowles, Mary Tyler. 1971. All male students and women's liberation. In *Female studies IV*, pp. 35–39.

Krouse, Agate Nesaule. 1972. A feminist in every classroom. In *Female studies V*, pp. 1–6.

Landy, Marcia. 1972. Women, education, and social power. In *Female studies V*, pp. 53–63.

Lauter, Paul, and Howe, Florence. 1970. *The conspiracy of the young*. Cleveland: World.

Lerner, Gerda. 1970. Teaching women about women. In *Female studies II*, pp. 86–88.

Lerner, Gerda. 1972. On the teaching and organization of feminist studies. In *Female studies V*, pp. 34–37.

Lewis, Eleanor J. 1972. What women's studies can do for women's liberation. Paper presented at the conference on Women and Education: A Feminist Perspective, November 5–7, 1971, sponsored by the University of Pittsburgh and the MLA Commission on the Status of Women.

Martin, Wendy. 1971. Teaching women's studies—some problems and discoveries. In *Female studies IV*, pp. 9–13.

Miller, Lindsay. 1972. Newest course on campus: Women's studies. *New York Post* (series): May 22–27.

Oltman, Ruth. 1970. Campus 1970: where do women stand? Washington, D.C.: American Association of University Women.

Reeves, Nancy. 1972. Feminine subculture and female mind. In *Female studies V*, pp. 84–93.

Reuben, Elaine. November 1971. Feminist criticism in the classroom, or "What do you mean *we*, white Man?" Paper read at Midwest Modern Language Association convention, Detroit.

Robinson, Lillian. 1970. The sexual order. In *Female studies II*, pp. 42–43.

Rossi, Alice. 1969. Sex equality: Beginnings of ideology. *The Humanist,* September/ October: 3–6, 16.

Salper, Roberta. 1971. Women's studies: San Diego State College. *Ramparts,* 10:56–60.

Salzman-Webb, Marilyn. 1972. Feminist studies: Frill or necessity. In *Female studies V,* pp. 64–76.

Schmidt, Dolores Barracano. 1972. Sexism in textbooks. In *Female studies V,* pp. 29–33.

Sherwin, Susan S. 1972. Women's studies as a scholarly discipline: Some questions for discussion. In *Female studies V,* pp. 114–116.

Showalter, Elaine. 1971a. Introduction: teaching about women, 1971. In *Female studies IV,* pp. i–xii.

Showalter, Elaine. 1971b. Women and the literary curriculum. *College English,* 32(8): 855–862.

Showalter, Elaine, and Ohmann, Carol (Eds.). 1971. *Female studies IV.*

Siporin, Rae (Ed.). 1972. *Female studies V.*

Somerville, Rose. 1971. Women's studies. *Today's Education,* 60:35–37.

Stimpson, Catharine R. 1972. Women as scapegoats. In *Female studies V,* pp. 7–16.

Strong, Brian. 1971. Teaching women's history experimentally. In *Female studies IV,* pp. 40–47.

Tobias, Sheila (Ed.). 1970a. *Female studies I.* Pittsburgh: KNOW, Inc.

Tobias, Sheila. 1970b. Female studies—an immodest proposal.

Tobias, Sheila. 1970c. Female studies for State University of New York. Paper read at Second Caucus on Women's Rights at State University of New York at Albany.

Tobias, Sheila, and Kusnetz, Ella. 1972. Teaching women's studies: An experiment at Stout State. *Journal of Home Economics,* 64(4):17–21; also published in *Female studies V,* pp. 100–113.

Trecker, Janice Law. 1971a. Women in United States history high school textbooks. *Social Education,* 35:619ff.

Trecker, Janice Law. October 16, 1971b. Women's place is in the curriculum. *Saturday Review,* 54:83–86, 92.

Trecker, Janice Law. March 1972. The amazing, invisible woman. Paper read at New York State Conference on the Social Studies, New York City.

Wallach, Aleta. 1972. Genesis of a "women and the law" course: The dawn of consciousness at UCLA Law School. *Journal of Legal Education,* 24(3):309–353.

West, Anne Grant. 1971. Women's liberation: or, exploding the fairy princess myth. *Scholastic Teacher Jr/Sr High,* November: 6–19.

White, Barbara A. 1971. Up from the podium: Feminist revolution in the classroom. In *Female studies IV,* pp. 28–34.

Chapter Eighteen

Internal Remedies for Sex Discrimination in Colleges and Universities

Margaret L. Rumbarger

SOME OF THE MOST conspicuous and controversial attacks on discrimination against women in higher education have come from agencies external to the academic community itself, specifically the federal government through the Department of Labor's Office of Federal Contract Compliance and HEW's Office for Civil Rights. Other chapters in this volume examine the laws which prohibit discrimination in employment on the basis of sex, and discuss the great number of individual and class action complaints filed by and on behalf of academic women with HEW over the past several years.

It is well known that certain members of the academic profession believe that the interference of governmental agencies in heretofore sacrosanct areas of faculty hiring and firing will compromise traditional prerogatives and academic standards (Seabury 1972; Hook 1972; *New York Times* 1972). The federal government has countered these claims with the contention that as government contractors, universities are no less obliged than other industries and businesses to take affirmative measures to eliminate practices that deny equal opportunity to women. Many academic women have argued that unless external pressures are brought to bear upon institutions and their faculties, discrimination will continue and may even increase as a reaction to women's political action. Others, however, have concluded that the elimination of discrimination can best be accomplished by the initiative and persistence of women themselves working within the academic community, through patient education of their male colleagues and the development of specific remedial mechanisms in their universities.

It is the argument of this chapter that institutional reform and the elimination of discrimination cannot be accomplished simply through the imposition of external requirements by governmental agencies, although these may be, in many cases, a precondition for change. If change does not come from within the institution itself, and if proposed reforms are not supported by the internal structures and resources of the university community, remedies imposed by external agencies will be superficial and will fail to reach the roots of discrimination against women. If these roots cannot be located and treated in our universities, it bodes ill for the success of efforts in other sectors of our society to achieve a lasting solution to the practice

425

and effects of discrimination against women in education, in employment, and in their personal lives. As the special task force of HEW noted:

> The unique role of higher education gives it extraordinary leverage to either help or hurt women's chances for equality of opportunity. When colleges and universities deny women the chance to gain skills and credentials, they increase the likelihood that women will not receive equal opportunities in all other social institutions for the rest of their lives.
>
> Higher education exerts another kind of leverage as well. Colleges and universities take upon themselves the task of forming and sanctioning the attitudes and practices which educated people will thereafter consider reasonable. If it is fairness which they sanction, all women are helped; but if it is discrimination they sanction, all women are hurt, educated or not (Newman 1971:51).

Contributing both to the difficulty and the urgency of improving the status of women and ending discrimination is the economic situation now confronting institutions of higher education (AAUP 1971e; Kurland 1972). Bertram H. Davis, general secretary of the American Association of University Professors, noted in his report to that association's 1971 annual meeting that while "a period of economic retrenchment affects us all, its heaviest impact is likely to be upon women" (AAUP 1971e: 182). A recent study points out one area in which women are particularly vulnerable:

> The over-supply of Ph.D.'s and the tight market for jobs has already had its impact on women teachers. For cutbacks in academic personnel always begin at the fringes, and this is where a large number of women have been employed. The expansive period of the sixties enlarged the opportunity for the part-time woman teacher. But with choices now having to be made as to using academic women as part-time teachers or graduate assistants working toward higher degrees, most departments will incline toward the latter. In addition, it will take strong pressures from the women themselves to offset the inclination to favor male applicants for admission to Ph.D. programs whose enrollments have been cut back (Eble 1971:110).

Thus, although institutional change regarding the role of women in academe has come to be understood as imperative, it is nevertheless difficult for colleges and universities to respond as they might have in the prosperous mid-1960s. The current generation of faculty women bears a special responsibility to press for reform within their institutions, not only to improve their own status but to assure greater opportunities for women who will follow them in the coming decades.

There are numerous areas which have been singled out by women as particularly obstructive to their entry and advancement in the academic profession. Traditional methods of recruiting and hiring for faculty positions, the absence of programs responsive to the nonprofessional roles which professional women are called upon to fulfill, and the criteria that determine how one achieves professional recognition, have attracted a good deal of attention.

Perhaps the most immediate and volatile problems arise when internal mechanisms of review and remedy of sex discrimination are either unavailable or not sufficiently responsive. The enormous number of complaints of discrimination which have been received by HEW's Office for Civil Rights attests to a failure on the part of institutions to develop systematic and equitable methods of dealing with sex discrimination particularly when complaints are registered by individuals. It is to this particular area of concern that this chapter will be devoted, with special attention to the role of the American Association of University Professors (AAUP) in developing effective grievance procedures.

THE AAUP AND FACULTY GRIEVANCES

Since its founding in 1915, the American Association of University Professors has been concerned to "increase the usefulness and advance the standards, ideals and welfare of the profession" (AAUP 1971b:288). In fulfilling this objective it has worked to protect the rights and responsibilities of individual faculty members and faculties as a whole, and to develop structures of government within institutions designed to meet this end. Through its Washington office staff and through its nearly 1,300 local chapters, the Association has often advised on the development of grievance procedures on a given campus, sometimes in the context of a particular problem, but more often in response to a generally felt need for an effective process through which individual faculty members can have their cases heard and judged on the basis of fair standards and procedures.

The body within the AAUP that bears primary responsibility for matters involving actions against individual faculty members is Committee A on Academic Freedom and Tenure. This committee has recommended that a faculty member who believes he or she has cause for grievance should be able to petition a faculty committee for redress of that grievance, whether it arises in the context of non-retention (and is thus of direct concern to Committee A), or whether it involves such matters as salary, promotion in rank, assignment of teaching duties, or propriety of conduct. Section 15 of Committee A's 1972 Recommended Institutional Regulations on Academic Freedom and Tenure states that a faculty committee should be appointed to hear a grievance, investigate the matter, seek to bring about a settlement, and report its findings to the grievant and the administrative or faculty body to which it is responsible (AAUP 1972a). Section 10 of this same document provides the same due process in cases where discrimination is alleged as a basis for non-reappointment as in cases where an issue of academic freedom is involved. The question of grievances relating to nonrenewal of appointment is addressed in more detail in the AAUP's 1971 statement on "Procedural Standards in the

Renewal or Nonrenewal of Faculty Appointments," which stresses the importance of adequate evaluation of academic services of nontenured faculty members, and states that an individual should receive upon request a statement of the reasons for nonrenewal and an opportunity for review by an impartial faculty committee (AAUP 1971c).

Most well-governed colleges and universities have a standing faculty grievance committee, most often established as a committee of the faculty senate or council, and responsible to that body. Where such a committee does not exist, and a case is brought to AAUP attention in which consideration by a faculty committee would seem the appropriate next step, the Association advises that such a committee be formed on an ad hoc basis. If an institution is unwilling to provide such a hearing, the Association staff reviews the information submitted by the individual and may seek to achieve a resolution. A Washington-based staff, however, generally is not in a position to reach substantive conclusions in cases involving alleged failures in professional performance. Where a faculty is itself unwilling or unable to hold an appropriate grievance hearing, it is often difficult for the Association itself to pursue the matter with any success. Without the benefit of faculty assessment, inquiry by an outside agency can lead at best to a tentative and untested judgment in the great majority of grievances. In the event of a finding on the contentions of the petitioner by a faculty grievance committee, the faculty as a whole, and the AAUP if necessary, has the basis for contributing to a resolution of the dispute between the individual and the administration or department.

COMMITTEE W AND GRIEVANCE PROCEDURES

In 1970, the AAUP reactivated its Committee on the Status of Women in the Profession,[1] signaling a formal recognition by the largest organization of professional academics of a need to devote increased attention to the special problems of faculty women.[2] One of the most important concerns of this committee was to

[1] Committee W's "reactivation" in 1970 came some forty years after the AAUP's original Committee on the Status of Women, one of the first committees established after the Association's founding, had been "excused from further service" in 1928. The early Committee W published two reports, in 1921 and 1924, which reflect many of the problems still facing women in the profession in the 1970s, and which make fascinating reading for their intrinsic as well as historical interest. See AAUP 1921 and AAUP 1924.

[2] In her first report to the Association's annual meeting, Committee W chairperson Alice S. Rossi noted the opportunities for the committee's work and its special responsibilities:

[T]he reactivation of Committee W in AAUP symbolizes the need to rise above disciplinary and institutional levels to broaden national focus on the issues and policy guidelines needed in hundreds of colleges and universities where women study and work.

Committee W has a unique responsibility, in my judgment, because the AAUP crosses the barriers of academic disciplines and of institutions. It is an enormous fa-

emphasize the need to establish grievance procedures to handle complaints of discrimination from women faculty. In her report to the 1971 annual meeting of the Association, the committee's chairperson, Alice S. Rossi, noted:

> I shall urge the Committee to recommend strongly that the Association make a firm demand that colleges and universities establish whatever grievance procedures are lacking on local campuses to facilitate the processing of complaints from women faculty members, with a strong recommendation that such grievance committees include women in proportion to their representation on the faculty, including all part-time, nontenured, and lower rank personnel where so many women have been kept (AAUP 1971d:217).

In 1972, a Committee on Discrimination established by the Association's council devoted an entire section of its report to a reiteration of Committee W's recommendation for grievance procedures, concluding that:

> The most appropriate mechanism for addressing and resolving cases of prejudicial treatment is effective institutional grievance procedures. We reiterate our concern that colleges and universities still lacking such procedures move promptly to develop them, so that grievances relating to discrimination can be heard and necessary corrective action can follow (AAUP 1972b:162).

During the fall of 1970, Committee W decided that it should not itself attempt to develop a special process to handle complaints of sex discrimination on either the national or local level, but that it should concentrate its energies in two directions. The first was to review existing policies and guidelines of the Association and to make specific policy recommendations which would assure equitable treatment of women in academe. Many of the policy revisions and new proposals would be implemented through Committee A by providing assistance to individuals suffering sex discrimination. The second direction was to urge local AAUP chapters to become active in educating faculty to the need to improve the status of women in academe.

THE ROLE OF THE AAUP CHAPTER

The national Committee W soon found it had little need to urge local campus action on the issue, for one of the most striking developments in the first year of

---

cilitation, unmatched by any other organization, to have an existing structure at the national, state and local levels, through which to reach and coordinate the efforts of individuals and groups sharing concerns for the problems faced by women in academe. Reports that reach me from hundreds of women and countless meetings across the country all share a common characteristic: the desire for a more sustained and systematic network through which academic women can be kept informed and through which our efforts can be coordinated. The existing structure of AAUP has given Committee W a good headstart in providing at least part of that coordination. (See AAUP 1971e).

its reactivated existence was the proliferation of local committees on the status of women. While a few chapters had shown interest in doing so prior to the spring of 1970, the academic year following the reactivation of the national committee saw the establishment of such committees in over a hundred AAUP chapters and state conferences, and many more were established during the academic year 1971–1972. These local committee W's undertook studies of the status of women on their campuses and in their states, gained the support of their chapters or conferences for effective campaigns against antinepotism regulations and in favor of maternity leave, advised individuals with complaints of discrimination, and developed recommendations for affirmative action programs to remedy patterns of inequality. The 1970–1971 Report of the national Committee W recognized the potential for change through the activities of these chapters.

> The long-standing permanent nature of local chapter organization makes the local AAUP chapter a natural locus to serve as monitor of any plans to effect changes in institutional procedures for however long it takes to achieve the goals of full equality for women in academe (AAUP 1971d:218).

Patterns of discrimination may be the more immediately appropriate focus of chapter energies since a chapter can work towards the development of remedial programs in local institutions. Where a senate, or other official faculty body that can assume this responsibility exists, a chapter can add its special perspective and information, as well as a sense of urgency.

Most chapters and their committees on the status of women also function in an advisory and mediative capacity regarding individual complaints, dealing for the most part with standards and with procedural questions rather than the substantive merits of a given case. Chapters can render valuable assistance in obtaining a competent academic advisor for a grievant, and see that proper grievance channels are made available to women. Some chapters have assisted women in the preparation and presentation of their cases. A chapter can be particularly effective in establishing and enforcing the principle that complaints of discrimination should be received, heard, and judged through an established procedure, and that individuals should have a fair opportunity to have their complaints adjudicated within their community by individuals who understand the pervasiveness and complexity of sex discrimination.

As in individual complaints involving matters other than discrimination, an AAUP chapter can and should be prepared to take a stand on clear issues of policy or fact which emerge from a given case involving an allegation of discrimination. In the absence of an alternative channel for the airing of grievances relating to sex discrimination, a chapter might report on individual cases brought to its attention and encourage the development of suitable review procedures. Many individual complaints never reach the Association's Washington office simply because chapter officers or committees are able to provide the required advice or mediation.

SEPARATE BUT EQUAL?

It has been suggested that colleges and universities should establish separate grievance procedures to handle complaints of sex discrimination, rather than process such complaints through channels that exist or that may be developed for general use. Government guidelines on affirmative action have not spoken to this point; indeed, at the time of this writing, they have not spoken at all to the question of institutional grievance procedures. Meanwhile, women on some campuses have pressed for such special procedures as grievance committees on which only women may sit, on the theory that women alone will be responsive to their complaints. It is doubtful that in the last analysis this would prove conducive to a wide-reaching and soundly based resolution of sex discrimination. Discrimination in any form is not consistent with the purposes of higher education, and its remedy should be the responsibility of all members of an institution. Furthermore, an integrated grievance committee can often serve as an important mechanism for informing male committee members of the problems faced by academic women and through this process contribute to a more informed and responsive faculty at large. In some cases, serving on such committees may encourage men to confront their own prejudices or to air their own ambivalences toward women in the academic community, and this too is a necessary step toward eliminating sex discrimination in academe. An all-women, like an all-black, committee runs the risk of being charged with bias and hence could jeopardize the acceptance of the procedures for all forms of grievance by all faculty members.

Grievance procedures, no matter how soundly formulated, are not in and of themselves sufficient to get to the root of the problem of discrimination, particularly those aspects of discrimination which have been permitted to exist unchallenged for generations. As the AAUP Council Committee on Discrimination has noted,

> The cultural conditioning which has permitted our profession, which in its teaching role should set the example for society in these matters to accept without question different standards of treatment for certain groups of people, may well impede fair consideration of the elements of an individual's situation within the context of a grievance hearing (AAUP 1972b:161).

It is important that those responsible for the review of sex discrimination grievances be aware of the long-entrenched patterns of discrimination and negative assumptions about the role and needs of women in order to approach such grievances in an informed and sympathetic fashion. They might better understand, then, the demands for the representation of women on grievance committees or requests for a final review by university administrative officers or task force personnel charged with the supervision of affirmative action programs.

In sum, it is essential that grievances involving sex discrimination be understood as legitimate, and reviewed and adjudicated according to established procedures within institutions. Moreover, an elected faculty committee should consider the faculty member's complaint. Complaints of discrimination have been shunted aside too often by faculty reluctant or unwilling to assert jurisdiction, or have received bare notice from a hearing committee which may have serious doubts as to their legitimacy, or have been reviewed by a body which lacks access to the necessary information upon which to base judgment.

SOME BASIC PRINCIPLES

The following is an outline of some basic principles that should govern consideration of grievances in general, and others that may be particularly relevant in cases of alleged sex discrimination. While some of these principles may seem self-evident to individuals at colleges and universities with a strong system of faculty government, it is surprising how much disagreement, at least in practice, there is on each one.[3]

1. A grievance may be defined as any circumstance, condition, or matter which any member of the faculty feels detrimental to her or his professional career. Narrow definitions of what a faculty member may and may not seek to appeal should be avoided.

2. Every effort should be made to resolve a grievance informally, and provision for such efforts should be made part of the regular grievance procedures. The chairperson of the grievance committee, or a panel of advisors and mediators under the auspices of the grievance committee might mediate at this stage through consultation and informal negotiation among the parties involved. If these efforts fail, the grievant should be permitted to proceed to the initial stages of consideration by the grievance committee. A grievant should be permitted academic counsel of her/his own choice at all stages of a grievance proceeding.

5. The entire procedure should be as expeditious as possible, largely because the prompt processing of complaints tends to facilitate resolution.

6. The grievant should have access to all information, including departmental recommendations and evaluations, which is not properly confidential and is deemed necessary for the preparation of the case.[4]

[3] It should be noted that these principles are intended to apply to grievances prior to the establishment of a *prima facie* case of discrimination; if a grievant succeeds in establishing a *prima facie* case of discrimination, it is incumbent upon those who made the decision to come forward with evidence in support of their decision. In this case, the procedures set forth in sections 5 and 6 of the 1968 Recommended Institutional Regulations on Academic Freedom and Tenure should be observed. See AAUP 1971a:15–19.

[4] The question of confidentiality of information relating to an individual's professional status is a difficult one, and one which cannot be adequately addressed in this chapter. It is sufficient to note that whether confidentiality can be considered legitimate grounds for refusing to disclose certain information may depend to some extent on the nature of the grievance and whether the information in question is deemed essential to the grievant's case.

7. At every step in the procedure some written record should be kept and made available to both complainant and respondent. In formal proceedings, a verbatim transcript or tape recording is often desirable. If the proceedings continue after a *prima facie* case of discrimination has been established, a verbatim record becomes an essential element of due process.

8. The grievance committee may ask to interview persons knowledgeable about the grievant's situation, and such a request should be denied only for compelling reasons. The administration of the institution should lend its assistance in procuring witnesses.

9. In cases involving an allegation of sex discrimination, women should be represented on the committee reviewing the complaint. A grievant should be allowed a limited number of peremptory challenges of members of the committee.

10. The burden of proof should rest upon the grievant, except in the following cases: dismissal of a tenured faculty member; dismissal of a nontenured faculty member prior to the expiration of a term appointment; or when *prima facie* evidence of a violation of academic freedom or *prima facie* evidence of discrimination has been established.

The procedure employed by a grievance committee may differ according to the nature of the grievance. For example, the complaint of an individual who alleges that she has been given notice of nonreappointment because of prejudice against women by the department chairman will call for a different approach from the complaint of an individual who alleges that her salary, like the salary of most women on the campus, is disproportionately low in comparison to those of her male colleagues of similar rank and length of service. The determination of approach should be essentially the responsibility of the grievance committee itself, which may choose in cases involving a possible pattern of discrimination to enlist the advice and assistance of an institution's affirmative action officer or commission on women.

FACULTY GRIEVANCE PROCEDURES: A MODEL

While the same specific grievance procedures are not applicable for all institutions, procedures recently adopted at Northern Michigan University provide a model for extended discussion (Northern Michigan 1972). In the paragraphs which follow, I shall point out some features of the University's procedures that may be particularly relevant to the concerns of women faculty.

Informal Resolution Procedures

The Northern Michigan procedures provide that a faculty member who feels that an injustice has been done normally will seek first to resolve the problem by informal means and/or through administrative channels, with "the right to prompt reply to his inquiries." The absence of a prompt response is sufficient reason for taking the problem to the next level of appeal. The grievant may seek the advice and assistance of the chairman of the Faculty Hearing Panel, who serves as an ombudsman for faculty. (At some institutions provision is made for a standing panel of grievance officers, from whose number a grievant may select one to serve as an academic advisor.) This advisor attempts to resolve the matter informally through negotiation and mediation, and, if unsuccessful, advises the complainant throughout the remainder of the grievance process.

The Northern Michigan procedures provide that "except under the most unusual of circumstances," administrative channels should be exhausted prior to the filing of a formal complaint:

> In general, when a grievance is generated by an action or inaction on the part of a member of the University, the initial steps should be to register the concern with him and then, if necessary, to appeal to his superior having immediate supervisory responsibility (Northern Michigan 1972: Section 4.1).

The Preliminary Hearing

If the difficulty which occasioned the grievance is not resolved informally, the matter will be turned over to a Preliminary Hearing Committee of three persons. The Preliminary Hearing Committee is appointed by the chairman of the Faculty Hearing Panel from a panel of twelve persons elected by the entire faculty, and including as many as four nontenured faculty members.

It is provided that a nontenured grievant may request that at least two of the three members of the Preliminary Hearing Committee be nontenured. A not unreasonable extension of this provision would be for a woman to be able to request that at least two of the three persons on the Preliminary Hearing Committee be women. If it is impossible to honor such a request, because of the composition of the Faculty Hearing Panel, the chairman of the panel asks the chairman of the academic senate to appoint sufficient ad hoc panel members from the faculty to honor the request.

The Preliminary Hearing Committee may recommend either that the complaint does not merit further action, resolve the grievance by negotiation, or determine that the complaint is justified and requires specific remedial measures, including, if necessary, a formal hearing. Appeal from a rejection of the complaint may be made only to the president of the university. (Provisions for appeal vary from institution to institution. One recommendation which might be made in cases involving alleged sex discrimination is that it be submitted for review to the administrative officer or advisory body responsible for the institution's affirmative action program.)

The Northern Michigan procedures provide that except where there is mutual consent to the contrary, no more than twenty-one days, exclusive of holidays, may pass between the time the matter is brought to the Preliminary Hearing Committee and the time that the concluding report and recommendations are made (Northern Michigan 1972:Section 5.3.7).

When a recommendation of the Preliminary Hearing Committee is not accepted by the president, written reasons are given to all parties to the grievance and to the committee.

The Formal Hearing

If no resolution of the complaint is forthcoming from the Preliminary Hearing Committee, and if the committee so recommends, it may be brought by the complainant to a formal hearing. A Formal Hearing Committee "will not negotiate or mediate. It will conduct a full and complete hearing, concluding with formal findings and recommendations" (Northern Michigan 1972: Section 3.3).

Membership on the Formal Hearing Committee is determined by the panel chairman, who selects five persons from the panel. A nontenured faculty member may request that two members of the committee be nontenured, and by analogy, a woman might request that two members of the committee be women. A grievant is permitted two peremptory challenges to the appointed membership of the committee, and members of the panel should withdraw if they deem themselves disqualified for bias or interest in the case.

The committee, in consultation with the president and the parties to the grievance, determines whether the hearing is to be public or private. During the proceedings the complainant and respondent(s) each are permitted to have academic counsel of their own choice. Each party is afforded an opportunity to obtain necessary witnesses and documentary or other evidence. The administration secures the cooperation of such witnesses, and makes available necessary documents and "other evidence within its control." In addition,

> The parties to the issue will have the right to confront and cross-examine all witnesses. Where the witness cannot or will not appear, but the committee determines that the interests of justice require admission of his statement, the committee will identify the witness, disclose his statement, and if possible provide for interrogatories (Northern Michigan 1972: Section 5.4.2.14).

There are additional provisions in the Northern Michigan procedures which govern a formal hearing (see also AAUP 1972a: sections 4, 5, 6). Procedures in cases involving dismissal differ from those in cases not involving dismissal (such as nonreappointment). In all cases, a decision of the Formal Hearing Committee is rejected by the administration or Board of Trustees only for compelling reasons stated in detail. Should the complainant consider the committee's decision unsatisfactory, or the recommendations not sufficiently far-reaching, she or he may appeal directly to the president.

PROVING DISCRIMINATION

The policy guidelines of the AAUP, which are reflected in most faculty grievance procedures, including the Northern Michigan procedures outlined above, provides that the burden of proof in grievances which do not involve the dismissal of a tenured faculty member, or of a nontenured faculty member prior to the expiration of the term of appointment, should be upon the complainant. This means, in effect, that an individual who wishes to appeal an action or condition which adversely affects his or her professional status or career is responsible for stating the grounds on which the allegations are based, and for providing clear and compelling evidence in support of those allegations. If a *prima facie* case is established, those responsible for discriminatory action are then obliged to come forward with evidence in support of their position. Only in cases involving dismissal must the institution itself from the outset bear the burden of proof.

Those who have been involved in cases of sex discrimination, whether as party to the injury, as advisor, or as sympathetic bystander, know how difficult it is for a woman to "bear the burden of proof." In most instances a woman either is the sole grievant who has experienced unfair or prejudicial treatment by informal means that are difficult to pinpoint or document, or she is one woman among many whose careers contribute to a pattern of underrepresentation, slower promotions, and lower salary for women.

In the case of an individual grievant, the burden of proving discrimination is in most instances a heavy one indeed. Not only are women hesitant to appeal prejudicial treatment, but they and their colleagues have tended to assume that women have a "harder time making it" in academe, that is, they must necessarily accomplish and endure more than their male counterparts. The difficulty of presenting proof of discriminatory treatment in many cases may be greater today than it was twenty years ago. Those who are biased against women in the profession perform strenuously to avoid doing anything that might constitute proof of sex discrimination. And although there are signs that faculty grievance committees are becoming more responsive to women, unless clearer and more precise standards of proper treatment and evaluation of faculty members are developed, the very latitude of operation of committees will result in inconclusive responses to women's grievances.

Complaints which involve a *pattern* of discrimination against women as a class are less difficult to document. Here the measure of a *prima facie* case can be made statistically, and the degree to which any individual complainant must bear the burden of proof thereby is lessened. For example, the pattern of representation of and rewards to women in the upper professorial ranks may be significant evidence in judging the complaint of a woman who claims to have been denied promotion for discriminatory reasons. It then becomes the responsibility of the administration —indeed it is their obligation—to take remedial action or to show cause why the individual's rewards are not equal to those of her male colleagues. While in many individual cases discrimination may be difficult to document, in a class complaint statistical evidence of a pattern of sex discrimination is not only easier to obtain, but shifts the burden of refuting or confirming the allegations to the institution.

In many academic institutions decisions on promotion and salary are made on the basis of undefined standards of scholarly competence, whose very vagueness permits their interpretation to favor male faculty members. Yet academe has committed itself, in theory, to fairness in evaluation of all aspects of an individual's contributions to the institution, educational program, students, and colleagues. It is now justly subject to demands that it put its theoretical commitment into operation.

CONCLUDING REMARKS

Grievance procedures such as the one established at Northern Michigan do not, of course, automatically guarantee that problems of discrimination will disappear, or that all individual cases will be successfully resolved. There is some basis for hope, however, that the university community is becoming aware of the problems of sex discrimination and beginning to demonstrate its willingness to work toward their resolution through affirmative action.

Government agencies and courts cannot by themselves effect a permanent and meaningful change in the situation of academic women. Channels within the university community can, however, be made to serve the needs of women if they are willing to work to strengthen them. Academic women have drawn upon the resources and spirit of the new feminism in exposing and eradicating the deeply entrenched cultural biases against the professional woman; they must also work to develop sound policies and procedures through which institutions of higher education will provide enhanced opportunities to women who wish to enter and succeed in the academic profession.

REFERENCES

American Association of University Professors (AAUP).

1921.   Preliminary report of Committee W on status of women in college and university faculties. *AAUP Bulletin,* 7:21–32.

1924.   Report of Committee W on status of women in college and university faculties. *AAUP Bulletin,* 10:65–72.

1971a.   *AAUP policy documents and reports.*

1971b.   Constitution of the Association. *AAUP Bulletin,* 57(2):288–290.

1971c.   Procedural standards in the renewal or non-renewal of faculty appointments. *AAUP Bulletin,* 57(2):206–210.

438   ACADEMIC WOMEN ON THE MOVE

1971d. Report of Committee W, 1970–71. *AAUP Bulletin,* 57(2):215–220.
1971e. Report of the General Secretary. *AAUP Bulletin,* 57(2):181–183.
1972a. Recommended institutional regulations on academic freedom and tenure. *AAUP Bulletin,* 58(4):428–433.
1972b. Report of Council Committee on Discrimination. *AAUP Bulletin,* 58(2): 160–163.

Eble, Kenneth E. 1971. *Career development of the effective college teacher.* Washington, D.C.: American Association of University Professors.
Hook, Sidney. March 1972. The road to a university "quota system." *Freedom at Issue,* 12:1–4.
Kurland, Jordan E. 1972. Reducing faculty positions: Considerations of sound academic practice. *Liberal Education,* 58(2):304–309.
New York Times (Editorial). March 2, 1972.
Newman, Frank (chairman). March 1971. *Report on higher education.* Washington, D.C.: U.S. Department of Health, Education and Welfare.
Northern Michigan University. 1972. *Faculty hearing panel: Policy and procedures.* Marquette, Mich. Author.
Seabury, Paul. February 1972. HEW and the universities. *Commentary,* 53(2):54–60.

Chapter Nineteen

A Little Help from Our Government: WEAL and Contract Compliance

Bernice Sandler

WHEN ACADEMIC women began to reexamine their status in the late 1960s, the need to rectify that status quickly became obvious. Many women assumed that sex discrimination was illegal, and were rudely surprised to find that legal remedies were not assured by existing federal statutes concerning discrimination. For example, Title VI of the Civil Rights Act of 1964 prohibits discrimination against the beneficiaries of federally assisted programs, but only on the basis of race, color, and national origin. It does not forbid sex discrimination. The first federal legislation forbidding sex discrimination against students was not passed until October 1971, when the Public Health Service Act was amended to cover sex discrimination in admission to medical schools and other health professional schools. The prohibition of sex discrimination in all federally assisted education programs did not occur until the passage of the Education Amendments Act in June 1972. Similarly, Title VII of the Civil Rights Act forbade sex discrimination in employment, but until March 24, 1972, when the act was amended, faculty were exempt from coverage.[1] In addition, the Equal Pay Act of 1963 did not cover administrative, executive and professional employees—i.e. faculty—until June 1972.

The Fourteenth Amendment to the United States Constitution which assures all persons "equal protection of the laws," is of potential use in combating sex discrimination in state supported institutions. However, no case concerning discrimination against women in education has ever been decided in favor of women by the Supreme Court.[2] Several cases which test the applicability of the Fourteenth

AUTHOR'S NOTE: The views expressed in this chapter are those of the author, and do not necessarily represent the views of the Association of American Colleges.

[1] The March 24, 1972, amendments to the Civil Rights Act forbid discrimination against all employees of all educational institutions, public or private, and regardless of whether or not an institution receives federal aid.

[2] It is perhaps instructive to compare efforts to combat race discrimination and sex discrimination under the Fourteenth Amendment. Racial segregation in our educational system was banned by the Supreme Court in 1954. Yet in 1960 the Supreme Court declined to hear a case in which the Texas Court of Civil Appeals upheld the exclusion of women from a state college. In 1971, the Court upheld the right of Winthrop College, a state-supported institution in South Carolina, to limit its admissions to girls only. Male students who were then attending

Amendment to discrimination in education are now in process but the outcome is not readily predictable. Even the United States Commission on Civil Rights had no jurisdiction concerning sex discrimination until October 1972.

Late in 1969 the Women's Equity Action League (WEAL)[3] discovered that there was indeed a legal route to combat sex discrimination. In 1965 former President Lyndon Johnson issued Executive Order 11246[4] which prohibited discrimination by all federal contractors on the basis of race, color, religion, and national origin. Executive Order 11375, effective October 13, 1968, amended the original order to include discrimination based on sex. Unlike the former Title VII, Executive Order 11375 does not exempt educational institutions. Universities and colleges receive over 3 billion dollars annually, much of it in federal contract money. Most institutions, other than the very small ones, have federal contracts, and as federal contractors, they are subject to the sex discrimination provisions of the Executive Order.

On January 31, 1970, WEAL launched a national campaign to end discrimination against women in education by filing a historic class action complaint against all universities and colleges in the country. The charges were filed with the United States Department of Labor under Executive Order 11375. Until that time, the Executive Order had been used almost exclusively in cases concerning blue-collar workers in the construction industry (most notably in the "Philadelphia Plan"). Although the Executive Order had covered sex discrimination since October 1968, there was virtually no enforcement by the government until WEAL began its campaign. Governmental compliance agencies simply ignored the sex discrimination provisions of the Executive Order.

In its initial complaint in January 1970, WEAL charged an "industry-wide pattern" of discrimination against women in the academic community. Dr. Nancy E. Dowding, then president of WEAL, asked that the Department of Labor investigate the following areas: admission quotas to undergraduate and graduate schools, discrimination in financial assistance, hiring practices, promotions, and salary dif-

---

the school were denied the right to continue at the college of their choice simply on the basis of sex. This decision conflicts with an earlier lower court decision concerning a similar case at the University of Virginia. In February 1970, a three-judge federal court dismissed as moot a class action in which women sought to desegregate sex-segregated public institutions of higher learning in Virginia: the court previously had ordered the University of Virginia at Charlottesville to consider without regard to sex the women plaintiffs' applications for admission.

[3] The Women's Equity Action League was incorporated in 1968 in Ohio for the purposes of promoting greater economic progress on the part of American women, and to establish solutions to economic, education, tax, and legal problems affecting women. It now has members in almost every state, and numerous state chapters.

[4] The first Executive Order dealing with discrimination and federal contractors dates back to 1941, with successive presidents revising and strengthening the government's non-discrimination requirements for contractors. Historically, Executive Orders have been stronger and more far reaching than concurrent civil rights legislation.

ferentials. More than eighty pages of materials documenting these charges were submitted with the complaint to the Secretary of Labor. WEAL requested an immediate "class action" and compliance review of all institutions holding federal contracts. At the same time, specific charges were filed against the University of Maryland. Charges against more than 250 other institutions (about 10 percent of the nation's institutions of higher education) were subsequently filed by WEAL as word went out to women throughout the academic community. Among the institutions charged by WEAL were the University of Wisconsin, the University of Minnesota, Columbia University, the University of Chicago, and the entire state university and college systems of California, Florida, and New Jersey. In October 1970, WEAL filed a class action against all the medical schools in the country. A similar class action against the nation's law schools also was filed by the Professional Women's Caucus in April 1971. The National Organization for Women (NOW) also filed charges against Harvard University and the entire state university system of New York. Additional complaints by individual women and women's campus associations have brought the number of formal charges filed against colleges and universities to more than 360 and the end is not in sight.

WHAT IS THE EXECUTIVE ORDER?

Executive Order 11246, as amended, forbids all contractors from discriminating in employment on the basis of race, color, religion, national origin, and *sex*. Until Title VII was amended in March 1972, this Executive Order was the *only* remedy for discrimination against academic women. The Executive Order is *not* law, but a series of rules and regulations that contractors must follow if they want to receive or maintain federal contracts. Essentially, it is an administrative rather than a legal remedy for discriminatory practices. (The order can also be suspended or amended at the pleasure of a particular administration.)

The order requires contractors to practice nondiscrimination in all aspects of their employment practices. Most important, contractors are required to

> take affirmative action to ensure that applicants are employed, and that employees are treated during employment, without regard to their . . . sex. Such action will include but not be limited to the following: employment, upgrading, demotion, or transfer; recruitment or recruitment advertising; lay-off or termination; rates of pay or other forms of compensation; and selection of training, including apprenticeship (*Federal Register* 1968).

As WEAL has pointed out, admission to undergraduate and graduate programs is analogous to the apprenticeship programs of industry.[5] Contractors also are re-

---

[5] Unfortunately, the government has interpreted the apprenticeship provisions more narrowly, limiting them to cases for which admission to graduate study is a prerequisite for employment. A ruling on this point was promised "within a few weeks" by Secretary Elliot Richardson of HEW in January 1971. As of this writing, the issue still was unresolved.

quired to take affirmative action wherever necessary *to remedy the effects of past discrimination.* Moreover, all contractors with fifty employees and a contract of $50,000 or more must develop a *written* plan of affirmative action. The plan must include an analysis of the contractor's current employment of minority and female workers, an evaluation of opportunities for increasing their numbers if they are "underutilized," as well as specific numerical goals and timetables for correcting existing discrimination.

The responsibility for the enforcement of the Executive Order is divided among various governmental agencies. The Office of Federal Contract Compliance (OFCC) of the Department of Labor is responsible for policy guidance and the supervision of federal agency enforcement. The Department of Health, Education and Welfare, through its Office for Civil Rights, has been designated by OFCC as the agency responsible for enforcement of the Executive Order for all contracts with universities and colleges (regardless of the agency from which the contract originated).

One of the most useful aspects of the Executive Order is that any individual or group can file a complaint, and the complaint can be filed on the basis of a pattern of discrimination. Of equal importance is the applicability of the Executive Order to the *entire* institution, even if only one department is involved in the contract. The complainant need not be the individual or group suffering discrimination. (A typical letter of filing appears in the Appendix to this chapter). In some instances complaints have been based on extensive reports; in others, simply the number and percentage of women at each rank in several departments of an institution has served as the basis of a complaint. Regardless of the data included, the complainant can request a complete investigation of all hiring practices and policies, salary inequities, nepotism rules, and so on. Although WEAL itself does not gather information, it assists groups or individuals who wish to do so. WEAL will file charges or assist individuals and groups who wish to file on their own. There is no charge nor is membership in WEAL necessary in order to receive assistance.

HOW WEAL CHANGED FEDERAL POLICY REGARDING ENFORCEMENT OF THE EXECUTIVE ORDER

When WEAL filed its initial charges in January 1970, it was well aware that merely filing a complaint would not lead to action on the part of either the Department of Labor or HEW. Therefore, personal notes were sent to numerous senators and representatives who were thought to be potentially helpful. Various materials describing sex discrimination in education were enclosed, and the accompanying note pointed out that although the Executive Order applied, it had never been enforced with regard to sex discrimination, particularly sex discrimination in universities and colleges. Each legislator specifically was asked to write a note to the secretary of labor, requesting that the Executive Order be enforced with regard to sex discrimination in the academic community. Within a few weeks, more than twenty members of the Congress contacted the Secretary of Labor. On March 9, 1970, Congresswoman Martha Griffiths gave a speech in the House of Representatives detailing sex discrimination in education, describing WEAL's complaint, and criticizing the government for not enforcing its own rules and regulations as contained in the Executive Order. Some three weeks after Representative Griffiths' speech, the first investigation concerning sex discrimination began at Harvard University.

As more complaints were filed, additional letters from WEAL and women in the academic community were sent to legislators, asking them specifically to contact the secretary of labor or the secretary of health, education and welfare.[6] At one point the Office for Civil Rights at HEW was receiving so much congressional mail that one person was assigned full-time to handle the correspondence. Similarly, at the Department of Labor more than 300 congressional letters were received within a short period of time. Letters to legislators serve a dual function: they sensitize congressional staffs to the problems of sex discrimination, and they are an effective prod to bureaucratic inaction. If anything moves the bureaucracy —and not much does—it's a series of inquiries from Capitol Hill. Five months after filing, in June 1970, there was a double payoff. HEW issued a memorandum to all field personnel requiring them to routinely include sex discrimination in all contract compliance investigations, regardless of whether or not there was a complaint involving sex discrimination. During the same month, the Department of Labor issued its long-awaited *Sex Discrimination Guidelines* for federal contractors. These guidelines, which deal with problems specific to women workers (such as maternity leave policies), had been in the works for nearly two years.

Equally important, investigations of college campuses began. When the first complaints were filed, there were no women in the contract compliance division of HEW's Office for Civil Rights. A woman investigator, Rose Brock, was hastily transferred from civil rights investigations and was given the responsibility of supervising compliance reviews concerning discrimination against women. Her dedication, experience, and persistence led to extensive documentation of sex discrimination charges in the early investigations, and she helped set the pattern for later compliance reviews.[7] Her findings also helped to convince some of the HEW staff of the extent of discrimination against women, and the blatant violations of the Executive Order on the campus.

When word of the investigations reached the academic community, many ad-

[6] Complaints may be filed with either the Department of Labor or the Department of Health, Education and Welfare. Most early complaints were filed with the Department of Labor because of their policy responsibility for the order, and because the writer was at the time a temporary employee of HEW.

[7] Subsequently, all sex discrimination investigations were integrated into the regular compliance reviews.

ministrators and faculty reacted with disbelief and denial. They were quick to rationalize: "There are *no* qualified women." "Women don't *want* to be promoted." "There is discrimination at *some* institutions, but not at ours." When the first investigation began at Harvard, a slight shiver ran throughout the academic establishment, a shiver that increased perceptibly when new government contracts totaling almost four million dollars were delayed for two weeks when Harvard refused to grant HEW investigators access to personnel files. The delay, coupled with the threat of the additional loss of existing contracts as well, was sufficient to cause Harvard to change its mind and open its files to HEW investigators. Threats to sue the government evaporated when Harvard lawyers discovered that access to personnel files is one of the terms of the agreement voluntarily signed by Harvard and all other federal contractors.

To date, nearly 200 universities and colleges have been investigated. Many of these investigations have been conducted in almost absolute secrecy, with HEW investigators coming and going without the knowledge of concerned women. On some campuses however, particularly those where organized women's groups exist, the HEW investigations have been more open, and usually more thorough.

WHAT HAPPENS TO COMPLAINTS?

Typically, enforcement works like this: A complaint is filed with the Secretary of HEW[8] who refers it to the Office for Civil Rights. It is then forwarded to one of HEW's ten regional offices. Initially, priority was given to complaints of individuals and to preaward compliance reviews (contracts involving more than a million dollars cannot be awarded without a prior investigation regarding nondiscrimination and the adequacy of affirmative action programs). As HEW began to be swamped with individual complaints, the department shifted its emphasis to pattern complaints while continuing its preaward reviews. Meanwhile, the department's priorities and schedules continue to be affected by political pressure from representatives and senators, as well as the work load of the particular regional office. Reviews are scheduled on a quarterly basis but delays and last minute changes are typical. Institutions have not been notified that a complaint has been filed against them until a few weeks before the investigation, despite requests from women's groups and educational associations that formal notification be given to institutions within thirty days after a complaint has been filed, and despite HEW's promise to do so. Since the time between filing and investigation may range from a few weeks to well over a year, valuable time is lost by not notifying institutions of charges— time that could well be used to reevaluate and assess policies long before HEW arrives on the scene. (One college labeled the charges a hoax because it had not received any formal notification from HEW.)

[8] Complaints filed with the Department of Labor are forwarded to HEW's Office for Civil Rights.

Requests for various kinds of information accompany the notice of an impending investigation by HEW. Until HEW finally sent out a memorandum to presidents of institutions of higher learning on October 4, 1972, to inform them of their responsibilities under the Executive Order (some four years after the order first went into effect) most institutions were surprised and caught unaware when they received notification of an investigation. Often, an institution will claim that the information HEW wants is "not available" for one reason or another. Negotiations with HEW and the threat of contract loss, as in the Harvard investigation, eventually produce the desired information, although often at the cost of postponed and delayed investigations.

The type of information requested has varied from school to school, depending upon the nature of the complaint, the particular investigator's predilections, the pressure (or lack of pressure) from Washington, the delay and avoidance tactics employed by the institution, and the activities of individual women and women's groups on campus. HEW has begun to codify the kinds of information it will require in all investigations of sex discrimination. At a minimum, they usually will ask for the following:

1. A listing of all employees (academic and nonacademic, full- and part-time, permanent and temporary, and student employees). The inventory must list employees by race, sex, ethnic origin, job category, rate of pay, status (e.g., full- or part-time; tenured, permanent, or temporary; and so on), number of hours if working part-time, date of hire, and date of last promotion. The data must be organized in two ways: by job category and organizational unit, such as academic departments.
2. A copy of the written affirmative action plan which details actions being taken to guarantee equal employment and any analysis or evaluation of the plan.
3. A listing of all persons hired (except in labor service categories) in a recent period (usually six months or a year depending upon circumstances), their job or position classification, date of hire, starting pay rate, race or ethnic origin, and sex.
4. Copies of tests and other criteria used in making selections for employment, upgrading, and promotion, and any validation studies which have been conducted on such criteria.
5. Copies of faculty manuals, administrative practices manuals, guides to personnel, or operational procedures or other issuances of the institution that describe matters affecting the employment or treatment of employees.

Investigators may request additional information that they believe to be pertinent. Sometimes these requests stem from suggestions made by concerned women on campus. The HEW team might also request a more detailed response to some of the items listed above. For example, they might ask to see the personnel files of a specific department in order to examine in greater detail the individual records of women and men applicants and employees. The review process may be completed in a whirlwind three weeks or drag on for many, many months.

Some institutions have balked at HEW's requests for personnel information, claiming that such requests are a "violation of privacy," "violation of academic freedom," and the like, despite the fact that each institution voluntarily agreed to supply such information upon signing the government contract. HEW has agreed that personnel information and statistics may be coded so that names are obscured. However, institutions *must* allow HEW to see all information related to hiring and promotion. In the summer of 1971 the University of California at Berkeley vigorously attempted to forbid HEW from viewing letters of recommendation in its files. After months of negotiation, HEW policy was clarified: an institution must make available all solicited letters of recommendation, whether solicited by the institution or the applicant. Information *not* relevant to employment (such as medical records, unsolicited information, and so on) can be withheld. All data examined or collected by HEW during the course of a compliance review are protected from public disclosure by the Freedom of Information Act (5 United States Code 552 [b] [7]).

During the investigation, the HEW staff may also select departments or organizational units other than those mentioned in the original complaint for further analysis. Department heads or supervisors may be interviewed as well as selected employees. Some women's groups on campus have found it easy to set up confidential interviews with HEW investigators; others have found it helpful, and in some instances, necessary, to ask their senator's assistance in this matter.

When the investigation is completed, a "letter of findings," detailing the results of the investigation is given to the institution, usually during a conference with the institution's head. The administrator may take exception to any or all of the findings if he or she can provide supporting data. In any event, the contractor must make a written commitment to correct "deficiencies" noted in the findings, and submit a written plan within thirty days. The plan then is reviewed by both the regional and Washington offices. The letter of findings is kept confidential by HEW, although the college or university is free to make its contents public if it wishes to do so. In actual practice, the delay between the letter of findings and HEW's acceptance of an affirmative action plan has dragged out in many cases to over a year. The delay has in part been caused not only by HEW staff shortages, conflicting policies, and other inefficiencies but also by the delaying tactics of the institutions.

HOW IS THE EXECUTIVE ORDER ENFORCED?

At any point during the compliance review, either before or after the letter of findings has been submitted, HEW can delay the awarding of *new* contracts if they find that the institution is in noncompliance and that reasonable efforts to secure compliance by conciliation and conference are not working. Such delays are for a specific number of days within which the institution must move into compliance if they want new contracts. About forty institutions have had new contracts delayed for short periods for such reasons as not providing access to information, not developing a satisfactory affirmative action plan, not adjusting a verified complaint, and the like. One large university claimed it could not compile the data necessary for setting numerical goals and timetables for women and minorities. After innumerable delays, negotiations between the institution and HEW collapsed, and HEW finally withheld a large contract that was about to be awarded, and froze all new hiring for sixty days, with the exception of new women and new minority employees. By the end of the sixty days, the institution had collected the data it previously had been unable to obtain, and the target goals for women and minorities were developed.

Procedures for the termination or suspension of *existing* contracts and debarment from future contracts are far more formal, involving hearings before such sanctions are imposed; and, indeed, they have been initiated in only one instance. In November 1971, after two years of negotiating with HEW, Columbia University was notified that proceedings for debarment of future contracts would be initiated by HEW. Shortly after receiving HEW's notice, Columbia University complied with their requests, and the debarment proceedings were dropped. Ordinarily, the threat of such hearings, plus the actual delaying of new contracts has been sufficient to bring about compliance.

NUMERICAL GOALS FOR WOMEN: ARE THEY QUOTAS IN REVERSE?

The affirmative action required by Executive Order 11246 includes the establishment of numerical goals for minorities and women. The concept of numerical goals (which often are confused with quotas), originated with the "Philadelphia Plan" which was aimed at eliminating discrimination against minority workmen in the construction industry. Under Revised Order No. 4 issued by the Department of Labor on December 4, 1971, such goals and timetables must be part of the affirmative action plan. Goals differ from quotas in a number of ways. Quotas are fixed, numerical limits with the discriminatory intent of restricting a specified group from a particular activity. Goals, in contrast, are numerical target *objectives* which a company or institution *tries* to achieve. The aim is not discriminatory but affirmative in intent: to increase the number of minority and women workers in a particular organization.

Failure to meet a goal does not automatically signify noncompliance, provided that good faith efforts (such as efforts to recruit, upgrade, promote and transfer women and minority employees) can be documented. HEW cannot force an employer to hire unqualified persons in order to meet stated goals. That clearly would be illegal, as was established in *Hughes* v. *Superior Court* (32 Cal., 2d 850, 198 p2d, 885, 1948). The contractor may not, in its efforts to achieve the goal, discriminate against any qualified applicant or employee on the basis of race, color, religion, national origin, or sex. Goals are established in line with aspects of the minority and female work force (e.g., number of available minority and female workers with requisite skills). They are a starting point in determining good faith compliance. If a contractor meets its goals, one can reasonably assume that it is in compliance. If the contractor does not meet the goal, this is not considered a violation per se. The contractor is given the opportunity to show that it made a good faith effort to do so. If it has, there are no consequences that follow from failure to meet the goal.

When goals are administered properly, they represent a plan of inclusion rather than exclusion. Preferential treatment is not the intent or outcome of numerical goals and is forbidden by Title VII of the Civil Rights Act of 1964. In March 1970 the United States District Court for the Eastern District of Pennsylvania ruled in a case brought by the Contractors' Association of Eastern Pennsylvania against the secretary of labor that numerical target goals do not conflict with Title VII or with the Fifth Amendment or Fourteenth Amendment. The decision was upheld by the United States Third Circuit Court of Appeals in March 1971, and by the United States Supreme Court in October 1971. Similarly, the courts have reaffirmed that the government does have the right to set the terms of its contracts with contractors, and that affirmative action requires more than the cessation of discriminatory practices and policies.

WHAT HAPPENS WHEN AN INSTITUTION IS INVESTIGATED?

The University of Michigan experience provides a good example of the kinds of problems that are encountered in the course of an investigation. Michigan was the first state university to be investigated. (Unlike many institutions which have kept HEW's activities and findings under wraps, Michigan openly publicized a good deal of its correspondence with HEW officials.) From its initial denial of discrimination at the university, Michigan administrators contacted officials at other institutions and educational associations to join with Michigan to sue HEW for violating the institution's rights. There were few, if any, takers, and the idea was dropped or postponed when attorneys realized that it would be difficult to establish a legal basis for such a suit.

Within a few days after HEW's investigation began, the compliance investigator publicly stated that there was no evidence of discrimination at Michigan because not one single woman had come forward to tell him how she personally had been discriminated against. This was a clear violation of HEW policy, and it ignored the fact that the complaint at Michigan was not an individual one, but a charge of a pattern of discrimination. WEAL immediately telegrammed the secretary of HEW demanding the investigator's resignation. While this was not forthcoming, he was removed from the investigation and a new person was assigned. The Michigan complaint was filed by a small but highly effective local feminist group called FOCUS. The act of filing encouraged campus women to band together in a new on-campus group called PROBE. FOCUS, PROBE, and WEAL together contacted every member of the Michigan congressional delegation as well as other members of Congress who were in a position to be of help.

Under the glare of congressional pressure, Washington subsequently monitored the Michigan investigation very closely, and a plan of affirmative action was adopted. It includes salary equity, back pay for women who have lost wages because of discriminatory treatment, revision of nepotism rules, increased recruitment of women for academic positions, and promotion of clerical and nonacademic women whose qualifications were equivalent to those of higher-level male employees. About one year after the plan was submitted, HEW notified the university that its plan was deficient in several respects.

Women's groups pointed out that Michigan's projections for additional women would increase the overall percentage of women on the faculty by only 2.5 percent after four years of so-called affirmative action. For example, the percentage of women at the rank of full professor at Michigan was 4.5 percent in 1970–1971, and projected to be 6.6 percent by 1973–1974—a mere 2.1 percentage increase, and still substantially below the current national figure of 8.7 percent. Once more the women protested, and HEW did not accept the numerical goals offered by the university.

When HEW insisted that the university recruit more women into its doctoral programs, the university protested strongly, and HEW retreated temporarily. HEW Secretary Elliot Richardson said in January 1971 that he would decide the issue "within a few weeks," and Michigan agreed to abide by his decision. As of June 1972, he had not yet issued any decision on this matter, nor is one expected. With the passage of the June 1972 Education Amendments Act, sex discrimination in admission to graduate programs is prohibited. The vigor of Michigan's struggle against admitting women on an equal basis suggests that the discrimination in admission must be far worse than women suspect.

Michigan personnel showed little sympathy to the issue. Fedele Fauri, one of Michigan's vice presidents was quoted as saying "We just want to get these bastards at HEW off our backs" (Zwerdling 1971:12). William Cash, the university's human relations director was quoted as saying "Once you let women know they've got you over a barrel they'll take everything they can get from you. Women just make life difficult"[9] (Zwerdling 1971:11). Such statements galvanized the women into action again. Although neither man was asked to resign, they and other officials

---

[9] One woman at Michigan bitterly commented that the university did not take sex discrimination as seriously as discrimination against minorities. She asked what would have happened to a university official if he had said, "Once you let *blacks* know they've got you over a barrel they'll take everything they can get from you. *Blacks* just make life difficult."

have begun to pay greater lip service to nondiscrimination, and have been much more cautious in their remarks to the press.

EVALUATION OF CONTRACT COMPLIANCE INVESTIGATION AND ENFORCEMENT

HEW officials, with notable exceptions, have been slow to understand the sex discrimination issue, and to accept it as part of HEW's responsibilities. Many men who joined HEW to work on civil rights simply do not see *women's* rights as part of that effort. When they speak of civil rights, they usually mean the rights of minorities only, and by minority, they often mean minority males. For example, the five-page letter of findings detailing the results of HEW's investigation at Harvard contained only *three paragraphs* that dealt with women. The rest dealt with male members of minority groups, although the investigation had been initiated to examine *sex* discrimination. None of the statistical data concerning women was included in the letter of findings, although a wealth of such data had been submitted with the official complaint. WEAL and several local groups actively dissented; letters went to HEW and to numerous senators and congressmen, whereupon HEW backtracked, saying that the letter of findings was only "preliminary" and that the study of discrimination against women was continuing. Similarly, when the Tufts plan of affirmative action was approved by HEW, WEAL quickly pointed out that there were no goals and timetables developed for women, although it was on the basis of a complaint of sex discrimination that Tufts had been investigated. Moreover, Tufts data were presented in such a way that the position of minority women was completely obscured: data were given for minority and nonminority employees in one column; in another column data were given for men and women faculty. There was no way of finding out if there were any minority women employed on the Tufts campus or what their status was. Under the Tufts plan every minority slot could have been filled with minority males, and Tufts nevertheless would have been in technical compliance. As a result of WEAL's pressure, the Tufts plan was amended to meet these criticisms.

WEAL and other groups have consistently asked that there be specific goals for minority women, in order to assure their fair treatment. Too often, minority recruiting has meant minority *males,* and too often, recruiting women has meant recruiting *white* women. In some instances, minority women are counted *twice* by the employer, once as minority and once as women, although only *one* salary is paid. Thus an employer with a goal of six slots for minorities, and six additional slots for women (or a total of twelve slots) could hire only six minority women, count them twice, and thereby fulfill the goals. Six of the original twelve slots would remain and could be filled by six white males. Unless goals are developed separately for minority females, either of the above evasions is likely to occur, both of which would be clear violations of the intent of the Executive Order.

Although the government was quick to praise its own efforts in the area of sex discrimination and hailed the Michigan affirmative action plan as a "landmark," WEAL and other women's groups were quick to point out the inconsistencies, inefficiencies, and blunders committed by both the Departments of Labor and HEW. A particular sore spot was Order No. 4, a set of guidelines issued for contractors by the Department of Labor in February 1970. This order details how affirmative action plans are to be written, and how goals and timetables are to be developed. The plan was clearly aimed at minorities, although there was no legal basis for excluding women. It had been developed without taking into account the sex discrimination provisions of the Executive Order; at the time of its writing, sex discrimination provisions of the order were not enforced (WEAL's first complaint had been filed just a few days prior to the issuance of Order No. 4). Women were quick to point out that affirmative action as detailed in Order No. 4 should apply to them as well. In fact, HEW campus investigations were proceeding on this assumption. The Department of Labor, through Arthur Fletcher, then assistant secretary of labor, assured women orally at several meetings that the order did indeed apply to them, but women were unable to obtain this statement in writing from any Department of Labor official. The department wavered, for at one point an internal memorandum was circulated within the department stating that Order No. 4 covered women workers; a few days later the memorandum was withdrawn, and Secretary Hodgson stated that Order No. 4 did *not* apply to women. Additional pressure from various members of the Congress and women's groups resulted in a new statement from the secretary on July 31, 1970. He stated that although the *concepts* of Order No. 4 applied to women, the *procedures* of the order did not, and that new procedures would need to be developed for women. He promised that the department would meet within a "few weeks" with women's groups and other interested parties to work out these procedures. The meetings were finally held, after much pressure, some nine months later in April and May of 1971. A Proposed Order No. 4 which includes women was issued for comment on August 31, 1971, again after much internal delay. On December 4, 1971, the Revised Order No. 4 finally was issued.

The Department of Labor, until late spring 1972, took the position that affirmative action plans did not have to be made public by the government or by contractors, although the latter were free to do so if they wished. In a letter to HEW dated June 10, 1971, Peter G. Nash, then solicitor of the Department of Labor, stated that "The contents of affirmative action programs would be useful to competitors with regard to contemplated changes in the contractor's processes, types of production, and overall business planning." Women's groups pointed out that it was difficult to see, for example, how Harvard's affirmative action plan (of which only part has been released) would be of help to its competitors. Some colleges and universities such as the University of Michigan have made their plans public. Others have released only part of their plans; many have refused to disclose them. WEAL's testimony before Representative William Moorhead concerning affirmative action plans and the Freedom of Information Act, undoubtedly played a role in the Department of Labor's change of policy which now makes these plans available to interested parties.[10] However, since the letter of findings also is kept confidential, it is all but impossible for women to find out what deficiencies exist on their campus, and what steps their institution is taking to correct these deficiencies.

Additional obstacles to full enforcement of the Executive Order are the understaffing of HEW's Office for Civil Rights and the relative lack of women on the contract compliance staff. Although the civil rights staff has expanded and additional positions have been requested, there is still an enormous backlog of cases and no end of new ones in sight. *More charges have been filed with HEW concerning sex discrimination than those of all the minority groups put together.* Yet there are very few women on the professional staff of HEW and virtually no women in policy-making positions. Nor are there enough women so that each compliance team has at least one woman. The director of the Office for Civil Rights has a special assistant for black affairs and a special assistant for Spanish-American affairs, but there is no special assistant to deal with the problems of women.

As mentioned earlier, an institution charged with discrimination is not notified until just before the investigation is scheduled. Charging parties have not been notified when investigations are begun nor when they are finished; during some investigations no women or women's groups were contacted by HEW compliance teams. Moreover, policies are not uniform from one institution to another. What is sanctioned by one regional office may be viewed as a violation by investigators in another region.

Women's groups claim that HEW has shown much more concern with the educational establishment than with women's groups. HEW has met in secrecy with representatives of various educational associations in Washington, and has conducted regional meetings with presidents, vice-presidents, and personnel administrators of major universities and colleges. Only after substantial pressure did HEW finally meet for the first time with representatives of women's civil rights groups in the fall of 1971. Consequently WEAL and the Professional Women's Caucus have called for a Congressional investigation of HEW's handling of the sex discrimination investigations.

WE MAY HAVE COME A LONG WAY, BUT THERE'S STILL A LONG WAY TO GO

Despite obstacles, delays, and frustrations, the HEW investigations have nevertheless played a major role in changing the shape of attitudes toward women in the academic community. For example, in June and July of 1970, Representative

---

[10] There is an hourly charge for the labor involved in duplicating the plan as well as a per page charge.

Edith Green held hearings concerning discrimination against women, particularly in employment and in education. The American Council on Education and other educational organizations declined to testify on the grounds that "sex discrimination was not a problem," or that "there really was no sex discrimination." A few months later these same groups were meeting with HEW and "offering their assistance" to develop ways of handling contract compliance on the campus. Many of these groups have since begun to work on the problem of sex discrimination. Several management consulting firms have even begun to hold high level seminars for university personnel to help them in developing affirmative action plans.

The very act of filing charges has helped to legitimize the issue and confirm the suspicion that "there really is discrimination." None of WEAL's charges of sex discrimination have ever been refuted, and the fact that a national organization has filed charges gives credence to the claim that the institution is indeed discriminating. As a result it has become far easier for women to band together both on the campus and in their professional organizations in order to fight sex discrimination. The very right to file charges frees women from being totally dependent upon the good will of their university to bring about change. Despite the image of the university as a just institution, it is far more likely to change as a result of pressure—pressure generated by the government and by women themselves.

As word has gone out to the academic community that their pocketbooks may well be endangered, campus administrators have begun to take a new look at women. Campus committees on the status of women are proliferating, and on many campuses, women themselves have begun to examine their status and to press for reforms. Before WEAL filed its first charges, there were only two known reports on sex discrimination in particular institutions: the University of Chicago and Columbia University. Less than two years later, there are reports on more than 100 institutions.

Several institutions have developed affirmative action plans without any charges ever having been filed. The University of Pennsylvania, for example, has had no charges filed against it, but on January 16, 1971, it announced a comprehensive program for women which will include among other things, equal pay, elimination of nepotism practices, and increased recruitment of women.The university's awareness of the Executive Order was contained in a statement by Martin Meyerson, president of the university: "Our action is less because of the Federal Government pressing us, but more because of the humaneness that universities stand for" (*New York Times* 1971) Women expect the "humaneness" of universities to show a marked increase as a direct result of HEW enforcement of the Executive Order.

Changes have begun to be made throughout the academic community. The University of Wisconsin, as a result of HEW's investigation, decided to give 870 staff and faculty women "equity raises." The University of Maryland, the University of Maine, and other schools have allocated special funds to provide raises to women who have been discriminated against in the past. Numerous institutions have begun actively to seek out women for placement, albeit sometimes in token positions. At Harvard, Stanford, and Princeton, rules for full- and part-time employment have been revised in order to allow women (and men) to achieve tenure while working part-time. Nepotism rules have been eliminated in the State University system of New York (SUNY), and have been rewritten in numerous other institutions.

Nevertheless, on many campuses little has changed, and women remain second-class citizens. It is still dangerous for women to raise their voices in protest against discrimination, and numerous women have had their contracts terminated or their jobs abolished when they actively sought to end discriminatory policies. Although such firings are a violation of the Executive Order, HEW has been notoriously slow in getting these women reinstated. At the University of Pittsburgh, women grew tired of HEW's inaction, and in July 1971 filed suit against the university on the basis of the Civil Rights Act of 1871, the Fourteenth Amendment, and the Executive Order. This is the first suit concerning discrimination against women faculty and it may well be a landmark case. Other suits have also been filed against the University of California at Berkeley and the University of Maryland.

Other developments on the legal front include congressional passage of the Equal Rights Amendment which, when ratified, will directly affect all publicly supported institutions, as well as serve as a model for private institutions. The constitutional amendment would insure that "Equality of rights under the law shall not be denied or abridged by the United States or by any State on account of sex." It would forbid laws or official practices (such as higher admission standards for women and inequalities in the administration of scholarship funds) that exclude women or limit their numbers in state colleges and universities. All students would have to be admitted to tax supported schools on the basis of ability, not on the basis of sex. Publicly supported schools and colleges that are restricted to one sex would have to allow students of both sexes to attend. Girls would be able to attend vocational high schools and take vocational courses when they are interested and qualified. The amendment would forbid discrimination in the employment of women in all publicly supported institutions. It would prohibit many of the discriminatory practices now engaged in by universities and colleges as well as elementary and secondary schools.

Dormitories would not have to be integrated under the Equal Rights Amendment. The lack of dormitories often is used as an excuse to limit or exclude women. Yale, for example, maintains a small quota for women, claiming lack of dormitory space. The real reason is that they simply do not want too many women; when Yale converted some of its men's dormitories for women, the only changes made were the addition of full length mirrors and new locks. Dormitories, like houses, hotels, and apartments are not built any differently for one sex than for the other; they can be used by either sex as determined by administrative fiat. The Equal Rights Amendment would insure that dormitory space, or the lack of it, would not be used to limit or exclude people from institutions on the basis of sex. Dormitory space may need to be reallocated and provided on an equal basis to both sexes, but the amendment would not require men and women students to share the same room. Coed or integrated dormitories are no longer a novelty, but an increasingly popular trend in campus housing; moreover, students who live off campus already live in "integrated housing," i.e., apartment buildings.

CONCLUDING REMARKS

What is particularly impressive is the speed with which the Congress has responded to the issue of sex discrimination in education. WEAL's charges of sex discrimination in January 1970 were followed by hearings that summer conducted by the Special Subcommittee on Education chaired by Representative Edith Green. In October 1971, discrimination in admission to medical schools and other health professional schools was outlawed by the passage of the Comprehensive Health Manpower Act. The Civil Rights Act, forbidding discrimination in employment, was extended in March 1972 to cover all educational institutions. Three months later, the president signed the Education Amendments Act which forbids discrimination in all federally assisted education programs, and extends the Equal Pay Act to cover faculty and other professional employees.

There is indeed a new hope on the campus as women discover that there are legal weapons to use in fighting discrimination. Women no longer need remain silent or grow bitter about the injustices of academe. Nevertheless, the Executive Order and other legislation are no panacea, and women will need to watchdog the activities of government enforcement agencies, and the activities of the university as it implements affirmative action plans. Women have taken the first long step on the hard and rocky road of equal opportunity, and American campuses will never be the same.

REFERENCES

Federal Register. May 28, 1968. 33(104):7806.
The New York Times. January 17, 1971.
Zwerdling, Daniel. March 20, 1971. The womanpower problem. *The New Republic,* 164(12):11–13.

Appendix A:
Typical Letter of Filing

The Honorable Caspar Weinberger
Secretary
Department of Health, Education and Welfare
Washington, D.C. 20201

Dear Mr. Secretary:

Please consider this letter as a formal charge of sex discrimination against
_____ University. These charges are filed under Executive Order 11246 as amended, which forbids *all* federal contractors from discriminating on the basis of sex.

The charges are based on information attached to this letter giving the number of women in various units of the university. The figures detail a consistent and vicious pattern of discrimination against women at _____. For example, of 172 faculty in the College of Liberal Arts, not one woman is a full professor. Only *two* are associate professors. The remaining 44 women are in the lower ranks, without tenure. In the Psychology Department, where one would expect a substantial number of women because 23 percent of the doctorates awarded nationally go to women, there are *no* women on the faculty of 12. In the College of Education where one would also expect to find substantial numbers of women, only 5 of the 48 assistant, associate and full professors are women, although at the lowest level, fully half of the instructors are women (4 out of 8). In administration, women are present but mainly at the lower levels. There are no women deans whatsoever, nor are any of the officers of the university female.

The Women's Equity Action League requests an immediate full-scale compliance review, and that such review include an investigation of admission policies, financial aid to women students, placement of graduates, recruiting, hiring and promotion policies for all women staff and faculty, and salary inequities. We also ask that all current contract negotiations be suspended until such time as all inequities are eliminated and an acceptable plan of affirmative action is implemented. Please notify us when the compliance review begins.

Sincerely,

NOTE: Typically, copies of the letter are sent to the Secretary of Labor, numerous Senators and Congressmen, such as those from the institution's state, members of House and Senate Committees that deal with education, women members of Congress, and others that might be helpful. In most instances, Senators and Congressmen are asked to help, with a specific request that they write the Secretary of Health, Education and Welfare for his assistance in scheduling a compliance review. Copies also can be sent to the student newspaper and various members of the press. Charges are also filed simultaneously under Title IX, Title VII, and the Equal Pay Act.

Appendix B:
Federal Laws[1] and Regulations Concerning Sex Discrimination in Educational Institutions[2]

October 1972

	Executive Order 11246 as amended by 11375	Title VII of the Civil Rights Act of 1964 as amended by the Equal Employment Opportunity Act of 1972	Equal Pay Act of 1963 as amended by the Education Amendments of 1972 (Higher Education Act)	Title IX of the Education Amendments of 1972 (Higher Education Act)[13]	Title VII (Section 799A) & Title VIII (Section 845 of the Public Health Service Act as amended by the Comprehensive Health Manpower Act & the Nurse Training Amendments Act of 1971[18]
Effective date	Oct. 13, 1968	March 24, 1972 (July 1965 for non-professional workers.) (Institutions with 15–24 employees are not covered until March 24, 1973.)	July 1, 1972 (June, 1964, for non-professional workers.)	July 1, 1972 (Admissions provisions effective July 1, 1973.)	Nov. 18, 1971
Which institutions are covered	All institutions with federal contracts of over $10,000.[7]	All institutions with 15 or more employees.	All institutions.	All institutions receiving federal monies by way of a grant, loan, or contract (other than a contract of insurance or guaranty).	All institutions receiving or benefiting from a grant, loan guarantee, or interest subsidy to health personnel training programs or receiving a contract under Title VII or VIII of the Public Health Service Act.[19]
What is prohibited[3]	Discrimination in employment (including hiring, upgrading, salaries, fringe benefits, training, and other conditions of employment) on the basis of race, color, religion, national origin or sex. Covers all employees.	Discrimination in employment (including hiring, upgrading, salaries, fringe benefits, training and other conditions of employment) on the basis of race, color, religion, national origin or sex. Covers all employees.	Discrimination in salaries (including almost all fringe benefits) on the basis of sex. Covers all employees.	Discrimination against students or others[14] on the basis of sex.[15]	Discrimination in admission of students on the basis of sex and against some employees.[20]
Exemptions from coverage	None.	Religious institutions are exempt with respect to the employment of individuals of a particular **religion** or **religious order** (including those limited to one sex) to perform work for that institution. (Such institutions are not exempt from the prohibition of discrimination based on sex, color and national origin.)	None.	**Religious institutions** are exempt if the application of the anti-discrimination provisions are not consistent with the religious tenets of such organizations. **Military schools** are exempt if their primary purpose is to train individuals for the military services of the U.S. or the merchant marine. **Discrimination in admissions**[16] is prohibited only in vocational institutions (including vocational high schools), graduate and professional institutions, and public undergraduate co-educational institutions.	None.

	Executive Order 11246 as amended by 11375	Title VII of the Civil Rights Act of 1964 as amended by the Equal Employment Opportunity Act of 1972	Equal Pay Act of 1963 as amended by the Education Amendments of 1972 (Higher Education Act)	Title IX of the Education Amendments of 1972 (Higher Education Act)[13]	Title VII (Section 799A) & Title VIII (Section 845 of the Public Health Service Act as amended by the Comprehensive Health Manpower Act & the Nurse Training Amendments Act of 1971[18]
Who enforces the provisions?	Office of Federal Contract Compliance (OFCC) of the Department of Labor has policy responsibility and oversees federal agency enforcement programs. OFCC has designated HEW as the Compliance Agency responsible for enforcing the Executive Order for all contracts with educational institutions. HEW's Office for Civil Rights (Division of Higher Education) conducts the reviews and investigations.	Equal Employment Opportunity Commission (EEOC).[9]	Wage and Hour Division of the Employment Standards Administration of the Department of Labor.	Federal departments and agencies which are empowered to extend financial aid to educational programs and activities. HEW's Office for Civil Rights (Division of Higher Education) is expected to have primary enforcement powers to conduct the reviews and investigations.[17]	HEW's Office for Civil Rights (Division of Higher Education) conducts the reviews and investigations.
How is a complaint made?	By letter to OFCC or Secretary of HEW.	By a sworn complaint form, obtainable from EEOC.	By letter, telephone call, or in person to the nearest Wage and Hour Division office.	Procedure not yet specified. A letter to Secretary of HEW is acceptable.	Procedure not yet specified. A letter to Secretary of HEW is acceptable.
Can complaints of a pattern of discrimination be made as well as individual complaints?	Yes. However, individual complaints are referred to EEOC.	Yes.	Yes.	Yes.	Yes.
Who can make a complaint?[4]	Individuals and/or organizations on own behalf or on behalf of aggrieved employee(s) or applicant(s).	Individuals and/or organizations on own behalf or on behalf of aggrieved employee(s) or applicant(s). Members of the commission may also file charges.	Individuals and/or organizations on own behalf or on behalf of aggrieved employee(s).	Individuals and/or organizations on own behalf or on behalf of aggrieved party.	Individuals and/or organizations on own behalf or on behalf of aggrieved party.
Time limit for filing complaints[5]	180 days.	180 days.	No official limit, but recovery of back wages is limited by statute of limitations to two years for a non-willful violation and three years for a willful violation.	Procedure not yet determined.	Procedure not yet determined.
Can investigations be made without complaints?	Yes. Government can conduct periodic reviews without a reported violation, as well as in response to complaints. Pre-award reviews are mandatory for contracts over $1,000,000.	No. Government can conduct investigations only if charges have been filed.	Yes. Government can conduct periodic reviews without a reported violation as well as in response to complaints.	Yes. Government can conduct periodic reviews without a reported violation, as well as in response to complaints.	Yes. Government can conduct periodic reviews without a reported violation, as well as in response to complaints.
Can the entire institution be reviewed?	Yes. HEW may investigate part or all of an institution.	YES. EEOC may investigate part or all of an establishment.	Yes. Usually the Wage Hour Division reviews the entire establishment.	Yes. HEW may investigate those parts of an institution which receive federal assistance (as well as other parts of the institution related to the program, whether or not they receive direct federal assistance). If the institution receives **general institutional aid**, the entire institution may be reviewed.	Yes. HEW may investigate those parts of an institution which receive federal assistance under Title VII and VIII (as well as other parts of the institution related to the program, whether or not they receive assistance under these titles).

	Executive Order 11246 as amended by 11375	Title VII of the Civil Rights Act of 1964 as amended by the Equal Employment Opportunity Act of 1972	Equal Pay Act of 1963 as amended by the Education Amendments of 1972 (Higher Education Act)	Title IX of the Education Amendments of 1972 (Higher Education Act)[13]	Title VII (Section 799A) & Title VII (Section 845 of the Public Health Service Act as amended by the Comprehensive Health Manpower Act & the Nurse Training Amendments Act of 1971[18]
Record keeping requirements and government access to records	Institution must keep and preserve specified records relevant to the determination of whether violations have occurred. Government is empowered to review all relevant records.	Institution must keep and preserve specified records relevant to the determination of whether violations have occurred. Government is empowered to review all relevant records.	Institution must keep and preserve specified records relevant to the determination of whether violations have occurred. Government is empowered to review all relevant records.	Institution must keep and preserve specified records relevant to the determination of whether violations have occurred. Government is empowered to review all relevant records.	Institution must keep and preserve specified records relevant to the determination of whether violations have occurred. Government is empowered to review all relevant records.
Enforcement power and sanctions	Government may delay new contracts, revoke current contracts, and debar institutions from eligibility for future contracts.	If attempts at conciliation fail, EEOC or the U.S. Attorney General may file suit.[10] Aggrieved individuals may also initiate suits. Court may enjoin respondent from engaging in unlawful behavior, order appropriate affirmative action, order reinstatement of employees, and award back pay.	If voluntary compliance fails,[11] Secretary of Labor may file suit. Aggrieved individuals may initiate suits when Department of Labor has not done so. Court may enjoin respondent from engaging in unlawful behavior, back pay and order salary raises, back pay and assess interest.	Government may delay new awards, revoke current awards, and debar institution from eligibility for future awards. Department of Justice may also bring suit at HEW's request.	Government may delay new awards, revoke current awards, and debar institution from eligibility for future awards. Department of Justice may also bring suit at HEW's request.
Can back pay be awarded?[6]	Yes. HEW will seek back pay only for employees who were not previously protected by other laws allowing back pay.	Yes. For up to two years prior to filing charges with EEOC.	Yes. For up to two years for a nonwilful violation and three years for a wilful violation.	Probably, to the extent that employees are covered.	Probably, to the extent that employees are covered.
Affirmative action requirements (There are no restrictions against action which is non-preferential)	Affirmative action plans (including numerical goals and timetables) are required of all contractors with contracts of $50,000 or more and 50 or more employees.[8]	Affirmative action is not required unless charges have been filed, in which case it may be included in conciliation agreement or be ordered by the court.	Affirmative action, other than salary increases and back pay, is not required.	Affirmative action may be required **after** discrimination is found.	Affirmative action may be required **after** discrimination is found.
Coverage of labor organizations	Any agreement the contractor may have with a labor organization can not be in conflict with the contractor's affirmative action commitment.	Labor organizations are subject to the same requirements and sanctions as employers.	Labor organizations are prohibited from causing or attempting to cause an employer to discriminate on the basis of sex. Complaints may be made and suits brought against these organizations.	Procedure not yet clear. Any agreement the institution may have with a labor organization can not be in conflict with the non-discrimination provisions of the legislation.	Procedure not yet clear. Any agreement the institution may have with a labor organization can not be in conflict with the non-discrimination provisions of the legislation.
Is harassment prohibited?	Institutions are prohibited from discharging or discriminating against any employee or applicant for employment because he/she has made a complaint, assisted with an investigation or instituted proceedings.	Institutions are prohibited from discharging or discriminating against any employee or applicant for employment because he/she has made a complaint, assisted with an investigation or instituted proceedings.	Institutions are prohibited from discharging or discriminating against any employee because he/she has made a complaint, assisted with an investigation or instituted proceedings.	Institutions will be prohibited from discharging or discriminating against any participant or potential participant because he/she has made a complaint, assisted with an investigation or instituted proceedings.	Institutions will be prohibited from discharging or discriminating against any participant or potential participant because he/she has made a complaint, assisted with an investigation or instituted proceedings.
Notification of complaints	Notification of complaints has been erratic in the past. HEW is proposing notifying institutions of complaints within 10 days. HEW notifies institutions a few weeks prior to investigation.	EEOC notifies institutions of complaints within 10 days.	Complaint procedure is very informal. Employer under review may or may not know that a violation has been reported.	Procedure not yet determined.	Procedure not yet determined.

	Executive Order 11246 as amended by 11375	Title VII of the Civil Rights Act of 1964 as amended by the Equal Employment Opportunity Act of 1972	Equal Pay Act of 1963 as amended by the Education Amendments of 1972 (Higher Education Act)	Title IX of the Education Amendments of 1972 (Higher Education Act)[13]	Title VII (Section 799A) & Title VIII (Section 845 of the Public Health Service Act as amended by the Comprehensive Health Manpower Act & the Nurse Training Amendments Act of 1971[18]
Confidentiality of names	Individual complainant's name is usually given to the institution. Investigation findings are kept confidential by government, but can be revealed during the investigation. Policy concerning government disclosure concerning investigations and complaints has not yet been issued. The aggrieved party and respondent are not bound by the confidentiality requirement.	Individual complainant's name is divulged when an investigation is made. Charges are not made public by EEOC, nor can any of its efforts during the conciliation process be made public by the commission or its employees. If court action becomes necessary, the identity of the parties involved becomes a matter of public record. The aggrieved party and respondent are not bound by the confidentiality requirement.	The identity of a complainant, as well as the employer (and union, if involved), is kept in strict confidence.[12] If court action becomes necessary, the identity of the parties involved becomes a matter of public record. The aggrieved party and respondent are not bound by the confidentiality requirement.	Identity of complainant is kept confidential if possible. If court action becomes necessary, the identity of the parties involved becomes a matter of public record. The aggrieved party and respondent are not bound by the confidentiality requirement.	Identity of complainant is kept confidential if possible. If court action becomes necessary, the identity of the parties involved becomes a matter of public record. The aggrieved party and respondent are not bound by the confidentiality requirement.
For further information, contact	Division of Higher Education Office for Civil Rights Department of HEW Washington, D.C. 20201 *or* Office of Federal Contract Compliance Employment Standards Administration Department of Labor Washington, D.C. 20210 *or* Regional HEW or DOL Office	Equal Employment Opportunity Commission 1800 G Street, N.W. Washington, D.C. 20506 *or* Regional EEOC Office	Wage and Hour Division Employment Standards Administration Department of Labor Washington, D.C. 20210 *or* Field, Area, or Regional Wage and Hour Office	Division of Higher Education Office for Civil Rights Department of HEW Washington, D.C. 20201 *or* Regional HEW Office	Division of Higher Education Office for Civil Rights Department of HEW Washington, D.C. 20201 *or* Regional HEW Office

SOURCE: Compiled by Project on the Status & Education of Women, Association of American Colleges, 1818 R Street, N.W., Washington, D.C. 20009.

NOTES TO APPENDIX B

General

1. State employment and/or human relations laws may also apply to educational institutions. The Equal Rights Amendment to the U.S. Constitution, passed by the Congress and now in the process of ratification would, when ratified, forbid discrimination in publicly supported schools at all levels, including students and faculty.

2. Unless otherwise specified, "institution" includes public and private colleges and universities, elementary and secondary schools, and preschools.

3. A bona fide seniority or merit system is permitted under all legislation, provided the system is not discriminatory on the basis of sex or any other prohibited ground.

4. There are no restrictions against making a complaint under more than one anti-discrimination law at the same time.

5. This time limit refers to the time between an alleged discriminatory act and when a complaint is made. In general, however, the time limit is interpreted liberally when a continuing practice of discrimination is being challenged, rather than a single, isolated discriminatory act.

6. Back pay cannot be awarded prior to the effective date of the legislation.

Executive Order 11246 as amended by 11375

7. The definition of "contract" is very broad and is interpreted to cover all government contracts (even if nominally entitled "grants") which involve a benefit to the federal government.

8. As of January 19, 1973, all covered educational institutions, both public and private, must have *written* affirmative action plans.

Title VII of the Civil Rights Act of 1964 as amended by the Equal Employment Opportunity Act

9. In certain states that have fair employment laws with prohibitions similar to those of Title VII, EEOC automatically defers investigation of charges to the state agency for 60 days. (At the end of this period, EEOC will handle the charges unless the state is actively pursuing the case. About 85 percent of deferred cases return to EEOC for processing after deferral.)

10. Due to an ambiguity in the law as it relates to public institutions, it is not yet clear whether EEOC *or* the Attorney General will file suit in all situations which involve public institutions.

Equal Pay Act of 1963 as amended by the Education Amendments of 1972
(Higher Education Act)

11. Over 95 percent of all Equal Pay Act investigations are resolved through voluntary compliance.

12. Unless court action is necessary, the name of the parties need not be revealed. The identity of a complainant or a person furnishing information is never revealed without that person's knowledge and consent.

Title IX of the Education Amendments of 1972
(Higher Education Act)

(Minority women are also protected from discrimination on the basis of their race or color by Title VI of the Civil Rights Act of 1964.)

13. Final regulations and guidelines for Title IX of the Education Amendments of 1972 have not yet been published. This chart includes information which is explicitly stated in the law, as well as how the law is likely to be interpreted in light of other precedents and developments.

14. The sex discrimination provision of Title IX is patterned after Title VI of the Civil Rights Act of 1964, which forbids discrimination on the basis of race, color and national origin in all federally assisted programs. By specific exemption, the prohibitions of Title VI

do not cover employment practices (except where the primary objective of the federal aid is to provide employment). However, there is no similar exemption for employment in Title IX.

15. Title IX states that: "No person . . . shall, on the basis of sex, be excluded from participation in, be denied the benefits of, or be subjected to discrimination under any education program or activity receiving federal financial assistance. . . ."

16. The following are exempted from the *admissions* provision:

Private undergraduate institutions.

Elementary and secondary schools other than vocational schools.

Single-sex public undergraduate institutions. (If public single-sex undergraduate institutions decide to admit both sexes, they will have 7 years to admit female and male students on a nondiscriminatory basis, provided their plans are approved by the Commissioner of Education.)

Note 1. *These exemptions apply to admissions only.* Such institutions are still subject to all other anti-discrimination provisions of the Act.

Note 2. Single-sex professional, graduate and vocational schools at all levels have until July, 1979, to achieve nondiscriminatory admissions, provided their plans are approved by the Commissioner of Education.

17. Under Title VI of the 1964 Civil Rights Act, which Title IX of the Education Amendments closely parallels, federal agencies which extend aid to educational institutions have delegated their enforcement powers to HEW. A similar delegation of enforcement power is expected under Title IX.

Title VII & Title VIII of the Public Health Service Act as amended by the Comprehensive Health Manpower Act & the Nurse Training Amendments Act of 1971

18. Final regulations and guidelines for Title VII and VIII of the Public Health Service Act have not yet been published. This chart includes information which is explicitly stated in the law, as well as how the law is likely to be interpreted in light of other precedents and developments.

19. Schools of medicine, osteopathy, dentistry, veterinary medicine, optometry, pharmacy, podiatry, public health, allied public health personnel and nursing are specifically mentioned in Titles VII and VIII. Regulations issued June 1, 1972, by the Secretary of HEW specify that *all* entities applying for awards under Titles VII or VIII are subject to the nondiscrimination requirements of the act.

20. HEW regulations state: "Nondiscrimination in admission to a training program includes nondiscrimination in all practices relating to applicants and to students in the program; nondiscrimination in the enjoyment of every right, privilege and opportunity secured by admission to the program; and nondiscrimination in all employment practices relating to employees working directly with applicants to or students in the program."

Chapter Twenty

Affirmative Action Plans for Eliminating Sex Discrimination in Academe

Lenore J. Weitzman

UNTIL RECENTLY, Executive Order 11246, as amended by Executive Order 11375, provided the sole legal means of rectifying sex discrimination in academe. The strongest tool in this order is the requirement for affirmative action. Affirmative action embodies two concepts: first, the elimination of all existing discriminatory conditions; and second, the institution of additional efforts to recruit, employ, and promote qualified women and minorities formerly excluded.

This chapter will focus on the nature and content of affirmative action programs. We shall first summarize the legal requirements for affirmative action; then suggest the most effective means of meeting these legal requirements and note programs that already have been developed by colleges and universities; and finally, we shall look at future legal prospects for academic women.

LEGAL REQUIREMENTS FOR AFFIRMATIVE ACTION

Executive Order 11375 requires an affirmative action plan from all businesses with government contracts of $50,000 or more and with fifty or more employees. When a college or university signs a contract with the federal government it agrees to the following equal opportunity clause:

1. Not to discriminate against any employee or applicant because of sex
2. To take affirmative action to ensure nondiscrimination
3. To comply with the regulations of the Department of Labor enforcing Executive Order 11375
4. To furnish information and reports necessary to ascertain compliance with these regulations

The Office of Contract Compliance (OFCC) of the Department of Labor has prime responsibility for enforcing the Executive Order and issuing regulations on affirmative action. However, OFCC has assigned the Department of Health, Education, and Welfare to enforce the Executive Order in educational institutions.

AUTHOR'S NOTE: I wish to acknowledge the valuable research assistance of Sheryl Ruzek, and to thank Carla Tate and William Goode for their comments on an earlier draft of this chapter.

HEW, through its Office for Civil Rights, oversees the implementation of affirmative action in colleges and universities by conducting compliance reviews.

To date, there have been three sets of regulations issued by OFCC. The first, the "Sex Discrimination Guidelines," issued in June 1970 (OFCC 1970), deals with specific policies required of government contractors to insure nondiscrimination in recruitment, wages, hours, and conditions of employment. These guidelines are especially important to academic women because prior to March 1972 they had not been covered by the Equal Pay Act and Title VII of the Civil Rights Act. The Sex Discrimination Guidelines were the first to establish the following regulations for educational institutions: sex, marital status, and parental status may not be used as a criteria for employment; women must be given leave for childbearing and must be reinstated in their original or similar positions without loss of seniority; wages may not be related to or based on an employee's sex; job classifications may not be restricted to one sex; and fringe benefits and retirement plans must be awarded women and men on an equal basis.

A second set of regulations, on "Employee Testing and Other Selection Procedures," was issued in October 1971 (OFCC 1971a). These regulations were issued by the Department of Labor to insure the elimination of selection procedures that had discriminatory effects. This order states that selection standards must be clear, applied equally to men and women (for example, men without doctorates may not be hired if women without doctorates are refused employment), and all selection standards must be shown to be "valid" job criteria (demonstrably related to job performance). Moreover, the order states that "no new selection standards may be imposed upon an individual or class of individuals who have been discriminated against in the past, and who, but for this prior discrimination would have been granted employment opportunity under less stringent standards" (OFCC 1971a:60–3.11). Thus, a department may not institute new selection standards when they begin to hire women (such as requiring publications of all new assistant professors) if men were hired under a less rigorous standard in the past.

The third and most recent set of regulations issued by the Office of Contract Compliance deals exclusively with affirmative action. Commonly referred to as Order No. 4 these regulations on "Affirmative Action Programs" were published in December 1971 (OFCC 1971b). In specifying the necessary components of affirmative action programs, Order No. 4 covers both women and minorities, and both academic and nonacademic employees of educational institutions. In this limited review, however, we shall confine ourselves to a discussion of how Order No. 4 affects academic women. Order No. 4 provides a series of specific guidelines for eliminating sex discrimination through affirmative action in individual institutions.

In October 1972, HEW issued a set of guidelines interpreting Order No. 4 as it specifically relates to institutions of higher education. These Higher Education Guidelines (HEW 1972) specify procedures to be followed in faculty recruitment and hiring, placement, conditions of work, salary, promotion, leave policies, and fringe benefits. They further include guidelines for antinepotism policies, employment policies relating to pregnancy and childbirth, back pay, child care, and grievance procedures.

Together, Order No. 4 and the Higher Education Guidelines provide academic institutions with the skeletal structure for an affirmative action program. However, these regulations also provide academic institutions with a challenge — the challenge of creating an affirmative action program that is both effective and uniquely suited to a specific college or university.

As outlined in the OFCC and HEW regulations, the eight essential components of an affirmative action program are as follows:

1. An Affirmative Action Policy and Written Program (OFCC 1971b, 60–2.13a and 60–2.20)

Each educational institution must reaffirm its equal employment opportunity policy by developing a written affirmative action policy and plan. The policy statement should include a statement of commitment from the president or chancellor; assign overall responsibility for the program; and provide for internal reporting and monitoring procedures. The written program should include, but not be limited to, insuring that decisions concerning recruitment, hiring, training, promotion, wages, benefits, layoffs, social and recreational programs are made without regard to sex.

Although private institutions were required to file an affirmative action program upon signing a government contract, public institutions (including state and city schools) were not required to file a written program until one was requested of them in a compliance review. However, on October 4, 1972, the Office of Federal Contract Compliance removed this distinction and now requires all educational institutions, both public and private, to maintain a written affirmative action policy and program.

2. Dissemination of Affirmative Action Program (OFCC 1971b: 60–2.13b and 60–2.21)

The university has the obligation to communicate its affirmative action program in writing to all persons responsible for its implementation. The provost, vice-presidents, deans, department chairpersons, members of recruitment and hiring committees, those on tenure review committees, and all other faculty involved in personnel decisions must know what the law requires, what the institution's compliance program is, and how to implement the program within their areas of responsibility. The regulations also require that the institution make available the specific information in the program that will "enable employees to know of and avail themselves of its benefits" (OFCC 1971b: 60–2.21, 11).

The university also is obligated to disseminate its program to community agencies, women's organizations, secondary schools, and the general public. The policy should be apparent in all official publications, such as the faculty handbook, student catalog, alumni magazine, and the campus newspaper; it must also be enunciated in recruiting communications to prospective employees.

The disclosure of affirmative action plans has been the subject of recent controversy, with women's organizations pressing HEW to require that compliance programs be made public. The new HEW guidelines "urge institutions to make public their affirmative action plans" (HEW 1972:17). They also state that the plans, once accepted by HEW, are subject to public disclosure under the Freedom of Information Act. Confidential information about employees, which might be contained in the plan, is exempted from disclosure. Whether or not institutions comply with HEW's urging that they disclose their plan before it is accepted by HEW, it is clear that they must continue to inform academic personnel within a college or department of the goals, timetables, and other policies for their division.

3. Responsibility for Implementing the Program (OFCC 1971b: 60–2.13c and 60–2.22)

Every college and university must appoint an executive to direct its affirmative action program. He or she should have the support of top university officials and necessary staff assistance. In light of the executive's responsibilities, we would suggest that she or he be appointed to the top administrative ranks of an institution, e.g. as provost, vice-president, assistant to the president, or dean. (Hereafter we will speak of "provost" in referring to this office.) The provost's responsibilities include, but are not necessarily limited to, developing affirmative action plans and evaluating their effectiveness. In developing affirmative action programs the provost might meet with department chairpersons to help them to identify problem areas and establish goals and programs. The affirmative action provost also is charged with periodic auditing of all hiring and promotion patterns; periodic review of the qualifications of all employees to insure that women are given full opportunities for promotions; and recommending remedial action when necessary.

In addition to evaluating departmental progress, individual department chairpersons and others who have responsibility for hiring and promotion are to be evaluated for their efforts in carrying out the directives of the compliance program. The affirmative action provost also serves as a liaison between faculty and administration and enforcement agencies, and as a liaison to women's organizations. Finally, the affirmative action provost should have the authority to act for the institution's president in the day-to-day administration of the affirmative action program.

4. Utilization Analysis of Female Employees by Department and Rank (OFCC 1971b: 60–2.11 and 60–2.23)

A utilization analysis is the official term for an examination of the absolute and relative employment of women on both a departmental and universitywide basis. It is designed to determine current deficiencies that will then become the basis for establishing goals and timetables.

In brief, the analysis should involve a three-step comparative treatment of women and men with regard to recruitment, selection, rank, salary, promotion, and conditions of employment. First, the current distribution of women and men in each of these areas is ascertained. Second, it is ascertained whether the number and percentage of women in each of these categories is fewer than reasonably should be expected. Third, if there are fewer women in a particular category than expected, the cause of this underrepresentation and the means to eliminate it should be explored.

If a college or university does not have current data on the distribution of women and men by rank, sex, and department in its central files, this data may be compiled at the department level and then computed for a college or the institution as a whole.

The second step involves a more complex analysis of the data. Once the current distribution of female employees has been ascertained, a department should have some standard for determining underutilization (defined by OFCC as having fewer women in a particular rank than would be reasonably expected from their availability). The question of what is a reasonable percentage of women faculty is a complex one, and currently there are no uniform standards for determining the "available pool." However, it may be useful to review several standards that are now being employed. Most are based on national data because it is still assumed that academic recruitment is conducted on a national market.

One standard for determining the "available pool" of women for faculty positions is the percentage of women among doctorates in a particular field.[1] Thus, for example, if women hold 17 percent of all doctorates in sociology, the expected percentage of women on the faculty of a sociology department would be 17 percent. This same percentage should hold for women at each professorial rank.

A second and more refined standard for estimating the available pool of women faculty takes into account differences in the proportion of doctorates granted to women over time. Thus the percentage of women full professors in a field might be expected to be low if a decade ago the percentage of women doctorates was low. If the percentage of women doctorates in that field is rising, we would expect a higher percentage of women assistant professors; moreover, goals should reflect the expected increase in the available pool of women at all ranks.

---

[1] Data on the number of Ph.D.'s by field for the last twenty-five years may be obtained from the Office of Education.

It is recognized that institutions vary in the pools from which they draw new faculty members. In some cases, the pool is national, while in others, colleges and universities hire from a group of "feeder" graduate schools. If the proportion of women in the feeder schools is higher than the national figures, it is expected that contractors will use the feeder school figures in determining availability of women, while if the feeder schools produce fewer women than the national average, contractors will use the national figures. If a particular department has a higher percentage of Ph.D.'s than the national average, HEW will often hold them to the higher percentage as their goal.

Other factors listed in the OFCC regulations that should be considered in estimating an available pool include the number of women doctorates in the geographic area, the number of women applicants, the greatly expanding number of women graduate students who soon could fill the positions, and the number of women within the institution who could be promoted and transferred. In the past, many qualified women doctorates have been relegated to marginal research positions or one-year renewable lectureships for most of their academic careers. As faculty wives or local residents who have found themselves in a restricted local job market, other women have settled for marginal employment. In addition, anti-nepotism regulations have often operated to deny or restrict the full employment of faculty wives. Women in each of these circumstances constitute a readily available and qualified source of faculty recruitment and should be included in the estimates of the available pool.

It may be useful to review standards for computing the available pool that are *not* allowed by HEW compliance reviewers. The HEW compliance staff does not allow departments to use different standards for women and men in estimating available pools of doctorates. For example, a department cannot calculate the available pool of women for faculty positions by taking the number of women doctorates, subtracting the number of such women who were not employed in academe and then using this reduced number of women to calculate the proportion of women in the available pool unless it also "corrects" the available pool of men faculty in the same manner.

In general, when a department uses a method of calculating the available pool that results in a percentage of women that is lower than the time-corrected overall percentage of women doctorates in a field, there is a stronger burden of proof placed on the department to justify the standards used in its calculations. Thus, if a department asserts that it recruits its faculty exclusively from the top five graduate departments in the country, and therefore estimates a much smaller pool of women than one based on all doctorates awarded nationally, it must submit data that establishes that each of its faculty was actually recruited from one of these five schools. OFCC regulations specifically state that "women cannot be expected to possess higher qualifications than those of the lowest qualified incumbent" (OFCC 1971b: 60–2.24f5).

An additional objection has been raised to using the standard of "top five departments" in computing the available pool. Just as many blacks were and still are excluded from elite educational institutions, women's exclusion from top institutions is clearly perpetuated when it becomes the basis of estimates of employment pools. The same doublebind is created when professional schools recruit faculty from a pool of eligibles with certain types of professional experience. For example, the pool for faculty members at Yale Law School consists primarily of persons who have clerked on the Supreme Court of the United States. However, since only one woman has clerked on the Court, this standard would effectively exclude women.

There has been no definitive ruling by either HEW or OFCC on the permissible standards for computing the available doctorate pool for faculty positions. However, compliance investigators have subjected the exclusionary standards we have just reviewed to strict scrutiny, and in several cases a department has been asked to broaden its basis for estimating the available pool.

Once a department or college has computed the available pool and estimated its underutilization of women, it turns to the third step in the utilization analysis: an examination of causes of underutilization and the development of effective action programs to correct them.

A department must consider if its sources and methods of recruitment give advantages to male candidates. Both the criteria and application of selection criteria must be examined. In addition, a department must examine the relative weight given to factors in determining salary and the extent to which they may operate to the disadvantage of women. For example, pay scales may properly be assigned by rank, yet women may be restricted by unfair requirements from moving up in rank. The standards for promotion, and the use of those standards, should be evaluated for possible sex bias. Finally, differences in conditions of employment, such as in teaching load, research assistance, or leave privileges should be examined.

Each of these areas require review on both the departmental level and on the collegewide or universitywide level, since the causes for underutilization may not be restricted to, or initiated by, a single department.

5. Establishing Goals and Timetables (OFCC 1971b: 60–2.12)

The next step in formulating an affirmative action program is to establish specific goals and timetables to eliminate the deficiencies found in the utilization analysis.

Goals are numerical targets established to eliminate the inequalities between women and men faculty, and to increase the proportional representation of women. Goals for *eliminating* inequities among presently employed women and men are easy to set, since the standard of parity required by HEW is clear. It is more difficult, however, to set reasonable goals to *increase* the representation of women on the faculty because of the complexities in establishing the standards of fair representation just reviewed. Roughly the same guidelines suggested in estimating the available pool for the utilization analysis should be used in establishing appropriate goals.

Goals should be established both by department and by the college or university as a whole in each of the areas covered in the utilization analysis: recruitment, selection, salary equity, rank equity, promotion, and conditions of employment. In some areas, such as recruitment, the universitywide goals will merely summarize the goals set by individual departments. But in other areas university goals may involve new programs which cannot be handled on the departmental level. For example, the goal of eliminating all salary inequities or the goal of establishing part-time tenure positions will probably have to be implemented through universitywide policies and procedures. Even in setting departmental goals, there must be some consultation and coordination with deans and affirmative action officials because departmental goals must take into account budgetary conditions, anticipated turnover, and the creation of new faculty positions.

Goals must be linked to specific target dates for their attainment. OFCC usually requires that goals be specified for a one-year period, although these yearly goals are expected to be part of a more comprehensive three–to five–year long-range plan. At the same time, goals that are set too far in the future, without yearly plans, are considered unreasonable and indicate the lack of a serious commitment to affirmative action.

In addition to requiring goals of both schools and departments, OFCC regulations require that all goals be specified by rank. Goals should be stated in numerical terms as well as in percentages. For example, a department may state that it wishes to increase the female faculty over a three-year period until it reaches 20 percent. It should specify that 20 percent of its faculty is equivalent to, say, six positions, and that to meet the long-range three-year goal, it will hire two new women faculty members each year.

When deficiencies exist, departments are required to establish separate goals for minorities and women, and to break down the goals for each minority group by sex. When this is done a department cannot count a minority female twice (as is typically done with black women) and thereby circumvent the spirit of the compliance program.

Goals have sometimes been confused with quotas. The important distinction between the two is explicated in a recent statement issued by J. Stanley Pottinger, Director of HEW's Office for Civil Rights, the compliance agency for educational institutions:

> Quotas, on the one hand, are numerical levels of employment that must be met if the employer is not to be found in violation of the law. They are rigid requirements and their effect is to compel employment decisions to fulfill them, regardless of qualifications, regardless of good faith efforts to fulfill them and regardless of the availability of capable applicants.

Goals, on the other hand, signify a different concept and employment practice. If, for example, an institution has been deficient in training, upgrading, promoting or otherwise treating employees without regard to . . . sex, goals are projected levels of hiring that say what an employer can do if he really tries. By establishing goals, the employer commits himself to a good faith effort that is most likely to produce results. Unlike quotas, goals are not the sole or even the primary measurement of a university's compliance. Good faith efforts remain the standard set by Executive Order 11246; goals are a barometer of good faith performance (Pottinger 1972:2).

Good faith efforts can be established by demonstrating that every reasonable effort was made by a department or university to achieve its goals. One indication of this is the extent to which a department or school has followed the compliance program that it has set for itself, to which we now turn. We will discuss the evaluation of good faith efforts in more detail in the section on review procedures.

6. A Program of Action to Attain Established Goals (OFCC 1971b: 60–2.24)

Perhaps the most important component of an affirmative action program is the concrete steps to be taken to achieve specified goals. Goals without concrete procedures for their attainment are merely hollow promises. Because detailed suggestions and references to existing programs will be discussed later, we shall confine our discussion in this section to a brief review of the types of programs enumerated by OFCC and HEW.

Action programs for recruitment include contacting women's organizations that can refer women with specific skills; including women in all phases of the recruitment process; active recruiting efforts at schools with large numbers of women students; and specific mention of women in recruitment letters, brochures, and job listings.

With regard to the selection process, OFCC regulations require the careful examination of selection criteria to "insure that the requirements in themselves do not constitute inadvertent discrimination" (OFCC 1971b:60–2.24b); validation of requirements that screen out a disproportionate number of women; a statement of standards for selection and promotion; the elimination of irrelevant selection criteria such as marital status, dependency status, or responsibility for minor children; and training of all personnel involved in the selection process to insure elimination of bias in the decisions.

Some faculty have feared any outside interference with the selection process, and have viewed the OFCC regulations as a threat to faculty autonomy and selection on the basis of merit. But it is clear that the above suggestions do not subvert merit standards, but rather strengthen them. In fact, they provide methods for furthering the goals which the faculty themselves have articulated. Rather than challenging merit criteria, these programs insure that it *is* merit, not such personal characteristics as sex or race, that will determine faculty appointments.

Turning to OFCC's regulations for insuring women equal opportunity for promotion, we also find procedures that strengthen merit standards. These include periodic review and evaluation of all female employees; validation of employment criteria to insure that women are not required to possess higher qualifications than those of the lowest qualified incumbent; a written justification from department chairpersons when apparently qualified women are passed over for promotions; and the open listing or announcement of all promotional opportunities.

With regard to establishing conditions of benefit to employees, OFCC's suggestions are more limited: the guidelines suggest offering child-care facilities, housing, and transportation programs where needed. OFCC does require that social and recreational activities be open to all.

7. Establishing Internal Audit and Reporting Systems (OFCC 1971b: 60–2.25)

Responsibility for establishing a means of monitoring all phases of the affirmative action program lies with the affirmative action official. To facilitate effective monitoring, Order No. 4 requires that periodic written progress reports be submitted to the official by department chairpersons and deans. These reports should include the department's utilization analysis, goals and timetables, description and evaluation of its action program, and complete supporting data.

Each report must be reviewed by the affirmative action official. Departments that have not made satisfactory progress are subjected to informal pressures by the affirmative action official to improve their performance. If this is not successful, the affirmative action official is charged with reporting lack of progress to the top university officials (the president or a committee set up for such reviews) and to provide recommendations to improve the department's performance. Specific recommendations or sanctions will be discussed in the second half of this chapter.

Failure to meet departmental goals does not, in itself, constitute unsatisfactory progress. The crucial indicator of departmental progress is good faith efforts to meet its goals. In order to demonstrate good faith efforts a department might show that it has followed all of the steps specified in its action program and done everything possible to meet its goals. Obviously departments and affirmative action offices will be spared cumbersome documentation of good faith efforts if they meet the goals and timetables specified in their affirmative action plans.

In order for the monitoring procedure to work effectively, departmental reports should be submitted biannually. This allows for a mid-year check on departmental personnel decisions, and for intervention when necessary, to forestall a charge of discrimination. By preventing a fait accompli in final departmental reports, the mid-year review may thus eliminate possible discriminatory decisions. A mid-year review may also allow the affirmative action staff to assist departments at difficult junctures in faculty recruitment, hiring, promotion, or termination.

An alternative to the time consuming biannual department reports is the continuing review process. Under this system, the signature of the affirmative action official is required on all departmental requests for an appointment, tenure, promotion, termination, or salary increase, or the denial of any of these. By withholding their signature, affirmative action officials may question or delay any recommendation that seems to violate a department's affirmative action goal.

In general, academic departments have been reluctant to allow administrative review of their personnel decisions for fear of interfering with important academic freedoms, even though affirmative action officials and committee members typically are drawn from the faculty. It is important to note, however, that academic freedom has never meant freedom to deny a qualified person a job or advancement on the basis of race or sex. Highly personal and subjective judgments often enter decisions concerning employment, and the review process suggested by OFCC simply insures that such judgments do not violate the faculty's own goals for hiring on the basis of merit.

8. Support for Other Action Programs with Special Attention to Increasing the Future Proportion of Women in Academe (OFCC 19971b: 60–2.13i and j and 60–2.26)

Educational institutions are obliged to encourage and train women for faculty positions and to expand the opportunities available to women in academe. Regulations apply primarily to programs for graduate training, but they also specify the need for career counseling and guidance programs for women at an earlier age.

With respect to high school women, Order No. 4 states that universities should assist secondary schools in programs designed to enable female graduates to compete with men on a more equitable basis, through summer school programs for promising female high school students; visits by university personnel and women faculty to high schools to discuss career opportunities for women; and guidance and counseling programs designed specifically for young women.

Similar guidance and counseling programs for female students are appropriate for undergraduate women as well. Other procedures to encourage the participation of women students, especially of older women students, might include the abolition of sex-based admission quotas, the loosening of regulations concerning part-time study, abolition of age or marital restrictions on financial aid, and other efforts to insure the equal training and support of women students at all levels.

In addition to the requirements we have just reviewed, Order No. 4 specifies that affirmative action programs should include policies which are consistent with the Sex Discrimination Guidelines and the Employee Testing Order. The Sex Discrimination Guidelines, discussed in the beginning of this chapter, specify nondiscriminatory policies on maternity leave, equal pay, job classifications, fringe benefits, and retirement plans (OFCC 1970). The Employee Testing Order, also reviewed at the beginning of this chapter, requires that employment criteria be specified and validated for each position, and prohibits the institution of new employment criteria which exclude women if women could have been hired under the old standards (OFCC 1971a).

These OFCC requirements for an affirmative action program provide merely the outline of the finished product. Specific programs designed to meet the needs of an individual college or university should be developed within this general framework. It is to these more specific programs that we now turn.

AN OVERVIEW OF CURRENT AFFIRMATIVE ACTION PROGRAMS

Most of the information to be presented has been culled from existing affirmative action plans and from interviews with college administrators responsible for affirmative action. Our sample admittedly is less than ideal. We requested from HEW a list of all schools that had submitted affirmative action plans as of spring 1971. This list was supplemented by additional plans as they became available, up to March 1972. Our requests for a copy of institutions' current affirmative action programs were sent to 105 institutions in March 1972.

Since Order No. 4 was published in December 1971 and did not go into effect until April 1972, the affirmative action plans we received may differ considerably from those now being developed. They do reflect, however, the provisions that institutions of higher education considered important in their first efforts toward developing affirmative action programs.

Table 20.1 presents an overview of the complete affirmative action plans we received as of March 1972. Between refusals to release plans and the many incomplete plans we received, only forty plans were complete enough to code for the factors listed in Table 20.1. As the table shows, a utilization analysis, numerical goals and timetables, affirmative search procedures, revision of antinepotism regulations, grievance procedures, and review procedures have been instituted in a number of schools. But even these provisions have been adopted by a very small percentage of the total number of schools reviewed. In addition, very few schools specified hiring procedures apart from the search procedures, and fewer still provided supportive services and programs for graduate students.

SUGGESTED AFFIRMATIVE ACTION PROGRAMS

In the following pages we will suggest a variety of possible action programs, drawing on many that have been instituted in colleges and universities. Our aim is to assist those who are committed to affirmative action in devising the most effective methods of achieving equality for women and men in higher education. The

TABLE 20.1. Key Action Components of Affirmative Action Programs

Key Component	Percentage of Schools with Component in Affirmative Action Program
Utilization analysis completed	55
Numerical goals for hiring set by college or school	40
Numerical goals for hiring set by departments	20
Timetables set for hiring goals	35
Action programs for hiring:	
Affirmative search procedures	60
Special funds provided	5
Antinepotism regulations revised	37.5
Provision for consideration of women in marginal positions	10
Inclusion of women on all hiring committees	20
Goals and timetable set for achieving salary equity	17.5
Goals and timetable set for achieving rank equity	7.5
Provision for back pay	2.5
Action programs for equity in conditions of employment:	
Provision of part-time ladder positions	15
Programs for equity in teaching and/or research conditions	0
Action programs for equity in fringe benefits:	
Child-care program	10
Health care program	5
Maternity leave and care	25
Extended contract/tenure decision for child-rearing leave	10
Grievance procedures	45
Provision for review of departmental hiring decisions	47.5
Sanctions for departmental compliance/noncompliance	5
Action program for graduate training:	
Aggressive search for women graduate students	30
Admission of older women/men students	7.5
Provision for part-time study	7.5
Nondiscrimination policy in awarding fellowships, research and teaching assistantships, scholarships	35

SOURCE: Classification and tally drawn from the affirmative action programs of the following schools: Amherst College, Auburn University, Baylor University, Brown University, California Institute of Technology, City University of New York, Dartmouth College, Duke University, Harvard University, Hofstra University, John Carroll University, Johns Hopkins University, Massachusetts Institute of Technology, Michigan State University, Ohio State University, Oklahoma State University, Oregon State University, Princeton University, Purdue University, Rice University, Rutgers University, San Diego State College, Southern Illinois University, State University of New York, Stanford University, Texas A & M, Tufts University, University of Arizona, University of California at Santa Barbara, University of Chicago, University of Maine, University of Maryland, University of Michigan, University of Minnesota, University of Pennsylvania, University of Pittsburgh, University of Southern Florida, University of Washington, University of Wyoming, and Vanderbilt University.

OFCC requirements we have enumerated may be viewed as a challenge to each educational community to design an action program that is both effective and uniquely suited to their institution.

The lack of progress at some schools with good affirmative action programs on paper clearly attests to the fact that a written program provides no guarantee of real affirmative action. However, a written plan is a necessary beginning and plans such as those suggested here, which provide for compliance reviews and sanctions, provide the mechanisms for concerned parties to challenge and pressure toward real progress.

In designing these action programs it is important to take into account the social position of women in American society. For example, we shall recommend that schools allow a delayed tenure decision for faculty who have taken a year's absence for childbearing and/or rearing. Although the option would be equally available to men, in the near future such policies will more directly benefit women faculty.

It is also important to emphasize the necessity for having people who are deeply committed to affirmative action goals involved in every stage of the process. OFCC regulations specify that all personnel involved in recruiting, screening, selection, and promotion should be carefully selected and trained to insure elimination of bias in personnel actions (OFCC 1971b:60–2.24d,1). The surest way to guarantee that the action plan is implemented is to allow those who are committed to it to play a crucial role.

The person with prime responsibility for the affirmative action program usually is appointed by and directly responsible to the president or chancellor. A number of schools appointed special search committees, with adequate representation of women, to recommend candidates for this office to the president.

In our interviews and review of existing programs we have noted that ineffective programs seem to suffer from one of three difficulties: the affirmative action official was not given sufficient rank and power; a nonacademic person was appointed to the position; or the affirmative action official lacked a commitment to improving the status of women.

With respect to rank, we recommend that the affirmative action official be given a rank equivalent to that of a provost or vice president. In a large university, each college or school might appoint an affirmative action dean to work with the universitywide affirmative action provost and to take direct responsibility for routine supervision of the program within their school or college.

The second difficulty has emerged with the appointment of a single affirmative action official with responsibility for both academic and nonacademic employees. A person trained in industrial "job analysis" does not have the experience or the knowledge to handle the problems of academic personnel. Because of the strong tradition of faculty autonomy, department chairpersons are likely to resent "directives" from someone who has little understanding of academic standards of professional competence. Similarly, a university professor usually has not had sufficient experience in dealing with nonacademic job classifications to supervise the non-academic employee compliance plan. For these reasons it seems advisable to appoint different officers to deal with academic and nonacademic personnel.

A third common reason for the failure in the university affirmative action office has been the appointment of individuals who are not sympathetic to or knowledgeable about the problems confronting academic women. To date, a majority of institutions have appointed black males to supervise affirmative action programs, and these men have often ignored the problems of faculty women. Again, it seems wise to have two separate programs, one for minorities and one for women, to prevent conflicts of interest and charges of favoritism within the program. Ideally, a person committed to improving the status of academic women should be appointed to a position of affirmative action provost for women.

In recommending that different persons be appointed to deal with women, minorities, academic, and nonacademic employees it might seem that we have restricted our recommendations to large universities. In fact, a school like Michigan State University is able to support an affirmative action staff of nine persons. However, we have not ignored the personnel limitations of small colleges. Affirmative action officials may have other administrative responsibilities in addition to affirmative action. Our recommendation is that different personnel of high rank be responsible for each employee category. In a small college these positions easily might be filled by college deans or by faculty members working part time on affirmative action.

The University of Vermont has solved the problem in another way by appointing a black woman to direct the affirmative action program for the entire university. The Vermont program has been particularly successful with minority women, who often are excluded from programs for both women and minorities because programs for women have concentrated on white women, while programs for minorities have concentrated on black or Chicano men.

As already noted in the regulations, the affirmative action provost has the overall responsibility for the implementation of the university plan. This typically includes establishing and implementing universitywide goals and timetables; assisting departments in conducting their own utilization analysis, establishing goals and timetables, and designing appropriate action programs; reviewing and evaluating progress reports and personnel recommendations submitted by departments; negotiating with departments that have not made satisfactory affirmative action progress and, where appropriate, recommending sanctions; and finally, issuing periodic reports on affirmative action progress.

Almost all affirmative action officers provide guidance to departments in the initial stages of the program—especially in helping them to conduct utilization analyses and providing them with data and assistance in setting appropriate goals and timetables in accordance with universitywide goals. At a later stage, affirmative action officials might assist departments in designing action programs to implement their goals. They can provide them with information on recruitment sources, guidelines for achieving salary equity, or special funds. The review and evaluation process is easier for both the department and the affirmative action official if good working relationships are established early in the program. If affirmative action officials are aware of the needs and problems of individual departments it will be easier for them to evaluate and assist departmental progress and good faith efforts. Acting as a resource for both information and guidance, the affirmative action official can have a profound impact on the direction and progress of an affirmative action program.

Because of the power and responsibility concentrated in the office of the affirmative action provost, several universities have established advisory committees to work with the officer in directing the affirmative action program. These committees include faculty with expertise in statistics, data processing, and law as well as significant representation from faculty and staff women, department chairpersons, and administrative personnel. In one university the advisory committee sent out guidelines to assist departments in establishing appropriate goals. In another it divided itself into small groups to meet with recalcitrant department chairpersons, and in a third, it issued directives for equalizing salaries. Whether the advisory committee takes an active role in program implementation, or defines itself as a committee to review the programs implemented by the affirmative action officer, it can provide an important service in facilitating affirmative action progress.

Although the most effective structures of affirmative action programs vary by the size, location, and orientation of the educational institutions, almost all schools benefit from having a high-ranking official responsible for implementing the affirmative action program for academic women, an affirmative action official in each organizational unit, and an advisory committee to oversee the implementation of the affirmative action program.

At this stage, it is impossible to recommend foolproof procedures for achieving affirmative action goals. Although any one of the following programs may be viewed as difficult, awkward, inconvenient, or too timid, it is hoped that some of them will be useful as they are, and that others will suggest modifications more suitable to particular institutions.

1. Programs for Recruitment

The recruitment process in academe has traditionally been referred to as the "old boy" or "buddy" system of hiring—that is, professors rely on contacts with friends in other universities for recommendations of promising graduate students. As the HEW guidelines state,

> the informality of word-of-mouth recruiting and its reliance on factors outside the knowledge or control of the university makes this method particularly sus-

ceptible to abuse. In addition, since women and minorities are often not in word-of-mouth channels of recruitment, their candidacies may not be advanced with the same frequency or strength of endorsement as they merit, and as their white male colleagues receive (HEW 1972:5).

Because women frequently are excluded by traditional recruitment networks, departments seeking women faculty will probably want to try new recruitment techniques designed specifically to locate women candidates. Therefore, on the departmental level, we recommend:

(a) *All recruitment communications should state that a department is actively seeking qualified women candidates.*

(b) *Contact professional women's organizations to request the referral of qualified candidates.* Most professional organizations have women's caucuses that will assist departments in recruitment. A list of these caucuses or commissions on women may be obtained from Ruth Oltman of the American Association of University Women.

(c) *List positions and job openings in professional journals.* Although many "prestige" departments have refrained from open listings in the past because they contended that they would be swamped by applicants, there is a growing recognition that anything less than open listings serve to maintain established exclusionary selection procedures. Last year at the meetings of the American Historical Association, prestigious history departments agreed to open listing of all positions. Some top departments in other fields have begun to announce vacancies in professional journals. The affirmative action group at the University of California at Davis has proposed that all University of California campuses adopt a policy of open listing for all faculty vacancies. This is currently the university-wide policy at the University of Minnesota.

(d) *List positions and job openings in women's journals and through women's organizations.* Women's journals, including *The Spokeswoman,* the *KNOW* newsservice, and *Women Today* will announce job openings, and women's organizations such as the National Organization for Women, or the Talent Bank of the Business and Professional Women's Organization will refer qualified women upon request.

(e) *Involve women in all phases of the recruitment process.* In addition to including women on the recruitment committee, departments should send them to national and regional professional meetings where recruitment is conducted. If a department does not have a woman on its faculty, it might ask a woman faculty member in a related discipline or a woman graduate student to serve on its recruitment committee.

(f) *Consult professional rosters and national directories of association memberships.* Most of these directories list members (both women and men) by area of specialty and provide information on awards and research interests. Some professional organizations publish a list of all prospective doctorates each year. For example, the American Sociological Association publishes information on each prospective doctorate, including the subject's dissertation topic, sponsor, field of interest, and degree-granting institution.

(g) *Consult regional and national rosters and referral services for academic women.* In contrast to the above sources, which list both women and men in academe, special referral services and directories have been established for academic women. The Regional Resource Center for Women in Higher Education at Brown University and the American Association for the Advancement of Science are developing national rosters of women scientists by field. Many regional rosters, such as the one being developed by the Boston Area Women in Social Science, are also in process.

(h) *Consult national and regional associations of black and Chicano professionals.* Efforts to locate minority women can be assisted by organizations such as the National Council of Negro Women, the National Chicano Foundation, and black women's sororities and service groups (such as Delta Sigma Theta, Alpha Kappa Alpha, and Zeta Phi Beta). Conferences such as the annual conference of black professionals in higher education also could be helpful. Similar referral organizations should be consulted for Asian women, native American women, and Puerto Rican women.

(i) *Solicit qualified applicants from schools that have large female populations.* Two examples are women's schools and schools in metropolitan areas. For minority women, the alumna office of such schools as Spelman College in Atlanta should be contacted, as well as schools in the urban north.

(j) *Invite the consultation of prominent women scholars.* Because of the increasing number of communication networks among academic women, a woman professor in art history at Yale, for example, is likely to be able to identify other women in her field.

(k) *Consider women who have held marginal positions in the department for regular faculty appointments.* Women who hold the title of lecturer, instructor, or research associate should be considered for ladder positions. Often women have been maintained in these positions because of nepotism rules, or because they lacked mobility. Departments have both a moral and a legal obligation to consider these women for new professorial positions. Michigan State University, and the Universities of Pittsburgh, Michigan, and Washington have specified that departments must consider marginal women for regular appointments. Duke University goes further and says that if two professionals are equally qualified, then the marginal person should be given priority in hiring.

(l) *Consider professional women working in independent research institutions, government agencies, private industry, or foundations for faculty appointments.*

(m) *Consider hiring the department's own doctorates.* Although many departments have informal rules against in-hiring, this may be an appropriate time to reconsider such regulations because they deprive many departments of a good source of new womanpower. If a department has certified a significant number of women as worthy professionals by granting them Ph.D.'s, such women may be worthy of consideration for a faculty position at the same university. Even if a department is reluctant to hire its own Ph.D.'s immediately after the degree is granted, it might maintain a list of its female doctorates for future consideration for faculty positions.

(n) *Consider unsolicited applications.* Although many departments have traditionally ignored unsolicited applications, one indication of good faith efforts is a willingness to consider applications from all women, whatever their source.

(o) *Consider tandem teams.* Husbands and wives typically have had great difficulty in finding employment in the same university because of antinepotism regulations. Good faith efforts might be indicated by a department's willingness to consider academic couples for employment.

There is some concern among women's groups that departments merely will go through the motions of using the above procedures but continue to hire persons recommended through informal networks. OFCC regulations require that departments maintain applicant flow data (the source of referral and the review procedures for each of the candidates considered) and applicant rejection ratios by sex. Such records may prove useful to the department for their own affirmative action analyses, as well as for documentation of good faith efforts.

Action programs for recruitment should be organized on both the departmental and universitywide basis. The affirmative action provost can assist departmental recruiting efforts by compiling information on recruitment sources or by maintaining their own registry of women scholars by field. Patricia Graham, a professor at Barnard College, compiled such a file while she was on leave at Princeton University. Graham combed available lists of scholars who had received National Institutes of Health or National Science Foundation grants, Woodrow Wilson Fellowships, Guggenheim awards, and so on. This list was used by the dean to stimulate recruitment in the following manner: when department chairpersons proposed male candidates they wished to hire, the dean asked if women had been considered. If the chairpersons contended that they had been unable to locate qualified women, they were referred to Graham's list. In addition to its use as a means of insuring that departments considered women scholars, the file soon became an effective recruitment aid for department chairpersons.

Another successful recruitment program was organized by Sheila Tobias, associate provost at Wesleyan University. Provost Tobias has a general fund to bring women scholars to the campus as lecturers. Since all departments are required to submit their recruitment priorities to the provost's office, Tobias can coordinate these lectures with recruitment efforts of departments. In this way, a department has an opportunity to review potential candidates, with no financial drain on department budgets, and students benefit greatly from the presence of visiting women scholars. Several women brought to the attention of departments through this program were eventually hired. Other universitywide programs, such as the one instituted at the California Institute of Technology, include workshops for faculty involved in recruiting. These give information about techniques to increase the representation of women on the faculty and encourage committment to affirmative action hiring.

One of the most effective universitywide programs to encourage the recruitment of women faculty is the provision of special university funds to be used for hiring women. The potential impact of this kind of stimulus is illustrated by the recent experience of the University of California at Davis. Two years ago the chancellor and the vice-chancellor for academic affairs sent strongly worded letters to department chairmen encouraging the recruitment of minority faculty. The letters were followed by other affirmative action appeals, but when departmental recommendations for new faculty appointments were reviewed, most department chairmen contended that they had not been able to locate qualified minority faculty. The following year, the chancellor established special funds for hiring minority faculty. These funds allowed departments to gain a new ladder position if they hired a minority scholar. Within one year, departments that previously had been unable to locate "qualified" minority persons suddenly found an abundance of outstanding black and Chicano scholars whom they wanted to hire.

Similarly, special funds for women faculty recruitment have been established at Stanford University and the California Institute of Technology. Such funding, administered by the affirmative action provost's office can be allocated in several ways. Funding for female faculty appointments can be available on a competitive basis to all departments in a university, and distributed among departments on the basis of the comparative merits of the women faculty they wish to hire. Or special funds can be provided to departments especially deficient in women faculty, or to departments who wish to exceed their affirmative action goals.

A university can also assist departmental recruitment efforts by making funds available for recruitment visits. Although most schools routinely provide funds for the department to invite candidates for campus visits, the current budgetary crises in schools has resulted in the elimination of campus visits for routine appointments. In these schools departments who wish to invite women candidates might be given priority.

A final suggestion involves university support for visiting professorships for women. In addition to providing departments with additional faculty appointments, this allows both students and colleagues increased opportunities for intellectual exchange with women faculty. These appointments might be especially useful when the department knows that it will have a permanent position open the following year and wants to persuade a female scholar to accept it. Postdoctoral fellowships and postdoctoral research positions can also be used to attract and evaluate potential female faculty.

Efforts to retain women who are already on the faculty are as important as recruitment efforts to improve the overall proportion of women faculty. The authors of the affirmative action plan at the University of Pittsburgh have noted that a crucial factor in attracting new women to the faculty is the current atmosphere and support given to women already on the faculty.

2. Programs for the Selection Process

Neither the criteria for faculty hiring, nor the procedures for applying these criteria should give an advantage to women or men candidates. However, applying egalitarian criteria is difficult, even when no bias is intended. Departments traditionally have relied upon the judgments of friends to assess the merits of candidates for junior faculty positions. These judgments are often affected by unconscious stereotypes about the interest and competence of women—e.g., that women are less committed to intellectual careers, that women are less able to deal with "high level theory," and so on. Because of the crucial role that such consciously or unconsciously biased assessments have played in the past, the increased pressures on departments to justify their hiring decisions (by making their selection criteria and procedures explicit) will probably have the positive effect of pushing all departments to develop more effective and sex–neutral means of evaluating a candidate's potential.

Given the wide variety of departments wishing to develop affirmative action programs, it is impossible to devise a set of uniform criteria and procedures that will fit the needs of every department. Thus, some of the following suggestions may not be applicable to certain departments, and others may have to be altered or changed to be effective. However, in the selection of faculty we recommend that:

(a) *Departments should specify their selection criteria for all faculty appointments.* It is important for selection criteria to be specified before individual candidates are considered. This will insure that ad hoc criteria are not being invoked to justify the selection of male candidates. Moreover, the *relative weight* given to letters of recommendation, teaching experience, area of specialization, graduate training, publications, and other factors should be established. The HEW guidelines state that,

> an employer must establish in reasonable detail, and make available upon request, the standards and procedures which govern all employment practices . . . including the criteria by which qualifications for appointment, retention, or promotion are judged (HEW 1972:4).

(b) *Departments should examine their selection criteria to insure that they are not sex biased.* Seemingly neutral standards may in fact eliminate prospective female candidates. For example, rigorous restrictions with regard to the prestige of the doctorate-granting institution or department, the amount of research support received, or expertise in some specialty area may exclude members of one sex more than the other. Because women have been systematically barred from entering some institutions, they should not be required to hold a degree from such an institution. Neither should women be rejected because of less auspicious records of research support, since they have had less access to research funds. Similarly criteria which emphasize active participation or office in professional associations, which have denied academic women equal opportunities in participation, may also serve to perpetuate sex bias.

On another level, the University of California at Santa Barbara has proposed substituting "equivalency criteria" since women and minorities have not had equal opportunities to complete advanced degrees. If equivalents were more widely adopted, the opportunities for women in both teaching and administration would be greatly increased. The policy statement at the University of Minnesota provides an excellent example in this area:

> In judging qualifications, the evaluators should look beyond formal credentials, which may themselves reflect the effects of past discrimination, and attempt to form judgments of probable overall promise—judgments of a candidate's abilities to contribute to the University's primary missions.

(c) *Departments may not raise or change hiring criteria when considering women candidates.* OFCC regulations specifically state that women should not be required to possess higher qualifications than those of the lowest qualified incumbent (OFCC 1971b, 60–2.24f5). For example, if a psychology department hired a male assistant professor in 1972 who had not published, it cannot decide that all its new female assistant professors in 1973 must have published books.

(d) *Departments must insure that women are not assigned a lower rank in hiring decisions.* The HEW guidelines state that,

> In hiring decisions, assignment to a particular title or rank may be discriminatory. For example, in many institutions women are more often assigned initially to lower academic ranks than are men. A study by one disciplinary association showed that women tend to be offered a first appointment at the rank of Instructor rather than the rank of Assistant Professor three times more often than men with identical qualifications. Where there is no valid basis for such differential treatment, such a practice is in violation of the Executive Order (HEW 1972:7).

(e) *Departments should insure that the academic work and recommendations of women candidates are processed in the same manner as those of men candidates.* The review process for candidates under serious consideration, including an examination of their written work, letters of recommendation, teaching experience, and a personal interview, should be identical for persons of both sexes. To insure impartial consideration, some schools have instituted a system of blind reading of candidates' written work. Another way of insuring an objective review might be to submit vitae and written work to outside consultants for a second reading and evaluation.

(f) *Departments should insure that irrelevant considerations such as marital status and the presence of dependent children are not part of the evaluation of a woman candidate.* Considerations of marriage and parenthood are specifically forbidden by OFCC regulations.

Even if such considerations are not raised directly, a woman's commitment or availability to students often is questioned. In other situations, it is assumed that family considerations would prevent a woman from moving, and she automatically is excluded from serious consideration. Departments should consider all women "available" for new positions unless they have been informed otherwise (by *her*). Departments should not assume that a married woman is less mobile or less committed to her career than a married man.

Other irrelevant social characteristics may intrude into a department's evaluations of women. Because members of the same academic department often become friends, many departments resemble a men's club, and hence women candidates are viewed as less suitable to become "one of the boys." Such irrelevant considerations as family background, athletic ability, congeniality, and political preferences have been used to exclude other minorities in the past, and they should be eliminated now in considering the academic competence of all candidates, including women.

(g) *Departments should afford women candidates the opportunity to present themselves and their work on recruitment visits.* An important indicator of good faith efforts is the number of women who have been invited to the campus for a recruitment visit. Equally important is the way in which they are treated on these visits. For example, one department did not schedule colloquiums for its women candidates because they allegedly did not want to put too much pressure on them. The result was that members of the department saw the women candidates only socially, and received the impression that they were less serious and less intellectually oriented than the male candidates.

(h) *Women should be involved in all stages of the selection process.* Such stages include establishing criteria, evaluating vitae, written work and letters of recommendation, and evaluating the relative merits of the candidates. By involving women in the selection process, a department may be better able to avoid the unconscious bias that often enters into judgments of merit. The Universities of Michigan, Pittsburgh, Pennsylvania, Arizona, and Harvard and Stanford have stated in their compliance programs that women should be included on hiring committees to insure fair evaluation of female candidates.

In addition to these procedures for insuring equal opportunities for women in departmental selection processes, some selection policies require revision on the college or universitywide level. *Antinepotism regulations,* which forbid the employment of members of the same family in faculty positions, often serve to restrict the employment of women. Although only some antinepotism regulations are overtly discriminatory (e.g., make reference to "faculty wives"), in practice almost all antinepotism regulations are interpreted to deny employment to wives of male faculty. The HEW Guidelines explicitly prohibit such regulations. HEW does allow, however, "reasonable restrictions" on an individual's participation in decisions involving a member of his or her family. The 1972 HEW Guidelines note that AAUP's policy on "Faculty Appointment and Family Relationship" is an example of a reasonable restriction. The AAUP policy suggests that when members of the same family are hired in the same department or unit they should be restricted from initiating or participating in an institutional decision involving a direct benefit (initial appointment, retention, promotion, or salary) to members of their immediate family (HEW 1972:9).

A number of major universities including the Universities of Arizona, California, Chicago, Michigan, Maryland, Pennsylvania, Pittsburgh, Washington, and the State University of New York, Oregon State, Ohio State, Michigan State, Duke, Stanford, and M.I.T., have lifted antinepotism regulations and many others are proposing similar action. Once antinepotism regulations have been abolished, departments might seek tandem teams or make special efforts to place the spouse of a candidate they wish to hire.

The positive effect of removing such rules is illustrated by recent events at the University of Washington. When the antinepotism rule was revised, a review was made of the status of women who held positions in the same departments as their husbands. The review resulted in a number of qualified women being recommended for promotion. One woman was appointed as a full professor, another was reclassified from an acting assistant professor position to regular assistant professor status. A woman lecturer became an assistant professor, and an instructor was appointed as an assistant professor. The University of Washington currently is reviewing women who hold positions outside of their husbands' departments, and is committed to make similar adjustments in appointments wherever woman have been given lower level or off-ladder positions because of the old antinepotism rule.

3. Programs to Achieve Salary Equity

Programs for achieving salary equity have two primary aims: the elimination of salary differences between women and men faculty of equal rank, experience, and contribution; and the awarding of back pay to women who have received lower salaries than men as a result of past discrimination. Some people have assumed that salary equity for women and men will result in the complete standardization of salary among faculty of the same rank. This is not so. Departments and universities will continue to determine the criteria for salary distinctions. Further, institutions are likely to vary in the relative emphasis placed on one or the other of such criteria as effective teaching, original research, service to the community, or seniority. Whatever the standards for salary distinctions, they should be clearly stated and applied equally to women and men. Salary equity with regard to sex precludes only salary distinctions made solely on the basis of sex; it does not preclude other distinctions deemed significant by a faculty.

The legal precedents for awarding compensation to victims of discrimination in salary have been clearly established in industry under the Equal Pay Act. Over 35 million dollars in back pay have been awarded under the Equal Pay Act since 1964, most of it to women who have been victims of past salary discrimination. Until 1972, academic employees of universities were exempted from the act, although some courts have ordered universities to grant back pay to nonacademic women. In *Hodgson* v. *Waynesburg College,* the college was found to be in violation of the Equal Pay Act in paying its female custodial workers lower salaries than its male janitors, and was ordered to increase the women's salaries and to award them back pay.

OFCC and HEW have held universities responsible for back pay to faculty women under the Executive Orders. After a long and bitter series of negotiations with HEW concerning back pay, the University of Michigan agreed to grant back pay to women faculty who had suffered from salary inequities. Over 200 faculty and staff received such awards in the spring of 1972.

In light of current financial problems in academe, some schools are expressing a reluctance to equalize salaries or to grant back pay to women. Yet, the moral and legal imperatives to do so are strong, and the pressure from organized women's groups is increasing. The programs reviewed below suggest that problems of funding can be solved once the commitment is made. As Martha Peterson, president of Barnard College and chairman of the American Council on Education urged in her keynote address before the ACE in October 1972:

> Of course budget considerations are tight and money must not be squandered. But once an institution knows it has an indefensible pay scale based on discrimination, it has no choice legally or morally except to right the inequities including whatever back pay is deemed reasonable by an unbiased mediator. . . . We have met other financial contingencies . . . (and) we probably can weather the additional cost of a reasonable amount of retroactive pay if we care enough.

Doubtless, an increasing number of schools will commit themselves to equity in this area without the threat of legal sanctions.

The following suggestions for salary equity plans are derived, in part, from those adopted at Stanford University, the California Institute of Technology, the Universities of Michigan, Oregon, and Massachusetts, and Michigan State University. Needless to say, differences in size, financial resources, and degree of past discrimination vary across institutions so these suggestions must be modified to meet local circumstances.

An action program for salary equity on the departmental level might involve the following steps:

(a) *Circulation of statement of departmental criteria for salary differentials.* Such a statement should specify the relative weight to be given to teaching, publications, original research, length of tenure, and service to the academic community and in administration.

(b) *The salaries of male and female faculty within the department should be compared for each rank.*

(c) *Where discrepancies are found, the department should examine the reasons for the difference.* If the salary differential is due to sex discrimination, then the department might recommend increasing the woman's salary to that of her male colleague.

(d) *If the department feels that the differential is justified, reasons should be given, in a written report, to the affirmative action provost.*

(e) *Departmental recommendations and justification for salary differentials would then be reviewed by the affirmative action provost or the appropriate affirmative action dean.* Certain justifications, such as the contention that a woman was hired at a lower salary, or that she had less outside bargaining power, are unacceptable. These justifications assume or build on differences by sex, perpetuate past discrimination, and violate the principle of equal pay for equal work. If the department considers a woman worthy of an associate professorship, then it must pay her accordingly. In contrast, an acceptable explanation would be, for example, that there was a difference in the length of total professional employment of the man and the woman.

(f) *When university funds are not provided for salary increases, departments should consider the most effective and equitable means of equalizing salaries within the department budget.* Financial constraints cannot be used as an excuse to continue salary discrimination. Most departments and schools committed to salary equalization have managed to find ways to achieve it. Three of the best programs in this area at Maine, Wisconsin, and Southern Florida will be briefly described in the following pages.

(g) *Women should be granted compensatory back pay for past salary discrimination.* HEW's policy for requiring back pay under the Executive Order has been to require back pay to October 13, 1968 (the date of Executive Order 11375) for salary discrepancies existing on or after that date. Back pay should consist of the difference between the woman's salary and the salary she would have received since October 1968. If the salary discrepancy was more recent, then the woman should be compensated from the date of the discrimination.

The most recent HEW Guidelines state that in the future HEW will pursue back pay awards only to employees who were not protected by Title VII of the Civil Rights Act of 1964, the Equal Pay Act, or the National Labor Relations Act at the time the violation occurred. Because faculty were not covered by this legislation until March 1972, back pay requests for 1968 to 1972 will remain under HEW jurisdiction. More recent cases of salary discrimination will now fall under the jurisdiction of the Equal Employment Opportunity Commission (which enforces Title VII and allows up to two years of back pay), and the Wage and Hour Division of the Department of Labor (which enforces the Equal Pay Act and allows up to two years of back pay for nonwillful violation, and three years of back pay for willful violation of the Act).

(h) *In the event of severe financial constraints, a department must show good faith efforts to award back pay by giving it priority over other salary and merit increases.*[2] In industry, court-awarded back pay has usually included 6 percent interest on the money due from the date of the discrimination. But thus far HEW has not made a decision on whether interest must be given on awards of back pay to faculty.

Many of these procedures for achieving salary equity have been adopted at Stanford University, the California Institute of Technology, and Universities of Michigan, Oregon, and Massachusetts, and Michigan State University. Of these schools only the University of Michigan has included specific timetables in their program (as required by OFCC regulations) and it is one of the few schools that has already granted back pay to women faculty from October 1968. No doubt the present lack of back pay awards is due to HEW's lax enforcement of this provision.

In addition to equalizing salaries within a department, some salary equalization between departments and schools may be necessary when women are concentrated in departments or schools with lower overall pay scales. For example, the University of Minnesota report states that

> since academic units with preponderantly women faculty have, over a long period, been penalized with respect to salaries, it is recommended that central and collegiate administrations make specific allocations to these units in order to improve this situation.

Accordingly, the central administration allocated $84,500 for upgrading salaries in the School of Nursing, the School of Home Economics, units of the Duluth campus, and the Office of Student Affairs.

Let us now consider three successful universitywide programs for eliminating salary inequity. At the University of Wisconsin, each department received a com-

---

[2] Statement of Owen Kiley (head of the Contract Compliance Staff, Office for Civil Rights, Department of Health, Education and Welfare, Washington, D.C.) in a personal interview in January 1972.

puter printout of faculty salary and rank-by-rank salary averages for women and men. The situation at the university was more complicated than most because faculty salaries are funded by two different sources—state funds and nonstate funds. Upon the recommendation of a department, salary increases for women paid from state funds were covered by the deans on a collegewide basis. This practice assured that departments with several women did not bear a disproportionate share of the burden of salary adjustment. Department chairpersons were asked to draw salary increases for women on nonstate funds from their department budgets. Departments were instructed to set salaries at appropriate levels and reduce the percentage of full-time employed to the level that could be funded. Confronted with this requirement, most chairpersons managed to bring salaries into line without reducing the size of their faculty. In addition to equalization, the University of Wisconsin established minimum salaries for positions in which large percentages of women had been employed at below average salaries.

The second successful program was at the University of Maine. Facilitated by a $900,000 appropriation for salary improvements allocated by its Board of Trustees, Maine adopted a two-phase program. First, minimal salaries were established for all ranks, and salaries falling below the rank minimum were raised to those levels. Although some male faculty received raises in this first stage, the most dramatic salary increases were awarded to women who had been greatly underpaid. Over $300,000 were awarded to faculty at this stage.

In the second phase of the program, inequities between male and female faculty were identified and corrected. Each department chairperson was responsible for reviewing the status and salary of all women academic staff members and nonfaculty professionals. Salary differences by sex that were not eliminated had to be justified in a written report to the president's office. In order to insure that equity adjustments were not regarded as a substitute for merit increases, each case was given a two-step review: the proper salary level for the individual (relative to male counterparts) was established, and a merit review was undertaken, using the adjusted salary as the base for a merit increase.

A third type of salary equalization program was instituted at the University of Southern Florida. This program, which also uses university funds, used a matching process to identify and correct inequities. The chairperson of each department was charged with locating a male counterpart for each female faculty member. The choice of a counterpart had to be agreed upon by both the woman under review and the chairperson. If an agreed-upon counterpart was identified, any difference in salary between the two was assumed to be the result of discrimination, and equity was restored. Where no counterpart was available, the woman's salary was compared with the average salary of men of comparable rank, experience, length of service, and academic qualifications (including teaching, research, and service) in the department. Any differences found between the woman's salary and the average salary of men were assumed to be the result of discrimination, and were changed accordingly. If there was reason to believe that salary differences were based on rank inequities, then rank as well as salary was changed. If department chairpersons were unable to identify an appropriate comparative group of male faculty, the standard of comparison was the salary offered a recruit with similar qualifications.

Where disagreement existed between the woman and the department chairperson, appeals were directed first to a departmental committee on faculty salaries, then to the dean of the college, and finally, to the academic vice-president. Of the affirmative action plans that we have reviewed, the one at the University of Southern Florida is the only one that includes a specific grievance procedure for disputes on salary.

4. Programs to Achieve Equity in Rank and Promotion

Salary and rank are closely linked. Inequities in salary per se are often minuscule in comparison to salary inequities that result from inequities in rank and promotion. As Astin and Bayer have demonstrated, women have been required to have higher qualifications for promotion than men and typically have remained at each faculty rank longer than their male colleagues (see Chapter Fifteen). To correct this situation, procedures should be established to review the rank of all women faculty, and to recommend promotions of those who have been victims of rank inequity. In addition, all future decisions concerning rank and promotion should be handled in a way to insure the elimination of sex–discriminatory processes.

In reviewing the rank distribution of current faculty and the departmental standards and procedures for promotion the following points should be covered:

(a) *A department should state its standards for promotion to each faculty rank by specifying the relative weight it will give to teaching, publication, research, service, administration, and length of service.* Criteria for tenure should also be specified.

(b) *A department should examine its criteria and procedures for promotion and tenure for possible sex bias.*

(c) *The rank of each woman faculty member should be reviewed.* Rank equity may be evaluated in two ways. First, one can compare the rank of women and men of the same "academic age" (that is, those who received their doctorates in the same year) within a department. In departments too small for such a comparison it is more useful to examine promotion rates by computing the average number of years that women and men have spent in each professorial rank. By this method, the promotion rate of a female faculty member would be compared with the average promotion rate for male faculty in the same department.

(d) *If a department feels that a lower rank for a woman is justified, it should submit a written report stating its reasons.* Acceptable reasons for a rank discrepancy should be based on departmental standards and might include an absence from professional work, or a lack of comparable scholarly productivity. The judgment of scholarly contribution often is complicated. In response to charges that their evaluation of the written work of women faculty is subjective and biased, some departments have considered instituting a *quantitative* system of evaluating "professional contribution." Such a system would devise quantitative standards for the number of books or articles required for promotion. Articles published in professional journals have already received assessment of their merit through editorial board review, which is therefore free of possible personalistic criteria when department members assess a colleague's work. Other checks on subjective evaluations would be to ask for an outside reading of a candidate's scholarly work, or to solicit letters of evaluation from leading scholars in the field, a pattern followed at many prestigious universities for many years.

(e) *When a department submits a justification for rank differences between women and men, it might also submit an analysis of the causes of the difference and, where appropriate, an action program for eliminating the causes.* If, let us say, a department justifies a rank differential on the grounds that a woman has published less than men of comparable academic age and university service, it should examine the reasons for the woman's lower productivity. If, for example, the department has given the woman a heavier teaching load or less research assistance in the past, then compensatory steps, such as increased research assistance, may be taken as part of the department's action program.

(f) *Women should be involved in every stage of the analysis of rank equity.* This includes determinations of departmental standards, analysis of rank differentials and their causes, decisions to recommend or not to recommend a promotion, and the recommendations concerning action program. In addition, women should be involved in every phase of decisions to grant tenure or promotion to women and men faculty.

(g) *Consideration for tenure appointments should not be restricted to persons currently employed in junior faculty ranks at that institution.* Such a restriction might perpetuate past discriminatory appointments. Although most college departments do not use national search procedures in tenure reviews, it might be advisable for them to adopt this practice for it would increase their acquaintance with women candidates whom they might not have otherwise contacted. National searches in tenure reviews are more common in large universities and could easily be expanded to seek out women candidates who might be more qualified than the incumbent for a tenure position.

Decisions on rank equity, tenure, and promotion begin with departmental recommendations and review of these decisions on a college or university level is crucial. All department personnel decisions should require the approval of the affirmative action provost, and affirmative action dean or a special faculty committee appointed to review departmental decisions with regard to affirmative action goals and regulations.

5. Programs to Achieve Equity in Conditions of Employment

In our review of OFCC regulations we noted that the utilization analysis required of each department included a comparison of the conditions of employment for male and female faculty. Employment conditions include teaching load, research facilities, research and teaching assistance, office space, secretarial assistance, and teaching assignments. They also include the type of faculty appointment and the opportunities and procedures for promotion just discussed.

A review might begin with a comparison of teaching conditions of male and female faculty over the past few years, examining the relative number of courses taught, the size of the classes, the number of graduate seminars taught, the hours the classes met, and the amount of teaching assistance received per size of course. If differences by sex are found, affirmative action may be warranted. For example, HEW's review at the University of Massachusetts included suggestions for reducing the teaching load of several women faculty members to the average load for men faculty, or redistributing the teaching load in specific departments.

Departments might establish two kinds of action programs. First, they could specify their standards and procedures for teaching assignments, and insure that these are applied equitably in the future. Second, they could establish compensatory programs to give women faculty who have suffered past discriminatory assignments a temporary priority in the assignment of classes and teaching load.

Departments should also consider conditions of employment with respect to research. They can compare the research assistants, research facilities, equipment, computer time, and the financial support for research that have been afforded women and men faculty. For example, the lack of comparable laboratory space and equipment for women faculty in the biological sciences was specifically noted in HEW's review of Rutgers University at Newark. Another area worthy of examination is the allocation of secretarial assistance among faculty. One often hears women faculty complain that their male colleagues seem to have priority in having their work typed or their course assignments prepared. Where such priorities are found, departments should take the necessary steps to correct this by establishing standards of priority (for example, preparation of course work should come before individual research papers) and insuring their implementation.

Responsibilities of faculty, such as serving on department committees, advising students, and supervising dissertations, should also be reviewed and divided equitably. Compensation for past misallocation of work may also be appropriate. For example, if a single woman faculty member has been carrying 50 percent of the undergraduate advisory responsibilities in a department, undergraduate advisees might be redistributed among men faculty and the woman given a temporary "leave" from this responsibility. In each of these areas, compensation should not be confused with reward. If a woman is compensated for past inequities by receiving a light teaching load, she should not then be saddled with advising because she has "more free time."

Although inequities in employment conditions may be corrected on the departmental level, it is clear that some of the compensatory programs would require universitywide support. Two kinds of action programs might be implemented on a college or university level. One program might be directed toward increasing research support for faculty women by giving them priority in obtaining faculty research funds. Some universities now give priority to junior faculty who otherwise would have more difficulty in obtaining outside research support. An ideal program would require only a simple application procedure, and funds awarded within a few weeks for research assistance, equipment and supplies, clerical assistance, and computer time. Such a program would greatly facilitate research by women faculty and would have a direct effect on their "productivity." Because women traditionally have obtained fewer grants from government and private sources, a side effect of this program might be to demonstrate that they are good "grant risks." The recently instituted "Provost's Development Fund" at the University of Pittsburgh is similar to the program we have suggested. This fund provides women and minority members with financial support to complete research projects (including preparation of findings for publication), or a degree program (including support of dissertation research for graduate students).

A second action program might be directed toward compensating women faculty who have carried unusually heavy or undesirable teaching loads in the past. (An undesirable teaching load might include anything from teaching at inconvenient hours to teaching courses outside of one's major areas of interest.) This program would provide for paid leaves from teaching obligations. Such leaves would be especially welcome to women who have devoted most of their time to teaching and would now appreciate having time for their research or writing. The woman could remain on campus, and fulfill other departmental obligations. Naturally, this type of leave would not be counted as a sabbatical. If the leaves are used for research (in contrast to writing) this program could be combined with the research support program to maximize productivity. The regents of the University of California are currently considering a plan to allow women and minority faculty who are coming up for promotion a paid semester without teaching obligations so that they may devote themselves to research and publication.

Either of these programs could be combined with summer support. In compensation women faculty could be given special grants for research, writing, assistants, or intensive study during the summer.

One of the most important universitywide programs for faculty women is the provision for *part-time faculty appointments* on the regular tenure ladder. A part-time faculty member normally would carry half of the regular teaching load, but would be considered a regular member of the department with full faculty privileges. She or he would serve on departmental committees, have a proportional share of departmental responsibilities and student advisees, and would receive prorated benefits (such as salary, medical coverage, retirement benefits, sabbatical leave). As first instituted at Princeton, part-time ladder faculty are allowed a proportionately longer period of time before review for tenure. Harvard, Princeton, Wisconsin, Stanford, and the University of California at Berkeley have established provisions for part-time ladder appointments. Harvard, Princeton, and Stanford have also revised their tenure rules so that part-time faculty are allowed delayed tenure reviews and can ascend the tenure ladder to the rank of full professor. These part-time appointments may be particularly suited to the needs of parents with small children. Such positions provide the department with a broader range of faculty specialties and may serve to increase the range of courses a department can offer.

6. Programs to Achieve Equity in Fringe Benefits

Universities and colleges are required by law to provide women and men with equal benefits of employment. Benefits that are directly related to work include sabbaticals, travel to professional meetings, faculty fellowships, summer salaries, and research grants. Since we have already reviewed many of these benefits, we simply reiterate that departments and schools should examine the distribution of benefits among women and men faculty, and take whatever steps are necessary to insure that they are awarded equitably.

Employment benefits that are not directly related to work include health and life insurance, retirement programs, and day-care. With regard to health care, the same type of coverage should be offered to all employees. Women should be accorded coverage for spouses and dependents if this is accorded to men employees. Policies for disabilities and leaves, including maternity and parental leaves, must also be equal. The University of Vermont has an extensive plan for both maternity leave and disability leave. All health plans should include coverage for gynecological and obstetrical services. Some schools may provide these services as part of a university health service while others may include such coverage in the medical plans to which they subscribe. Yale University, which has one of the best plans for health and maternity coverage, allows a faculty woman her choice of these options. Many of the action programs we have reviewed in this area are excellent, and cover birth control information, abortion, and full maternity services. For example, Catonsville (Maryland) Community College has initiated a wide variety of services for women including family planning, venereal disease and pregnancy testing, cancer prevention, and infertility counseling.

Women should be allowed maternity leave, and the right to return to their job (or a job of like status and pay) after maternity leave. Optional extended leave, without pay, should also be provided. Some schools, such as Princeton and Stanford, extend faculty women's contracts and postpone tenure decisions one year for each year taken off for childbearing and/or rearing, up to two years. These benefits could easily be extended to male faculty willing to assume equal responsibility for child rearing. The University of Maine has instituted a program of granting both women and men faculty leave for child-rearing purposes for periods up to two years.

Retirement plans for women must also be equal to those for men: in regard to age at which one can retire, payment schedules, and support for a surviving spouse.

Day care which is suggested in OFCC regulations, is an important fringe benefit for many faculty women because it often has a direct effect on their professional activities and contributions. To show good faith efforts, a college or university might institute several alternative provisions for day care. For schools with limited funds and resources, a voucher system might be most useful. This would allow faculty to purchase the type of child care arrangement they want with financial assistance from the school. This type of program has been established at the Ford Foundation in New York with a sliding scale of payments linked to family income. Michigan State University, the Universities of Michigan, Pittsburgh, and California at Berkeley have included university-sponsored day-care in their affirmative action programs. Ideally, child care could be available twenty-four hours a day on a sliding scale fee basis. It is essential that faculty parents have child care services available beyond the usual nine-to-five workday. Some schools have already established 8 A.M. to 8 P.M. child-care facilities. Others are working toward a separate overnight facility for children. The existence of twenty-four hour child care does not imply that university women will drop their children off for days at a time. It does, however, provide the flexibility needed to give adequate child-care coverage for those whose study or work often extends into the evening hours or takes them away from the community to attend professional meetings.

In addition to the fringe benefits we have reviewed, faculty may be provided with meals, housing, transportation, or recreational opportunities and facilities. Each institution should examine the full range of fringe benefits available to their faculty to make sure that they contain no inequality. For example, HEW's report of findings to Brown University indicated that such fringe benefits as moving expenses for new faculty, and housing and maid service for administrators, were granted to men more often than to women staff members.

7. Programs to Achieve Equity in the Training of Future Women Faculty

The most direct and profitable way a university can expend time and money to increase the number of women available for faculty positions is to insure the equal training of women graduate students. A full discussion of the situation of women graduate students is beyond the scope of this chapter, but a few examples of affirmative action plans for graduate students suggest the direction they might take:

(a) *A college, university, or department should actively recruit female graduate students.*

(b) *Age restrictions for admissions to graduate school should be reconsidered* and the admission of older women who have taken time out for child-rearing could be encouraged.

(c) *Special efforts can be made to locate, readmit, and assist financially, women who have completed everything but their dissertations.*

(d) *All admissions quotas should be abolished, with students admitted on a merit basis only.* Medical and law schools are in particular need of improvement in this regard.

(e) *A university should ensure the elimination of sex bias in the granting of fellowships, teaching or research assistantships, and other forms of financial aid awarded to graduate students.* Age restrictions for these awards should also be abolished.

(f) *The university might provide for part-time study and part-time financial support for women and men with family responsibilities that preclude full-time study.*

(g) *Departments should insure that there is no sex bias in the dissertation support and guidance given to women and men graduate students.*

(h) *Departments might give more assistance to their women doctorates in obtaining employment.*

One especially extensive program for women graduate students is provided by M.I.T. Women graduate students are actively recruited, supported, and some are guaranteed assistant professor positions in the department when they finish their doctorates.

8. Other Action Programs to Achieve Equity for Academic Women

The wide range of programs and activities within a university has the cumulative effect of making faculty women feel either very welcome or totally excluded from the university community. We offer a few suggestions for improving the overall position of women in the academic community. The college or university might take action to provide for:

(a) *Representation of women in crucial decision-making positions throughout the university.* In addition to reviewing the representation of women at all levels in the university administration, the provost might appoint a special committee to review the representation of women in decision-making positions throughout the university (e.g. on the board of trustees, the budget committee, the educational policy committee, and so on).

(b) *Support for women's programs and activities.* Examples are a woman's center, lectures by academic and professional women, a film series on women, women's athletic programs, guidance and career counseling, or a women's newsletter. The affirmative action provost might further review the representation of women throughout the university community, in considering the recognition accorded women as commencement speakers, as recipients of honorary degrees at commencement, as invited public university lecturers, and as the president's or dean's representative at outside functions.

(c) *A woman's studies program and the institution of courses and research on women.* Both women faculty and students should be afforded the opportunity to study their own history, biology, psychology, sociology, art, literature. The existence of courses and seminars on women will provide added stimulus to faculty research in these areas and may provide both women and men faculty with new analytic tools (see Chapter Seventeen). Historical and current library materials on women, and other research supports should be provided when possible.

(d) *An ombudsman for women.* The duties of an ombudsman are usually flexible, and the person is empowered to do whatever is necessary to assist in resolving individual complaints. An ombudsman for women might assist in individual complaints of sex discrimination by attempting to resolve the case informally through negotiation with department chairpersons and faculty, or she might represent the complainant in a grievance committee hearing. The ombudsman also might handle requests by individual women for assistance in other areas, such as obtaining health care insurance, arranging a sabbatical year abroad, obtaining research facilities, securing day-care assistance, and so on. The university ombudsman at Cornell University provides a model for this position. There the ombudsman is appointed for a term of five years so that she or he will be relatively free of administrative and faculty pressures. The ombudsman typically is allowed access to confidential records and information, and is accorded a "privileged" status within the university hierarchy.

9. Action Programs to Insure Faculty Members a Means of Appeal of Department Decisions

An essential component of any action program is the establishment of internal grievance procedures. Such procedures should provide for an impartial review of individual complaints of sex discrimination, as well as for a review of general complaints about the implementation of the affirmative action program. Procedures should be adequate to deal with complaints about recruitment, selection, hiring, salary, rank, promotion, tenure, and termination decisions. The University of Hawaii and Michigan State University have developed excellent internal grievance procedures (see Chapter Eighteen for further discussion of grievance procedures).

10. Action Programs for Reviewing and Sanctioning Affirmative Action Progress

As noted earlier, OFCC requires that departments submit periodic reports of their progress in meeting affirmative action goals. In addition, departments may have to demonstrate "good faith efforts" by providing documentation to show that they have followed the procedures outlined in their action program.

Two means of reviewing departmental progress were suggested: biannual departmental reports to allow a review of intended personnel decisions before they are approved; and provisions for the review of *all* departmental personnel decisions at the time they are recommended before a department can make an offer of an appointment. Such a review might be conducted by the affirmative action provost, the affirmative action dean of the college, or a special faculty committee with adequate representation of women. This type of review of all personnel decisions is now required at Columbia University, Brown University, Northwestern University, and the University of California at Berkeley. At Columbia, for example, the signature of the vice-president for academic affairs is required before a department can make an offer of an appointment. At Brown University the review begins even earlier, as all vacancies and recruitment aims must be filed with the affirmative action office which monitors departmental progress in filling each position.

A review of departmental decisions and progress is an essential part of any action program. It serves to demonstrate good faith efforts on the part of the university in monitoring the effectiveness of its program. In addition, it allows the administration to sanction compliance and noncompliance with the affirmative action goals. Compliance does not depend on attaining the goals of an affirmative action program, but rests on documented evidence of good faith efforts. Here we wish to suggest how universities might cope with departments that neither achieved their affirmative action goals nor documented that they made good faith efforts to do so.

The first step in dealing with such departments would focus on negotiation and persuasion, through special meetings with the chairpersons and faculty to assist them in improving their action program, and strengthening their commitment to affirmative action goals. The OFCC regulations do not specify what steps might be taken if negotiation and persuasion do not work; they only specify that other recommendations should be provided. This is of critical importance, however, since without concrete sanctions to enforce an affirmative action program, the plan becomes a series of hollow promises. Good faith efforts on the part of a college or university mean that the institution will do everything possible to insure compliance with its action program.

Although it is theoretically possible to distinguish between negative and positive sanctions and to assert that positive sanctions are always preferable to negative ones, in practice it is often difficult to make the distinction. For example, in a tight economic situation departments may be asked to cut operating costs by 15 percent. As a positive sanction, departments that filled or exceeded their affirmative action goals could be allowed their previous operating budgets. This same option could be seen as a negative sanction by those departments *not* meeting affirmative action goals, who become subject to a 15 percent cut in operating cost. This type of sanction is in operation on at least two campuses. San Diego State College has stated that if departments fail to make progress in meeting goals, a review will be made of budgetary allocations; Southern Illinois University has stated that a freeze may be placed on hiring in non-compliant departments. Other schools, such as the University of Minnesota, have instituted nonfinancial sanctions such as subjecting all departmental personnel decisions to intensive review by a central administrative body.

To insure compliance with affirmative action goals, a school might consider the following positive and negative sanctions:

(a) *Publicizing departmental success or failure in meeting goals in periodic reports in the campus newspaper, and alumni bulletins.*

(b) *Providing special funds to departments for affirmative action hiring.*

(c) *Rewarding departments by allowing them to retain the ladder positions given to them for affirmative action hiring.* (However, if a position is not continuously filled by affirmative action hiring, it might revert back to the affirmative action provost for reallocation to another department.)

(d) *Linking increases and decreases in departmental operating budgets to progress in meeting affirmative action goals.*

(e) *Linking all faculty appointments to affirmative action progress.* A department that has not met its affirmative action goals or documented good-faith efforts might not be allowed to hire any new faculty until it meets its affirmative action goals.

(f) *Instituting a strict review of all departmental decisions in problem departments.* At the University of Minnesota,

> if a unit of the university fails to correct existing inequities in regard to women and is unable to demonstrate that the reasons for failure are beyond its control, all of its personnel decisions become subject to college-level or central administrative review until such time as the unit appears capable of eliminating discrimination by itself.

(g) *Linking university travel funds to affirmative action progress.* Travel allowances for members of departments that have not met affirmative action goals might be limited. (An exception would be travel for recruitment purposes.) If there are sufficient funds, members of compliant departments might be allowed two scientific meetings a year (instead of only one) or other increased travel support.

(h) *Linking salary and merit increases to affirmative action progress so that salary increases or merit increases might not be granted in departments that have not met affirmative action goals, especially those for salary equity.*

(i) *Linking budget decisions on the expansion and contraction of departments to affirmative action progress.*

(j) *Linking university research grants to departments' affirmative action progress.*

(k) *Linking university approval of outside grant applications to affirmative action progress.*

(l) *Recommending that a department chairperson be replaced by a new chairperson more sympathetic to affirmative action.*

The extent to which individual faculty members of a department should be penalized for the failure of a department as a whole to meet affirmative action goals is a difficult issue. However, we believe that all departmental faculty should share the responsibility for affirmative action. By instituting individual as well as collective sanctions for the goals, the chances of insuring commitment of all faculty are maximized. It is important to structure the situation so that individuals as well as departments are rewarded for meeting affirmative action goals, and so that those who remain in opposition to the goals will most probably lose their power in a department, or be isolated by their departmental colleagues as deviants. This kind of structure contrasts sharply with the current situation in most departments in which a faculty minority can greatly retard and hamper a majority committed to affirmative action. Because academic decisions often require consensus for new faculty hiring (or, in many cases, give all senior faculty veto power), a recalcitrant minority may make affirmative action hiring impossible. Only when those who are opposed to affirmative action are penalized will discriminatory practices cease to exist. Without sanctions affirmative action plans remain paper tigers; with sanctions, they are turned into forceful directives for necessary social change.

CONCLUDING REMARKS

Until recently the Executive Order and its requirements for affirmative action provided the only legal basis for combating sex discrimination in academe. Legislative changes have, however, provided academic women with a different set of legal options for the future. It thus may be useful to briefly note the direction of current legislation that may provide additional or supplementary tools to rid academe of sex discrimination.

Title VII of the Civil Rights Act of 1964 was amended by the Equal Employment Opportunity Act of 1972 to include professional employees and employees of state and local governments. Thus faculty women in both public and private educational institutions are now covered by the powerful compliance provisions of Title VII. Title VII is enforced by the Equal Employment Opportunities Commission (EEOC), which has the power to review individual and class complaints of sex discrimination, issue findings, grant injunctive relief, and seek a court order to enforce its decisions.

Two examples of recent court decisions on Title VII cases indicate the broad range of protection that is now available to academic women. In *Weeks* v. *Southern Bell* the court ordered Southern Bell to pay Lorena Weeks more than $30,000 in back pay to compensate for a promotion that she had been illegally denied. This sum represented back pay with interest, including the overtime pay earned by the man promoted to the job that Weeks had been denied (East 1971:2). In a second Title VII case, the court ruled that men at Libby-Owens-Ford Company, who had been hired by a process that discriminated against women, had to be replaced by women. These and many other Title VII decisions in industry have established strong legal precedents for future cases involving academic women.

Even where similar rulings should be expected under Order No. 4, as in the case of back pay, individual victims of sex discrimination will probably obtain more effective enforcement of the law through complaints to EEOC. This is because Order No. 4, like other regulations issued under the Executive Order, is enforced through an examination of institutional patterns of compliance, rather than through attention to specific areas (such as salary) or individual complaints. Thus an individual complaint under Order No. 4 is likely to be incorporated into a compliance review, which is a time consuming examination of all institutional patterns that is typical of most university reviews. Although several suits are currently asserting an individual right to sue a university in federal court (under the Executive Order) there has not yet been a favorable ruling on this.[3] In contrast, a complaint to EEOC will result in a review of the individual case and the specific concern (e.g., of back pay). Since its establishment in 1965, EEOC has concentrated on individual complaints and specific discriminatory policies (although it will also handle class action complaints).

In addition to responding to complaints, the EEOC has issued several sets of forceful policy guidelines outlining prohibited employment practices. The most recent, entitled "Guidelines on Discrimination Because of Sex" (EEOC 1972), included the strongest policies on pregnancy and fringe benefits to be issued by any

---

[3] One suit was filed against the University of Pittsburgh in Federal District Court in August 1971. The second suit was filed against the University of California at Berkeley in Federal District Court in February 1972. Both suits assert a right to individual and class action suits under the Executive Order, and seek injunctive relief against specific discriminatory practices of the universities involved, reinstatement of individual plaintiffs and a court-ordered affirmative action program. In contrast to this type of sanction, a complaint to HEW, if successful, could possibly result in the termination of federal contracts to the university.

enforcement agency to date. These new EEOC guidelines prohibit discrimination in hiring or employment practices based on pregnancy, and require that pregnancy and maternity leave be treated like any other "temporary disability" in the granting of leave, the duration of leave, availability of extensions, seniority, reinstatement, pay during leave, and medical benefits provided. The new EEOC guidelines on fringe benefits are equally stringent in prohibiting any differences in benefits to women and men employees, or to the spouses of women and men employees. In addition, the guidelines state that the greater cost of providing benefits for members of one sex will not be allowed as a defense by an employer. Thus, these EEOC guidelines provide even stronger directions to educational institutions in formulating nondiscriminatory policies in this area than those issued by OFCC or HEW.

The New Higher Education Act and the Comprehensive Health Manpower Training Act of 1971 will also effect educational policy, especially admissions policies in graduate and professional schools. Both Acts prohibit discriminatory admission policies (and therefore related practices such as the awarding of scholarships, fellowships, and assistantships) in institutions receiving federal funds. Thus government grants, loans, research funds, subsidies, and contracts will be given only to schools which affirm and demonstrate nondiscriminatory admissions policies.

A second recent legislative change will provide an additional avenue for combating sex discrimination in academe. The Education Amendments Act of 1972 amended the Equal Pay Act of 1963 to cover executive, administrative, and professional employees. Thus for the first time the Equal Pay Act covers professional employees in higher education. The Equal Pay Act is enforced by the Wage and Hour Division of the Employment Standards Administration of the Department of Labor. The enforcement of this act has resulted in orders for a total of 35.6 million dollars in back pay since it went into effect in June 1964 (East 1971). This figure represents back pay to nearly 88,000 employees, most of whom were women. Complaints under the Equal Pay Act have the advantage of relatively swift resolution (because of the comparatively large compliance staff) and of anonymity for the complainant. A person who files a complaint does not have her or his name revealed to the employer, as the investigation is conducted for all employees in that job category. This will help to eliminate the threat of reprisals against individual women faculty who file complaints of sex discrimination. Reprisals or the threat of reprisals against women who complain of sex discrimination have prevented some complaints in the past, and is currently at issue in the suit of *Braden* v. *University of Pittsburgh.*[4]

[4] According to Sylvia Roberts, Ina Braden's attorney, Braden was active in the faculty women's group that compiled evidence against the University of Pittsburgh and filed the sex discrimination complaint with HEW. It was only after Braden had been identified as a leader of the women's group, and a vocal opponent of sex discrimination, that her contract was terminated. The suit charges the University of Pittsburgh with denying Dr. Braden "her exercise of free speech by their reprisals for her action." It further charges that the university has harrassed the plaintiff and dismissed her from her university position because she spoke out against the university (Personal communication, March 1972).

Finally, the position of academic women will be affected by the passage of the Equal Rights Amendment to the United States Constitution. By declaring that "equality of rights under the law shall not be denied or abridged by the United States or by any State on account of sex" the amendment will marshal the full weight of the law toward eliminating sex discrimination in academe. Until now the Supreme Court has refused to consider sex discrimination in academe a violation of constitutional equality for women, but with the new constitutional amendment women can expect increased support in federal court and from the Supreme Court itself.

Thus, in the future, academic women seeking recourse for sex discrimination will find their options greatly increased, and the legal support for their grievances both broader and stronger. However, it is important to note the crucial difference between the most effective remedy for an individual complaint, and the most effective methods for creating institutional change. While the options for individual grievants will increase, women as a collectivity will continue to derive the most benefit from changes in basic institutional patterns of admission and employment and thus from affirmative action in these areas.

In sum, affirmative action will remain a crucial legal remedy for academic women, because it is the only remedy that is oriented toward changing institutional structures. It is change on this fundamental level, on every college campus, that will eliminate institutionalized sex discrimination in academe.

REFERENCES

East, Catherine. October 1971. What the government will require. Washington, D.C.: The Citizens Advisory Council on the Status of Women. Mimeographed.

Equal Employment Opportunities Commission. April 5, 1972. Guidelines on discrimination because of sex. *Federal Register,* 37(6835).

Office of Federal Contract Compliance, U.S. Department of Labor. June 9, 1970. Sex discrimination guidelines. *Federal Register,* 35(111).

Office of Federal Contract Compliance, U.S. Department of Labor. October 2, 1971a. Employee testing and other selection procedures. *Federal Register,* 36(192).

Office of Federal Contract Compliance, U.S. Department of Labor. December 4, 1971b. Affirmative action programs (commonly referred to as Order No. 4). *Federal Register,* 36(234).

Pottinger, J. Stanley. May 1, 1972. Goals yes, quotas no. *Women Today,* 2(9):2.

United States Department of Health, Education and Welfare. October 1, 1972. Higher Education Guidelines (for Executive Order 11246).

Chapter Twenty-One

Summary and Prospects

Alice S. Rossi

A SUMMARY chapter to a volume that reviews many facets of a topic in depth must, of necessity, be highly selective. This summary will emphasize the highlights of the preceding review chapters on research and political action, particularly those with important policy implications, and will explore the potential impact of present economic and political circumstances in higher education on the efforts now underway to rectify sex discrimination in academe.

Four specific topics will be covered, drawing predominantly on the chapters indicated in brackets: (1) a brief overview of the political revolt of academic women during the past five years and the direction this movement may take in the coming years [Chapters One, Sixteen, Seventeen, and Nineteen]; (2) an overview of the major research findings on differences between women and men students in higher education [Chapters Two, Three, Four, Eleven, and Thirteen]; (3) a summary of the major results of research on the career development and status of women faculty compared to that of men [Chapters Seven through Fifteen]; and (4) a discussion of the current economic and political scene in academe as it bears upon the future status of academic women [Chapters Eighteen, Nineteen, and Twenty].

POLITICAL REVOLT OF ACADEMIC WOMEN

Klotzburger has traced the history of academic feminist activism from 1968, when the first organizing of women took place in higher education, to the present (Chapter Sixteen). There have been three major arenas of feminist activity among academic women during the past five years. The earliest was the *professional association,* as activist caucuses and then advisory committees and commissions were established to conduct studies and make recommendations aimed at the improvement of women's position in the associations and disciplines themselves. If academic disciplines were ranked on a continuum from radical to conservative, a flow-chart of feminism as it rippled through academic disciplines could be approximated. The pioneer activists in 1968 were in disciplines known for liberal-to-radical political orientations for more than a decade—sociology, political science, psychology, and literature. Over the past five years, activism has rippled out into other humanities, history, mathematics, and the sciences. More recently, organized efforts by women have surfaced in such professional fields as law, medicine, education, library science, and the more conservative disciplines of economics and philosophy. As Klotzburger has shown, the early discipline-based groups tended to be of the political activist sort, whose resolutions to the professional associations led to the establishment of advisory bodies; the more recently formed groups bypassed the activist caucus stage and immediately established advisory bodies to investigate the status of women in their disciplines and professions.

A similar sequence was exhibited in the second arena of academic feminist activism: *the institutional context*. The first feminist groups were formed at those prestigious universities with the greatest degree of political activism and student unrest—Columbia, Berkeley, Harvard, and Chicago, followed by the elite four-year private colleges, then four-year state and two-year community colleges. In the early stage of institutionally-based activity, organizations took the form of departmental women's caucuses, like those formed in political science and sociology at the Los Angeles and Berkeley campuses of the University of California; or they took the form of cross-disciplinary coalitions, the purpose of which was to file individual or class action complaints of sex discrimination with the Office for Civil Rights of HEW. In the past year or so, these groups have been supplemented by coalitions of women students, employees, and faculty members pressing for affirmative action plans or the monitoring of existing affirmative action plans.

The third arena of activism has been the *classroom* itself, where academic women have begun to reassess the assumptions of their disciplines concerning sex roles. The women's liberation movement is essentially a teaching movement, and participation in consciousness-raising groups by women students and faculty members quite naturally led them to a critique of the academic curriculum. Before long there were demands for new courses on the psychology and sociology of women, and on the role of women in politics, history, art, and literature. As Howe and Ahlum have shown, the early women's studies courses typically were cross-disciplinary and team-taught, while more recently courses have concentrated on in-depth explorations of the significance of sex roles in the analysis of traditionally-defined inquiries (Chapter Seventeen). The same ripple-out process we noted in the emergence of activism in professional associations has occurred in the subject areas in which women's studies courses have developed. The fields in which activism first developed in the professional associations are the same disciplines in which women's studies courses were first offered. We might well expect an increasing number of such courses to develop over the next few years in disciplines only now initiating political activity: law, medicine, economics, business, education, and the health professions.

Four years of political activity, research on the status of academic women, and growing numbers of women's studies courses produced the large volume of material reviewed in chapters of this book. Morlock's review of discipline studies is based on thirty studies on the status of women in fourteen academic disciplines; Robinson's review is based on more than 100 reports on the status of women in institutions of higher education; Howe and Ahlum report close to 1,000 courses in women's studies across the nation, and increasing numbers of institutions at which discussions about women's studies programs are underway. Since the summer of 1972, numerous high school courses in women's history or women's movements have been developed. In the fall of 1972, for example, I met with students from a local high school who were working on a project on the treatment of the women's movement by the media. The meeting had been arranged by telephone with their instructor, and to my surprise the students who visited me were young men—students at an all-male Catholic high school in Baltimore taking a course in women's history taught by a male instructor! Another spin-off has been the formation of over 200 local Committee W's in AAUP chapters across the country, and numerous state conferences of AAUP which have helped to bring together local Committee W members from across the state for special meetings on their common problems.

In planning this volume, we were aware that we would be reporting on and summarizing an ever-changing movement. In the years immediately ahead, there will be continued political activity, research, and increasing numbers of women's studies courses and programs. In the view of many academic observers, the movement among academic women has not even crested. Most of the review chapters carry the story of this development only to the summer of 1972. Since then there have been several new developments worth noting. One is the city, state, and regional conferences and organizations which establish intellectual, social, and political ties among academic women that cross discipline and institutional lines. In sociology, for example, SWS members in San Francisco called an area-wide meeting which attracted seventy women sociologists from the Bay area, while a similar meeting in New York City drew 100 women sociologists. Such meetings permit women to share experiences, find other women with similar intellectual and political interests, and facilitate political effectiveness in regional professional societies. In Maryland, a cross-college coalition of feminists sponsored a series of three conferences on women in higher education during the 1972–1973 academic year that drew several hundred academic women from two dozen campuses across the state. Such conferences may stimulate the formation of political coalitions concerned with state legislation that affects women, and informal social networks of potential utility in recruiting women students and staff, as well as in organizing around political and professional issues of concern to academic women in the state. The affirmative action guidelines released by HEW in October 1972 have stimulated the formation of still other locally-based coalitions of women to press for the development of affirmative action plans for their institutions, or to monitor the implementation of existing plans. Private foundations and federal agencies have begun to review their grant and fellowship programs and may well announce new policies of special interest to academic women by the time this book goes to press.

Even more recently, academic women's concerns are affecting the demands of collective bargaining agents representing faculties. This is an important development because collective bargaining carries with it the leverage of a large body of labor law and precedent. Labor law gives the bargaining agent access to accurate information on salaries, titles, job definitions, dates of employment, and other information necessary for estimating the extent of discrimination and the cost of remedying it. Through this route, the Rutgers University Council of AAUP Chapters in New Jersey, representing 3,600 faculty members and graduate assistants, successfully negotiated a procedure for remedying pay discrepancies by sex within rank, and for revising maternity and nepotism policies of the university (Smith 1972). Georgina Smith, a labor economist on the Rutgers faculty and chairman of the bargaining team for the Rutgers Council, reported an interesting change in campus response to women's demands over the course of the first year of bargaining negotiations: in the fall of 1971 the university senate received the preliminary report of its own ad hoc committee on women with smug and humorous comments, but by the end of that academic year, the same senate listened gravely and unanimously accepted far-reaching recommendations regarding the review of salary, promotion procedures, and personnel practices as they affected women.

More importantly, the Rutgers University administration secured a special appropriation from the state legislature to remedy inequities against women and minority group members. Through negotiation with the bargaining agent, the amount was increased from $190,000 to $250,000, a sum arrived at through a multivariate regression analysis of survey data on pay and qualifications which showed an average salary inequity of $500 per woman among the 500 women on the faculty. Paid maternity leave became university policy through the same procedure of negotiation: the university first proposed that *unpaid* leave be available to all pregnant women requesting it, but the Rutgers AAUP bargaining agent successfully won *paid* leave at the bargaining table by pointing out that EEOC guidelines directed that maternity leave be treated for all job-related purposes as a temporary disability, hence warranting paid leave.

The Rutgers experience is an interesting example of the responsiveness of state legislatures to pressure from federal agencies under the threat of termination of federal contracts to state universities. As more and more studies establish the extent of salary inequities by sex and affirmative action plans call for the redress of such inequities, college and university administrators may find far less resistance to special appropriation requests by their state legislatures than they now expect. A quarter of a million dollars for the redress of salary inequities may not seem so high a price to pay when several million dollars of federal support are at stake.

Financial acumen, if not an ethic of justice, may convince many state legislative bodies to follow the New Jersey example.

It is ironic that the institutions at which protest by academic women first began may not be the first institutions to rectify sex discrimination, to accept women's studies programs, or to adopt new policies concerning parental leave or part-time status. In fact, the greatest resistance to affirmative action, redress of salary grievances, and women's studies has been exhibited by the major private universities with the most prestigious graduate and professional schools, while the community colleges and four-year state colleges are becoming the pacesetters in adopting new programs and responding to charges of sex discrimination. By late 1972, many pioneer activist women in major universities felt that little progress had been made, while the latecomer activists on less prestigious campuses were optimistic with the progress being made on their campuses. Why this should be the case is a complex question. It may be that protest typically is initiated in institutions with the most serious patterns of discrimination and the most entrenched assumptions about male leadership and intellectual superiority. Professorships at Harvard, Berkeley, and Chicago carry with them not only intellectual recognition of substantive professional contributions to knowledge but also access to power and prestige that extend far beyond academe itself. Prestige hierarchies are also political dominance hierarchies, and men at the top of these ladders may exclude women from their ranks as detractors from their own prestige and dominance. Men will not explain this in such terms; rather they will indicate willingness to accept women, if only women as "extraordinarily bright, competent, and powerful" as themselves were available. Women students and junior faculty members are more apt to feel unwelcome, put down, or kept out at prestigious universities than at the less prestigious ones. One would expect, then, to find at the most prestigious institutions the greatest amount of sex discrimination and the highest levels of motivation among women to seek change, yet the lowest probability of a quick and easy redress of their grievances because the male leadership will strongly resist such change.

There is some support for this interpretation in studies of field and institutional variations in the status of women. Robinson shows that women fare worst in the most prestigious universities, and Morlock shows that women fare worst in political science and sociology—the same institutions and fields in which the revolt of academic women began. Added to this is the fact that community colleges represent the major growth sector of higher education, and have a tradition of meeting the diverse educational needs of community members. As a result, finances are not nearly so short as in the universities, and consequently male faculty and administrators not nearly so resistant to women's demands. Thus, an English department at an elite institution may object to a new course on "women novelists" because it disturbs the traditional chronological symmetry of its curriculum, while a counterpart department at a community college may view such a course as an appealing means to stimulate the interest of their students in a serious reading of literature.

Precisely because our review has cut into an ongoing process of protest and change in academe, it is difficult to predict the course of events over the next few years. Suffice it to say that a mere five years of political revolt has produced rising expectations among academic women; stimulated research of both theoretical and political significance; instigated a serious reexamination of assumptions concerning gender and sex roles; and sparked a growing number of innovative courses on women that cut across traditional disciplines and provide a focal point for collaboration among academic women. These courses seem, in turn, to have stimulated a remarkable wave of intellectual curiosity and a rising level of aspirations among undergraduate women. A pressing need that undoubtedly will be met during the next few years is research concerning the impact of women's studies courses on the self-confidence and aspirations of women students. Many academic women who are in daily contact with undergraduate students already sense such a change. At Goucher College, for example, we have noted a sharp increase in the number of women seniors applying to law schools and we expect a similar upturn in applications to medical schools within the next few years. We need to know how extensive this change is on a national basis, where it is strongest, and what specific influences have stimulated this increase in young women's aspirations. We do not know how much to attribute to the influence of certain feminist teachers, to women's studies courses, or to publications of a feminist nature that students may be reading quite apart from the college curriculum. It is tempting to attribute a good deal of influence to courses and teachers, since that emphasizes the contribution of feminist women in academe, but it is very likely that a good part of such influence has come from a more free-floating exposure to feminist ideas. While humbling to think that feminists outside academe have more impact on the young than feminists inside academe, this is quite possibly the case, since there are hardly enough academic feminists to have stimulated such a general rise of aspirations among women students. In any event, the issue calls for scientific inquiry.

RESEARCH ON CONTEMPORARY ACADEMIC WOMEN

Research on academic women comes from diverse sources, but is essentially of three types. Under the stimulus of political activists, a great number of institutional and discipline studies on the status of women have been conducted, focused largely on economic and status characteristics of women compared to men: their distribution in the rank structure of a profession or institution, promotion and tenure rates, salary, distribution of work time, and productivity in publications. Data have been gathered either from survey samples of women and men faculty members or institutional records at the departmental or administrative level.

A second type of research includes large national surveys of graduate students or faculty. The best example of this type of research is the 1969 national survey of some 60,000 women and men faculty members which was conducted by the Carnegie Commission on Higher Education in cooperation with the American Council on Education. Properly weighted to correct for sampling and response biases, these data produced national norms for all American college and university teaching faculty. National estimates from these data indicate that 19 percent of all teaching faculty in 1969 were women, 81 percent men. During December 1972, the American Council on Education launched a second national survey of faculty members to supplement the 1969 data and to explore, among other things, whether any significant change has taken place in the status of academic women during the course of the past three years.

The third type of research concerns special cohorts of advanced degree holders, a large proportion of whom are employed by academic institutions. Pioneer studies of this type were conducted by Lindsey Harmon at the National Academy of Sciences, based on the doctorate records file in the Office of Scientific Personnel. This extensive data bank has yielded numerous studies on trends in the fields in which doctorates are earned; which colleges have high proportions of graduates who go on to earn a doctorate; career patterns of doctorate holders; and employment plans of recent doctoral candidates. The most relevant aspects of these studies to the present volume have been reviewed by Astin in Chapter Seven. Other studies of this type include Ginzberg's follow-up study of women who held graduate fellowships at Columbia University between 1945 and 1951 (Ginzberg 1966), and Astin's study of women who earned the doctorate in 1957–1958 (Astin 1969). A major study of this type, to be launched by the Educational Testing Service in 1973, will match 4,000 women and men doctorates by field, institution, and year in which the doctorate was earned.

To cut through the complex set of research data reviewed in the preceding chapters, I shall summarize the findings in respect to women graduate students as distinct from findings regarding women faculty. While the major focus will be on a summary of what has been reported in this volume, new materials will be introduced where they are critical to understanding current trends in higher education as they affect women.

Graduate and Professional Education

Admissions and Stipends. The research on women in graduate education which was reviewed in Chapters Two, Three, and Four do not permit us to draw up a balance sheet that indicates the extent to which women's exclusion from advanced training is the result of sex discrimination as compared to the extent to which their exclusion is self-imposed; that is, the result of sex role socialization that inhibits their aspirations. A review of admissions and stipend policies shows that sex discrimination is greater in law and medical schools than in graduate schools of arts and sciences (Chapter Two). Medical schools have been notoriously guilty of sex discrimination over the years, often with overt sex quotas. Some professional schools have applied what is called an "equal rejection" theory to applicants, publicly known because those who have used it thought it a "fair" procedure. By this device women applicants are separated from men applicants and an equal proportion of applicants in each category is accepted, say 10 percent. But this is implicitly discriminatory because women generally have better academic records than men, and in such traditionally masculine fields as medicine and law only the very best women even apply. Testimony at the 1970 House of Representatives hearings before the Committee on Labor and Education reported that studies of medical school admission policies indicate that the women rejected from their smaller applicant pool were equal to or better than men the schools accepted, and that the women were rejected simply because their sex quota was filled, not because they were unqualified to undertake medical training.

Financial Support. Studies of the financing of graduate training do not support the view that women are discriminated against in the granting of stipends. Slightly more than a third of both women and men graduate students receive stipends from their institutions (Chapter Two). But, as numerous studies of both college and graduate school students have shown, women's academic performance is uniformly superior to that of men. If academic merit is the basis for granting stipend support, one should expect a higher proportion of institutional stipends to be granted to women. That there is no difference between the sexes in the extent of support does not mean, therefore, that no sex discrimination is operant; but we have found no data that permit us to explore this problem further.

The critical difference between the sexes in financial support of graduate studies is the greater tendency for women to rely on parents or spouse for help, and for men to rely on employment. Roby points out that graduate student men have access to better-paying jobs than women, which makes part-time employment more feasible for men. She cautions that we need to know more about the psychology of dependency that may be encouraged in women graduate students who rely on parents and spouses for such support. Roby also notes that the restriction of stipend support to full-time students not only works a special hardship on married women, but reduces the opportunity for both men and women married students to work out more egalitarian relations in coping with home, family, and school responsibilities.

During the past year there has been much discussion about probable cutbacks in federal financing of graduate education with a major shift from stipends to loans. This is bound to work a hardship on women students who are more hesitant than men to borrow against future earnings. With the general level of support declining at the same time women's aspirations are rising, more than ever women graduate students will have to be dependent on parents and spouses for financial aid.

Attrition. The variable that most sharply differentiates the sexes in graduate training is attrition rate, at both the master's and the doctorate levels (Chapter

Four). In psychology, to cite a typical example, one 1970 study showed that 53 percent of the graduate students *seeking* a master's degree were women, but only 38 percent of those *awarded* the master's degree were women; among doctoral students, 35 percent were women, but only 22 percent of the Ph.D.s awarded went to women (Chapter Thirteen). In a study of Woodrow Wilson fellows rated by graduate faculty members as "excellent" students, 32 percent of the men, but 58 percent of the women dropped out of graduate school before completing their degree requirements (Chapter Four).

Poor academic performance is not a likely explanation of the higher attrition rate among women since numerous studies show that women perform better than men both as undergraduate and graduate students. Among the students themselves, men report higher anxiety levels about academic performance than women, while women more often than men cite emotional strain as a consequence of graduate study. Part of the strain graduate women experience may be linked to a lack of social support from members of their own sex, or from their sheer lack of numbers in graduate school. One study in progress conducted by Sells suggests that lack of social support may be related to the sex differential in graduate attrition rates. Sells compared the dropout rate by sex in the Berkeley graduate department of sociology for three years in the early 1960s with the rates for the years 1968 through 1970. She shows that during the years before the women's caucus was formed in the department in 1968, the dropout rate of men was 53 percent, and of women 70 percent. For the three years since the formation of the caucus, the dropout rate of men has been 36 percent, and of women 33 percent (Sells 1972:20). That the more recent rates are lower may be explained, in part, by the fact that the time interval has not been long enough to permit the full attrition rate to show for the more recent cohorts of entering students. But the fact that the decline in attrition rate wiped out all differences by sex suggests that the women's caucus provided entering women graduate students with easier and more frequent access to the help and support of older women graduate students and women faculty. More generally, the women's movement may have contributed not only to the rise in women's aspirations, but to their ability to cope with the hurdles they face in reaching their goals.

Sexual alliances, real or fancied, between women students and male faculty members are another possible determinant of attrition rate that deserves attention. We do not know to what extent women leave graduate school for fear of developing entangling sexual alliances, because of the disastrous consequences of being involved in such an alliance, or even whether such alliances contribute to or detract from the career advancement of graduate women. A sexual alliance may provide the woman student with an inside track to the politics of a graduate department, or it may provide her with an extra, personalized edge of professional training in her field. On the other hand, such departures from strictly professional mentorship sow the seeds of doubt in the woman that her progress or degree was earned on the grounds of merit and not favoritism. When the times comes for referrals for appointments elsewhere, there is always the possibility that her professor-lover may be reluctant to give a high recommendation even if her work warrants it, either because she would be useful to retain as his professional assistant, because he is not emotionally ready to see her depart, or because high praise might be misinterpreted by his male colleagues at other institutions. If the liaison ends before the woman has obtained her degree, she may hesitate to seek, and he to grant, help in the final stages of her dissertation work and her transition to a professional career.

Short of any research on the topic, sexual alliances can only be viewed as possibly significant factors in the comparatively higher dropout rate of women graduate students. There is no need, however, to wait for the results of such studies before graduate women explore the subject among themselves. They may be able to lend significant help to entering women students in facing not only the academic hurdles of graduate training, but the sexual hurdles as well.

Recruitment Pool for Women Graduate Students and Faculty

A persistent theme throughout this volume has been that academic women have lost rather than gained ground in American higher education in recent decades. We have seen that women earned a smaller proportion of advanced degrees in the early 1960s than they did during the 1930s and early 1940s, and that they represent a smaller proportion of college and university faculties now than they did thirty years ago. What has not been examined in detail are a number of economic and demographic characteristics of the past fifty years which have profoundly affected the size of the undergraduate women pool from which graduate students and faculty members are drawn. Since some of these same characteristics will be relevant in the future, they merit careful review.

From the turn of the century to the beginning of World War II, the proportion of women among bachelors' degree recipients doubled from slightly under 20 percent to a little over 40 percent. The wartime service of men gave women students a temporary numerical edge, and by 1944 they had increased to over 50 percent of all bachelors' degree recipients. This peak was followed by a precipitous decline: in just six years, from 1944 to 1950, women students declined from 50 to 30 percent of all resident college enrollees, and it has taken the past twenty years for the proportion of women among college graduates to reach the 1940 level of 43 percent (Roby 1972).

Two new factors which entered the postwar picture in higher education had a direct impact upon the relative position of women among college and graduate students and, eventually, upon faculty of our colleges and universities. For one, the G.I. Bill gave a decided boost to the educational opportunities of American veterans. Bright young men, who might never have entered, much less completed, college did so and moved on to graduate school to earn advanced degrees. What was a boost for the men put women at a great disadvantage, particularly working and lower class women, since the G.I. Bill simply reinforced the preference parents typically show in more often supporting their sons' than their daughters' educational aspirations, particularly lower middle class and working class parents (Sewell 1971). Secondly, there was a sharply rising infusion of federal money into American graduate education to support research and training in the natural and social sciences, creating stipends and jobs for thousands of additional students and staff members in universities across the country. Since this expansion was greatest in fields with low proportions of women, the overall impact of federal funding was to lower the proportion of women among students, researchers, and faculty members in academe.

Figure 21.1. Proportion of Doctorates Earned by Women, 1920–1969

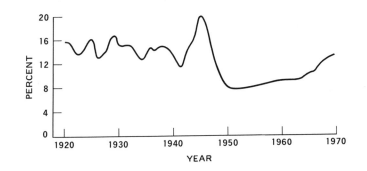

SOURCE: See Chapter Two, Table 2.2.

Figure 21.1 presents a graphic profile of the fifty-year trend in the proportion of women doctorates, an overview of the extent to which women lost ground during these decades. As shown in statistics published by the National Academy of Sciences and the American Council on Education, women earned about 16 percent of the doctorates granted in the United States from 1920 to the beginning of World War II. During World War II women gradually earned an increasing proportion of all advanced degrees granted, reaching a peak of 20.4 percent in 1945. The infusion of federal money in research and training programs was most dramatic in those fields in which women were traditionally underrepresented—the physical and biological sciences and engineering. When returning veterans swelled the ranks of graduate students, and graduate stipends increased in the hard sciences, the proportion of doctorates earned by women declined to a low of 9 percent in 1954. There was little change in the proportion of women earning the Ph.D. from 1954 until the mid-1960s, when a slight upward trend began. Even by 1970, however, women still represented a lower proportion of all doctorates than they had forty years earlier. More men received the Ph.D. in the single year of 1971 than women received during the twenty-year period from 1950 to 1969.

Trend data on the relative position of a group that has always comprised a small minority can be very misleading and any interpretation of their position must also take into account whether their *absolute numbers* have declined as well as their *relative proportion*. Figure 21.2 shows that for the past fifty years there has been a steady increase in the number of women who earned the doctoral degree. It is striking that the number of degrees granted to women continued to climb during the 1950s and 1960s despite the great pressure on women to live in conventional domesticity. What is especially important is that there was a dramatic increase in women's numbers in the late 1960s, that is, *before* academic women became actively concerned about their position in higher education. In other words, political action may escalate a trend but it rarely serves as a primary stimulant.

Figure 21.2. Annual Production of Women Doctorates, 1920–1969

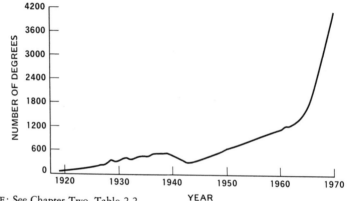

SOURCE: See Chapter Two, Table 2.2.

Table 21.1 presents the trend data on women doctorates in yet a third way by examining the differences between women and men in the proportionate increase by decade in their numbers earning the doctorate. In the 1930s the number of women who earned the doctorate was slightly more than double the number who had earned the degree in the 1920s (an increase of 107 percent), while for men the percentage increase was slightly less (90 percent). As a consequence of the war, the rate of increase slackened for the decade of the 1940s, although the postwar expansion of higher education and veterans' benefits gave an edge to men. The decade increase in the 1950s was 100 percent for women while it reached an all-time high of an 187 percent increase for men. During the 1960s, however, the trend showed a greater rate of increase for women (131 percent) than for men (92 percent).

Some of the historical circumstances that might have affected an increase in

TABLE 21.1. Decade Increase in Production of Doctorates, 1920–1969
(In percentages)

Decade in which Doctorate was Earned	Number of Doctorates		Percentage Increase over Previous Decade		Decade of Birth[a]	Decade of Adolescence[b]
	Women	Men	Women	Men		
1960–1969	18,986	144,959	+131	+91	1930–1939	1946–1954
1950–1959	8,214	75,333	+100	+187	1920–1929	1936–1944
1940–1949	4,101	26,204	+9	+20	1910–1919	1926–1934
1930–1939	3,763	21,823	+107	+90	1900–1909	1916–1924
1920–1929	1,816	11,458			1890–1899	1906–1914

[a] Based on an assumption that the average age when the Ph.D. was earned was 30.
[b] Based on the assumption of the average of the years of birth for each decade cohort (e.g., 1933 as the year of birth for women who earned the Ph.D. between 1960 and 1969), and a definition of adolescence as 12 to 20 years of age.
SOURCE: Computed from data in Chapter Two, Table 2.2.

the number of women who obtained the doctorate during the past thirty years are suggested by reconstructing the periods in which the doctorate earners were born and spent their adolescent years. This requires an assumption that the average age at which the doctorate is earned is 30. The last two columns of Table 21.1 show that women who earned their doctorates in the 1960s were born during the depression years of the 1930s and spent their adolescent years in the postwar period. Since the birth rate was very low during the 1930s, the increase in the number of doctorates earned by women from the 1930s birth cohort is all the more significant. Many of them were reared by women who experienced acute financial difficulties early in their marriages, and undoubtedly many either worked during the war or returned to the labor force in the 1950s when their daughters were adolescents. The message to many of the daughters may have been a warning that women needed job training if they are to cope with fluctuations in the economy and the uncertainties of world circumstances.

The great expansion during the 1950s in the proportion of young people attending college, particularly public institutions, also meant that many vocationally-oriented young women from the lower middle class and working class were the first women in their families to attend college. Once they reached the campus they had an opportunity to expand their occupational aims to more prestigious goals. They did not take college attendance for granted as the proper thing for a young woman to do, as increasing numbers of upper middle class families did in the postwar period. Consequently, their energies might have been concentrated on doing well in their studies. We know from Astin's research on woman doctorates that bright women from less well-off families are overrepresented among high achieving women. Though far smaller in number than their veteran brothers who earned advanced degrees with the help of the G.I. Bill, many bright women from

outside the upper middle class may have seized upon the new opportunities to secure the advanced training that would provide the protection against financial
duress that their mothers had not had when they faced the need to work.

Although Table 21.1 shows an even greater proportionate increase in the number of doctorates earned by women than by men in the 1960s, this did not increase the visibility of women on campuses during the 1960s because of the even
greater expansion of higher education to absorb the postwar baby boom generation
that reached college age in the early 1960s. Male faculty were already in plentiful
supply because of the sharp increase in degree production in the 1950s and these
men were rapidly promoted up the academic hierarchy. Thus, while the sheer number of doctorate women increased during the 1960s, it is not surprising that they
remained in comparatively low visibility positions.

Nevertheless, this increase in women's numbers on campus represented a factor
—what might be called a "social density" threshold—that paved the way for their
political activity in the late 1960s. The Berkeley faculty, for example, more than
doubled between 1951 and 1968, from about 700 to more than 1,600 members. To
be one of, say, three women on a faculty, is very different from being one of thirty
women on a faculty. Among a group of thirty women there is a greater potential
for social interaction and mutual social and emotional support, and this may generate a strong confidence in challenging sex discrimination. Just what the threshold
size of a minority group must be to stimulate such interaction is unknown, although there are precedents which support the importance of the social density
factor itself. It has been found, for example, that black students exhibit higher
retention rates and higher morale at colleges in which they represent more than 10
percent of the student body than at colleges with smaller proportions of black students. Though small as a proportion of the total, an absolute increase in the number
of women students in a graduate department may raise the women's morale and
increase their retention rate in graduate school. A similar increase in the number of
women on the faculty may encourage them to exert political pressure for improvement in the status of women once the political climate is ripe.

The same social density factor may help to explain the early emergence of political action among women in such fields as psychology, sociology, and modern languages, where women were earning at least 20 percent of the advanced degrees.
The science in which women first organized was that of biology, which has the
highest proportion of women of all the sciences. That women first organized at
annual conventions of their professional associations may also reflect the influence
of social density. In their own departments women rarely have more than one or
two, if any, women colleagues. Coming together at an annual convention they
represent a sizable number of women, and such meetings may generate the elements
of confidence and solidarity that stimulate political action.

As noted previously, the proportion of women faculty declined in the last decade.
This is rooted in the fact that a minority always suffers a decline in occupations

undergoing rapid expansion. Hiestand has shown in his studies of changes in the labor force between 1900 and 1960 that any occupation undergoing a sharp rate of expansion draws more heavily upon the majority group in the labor force—white males—than on any minority (Hiestand 1964). Suppose for example, that in the early 1960s, there was a sharp increase in available jobs in a particular scientific specialty. In those years, there were 370 women among every 1,000 college graduates; but only 7 percent of the women who earned bachelor's degrees in the early 1960s majored in *any* science, while 30 percent of the men graduates had such majors. Out of every 1,000 college graduates, then, there were 183 men, but only 23 women science majors to recruit from. A good employment market in one science specialty might motivate those in a related science to shift over, or to remain in the scientific occupation rather than pass on to management or administration. The sheer contrast between the sexes in the potential numerical recruitment base sets the stage for an increasing proportion of a growing specialty to consist of white males. This was the situation a decade ago not only in such traditional masculine fields as science and engineering, but also in fields that traditionally were female in composition. Even when married women were induced to return to teaching during the 1950s, high school teaching from 1950 to 1970 changed from an occupation with a majority of women to one with a male majority.

Academe was a high growth profession during the 1950s and 1960s, and this represented an unparalleled opportunity for white male professionals to obtain academic employment and to experience rapid promotion and higher wages than ever before in the history of higher education. That the proportion of women on college faculties declined during these years reflects, therefore, several processes quite apart from sex discrimination: women lost relative status as an unintended consequence of national policies to compensate veterans for wartime service through educational benefits; more stipends and research assistantships in the sciences meant men graduate students could marry and raise a family before their degrees were completed; and an expanding profession with high status job openings gave an edge to the more geographically mobile male members of the profession.

Looking ahead to the future, this economic and demographic analysis has an important implication. A decrease in the rate of expansion in college enrollment or academic employment does *not* mean necessarily that women will lose ground in terms of status relative to men. In fact, a tightening labor market in academe may lead men to turn from the academic profession toward business and government employment, leaving room for an increase in the proportion of women in academe in the years ahead.

To stress the demographic and economic factors at work over the past several decades that reduced the recruitment pool of academic women does not mean there were no overt and covert attempts to exclude women from entry to the professions. The issue of sex discrimination concerns not simply women's proportionate representation, but the treatment they receive once they join a faculty: their rank distribution, salary, and rate of promotion compared to men. Questions such as these have been reviewed by Robinson, Morlock, Astin and Bayer, and Loeb and Ferber in the central chapters of this volume.

The Career Profile of Women Faculty Members

Several studies examined the career profile of academic women before women began to articulate their criticisms of the way they were being treated in academe. Harmon's studies of doctorates showed that a higher proportion of women than men had exceptionally high aptitude scores in high school and superior academic records in undergraduate and graduate school (Harmon 1965). Astin showed that the same proportion of women as men doctorates received their degrees from the top ten universities (29 percent), that few women doctorates withdrew from the labor force, and when they did so, it was for very short periods of time—an average of fourteen months (Astin 1969 and Chapter Seven).

On the basis of this profile, women doctorates might be expected to exceed men in a range of career characteristics: appointments to universities rather than colleges, more rapid advancement, at least equal pay, and "ladder" rather than peripheral or "permanent temporary" appointments. But as Chapters Seven through Fifteen show, none of these expectations have been fulfilled, for on all such career characteristics women fare worse than men.

The most sophisticated analyses of the differences by sex in academic career profiles are those conducted by Astin and Bayer based on ACE national data on faculty members (Chapter Fifteen), and Loeb and Ferber with University of Illinois faculty data (Chapter Twelve). Both studies conducted regression analyses to ferret out the contribution sex per se made to salary, rank, and promotion, over and above many other variables which were themselves sex-linked. Astin and Bayer found that sex was a better predictor of salary than such factors as numbers of years of professional employment or whether one has the doctorate. Loeb and Ferber found an unstandardized regression coefficient of $846 which they define as the "yearly dollar value of masculinity" at their university. In a review of about 100 institutional reports, Robinson found considerable variation among institutions in the extent to which men's average salaries exceeded women's: the range was from $64 to about $4,000 (see Chapter Eleven). Morlock reports that while women fare better in certain academic disciplines (physics and anthropology, for example) than in others (sociology and political science), in none do they do as well as men (see Chapter Thirteen).

In one of the most interesting analyses conducted for this review, Astin and Bayer compared women's actual and predicted rank and salary levels. They reasoned that by applying the regression weights of predictor variables which emerged in an analysis of men faculty to the data on women faculty, they could establish a minimum estimate of sex discrimination. They found that to award women the same salary as men of similar rank, background, achievement, and work setting would require an average compensatory raise of more than $1,000. Their estimates of the extent of sex discrimination in academe are extremely conservative, since the analysis necessarily accepts all preceding discrimination against women as nonsex-related, and thus underestimates the impact of discriminatory factors which have operated against women since their childhood (Chapter Fifteen).

One further finding, from the Loeb and Ferber study, is of particular interest in respect to the rank distribution of academic women. They found no overall differences between women and men faculty at the University of Illinois in publication productivity when highest degree, date of degree, and years of employment were introduced, but they did find interaction effects between career variables and sex: among young faculty members with recent degrees, women published more than men, while among older faculty, men published more than women. If merit rather than sex determines promotion and salary, it follows that at the early stages of their academic careers, women should be promoted more rapidly than men, but this has not been found in any studies we have examined. Academic women typically spend a longer time than men in each rank before promotion, and consistently earn less than men at all ranks.

Further suggestions that factors other than career or merit considerations affect promotion and salary are illustrated by Astin and Bayer's finding that being married and having children is linked to higher rank and higher salary for men, but not for women. It is possible that marriage and increasing family size may involve greater motivation on the part of men to perform in ways that earn them promotions and salary increases. Married academic women less often carry heavy financial responsibilities, and increased family size may, in fact, curtail their academic productivity. It is also possible, however, that in the male "buddy system," it is socially acceptable for a man to approach his chairman or dean for a salary increase on the grounds of increased family need, while academic women accept the public definitions of their professional role which requires that they act as if they had no financial or family responsibilities at all. The analysis does not permit us to choose between these interpretations, but the findings are sufficiently important and interesting to call for further research on the influence of nonprofessional factors on the status and career development of men. For too long it has been assumed that personal and family circumstances have both theoretical and practical significance for women only. A decade of research on women clearly substantiates the fact that personality, marriage, and family status are indeed determinants of women's career development. But until more research has been conducted on the work and family roles of men, there is little firm evidence to support the observation of many women that family factors affect the work careers of men as well as women.

Remedies for Sex Discrimination

Our review concluded that sex inequities in hiring, salary, rank, fringe benefits, and promotion are pervasive in the academic world. What is being done or could be done to remedy the grievances of academic women has been the focus of the chapters by Rumbarger, Sandler, and Weitzman (Chapters Eighteen through Twenty). The choice of remedy depends on the one hand, on whether the complaint is made on an *individual* or a *class* basis; and secondly, on whether the procedure is *internal* or *external* to the employing institution. A woman may take a complaint of sex inequity in salary through the internal route of discussion with her departmental chairman, academic dean, or affirmative action officer. If this does not settle the matter, she might contact a faculty grievance committee or her local AAUP chapter. Should none of these internal routes succeed, an individual complainant could then try such external routes as filing a complaint with the EEOC, the Wages and Hours Division of the Employment Standards Administration, the discrimination committee of a women's caucus or organization if one exists in her discipline, or Committee A on Academic Freedom and Tenure of the national AAUP.

In contrast, class complaints of sex discrimination assume some coalition of women that cuts across departments or categories of personnel within an institution. Class actions that concentrate on internal procedures for the rectification of sex discrimination grievances might involve a local Committee W of an AAUP chapter, or where the faculty has so opted, a collective bargaining representative of the faculty. Class action through the external route of contract compliance procedures (Chapter Nineteen), and the affirmative action plans they entail (Chapter Twenty) has been a predominant mode of remedy in recent years. These procedures were the only external routes for the redress of sex discrimination until 1972. That academic women have had to use them reflects the basic intransigence and preoccupation with other issues of the academic community. It would not have been necessary for women to use these external routes had there been any recognition of the position of women in academe and a willingness to rectify it internal to academe itself.

Since the spring of 1972, several pieces of federal legislation have broadened the external routes through which academic women can seek redress. In March 1972, Title VII of the Civil Rights Act of 1964 (which forbad sex discrimination in employment, but exempted educational institutions) was extended to cover all public and private educational institutions regardless of whether or not they receive federal aid. In July 1972, an amendment of the Equal Pay Act of 1963 extended the coverage of the act to executive, administrative, and professional employees, so that faculty members may now seek redress of salary inequities under the Fair Labor Standards Act. In October 1972, the jurisdiction of the United States Commission on Civil Rights was extended to cover cases of sex discrimination. And as of July 1973, women applying to graduate and professional schools will have strong legal support for redress under a provision of the 1972 Educational Amendments Act which forbids sex discrimination in admissions policies and practices in graduate and professional schools.

These legal protections will be particularly important in the years ahead if the present administration does not appropriate sufficient funds to process the several hundred class action complaints already on file with HEW. A special *New York Times* report in December 1972 suggested that the present administration has "all but abandoned" efforts to force federal contractors to hire more blacks and women. The reporter, Philip Shabecoff, claims a survey of officials in the Office of Federal Contract Compliance indicates the agency is "now receiving virtually no support and direction from the Administration" (*Spokeswoman* 1973:8).

Those concerned with the autonomy of higher education have a clear mandate: to the extent that the academic community puts its own house in order by remedying past bias against women, enlarging the opportunities for women on an equitable basis with men, and establishing effective and responsive mechanisms for the internal redress of grievances, there will be little need for women and minority group members to utilize external grievance routes. As Martha Peterson, president of Barnard College, pointed out at the ACE annual meeting in 1972, "the disgrace of 'affirmative action' is that HEW had to get into it at all" (*Chronicle of Higher Education* 1972:3).

LOOKING AHEAD

In much of the recent discussion of financial troubles in academe, there is an assumption that we are only passing through a short-run period of trouble and that somewhere just around the corner we shall return to "normal." This is in all likelihood a delusion on several counts, three of which we will discuss since they have the most direct implications for the position of women in academe.

The first factor concerns the consequences of fluctuations in the American birth rate. We already have noted that the expansion of higher education in the early 1960s was, in part, a function of the baby-boom generation grown to college age. On the basis of a moderate population predictor model, educational planners in the late 1960s predicted that the college-age population would grow from 10 million in 1969 to about 24 million by the year 2000 A.D. As it turns out, however, the fertility rate which began to decline in 1958 has dropped at an even sharper rate in the past five years than it did early in the 1960s. As a result, the prediction of 24 million has been altered to 17 million. Higher education will feel the impact of this decline, however, long before the end of the century. Cartter (1970:9) has shown that the aggregate high school class of 1986 will be 25 percent smaller than the class of 1979. Another example of the changes taking place can be seen in the fact that there were 20 percent fewer 2-year olds (born in 1968) than 12-year olds (born in 1958) when the census was taken in 1970. These recent trends suggest that quite apart from any other factors affecting the educational plans of young people, college enrollment will be expanding at a steadily decreasing rate through the 1970s, and by the 1980s there will be an absolute decline in the number of eligible students.

All such projections of the size of the college-age population in future years take no account of changes in economic circumstances, in views toward the necessity of higher degrees, or in national policies of financial support for higher education. For the past several years, cutbacks in federal support coupled with rising inflation have seriously lowered college enrollment figures. At the same time two very basic assumptions concerning higher education have been challenged. One assumption has been that education pays off handsomely in higher paychecks and higher work morale. Berg (1970) has shown that the better educated may indeed receive higher starting salaries, but by any measure of job performance, they do not necessarily perform better than less educated workers. Being "over-educated" for a job can lead to low morale, low productivity, high absenteeism, and high labor turnover. Berg has demonstrated the fallacy of assuming that the reason better educated workers get higher wages is because they perform better on the job. In fact, in many occupations workers with less education have been shown to perform their jobs better than workers with higher levels of educational attainment.

The second assumption has been that an expansion of educational opportunities will erase social inequalities. From the Coleman report (1966) to Jencks' recent study (1972), researches have shown that equal educational opportunities do not close the gap between rich and poor: the poor may be less so than thirty years ago, but the gap between the socioeconomic classes has not narrowed. Debate about these assumptions will probably increase in the next several years. Coupled with rising tuition fees and continuing inflation, many parents and young people may conclude that college and graduate training give no real assurance of better paying jobs and more interesting work.

The third factor of concern is that we have created a graduate education and research establishment that is at least 30 percent larger than what will be needed in the 1970s and 1980s. This is not news to those who have followed manpower predictions, but it is startling to realize how very recently one still heard the old cry of teacher shortage in academic circles. Just a few years ago leading graduate deans predicted that the percentage of college teachers with the doctorate would decline from the 40 percent level in 1957 to 20 percent or less by 1970. In 1964, the Office of Education predicted a cumulative deficit of 125,000 Ph.D.s by 1974, and even in the fall of 1968, the Office of Education was claiming that faculty shortages would continue to exist "as far into the future as prudent men can see." As it turned out, they were not very prudent men.

Yet in 1964 Cartter predicted an emerging surplus of Ph.D.s which would begin to show itself by 1969, will become significant in the 1970–1974 period, and will be very serious indeed by the last half of the 1970s. In a paper he submitted to the Joint Economic Committee of the Congress in 1969 (Cartter 1969), he predicted that the demand for new Ph.D.'s in 1970–1971 would be down about one-third from its 1968–1969 level, while the supply would have increased by at least 16 percent. By 1975 there may be an oversupply of Ph.D.'s in the order of magnitude of 30 to 50 percent. This oversupply was first felt at annual conventions in scientific fields, but by 1970 history and modern language associations also understood that job seekers far outnumbered jobs in those fields. Since roughly 90 percent of doctoral degree recipients in such fields as English and history traditionally enter college teaching, the impact of surplus doctoral production on employment in these fields is direct indeed. Even in the scientific professions, the golden decade of federal research and development support ended by 1966. From 1956 to 1966, the annual rate of increase in federal expenditures was 14 percent a year, but since 1966 such expenditures averaged a 2 percent annual decline. The current reduced level of federal support does not appear to be a temporary measure, but a long range trend, which means that both academic and nonacademic scientists and engineers will continue to be underutilized.

To gauge the future situation in higher education, manpower predictions of doctoral production must be viewed together with predicted rates of increase in college enrollment. Clearly there has been an enormous increase in college enrollment over the past twenty years: in 1950 some 2.3 million students were enrolled in college while in 1971 Census reports recorded 8.1 million students. During the same twenty-year period, however, the annual doctorate production underwent a five-fold increase, from about 7,000 in 1950 to roughly 31,000 in 1970. Yet most students spend only an average of four years in higher education while Ph.D. recipients who join college and university faculties stay more than thirty years. Consequently, the rate of increase in the production of college teachers only has to be a fraction of the rate of increase in student enrollment. Recent data from the Office of Education and the National Science Foundation have shown that the annual rate of increase in doctoral output has been 14 percent a year—a figure close to Cartter's prediction. Assuming the same rate of increase, the annual number of doctorates awarded in 1980 would be 60,000, double the 1970 number.

There are signs that graduate schools, professional associations, and government agencies have removed their rose-colored glasses and begun to look soberly at the implications of these trends. In a recent survey of sociology graduate department chairmen, Habenstein found a trend toward restricting enrollment. As he put it:

> if it has been the case that the already restrictive "top ten" departments have been the first to cut back, the rest of the departments, for whatever reasons dimly or clearly perceived, are beginning to restrict entry also (Habenstein 1972:5).

There is no reason to anticipate basic changes in the most recent predictions concerning the surplus of doctorate degrees in this decade. At the moment the major universities are feeling the greatest economic pinch from federal cutbacks. Assessments of the doctorate surplus are underway in a number of academic disciplines, and more surely will follow in the next few years. It is quite likely that before long academic women will realize their indebtedness to legislative reformers in such women's organizations as NOW and WEAL who lobbied successfully for the passage of legislation proscribing sex discrimination in admissions policies in graduate and professional schools. Were it not for such legal protection, there could well have been pressure to cut back graduate enrollment and faculty by excluding more women than men.

Those of us dedicated to ridding academe of sex discrimination and widening women's aspirations and opportunities must reckon with these trends. Let us construct a hypothetical case that illustrates the choices that lie ahead. A graduate department has been admitting 100 doctoral students (eighty men and twenty women) annually for several years. Faced with pressure from the women's movement and pressure to cut back on the number of doctoral degrees, two alternatives are considered. Under Alternative A, the total number of students admitted would be cut back; there would be no change in the proportion of women among the entering classes. Under Alternative B, the total size of entering classes would be cut back and the proportion of women increased. The distribution of women and men students under the two plans and the present pattern would be as follows:

	Number of Women	Number of Men	Total Number
Past Pattern	20	80	100
Alternative A	12	48	60
Alternative B	24	36	60

The anticipated change in the situation for men and women under Alternative A compared to Alternative B would be as follows:

	Women	Men
Alternative A		
Percent change in absolute numbers	−40%	−40%
Percent change in relative proportion of sexes	0%	0%
Alternative B		
Percent change in absolute numbers	+20%	−55%
Percent change in relative proportion of sexes	+100%	−25%

Under Alternative A, both sexes would experience cutbacks equally. Under Alternative B, the number of women would increase slightly but the number of men would decline more than 50 percent.

Under the latter alternative, then, there would be a great improvement for women. With only a slight overall increase in the number of women—in the example above, only four more women than in the past—women's representation would increase from a very small to a significant minority approaching equity. As such women earn their degrees and take their place in academe, a policy like that described under Alternative B would provide a steady, but slow rate of change in the sex distribution of the academic hierarchy. For men, there would be a very sharp decline in both proportion and absolute numbers, with less than half as many men students entering graduate departments. The "sting of change" will indeed be sharp for men if in the coming decade there is both an overall contraction of graduate education and an improvement in the status of women. Yet this is precisely what must happen if we are to solve the problem of oversupply of doctorates, as well as improve the position of women in academe.

What are the implications of this shape of the future for women? For one, there will be increasing outcries from men against the demands by women for equity in admissions, hiring, and promotion. These responses will not necessarily be instances of sexism, but simply responses to pressure on academe to begin some rational contraction. While some will be pleased to see greater equity for women, many people also feel concern for brothers and sons—they will not simply be against women. Not all recent outcries about "quotas" are antiwomen responses to women's political actions, but alarms sounded against a tightening market for sons and male students—responses by a generation of men whose expectations were formed during the "golden" era of expansion in higher education. The readiness with which academic men translate the "goals" of affirmative action into "quotas" should be seen as nervous confusion as they face an uncertain future unlike their own past, and not simply as resistance to the legitimate claims of academic women. Had the feminist renascence taken place in the late 1950s, and were we developing affirmative action plans in the early 1960s rather than the 1970s, there probably would have been considerable support from the now protesting men since they would view women as a source of labor to ease the teacher shortage. This is in fact what happened in the 1950s when it became necessary to cope with the baby-boom generation entering grade school. The hundreds of school superintendents who had to woo married women back to the classroom did not suddenly undergo a great conversion to the cause of women; they simply needed women's skills in the classroom. But this is *not* the social–historical context academic women face in the 1970s. We are placing sharp demands on academic institutions in a period when the best will in the world will not yield easily to them. We must be alert to the nonsexist and very real economic issues confronting higher education. It is just possible that the expression of genuine concern by academic women for the future careers of their male students also might stimulate more enthusiasm in their male colleagues for the opportunities opening for women students.

We should be extremely cautious not to dampen the legitimate aspirations of our competent women students, but we must at the same time warn them about discouragement from men and the sources of men's response. If a student is white and male, he will confront sharp competition for fewer places in graduate education and in technical and professional occupations than he would have until very recently. But the student who is female, white or black, will find doors open to her that typically were closed. There will be greater opportunities for women in academe as well as in other sectors of the economy, since affirmative action guidelines affect all organizations under federal contract. Business corporations and government agencies have joined academic institutions in seeking out women to hire and to promote in order to improve the representation of women and minority group members at all levels of their organizations.

Our review of research, political action, and economic and demographic problems confronting higher education in the 1970s yields a mixed outlook for academic women. While there has been a great deal of progress since 1968, there are serious hurdles ahead that will challenge academic women and men dedicated to the removal of sex discrimination from academe and the transformation of our colleges and universities into more humane social institutions. Such change will require persistent political effort, hard work, and resistance to short-run discouragements and rebuffs. It will require extra effort by women faculty and advanced graduate students to provide the social and psychological support our women undergraduate and entering graduate students desperately need. It will require that we not simply invoke but practice sisterhood and solidarity by suppressing the temptation to fight factional battles within our ranks that divide black women from white women, women students from women faculty, and junior staff women from senior staff women. We must no longer reject women as "elitists" when they secure their doctorates, publish widely, and accept appointments of responsibility —a rejection that, in fact, equates womanliness with powerlessness. We need as many women in positions of power and prestige as can possibly achieve those positions. With such efforts it is realistic, I think, to view the future for women in academe with at least a moderate degree of optimism.

REFERENCES

Astin, Helen S. 1969. *The woman doctorate in America.* New York: Russell Sage Foundation.

Berg, Ivar E. 1970. *Education and jobs: The great training robbery.* New York: Praeger.

Cartter, Allan M. Summer 1966. The supply of and demand for college teachers. *Journal of Human Resources.* 1 (1):22–38.

Cartter, Allan M. December 27, 1970. Scientific manpower trends for 1970–1985 and their implications for higher education. Paper presented to the A.A.A.S. meeting, Chicago, Illinois. Mimeographed.

Cartter, Allan M., and Farrell, Robert L. 1969. *Academic labor market projections and the draft: The economics and financing of higher education in the United States.* Joint Economic Committee, Congress of the United States. Washington, D.C.: U.S. Government Printing Office.

Chronicle of Higher Education. October 16, 1972. 7 (4):3.

Coleman, James S. 1966. *Equality of educational opportunity.* Washington, D.C.: U.S. Government Printing Office.

Ginzberg, Eli. 1966. *Life styles of educated women.* New York: Columbia University Press.

Habenstein, Robert W. 1972. Recent trends in graduate training: Preliminary results of a survey. *The American Sociologist,* 7:3, 5.

Harmon, Lindsey R. 1965. *High school ability patterns: A backward look from the doctorate.* Washington, D.C.: Academy of Sciences, Office of Scientific Personnel, Scientific Manpower Report No. 6.

Hiestand, Dale L. 1964. *Economic growth and employment opportunities for minorities.* New York: Columbia University Press.

Jencks, Christopher. 1972. *Inequality: A reassessment of the effect of family and schooling in America.* New York: Basic Books.

Roby, Pamela. 1972. Women and American higher education. *The Annals of the American Academy of Political and Social Sciences,* 404:118–139.

Sells, Lucy W. 1972. Convention Notes. *SWS Newsletter,* 2(5):20.

Smith, Georgina M. 1972. *Faculty women at the bargaining table.* Mimeographed.

Sewell, William M. 1971. Inequality of opportunity for higher education. *American Sociological Review,* 36(5):793–809.

The Spokeswoman. January 15, 1973. 3(7):8.

Notes on Contributors

Carol Ahlum is coordinator of the Western Massachusetts Task Force on Sexism in Education, Valley Women's Center, Northampton, Massachusetts. Her publications include *Female Studies III* (with Florence Howe, KNOW 1971), and *New Guide to Current Female Studies* (with Florence Howe, KNOW 1971).

Helen S. Astin is Director of Research and Education at the University Research Corporation, Washington, D.C. Her major publications are *The Woman Doctorate in America* (Russell Sage Foundation 1970), and *Women: A Bibliography on their Education and Careers* (Human Service Press 1971). Since January 1971 Dr. Astin has served as Chairperson of the Task Force on the Status of Women in Psychology of the American Psychological Association. She is currently at work on a review of research literature on sex roles. She also has conducted research in the areas of educational and occupational development of disadvantaged students, open admissions, and educational and career development of college graduates.

Alan Bayer is Associate Director of Research at the American Council on Education, Washington, D.C. He is the co-author of *Human Resources and Higher Education* (with John K. Folger and Helen S. Astin, Russell Sage Foundation 1970), the author of *Survey of College and University Faculty and Staff* (American Council on Education, forthcoming), and he recently completed a study on "Nurses for Our Future: Characteristics of New Student Nurses." In 1972 he served as a member of the advisory committee to establish a National Academy of Sciences Commission on Minorities in the Sciences and Engineering.

Ann Calderwood is publisher and an editor of *Feminist Studies.*

Jean Campbell is Director of the University of Michigan Center for Continuing Education of Women. As a member of the University's Commission for Women she has been instrumental in developing new university complaint appeal and review procedures in investigating alleged sex discrimination. Her research concerns primarily have been in the areas of administrative program design and evaluation, adminstrative style, and career development of women.

Constance M. Carroll is Assistant Dean of the College of Liberal Arts, University of Maine at Portland-Gorham. She has served as a member of the Chancellor's Advisory Council on Women's Opportunities at the University of Pittsburgh, and as Associate Director of the U.S. Office of Education Institute, "Challenge: Women in Higher Education." She recently was appointed Co-Chairperson of the Higher Education Commission of the National Council of Negro Women. A classics scholar specializing in tragedy and Greek lyric poetry, she is currently at work on a study of the Homeric depiction of women.

Marianne A. Ferber is a member of the faculty of the Department of Economics, University of Illinois at Urbana-Champaign, and is a member of the university's Committee on the Status of Women. She is the co-author (with Jane Loeb) of "Sex as

Predictive of Salary and Status on a University Faculty," *Journal of Educational Measurement* (8:235–244), and "Performance, Rewards, and Perceptions of Sex Discrimination of Male and Female Faculty Members," *American Journal of Sociology* (78(4): 995–1002).

Jo Freeman is a doctoral candidate in political science at the University of Chicago where she is writing a dissertation on women's liberation. Ms. Freeman has been active in the women's movement since its inception and has written extensively on the subject. She is currently editing a book on women from a feminist perspective.

Patricia Albjerg Graham is a member of the history and education faculty at Barnard College and Teachers College, Columbia University. From 1969–1971 Dr. Graham was a member of the American Historical Association Ad Hoc Committee on the Status of Women Historians, and from 1971–1972 served as Chairperson of the AHA Standing Committee on the Status of Women Historians. She is the author of *Progressive Education: From Arcady to Academe* (Teachers College 1967); "Women in Academe," *Science* (September 25, 1970); *Community and Class in American Education* (John Wiley 1973); and a history of women and higher education (in progress).

Judith Dozier Hackman is a member of the research staff of the Office of Institutional Research, Yale University, and is currently involved in research on criteria for college performance.

Florence Howe is Professor of Literature and Education at the State University of New York/College at Old Westbury. From 1969–1971 she served as Chairperson of the Modern Language Association's Commission on the Status of Women and has lectured and consulted on women's studies curriculum since 1970. Her publications include *The Conspiracy of the Young* (with Paul Lauter, World 1970); *Female Studies III* (with Carol Ahlum, KNOW 1971); *No More Masks: An Anthology of Women's Poems* (with Ellen Bass, Doubleday and University of Massachusetts Press 1973). Ms. Howe also plays a major role in The Feminist Press and the Clearinghouse on Women's Studies, Old Westbury, L.I., N.Y.

Joan Huber is a member of the faculty of the Department of Sociology at the University of Illinois, Urbana-Champaign. From 1970–1971 she served as treasurer of Sociologists for Women in Society and is currently the president of SWS and a member of the University of Illinois' women's caucus. She was special editor of the January 1973 issue of *The American Journal of Sociology,* "Changing Women in a Changing Society." She has published numerous articles and is co-author of a forthcoming text-reader.

Katherine M. Klotzburger is a doctoral candidate in political science at New York University. She is currently Project Director of the Chancellor's Advisory Committee on the Status of Women of the City University of New York. She is an active member of the National Organization for Women, the Professional Women's Caucus, and the Women's Caucus for Political Science. From 1969–1972 she served as a member of the Committee on the Status of Women in the Profession of the American Political Science Association. She is author of *Keynote Guide to American Government* (Barnes and Noble 1973).

Janet Lever is a doctoral candidate in sociology at Yale University. She is co-author (with Pepper Schwartz) of *Women at Yale* (Bobbs-Merrill 1970) and has conducted research and published articles on sex-role socialization in children's games and play. She is presently working in Brazil, conducting comparative research on sex-role socialization in children, and research on the integrative and disintegrative powers of soccer.

Jane Loeb is Director of Admissions and Records, University of Illinois at Urbana-Champaign. She is conducting research on salary and rank differences by sex; student personnel and applications of multivariate statistics.

Laura Morlock is a Research Associate in the Department of Social Relations, Johns Hopkins University. She is co-author (with Florence Howe and Richard Berk) of "The Status of Women in Modern Language Departments: A Report of the Modern Language Association Commission on the Status of Women in the Profession," *PMLA* (86:459–468); and co-author (with the MLA Commission on the Status of Women in the Profession) of "Affirmative Action for Women in 1971," *PMLA* (87:530–540). She is currently analyzing data on power structures and black communities from a study of 93 northern American cities.

Katherine Nelson is a member of the Department of Psychiatry, Yale University. As a member of the Yale Faculty and Professional Women's Forum, she has been concerned with alternatives of part-time study and employment, the status of research associates, employment of faculty wives, and day-care programs. She has published several articles in the area of cognitive and language development in young children.

Michelle Patterson is Assistant Professor of Sociology, Brandeis University, on leave as Visiting Assistant Professor of Sociology at the University of California, Santa Barbara, 1972–1973. She has served as secretary of Sociologists for Women in Society and has been active in Boston Area Women Social Scientists. She is a Research Fellow on The Impacts and Benefits of Higher Education on Women, National Research Council, 1972–1973. Although her major sociological field of research is comparative systems of higher education, she has published and is continuing research on women and education.

Cynthia Sterling Pincus is Director of the Information and Counseling Center for Women, Yale University Women's Organization. She has published several articles on the growth of counseling centers for women in the United States and on the needs of educated women. She recently completed research in collaboration with the Yale Department of Psychiatry on the relationship between mood and life style among educated women.

Brigitte A. Prusoff is a statistical consultant in psychiatric studies and is with the Department of Psychiatry, Yale University.

Lora Hnizda Robinson is a member of the Staff of the ERIC Clearinghouse on Higher Education. She is the author of *The Status of Academic Women* (ERIC 1971), and "The Emergence of Women's Courses in Higher Education," *Research Currents and College and University Bulletin* (September 1972). She is a member of the Northern Virginia Chapter of the National Organization for Women and directs chapter efforts toward ratification of the ERA in Virginia. She also has published articles on student participation in academic governance, and on the measurement of campus and student morale.

Pamela Roby is a member of the faculty of The Florence Heller School for Advanced Studies in Social Welfare and the Department of Sociology, Brandeis University. Her publications include: *The Future of Inequality* (with S. M. Miller, Basic Books 1970); *Child Care—Who Cares? Foreign and Domestic Infant and Early Childhood Develop-*

ment Policies (Basic Books 1972). She is currently at work on a political and economic history of the development of laws and policies concerning prostitution in the United States. Ms. Roby served as Chairperson of the Eastern Sociological Society Committee on Women 1971–1972, and is an active member of the National Women's Political Caucus and Sociologists for Women in Society.

Alice S. Rossi is Professor and Chairperson of the Department of Sociology and Anthropology at Goucher College, Baltimore, Maryland. She has served as a research sociologist at Cornell University, Harvard University, University of Chicago, and Johns Hopkins University prior to her teaching appointment at Goucher College. Special areas of research interest in which she has published include the sociology of the family, career development, sex roles, sexuality, and the history of feminism. She is national chairman of Committee W on the Status of Women in the Profession in AAUP and serves on the boards of the Schlesinger Library at Harvard-Radcliffe, the Social Science Research Council, and the American Council on Education. In addition to editing *Academic Women on the Move,* Dr. Rossi has a book on feminist lives and works which will be published by Columbia University Press and Bantam Books in 1973.

Margaret Rumbarger is Associate Secretary of the American Association of University Professors. As a staff advisor to the Association's Committee on the Status of Women she has focused on the particular problems faced by women in higher education and the formulation of Association policy positions that may lead to their resolution. When on leave from 1971–1972 to the Office for Civil Rights, Department of Health, Education and Welfare, Ms. Rumbarger was instrumental in developing policy decision papers regarding the enforcement of executive orders and the obligations of federal contractors.

Bernice Sandler is an Executive Associate with the Association of American Colleges, Washington, D.C. She is a past chairperson of the Action Committee for Federal Contract Compliance of WEAL, and as a former Education Specialist for the United States House of Representatives Special Subcommittee on Education, she was the first person ever appointed to the staff of a congressional committee to work specifically in the area of women's rights. She also was responsible for the preparation of the hearings conducted by Representative Edith Green entitled *Discrimination Against Women,* the first comprehensive congressional hearings to be held concerning discrimination against women in education and employment. She is currently directing a project aimed at improving the status of academic women.

Pepper Schwartz is a member of the faculty of the Department of Sociology, University of Washington. She is currently a member of the university's Woman's Commission, and is the west coast chairperson of Sociologists for Women in Society. Her publications include *Women at Yale* (with Janet Lever, Bobbs-Merrill 1970), *A Feminist Interpretation of Human Sexuality* (Rand-McNally, forthcoming), and "Female Sexuality and Monogamous Marriage," in R. Whitehurst and L. Libby (Eds.), *Critiques of Marriage* (Consensus forthcoming). She is currently at work on research on sex roles and marital roles in relation to self-esteem and professional achievement.

Lucy W. Sells is a doctoral candidate in sociology at the University of California, Berkeley, and is working on a dissertation entitled "Disciplines and Sex-Differences in Doctoral Attrition." Since 1971 she has served as a member of the Chancellor's Advisory Committee on the Status of Academic Women. Ms. Sells is the author of two bibliographies, "Current Research on Sex Roles" (1971, 1972), compiled for Sociologists for Women in Society.

Myrna M. Weissman is an Assistant Professor in the Department of Psychiatry, and a doctoral student in epidemiology at Yale University School of Medicine. She has published extensively and is continuing research on women and depression. Ms. Weissman is also Co-Director of the Depression Research Unit at Yale.

Lenore J. Weitzman is Assistant Professor of Sociology at the University of California at Davis where she also teaches a course on sex discrimination in the School of Law. Her research interests are in the areas of sex role socialization and the sociology of law. Her current research concerns the impact of the no-fault divorce and the family reform act in California.

Author Index

Achbar, Francine, 227, 230, 232, 233, 234, 235, 236, 237
Addis, M. E., 96, 102, 103, 109, 119
Ahlum, Carol, 393, 398, 402, 406, 410, 412, 416, 417, 418, 420, 421, 422, 506, 507, 531, 532
Albro, Mary D., 112, 123
Alexander, Anne, 233
Allen, Pamela, 31
Allen, Priscilla, 410
Amber, R. B., 231
Anderson, Charles J., 354, 356
Anthony, Susan B., 128
Arnesen, Nancy, 421
Astin, Alexander W., 79, 81, 82, 83, 88, 90, 333, 346, 355, 356
Astin, Helen S., 50, 55, 116, 119, 139, 143, 145, 146, 147, 149, 151, 152, 154, 155, 156, 157, 161, 166, 167, 172, 195, 263, 275, 278, 287, 293, 304, 305, 333, 341, 354, 356, 369, 491, 511, 517, 520, 521, 528, 531
Austen, Jane, 408

Babey-Brooke, Anna M., 231
Bain, Beatrice, 411
Barach, Peter, 370
Barauch, Grace, 421
Barker, R., 314, 331
Barrnett, Elizabeth, 187
Bart, Pauline B., 421
Bass, Ellen, 532
Bates, Jean M., 119
Batten, James K., 229
Baxter, Annette, 397, 413
Bayer, Alan E., 55, 79, 84, 88, 90, 150, 154, 155, 157, 161, 202, 203, 207, 208, 219, 220, 228, 258, 259, 264, 268, 274, 275, 278, 280, 283, 286, 304, 305, 333, 334, 335, 346, 355,

Bayer, Alan E. (cont.)
356, 491, 520, 521, 531
Bazell, Robert J., 229
Beal, Frances M., 180, 181, 184
deBeauvoir, Simone, 405, 406, 408
Beazley, Richard, 209, 228
Beecher, Catherine, 395
Bem, Daryl J., 330, 331
Bem, Sandra L., 330, 331
Benson, Ruth Crego, 421
Benston, Margaret, 405
Berg, Ivar E., 524, 528
Berger, Alan S., 84, 90
Berger, Caruthers, 11, 84, 90
Berk, Richard, 259, 260, 261, 267, 269, 270, 272, 273, 274, 281, 282, 288, 289, 306, 533
Bernard, Jessie, 61, 76, 156, 161, 202, 209, 214, 218, 223, 228, 260, 263, 292, 305, 333, 356
Bernstein, Judi, 15, 31
Berry, Jane, 99, 112, 119, 124
Berry, Sara, 233
Bethune, Mary McLeod, 173
Bettelheim, Bruno, 76
Bird, Caroline, 6, 31, 315, 331
Bishop, Pam, 227, 230, 232, 233, 234, 235, 236, 237
Blankenship, W. C., 304, 305
Bloom, Samuel, 331
Booth, Heather, 17
Boring, Phyllis, 236
Boyer, Elizabeth, 25
Braden, Ina, 503
Brewster, Kingman, 124, 187
Brock, Rose, 443
Brown, David G., 305
Brown, Judith, 17, 275, 286, 292
Bunting, Mary I., 94, 97, 112, 119
Burkom, Selma, 409

Burton, Lisbeth K., 115, 119
Bynum, Caroline W., 232

Cain, Louise G., 98
Calabrese, Maureen, 238
Calderwood, Ann, 531
Campbell, Jean W., 93, 116, 119, 531
Campbell, Rex, 88, 90
Card, Emily, 231
Carey, Robert C., 240, 254
Carmichael, Stokeley, 15
Carr, Ronald G., 236
Carroll, Constance, 173, 531
Carroll, Rebecca, 173
Cartter, Allan, M., 37, 55, 157, 161, 354,
    356, 523, 524, 525, 528
Cash, William, 449
Chamberlain, Kathleen, 421
Chandler, Marjorie O., 206, 228, 243,
    254, 257, 258, 306
Chapman, Gretal, 421
Chisholm, Shirley, 173, 176
Chmaj, Betty E., 281, 284, 293, 294, 300,
    304, 305, 421
Chopin, Kate, 410
Clarenbach, Kathryn, 7, 98, 421
Clark, Shirley M., 172, 218, 228, 254,
    271, 272, 278, 283, 286
Clemente, Frank, 283, 305
Cless, Elizabeth, 98, 99, 122
Cohen, Audrey, 101, 120, 421
Coleman, James S., 80, 90, 524, 528
Collins, J., 229
Converse, Jean M., 277, 279, 284, 291,
    294, 295, 297, 298, 304, 306
Converse, Philip E., 277, 279, 284, 291,
    294, 295, 297, 298, 304, 306, 370
Cowan, Ruth, 413
Crane, Stephen, 410
Creager, John A., 42, 46, 50, 52, 55, 86,
    88, 90
Cullen, Dallas M., 264, 293, 304, 306

Dahl, K., 238
David, Opal D., 94, 120
Davis, Ann E., 305, 306

Davis, Bertram H., 426
Davis, Caroline, 7
Davis, Devra Lee, 421
Davis, James A., 44, 49, 55, 88, 90
Davis, Natalie Zemon, 115, 120
Deering, A., 331
Dennis, Lawrence E., 95, 96, 120
Dinerman, Bernice, 44, 55, 315, 319, 331
Dinnerstein, Dorothy, 238
Dixon, Marlene, 17
Doely, Sarah Bentley, 27, 31
Dohrn, Bernadine, 17
Douvan, Elizabeth, 94
Dowding, Nancy E., 109, 120, 440
Drake, St. Clair, 185
Driver, Anne, 413
Dubois, W. E. B., 185
Dutton, Jeffrey E., 333
Dweck, Susan, 119, 356

East, Catherine, 504
Eastwood, Mary, 11
Eble, Kenneth, 426, 438
Edelsberg, Herman, 6, 31
Edisen, Adele, 304, 306
Ehrlich, Carol, 409
Eisler, Riane, 411
Eliot, George, 408
Elkes, Charmian, 122
Ellison, Sylvia, 11
Engels, Friedrich, 405, 407
Epstein, Cynthia Fuchs, 58, 75, 76, 99,
    308, 320, 331, 341, 356
Epstein, Sandra, 119
Erenburg, Mark, 233
Euripides, 182, 184
Eyde, Lorraine, 112, 123

Fagerburg, J. E., 108, 115, 120
Fagin, Margaret C., 99, 120
Farians, Elizabeth, 421
Farrell, Robert L., 528
Farson, Richard, 2, 31
Fauri, Fedele, 449
Fava, Sylvia, 305, 306
Feig, Konnilyn, 173, 185

Feldman, Kenneth A., 79, 90
Ferber, Marianne A., 233, 239, 249, 254, 520, 521, 531
Ferguson, Mary Anne, 421
Ferris, A., 185
Fidell, Linda S., 212, 218, 228, 293, 304, 306
Firestone, Shulamith, 413
Fischer, Ann, 274, 284, 304, 306
Fixter, Deborah, 116, 123
Fletcher, Arthur, 451
Flexner, Eleanor, 408
Flint, Arden A., 122
Flory, Maureen B., 413
Folger, John K., 79, 88, 90, 157, 161, 346, 356, 531
Foster, Ginny, 421
Fought, C. A., 120
Fox, Greer Litton, 305, 306
Francis, Barbara, 232
Freeman, Jo, 1, 9, 32, 232, 532
Freud, Sigmund, 407
Friedan, Betty, 2, 5, 6, 7, 12, 32, 54, 55, 59, 64, 76, 326, 331, 406, 408
Fuller, Margaret, 408

Galway, Kathleen, 172, 218, 228, 271, 272, 278, 283, 286
Gardner, John, 112
Garland, Hamlin, 410
Gilman, Charlotte Perkins, 405
Gilotti, Susan S., 122
Ginsburg, Ruth Bader, 421
Ginzberg, Eli, 511, 528
Glancy, D. J., 320, 321, 331
Goffman, Erving, 314, 315, 331
Golde, Peggy, 274, 284, 304, 306
Goldfield, Evelyn, 17
Goldman, Freda, 99
Goode, William, 463
Gordon, Chad, 80, 90
Gordon, Linda, 408, 422
Gottlieb, David, 84, 91
Graham, Patricia A., 163, 195, 481, 532
Green, Edith, 59, 71, 76, 453, 455, 534
Greenwald, Maurine, 421

Greenwood, Nell, 99
Gribben, Suzanne, 87, 90
Griffin, Verna E., 316, 331
Griffiths, Martha, 6, 32, 443
Grimm, James W., 281, 304, 306
Grimshaw, J., 120
Grouchow, Nancy, 229

Habenstein, Robert W., 525, 528
Hackman, Judith, 187, 195, 532
Haller, Archibald O., 80, 91
Hardaway, Charles W., 233
Hare, Nathan, 415, 422
Hargens, Lowell L., Jr., 218, 228
Harmon, Lindsey R., 140, 145, 149, 151, 152, 161, 166, 167, 172, 263, 278, 280, 286, 306, 511, 520, 529
Harris, Ann Sutherland, 51, 55, 73, 75, 76, 203, 223, 228, 231
Harris, Louis, 31, 32
Harte, Bret, 410
Hawkes, Anna, 94
Hawkins, Ruth R., 229
Hayden, Casey, 15, 32
Heide, Wilma, 13
Henderson, Jean C. G., 202, 203, 218, 224, 228, 274, 275, 276, 278, 287
Henderson, Virginia, 98
Hernandez, Aileen, 13
Hiestand, Dale L., 519, 529
Hochschild, Arlie, 403
Hoffman, D. T., 271, 279, 284, 300, 304, 306, 325, 331
Hoffman, Nancy, 409, 422
Hole, Judith, 9, 11, 26, 27, 33
Hook, Sidney, 425, 438
Hooper, Mary E., 206, 228, 243, 254, 257, 258, 306
Horch, Dwight, 46, 55
Horner, Matina A., 59, 68, 76, 80, 81, 90, 115
Hortenstine, Anne, 101, 121
Houston, Susan, 235
Howe, Florence, 236, 259, 260, 261, 267, 268, 269, 270, 272, 273, 274, 281, 282, 288, 289, 304, 306, 393, 396,

Howe, Florence (*cont.*)
    399, 400, 402, 406, 409, 410, 412,
    413, 415, 416, 417, 418, 420, 421,
    422, 506, 507, 531, 532, 533
Howells, W. D., 410
Hruby, Norbert, 103, 108, 121
Huang, Alice S., 263, 264, 304, 306
Huber, Bettina, 331
Huber, Joan, 125, 324, 532
Hutchinson, Anne, 408

Ibsen, Henrik, 405
Ilchman, Warren, 370
Irish, Marion, 370
Irwin, Inez Haynes, 3, 32
Iverson, Mary, 98

Jackson, Jacqueline J., 174, 176, 177,
    184
Jackson, Priscilla, 98
Jacobson, R. F., 51, 96, 109, 121
Jaffe, Naomi, 17
Jancek, Camilla, 236
Jaquette, Jane, 304, 306
Jencks, Christopher, 524, 529
Johnson, Lyndon B., 8, 25
Johnson, Virginia, 407
Jones, Beverly, 17
Joreen, 24, 32
Joseph, Charlotte B., 84, 85, 90

Kahne, Hilda, 116, 121
Kaplan, Harold I., 44, 293, 304, 306
Kashket, Eva, 263, 264, 304, 306
Katz, David A., 254
Kaynor, Betty, 100
Keiffer, Miriam J., 264, 293, 304, 306
Kelsall, Ann, 109, 121
Kennedy, John F., 5, 95
Kent, Laura, 333
Kern, Kenneth K., 124
Kiley, Owen, 489
King, Coretta, 173
King, Mary, 15, 32
Klaus Michelle S., 233
Kline, Caryl, 99

Klotzburger, Kay, 359, 370, 505, 506,
    532
Knauss, Jenny, 413
Knowles, Mary Tyler, 403, 422
Kohn, Melvin L., 80, 90
Komarovsky, Mirra, 75, 76
Komisar, Lucy, 8, 32
Kott, E., 331
Kraditor, Aileen, 408
Kramer, Noel Anketell, 304, 306
Kreps, Juanita, 314, 331
Kronus, Carol L., 281, 300, 304, 306
Krouse, Agate Nesaule, 422
Kurland, Jordan, 426, 438
Kusnetz, Ella, 423

Ladner, Joyce, 178, 184, 405
Lander, Patricia Slade, 259, 276, 281,
    293, 294, 304, 307
Landy, Marcia, 259, 422
La Sorte, Michael A., 261, 267, 268,
    269, 270, 271, 273, 281, 289, 291,
    305, 307, 334, 356
Laurance, Margaret, 304, 307
Lauter, Paul, 396, 415, 422, 532
Lee, Calvin B. T., 354, 356
LeFevre, Carol, 115, 121
Leive, Loretta, 166, 172, 261, 267, 270,
    272, 279, 280, 281, 288, 291, 304,
    307
Leland, Carole, 109, 110, 116, 121
Leoffler, Dorothy, 122
Lerner, Gerda, 93, 117, 121, 406, 408,
    422
Lessing, Doris, 405, 408
Lever, Janet, 57, 532, 534
Levine, Ellen, 9, 11, 26, 27, 32
Levy, Joan, 178, 184
Lewis, Eleanor J., 422
Libby, L., 534
Likert, Jane, 115, 121
Lippmann, Walter, 315, 331
Lloyd, Betty Jane, 98, 121
Loeb, Jane W., 233, 239, 249, 254, 520,
    521, 531, 532
Loewenberg, Bert, 99

Logan, Albert A., Jr., 229
Lombard, Frederica, 319
Loring, Rosalind, 100
Lozoff, Marjorie M., 116, 121
Lubkin, Gloria B., 304, 307
Lucas, Rex A., 102, 121
Luria, Zella, 413
Lyons, Mary, 395

Maccoby, Eleanor, 62, 76, 115
MacKay, E. M., 232
Manchak, Barbara, 304, 307
Mandell, E., 120
Mantini, Barbara K., 122
Marcuse, Herbert, 407
Markus, Hazel, 108, 121
Martin, Janet M., 232
Martin, Joanna Foley, 32
Martin, Wendy, 20, 408, 409, 413, 422
Masters, William, 407
Mattfeld, Jacquelyn A., 111, 121
Mayhew, Harry C., 102, 103, 121
McCarthy, Eugene, 72, 119
McCarthy, Mary, 405
McCarty, Edward R., 119
McCune, Cornelia W., 122
McGuigan, Dorothy G., 93, 121
McLean, Catherine D., 102, 121
Mead, Margaret, 407
Medsker, L. L., 79, 91
Meleney, Elaine K., 124
Merideth, Elizabeth, 117, 121
Merideth, Robert, 117, 121
Merton, Robert K., 314, 317, 331
Metzler, Cindy, 235
Meyerson, Martin, 453
Milburn, Josephine, 370
Mill, John Stuart, 405, 407
Miller, Albert, 185
Miller, Lindsay, 422
Miller, Susan B., 229
Millett, Kate, 405, 406, 408
Miner, Anne S., 238
Miniace, Dorothy, 98
Minturn, Leigh, 232
Mintz, Benjamin, 10

Mitchell, Janet, 79, 304
Mitchell, Joyce M., 307, 370
Mooney, Joseph D., 84, 85, 86, 87, 88, 89, 91
Morehead, William, 452
Morlock, Laura, 255, 259, 260, 261, 265, 266, 267, 268, 269, 270, 272, 273, 274, 277, 281, 282, 288, 289, 304, 306, 307, 506, 509, 520, 533
Mott, Lucretia, 408
Muirhead, Peter, 42, 43
Mulvey, Mary Crowley, 156, 161
Munaker, Sue, 17
Murdoch, Iris, 182, 183, 184
Murray, Pauli, 43, 50, 55, 230
Myint, Thelma, 143, 161
Myrdal, Gunnar, 405

Nash, Peter G., 451
Nelson, Katherine, 187, 195, 533
Newcomb, Theodore M., 79, 90, 115
Newman, Frank, 426, 438
Nixon, Richard M., 16, 26
Noble, Jeanne, 176, 178, 184
Norris, Frances S., 43, 304, 307
Norris, Frank, 293, 410
North, Sandie, 20, 32

O'Driscoll, Pattie, 182
Ohlendorf, George, 80, 91
Ohmann, Carol, 402, 421, 423
Olsen, Tillie, 408
Oltman, Ruth M., 67, 77, 109, 122, 223, 228, 265, 266, 280, 308, 360, 401, 422, 479
O'Neill, William, 406, 408
Oppenheimer, Valerie, 93, 122, 314, 331
Osborn, Ruth H., 98, 122

Packer, Barbara, 61, 77
Panos, Robert J., 79, 81, 90
Parrish, John B., 203, 209, 228, 308
Parsons, Talcott, 54, 55
Patterson, Michelle, 79, 259, 264, 270, 271, 274, 278, 282, 305, 308, 313, 324, 325, 331, 533

Paul, Alice, 2, 3
Pease, John, 84, 91
Pennell, Maryland Y., 316, 317, 318, 331
Pennington, Jean, 99
Peterson, Esther, 5
Peterson, Martha, 170, 487, 523
Pietrofesa, John S., 124
Pincus, Cynthia, 187, 195, 533
Plath, Sylvia, 408
Porter, Elsa, 112
Portes, Alejandro, 80, 91
Pottinger, J. Stanley, 470, 471, 504
Prentice, A. S., 120
Prestage, Jewel, 371
Pringle, Marlene, 112, 122, 124
Prusoff, Brigitte, 187, 195, 533

Quigg, Lillian, 359

Raines, M. R., 103, 122
Raushenbush, Esther, 97, 112, 122, 124
Reeves, Nancy, 422
Reich, Wilheim, 407
Renshaw, Josephine E., 316, 317, 318, 331
Reuben, Elaine, 422
Richardson, Elliot, 441, 449
Richter, Melissa L., 97, 103, 122
Riffe, Nancy L., 234
Rioch, Margaret J., 101, 122
Robbins, Mary Louise, 304, 305
Roberts, Joan, 406
Roberts, Sylvia, 503
Robinson, Lillian, 403, 406, 407, 422
Robinson, Lora, 71, 77, 199, 204, 206, 209, 221, 228, 255, 275, 278, 287, 292, 308, 334, 356, 403, 507, 509, 520, 533
Roby, Pamela, 37, 333, 356, 512, 514, 529, 533, 534
Rogoff, Natalie, 331
Rogoff, Regina, 237
Roose, Kenneth D., 354, 356
Rosenblatt, Aaron, 284, 305, 308
Rosenthal, Evelyn, 51, 208, 211, 214, 228, 266

Rossi, Alice, S., 93, 115, 122, 208, 228, 255, 256, 259, 260, 261, 270, 271, 272, 273, 281, 282, 305, 308, 380, 381, 382, 384, 398, 422, 428, 429, 505, 534
Royer, Jeannie, 333
Ruben, Alan Miles, 231, 235
Rudolph, Susanne, 371
Rumbarger, Margaret L., 360, 425, 522, 534
Ruzek, Sheryl, 463

Sager, Lawrence, 98, 123
Salper, Roberta, 422
Salzman-Webb, Marilyn, 17, 422
Sandler, Bernice, 234, 439, 522, 534
Sanford, Nevitt, 94, 122, 396
Sassower, Doris L., 304, 308
Scally, B., 331
Schifer, Margaret H., 122
Schiller, Anita R., 263, 304, 308
Schleman, Helen, 99
Schletzer, Vera M., 97, 98, 115, 122
Schlossberg, Nancy, 111, 122, 124
Schmidt, Dolores Barracano, 422
Schneider, Liz, 59, 60, 74, 77
Schneir, Miriam, 408
Schuck, Victoria, 203, 208, 228, 256, 259, 261, 267, 268, 284, 304, 308, 371
Schwartz, Felice N., 100, 122
Schwartz, Jane, 112, 122
Schwartz, Pepper, 57, 532, 534
Scott, Ann, 8, 13, 14, 32, 235
Scully, Malcolm G., 220, 228
Seabury, Paul, 425, 438
Selick, Barbara, 236
Sells, Lucy W., 79, 513, 529, 534
Senders, Virginia L., 98, 112, 123
Sewell, William M., 44, 49, 56, 80, 91, 529
Shabecoff, Philip, 523
Shapiro, Linn, 359
Sherwin, Susan S., 423
Shortridge, Kathleen, 234

Showalter, Elaine, 51, 56, 401, 402, 421, 423
Siegel, Alberta E., 236
Sigworth, Heather, 230
Silverberg, Marjorie, 112, 123
Simon, Rita J., 166, 172, 208, 211, 214, 218, 228, 244, 266, 271, 272, 278, 283, 286, 308
Simmons, Adele, 244, 413
Simpson, Lawrence A., 211, 228, 292
Siporin, Rae, 402, 421, 423
Skinner, Alice B., 112, 123
Slacker, Francis, 359
Slaughter, Diane T., 185
Slesinger, Tess, 410
Smith, Alice, 99
Smith, Constance E., 97, 123
Smith, Georgina M., 236, 508, 529
Smith, Howard W., 6
Somerville, Rose, 423
Starr, Rachel, 304, 307
Stead, Christina, 410
Stimpson, Catherine, 423
Stokes, Sybil L., 304, 308
Strauss, Deja, 359
Strawn, Dorothy, 99
Strong, Brian, 423
Suniewick, Nancy, 119, 356

Tangri, Sandra, 116, 123
Tate, Carla, 463
Taylor, Charles H. Jr., 187, 195
Taylor, Harold, 94
Terrell, Mary Church, 173, 176
Terrill, Hazel J., 119
Thomas, M. Carey, 395
Thomas, Norman, 134
Thompson, Clarence H., 98, 124
Thompson, Marian L., 123
Thorne, Barrie, 410
Threinen, Constance, 99
Tifft, L. L., 218, 228, 254
Tinker, Irene, 371
Tobias, Sheila, 402, 423, 481
Torrey, Jane W., 256, 258, 260, 267, 272, 273, 274, 304, 308

Tousey, Walter C., 239, 241, 242, 244, 254
Trecker, Janice Law, 401, 423
Trent, J. W., 79, 91
Troll, Lillian E., 111, 123
Truax, Anne, 322, 327, 328, 329, 331
Truth, Sojourner, 408
Tucker, Allan, 84, 91

Van Doren, Ruth, 100
Van Fleet, David, 230
Vance, Carole, 259, 260, 261, 269, 270, 279, 280, 304, 309, 331
Vetter, Louise, 124

Waggoner, Karen, 61, 77
Wallach, Aleta, 411, 423
Warkentin, G., 120
Wasserman, Elga, 72, 73, 77, 187
Weeks, Lorena, 502
Weinberger, Casper, 456
Weisberg, Gerard M., 9
Weisman, Martha, 412
Weissman, Myrna M., 187, 195, 535
Weitzman, Lenore J., 463, 522, 535
Wells, Audrey, 359
Wentworth, Eric, 229
Werts, Charles E., 79, 91
West, Anne Grant, 423
Westervelt, Esther M., 103, 116, 123
Wheeler, Elliot S., 238
Whipple, Jane B., 97, 103
White, Barbara A., 423
White, James J., 44, 56, 309, 314, 318, 319, 320, 321, 331
White, Martha, 123, 304
Whitehurst, R., 534
Wilcox, Thomas, 203, 208, 228, 261, 268, 292, 304, 309
Willard, Emma, 395
Willie, Charles, 178, 184
Willis, Betty J., 231, 235
Wilson, Margaret, 259, 269, 270, 304, 309
Winch, Robert, 54, 56
Withycombe-Brocato, C. J., 115, 124

Wolf, Charlotte, 54, 56
Wollstonecraft, Mary, 407, 413
Woolf, Virginia, 407, 408
Wright, Doris, 180, 184
Wulp, Patricia, 103, 124

Wylie, Philip, 1, 32

Zelditch, Bernice, 409, 410
Zissis, Cecilia, 99
Zwerdling, Daniel, 449, 455

Subject Index

Abortion services. *See:* Health services

Academic field. *See:* specific discipline entries

Academic performance, in college, 40, 42, 61–62, 83–84; in graduate and professional school, 40, 52–53; in high school, 39, 41; of woman doctorates, 143–144

Academic rank, 336, 339–342, 346–348; discipline variation, 260, 271, 302–303, 310, 311; discipline variation and degree held, 269–271, 310, 311; discipline variation and marital status, 263–264, 310, 311; institutional variation, 207–212, 239, 251–252; programs to achieve rank equity, 491–493; by race, 174–176

Adelbert College, 97, 120

Administration, institutional variation, 223–225; proportion of women on college committees, 243–244; transition from faculty to, 169–172

Administration, discipline of, 105, 141, 243, 322, 362, 390

Administration, women in, 169–172

Admission, to college, 38–42, 440, 441, 454, 462, 473–474; to graduate school, 42, 51–53, 75, 440, 441, 454, 462, 473–474, 511–514; to professional school, 43–44, 75, 439, 440, 441, 454, 462, 473–474, 511–514

Affirmative action, 187, 239, 425–426, 430, 441, 445, 450–451, 463–504, 507. *See also:* Contract compliance

Affirmative action, legal and administrative requirements, 463–474; audit and reporting systems, 472–473; current program overview, 474; dissemination of plans, 465–466; goals

Affirmative action (*cont.*)
and timetables, 469–471, 527; long-range programs, 473; policy and written plans, 465; program to attain goals, 471–472; responsibility for program implementation, 466; utilization analysis, 467–469

Affirmative action, suggested programs, 474–501; assessment of progress, 499–501; to achieve equity in conditions of employment, 493–495; to achieve equity in fringe benefits, 495–496; to achieve rank and promotion equity, 491–493; to achieve salary equity, 486–491; characteristics of ineffective programs, 476–477; for recruitment, 478–483; for selection process, 483–486; training of future women faculty, 496–497

African Studies Association (ASA), informal women's caucus, 364; Women's Steering Committee, 389

African studies, discipline of, 362, 364, 389

Agriculture, discipline of, 141, 241, 242, 244, 322

Akron, University of, 204, 222, 230

Alverno College, 115

American Anthropology Association (AAA), Committee on the Status of Women in Anthropology, 323, 331, 375, 389; informal women's caucus, 365

American Association for the Advancement of Science (AAAS), 480; Women's Caucus of, 389

American Association of Immunologists, Committee on the Status of Women, 300

American Association of Law Schools

American Assoc. of Law Schools (*cont.*) (AALS), Committee on Women in Legal Education, 304, 389

American Association of University Professors (AAUP), 93, 94, 95, 102, 109, 111, 222, 236, 360, 426–431, 435, 436, 437, 486, 507, 508, 522, 534; Committee W (National), 29, 389, 428–430, 534; Committee W's (local), 430, 507, 522; Council committee on discrimination, 431

American Association of University Women (AAUW), 113, 114, 119, 132, 133, 205, 223, 360, 401, 479

American Association of University Women Educational Foundation, 109, 119

American Chemical Society, Women Chemists Committee, 389

American College Personnel Association (ACPA), Women's Task Force, 231, 389

American Council on Education (ACE), 39, 41, 86, 93, 94, 95, 115, 143, 161, 175, 184, 333, 335, 453, 487, 511, 515, 520, 523, 531, 534

American Economics Association (AEA), Informal Women's Caucus, 389

American Historical Association (AHA), Committee on the Status of Women in the profession, 300, 365, 366, 369, 387, 389, 532

American history. *See:* History, discipline of

American Library Association (ALA), Social responsibilities round table, Task Force on Women, 300–301, 389

American literature, discipline of. *See:* English language and literature, discipline of

American Mathematical Society (AMS), Association of Women Mathematicians, 365; Committee on the Status of Women, 389

American Medical Association (AMA), 316

American Medical Women's Association (AMWA), 363

American Newspaper Publishers Association (ANPA), 9

American Personnel and Guidance Association (APGA), 111

American Philosophical Association (APA), informal women's caucus, 365; Subcommittee on the Status of Women in the Profession, 369, 387, 389

American Physical Society (APS), Committee on Women in Physics, 277, 300, 304, 305, 390

American Political Science Association (APSA), Committee on the Status of Women in the Profession, 294, 300, 359, 360, 366, 368, 369, 374, 387, 390; Women's Caucus for Political Science, 532

American Psychological Association (APA), Association for Women in Psychology (AWP), 304, 305, 325, 326, 359, 365, 366, 375, 387; Task Force on the Status of Women in Psychology, 365, 390, 531

American Society for Microbiology (ASM), Committee on the Status of Women Microbiologists, 390

American Society for Public Administration (ASPA), 390

American Society for Training and Development (ASTD), Women's Caucus, 390

American Sociological Association (ASA), 480; Ad Hoc Committee on the Status of Women in Sociology, 283, 300, 305, 366, 377, 382, 383, 390; Sociologists for Women in Society (SWS), 299, 324, 359, 375, 376, 379–384, 507, 532, 533, 534, 535

American Speech and Hearing Association (ASHA), Subcommittee on the

American Speech & Hearing Assoc. (*cont.*)
Status of Women, 365, 390
American Statistical Association (ASA),
Women's Caucus, 390
American Studies, discipline of, 304, 396;
advanced degrees earned in, 257,
310; attrition in graduate departments of, 257; graduate enrollment
in, 256, 310; political activity of
women in, 362, 390; productivity
of women in, 283, 284; specialization in, 322; status of women in,
281, 284, 293, 294, 300, 311, 312;
undergraduate majors in, 257, 310.
See also: Discipline variation; Field
specialization
American Studies Association (ASA),
Commission on the Status of
Women, 300–301, 390
American University, 53, 370
Anatomy, discipline of, 141, 158, 159,
329
Anthropology, discipline of, 201, 304;
advanced degrees earned in, 141,
243, 257, 262, 263, 310; attrition
in graduate departments of, 257;
employment trends in, 158, 159,
274; graduate enrollment in, 256,
310; political activity of women in,
362, 364, 365, 374, 389; productivity of women in, 283, 312;
specialization in, 322, 323–324;
status of women in, 201, 243, 259,
260, 261, 262, 263, 269, 276, 278,
279, 280, 281, 287, 293, 294, 302,
303, 310, 311, 312, 520; undergraduate majors in, 257, 310. *See
also:* Discipline variation; Field
specialization
Architecture, discipline of, 54, 106, 177,
405
Arizona, University of, 200, 201, 230,
475, 485, 486
Art, discipline of, 187; advanced degrees
in, 141, 243; status of women in,
241, 242, 243, 244, 343, 344, 351,

Art (*cont.*)
401; women's studies courses in,
405, 412, 498, 506. *See also:*
Discipline variation
Aspiration levels, 44, 179, 400. *See also:*
Barriers in higher education;
Success avoidance
*Assembly on University Goals and
Governance,* 117, 119
Association for Women in Mathematics,
304, 305
Association for Women Psychologists
(AWP), 304, 305, 325, 326, 359,
365, 366, 375, 387
Association of American Colleges (AAC),
534; Project on the Status and Edu-
cation of Women, 43, 390
Association of Asian Studies (AAS),
Committee on the Status of Women
in Asian Studies, 390
Association of Women in Science
(AWIS), 284, 300, 305, 365, 366
Assumption College, 230
Atomic Energy Commission, 112
Attrition, 75, 79–91, 93–124, 512–514;
and academic performance, 82–83,
86, 513; in college, 81–84; by
disciplines (*See:* entries under
specific disciplines); and financial
problems, 88–89; in graduate
schools, 84–89, 400; and marital
status, 86–88, 106; and social class,
86; withdrawal and return, 93–124,
125–134
Auburn University, 475
August 26 Strike, 12–13, 21

Baldwin-Wallace College, 204, 230
Barnard College, 73, 75, 100, 101, 119,
170, 171, 397, 413, 418, 481, 487,
523, 532
Barriers in higher education, institutional,
37–56, 57–76; in campus regula-
tions and services, 53, 74–75; in
counseling, 50–53; in curriculum,
53–54; entry barriers, 37–50, 165.

Barriers in higher education (*cont.*)
  See also: Admissions; Financial aid
Barriers in higher education, psycho-
    logical, 57–76; in aspirations, 58–
    62, 133–134; role conflict, 67–69,
    75–76; in student-faculty relations,
    69–73, 108, 133, 134, 165
Baylor University, 475
Bennett College, 176
Bennington College, 76
Biochemistry, discipline of, 141, 146,
    158, 159, 329
Biology, discipline of; advanced degrees
    earned in, 141, 206, 207, 257, 310;
    attrition in graduate departments of,
    257; employment trends in, 152,
    158, 159; political activity of women
    in, 366, 391, 518; productivity of
    women in, 283, 284, 312; specializa-
    tion in, 327–328, 329; status of
    women in, 206, 207, 274, 284, 287,
    289, 291, 300, 311, 312, 340, 342,
    515; undergraduate majors in, 257,
    310; women's studies in, 405, 406,
    498. *See also:* Discipline variation;
    Field specialization
Biophysics, discipline of, 141, 146, 158,
    159, 329
Birth rate, 523–524. *See also:* Family
    size
Black Studies, 117, 178, 181, 396, 398,
    399, 415
Black women in academe, 173–184, 450,
    477, 480; career advancement, 176,
    177; career choice of college
    graduate, 176; professors and ad-
    ministrators, 178–180; undergrad-
    uate students, 177–178
Boston Area Women in Social Science
    (BAWSS), 480, 533
Boston College, 230
Boston University, 230
Botany, discipline of, 141, 159, 329
Bowe v. *Colgate Palmolive,* 11
Bowling Green College, 396

Braden v. *University of Pittsburgh,* 503
Brandeis University, 61, 65, 230, 533
Bridgeport, University of, 230
Brooklyn College, City University of New
    York, 231
Brown University, 213, 231, 475, 480,
    496, 499
Bryn Mawr College, 60, 73
Business, discipline of, 342, 343, 345,
    351, 355, 363, 506
*Business and Professional Women's
    Organization* (BPWO), 479

California Institute of Technology, 475,
    482, 487, 489
California State Colleges; California
    Polytechnic-Pomona and San Luis
    Obispo, 231; Chico State, 231;
    Dominquez Hills, 231; Fresno
    State, 231, 403, 417; Fullerton,
    231; Hayward, 231; Humboldt
    State, 231; Kern County, 231; Long
    Beach, 231, 417; Los Angeles, 231;
    Sacramento State, 212, 231, 236,
    416, 417, 418, 419; San Bernadino,
    231; San Diego State, 231, 236,
    293, 419, 475, 500; San Fernando
    State, 231; San Francisco State, 231,
    393, 396, 398, 411, 417, 420;
    San Francisco State Experimental
    College, 415; San Jose State, 231;
    Sonoma State, 231; Stanislaus State,
    231
California, University of, 441, 486;
    Berkeley, 29, 87, 145, 204, 217,
    218, 225, 231, 370, 446, 454, 495,
    496, 499, 502, 505, 509, 518, 534;
    Davis, 231, 479, 482, 535; Irvine,
    231, 405; Los Angeles, 100, 123,
    145, 231, 411, 505; Riverside, 231;
    San Diego, 231; San Francisco, 231;
    Santa Barbara, 231, 475, 484, 533;
    Santa Cruz, 231
Career commitment, 51–52, 156; and
    family size, 127; fear of, 58–61

Career development, 94, 115–16, 139, 147–161, 165

Carnegie Commission on Higher Education (CCHE), 55, 86, 117, 119, 333, 335, 511

Carnegie Corporation, 97

Carnegie-Mellon University, 231, 238

Case Western Reserve University, 231

Catalyst-on-Campus, 100, 113, 119, 120

Catholic colleges, 175, 340

Catonsville (Maryland) Community College, 495

Cell biology, discipline of, 362, 363, 391

Chemistry, discipline of, 187; advanced degrees earned in, 141, 206, 243, 257, 310; attrition in graduate departments of, 257; employment trends in, 158, 159; political activity of women in, 363, 389; productivity of women in, 218; specialization in, 326–327, 329; status of women in, 206, 243, 287, 289, 312; undergraduate majors in, 257, 310. *See also:* Discipline variation; Field specialization

Chicago, University of, 29, 51, 71, 145, 204, 211, 214, 224, 231, 371, 441, 453, 486, 505, 509, 532, 534

Child-bearing leave, 225, 430, 443, 464, 476, 495–496

Child-care services, 53, 113, 495–496

Church Women United (CWU), 27

Civil Rights Act of 1964, 439, 448, 457, 458, 459, 460, 461, 464, 489, 501, 522

Civil rights movement, 2, 31; dilemma of black women in, 173–175, 180–184

Clark University, 232

Classical language and literature, discipline of, 141, 158, 159, 181, 412

Coeducation, at Yale, 57–76

Coeducational colleges, 175, 204

Collective bargaining, 508–509

College Administration. *See:* Administration, discipline of

College admission. *See:* Admission, to college

College attendance. *See:* College enrollment

College enrollment, 37, 139, 523–527; and academic performance, 79–80; by race, 174; and social class, 48–49, 79–80

Colorado, University of (Boulder), 232

Columbia University, 145, 169, 200, 201, 202, 212, 232, 441, 447, 453, 499, 505; Teachers College, 532

Commission on Non-Traditional Education, 117, 120

Comprehensive Health Manpower Training Act of 1971, 503

Congress to Unite Women, 12

Congressional Union for Women's Suffrage (CUWS), 2

Congressional women's caucus, 25–26

Connecticut College, 215, 232

Consciousness-raising groups, 22–24, 61, 111–112

Continuing education, centers for, 95–102; profile of returning student, 104–109, 194–195; program evaluation, 102–104, 114–115; scope of programs, 109–110; themes in programs, 110–117. *See also:* Attrition, withdrawal and return

Contraception services. *See:* Health services

Contract compliance, 439–462; compliance reviews, 443, 465; enforcement, 446–447; evaluation of, 450–452; goals v. quotas, 447–448, 469–471, 527; individual v. class complaints, 442; problems during investigation, 448–450; processing of complaints, 444–446; requirements under executive orders, 441–442, 464; role of WEAL in enforcement, 442–444. *See also:* WEAL; Affirmative action

Cornell College, 145, 204, 232

Cornell University, 50, 232, 393, 405, 498, 534

Council of Graduate Schools, 116, 117

Counseling services, to returning students, 109, 112

Cytology, discipline of, 141, 150, 159, 329

Danforth Foundation, 114

Dartmouth College, 74, 403, 475

Day-care. *See:* Child-care services

Degree aspirations, doctoral degrees, 84–85

Degrees earned, bachelor's degrees, total, 41, 79, 89, 139, 256–257; bachelor's degrees by major, 257; doctoral degrees, total, 37–38, 40, 41, 75, 79, 84, 89–90, 93, 139, 142, 163, 256, 335, 511, 514–519; doctoral degrees by field, 243, 257; master's degrees, total, 41, 79, 256, 335; master's degrees by field, 257

Delaware, University of, 238

Detroit, University of, 232

Discipline, academic. *See:* specific discipline entries

Discipline variation, graduate school enrollment, 258, 312; initial appointment, 275–278, 311; job functions, 281–282, 311; nonladder appointments, 272–273, 311; part-time appointments, 271–274, 310; participation in professional associations, 299, 312; participation rate, 258–260, 310, 509; perception of discrimination, 292–299, 312; productivity, 154–155, 283–286, 312; promotion rate, 278–280, 311; rank, 260–271, 302–303, 310, 311; rank and degree held, 269–271, 310, 311; rank and marital status, 263–264, 310, 311; salary, 286–292, 302–303, 311, 312; tenure, 274–278, 310, 311. *See also:* specific discipline entries; Field specialization

Doctoral degrees earned. *See:* Degrees earned

Double-bind, 58–61, 80–81

Drop-Out. *See:* Attrition

Dual career management, 167–168

Duke University, 475, 480, 486

Earth sciences, discipline of, 141, 287, 328

East Carolina University, 231

Eastern Sociological Society, Committee on Women, 534

Economics, discipline of, 304; advanced degrees earned in, 141, 206, 257; attrition in graduate departments of, 257; political activity of women in, 363, 366, 389, 506; specialization in, 322; status of women in, 54, 206, 287; undergraduate majors in, 257; women's studies courses in, 394, 405, 407, 410, 506. *See also:* Discipline variation

Education, discipline of, 146; advanced degrees earned in, 141, 206, 243, 257, 310; attrition in graduate departments of, 257; employment trends in, 158, 159, 278; marital status of those in, 167; political activity of women in, 362, 363, 364, 365, 391, 506; productivity of women in, 155; specialization in, 59, 100, 105, 142, 143, 144, 163, 177, 314, 335; status of women in, 176, 206, 207, 221, 223, 241, 242, 243, 244, 278, 286, 312, 342, 519; undergraduate majors in, 257, 310; women's studies in, 406, 411, 412, 506

Education Amendment Act, 439, 455, 457, 458, 459, 460, 461, 503, 522

Educational Testing Service (ETS), 511

Eisenstadt v. *Baird,* 25

Embryology, discipline of, 141, 158, 329

Engineering, discipline of; employment trends in, 108, 152, 525; political activity of women in, 362, 363, 390; specialization in, 61, 105, 205,

Engineering (*cont.*)
335; status of women in, 54, 340,
344, 345, 347, 351, 355, 515, 519.
See also: Discipline variation; Field
specialization
English language and literature, discipline
of, 146, 187, 281, 398, 399;
advanced degrees earned in, 141,
243, 257, 262, 310; attrition in
graduate departments of, 257;
employment trends in, 159, 525;
political activity of women in, 505;
status of women in, 54, 165, 201,
223, 241, 243, 261, 262, 268, 269,
292, 312, 401; undergraduate
majors in, 257, 310; women's studies
courses in, 394, 402, 404, 405, 406,
407, 408–410, 413, 498, 506. *See
also:* Discipline variation; Field
specialization
Enrollment. *See:* College enrollment;
Graduate school enrollment
Entomology, discipline of, 141, 158, 159,
329
Equal Employment Opportunity Act of
1972, 501
*Equal Employment Opportunity Com-
mission* (EEOC), 6, 7, 8, 9, 13, 21,
489, 502, 504, 522; "Guidelines
on Discrimination Because of Sex,"
502–503, 508
Equal Pay Act of 1963, 455, 457, 458,
459, 460, 461, 464, 487, 489, 503,
522
Equal Rights Amendment (ERA), 3, 4,
10, 26, 76, 454, 504
ERIC Clearinghouse on Higher Education,
116, 199, 230, 238, 533
Executive Order 11246, as amended, 439–
462, 463–504. *See also:* Affirmative
action; Contract compliance; WEAL
Executive orders, 440

Faculty wives, 187–195; compared with
women faculty, 191–193; with advanced degrees, 191–193; educa-

Faculty wives (*cont.*)
tional status and interests, 188–190;
employment status and interests,
190–191
Fair Labor Standards Act, 522
Family size, and career commitment, 127,
169; and depression years, 129–130,
517
Federally Employed Women (FEW), 4,
26, 113
*Federation of American Societies for
Experimental Biology* (FASEB),
366
Fellowships, 84, 85, 146, 200, 201, 275.
See also: Financial Aid
Female Studies. *See:* Women's studies
Feminist organizations, 25–30
Feminist Studies. *See:* Women's studies
The Feminists, 11
Field specialization, 313–331; in anthropology, 322, 323–324; in biological sciences, 327–328, 329; in
languages and literature, 326, 327;
in law, 60, 61, 105, 176, 314, 315,
316, 318–321, 328, 330; in medicine, 54, 59, 105, 176, 313, 314,
316–318, 320, 328, 329; in physical
sciences, 326–327; pressure vs.
preference, 328–330; processes to
cope with sex typing, 314–316; in
psychology, 144, 325–326; sex
typing of occupations, 313–316; in
social sciences, 321–322; in sociology, 322, 323, 324–325, 329
Financial aid, in college, 44–46, 108,
113–114; in graduate and professional schools, 47–48, 49–50, 108,
113–114, 145, 340–342, 511–512;
postdoctoral fellowships, 145–146
Financial dependency on family, 48, 130
Fisk University, 232
Florida, State University of; Florida
A & M University, 232; Florida
Atlantic University, 232; Florida
International University, 232;
Florida State University, 232;

Florida, State University of (*cont.*)
Florida Technological University,
232; University of Florida, 232;
University of Northern Florida, 232;
University of South Florida, 210,
232; University of West Florida, 232
FOCUS (campus feminist group), 449
Ford Foundation, 496
Freedom Socialist Club, 15

General Federation of Women's Clubs
(GFWC), 2
Genetics, discipline of, 141, 158, 159,
329
Georgetown University, 232
George Washington University, 98
Goddard College, 408, 418, 419
Goucher College, 403, 510, 534
Graduate School Admission. *See:* Admissions
Graduate school enrollment, 258, 312
Grievance procedures; AAUP chapters
and committees' role in, 430–431;
basic principles for, 432–433;
formal, 433, 435–436, 491, 523;
individual v. patterned discrimination, 436–437; informal, 433–
434; internal to academe, 425–438,
498–499, 523; model for, 433–
436; preliminary hearing, 434–435;
specialized for sex discrimination v.
for all faculty grievances, 431–432

Harvard University, 42, 97, 113, 120,
145, 204, 208, 212, 213, 232, 321,
441, 443, 444, 445, 450, 454,
485, 495, 505, 509, 534
Haverford College, 73, 74
Hawaii, University of, 498
Health Sciences, discipline of; advanced
degrees earned in, 141; employment
trends in, 159; graduate enrollment
in, 455; political activity of women
in, 363; specialization in, 105, 163,
176, 328, 329; status of women in,
224, 342, 347, 348, 349, 351;

Health Sciences (*cont.*)
women's studies courses in, 506.
See also: Discipline variation
Health Services, 53, 57, 495–496
History, discipline of, 187, 201, 304,
398, 399; advanced degrees earned
in, 141, 206, 243, 257, 262, 310;
attrition in graduate departments of,
257, employment trends in, 159,
311, 525; political activity of
women in, 361–362, 364, 365, 366,
369, 387, 389, 391, 505; specialization in, 322; status of women in,
54, 201, 206, 259, 261, 262, 267,
276, 294, 300, 310, 311, 312, 401;
undergraduate majors in, 257;
women's studies courses in, 394,
402, 404, 405, 406, 407–408, 413,
498, 506. *See also:* Discipline
variation
Hodgson v. *Waynesburg College,* 487
Hofstra University, 475
Holy Cross College, 233
Home economics, discipline of, 163, 205,
223, 224, 241, 412, 489
Hoyt v. *Florida,* 3, 32
Hughes v. *Superior Court,* 447
Humanities. *See:* Specific discipline entries
Human Rights for Women (HRW), 12,
25

Illinois State University, 238
Illinois, University of, 145, 243, 245,
253, 520, 521; Champaign-Urbana,
233, 531, 532, 533
Illinois Wesleyan University, 238
Illinois University (Eastern), 210, 233
Illinois University (Southern), Carbondale, 233
Illinois University (Western), 233
Immunology, discipline of, 274, 283,
284, 300, 311, 312
Indiana State University, 204, 205, 209,
216, 233
Indiana, University of, Bloomington, 215,
222, 233

Institute of Electrical and Electronics Engineers (IEEE), Committee on Professional Opportunities for Women, 390

Institutional barriers. *See:* Barriers in higher education

Institutional variation; academic rank, 207–210, 509; administration, 223–225; elite v. nonelite, 204, 509; initial appointment rank, 210–212; marginal appointments, 212–214; promotion, 214–218, 226; proportion of black students, 174–175; salary, 219–223, 335–336; sex composition of faculty, 200–205; sex composition of faculty by department, 205–207; tenure, 219, 226

John Carroll University, 475
Johns Hopkins University, 233, 475, 533, 534
Johnson Foundation, 114

Kansas State Teachers College, 220, 233
Kansas, University of, 221, 222, 233
Kellogg Foundation, 114
Kentucky University (Eastern), 204, 233
Kentucky, University of, 224, 234
Kirkland College, 409

Labor force participation; trends, 126, 518–519; of woman doctorates, 156
Law, discipline of, 187, 304; advanced degrees in, 174, 257, 310; graduate enrollment in, 256, 310, 510, 511, 512; political activity of women in, 362, 389, 506; specialization in, 60, 61, 105, 176, 314, 315, 316, 318–321, 328, 330; status of women in, 49, 177, 259, 260, 261, 268, 269, 310, 441; women's studies courses in, 394, 404, 405, 411–412, 506. *See also:* Field specialization
League of Women Voters (LWV), 3
League of Academic Women (LAW), 29

League of American Working Women (LAWW), 27, 28
Library science, discipline of, 304; degrees earned in, 243, 256, 257; attrition in graduate departments of, 256, 257; employment trends in, 263; political activity of women in, 362, 364, 389, 506; specialization in, 105, 163; status of women in, 241, 242, 243, 281, 300; undergraduate majors in, 257
Louisiana State University, 234
Loyola University, 234

Maine, University of, 453, 475, 488, 490, 496, 531
Margaret Morrison Carnegie College, 98
Marginal appointments, discipline variation in, 272–273, 311; institutional variation in, 212–214
Maryland, University of, 441, 453, 454, 475, 486; Baltimore County, 201, 234; College Park, 234
Massachusetts Institute of Technology, 234, 403, 409, 475, 486, 497
Massachusetts, University of, 487, 489, 493; Amherst, 230, 234, 475
Maternity leave. *See:* Child-bearing leave
Mathematics, discipline of, 187, 188, 304; advanced degrees earned in, 141, 206, 243, 257, 310; attrition in graduate departments of, 257; political activity of women in, 362, 364, 365, 389, 390, 505; productivity of women in, 218; specialization in, 105; status of women in, 206, 241, 243, 244, 287, 289, 312; undergraduate majors in, 257
Mather College, 97
Medicine, discipline of, 187, 304; advanced degrees in, 141, 174, 257, 310; employment trends in, 158, 159; graduate enrollment in, 43–44, 256, 310, 455, 510, 511–512; political activity of women in, 363, 506; specialization in, 54, 59, 105,

Medicine (*cont.*)
176, 313, 314, 316–318, 320, 328, 329; status of women in, 54, 177, 293, 310, 311, 312, 441; women's studies courses in, 411, 412, 506. *See also:* Discipline variation; Field specialization
Menglekock v. *State of California,* 11
Miami-Dade Junior College, 100
Miami, University of, 234
Michigan State University, 98, 212, 213, 234, 410, 475, 477, 480, 486, 487, 489, 496, 499
Michigan, University of, 98, 101, 103, 104, 108, 110, 145, 234, 256, 370, 448–450, 475, 480, 485, 486, 487, 489, 496, 531
Microbiology, discipline of, 304; advanced degrees earned in, 141; employment trends in, 158, 159, 263, 264; marital status of those in, 264, 310; political activity of women in, 362, 363, 390; specialization in, 329; status of women in, 261, 268, 270, 271, 272, 288–289, 291, 310, 311, 312
Mills College, 73
Minnesota, University of, 97, 113, 210, 211, 217, 475, 479, 484, 487, 500; Twin Cities, 234
Missouri, University of, Kansas City, 99, 112, 234; St. Louis, 99
Modern Language Association (MLA), Commission on the Status of Women, 374, 377, 391, 393, 532; Women's Caucus, 359, 365, 366
Modern languages, discipline of, 201, 304; advanced degrees earned in, 141, 243, 257, 262, 263, 277, 310; attrition in graduate departments, 257; employment trends, 152, 158, 159, 265, 266; graduate enrollment in, 256, 310; political activity of women in, 359, 362, 363, 364, 365, 366, 374, 377, 391, 518; specialization in, 326, 327; status of

Modern languages (*cont.*)
women in, 201, 223, 243, 258, 259, 260, 261, 262, 263, 267, 268, 269, 270, 271, 272, 273, 274, 275, 281, 282, 287, 288, 289, 290, 302, 310, 311, 312; undergraduate majors in, 257, 310; women's studies courses in, 412. *See also:* English, discipline of; Discipline variation; Field specialization
Molecular biology, discipline of, 141, 146, 159
Mount Holyoke College, 73, 234, 370, 371, 413
Mueller v. *Oregon,* 8
Mundelein College, 108, 413
Music, discipline of, 141, 206, 207, 243, 401

National Academy of Sciences, National Research Council, 307, 511, 515, 531, 533
National American Women's Suffrage Association (NAWSA), 2, 3
National Association for the Advancement of Colored People (NAACP), 11, 177
National Chicano Foundation, 480
National Coalition for Research on Women's Education and Development (NCRWED), 114, 120
National Coalition of American Nuns (NCAN), 27
National Council of Negro Women, 480, 531
National Council on Family Relations (NCFR), Task Force on Women's Rights and Responsibilities, 391
National Educational Association (NEA), Temporary Committee on the Status of Women, 286, 288, 307, 391
National Institutes of Health (NIH), 481
National Labor Relations Act, 489
National Manpower Council (NMC), 122
National Organization for Women

National Organization for Women (cont.)
(NOW), 4–15, 18, 21, 24, 25, 27,
29, 117, 231, 365, 400, 441, 479,
532, 533
National Science Foundation, 307, 481,
525
National Vocational Guidance Association
(NVGA), Commission on the Oc-
cupational Status of Women, 391
National Women's Party (NWP), 2, 3, 4
National Women's Political Caucus
(NWPC), 26, 534
Nepotism rules, 134, 167, 194–195, 225,
265–266, 486
"New Careers" programs, 100–101, 112
New Hampshire, University of, 234
New Haven College, 69
New Higher Education Act, 503
New Jersey, State University of, 441;
Douglass College, 235, 417;
Livingston, 235; Rutgers, 235, 417,
475, 493, 508
New Mexico, University of, 417
New York, City College of, 412
New York, City University of, 475;
Richmond, 417
New York Human Rights Commission,
405
New York Radical Women (NYRW),
18
New York, State University of (SUNY),
441, 454, 475, 486; Buffalo, 14,
199, 235, 403, 412, 417, 419, 420;
Old Westbury, 406, 413, 532;
Stonybrook, 413
New York University, 49, 99, 122, 370,
532
Nonsectarian colleges, 175
North Carolina, University of (Chapel
Hill), 43
Northeastern University, 235
Northern Michigan University, 433, 434,
435, 436, 437, 438
Northwestern University, 235, 416, 499
Notre Dame University, 235
Nursing, discipline of; political activity of

Nursing *(cont.)*
women in, 364; specialization in,
105, 163, 205, 313; status of women
in, 223, 224, 489; women's studies
courses in, 411, 412. *See also:*
Discipline variation

Oakland University, 113
Office for Civil Rights (OCR). *See:* U.S.
Department of Health, Education
and Welfare
Office of Federal Contract Compliance
(OFCC). *See:* entries under U.S.
Department of Labor
Ohio State University, 235, 238, 475, 486
Oklahoma State University, 475
Ombudsman. *See:* Grievance procedures
Oregon State University, 475, 486
Oregon, University of, 204, 208, 214,
235, 487, 489
Organization of American Historians
(OAH), Committee on the Status of
Women, 391

Pace College, 235
Part time v. full time, employment, 112,
193–195, 212–213, 225–226, 271–
274, 310, 509; study, 50, 59, 112,
193–195
Pennsylvania State University, 43, 98, 235
Pennsylvania, University of, 201, 204,
235, 396, 453, 475, 485, 486
Phillips v. *Martin Marietta,* 25
Philosophy, discipline of, 146, 201, 304;
advanced degrees earned in, 141,
206, 243, 257, 310; attrition in
graduate departments of, 257; employment trends in, 158, 159;
graduate enrollment in, 310; political activity of women in, 362, 365,
389, 506; status of women in, 201,
206, 243, 259, 269, 310, 311, 312;
undergraduate majors in, 257, 310;
women's studies courses in, 407. *See
also:* Discipline variation
Philosophy of Education Society (PES),

Philosophy of Education Society (*cont.*)
Committee on the Status of Women, 391

Physical education, discipline of, 223, 241, 242, 244

Physics, discipline of, 304; advanced degrees earned in, 141, 206, 256, 257, 262, 263, 310; attrition in graduate departments of, 256, 257; employment trends in, 152, 158, 159, 263, 265, 277, 311; graduate enrollment in, 256, 310; marital status of those in, 264, 302, 310; political activity of women in, 362, 390; specialization in, 59, 328; status of women in, 206, 207, 259, 260, 261, 262, 263, 264, 267, 268, 269, 270, 271, 272, 273, 281, 287, 288, 289, 293, 299, 300, 302, 303, 310, 311, 312, 342, 343, 349, 355, 515, 520; undergraduate majors in, 257, 310. *See also:* Discipline variation; Field specialization

Physiology, discipline of, 141, 146, 159, 329

Pittsburgh, University of, 99, 174, 177, 179, 182, 210, 225, 235, 402, 405, 416, 454, 475, 480, 485, 486, 496, 502, 503, 531

Political action, among academic women; advisory v. activist groups, 359–360, 364–365; campus-based, 28–30; current trends in, 384–388, 505–506; emergence of, 360–366, 453. *See also:* Political activist groups; Political advisory groups

Political activist groups, among academic women; activities of, 377–379; budget of, 373–374; case study (SWS), 379–384; founding of, 366; leadership of, 368–373; membership in, 367; size of, 367

Political advisory groups; activities of, 377–379; budget of, 373–374; founding of, 366–367; membership in, 367–368; size of, 367;

Political advisory groups (*cont.*)
structure, 374–376

Political Science, discipline of, 187, 201, 304, 399; advanced degrees earned in, 141, 243, 257, 262, 310; attrition in graduate departments of, 256, 257, 258; employment trends in, 277, 311; graduate enrollment in, 256, 258, 310; political activity of women in, 303, 359, 360, 361, 362, 366, 368, 369, 370, 371, 374, 375, 387, 390, 505, 506; productivity of women in, 218, 283, 284, 285–286, 312; specialization in, 106, 107, 322, 329; status of women in, 201, 243, 259, 261, 262, 267, 268, 272, 278, 284, 287, 291–292, 294–298, 300, 302, 303, 310, 311, 312, 401, 509, 520; undergraduate majors in, 257, 310; women's studies courses in, 405, 407, 410, 506. *See also:* Discipline variation; Field specialization

Population Association of America (PAA), Committee on the Status of Women in the Profession, 391

Portland State University, 409, 416, 418, 419

President's Commission on the Status of Women, 5

Princeton University, 51, 74, 235, 454, 475, 495, 496

PROBE (campus feminist group), 449

Productivity, by discipline, 154–155; and professional experience, 247–248; publications, 155, 218, 245–246, 283–286, 312; and salary, 249; and teaching effectiveness, 247

Professional and Executive Corps, 112

Professional Women's Caucus (PWC), 4, 27, 365, 366, 441, 452, 532

Promotion, and discipline variation, 278–280, 311; institutional variation, 214–218, 226; mean time in rank before promotion, 241–242; programs to achieve equity in, 491–493

Protective legislation, 8

Psychological barriers in higher education. *See:* Barriers in higher education

Psychology, discipline of, 187, 188, 304, 399; advanced degrees earned in, 141, 145, 206, 243, 257, 310; attrition in graduate departments of, 256, 257, 258, 513; employment trends in, 158, 159; graduate enrollment in, 256, 258, 310; marital status of those in, 264, 302, 310; political activity of women in, 359, 362, 363, 364, 365, 366, 369, 375, 387, 390, 391, 505, 518; productivity of women in, 155, 218, 283, 284, 312; specialization in, 144, 325–326; status of women in, 54, 206, 207, 212, 243, 259, 260, 267, 271, 272, 273, 274, 278, 279, 284, 287, 289, 293, 294, 310, 311, 312, 401; undergraduate majors in, 257, 310; women's studies courses in, 406, 407, 410, 413, 498, 506

Public administration. *See:* Administration, discipline of

Public Health Service Act, 457, 458, 459, 460, 462

Purdue University, 99, 108, 224, 235, 475

Quo Vadis School of Nursing (Canada), 101

Radcliffe College, 43, 65, 73, 94, 97, 99, 112, 113, 115

Radical Women, 18

Rank. *See:* Academic rank

Rank advancement. *See:* Promotion

Rap Groups. *See:* Consciousness-raising groups

Regional Resource Center for Women in Higher Education, 480

Religion and theology, discipline of, 141, 401, 411

Rhode Island, University of, 99, 235, 370

Rice University, 475

Rockefeller University, 235

Rockland County Community College, 103

Role conflict, 67–69, 75–76, 80–81, 128–130; of black women in academe, 183–184. *See also:* Barriers in higher education, psychological

Role models, 71–72, 73, 109

Roosevelt University, 101

Rosenfeld v. *Southern Pacific,* 25

Russell Sage Foundation, 531

Salary, 249–250, 334, 336, 342–346, 350–352; compensatory back pay, 488–489; discipline variation, 286–292, 302–303, 311, 312; institutional variation, 219–223, 239, 241

St. Joan's Alliance, 27

Salem State College, 236

Sarah Lawrence College, 94, 97, 99, 100, 103, 393, 408

Seattle, Free University of, 397

Science. *See:* specific discipline entries

Sex discrimination; administrative remedies for, 441–462, 521–522; contract compliance to combat, 439–462; extent of, 353–354, 453; guidelines (*See:* Affirmative action; Contract compliance); individual v. patterned, 436–437; legal protection against, 439–440, 455, 502–504, 521–522; perception of, 292–299, 312, 453; resolution through internal grievance procedures, 425–438

Sex role socialization, 57–76, 127–129, 333

Sex typing of occupations. *See:* Field specialization

Sexual status, as complication in advanced training, 70, 513–514

Simmons College, 220, 226, 236, 370, 413

Single-sex colleges, 66, 67, 73–74, 175, 204

Smith College, 65, 73, 236
Social movements, general, 1–5, 30–31. *See:* special entries for specific social movements
Socialist Workers Party (SWP), 15
Social Science. *See:* specific discipline entries
Social Science Research Council, 534
Social work, discipline of, 304; productivity of women in, 283, 284, 312; specialization in, 59, 100, 105, 163, 176, 177, 322, 333; status of women in, 284; women's studies courses in, 411, 412
Society for Cell Biology (SCB), Task Force on Women in Cell Biology, 391
Sociologists for Women in Society (SWS), 359, 375, 376, 379–384, 507, 532, 533, 534, 535
Sociology, discipline of, 304, 361, 399; advanced degrees earned in, 141, 206, 243, 257, 262, 263, 310; attrition in graduate departments of, 256, 257, 258, 513; employment trends in, 159; graduate enrollment in, 256, 258, 310, 525; marital status of those in, 264, 279, 302, 310; political activities of women in, 299, 303, 359, 361, 362, 363, 364, 366, 375, 376, 377, 379–384, 390, 505, 506, 507, 513, 518; productivity of women in, 283, 284, 312; specialization in, 322, 323, 324–325, 329; status of women in, 54, 206, 207, 243, 259, 260, 261, 262, 263, 264, 267, 268, 269, 270, 271, 272, 273, 274, 275, 278, 281, 282, 284, 287, 289, 299, 300, 303, 310, 311, 312, 334, 509, 520; undergraduate majors in, 257, 310; women's studies courses in, 394, 402, 403, 405, 406, 410, 506. *See also:* Discipline variation; Field specialization
South Carolina, University of, 236

South Jersey, the College of; Rutgers-Camden, 235; Rutgers-Newark, 235
Southern Florida, University of, 475, 488, 490
Southern Methodist University, 236
Southern Illinois University, 475, 500
Southern University, 371
Speech, discipline of, 141; advanced degrees earned in, 141; employment trends in, 159; political activity of women in, 362, 365, 390; status of women in, 206, 207, 241, 243; women's studies courses in, 412
Spelman College, 480
Stanford University, 118, 145, 208, 236, 238, 454, 475, 482, 485, 486, 487, 495, 496
Statistics, discipline of, 287, 362, 390
State Commissions on the Status of Women, 5, 14, 25
Status transitions, faculty to administration, 169–172; student to faculty, 165–169; undergraduate to graduate student, 256
Stipends. *See:* Financial aid
Student Non-Violent Coordinating Committee (SNCC), 15
Students for a Democratic Society (SDS), 14, 15, 16, 396
Success avoidance, 59, 68–69, 80–81, 167
Suffrage movement, 2–3
Syracuse University, 98, 238

Temple University, 370
Tennessee State University (middle), 236
Tennessee, University of, Knoxville, 236
Tenure, 336, 342, 348–350; discipline variation, 274–278, 310, 311; institutional variation, 219, 226
Texas A & M, 475
Texas, University of, Austin, 236
Tufts University, 413, 450, 475; Jackson College, 237

Undergraduate v. graduate teaching, 335, 493

Utilization Analysis. *See:* Affirmative action
Unitarian-Universalist Women's Federation (UUWF), 27
United Auto Workers (UAW), Women's Committee, 7, 10, 27; network for economic rights, 28
United Glass and Ceramic Workers of North America, 9
U.S. Commission on Civil Rights, 522
U.S. Department of Health, Education and Welfare (HEW), 116, 123, 163, 179, 183, 253, 443, 456, 463–504, 523; Office for Civil Rights, 425, 427, 442–452, 489, 506, 534; Office of Education, 307, 308, 524; Women's Action Program, 115
U.S. Department of Labor, 443, 450–451; Office of Federal Contract Compliance, 8, 14, 425, 442, 463–504, 523; Wage and Hour Division, 489, 503, 522; Women's Bureau, 5, 95, 109, 110, 111, 123, 124, 314, 316, 318, 321, 331
United States v. *Vuitch,* 25
Urban League, 177

Vassar College, 60, 67, 73, 94
Vermont, University of, 477, 495
Virginia Public Colleges, 237
Virginia, University of, 43, 237, 440
Vocational guidance. *See:* Psychology, discipline of
Volunteerism, 131–133

Washington University, 99
Washington, University of, 99, 210, 215, 237, 396, 416, 417, 418, 475, 480, 486, 534
Wayne State University, 111, 237, 319, 403
Weeks v. *Southern Bell,* 502
Wellesley College, 66, 71, 72, 73, 75, 99, 100, 171, 237
Wesleyan University (Connecticut), 481
William and Mary College, 237

Willamette University, 237
Winthrop College, 439
Wisconsin, University of, 98, 99, 406, 407, 453, 488, 489, 495; Madison, 237, 403; Whitewater, 403
Woman doctorates, 139–161, 511, 517, 520–521; academic achievements, 154–156, 160, 166; academic status (rank), 152–154, 160, 165–166; early experiences, 143–144, 160; employers of, 147–150, 160; field choices of, 141–143, 160; graduate training of, 144–145; job functions, 150–152, 160; job mobility, 147–150, 160; personal characteristics, 150, 166; salary, 152, 160, 166; trends in employment of, 157–160, 244
Women's Caucus for Political Science (WCPS), 359, 375, 387
Women in Legal Education, Association of American Law, 319
Women, Inc., 28
Women's Board of the Methodist Church (WBMC), 27
Women's Christian Temperance Union (WCTU), 2
Women's colleges. *See:* Single-sex colleges
Women's Educational and Industrial Union, 112
Women's Equity Action League (WEAL), 4, 8, 11, 25, 29, 117, 232, 365, 439–462, 534
Women's liberation movement, 1–32; and black women, 180–184
Women's studies, 55, 76, 114, 182–183, 393–423, 498, 506–507, 509, 510; origins in educational reform, 399–402; origins in student movement, 396–399
Women's studies courses; current trends, 412–414; disciplinary courses, 407–411; growth of, 393–394; interdisciplinary v. general courses, 404–406, in professional schools, 411–412

Women's studies programs, 394–395, 414–421

Women's Talent Corps, 101

Women's Trade Union League (WTUL), 2

Woodrow Wilson Fellowship, 84, 85, 200, 201, 205, 275, 481, 513

Wyoming, University of, 475

Yale University, 29, 42, 57, 62, 63, 64, 65, 66, 67, 68, 69, 71, 72, 73, 74, 75, 145, 187, 188, 193, 212, 213, 237, 383, 454, 480, 495, 532, 533, 535; Law School, 469

Zoology, discipline of, 141, 152, 159, 243, 329